THE ROUTLEDGE HANDBOOK
OF FOOD ETHICS

While the history of philosophy has traditionally given scant attention to food and the ethics of eating, in the last few decades the subject of food ethics has emerged as a major topic, encompassing a wide array of issues, including labor justice, public health, social inequity, animal rights, and environmental ethics. This Handbook provides a much needed philosophical analysis of the ethical implications of the need to eat and the role that food plays in social, cultural, and political life. This text integrates traditional approaches to the subject with cutting edge research in order to set a new agenda for philosophical discussions of food ethics.

The Routledge Handbook of Food Ethics is an outstanding reference source to the key topics, problems, and debates in this exciting subject and is the first collection of its kind. Comprising 40 chapters by a team of international contributors, the Handbook is divided into 7 parts:

- the phenomenology of food
- gender and food
- food and cultural diversity
- liberty, choice, and food policy
- food and the environment
- farming and eating other animals
- food justice.

Essential reading for students and researchers in food ethics, it is also an invaluable resource for those in related disciplines such as environmental ethics and bioethics.

Mary C. Rawlinson is professor and chair in the Department of Philosophy at Stony Brook University, USA. She is author of *Just Life* (Columbia University Press, 2016) and editor of many volumes. She is also the editor of the *International Journal of Feminist Approaches to Bioethics*.

Caleb Ward is an instructor and PhD student in philosophy at Stony Brook University, USA. He is editor of *Global Food, Global Justice: Essays on Eating under Globalization* (with Mary C. Rawlinson, 2015).

Routledge Handbooks in Applied Ethics

Applied ethics is one of the largest and most diverse fields in philosophy and is closely related to many other disciplines across the humanities, sciences and social sciences. *Routledge Handbooks in Applied Ethics* are state-of-the-art surveys of important and emerging topics in applied ethics, providing accessible yet thorough assessments of key fields, themes, thinkers and recent developments in research.

All chapters for each volume are specially commissioned, and written by leading scholars in the field. Carefully edited and organized, *Routledge Handbooks in Applied Ethics* provide indispensable reference tools for students and researchers seeking a comprehensive overview of new and exciting topics in applied ethics and related disciplines. They are also valuable teaching resources as accompaniments to textbooks, anthologies and research-orientated publications.

Forthcoming:

The Routledge Handbook of Global Ethics
Edited by Darrel Moellendorf and Heather Widdows

The Routledge Handbook of the Ethics of Consent
Edited by Peter Schaber

The Routledge Handbook of End-of-Life Ethics
Edited by John Davis

The Routledge Handbook of Neuroethics
Edited by Syd Johnson and Karen S. Rommelfanger

THE ROUTLEDGE HANDBOOK OF FOOD ETHICS

Edited by Mary C. Rawlinson and Caleb Ward

LONDON AND NEW YORK

First published 2017
by Routledge
2 Park Square, Milton Park, Abingdon, Oxon, OX14 4RN

and by Routledge
711 Third Ave., New York City, NY 10017

Routledge is an imprint of the Taylor & Francis Group, an informa business

© 2017 Mary C. Rawlinson and Caleb Ward, selection and editorial matter; individual chapters, the contributors

The right of Mary C. Rawlinson and Caleb Ward to be identified as the authors of the editorial material, and of the authors for their individual chapters, has been asserted in accordance with sections 77 and 78 of the Copyright, Designs and Patents Act 1988.

British Library Cataloguing in Publication Data
A catalogue record for this book is available from the British Library

Library of Congress Cataloging in Publication Data
Names: Rawlinson, Mary C., editor. | Ward, Caleb, editor.
Title: The Routledge handbook of food ethics / edited by Mary C. Rawlinson and Caleb Ward.
Description: 1 [edition]. | New York : Routledge, 2016. | Series: Routledge handbooks in applied ethics | Includes bibliographical references and index.
Identifiers: LCCN 2016000808| ISBN 9781138809130 (hardback : alk. paper) | ISBN 9781315745503 (e-book)
Subjects: LCSH: Food—Moral and ethical aspects.
Classification: LCC TX357. R68 2016 | DDC 178—dc23
LC record available at http://lccn.loc.gov/2016000808

ISBN: 978-1-138-80913-0 (hbk)
ISBN: 978-1-315-74550-3 (ebk)

Typeset in Bembo
by Apex CoVantage, LLC

Printed and bound in Great Britain by
TJ International Ltd, Padstow, Cornwall

CONTENTS

Contents

Contents

Contents

Contents

CONTRIBUTORS

Marko Ahteensuu works as a collegium researcher at the Turku Institute for Advanced Studies and in the Philosophy unit at the University of Turku, Finland. He has published papers on the precautionary principle and public engagement in the context of modern agricultural biotechnology.

Sandra Albert MD, DNB, DrPH is a dermatologist and public health professional with the Public Health Foundation of India. She is the Director of the Indian Institute of Public Health, Shillong, in Meghalaya, India.

Matteo Bonotti is a lecturer in political theory at Cardiff University, UK. His research interests include political liberalism, the normative dimensions of partisanship, free speech, religion and political theory, language and political theory, and the political theory of food policy. His work has appeared or is forthcoming in such journals as the *American Political Science Review, European Journal of Political Theory, Philosophy & Social Criticism*, the *Critical Review of International Social and Political Philosophy*, the *Kennedy Institute of Ethics Journal*, and *Res Publica*.

Lynette Carter is from the New Zealand Māori tribal group of Kai Tahu. Her main research area is environmental literacy, focusing on Indigenous development and sustainability. Lynette teaches in Indigenous Studies at the University of Otago, New Zealand.

Emanuela Ceva is an associate professor of political philosophy at the University of Pavia (Italy). She has held several visiting positions at, among others, the Center for Human Values of Princeton University, Nuffield College (Oxford), Hitotsubashi University (Tokyo), University of St. Andrews, and Université de Montréal. Her research focuses on issues of value conflict and procedural justice, democracy, corruption, and the treatment of minorities. Her most recent publications have appeared in such journals as the *Journal of Social Philosophy, Social Theory and Practice, Journal of Applied Philosophy, Politics, Philosophy & Economics*, and *European Journal of Philosophy*.

M. Jahi Chappell is a senior staff scientist at the Institute for Agriculture and Trade Policy (IATP) in Minneapolis, Minnesota (USA). There he leads IATP's work on agroecology and food sovereignty, and he provides scientific input for all of IATP's programs. He has consulted for organizations such as the Food and Agriculture Organization of the United Nations and the international peasants' movement La Vía Campesina. He is past chair of the Agroecology Section of the Ecological Society of America and serves on the board of the Open Source Seed Initiative. He holds a PhD in ecology and evolutionary biology from the University of Michigan.

Anna Charlton is an adjunct professor of law at Rutgers University School of Law (USA). She served as director of the Animal Rights Law Clinic at Rutgers from 1990–2000.

Kayla Del Biondo graduated with a bachelors degree in sociology and a minor in visual arts from Purchase College (State University of New York, USA). Her senior thesis examined why people photograph their food, and why these photographs have come to be called "food porn" on social media.

Wiwik Dharmiasih is a lecturer at the Department of International Relations, Universitas Udayana, Indonesia. She holds an MA in politics with a specialization in international relations from Jawaharlal Nehru University, India. She provided social and legal analysis for the UNESCO nomination of the Cultural Landscape of Bali Province and is currently active in the monitoring and evaluation of its management system under the Subak Research Center, Universitas Udayana.

Kendall J. Eskine received his doctorate in psychology from the CUNY Graduate Center (USA), where he studied the representation and processing of abstract conceptual domains. He currently works in program and grant evaluation.

Francesco Ferraro received his PhD in legal philosophy and jurisprudence at University of Milan, Italy. His research interests have included the legal theory of Jeremy Bentham and the analysis of moral and legal rights within a utilitarian perspective. At the time of writing he is a visiting fellow at the University of Girona (Spain).

Gary L. Francione is Board of Governors Distinguished Professor of Law and Nicholas deB. Katzenbach Scholar of Law and Philosophy at Rutgers University School of Law (USA). He is co-editor (with Gary Steiner) of a series, *Critical Perspectives on Animals: Theory, Culture, Science and Law*, published by Columbia University Press. He blogs at www.abolitionistapproach.com.

David Fraser is a professor in the Animal Welfare program at the University of British Columbia in Vancouver, Canada. His scientific research has focused on the welfare of farm, companion, and wild animals.

Margaret Gray is an associate professor of political science at Adelphi University (USA). Her research focuses on farmworkers, immigration, and labor dynamics. She is author of *Labor and the Locavore: The Making of a Comprehensive Food Ethic* (University of California Press, 2014).

Craig K. Harris is an associate professor in the Department of Sociology at Michigan State University (USA), with appointments in the Center for Regional Systems and Michigan AgBio Research. He has conducted research on technological change in the fisheries of the North American Great Lakes, on the impacts of introduced species in East African Great Lakes, and on the development of shrimp aquaculture in Taiwan. In addition to the social dimensions of seafood, he has written about the ethical dimensions of cacao and chocolate and about food safety and pest management in the US agrifood system. His current research is on the food–energy–water nexus in regional food systems in western Michigan and northern Mexico.

Thomas C. Hilde is a research professor at the University of Maryland School of Public Policy (USA), where he focuses on international development and environmental policy, governance, and ethics. He also directs the Indonesia and Peru programs at the School of Public Policy, taking 20 graduate students each year to Bali, Sumatra, Java, and the Peruvian Amazon. He is editor of *The Agrarian Roots of Pragmatism* (with Paul B. Thompson), editor of *On Torture*, and co-author of a forthcoming book on organized environmental crime.

Sabine Hohl is an assistant professor in political philosophy at the University of Graz, Austria. She studied for a PhD at the University of Zurich, Switzerland. Her PhD thesis deals with the question of individual responsibility for collectively caused harm.

Elena Irrera (PhD) is a research fellow in political philosophy at Bologna University (Department of History, Cultures, and Civilization), in Italy. She is member of the research project *Feeding Respect: Food Policies and Minority Claims in Multicultural Societies*, run by the University of Pavia.

Simon Jenkins is a teaching fellow in the Department of Medicine, Ethics, Society and History, at the University of Birmingham, UK. He writes on a broad range of ethical issues, including environmental ethics, social robotics, and reproductive technology.

Marion Johnson is a senior researcher at the Future Farming Centre, Lincoln, Aotearoa (New Zealand). From a farming background, her research interests encompass agroecology and ethnoveterinary practices.

David M. Kaplan is an associate professor in the Department of Philosophy and Religion at the University of North Texas. He is editor of *The Philosophy of Food* (University of California Press, 2012), *Readings in the Philosophy of Technology* (Rowman and Littlefield, 2003), and co-editor with Paul B. Thompson of the *Encyclopedia of Food and Agricultural Ethics* (Springer, 2014). His book *Food Philosophy* is forthcoming from Columbia University Press. He also manages the Philosophy of Food Project: www.food.unt.edu.

Michiel Korthals is an emeritus professor of applied philosophy, Wageningen University and Free University, Netherlands. His main research focuses on the ethics of agriculture, food, environment, intellectual property, global warming, and hunger and malnutrition. His academic interest covers bioethics (in particular food, animals, and the environment), deliberative and democratic theories, and pragmatism. His main publications include *Before Dinner* (Springer, 2004) and *Ethical Traceability* (Springer, 2010, with C. Coff and D. Barling, eds.).

Michele Loi has a BA–MA Degree ("*laurea quadriennale*") in philosophy from the University of Cagliari (Italy) and a doctorate in political philosophy from the Libera Università degli Studi Sociali (LUISS) in Rome. As a postdoctoral researcher he specializes in the ethical and political implications of genetics, social justice in public health, epigenetics, and biomedical enhancement.

Clement Loo is an assistant professor in the Environmental Studies program at the University of Minnesota, Morris (USA). He works mainly in environmental philosophy and philosophy of ecology.

Christopher Mayes is a postdoctoral research fellow in the Centre for Values, Ethics and the Law in Medicine at the University of Sydney (Australia). He is the author of *The Biopolitics of Lifestyle: Foucault, Ethics and Healthy Choices* (Routledge, 2015).

James McWilliams, a professor of history at Texas State University (USA), is the author of numerous books on food and agriculture, including *Just Food* (2009) and *The Modern Savage* (2015). His writing on animals and ethics has appeared in the *New York Times*, *The American Scholar*, *The Virginia Quarterly Review*, and online at *The Atlantic*. He writes *The Things We Eat* column for *Pacific Standard*.

Josh Milburn is a PhD candidate in the School of Politics, International Studies and Philosophy at Queen's University Belfast, United Kingdom. His research focuses on applied moral and political theory, especially animal ethics. His work has appeared in a variety of places, including the *European Journal of Political Theory*, *Res Publica*, and the *Journal of Social Philosophy*.

Miranda Mirosa is a senior lecturer in the Department of Food Science at the University of Otago, New Zealand. Miranda is an interdisciplinarian with a research focus on consumer behavior and sustainable food consumption.

Lisa Jean Moore is a medical sociologist and professor of sociology and gender studies at Purchase College (State University of New York, USA). Her most recent books are *The Body: Social and Cultural Dissections* (Routledge, 2014) with Monica J. Casper, and *Buzz: Urban Beekeeping and the Power of the Bee* (NYU Press, 2013) with Mary Kosut.

Morten Ebbe Juul Nielsen is an associate professor in applied philosophy at Copenhagen University (Denmark), associated with the Philosophy Department and the Institute for Food and Resource Economics. He has published extensively in political philosophy, bioethics, business ethics, and legal philosophy. He is currently working on two interdisciplinary research projects, Governing Obesity (on personal responsibility and obesity policies) and Global Genes, Local Concerns (on the ethics of bio-banking). His other key research topics are legitimacy and pluralism, health, consent, and liberty.

David Pearson is a professor in communication at the University of Canberra (Australia). His research is on the policy and practice of communication in achieving positive social change. In recent years this has focused on environmental sustainability and human health in the global food system.

Rory Pearson is currently working on a Bachelor of Science degree at the University of Queensland in Australia. He is passionate about encouraging individuals to take responsibility for looking after their physical and mental health by creating a healthy lifestyle built on nutritious food and regular exercise.

Corine Pelluchon is a full professor in political philosophy and applied ethics at the University of Franche-Comté (France). She is the author of several books: *Leo Strauss and the Crisis of Rationalism: Another Reason, Another Enlightenment* (SUNY Press, 2014); *L'autonomie brisée. Bioéthique et Philosophie* (PUF, 2009/2014); *Eléments pour une éthique de la vulnérabilité. Les hommes, les animaux, la nature* (Le Cerf, 2011), winner of the Prize Moron of the French Academy; and *Les Nourritures. Philosophie du corps politique* (Le Seuil, 2015), awarded the Prize Edouard Bonnefous of the French Academy for Moral and Political Sciences. Her website is http://corine-pelluchon.fr.

Thomas E. Randall is a PhD political science student at the University of Western Ontario, Canada. His research focuses on feminist care ethics and political theory.

Mary C. Rawlinson is a professor and chair in the Department of Philosophy at Stony Brook University (State University of New York, USA). She is author of *Just Life* (Columbia University Press, 2016) and editor of many volumes, including most recently *Global Food, Global Justice: Essays on Eating under Globalization* (with Caleb Ward, Cambridge Scholars Publishing, 2015) and *Engaging the World: Thinking after Irigaray* (SUNY Press, 2016). She is also the editor of the *International Journal of Feminist Approaches to Bioethics*.

Matthew R. G. Regan is a doctoral student at the University of Maryland's School of Public Policy (USA), where he is researching a dissertation on democracy and culture in Southeast Asia. He holds a BA in history and an MA in modern European history from the Catholic University of America in Washington, DC, where his research focused on the history of the social sciences and European interpretations of Asian thought and culture.

Alison Reiheld is an associate professor in the Philosophy Department at Southern Illinois University–Edwardsville (USA). Dr. Reiheld also serves as director of the Interdisciplinary Women's Studies program at the university. She has written as a scholarly public intellectual as well as produced traditional scholarly works on food ethics, medical ethics, caregiving, and civility in a morally diverse society.

David Reynolds is a Masters student in the Centre for Sustainability and the Department of Sociology, Gender and Social Work at the University of Otago, in Dunedin, New Zealand. He has been involved in research on a number of topics within the sociology of food, including food insecurity, food waste, entomophagy, and pathways of agricultural intensification.

Bernard E. Rollin is University Distinguished Professor of Philosophy at Colorado State University (USA), where he is also professor of Animal Sciences, professor of Biomedical Science, and University Bioethicist. He is a pioneer in animal ethics and the author of twenty books.

Mindi Schneider is an assistant professor of Agrarian, Food and Environmental Studies at the International Institute of Social Studies (ISS), in The Hague, Netherlands. Her research centers on global agrifood politics, agrarian and environmental transformation in contemporary China, and capitalist natures more broadly. She holds a PhD in development sociology from Cornell University.

Graeme Sherriff is a research fellow and associate director of the Sustainable Housing and Urban Studies Unit (SHUSU) at the University of Salford, UK. His research is focused on social science aspects of environmental sustainability, including urban food, energy use in the built environment, fuel poverty, active travel, and sustainable transport.

Helena Siipi works as a collegium researcher at the Turku Institute for Advanced Studies and the Philosophy unit, University of Turku, Finland. Her research interests include ethics of food, environmental philosophy, and ethics of new biotechnologies.

Robert A. Skipper, Jr. is a professor in the Department of Philosophy at the University of Cincinnati (USA). He works mainly in philosophy of biology.

Karyn Stein is a PhD student at the University of Otago, in Dunedin, New Zealand. She worked with Indigenous organizations and communities for five years in Latin America (Belize and Guatemala) on projects related to sustainable development and human rights.

Ileana F. Szymanski is an associate professor of philosophy at the University of Scranton (Scranton, Pennsylvania, USA). Her most current work bridges the areas of philosophy of food and ancient philosophy. She has also worked on feminist philosophy and Kierkegaard's *Fear and Trembling*.

Chiara Testino is a research fellow in political philosophy at the University of Pavia (Italy) on a project entitled "Feeding Respect." She has been a visiting scholar at San Diego State University (USA). Her research interests include public reason and public justification, toleration and respect, and minority and group rights. Her most recent articles have appeared in *Politeia, Politics in Central Europe*, and *Ragion Pratica*. She has written a monograph on public reasons and justification.

Paul B. Thompson holds the W. K. Kellogg Chair in Agricultural, Food and Community Ethics at Michigan State University (USA). His most recent book is *From Field to Fork: Food Ethics for Everyone*, published by Oxford University Press in 2015.

John Vandermeer is Asa Grey Distinguished University Professor of Ecology and Evolutionary Biology, University of Michigan. Vandermeer has been involved in questions of biodiversity conservation in agricultural landscapes for the past several decades and has written extensively on the subject, including six books and many publications. His work currently is on the coffee agroecosystem in the American tropics, especially with regard to the ecosystem services provided by biodiversity.

Caleb Ward is an instructor and PhD student in philosophy at Stony Brook University (State University of New York, USA). He is editor of *Global Food, Global Justice: Essays on Eating under Globalization* (with Mary C. Rawlinson, 2015). His current work deals with feminist ethics, sexual ethics, and the environment.

Ian Werkheiser is an assistant professor in the Department of Philosophy at University of Texas Rio Grande Valley (USA). He works on issues in environmental justice and food justice, social epistemology, and social and political philosophy. His research and activism focus on marginalized or oppressed communities' responses to problems in their environment and food systems.

Kyle Powys Whyte holds the Timnick Chair in the Humanities and is an associate professor of philosophy and community sustainability at Michigan State University. Kyle's primary research addresses moral and political issues concerning climate policy and Indigenous peoples and the ethics of cooperative relationships between Indigenous peoples and climate science organizations. He is an enrolled member of the Citizen Potawatomi Nation.

Federico Zuolo is Alexander von Humboldt Foundation Senior Research Fellow at the Freie University of Berlin and University of Hamburg (Germany). He has been visiting scholar at the Universities of Cambridge (UK) and Pompeu Fabra (Barcelona, Spain). His research focuses on issues of animal ethics, disagreement, toleration, respect, and the treatment of minorities. He has published several papers in such journals as the *Journal of Social Philosophy, Journal of Applied Philosophy, European Journal of Political Theory, Philosophical Papers*, and *Les Atelier de L'Ethique/The Ethics Forum*.

INTRODUCTION

Mary C. Rawlinson

> *The spirit of pride in community and of cooperation in the work of farming is what made Freetown a very wonderful place to grow up in. . . . The farm was demanding, but everyone shared in the work – tending the animals, gardening, harvesting, preserving the harvest, and, every day, preparing delicious foods that seemed to celebrate the good things of the season. . . . Over the years since I left home and lived in different cities, I have kept thinking about the people I grew up with and about our way of life. Whenever I go back . . . I realize how much the bond that held us had to do with food.*
> —Edna Lewis, *The Taste of Country Cooking*, xx–xxi

For the most part, philosophers have not paid much attention to food. Beyond a concern with temperance or moderation that remains relevant today in the epoch of the supersized soda, philosophers have remained mostly silent on the knowledges and practices embedded in food, preferring to characterize the human by rational agency, rather than by the need to eat, even though humans, unlike other animals, are not determined in their eating habits by the *differentiae* of tooth and claw, but face eating as an ethical challenge. Philosophy has not made a human's dependency for his sustenance on other living beings, plants and animals, central to human identity, nor has it included the labor of producing and serving food among the privileged activities of reason.

In the last thirty years interest in food and food ethics has mushroomed. Malnutrition, both undernutrition and a burgeoning global obesity epidemic, as well as environmental damage and social dislocation related to agribusiness and processed food, have emerged as pressing public concerns. This volume not only addresses these timely issues, but also the necessity of situating them within a new conceptual frame. Though a few authors, like the philosopher Lisa Heldke and the anthropologist Penny van Esterik, approached food from the beginning as a network of social relations,[1] the discourse of food ethics regularly fails to interrogate the definition of food as a commodity, at the same time that it focuses narrowly on the ethics of individual choice or apparent conflicts between liberty and state paternalism. Given global distribution systems and marketing forces, however, food choice is often severely limited.[2] Individual choices occur in a specific culture of possibilities that makes healthy eating difficult or impossible. Centering food ethics on individual choice ignores the structural determinants of what and how we eat and defers the necessity of structural change. A single mother working a low-wage job with several children to feed will not find it easy to provide healthy home cooking. At the same time, the state is already extensively involved in determining what and how people eat. Globally, food policy favors transnational actors over local, indigenous farmers, and many states, and the US in particular, collaborate with global agribusiness, through both subsidies and "development" projects. State policies to promote healthy eating would be a different, but not new, incursion into food choice.

The current volume addresses these issues of liberty, food choice, and public policy, but it situates them within the larger horizons of, on the one hand, a phenomenology of food, and, on the other, the question of food justice. Discussions in food ethics need to be informed by a robust account of the role of food in constituting and sustaining both identity and community. Lévi-Strauss identifies cooking as the transformative act that inaugurates culture, as well as an infrastructure necessary to sustain social bonds.[3] Further, the historian Massimo Montanari argues that,

> Like spoken language, the food system contains and conveys the culture of the practitioner; it is the repository of traditions and of collective identity, to be sure, but also the first way of entering into contact with a different culture.
>
> (2006: 133)

Before and in spite of its transformation into a commodity, food, as well as the labor required to produce and serve it, provides the original embodiment of personal and cultural identity. It combines, as Montanari suggests, an infrastructure of singularity or identity with the possibility of cosmopolitanism and cultural exchange. The first section of this volume develops an account of the experience of food and of its role in sustaining both singularity and solidarity. From multiple perspectives – social relations, differentiated bodies, language, technology – these essays demonstrate the necessity of taking account of food in any account of human identity and agency.

The second section of the volume takes up this theme in relation to sexual difference and the gender division of labor. As these essays demonstrate, the identities of sexual difference, masculinity and femininity, are constituted in part in relation to food, and every relation to food is marked by sexual difference.[4] This section also makes visible the invisibility of women's labor under global capital. Women's knowledge and experience gained in the long history of feeding their men and children remains largely unarticulated in the discourse of food ethics. Food ethics ought not to ignore it, as the history and experience of the home cook may provide not only a healthier way of eating, but also important evidence for philosophy and new exemplars for ethics.

The third section of the volume continues to explore food as an infrastructure of community and identity by analyzing the relationships between food and cultural diversity. The essays demonstrate the need in pluralistic societies to take cultural diversity into account and the way in which dietary pluralism may challenge cultural norms, community standards, or public policy.

Sections four through six of the volume advance contemporary discussion in food ethics by providing new analyses of its three major issues. The essays in section four address the limits and scope of individual choice in relation to state policy and the structural determinants of choice. Section five explores the structural effects on the environment, including the social environment, of how we eat. These essays make clear the implication of culinary practices in environmental injustice. The authors in section six debate the question of the ethics of eating other animals. This is, perhaps, the most contentious section of the volume. The authors stake out positions ranging from several reluctant considerations of the possibility of a humane animal agriculture to an uncompromising call for veganism as an ethical imperative.

The final section of the volume includes essays that articulate a concept of food justice, both from a theoretical perspective and through the analysis of case studies. The section begins with a study of the Balinese *subak* or water irrigation societies that are responsible for maintaining the vitality of the famous Balinese rice terraces through the intelligent management of water. This agricultural formation perfectly illustrates Plato's idea of justice: justice exists in a complex whole when all of its parts are playing their proper role or "minding their own business" (Plato 1935: Book IV, l. 433a).[5] The *subak*, as the authors indicate, is much more than an agricultural guild, as it also intersects with and participates in political and religious practices and authorities.

> Rather than "simply" a traditional way of growing rice, the subak system incorporated a whole range of concepts and relationships, summarized into what the Balinese call *tri hita karana* – the three sources of goodness, understood as harmonious relationships between humans and the spiritual realms (*parhyangan*), between humans and other humans, and between humans and nature (*palemahan*).
>
> (Hilde et al. 2016: 332)

Like the essays in this section, the *subak* illustrates how justice requires respect for the role of food in establishing and sustaining identity and community, respect for the labor that produces and serves food, respect for the earth and climate on which all life depends, and respect for other animals. In developed countries under global agribusiness, the means by which food is produced are not only invisible, but they are also actively hidden.[6] The consumer does not see the suffering of the cattle in the package of shrink-wrapped beef and takes for granted the privilege of being served by a fast-food worker. This culture of possibilities makes it difficult to take responsibility for how one eats and to show the required respect for the others – other humans, other animals, the environment – implicated in the infrastructures of food.

The example of the *subak*, then, also teaches how important it is in food ethics, or in any ethics or philosophy, to approach another culture with an attentive ear and with the expectation that it might embody knowledges and practices that are not already anticipated by globalization or Western reason. Discussions of "development" often proceed without questioning whether the transfer of Western technologies to other countries is an unalloyed good and as if the indigenous cultures did not provide their own ideas, solutions, and ethical figures. Clearly, a culture whose eating habits have produced an obesity epidemic, food insecurity, labor injustice, degradation of the environment, and loss of biodiversity, as well as contributing significantly to catastrophic climate change, might have something to learn from the *subak*. This essay, like so many in the volume, demonstrates the need for structural change, not only in what and how humans eat, but also in the disposition of power and decision-making under global capital.

The epigraph of this introduction is taken from *A Taste of Country Cooking* (2015), by Edna Lewis, one of America's most famous home cooks and a descendant of emancipated slaves. Her book conveys the role in her community played by farming and cooking in establishing both personal dignity and solidarity with others. Thinking ethically about food requires an acknowledgement of the injustices of the current infrastructures of gender and race. It requires attention to the environmental injustice in the effects of global food on the climate and in the distribution of toxic waste. Thinking ethically about food requires an admission of the ethical claims of other animals, claims that have the most purchase on the most privileged, who, at the very least, must eat less meat. Thinking ethically about food requires respect for indigenous populations and a critical attitude toward development policies that would dispossess them of their knowledges and practices, as well as their land. It requires a receptivity to indigenous knowledges and practices that may provide a field of discovery for new universals in food ethics. Most importantly, as in this volume and Miss Edna's cookbook, debates in food ethics need to be situated between, on the one hand, an appreciation of food as an infrastructure of singularity and solidarity, and, on the other, a reciprocating respect for the labor and life on which the production of food depends. To whatever extent these essays contest the same terrain – and they do – still, they all advance the ethical claim that the privilege of being served ought never to be taken for granted.

Notes

1 See, e.g., Curtin and Heldke (1992); see, also, Heldke (2003). Additionally, see, e.g., Counihan and van Esterik (1997). See, also, van Esterik (2008).
2 See Nestle (2007).
3 See, e.g., Lévi-Strauss (1978), part seven, section 2.
4 Any thorough analysis of food and gender would need to take account of the significant differences in the experiences of heterosexual and same-sexed households. It should also avoid taking the nuclear family as normative for any food community.
5 Plato envisions a state committed to educating all its citizens, male and female, so that they may flourish according to their talents and capacities – something that cannot be deduced from a person's sex   for the benefit of each and all.
6 On US "ag-gag" laws, see Landfried (2013).

References

Counihan, C. and P. van Esterik. (1997) *Food and Culture*, New York: Routledge.
Curtin, D. W. and L. Heldke. (1992) *Cooking, Eating, Thinking: A Transformational Philosophy of Food*, Bloomington, IN: Indiana University Press.
van Esterik, P. (2008) *Food Culture in Southeast Asia*, Westport, CT: Greenwood Press.
Heldke, L. (2003) *Exotic Appetites: Ruminations of a Food Adventurer*, New York: Routledge.
Hilde, T. C., M. R. G. Regan, and W. Dharmiasih. (2016) "Saving a Dynamic System: Sustainable Adaptation and the Balinese Subak," in M. C. Rawlinson and C. Ward (eds.), *Routledge Handbook of Food Ethics*, New York and Abingdon: Routledge, pp. 331–343.
Landfried, J. (2013) "Bound and Gagged: Potential First Amendment Challenges to 'Ag-Gag' Laws," *Duke Environmental Law & Policy Forum* 23(2): 377–403.
Lévi-Strauss, C. (1978) "A Short Treatise on Culinary Anthropology," in *The Origin of Table Manners*, trans. by J. Weightman and D. Weightman, vol. 3 of *Introduction to a Science of Mythology*, New York: Harper Colophon Books, pp. 471–495.
Lewis, E. (2015) *A Taste of Country Cooking*, New York: Knopf.
Montanari, M. (2006) *Food Is Culture*, New York: Columbia University Press.
Nestle, M. (2007) *Food Politics: How the Food Industry Influences Nutrition and Health*, Berkeley: University of California Press.
Plato. (1935) *Republic*, trans. by Paul Shorey, Cambridge: Harvard University Press.

PART I
The phenomenology of food

1

WHAT IS FOOD?

Networks, not commodities

Ileana F. Szymanski

This study aims at providing an alternative avenue for our critical evaluation of moral actions with respect to food. It is based on a metaphysical account of food that takes it to be not a commodity but, rather, an active and multi-directional network.

Food is present in many aspects of our lives. Perhaps the first thing that comes to mind when we try to describe food is that it is what sustains us physically to go about our activities. Beyond this role, food is also in many ways a topic of national and international political debate. It is the lifeline of restaurants, chefs, waiters, food critics, farmers, supermarkets, and other food outlets, as well as that of cooking schools, food scientists, institutes of agricultural policy, many health institutions, and health professionals ranging from physicians and nutritionists to dieticians and counselors. Food is also a stronghold of practices that reaffirm and showcase the identities of specific cultures, religions, ethnicities, and other groups. It gives power to those who can prepare it skillfully; it also gives power to those who eat it or refuse to do so for a variety of reasons, such as political protesting, revenge, health, and abstinence. It is the subject of advertisements, films, television shows, photographs, paintings, and other media; it is an object of private and public trade and consumption. Food can be a lifeline, or a road to debt, illness, poverty, and hunger. It can be divisive of families and friendships; it can be the foothold of exploitation, extortion, and oppression of countless human and animal lives, or it can be their redemption.

The quasi-omnipresence of food in people's lives would have us believe that its paramount role is reinforced by a strong account of what food *is*, i.e., a strong metaphysics of food. However, this is not the case even though it seems that it should be. A generally accepted account of food is that it is what people eat. There are at least three significant problems with this account. The first is its centeredness on humans; the second is its emphasis on food as a thing, i.e., as radically separate and different from the person who eats it; the third (a consequence of the second) is its emphasis on food as food *items*, thus preventing a clear understanding of food beyond its role in feeding.

It is possible to think that the term "food" is human-centered because there is another term to describe animal food, namely, "feed." While this is true in many cases (e.g., when we speak of cattle feed and chicken feed, etc.) it is not always the case: the terms "dog food" and "cat food" are two salient examples. Perhaps we are comfortable with the category "dog food" (or any other type of pet food) and not "cattle food" because we ascribe human-like qualities to companion animals. Or perhaps it is because those companion animals are kept mostly in a human home, and, therefore, we may be inclined to think that their eating is vastly different from that of other animals, many of whom humans (and our pets) also eat. There is, thus, a gradation of species (strongly influenced by their domestication and our particular appreciation of them) implicated in our understanding of food that can be used to justify our turning a blind eye to the suffering of many animals raised for consumption.[1]

When food is viewed as a *thing*, i.e., a commodity, it becomes confusing to claim that at the same time, as it is commonly said, "we are what we eat." Personal identity, indeed, is not reducible to things such as the items we consume; nevertheless, our identity is greatly affected by the processes that facilitate our eating what we eat (as well as when, where, how, and at what cost), and by the people, institutions, animals, products, and living conditions that enact, interrupt, alter, diversify, or stop those processes. The concept of food exceeds the limits of a commodity. The account of food as a commodity, while not patently false (we do indeed buy and sell food), is nevertheless reductive of what food *is*, because, on its own, it is unable to explain why food, beyond the necessity of feeding our physical bodies, is central in our lives and our development.

Underlying the above-mentioned problems is a metaphysical architecture that categorizes eater and eaten as separate and mostly unrelated entities: one is a person, the other a thing; one is rational, the other is not; one is special and unique, the other is repeatable and easily substituted by another of its kind. The only link between these entities is the activity of eating (and, perhaps, the preparation towards eating), which is impermanent, and not always significant for the subjects involved. In my view, this metaphysics does not address the richness of the relationships that join eater and eaten and, most importantly, it ignores that the eaten is not primarily a *thing*. It is rather an active and multi-directional *network* of forces, events, institutions, etc. It also ignores the relationships that, while being about food, do not always or primarily involve the act of eating.

In his article "Food and Memory," Jon D. Holtzman (2006: 364) tells us, "food – like the family, gender, or religion – must be understood as a cultural construct in which categories rooted in Euro-American experience may prove inadequate." These categories seem to be those responding to a binary logic of domination that finds its home in a substance-based metaphysics, where there is a sharp divide amongst entities based on the properties of their substance (person/thing, man/woman, native/foreign, culture/nature, etc.). The tradition of this kind of metaphysics is long and tortuous, and it has been challenged many a time. For example, in his work "Convivialism: A Philosophical Manifesto," Raymond Boisvert (2010) proposes a theoretical framework for reinterpreting Western philosophy (particularly modern metaphysics)[2] through the use of the preposition "with." His account is based on William James and Michel Serres, who propose a "rearranging" of philosophy and the categories it uses to explain the world through this very focus. Boisvert believes that in the area of metaphysics, if philosophy were to include the use of the particle "with" in its analyses of reality (that is to say, if it were to focus on the connections between entities as opposed to their separateness and autonomy), the examination of existence would move from being dominated by the category of autonomy into the category of *convivialism*, i.e., "accepting an orientation built around the slogan 'to be is to always be with'" (2010: 60).

This approach to convivialism fuels a metaphysical analysis sharply focused on food, and a re-evaluation of specific categories that we use to address issues surrounding this topic. In *I Eat, Therefore I Think: Food and Philosophy*, Boisvert (2014) uses a metaphysical approach to reconsider the notion of "para-site": "It literally means the one who eats [*sitos*] next to [*para*] another." A "parasite" could then be considered a "tablemate," a "co-eater," even a "companion" (2014: 45). The nature of the parasite is, thus, to be with others – this is what its being is. It can be adopted as a "prototypical metaphysical figure" (2014: 50) that shows us that all beings are, at their very core, relational. When we allow for the intromission of another in our lives, there is potential for harmony: "A dinner table with no new guests is a safe place. It is also the place for redundancy and stagnation. The most vibrant system is hospitable to parasites" (2014: 51).

Boisvert's original idea about metaphysics is highlighted by Lisa Heldke in her article "An Alternative Ontology of Food: Beyond Meataphysics" (2012). Based on the work of Boisvert and Kelly Oliver, Heldke suggests, "we root our ethical decisions about our food *in* the tangle of relationships that, together, bring foodstuffs into existence" (2012: 79). She develops the metaphor of a *conceptual barn* where many different entities live under the same roof based on multiple relationships. The conceptual barn highlights that the decisions we make about what to eat (these being grounded on considerations beyond the biological categories in which we place different kinds of food, e.g., animal/not animal) are interconnected: "all the things we eat are the products of multiple relationships" (2012: 81).

In Heldke's view, a metaphysics based on relationships works particularly well with food:

> [T]o *be* food is to be (defined as) something that can be eaten by something else, and eating is, of course, a relationship. But the relational character of food extends far beyond the stage at which it is actually consumed. To *become* food – to be rendered edible, palatable, delicious – means that a living thing has been part of scores of relationships, both natural and cultural: with the soil in which a plant is grown and the sun and rain that enables its growth; with the factory workers who process a raw material . . . with the heat and the metal pan that turn an ingredient into a "dish" in someone's home.
>
> (2012: 82)

These relationships form the basis of Heldke's alternative ethical approach to food issues: "When it comes to making moral decisions about whether or not to purchase and eat some particular food, all of these 'withs' are (at least potentially) relevant, and all are operating in relation to each other" (2012: 84). The relationships that she considers are not only amongst eaters, but also amongst eaters and the food they eat, and those people, institutions, parts of environment, etc., that make that food possible. In "Food Politics, Political Food" (1992), Heldke focuses on the self as relational to draw attention to our connections with food. She develops an ontology of the self that she calls the "Coresponsible Option" (1992: 311). This ontology of the self includes awareness of the relationships that humans form not only with other humans "but also with other animals, plants, soil, air, and water" (1992: 314).

In Heldke's Coresponsible Option theory it is emphasized that regardless of the challenges that accompany the relationships with humans, non-human animals, and the environment (e.g., their asymmetry, the fact that it may make us uncomfortable to know that we are complicit in the suffering of others, etc.) it is clear that being a part of those relationships is not a matter of choice: "it is not a matter of *deciding* to become involved with others' lives, but of recognizing the way in which I am inevitably a part of them – and of understanding how their problems are also my own" (1992: 319). According to Heldke, "[t]he interrelations in which food involves us provide powerful examples of the fact that our relations to others are not optional" (1992: 320). The point is underscored once more in her conclusion:

> a food-focused coresponsible model for action challenges me to act in ways that will illuminate rather than mystify my relationality, that will highlight the many ways in which those relations involve food, and that will work toward the elimination of the pathological asymmetry that characterizes many of those relations.
>
> (1992: 322)

Heldke's Coresponsible Option is very convincing. She is able to illuminate our inextricable link to others and to food. Boisvert's work goes in tandem with this and provides further support to the idea that it is not only not optional to "be with" others but, also, being with others is a source of vitality and harmony. Much like these two projects, my proposal underscores a connection between metaphysics, ethics, and politics. There are, however, two key aspects that differentiate my view.

First, I am focusing on the metaphysics of food as opposed to making a larger metaphysical claim about other aspects of reality that can also be seen as relational. Second, I bring food and not the eater or even the activity of eating into the center of my discussion. My claim is that food can be understood in two ways: food *items* are tokens of a food insofar as it is a larger *network* of relationships (perhaps akin to Heldke's "conceptual barn"). Conceived in this theoretical framework, food includes acts of not eating, both as the rejection of food and as actions existing outside of the sphere of ingestion or digestion (e.g., cultural heritage preservation); national and international trading policies; animal husbandry methodologies; the ethical treatment of animals, farm workers, and their surrounding communities; the environmental impact of growing certain kinds of foods using specific agricultural technologies; practices of disposing of food items, etc. Conceiving of food as having two related meanings offers clarity in that (a) food is sometimes a commodity and, at the same time, a marker of personal identity of the human eater; (b) the same process of carving our personal identities can occur when food items are not present (even if these are seen as more than just commodities); and (c) this provides yet another avenue for moral agents to consider the relationships of which they are already a part, and to which they need to offer an ethical response. In the case of Heldke, the ethical responses that she is looking to examine are those that answer the question, "How are we to eat?" (2012: 69). I wish to offer an approach that helps answer those questions and others, such as, who do I become when I eat in such-and-such way? What vision of the world do I perpetuate because of my actions? What use do I make of the democratic means available to me to create a vision of the world where my thoughts and actions cohere?

It may be surprising that I have chosen to conceive of food using the trope of an active, multidirectional *network*. I do not mean to be clever or to overcomplicate things. I rather see the need to create a new term to express my ideas. Much like Judith Butler,

> [i]t's not that I'm in favor of difficulty for difficulty's sake; it's that I think there is a lot in ordinary language and in received grammar that constrains our thinking . . . and that I'm not sure we're going to be able to struggle effectively against those constraints or work within them in a productive way unless we see the ways in which grammar is both producing and constraining our sense of what the world is.
>
> (2004: 327–328)

When privilege allows us to think about food as a commodity, then moral responsibility is eschewed; suffering ceases to be palpable; injustice seems illusory. The language of commoditization allows us to depersonalize our relationship to food; it paints a landscape where food items are static, replaceable, and the product of some process of mechanized activity that we imagine to be aseptic, regulated, and scientific. Our actions with respect to food (how we grow it, buy it, dispose of it, eat it, ban it, promote it, etc.), thus, are many times the result of an uncritical and indifferent thought process.

With the advent of information technologies and the relative abundance (compared to the past forty years or so) of books, academic and popular articles, films, undercover video footage, television shows, pamphlets, etc., that inform consumers about the physical, ethical, and political dangers that ensue in the status quo of food in the world, it is astonishing that a change towards a more responsible way of interacting with food has not been adopted more decisively by consumers. It thus seems that abundant information about the effects of our decisions is not the solution for change towards the better. The types of media used to disseminate the information in question, and the frequency of dissemination, also do not seem to be the problem.

When food is seen exclusively as a commodity, moral obligations towards the different parts of the food system are, at best, relegated to being optional and, at worst, not even a part of the landscape of our interactions. This is plain when our thoughts about food and our behavior towards it are not coherently connected. Consider the following: (1) Loving animals and wishing to protect them, some people experience feelings of compassion when confronted with information about animal abuse; however, this information does not prevent them from eating meat from animals farmed in CAFOs, whose lives are the very expression of the suffering these people perceive as abominable; (2) Advocating verbally for the fundamental dignity of people does not seem to prevent some from purchasing products from companies with documented records of poor working conditions; (3) Claims expressing concern about personal health do not seem to illuminate how people's diets (usually based on aesthetic preferences rather than nutritional ones) connect them to unnecessary health risks that increase taxation and debt in their community, and how those same choices are examples of selfish and careless life practices.

When a moral agent faces conflicts such as the ones mentioned above, it is evident that thoughts and actions about food do not always dovetail. The reason for this is that those actions are strongly influenced by an understanding of food as a commodity, which does not address, but rather reduces, the richness of what food is. In highlighting a much richer understanding of food (namely, food conceived as an active, multi-directional network), we open alternative avenues of critical examination to those willing to change their relationship to food in a more responsible way. Also, awareness about the responsibilities that already exist in our relationship with food is underscored, as is the process of reciprocal shaping that exists between food and those who engage with it in a variety of ways.

I conceive of a network as a confluence of several "points," each of which can be an event, a person, a trend, a community, an institution, a practice, a memory, an artifact, a story, a commodity, a space, a living being, etc. The points have a relationship to each other, although not all points have to be necessarily related to all others in the same way or in the same direction. A community is a network of many points, connected in many different directions: the environment; the living beings that inhabit it; the institutions that govern their practices; the cultural artifacts they produce, reproduce, and record; the practices they encourage and discourage, etc.

The behavior of one of the points in the network can have an effect of varying degrees on other points. In a community, the environment shapes its inhabitants, and the inhabitants shape the environment; cultural artifacts shape those who created them and also the environment; institutions shape living beings and their artifacts, and, as a consequence, environments and institutions morph, are created, or cease to exist based on similar relationships. The behavior of one point produces an effect on all others.

What I call food is this very kind of network. It is not only part of a network as one of its points; it is a network unto itself. Food items are part of this network. Other parts include, to name a few, animals and humans who eat food items, who refuse to eat them, and who cannot eat them; inanimate objects, animals (and, yes, in some cases, humans) who are used as food items; the practice of agriculture; the political institutions at local and global levels that regulate the practice of agriculture; the academic area of food science; the religious institutions and practices that regulate the preparation and consumption of food items; the economic structures of global and local food markets; advertising and media; professionals and institutions regulating the relationship of food and health; cultural practices about the acquisition, preparation, consumption, and disposal of food items, as well as their preservation and transmission; international organizations that oversee food aid. All of these are the participants of the network, and they include past, present, and, in some cases, also future participants (e.g., when we consider the future environmental impact of specific agricultural practices).

All of the above points of the network *are* food or, in other words, they are participants in the network of food. This means that to be *in* the network is to be the network – in other words, there is no network outside of the points, and the points achieve their full significance when seen in their mutual connection. The relationship between the points of the network and the network itself is one of active and multiple directions. Not one of the points ever remains static and unchanging: food items rot and become stale; species become extinct; varieties of vegetables and other agricultural products get introduced or die out; cultural practices are modified; religions fragment into sects; rules and their applications get diluted or strengthened; crops fail or succeed; companies cease to exist, or they are created, or they are sold; the environment is polluted, or it is improved, or it is modified for specific purposes; regulatory bodies develop more or less of a foothold in society; advocacy groups arise or disperse, etc. Each one of these points in the network affects the others, and further variation of relationships is being constantly generated. If the points of the network are not static, then the network itself is also not static; as a result of the many variables and their volatility, there is a certain degree of unpredictability in the network. When we conceive of our moral response to food, we benefit from framing our actions in this changing landscape because the widespread consequences of our practices become more palpable.

My preference that the name *food* should apply to the network as opposed to only the food items within the network expresses my concern with the idea that food items owe their identity to other points in the network. Indeed, food items are not a natural kind; nothing just *happens to be* food. Food items are taken from the world and chosen as something to be eaten, and, thus, they are made into food items. Food is *made to be* an object of consumption, trade, affection, oppression, etc. Food is made to be what it is by those who eat it, trade it, exchange it, gift it, reject it, etc., and by the policies and mechanisms that underlie and oversee those events, be they social, political, ethical, aesthetic, etc. Whatever items fall into the category of food, they are there because they have been brought into it. Thus, we can identify agency on the part of all whose lives intersect food in different ways; this agency provides food with some of its identity. It is evident that not everyone eats the same things, and that not everyone considers certain items to be edible. Indeed, not everything that is considered food by specific groups or individuals needs to be nutritious, or have caloric value, or be healthy, or be natural.[3] A few examples of foodstuffs that are not always accepted as food are insects, junk food, animal flesh, meal-replacement bars and shakes, and artificially produced food substitutes (e.g., "fake" dairy products, "lab-grown" meat, etc.). The participants of the network collaborate in carving the identity of such items by making them into "food," and, as will be shown below, this relationship is reciprocal, and food items (as well as other points in the network of food) help our identities develop.

At the beginning of this article it was mentioned that a generally accepted account of food is that it is what we eat. From this perspective, there is no eating unless there are food items to be consumed. The reverse, however, need not be true. Food items may exist, but eating does not have to ensue. Indeed, there are phenomena in the network of food whose existence depends on the very absence of food items, and this absence is as powerful (and sometimes even more powerful) than the actual presence of food items.

Where hunger exists (that is, where food items are scarce or not plainly present), food as a network is still present and palpable in its *failure* to deliver a basic human need. It is also present in the memories of items that do not exist anymore (e.g., extinct varieties of fruits and vegetables; items not produced anymore because of the closure of a company, or because the way to obtain such products was harmful); in their companion items (e.g., their packaging, transportation, and preservation technologies, the instruments used to serve them, etc.); in their artistic representations; in their representatives, advocates, detractors, etc. Food items need not be abundant for the continuous activity of food as a network. Eating does not need to occur frequently or at all for food as a network to unfold at least partially. The following example will help clarify what I mean.

In the Terezin World War II concentration camp, some women prisoners engaged in what they called "cooking with the mouth": after long days of work they would gather at night to discuss recipes; they had no ingredients, no way of cooking, perhaps not even the hope of one day cooking again, and they were very hungry. Despite all of this, they continued cooking by verbalizing the recipes, writing them down wherever and whenever they could, thus reaffirming their identity as cooks, as members of a family, as members of a religion, as born in a certain region where a specific dish is done in a certain way, as preservers of traditions, as story-tellers, etc. (Szymanski 2014).[4] In the absence of food items and the activity of eating them, food still allowed those women to develop a sense of self. If we are what we eat, we also are what we do not eat. This is not a word game. The absence of edible items may allow for the reaffirming of personal identity, as it did for those women in Terezin. We are what we eat only if "what we eat" really means "what we eat even when we are not eating it." The statement should not be read as a contradiction: personal identity is underscored, carved, and molded because of many factors, among them, what, why, where, and how we do *not* eat. The refusal of food is what makes a hunger-striker; it is what can make someone a victim of suicide; it is what can cancel, modify, and challenge a marker such as *prisoner*, and exchange it for *survivor, cook, creator, archivist*, etc.

Indeed, we speak of food as possessing certain qualities or properties with which we connect as both agents and patients. The network of food does something to us as much as we do something to it, and this reciprocal affection goes beyond physical and chemical changes in the food consumed and in the body of the eater. To be what one eats implies not only that the nutrients (or lack thereof) of a foodstuff allow one's body to extract energy and vital substance in order to live. To be what one eats implies, further, that a specific identity is carved for the eater: vegan, vegetarian, pescatarian, lacto-ovo vegetarian, carnivore, omnivore. It implies also that one may be, perhaps, a discerning eater, allergic to certain things, and observant of certain rules, be these of etiquette, law, morality, or religion – even on pain of death. That is to say, the identity we seek to preserve by eating can also be preserved by *not* eating. This point is illustrated in the story of the survival of Jonathan Safran Foer's grandmother in World War II (Foer 2009). This is the dialogue they had when she told him the story:

> "The worst it got was near the end. A lot of people died right at the end. And I didn't know if I could make it another day. A farmer, a Russian, God bless him, he saw my condition, and he went into his house and came out with a piece of meat for me."
> "He saved your life."
> "I didn't eat it."
> "You didn't eat it?"
> "It was pork, I couldn't eat pork."
> "Why?"
> "What do you mean why?"
> "What, because it wasn't kosher?"
> "Of course."
> "But not even to save your life?"
> "If nothing matters, there is nothing to save."

(16–17)

Further, to be what one is in and through food (or its absence) also implies that one's practices engage with categories such as picky, voracious, convivial, etc. And, whether one is aware of this or not, it also implies that one supports certain types of agriculture, certain living wages and conditions for farm workers and their neighbors (domestic and global), certain ecological impact on the environment (due, for example, to transportation costs, air and water pollution, etc.), certain companies that sell their products, certain methodologies and goals for science, and the politicians who stand behind the policies and procedures used to arrive at, market, and sell the final product ("food").

Food conceived as an active and multi-directional network allows us to engage with all of these issues and provide a foothold for further examination of our ethical relationship with each of them. We are already involved in these relationships expressed in the network of food; what is now required is a critical response to them. This critical response can indeed include a re-definition of food such as the one I have attempted in this project.

In 2008, Michael Pollan published in *The New York Times Magazine* a letter addressed to the President-Elect of the United States. In that letter he provides a series of recommendations. One of them is the creation of a federal definition of food. The context of this recommendation was that many items are federally counted as food – and therefore able to be purchased with food stamps and eligible for exemption of local sales tax – when they are in fact harmful to consumers. Pollan states, "We need to stop flattering nutritionally worthless food like substances by calling them "junk food" – and instead make clear that such products are not in fact food of any kind." In 2009, in his piece "Rules to Eat By," also published in *The New York Times Magazine*, Pollan revives the question of what counts as food, and he suggests that "it is not easy" to know what counts as food and what does not in an environment where the food industry makes tantalizing claims about new products.

I find Pollan's prompts to consider a new definition of food quite provocative. His strategy, as well as the present study, faces several challenges. First, searching for a federal definition of food *might* seem like a pursuit that has fewer immediate consequences for the foodscape than, say, instituting laws that would more closely regulate the food industry. In other words, it seems like a definition of food would be ineffective at producing rapid – and much-needed – change in the network of food. The second reason is that answering the question "What is food?" seems to be intuitively accessible to some individuals, and, consequently, its further consideration seems like a futile and elitist exercise. Thirdly, even when one is willing to entertain the question, this seems to be a rather unassailable topic, because its answer may be relative to an individual's culture. Moreover, it is possible that only a dominant culture's voice may be taken as representative of everyone.[5]

From this perspective, looking for a definition of food seems like an exercise in abstraction that can easily appear superfluous, presumptuous, and possibly exclusive of certain groups, whether ideological, ethnic, religious, etc. As I mentioned above, this perspective can also be applied to the appeal for a metaphysics of food. While the intention of the metaphysics I propose is to seep into the ethical deliberation of moral agents, it can nevertheless be perceived as ineffective. As I have endeavored to show, moral agents espouse an underlying commitment to some account of food that, while perhaps tacit, is there and guides our behavior in the relationships we sustain in multiple networks of food. Promoting critical awareness of the putative account of food may not be *enough* to achieve political change at a federal level, yet this does not mean that it cannot produce *any* change and, thus, there is no reason why it should not be attempted.

Pollan's suggestion is that whatever receives the name *food* should be "an edible substance [that] must contain a certain minimum ratio of micronutrients per calorie of energy" (2008). Certainly, the meanings of "edible" and "certain minimum ratio" would be subject to interpretation, and it would be fair to ask questions about the source of the funding for the science that would oversee the studies to determine it. Moreover, it would be fair to ask whether a federal definition of food is only a definition about food *items* or whether it should include (as perhaps it already, tacitly, does) aspects related to cultural preservation and development. My proposal is, in a way, modest compared to Pollan's, because the outcome he desires is very specific. I am operating on the assumption that those who will contemplate my proposal for a new metaphysics of food will consider it as yet another avenue for evaluating their individual moral behavior, and that the impact of one person's change will be reflected in and examined throughout the community – resulting, potentially, in incremental changes in ethical practices concerning food. One such outcome could be engaging with what a federal definition of food might be in the United States, and what it might be globally, as a fundamental human right.

Notes

1 In *Eating Animals* Jonathan Safran Foer (2009: 21–29) offers a compelling discussion on the special treatment of companion animals.
2 "For a variety of cultural, historical and personal reasons, Modern metaphysics, the generic description of what things are, focused on a particular starting point: self-standing, nondependent, non-needy entities....The 'with' dimension got relegated to cold storage. Relations, interconnections, conjunctions, and spatial and temporal locations were not defining ingredients of entities" (Boisvert 2010: 58).
3 In *Animal, Vegetable, Miracle*, Barbara Kingsolver recalls a touching anecdote where her husband Steven showed one of the neighborhood kids that carrots came from the earth. When other children gathered around to see, he asked if they knew other vegetables that could also be roots; their final answer was spaghetti (2007: 12).
4 The story is told in full in Cara de Silva's *In Memory's Kitchen* (1996).
5 The question remains, is it at all possible to determine what is food regardless of cultural associations? Or, more pointedly, *should* one do this? And, if one does, have we in fact erased a valuable trait of food? Moreover, what aspects about food are left out of its definition when it does not transcend the act of eating?

References

Boisvert, R. D. (2010) "Convivialism: A Philosophical Manifesto," *The Pluralist* 5(2): 57–68.
———. (2014) *I Eat, Therefore I Think: Food and Philosophy*, Lanham: Fairleigh Dickinson University Press.
de Silva, C. (1996) *In Memory's Kitchen. A Legacy from the Women of Terezin*, Lanham: Rowman & Littlefield Publishers, Inc.
Foer, J. S. (2009) *Eating Animals*, New York: Little, Brown and Company.
Heldke, L. (1992) "Food Politics, Political Food," in D. W. Curtin and L. M. Heldke (eds.), *Cooking Eating Thinking: Transformative Philosophies of Food*, Bloomington and Indianapolis: Indiana University Press, pp. 301–327.
Heldke, L. (2012) "An Alternative Ontology of Food: Beyond Meataphysics," *Radical Philosophy Review* 15(1): 67–88.
Holtzman, J. D. (2006) "Food and Memory," *Annual Review of Anthropology* 35: 361–378.
Kingsolver, B. (2007) *Animal, Vegetable, Miracle*, New York: Harper Perennial.
Pollan, M. (2008) "Farmer in Chief," viewed 31 May 2015, http://michaelpollan.com/articles-archive/farmer-in-chief/.
———. (2009) "Rules to Eat By," viewed 31 May 2015, http://michaelpollan.com/articles-archive/rules-to-eat-by/.
Salin, S. and J. Butler. (eds.) (2004) *The Judith Butler Reader*, Malden: Blackwell Publishing, Ltd.
Szymanski, I. (2014) "The Metaphysics and Ethics of Food as Activity," *Radical Philosophy Review* 17(2): 351–370.

2

INTERACTIONS BETWEEN SELF, EMBODIED IDENTITIES, AND FOOD

Considering race, class, and gender

Lisa Jean Moore and Kayla Del Biondo[1]

Unique appetites, social cravings

When organizing a social gathering in New York City in 2016, the host almost automatically sends out an email asking guests to list their allergies, dietary preferences, and restrictions.

> *So I'm a vegan who will sometimes eat eggs for protein. And, you know, Bill is in recovery so I try not to cook with alcohol, but he eats everything and he is used to it if you serve wine or beer. I think Maddie is still doing Atkins, so that might be tricky with the menu, but I'm sure you'll figure it out. And you know her son has that nut allergy.*
>
> —Response to a dinner invitation

As the above response attests, some people can be quite specific about their diets. These nutritional revelations, often couched in discourses of health and illness alongside environmental and sustainability concerns, also provide ample information about selves. Through our commonplace replies about diet, we also share intimate details of our own cultures, habits, vices, illnesses, and vulnerabilities. Furthermore, our food identifications are not stable over time but rather change with trends of food culture, migration, aging, and shifts in the marketplace. Not unsurprisingly, then, there seems to be an ever-expanding number of terms used to specify one's relationship to food, based on ingredients, food sensitivities, geographies, religions, class locations, and trends: gluten-free, lactose intolerant, free lunch, nut-free, vegetarian, vegan, lacto/ovo vegetarian, halal, kosher, pescatarian, macrobiotic, paleo, Ayurvedic, locavore, organic, free-range, artisanal, raw food, whole grain, etc.

In this article, we examine the ways in which people come to know themselves and their bodies through their patterns of dietary consumption. This intense identification with food adds depth to the statement, "you are what you eat," or "you are what you don't eat," and perhaps even "you eat what you are." As we age, humans continuously express themselves through a socially and culturally mediated relationship with food. Although we might behave as if our relationships with food are highly personal, even unique, our food practices are also deeply economically, socially, and culturally constructed. We come to know and identify ourselves as members of communities, appropriately gendered beings, citizens of nations, and ethically situated through our consumption of food and nutritional behaviors. In fact, the traffic between these ideas of individual preferences and the socialization of one's diet co-constitute our sense of being in the world.

Through a survey of the contemporary social science literature about food and identity, we explore how embodiment, race, gender, class, culture, and food movements are all factors that play a part in determining what an individual will eat, how the individual will see his or her body in the world, as well as how others will perceive him or her. We examine aspects of food and bodily identity, tracing the growth of scholarship in the phenomenology of food and investigations of linkages between food and identity formation. After a brief explanation of theories of identity based in symbolic interactionism, we present a theoretical backdrop of bodies and embodiment. Moving to the palate, we describe how this body part is not merely biologically but also *socially* mediated. We then explore contemporary empirical studies of food and current food movements and trends to see where the discussion on food and identity issues is headed, and the continuing relevance of gender, race, class, and cultural norms for the conversation.

Identities, selves, and bodies: expressions of social location

In order to understand how identity is formed, it is useful to consider the work of symbolic interactionists, a group of social scientists who argue that for humans, reality is developed in interaction with others. In opposition to a sense of the human self as a stable, essential unfolding of internal drives, George Herbert Mead (1934/1962: 164) claims that "selves can only exist in definite relation to other selves." The self emerges in this ability to incorporate the perspectives of others into one's presentation, self-concept, and performance of the self. Mead (1934/1962: 182) defined the self as "a process in which the individual is continually adjusting himself in advance to the situation to which he belongs and reacting back on it." With respect to our relationship with food, our shared essential need to eat is as common to our species as the need for shelter or water. However, we are not limited to a merely biological interpretation of dietary practices. It is perhaps more precise to say that while humans must consume food to live, their selves and identities are organized around the actual (gendered) harvesting, gathering, preparing, and eating of food, and thus we become selves through interacting with food. As food anthropologist Robin Fox writes, "All animals eat, but we are the only animal that cooks" (2002: 1). This supports the notion that humans construct identities organized around food preparation. Fox lists timing, setting, ceremonial eating, religious eating, and dieting as among the innumerable ways by which people separate themselves from others, knowingly or unknowingly, through their eating habits and customs.

Mead's contemporary, Charles Cooley (1994), coined the term *the looking-glass self* to describe a process where individuals self-regulate their own actions based on the reflective evaluations of others – in other words, we adjust our behaviors and appearances to meet what we imagine is expected. Since individuals do not exist in a vacuum, we make meaning of our lives by being socialized by and within groups. Using our bodies, including facial expressions and bodily comportment, we modify our physical appearance and affect to transmit meaning to others and in turn receive feedback about our belonging. Furthermore, one's *self* becomes knowable through how we identify – our publicly displayed *identities*. Identity is tied to some social group or social position. For example, one's identity can be that of a father, professor, or Latino. *Self* is the ability to be reflexive and look back on your own behaviors and performances. So, while an identity might be that of a middle-aged lesbian, a self involves the considerations, thinking about and mulling over of these identity positions. To treat yourself as an object means you are self-aware – "I am an Italian vegetarian" means this individual identifies with these groups and manipulates objects and symbols to signify these identifications. Just as you can manipulate, alter, reflect, and evaluate some external object or person in the world, having a self means you can manipulate, alter, or reflect and evaluate yourself as an object.

Our ability to interact in social groups and achieve desired outcomes within a specific social context depends upon the management of our bodies. One of the central themes running through Erving Goffman's (1959) work is his treatment of appearance as a central component in mundane everyday encounters among people. According to Goffman, any successful social performance hinges on expressive control to keep inconsistent moods and signs from disrupting it. In order to achieve a semblance of reality or authenticity, one must master the art of "impression management," a highly nuanced technique of constant reflexive self-examination. To prevent embarrassment and disruption in social interaction, we must learn to manage our embodied presentations of self, including its demeanor, noises, smells, and facial expressions. Eating and digesting involve minute management of bodily processes in addition to signaling membership in specific communities.

Embodiment is the quality of having a body and perceiving and being in the world through the body. The body is the medium through which we navigate the world, and it is also an entity that is invested with meaning conveying statuses, ranks, and relationships (Kosut and Moore 2010). Corporeality is not sui generis, even when bodies appear to have obdurate and consistent physical characteristics. In other words, as actual physical bodies exist, our understandings of these bodies, our interpretations and explanations of bodily processes, give meaning to their materiality. Body image is defined as a person's self-perception of their own body. Internal body image refers to the way someone feels about their body, or the way we see ourselves; this is social and psychological. External body image is how others perceive and react to our bodies; this is sociological. It is important to consider the interaction between the psychological and sociological perspectives of body image. Though these two body images are inextricably linked, a person's internal body image can be vastly different from their external body image. In other words, the way you see yourself can be incongruent with how others see and assess your body.

Among those taking up the question of bodies and knowledges as political objects is French sociologist and public intellectual Pierre Bourdieu. His notion of *habitus*, or a "structuring structure" of everyday knowledge about the world contained in habitual patterns of action is contingent on "a past which survives in the present and tends to perpetuate itself into the future by making itself present in practices structured according to its principles" (Bourdieu 1977: 82). These practices, forming dispositions and inclinations, are embodied through repetition and habit, connecting the individual to both historical and social structures. Habitus is the making of the world through bodily practice and the making of the body through worldly practice. In other words, habitus is the medium for traffic between the social environment and the embodied lived experience. Habitus is the basis for performing the self in social circumstances such as generational differences in preferences for food or cultural differences in etiquette associated with consumption. Habitus is thus a crucial medium through which social status and class position are reproduced. Class becomes embodied through the deployment of certain social markers of one's position within social structures: tastes and dispositions. One's bodily experience is thus simultaneously understood and performed through class-based cultural markers. An individual's diet, weight, table manners, and gait function as signs within a larger system of social positions. In some countries where food is scarce, being fat is sometimes envied as a sign of wealth or economic status.

Taken together, the foregoing concepts of the selves, identities, reflections, embodiment, presentation of self, impression management, and habitus enable us to see how food is integral to one's perpetual socialization as an individual and member of a collective. Our relationship with food shapes the way we look at ourselves, how our body looks and performs, and how people perceive us. We all need to eat, or as sociologist Georg Simmel put it, "Food encapsulates . . . complete universality" (Probyn 1999). While humans do prepare foods and view their bodies in differing ways, fabricating what they think are unique identities, they are in reality reproducing patterns of dietary socialization. What follows is a close examination of the linkages of food to individuality, race, class, culture, and gender.

Developing a palate

The *palate* refers to one's sense of taste, and there are variations in palates across the lifespan, among individuals, and across geographies that reveal the social bases of taste. Sometimes when sampling different foods, a palate cleanser might be used to clear the sense of taste and wipe out any remaining lingering flavors. A tradition in France is to use a sorbet as a palate cleanser between courses of an elaborate meal. Furthermore, having a good palate indicates that an individual has a refined appreciation for taste or flavor. In keeping with Bourdieu's discussion of habitus, an individual's sense of taste signals a location in a social stratification. We judge and stratify one another and ourselves by the specificity of our ability to literally taste food.

Children also have a specific type of palate – sour gummy worms, for example, are often an age-specific delicacy, and one's palate changes over one's lifespan. Literary critic Samira Kawash (2013) has coined the term *hyperpalatability* to describe the extreme yumminess that makes junk food, like candy, so irresistible. Interestingly, she writes that candy is a tricky food to describe, because it is characterized by opposites. We know that candy is not good for us (it is caloric and practically all sugar), but on the other hand, when we eat it we feel a distinct pleasure and experience old memories: "cotton candy at a state fair, the birthday party piñata, the overflowing Easter baskets and Halloween" (2013: 8). To add to the "dangers of candy" argument, Kawash makes the point that we are taught to never take candy from strangers, and to always brush our teeth after eating candy or else our teeth will rot. Clearly, candy is a contradictory treat that defines one's past and makes one worry about his or her future.

As a means of resisting the hyperpalatability of unhealthy foods, feminist geographers Hayes-Conroy and Hayes-Conroy (2008) call for a *visceral politics*, meaning that we must unravel how it is that certain people develop food preferences and tastes that might not create the best health outcomes for individuals. The researchers explore the concept of "taking back taste," and demonstrate using an experiment of grade-school-aged Australian children being taught in school to appreciate the taste of homemade jam over store-bought jam. Expanding the palate can be done by providing individuals with food choices and an explanation of why certain choices might be preferable over others.

Men eat meat, women eat salad

Men and women eat differently, and this cannot be simply explained by biological differences. For example, in the Global North, women tend to eat less and are more likely to be vegetarians or vegans. Throughout history, women have been denied food as a way of limiting their power (Lupton 1996). Women have also limited their own intake of food to conform to the ideal feminine body type: small, thin, toned yet not overwhelmingly muscular (Caplan 1997). Oppositely, men often eat more meat and are more likely to follow protein-based diets (Adams 2004; Lockie and Collie 1999: 255–273; Rogers 2008). Men are expected to be larger than women, which results in men eating greater amounts of food. Additionally, men are shown and expected to eat more meat because of what animal flesh symbolically represents. Eating meat has come to represent humans' superiority over other animals, specifically men's because of its representation as a masculine food (Adams 2004). Eating animal flesh is used in the media as a display of power over other animals, supposedly proving human strength (Fiddes 1991). Though these ideas are still perpetuated daily, new research has called them into question. Meat as a representation of masculinity, power, and strength contrasts with what meat actually does to the human body. And despite the preponderance of evidence that connects the consumption of red meat to coronary heart disease, eating meat is still dominantly considered by many a path to strength, health, and virility (Lockie and Collie 1999; Nath 2011).

Originating with prehistoric ideas of men as hunters and women as gatherers (Sobal 2005), eating habits and ideas are communicated through generations. Children often mimic the performances that adults around them find favorable, and this collective imitation continues into adulthood. Within an age group, we often mimic the performances that the people around us find favorable, and we eat accordingly. These emulations include family members and friends, and may result in generations of similar performances (Goffman 1959).

Perhaps nowhere is a strict gender divide more evident than in food advertising, which is deeply reliant upon gendered tropes to showcase its products. For example, Taco Bell claims in its latest commercial, "If you need to be told how to be a man, Taco Bell's triple steak stack isn't for you." Conversely, a Yoplait yogurt commercial from early 2012 depicts a slim woman who is able to fit into an "itsy bitsy teenie weenie yellow polka dot bikini" after eating yogurt. The presentation of self, as a normatively gendered man or woman, then involves making gender-coded food choices – yogurt for females and steak tacos for males. In addition to commercials, there are also deeply gendered television shows in mainstream American culture. The television series *Man v. Food* showcases a main protagonist, Richman, as he eats his way through gigantic, meaty meals, in speedy, competitive styles, often against opponents. Athleticism, fighting and conquering, gorging, toughness, appreciation of the female body – these are all prominent themes in the show, and they help their audience get a sense of what it means to eat "like a man" (Calvert 2014).

Statistically, women and children are most susceptible to hunger and malnourishment, so what does this say about their relationship to food? Hunger and food security have not often been considered in their gendered dimensions. Food advocates and researchers Carolyn Sachs and Anouk Patel-Campillo (2014) suggest that it is the United Nations' job to implement woman-friendly solutions. As Sachs and Patel-Campillo state, "Understanding how interlocking systems of class, race, gender, and ethnicity intersect in cross-border dynamics is essential as we attempt to address issues of food security and food sovereignty," which affirms the ongoing argument of this paper: what a person eats is always connected to how he or she identifies in regards to gender, race, etc. Furthermore, Sachs and Patel-Campillo reject the Food and Agriculture Organization's (FAO) traditional focuses when dealing with food insecurity, availability, access, utilization, and stability. Instead, they promote feminist food justice, which would involve supporting food production at multiple scales, revaluing food work that feeds families, and providing good food for all (2014). While gender often determines the accessibility of healthy food alternatives, this is also bound up with questions of economic justice. Unequal pay for equal work goes hand in hand with women's inability to put food on the table (Sachs and Patel-Campillo 2014).

Some scholars argue that access to healthy foods has less to do with gender and more to do with one's environment. Anna Kirkland, a professor of Women's Studies at the University of Michigan, describes the current environmental approach to fighting obesity, which typically consists of shutting down fast-food restaurants that serve unhealthy food, and what she calls *responsibilization*, or the notion that individuals must take care of themselves so that they do not become society's burden (Kirkland 2011). Kirkland shares British Health Secretary Alan Johnson's view – "modern life makes us overweight" – and she urges people to first seek collective solutions to the obesity epidemic. Unlike responsibilizing, this requires a closer look at the bigger social and economic factors that surround obesity. In other words, shutting down a restaurant here and there is not going to address and solve a nation's problems. To Kirkland, obesity is a purposefully hyped-up issue, whose hype hides the structural issues that need more attention. These hidden issues include poverty, lack of universal health care, and inadequate public transportation. Once solved, obesity will lessen. Clearly, the discussion over what people eat and how it affects their bodies is political as well as personal.

Cross-cultural eating: American Jews and Chinese food

How does cultural identity relate to an individual's relationship with food, eating habits, and preferences? There are deeply held, stereotypical beliefs about how an individual eats and whether or not that calls the legitimacy of their ethnic identity into question. Delicia Dunham, author of *Sistah Vegan: Black Female Vegans Speak on Food, Identity, Health, and Society*, explains how she feels conflicted in her eating style. She shares:

> Our culture . . . [is] typically far from supportive of the life we have been called to lead. So we find our vegan selves existing in a state of duality, conflicted and torn, wearing masks over our faces as we try to fit in . . .
>
> (2010: 42)

Dunham shares her alienation from some aspects of black pop culture: hip-hop lyrics often include references to fur coats and leathers, so she, as a black female, feels even "less black" being a vegan. Dunham's work calls for black vegans to let the rest of the world know that being vegan is not a "white thing" but the right thing, and that a diet consisting of soul food – a mainly flesh-food diet lacking fruits and vegetables historically associated with the African-American community – negatively affects people's health (2012: 42–46). However, to stray from a traditional soul-food diet (like Dunham) feels wrong to the majority of the African-American community. In *Black Hunger*, sociologist Doris Witt shares, "the emergence of soul food should be construed not just synchronically but also diachronically, as a part of an ongoing debate among African Americans over the appropriate food 'practices' of blackness" (2004). The word "diachronically" is significant here, and Witt uses it to argue that soul food is forever a part of black peoples' twofold history: its preparation and ingredients are partially representative of what was eaten in Africa before and during the slave trade, and these same foodstuffs were consumed by blacks living in America after their emancipation. Clearly, by this view, because veganism is both a trendy lifestyle in many predominantly white communities today and a contradiction to a historical soul-food diet, veganism challenges authentic black identity.

If being vegan is a "white thing" to many, what is the cultural identity of a Jewish person who loves Chinese food? Symbolic interaction applies to food and identity because specific foods can mean something to one culture and something completely different to another culture. In her study, food historian Hanna Miller (2006) sets out to discover when and where American Jews began eating Chinese food, and how the affinity became an aspect of Jewish identity. Miller begins by explaining how kosher foods, or foods that conform to the guidelines set out by *kashrut*, are "endlessly symbolic, representing the human relationship to God" for Jews. She then describes kashrut as an intricate set of dietary restrictions and food preparations codified in the Torah that Jews slowly drifted away from after immigrating to America. One explanation that Miller explores for the affinity of American Jews for Chinese food is historical location. American Jewish neighborhoods in New York, such as those located in the Lower East Side of Manhattan, were historically close to many cafes and restaurants. Additionally, low prices made many American Jews fond of going out to eat frequently. Furthermore, while Chinese food was consumed by members of every class, racial, and religious group, Miller claims that American Jews ate it and still eat it the most because they wanted to "identify down." This means that because Jews had a history of oppression, they inherently felt like outsiders, and wanted to participate in something that made them feel different from the rest. According to Miller, American Jews love Chinese food based on a combination of reasons related to location, economic status, and cultural desires, revealing a culturally rich and cross-pollinated Jewish identity.

Another noteworthy example of cross-cultural eating is Japanese sushi made in America. Paige Edwards, a cultural anthropologist, explores how globalization can be examined through foods. She addresses the question of how sushi, associated with Japanese cultural heritage, has become Americanized. In some cases, adding regional flair creates comfort for individuals to try different types of food. Certain rolls, like the Philadelphia roll, received their name after being created by a Japanese sushi chef who was trying to satisfy the Philadelphian taste buds by adding cream cheese. Changing the size or shape of a portion also creates more familiarity with foods. Sushi rolls are typically a lot larger in America than in Japan, and before being rolled up in seaweed and rice, fish is fried more frequently in America, too. Finally, Edwards interviews American sushi "virgins" to see what they think of the cuisine: some interviewees feel a sense of culture shock when served sushi and refuse to touch it, while others want to experience what they (wrongly) believe to be pure Japanese culture and cuisine (2012). When one culture manipulates another culture's food norms, the former culture's identity transforms the cuisine. When African Americans become vegans, Jewish Americans eat Chinese food, and Americans in general see sushi as an integral part of their diet, it becomes clear that people create an identity by participating in culturally contrasting patterns of dietary consumption.

Immigration and eating

The familiar expression "home-cooked meal" brings to mind a feeling of belongingness and peacefulness when a favorite meal is prepared and consumed in the comfort of one's own home. But when people emigrate from one country to another, cooking and serving what is, to them, a home-cooked meal is a bit harder than one would think. Psyche Williams-Forson (2014), professor of African American Studies and Women's Studies at the University of Maryland, uses participant observation, food narratives, and interviews to discover how Ghanaian immigrants strive to maintain their cultural identity amidst the diverse foodscapes of America. Williams-Forson defines foodscapes as "spaces defined by the intersections of geography, environment, ethnicity, economic status, gender, social organization, and various cultural practices . . ." and stresses how food has emotional and psychological meaning no matter where you are from and where you are immigrating. Ghanaian immigrants' tips and strategies for maintaining a Ghanaian identity through food in America include: shopping at ethnic grocery stores, substituting foods like peanut butter for fresh groundnut, and buying vegetables from discount food stores, since many immigrants do not have a farm or garden like they did in their home country. Feeling out of place because culturally symbolic foods are unavailable is a struggle for many immigrants, and the pursuit of finding substitutes or having spices shipped from home affirms the notion that food is a part of one's cultural identity.

Supporting this idea are the findings of anthropologist Teresa Mares, who studies Latino/a immigrants living in Seattle, Washington, and claims, "There is a rich tradition in the humanities and social sciences of exploring connections between food and cultural identity, especially for racial and ethnic minorities living in the United States" (2012). She defines *foodways* as "the eating habits or food practices of a community, region, or time period." Mares conducted several interviews – thirteen with people who work in food policy, and forty-six with first-generation immigrants – which led her to conclude that immigration disrupts one's foodways. Mares asked interviewees about their favorite foods and the availability of them in America and found that although only four interviewees were tending home gardens, thirty-seven had grown food before migrating to the United States. Most interviewees were not growing their own foods because of their job constraints; many worked in service-sector jobs, as domestic workers, or as day laborers in construction and landscaping projects (Mares 2012). As with the Ghanaian immigrants, this community testifies to the ways in which immigration disrupts one's foodways and, therefore, their cultural identity. This research reveals the importance of sustenance and its impact on the self.

Ethnographer Megan Carney's work examines how state practices around food affect the minds and bodies of migrants (Carney 2013). Carney spends time with twenty-five unauthorized migrant women who had spent anywhere from three months to thirty years living in the United States and who had been detained at some time in their lives for being undocumented citizens. Pilar – Carney's key informant – shares that while she was in a detention center on the border of Mexico and California for four months, the food served to her was contaminated with maggots and/or mold, or that she was not fed at all. Unfortunately, detention centers use feeding rituals as a key instrument to elicit compliance; food is a tool employed to obtain social control. Carney argues that this institutionalized abuse can lead to disordered eating for life, and that detention centers must revisit and abide by the food service standards outlined by the Immigrant Customs Enforcement (ICE) and the Department of Homeland Security (DHS). After all, access to food and water is a human right. Being unable to eat foods one is used to preparing in his or her home country, or not being able to eat substantial food in the case of detainment, robs migrants of a central part of their cultural identity. In the absence of culturally symbolic foods, immigrants find it hard to connect with their own selves (the persons they were in their home country), with others, and with their new environments.

Food and identity: singularity or pluralism?

Singularity in eating

Most humans in the Global North have a choice about what they put in their bodies once they enter adulthood, and with this choice comes a sense of individuality, power, and pride. When a teen reaches a certain age, his or her mother or father may finally give up on the "eat your vegetables" fight; however, for those young adults with disabilities, a different set of norms is followed, or even enforced. Welsh sociologist Charlotte A. Davies (2007) conducts ethnographic fieldwork in group homes and private homes with young adults with disabilities to see just how much their palate and eating choices are affected by those around them. Davies interviews young adults with learning disabilities and finds that much of what they do and do not eat can be attributed to their parents' authority – candy and cakes being the ultimate taboo. Interestingly, some parents wanted their adult son or daughter with disabilities to drink alcohol, because it is an adult drink, while other parents did not let their of-age children drink alcohol, for fear of how their children would react. Davies finds that a lot of young adults with learning disabilities eat a simplistic, restricting diet, resulting in stunted adult identities (2007). Stunted adult identities are the result of restricted eating habits because, as the aforementioned social science literature attests, what you decide to eat says a lot about who you are. Hence, when a person does not decide on his or her own what to eat, knowing oneself can be difficult, an individual's identity becomes damaged, and he or she is likely to feel powerless.

On the other hand, some people feel that their eating habits make them powerful and unique. Sociologist Joanne Finkelstein (2014: 62) writes, "The idea of self-identity is paradoxical; it supposedly encapsulates individuality, of how we feel different and separate from others, but it also inserts us into a collective identity that provides a sense of belonging." This myth of individuality applies perfectly to one's eating habits because, while a person may feel unique in his or her new eating style – becoming a vegan, for example – the person has just joined a group of people like him or her: other vegans. Furthermore, Finkelstein explains that restaurants, as businesses, must keep up with "fashion trends" in the food world to compete in the cutthroat consumer culture currently underway. Clearly, people ingest certain foods to construct what they perceive to be an individualistic identity for themselves.

Plural eating: food movements and trends

While food can be used to express or frustrate a sense of individuality, food also offers an opportunity for shared group membership through social movements. Eating has become more of a lifestyle than an inclination, particularly among those considered part of an urban hipster community. James Cronin et al. (2014), of the Department of Food Business and Development at University College Cork, have studied how hipsters – urban 20-somethings who reject parts of mainstream culture – express their identity through their food choices. The researchers found that the following themes emerged in regards to hipsters' eating behaviors: (1) de-commodification practices, (2) brand choices and brand avoidances, (3) vegetarian or vegan choices. In detail, de-commodification practices refer to stripping corporate food of its labels and packaging, so that you cannot see the brand or price; but rather, a simple box or jar of food. Next, hipsters practiced brand avoidances because they felt that popular global brands and businesses did not serve their community, especially those corporations who mass-produced ready-to-eat meals which involved no true cooking or preparation. Finally, vegan and vegetarian choices were frequent among the hipster community because hipsters sought to reject mainstream tastes – tastes they feel the meat industry successfully trained consumers to have (2012). Interestingly, the researchers found that if a hipster did buy something cheap, of low quality, and/or name-brand, they ripped the label off or added ingredients from farmer's markets to make it their own. Maintaining a sense of DIY, or "do it yourself," culture communicates people's distaste for mass-produced products, and their desire to bring creativity and individuality back into the kitchen.

More often than not, when transgressive subcultures, such as vegan hipsters, emerge, the biggest concern is the cooptation of their mission. Sociologist Alison Alkon (2014) states that a major struggle shared by many food justice movements involves making sure neoliberal and capitalist motives do not arise, take over, or dilute the strength of movements resistant to corporate food ownership. In other words, leaders of food justice movements must make sure that small-scale projects with good intentions do not become large-scale projects with capitalistic motives. Alkon writes, "Supporters of local/organic food mainly seek to create and support market-based alternative food systems, and community food security and food justice activists work to make these alternatives accessible to low-income communities and communities of color," but she also discloses that there are "bad actors," or people primarily interested in accumulating profit, rather than providing fresh food (Alkon 2014: 34). Alkon urges that instead of merely critiquing neoliberal cooptation, food justice activists can look to restructure food projects so that they can resist being a part of the capitalist market. Worker cooperatives and food workers' movements are positive programs where people can work together. Most importantly, Alkon calls for food and its multifaceted connection to culture, identity, personal and public health, environmental issues, education, and more, to be further explored in these food justice movements – a call that captures the essence of the social science literature we have explored throughout this article.

A larger movement that still stays true to its small-movement motives is the Slow Food Movement started by Carlo Petrini (2003). In his book *Slow Food*, Petrini describes the movement he started in Bra, Italy, dedicated to making sure food was good, clean, and fair. Petrini discloses the four main themes of the movement: (1) to get to know the material culture of food (for example, the smell of good bread), (2) to preserve the agricultural aspect of food production, (3) to protect and inform the consumer about what he or she is eating and its quality, and (4) to research and promote the pleasures of gastronomy. This movement towards reclaiming good taste did not directly arise in opposition to a McDonald's being built in Rome; but at the same time, the movement does not agree with the standardization and taste of McDonald's foods. Those who support the Slow Food Movement, veganism, and the resistance of neoliberalism through food co-ops and farmer's markets, come together and share something of a group identity. The careful selection of what the collective eats, and the valorization of how it is produced and grown, says a lot about how certain people want to love and nourish their bodies, and respect the world they live in – all through meditated food choice.

Conclusion

Eating is necessary, but eating habits are rarely coincidental; and for most people, the palate is not very malleable. In other words, what one chooses to eat is typically a part of one's personal history that has persisted through time, and was either introduced by a family member, or in the above cases of detainees and those people with disabilities, forced on them. On the other hand, eating trends and the birth of new movements and communities such as Slow Food and hipster veganism can suddenly emerge to have immense influence over people's eating habits.

While eating is a biological process needed for survival, it is also a social process: people usually eat together, and what you eat is then interpreted by those around you. To be a woman and eat salad, to be a man and eat meat, to be an African-American vegan, to be a Chinese-food-loving American Jew, to be a disabled adult denied sweets and permitted alcohol, to be a Ghanaian immigrant who no longer has a garden, to participate in the Slow Food Movement – all of these voluntary or involuntary food choices foster emotions that allow people to get to know their self-constructed and socially constructed bodies on a deeper, more intimate level. Food is a meaningful and observable form of self-expression.

Note

1 We would like to acknowledge the helpful comments of Monica J. Casper, Tara Melfi, Patricia Howells, and Casey Saunders.

References

Adams, C. J. (2004) *The Pornography of Meat*, New York: Continuum.
Alkon, A. H. (2014) "Food Justice and the Challenge to Neoliberalism," *Gastronomica* 14(2): 27–40.
Bourdieu, P. (1977) *Outline of a Theory of Practice*, Cambridge, MA: Cambridge University Press.
Calvert, A. (2014) "You Are What You (M)eat: Explorations of Meat-eating, Masculinity and Masquerade," *Journal of International Women's Studies* 16(1): 18–33.
Caplan, P. (1997) *Food, Health and Identity: Approaches from the Social Sciences*, New York and London: Routledge.
Carney, M. A. (2013) "Border Meals: Detention Center Feeding Practices, Migrant Subjectivity, and Questions on Trauma," *Gastronomica* 13(4): 32–46.
Cooley, C. (1994) "Looking-Glass Self," in Peter Kollock and Jodi O'Brien (eds.), *The Production of Reality: Essays and Readings in Social Psychology*, London: Pine Forge Press, pp. 293–296.
Cronin, J. M., M. B. McCarthy, and A. M. Collins. (2014) "Covert Distinction: How Hipsters Practice Food-based Resistance Strategies in the Production of Identity," *Consumption Markets & Culture* 17(1): 2–28.

Davies, C. A. (2007) "Food and the Social Identities of People with Learning Disabilities," *Disabilities Studies Quarterly* 27(3): 21–35.

Dunham, D. (2010) "On Being Black and Vegan," in A. B. Harper (ed.), *Sistah Vegan: Black Female Vegans Speak on Food, Identity, Health, and Society*, New York: Lantern, pp. 42–47.

Edwards, P. A. (2012) "Global Sushi: Eating and Identity," *Perspectives on Global Development and Technology* 11(1): 211–225.

Fiddes, N. (1991) *Meat: A Natural Symbol*, New York: Routledge.

Finkelstein, J. (2014) *Fashioning Appetite: Restaurants and the Making of Modern Identity*, New York: I. B. Tauris & Co.

Fox, R. (2002) "Food and Eating: An Anthropological Perspective," *Social Issues Research Center*, viewed 16 May 2015, http://www.sirc.org/publik/foxfood.pdf.

Goffman, E. (1959) *The Presentation of Self in Everyday Life*, New York: Doubleday.

Hayes-Conroy, A. and J. Hayes-Conroy. (2008) "Taking Back Taste: Feminism, Food and Visceral Politics," *Gender, Place & Culture* 15(5): 461–473.

Kawash, S. (2013) *Candy: A Century of Panic and Pleasure*, New York: Faber and Faber.

Kirkland, A. (2011) "The Environmental Account of Obesity: A Case for Feminist Skepticism," *Signs* 36(2): 463–485.

Kosut, M. and L. J. Moore. (2010) "Not Just the Reflexive Reflex: Flesh and Bone in the Social Sciences," in L. J. Moore and M. Kosut (eds.), *The Body Reader: Essential Social and Cultural Readings*, New York: New York University Press, pp. 1–30.

Lockie, S. and L. Collie. (1999) "'Feed the Man Meat': Gendered Food and Theories of Consumption," in D. Burch, J. Goss, and G. Lawrence (eds.), *Restructuring Global and Regional Agricultures: Transformations in Australasian Agri-food Economies and Spaces*, Burlington, VT: Ashgate, pp. 255–273.

Lupton, D. (1996) *Food, the Body and the Self*, London: Sage Publications.

Mares, T. (2012) "Tracing Immigrant Identity Through the Plate and the Palate," *Latino Studies* 10(3): 334–354.

Mead, G. H. (1934/1962) *Mind, Self and Society: From the Standpoint of a Social Behavioralist*, Chicago: University of Chicago.

Miller, H. (2006) "Identity Takeout: How American Jews Made Chinese Food Their Ethnic Cuisine," *The Journal of Popular Culture* 39(3): 430–465.

Nath, J. (2011) "Gendered Fare?: A Qualitative Investigation of Alternative Food and Masculinities," *Journal of Sociology* 47: 261–278.

Petrini, C. (2003) *Slow Food: The Case for Taste*, New York: Columbia University Press.

Probyn, E. (1999) "Beyond Food/Sex: Eating and an Ethics of Existence," *Theory, Culture & Society* 16(2): 215–228.

Rogers, R. A. (2008) "Beasts, Burgers and Hummers: Meat and the Crisis of Masculinity in Contemporary Television Advertisements," *Environmental Communication* 2(3): 281–301.

Sachs, C. and A. Patel-Campillo. (2014) "Feminist Food Justice: Crafting a New Vision," *Feminist Studies* 40(2): 396–410.

Sobal, J. (2005) "Men, Meat, and Marriage: Models of Masculinity," *Food and Foodways* 13: 135–158.

Williams-Forson, P. (2014) "'I Haven't Eaten If I Don't Have My Soup and Fufu': Cultural Preservation through Food and Foodways among Ghanaian Migrants in the United States," *Africa Today* 61(1): 70–87.

Witt, D. (2004) *Black Hunger: Soul Food and America*, Minneapolis, MN: University of Minnesota.

3

METAPHORIC DETERMINANTS OF FOOD AND IDENTITY

Kendall J. Eskine

It would seem that our relationship with food ought to be simple. After all, what is food if not a nutritive base, energizing the bits and pieces comprising bodies of all sorts? But this is hardly the case. In many ways, the representational nature of food extends well beyond its capacity for sustenance and projects itself onto some of our most abstract domains, ranging from identity formation to foreign diplomacy. We even conceptualize and describe people in terms of food metaphors: he's *spicy*, she's *sweet*, the congressman showed *unsavory* behavior, the sales clerk had a *bitter* attitude, and so on. Are these mere linguistic conventions, or do our sensory and perceptual experiences with food meaningfully animate how we understand others? In what follows I will first explore how food finds homes in such curious places in human culture and craft something of a tasting menu to survey the extant empirical research. Second, I will explore a potential mechanism for these effects by drawing from contemporary theories in conceptual metaphor.

The representational structure of food

Discovering viable food sources is arguably one of the most pervasive instincts across the natural world. From heterotrophic prokaryotes to newborn human infants, locating nutrition externally is an immediate, life-affirming goal. A clear example of this behavior takes form in an infant's rooting reflex. Here, when an infant's cheek is stroked, she naturally turns her head toward the stimulus until it reaches her mouth. Indeed, before young ones possess the dexterity to manipulate objects with their hands, they use their mouths to learn about an object's properties. Is this hard or soft, rough or smooth, edible or not? And further still: Is this edible and delicious, edible and disgusting, or something more equivocal, like the strange allure of pickled ginger (certainly more alluring for adults than infants)? In some ways, mouthing objects is an infant's first meaningful journey into metaphysics as she discovers the principles that govern her reality. Based on the particulars and category exemplars[1] she encounters, she will gain insight into how the world is structured and begin to form nascent categories to help organize and process these stimuli, including both the novel and the repeats. There are similar ways in which all of these objects take up space, vary in mass, roll or bounce according to some physical principles, and so on, and these are called primary qualities because they occur independent of an observer. However, objects also deliver more subjective properties onto their observers, like color and taste, which are termed secondary qualities because they are constructed *through* individuals' unique sensori-perceptual systems (Locke 1979 [1690]).

It is worth noting that there has been considerable debate about the extent to which any claims can be made about the nature of objects' primary qualities and whether we can know anything "objective" that isn't colored by our senses. Either way, food, like many other classes of objects, is somewhat interesting because it holds qualities at primary levels (size, macronutrient content, etc.) and secondary levels (taste and preference). However, what makes food an exceptionally privileged category is its impressive link to our learning and appetitive motivational systems. Appetitive motivational systems refer to a complex array of adaptive, approach-related behaviors that help organisms survive (Lang and Bradley 2013). In this way, hunger is motivational because it urges organisms to seek food in a manner that clearly promotes survival. The same can be also said of sex drives and defensive appetitive behaviors like fighting off a threatening other. These behaviors are psychologically and behaviorally privileged because they were naturally selected for and are hence uniquely tethered to our learning systems, which represent a pattern of distributed neural processing that includes information from our affective (i.e., emotional) and memory systems. In terms of neural coding, food is also special because it enjoys substantial cortical and subcortical processing, from food-craving instincts that engage seeking behavior, taste perception that combines insights across a variety of sensory processing regions (touch, taste, vision, etc.), emotional payoffs and backlashes after locating food (both positive and negative outcomes are equally important), and immediate encoding and long-term storage in memory systems that remind organisms of these outcomes. To this end, the feeling of delight during the discovery of a tasty new treat is immediately interwoven into the neural circuitry that envelops positive affect, behavioral motivation, etc. Overall, the processes involved with food signify a massive effort on behalf of the brain and body to "understand" the relationship between food and what could be considered a *self*, particularly if we juxtapose it with its cognitive and behavioral outcomes.

Historically, philosophers and psychologists have made a significant scholarly investment in understanding the self, an idea that has been breathed into innumerable lectures and inked on as many pages. In fact, a quick search on PSYC INFO (a major search database for psychological research) reveals more hits on the topic of the self than nearly any other search query. Given its primacy across various research programs, it's no surprise that scholars conceptualize the self differently. The present analysis will consider the self along traditional definitions that define it as a distinct constellation of features that express what it's like to be one particular individual and not another, a distinction that can be framed at both neural and phenomenological levels. Although it is not the intent of this work to discern a location for the self – be it in the brain, body, or more radical alternatives that project it into the environment itself (Clark and Chalmers 1998) – I will nonetheless suggest that the self can be distributed beyond the confines of the skull. By focusing on the representational structure of food and how people help construct and relate to it in a way that influences their self-understanding and social cognition, we might arrive at a junction where one's identity *emerges* as a dynamic property of these complex interactions between food, cognition, affect, and biological homeostasis. And while we remember all kinds of events and objects, food is unique because it accosts us every few hours by projecting itself into our consciousness and working memory via our complex, biologically based motivational systems. Food takes on meaning through its outcomes in our bodies and specifically our memory and representations of them.

It is a truism in cognitive science that memory works best with "hooks." Whether through mental imagery or explicit elaboration, connecting new, fragile memories with old, crystallized ones creates hooks that help strengthen the fledgling neural pathways that represent some object, event, or idea that ultimately *becomes* its representational structure. In general, representations refer to any state or system that carries information about something else. For example, Dretske (1995) argued that representation occurs only when information is carried in a law-like manner *and* when it is the primary function of the representation to carry information about its referent. Thermometers and teakettles equally convey information about temperature through rising mercury or whistles, respectively, and it is their primary function to do so. But the representational structure of food is more intricate than that because its use in organisms' bodies occurs as a purely secondary quality: salt, vitamin D, and raw meat do very different things to different creatures. Therefore, how food becomes linked to a creature's unique affective and motivational systems provides a first glimpse into a food's representational structure. As this nascent pattern of neural activity begins to represent a food, it *necessarily* includes our relationship to it through its distributed neural activation and processing. After several trials, this neural pathway becomes more crystallized and thus available to become connected to other types of stimuli. In this way, food can take on multiple meanings as it becomes neurally connected to various aspects of one's experience.

To summarize the foregoing, food has been described as a stimulus that we represent through multiple neural channels. Our biological programming is such that our food experiences are fundamentally tethered to affective, memory, and motivational systems that help us form representational structures of food in an immediate, survival-inducing way. Though physiological and pre-conscious in one sense, these structures ultimately become expressed phenomenally as properties of subjective experience (e.g., he *loves* creole tomatoes and she *loathes* licorice). These experiences help the representations carry information about how one will come to interact with food through appetitive or defensive motivations. These activity patterns, reactivated continuously and over time, become truly learned. The food-relevant neural pathways then become available as crystallized knowledge that can be used as hooks for new information, which increases their capacity to represent additional complex stimuli in newly forming representational structures.

But how are these processes specifically related to identity? Although there is no part of the brain that signifies identity, it will be treated as any other advanced psychological construct: as the emergence of a dynamic pattern of neural activation across several brain regions (Anderson 2010). Given that the self is arguably a *social* construct, we will therefore consider self-identity as a (re) construction that occurs during social cognition.

Locating types of value in food

Meals are important – not just for biological sustenance, but also for providing social satiety. Family dinners, coffee dates, and tasty celebratory delights of all types bring people together on the pretext of filling their guts. In this way, food goes beyond its nutritional content to represent more complex social events. Meals can be deconstructed and reconsidered as a window into a family's history. Imagine how great-grandmother's special recipe conveys specialized information about her family, including traits related to their geography and ecology (via recipes comprising local ingredients that are readily available and ultimately have environmental implications); their nutritive needs, allergies, and similar biological constraints; their connections to their community; and their history of taste preferences. Recipes can even be construed through the lens of personal empowerment. For example, Ferguson (2012) explores community cookbooks as a mechanism that helps build and unite communities by instantiating a sense of belonging on the basis of gender, socioeconomic status, race, and other demographic traits. The ingredients comprising meals express shared tastes that signify shared cultural values and thus structure communities along similar goals (e.g., budget-centered cookbooks signify class through the goal of saving money). Ferguson goes on to explain how the emergence of female identities is often tethered to cooking and other domestic happenings, which complements a significant and growing body of research in feminist food studies (Inness 2001).

Further empirical evidence supports the view that people represent food as social signifiers. Trisoli and Gabriel (2011) investigated the relationship between comfort food and social ostracism. In one study, all participants were asked to recall an interpersonal conflict with another and subsequently taste a potato chip. The researchers found that some participants were more likely to rate a potato chip as tastier following the interpersonal skirmish, and this depended on the extent to which they possessed secure attachment styles (i.e., they were generally able to form strong and positive emotional bonds with others). In effect, activating conceptual representations involved with social conflict induced people to perceive a prototypical comfort food as tastier, but only when they experienced social-psychological distress. This pattern suggests that food was transformed into a social device to help them recover from their interpersonal woes. For those who did not possess secure attachment styles, we wouldn't expect there to be any meaningful social distress to overcome, and hence the chips need not take on a special taste. In another study, researchers observed that exposure to comfort foods like chicken noodle soup alleviated feelings of loneliness after participants were socially ostracized, though this effect was only salient for those who perceived the soup as a personal comfort food. Together, these findings suggest that people experience conceptual overlap between social relationships and comfort food, and that the latter can indeed be treated as a kind of social surrogate in different contexts. This view is in line with the present thesis that food stimuli can represent social information in a way that contributes to how people understand their own self-identities and even how they experience physical taste.

Foods also carry information about people's values across broader cultural domains, such as foreign diplomacy. Consider Hillary Clinton's remarks in the *New York Times* (Burros 2012): "Showcasing favorite cuisines, ceremonies and values is an often overlooked and powerful tool of diplomacy" and that "the meals that I share with my counterparts at home and abroad cultivate a stronger cultural understanding between countries and offer a unique setting to enhance the formal diplomacy we conduct every day." Here, Clinton argues for a food-enriched view of international relations, what some now call *gastrodiplomacy* (Nirwandy and Awang 2014). To this end, a recent study found that over half of its participants who tried another country's cuisine were more likely to have changed their opinions about that country as a whole (Ruddy 2014). In the related construct of "gastronationalism," DeSoucey (2010) considers the bidirectional relationship between food and nations through several perspectives. For example, she argues that nationalist ideologies can influence the manner in which foods are produced, marketed, and treated in business settings. On the other hand, DeSoucey notes that food production and consumptive practices affect how individuals within a community develop national sentiments and taste preferences for particular foods, like France's identity-laden admiration of foie gras. These are budding areas of research that indicate how food production, distribution, and consumptive practices influence our sense of self and judgment towards others and communities at large. From the perspective of cognitive science, these findings reveal how the availability, proximity, and socioeconomic practices surrounding food politics affect how people represent and process *food* categories in a way that connects them to *social* categories. Here, the authenticity of food highlights nationalist identities, much in the way that the growing movement involving organic food production and consumption highlights moral, ethical, and health identities.

The organic food industry has blossomed into a billion-dollar empire. Marketed to those expressing unequivocal concern for personal health and nutritive purity, organic foods inspire people to pay top dollar even though the evidence is mixed in terms of the actual nutritive content of many such products. For example, a large meta-analysis (including data from over 200 studies) concluded that there were no significant differences in vitamin, fat, or protein content across a large sample of different foods (with the exception of higher phosphorus in some organic produce) (Smith-Spangler et al. 2012). Most of the organic benefits were found in meat and dairy products (e.g., organic milk possessed significantly higher levels of omega-3 fatty acids). While this might not be a revelation to some, many instead focus on the benefits of organic foods through their eschewal of pesticides. However, results revealed that most organic foods only had about a 30% lower amount of pesticide relative to conventionally grown foods, a far cry from the 100% pesticide-free expectation that most consumers likely possess. The researchers conclude by encouraging consumers to focus more on simply eating more servings of fruits and vegetables (organic or conventional) if health is their primary concern.

Going beyond the nutritive content of organics, social and behavioral scientists have also investigated its psychological content. For example Schuldt and Schwarz (2010) found that participants judged organic cookies to contain fewer calories than non-organic alternatives, and they saw it as more permissible to overindulge in the former than the latter, a phenomenon termed *organic obesity*. In a separate study, researchers observed that individuals with salient weight-loss goals who failed to exercise were judged more favorably when they consumed an organic as opposed to conventional dessert. While these findings attest to the nutritive health halo people associate with organic food, further experiments have extended similar findings to foods offering other ethical claims. Across two studies, researchers learned that participants were significantly more likely to judge a candy bar to contain fewer calories (and hence be more permissible to overindulge in) when it was labeled "fair trade" (Study 1) and when it came from a company that treated its workers ethically (Study 2) (Schuldt et al. 2012). Although no one would deny the value of positive ethical treatment towards a company's employees, this moral virtue does not necessarily enhance food quality.

These results show how food can become cognitively interleaved with social and moral spheres. Indeed, other research programs have observed that consumers whose self-identities converge with an appreciation for natural, simple products and technologies were more willing to purchase environmentally and ethically sound products, and that those with organic-laden self-identities were significantly more likely to possess similar purchase intentions (Bartels and Onwezen 2014). Similar findings have been obtained through qualitative interviews investigating how personal identities and social categories predict food choices, yet participants were sometimes unaware of this relationship (Bisogni et al. 2002). This indicates that food and identity do not necessarily share a conscious relationship but rather operate more implicitly, like appetitive and defensive motivational systems that share and express information more neurally than phenomenologically.

In some ways these results seem reasonable and expected. But they are also important because they further spotlight how self-identity is an important predictor of the way in which one consumes food. It becomes a representational structure that carries information about personalities, ethics, and ideas more broadly. And how we interact with and consume these nutrient-dense social signifiers can potentially influence what kind of people we become and how we represent the world. However, can one's ethical and social taste translate into actual taste? Is it possible that such rich social information can intervene during the biological processes underlying taste perception?

In this vein, Schuldt and Hannahan (2013) explored the extent to which ethical food claims affected taste perception. In one study, the researchers directed participants to rate how healthy and tasty (in two separate questions) they believed organic foods to be compared to "other foods." While all participants generally rated organics as the healthier option, they differed in their assessment of taste judgments, which varied as a function of participants' individual differences in environmental concern. Specifically, results showed that those low in environmental concern believed organic foods would taste significantly worse than other foods. There are several reasons why this might be the case. This class of participants may naturally associate healthy foods with poorer taste more generally, may have limited exposure with organics due to their ethical preferences, or could be justifying their decisions not to indulge in these products by discrediting their taste a priori. Further, it is also possible that this effect was driven by the pro-environmental concern participants, who perhaps ascribe positive value to organics because of their general preferences for environmentally friendly products. While this research reveals a negativity bias for organic taste, it is important to note that this work does not explicitly study *actual* taste but instead *potential* taste. Second, the findings are actually mixed in this regard. For example, Sörqvist et al. (2013) found that participants judged coffee labeled as "eco-friendly" to taste significantly better than its counterpart, and that they were willing to pay more for it, though the two products were in fact the same. Further, in other variations of the research program, when participants were experimentally told that they actually preferred the non-eco-friendly coffee, they were still willing to pay more for it, which indicates that choosing environmentally friendly and organic products is only partially involved with taste.

The research reviewed thus far shows how people consciously and non-consciously associate food with different aspects of their identities, values, and social judgments about the world. But food can also be a vehicle for understanding *others* in terms of their cognitive abilities and values. In a clever study, Bastian et al. (2012) explored how people estimated the cognitive capacity of non-human animals. They found that meat eaters vary significantly in their judgments of cognitive capacity and ultimately moral status depending on whether they ate those animals regularly. In particular, moral status is often ascribed to creatures as a function of whether they have the cognitive capacity to feel pain, possess emotions, etc. Results showed that people who ate pigs and cows estimated their mental capacity to be significantly lower than other animals they didn't eat, like cats and horses, and the effects were transposed accordingly for those who ate different animals. The results were particularly strong when participants were reminded of potential animal suffering – that is, they were more likely to deny mental capacities to their future meals. The authors explain these effects through cognitive dissonance reduction, which occurs when one alters their attitudes to better correspond to their behaviors.

In addition to impacting how we judge non-human animals, food and meals also affect how people judge other people. (Over)weight stigma is a particularly salient effect. Puhl and Brownell (2001) found that parents provided significantly less college support to their overweight children relative to their leaner counterparts, and that 24% of nurses admitted feeling "repulsed" by their obese patients. The authors also detailed the discrimination overweight individuals suffered in terms of employment status; they experienced severe disadvantages in hiring, promotion, job termination, etc. As obesity rates have increased in America over the years, a spotlight has been placed on weight reduction. While this rising legislative attention has undoubtedly helped many find their way to programs and lifestyles that improve their physical health, it may have also inadvertently exasperated weight stigma. To empirically investigate this possibility, Major et al. (2014) asked women to read one of two possible mock articles from the *New York Times*, "Lose Weight or Lose Your Job" or "Quit Smoking or Lose your Job." All participants were then directed to explain the major points of the article to someone unfamiliar with it. Afterwards, they were ushered into a "waiting room," which had snacks such as M&Ms, Goldfish crackers, and other blatantly non-healthy treats available (all of which were pre-weighed so researchers could determine how much was consumed). After the waiting period, participants were then asked about their willpower and general ability to control their eating habits. The results were surprising. Overweight females were significantly *more* likely to overindulge in the unhealthy snacks and significantly *less* likely to feel like they had any self-control over their eating habits. This is an important finding because it demonstrates that while attention should be given to weight issues, too much attention could induce a kind of cognitive helplessness/hopelessness in overweight individuals. To complement these results, other research programs have found that threats to people's self-identities could induce unhealthy eating practices and risky decision-making (Inzlicht and Kang 2010). Together, these findings suggest that our self-identities are fragile and intricately linked to our relationships with food. This should be considered against the backdrop of ubiquitous social media, advertising, and television programming depicting food and bodies. The implications cannot be overstated, although food's relationship to media is multivariate – and such media have also helped food achieve new significance in many ways.

Since the proliferation of popular reality television programs showcasing various aspects of the culinary arts (*Top Chef, Masterchef, Chopped*, etc.), food preparation now seems commonly regarded as equally creative and aesthetic as more traditional artistic domains like performance and visual arts. Along these lines, Michel et al. (2014) designed a Kandinsky-infused salad to present to customers at a restaurant. They created three versions of the salad, all of which contained the same ingredients and portions: simply tossed and plated, organized neatly (but not artistically), and designed to mimic a Kandinsky painting. After consuming one of the three possible salads, customers all rated their dining experience in terms of how much they enjoyed the taste, how much they'd be willing to pay for it, how complex it seemed, and similar questions assessing how much they liked the salad. The Kandinsky salad outperformed the other two on all measures of liking, indicating that more "aesthetic" foods can deliver more pleasurable gustatory experiences.

While these results reveal how traditional aesthetics and food domains can converge to produce beauty and creativity, they also seem to affect taste, which is a more complex physiological process than traditionally believed. In terms of cortical and subcortical processing, taste perception is informed by several brain regions, including the frontal operculum cortex (taste processing), piriform cortex (smell processing), inferotemporal lobe (visual processing specific to objects' identities), somatosensory cortex (touch and tactile processing), amygdala (emotion processing), orbitofrontal cortex (contains multisensory bimodal neurons), and other higher-order processing centers (recall, for example, the taste effects that accompany environmentally friendly foods). In short, even an evolutionarily aged process like taste enjoys significant multimodal processing, which provides a glimpse into the metaphorical nature of cognition.

Conceptual metaphors and food identities

Metaphors come in different varieties. Linguistic metaphors compare seemingly unrelated concepts by expressing one concept in terms of another (Glucksberg 2003). In stating that *life is a bumpy road*, the speaker uses a source domain (bumpy road) to explain a target domain (life), and listeners will understand this metaphor to the extent that they understand what bumpy roads are. But metaphors aren't just clever literary devices; they also help us identify and understand new target concepts through more familiar source domains. Imagine a common situation in which one colleague whispers to another, "David is a far cry from a sweetie." The two source domains (*far cry* and *sweetie*) convey two important bits of information about the target domain (David): we now know that David is potentially unpleasant (*sweetie* domain) and this is by a considerable amount (*far cry* domain). But how do physical properties like taste and distance via *sweetie* and *far cry* references, respectively, represent abstract qualities like pleasantness and severity in the first place?

Unlike linguistic metaphors, conceptual metaphors refer specifically to how the mind and brain process information. In this sense, conceptual metaphors aim to illuminate the underlying cognitive architecture of the mind. As Ritchie (2008) noted, "[M]etaphor is primarily conceptual, and the linguistic expressions we usually think of as 'metaphors' are expressions or manifestations of underlying conceptual metaphors" (176). Thus, conceptual metaphors explore how we represent *new* concepts and information in terms of *old* ones.

Arguably some of the most celebrated ideas on this topic come from Lakoff and Johnson's works, *Metaphors We Live By* (1980) and *Philosophy in the Flesh* (1999). They advance the hypothesis that embodied information taken in by the senses forms a concrete informational wellspring that forms the foundational conceptual structure for more abstract concepts. In other words, "low-level" sensorimotor states that naturally accompany perceptual experience provide the basic material from which concepts are developed, organized, represented, and ultimately processed in the mind and brain. Consider the following expression: *Marian is a warm person.* To most native English speakers, Marian's warmth is not literal, yet it conveys her caring interpersonal nature. According to conceptual metaphor theory, our early embodied experiences of warmth are often naturally accompanied by positive experiences with nurturing caregivers – one is being cradled, held, and so on. These embodied experiences of warmth (source domain) provide foundational data that subsequently help shape individuals' understanding of positive qualities (target domain) in others. Over repeated trials that pair physical warmth and interpersonal caring, the latter becomes structured (represented) and understood (processed) *through* the former. However, an alternative account would contend that warmth became associated with specific personality traits through language conventions and similar linguistic co-occurrences. A stronger test of the conceptual metaphor hypothesis would show that embodying warmth could promote the corresponding feelings in a causal manner, thus revealing that embodied experiences are in fact *part* of this conceptual domain. In a clever experiment, Williams and Bargh (2008) showed that participants who experienced physical warmth (holding a hot vs. iced cup of coffee) were more likely to judge unknown target individuals as more caring, generous, etc., than participants who experienced coldness. In short, literal warm feelings engendered figurative warm feelings through metaphorical processes.

For Lakoff and Johnson, embodied information is crucial to the development of more abstract and complex concepts (like kindness) for which there are no unified or structured sensory experiences. In these cases, low-level features that are biologically rooted in organisms are good candidates for acting as metaphorical source domains for abstract concepts, because abstract concepts must first be *framed* in terms of something understandable before they can be comprehended.

Given the theme of this contribution, sensory and perceptual experiences involved with food seem like especially strong candidates for conceptual metaphor for at least two reasons. First, the processes involved with linking food to human animals are evolutionarily privileged to promote survival; thus, food is uniquely tethered to affective, memory, and motivational systems to facilitate quick learning to further help ensure survival. Second, and perhaps more importantly, food is processed in a multimodal format, receiving sensory signals from across the brain, which helps us form representational structures of food in an immediate and far-reaching manner. Therefore, food takes up a lot of real estate in the brain, and metaphorical processes seem to operate best when representational structures are (1) *available* as potential source domains that can be projected onto new, more abstract target domains, and (2) rooted in low-level mechanisms related directly to survival or our more basic senses.

There is increasing evidence for this view. Meier et al. (2012) found that participants were more willing to help others after tasting something sweet compared to control conditions, which helps explain where terms of affection (*sweetie, sweetheart, sugar*, etc.) get their embodied meaning. Their analyses also confirmed that the results were not due to positive affect or other emotional cues, hence placing the causal spotlight on the metaphorical power of sweet tastes. Chapman et al. (2009) provided strong evidence that moral disgust is actually processed quite similarly to physical disgust in the brain, which reveals how embodied experiences with oral disgust could be metaphorically projected onto abstract domains like moral disgust. This thesis has been born out in several research programs, with some experiments observing that participants who ingest a disgusting taste unknowingly judge targets as more morally disgusting than those who consumed other tastes (sweet or water) (Eskine et al. 2011). Other lines of research have established metaphorical links between spicy tastes and personality traits like anger (Ji et al. 2013), showing specifically that participants higher in trait anger were more likely to enjoy spicy foods and that participants judged spicy-taste aficionados to possess significantly greater tempers than non-spicy consumers.

These results indicate a potential metaphorical relationship between food, social cognition, and self-identities. Conceptual metaphors are also consistent with some of the latest findings in cognitive neuroscience. According to Anderson's (2010) neural reuse hypothesis, evolutionarily "older" neural circuitry is more likely to be co-opted and redeployed for new use, a more economical approach than creating entirely new and highly specialized circuitry, which would require significant time, energy, and selective pressures. To support his theory, Anderson conducted a meta-analysis of over 1,400 fMRI studies and observed that evolutionarily older regions of the brain were more likely to be activated in later-developed functions (like higher-order reasoning, etc.) and similarly that more advanced cognitive processes were more widely distributed across various brain regions. This work can be viewed as the neural mechanisms that support conceptual metaphor. Older neural circuitry (metaphorical source domains) are reused and activated in more abstract cognitive functions (metaphorical target domains), which ultimately outline representational structure. Buttressing this view, recent findings show that hunger, historically viewed as a specialized process, can activate motivation towards non-food objects and domains (Xu et al. 2015). Together, these findings help explain how identities and food become merged in the mind and brain to create a self.

Conclusion

The purpose of this work was to provide an empirically motivated account that reveals the psychological impact of food. Contemporary research across the cognitive sciences frames food not as a culinary artifact or mere means to survival but rather as a foundation of sensory and perceptual information that helps shape our future cognitive architecture. Grounded in evidence from contemporary cognitive neuroscience, conceptual metaphor provides a glimpse into understanding how the brain re-tools itself to form new concepts by bridging older, more familiar domains with newer, murkier ones. The sensori-perceptual processes involved with food representational structures can therefore offer the cognitive capital to construct a food-infused social cognition that influences one's identity, politics, and person perception, among other arenas.

Given the diverse array of potential food experiences and the impressive role that social forces play in cognitive processing and brain development, future research in metaphor would do well to consider the extent to which metaphorical processes are affected by culture. To this end, perhaps "sweet" is not universally regarded as a linguistic token for interpersonal kindness. Though some work has begun on this topic (Lee et al. 2015), much more is needed to delineate how bodies, brains, and culture come together to inform our identities and social cognition more broadly.

Note

1 The terms "particulars" and "category exemplars" are more or less synonyms but reflect the different vernaculars of philosophers and cognitive scientists, respectively.

References

Anderson, M. L. (2010) "Neural reuse: A fundamental organizational principle of the brain," *Behavioral and Brain Sciences* 33(4): 245–66.

Bartels, J. & Onwezen, M. C. (2014) "Consumers' willingness to buy products with environmental and ethical claims: The roles of social representations and social identity," *International Journal of Consumer Studies* 38(1): 82–9.

Bastian, B., Loughnan, S., Haslam, N., & Radke, H. R. (2012) "Don't mind meat? The denial of mind to animals used for human consumption," *Personality and Social Psychology Bulletin* 38(2): 247–56.

Bisogni, C. A., Connors, M., Devine, C. M., & Sobal, J. (2002) "Who we are and how we eat: A qualitative study of identities in food choice," *Journal of Nutrition Education and Behavior* 34(3): 128–39.

Burros, M. (2012) "Diplomacy travels on its stomach, too," *New York Times*, 2 July, viewed 1 July 2015, <http://www.nytimes.com/2012/07/04/dining/secretary-of-state-transforms-the-diplomatic-menu.html?nl=us&emc=edit_cn_20120703&_r=1>.

Chapman, H. A., Kim, D. A., Susskind, J. M., & Anderson, A. K. (2009) "In bad taste: Evidence for the oral origins of moral disgust," *Science* 323(5918): 1222–6.

Clark, A. & Chalmers, D. J. (1998) "The extended mind," *Analysis* 58: 10–23.

Desoucey, M. (2010) "Gastronationalism: Food traditions and authenticity politics in the European Union," *American Sociological Review* 75(3): 432–55.

Dretske, F. (1995) *Naturalizing the Mind*, Cambridge: MIT Press.

Eskine, K. J., Kacinik, N. A., & Prinz, J. J. (2011) "A bad taste in the mouth: Gustatory disgust influences moral judgment," *Psychological Science* 22(3): 295–9.

Ferguson, K. (2012) "Intensifying taste, intensifying identity: Collectivity through community cookbooks," *Signs: A Journal of Women in Culture and Society* 37(3): 695–717.

Glucksberg, S. (2003) "The psycholinguistics of metaphor," *Trends in Cognitive Science* 7: 92–6.

Inness, S. A. (2001) "Introduction: Thinking food/thinking gender," in S. A. Inness (ed.), *Kitchen Culture in America: Popular Representations of Food, Gender, and Race*, Philadelphia: University of Pennsylvania Press, pp. 1–12.

Inzlicht, M. & Kang, S. K. (2010) "Stereotype threat spillover: How coping with threats to social identity affects aggression, eating, decision making, and attention," *Journal of Personality and Social Psychology* 99(3): 467–81.

Ji, T., Ding, Y., Deng, H., Jing, M., & Jiang, Q. (2013) "Does 'spicy girl' have a peppery temper? The metaphorical link between spicy tastes and anger," *Social Behavior and Personality: An International Journal* 41(8): 1379–86.

Lakoff, G. & Johnson, M. (1980) *Metaphors We Live By*, Chicago: University of Chicago Press.

———. (1999) *Philosophy in the Flesh: The Embodied Mind and its Challenge to Western Thought*, New York: Basic Books.

Lang, P. J. & Bradley, M. M. (2013) "Appetitive and defensive motivation: Goal-directed or goal-determined?," *Emotion Review* 5(3): 230–4.

Lee, S. W. S., Tang, H., Wan, J., Mai, X., & Liu, C. (2015) "A cultural look at moral purity: Wiping the face clean," *Frontiers in Psychology* 6: 577.

Locke, J. (1979 [1690]) *An Essay Concerning Human Understanding*, Nidditch, P. H. (ed.), Oxford: Oxford University Press.

Major, B., Hunger, J. M., Bunjan, D. P., & Miller, C. T. (2014) "The ironic effects of weight stigma," *Journal of Experimental Social Psychology* 51: 74–80.

Meier, B. P., Moeller, S. K., Riemer-Peltz, M., & Robinson, M. D. (2012) "Sweet taste preferences and experiences predict prosocial inferences, personalities, and behaviors," *Journal of Personality and Social Psychology* 102(1): 163–74.

Michel, C., Velasco, C., Gatti, E., & Spence, C. (2014) "A taste of Kandinsky: Assessing the influence of the artistic visual presentation of food on the dining experience," *Flavour* 3: 7.

Nirwandy, N. & Awang, A. A. (2014) "Conceptualizing public diplomacy social convention culinary: Engaging gastro diplomacy warfare on economic branding," *Procedia* 130: 325–32.

Puhl, R. & Brownell, K. D. (2001) "Bias, discrimination, and obesity," *Obesity Research* 9(12): 788–805.

Ritchie, L. D. (2008) "X is a journey: Embodied simulation in metaphor interpretation," *Metaphor and Symbol* 23: 174–99.

Ruddy, B. (2014) "Hearts, minds, and stomachs: Gastrodiplomacy and the potential of national cuisine in changing public perception of national image," *Public Diplomacy Magazine* 11: 29–32.

Schuldt, J. P. & Hannahan, M. (2013) "When good deeds leave a bad taste: Negative inferences from ethical food claims," *Appetite* 62: 76–83.

Schuldt, J. P., Muller, D., & Schwarz, N. (2012) "The 'fair trade' effect: Health halos from social ethics claims," *Social Psychological and Personality Science* 3(5): 581–9.

Schuldt, J. P. & Schwarz, N. (2010) "The 'organic' path to obesity? Organic claims influence calorie judgments and exercise recommendations," *Judgment and Decision Making* 5(3): 144–50.

Smith-Spangler, C., Brandeau, M.L., Hunter, G.E., Bavinger, J.C., Pearson, M., Eschbach, P.J., Sundaram, V., Liu, H., Schirmer, P., Stave, C., Olkin, I., & Bravata, D.M. (2012) "Are organic foods safer or healthier than conventional alternatives?: A systematic review," *Annals of Internal Medicine* 125(5): 348–66.

Sörqvist, P., Hedblom, D., Holmgren, M., Haga, A., Langeborg, L., Nöstl, A., & Kågström, J. (2013) "Who needs cream and sugar when there is eco-labeling? Taste and willingness to pay for 'eco-friendly' coffee," *PLoS ONE* 8(12): e80719.

Trisoli, J. D. & Gabriel, S. (2011) "Chicken soup really is good for the soul: 'Comfort food' fulfills the need to belong," *Psychological Science* 22(6): 747–53.

Williams, L. E. & Bargh, J.A. (2008) "Experiencing physical warmth promotes interpersonal warmth," *Science* 322(5901): 606–7.

Xu, A. J., Schwarz, N., & Wyer, R. S. (2015) "Hunger promotes acquisition of nonfood objects," *Proceedings of the National Academy of Science* 112(9): 2688–92.

4

FOOD AND TECHNOLOGY

David M. Kaplan

Everything we eat has been grown, raised, or processed using technologies. Even ancient forms of farming and ranching used man-made things to transform plants or animals into food. Foraging for food without technologies is, of course, possible – but unless eaten raw, we require some technology. The diet of a typical city-dweller, a group that includes over half the world's population, would be impossible without technologies of production, distribution, and preparation. It is safe to say that without some kind of technology everyone in the world would starve to death. Yet technology and food are like chalk and cheese, at least according to common perception. They represent the poles along a continuum of life: one is organic, the other inorganic; one is natural, the other artificial; one is edible, the other inedible; one is wholesome, the other corrupting. Technology, on this reckoning, is viewed as the antithesis of everything having to do with food. The more technology is involved in our food, the worse it is; the less it is involved, the better.

The question is, which technologies are acceptable and which are problematic? Which should we endorse and which should we oppose? And what exactly is wrong with technologically mediated food: measurable effects on health, safety, and the environment, social-political problems, or something less determinate and more visceral? This chapter attempts to sort through different frameworks for understanding what technologies are, and how they relate to the food we produce and consume. The argument is that basic assumptions of the nature of technology color our perception of how it affects our food. First, we will consider different theories of technology; then we will apply each theory to food production and food consumption.

Three theories of technology

There are three main theories on the relationship of technology to society: *neutrality*, *autonomy*, and *social construction*. That is to say, philosophers have interpreted technology either as: (a) a neutral tool that is independent of values, ends, or purposes; (b) an autonomous force of social change that is increasingly beyond our control; or (c) a man-made thing that influences the social and natural worlds which, in turn, influence the course of technological development. Most of us believe in one or some combination of these theories. Let us briefly consider each in order.

Technological neutrality

The theory of technological *neutrality* defines technology in terms of its technical properties. Technology is seen as applied science. It embodies a pure, abstract, universal rationality, i.e., a rationality governed only by natural laws and technical considerations that are independent of social forces. What matters most in a technology is that it works, so this line of argument goes, and what works can be determined objectively according to universally valid and scientifically established principles. The technology itself is simply a tool. It can be used for a variety of human ends and purposes. It is neutral with respect to values and purposes. There is no such thing as morally good or bad technology, only good or bad users. The technology itself obeys only value-free, context-free principles. It is precisely this indifference to ends that makes technology so practical: when it works, it works everywhere, and when it breaks down, it can be fixed the same way, by anyone with the right technical know-how. The same standards, the same rules, the same techniques, and the same concept of efficiency govern the creation and use of technologies.

The theory of technological neutrality states that artifacts are independent of values. Things are mere instruments for human activities. Technology is value-neutral; human users are not. According to the theory of neutrality, devices are subservient to human choices. They are mere means to our human ends. The neutrality of technology assumes a complete separation of (technical) means and (human) ends. Technical objects and human values have nothing to do with one another.

Technological autonomy

Next is the theory of *autonomous* technology, the idea that technology is out of control. According to this theory, humans no longer control technology – instead, it controls us. It is an independent force that follows its own rules and imperatives. Humans merely respond, adapt, and conform. Technology imposes a way of life on a society: everything is *technicized*. Technical efficiency is the only end in a technological society. In fact, that end is built into things so that users have no choice but to adopt a technicized lifestyle. Technology constitutes a new cultural system that restructures the entire social world as an object of control. It is an independent cultural force that overrides all traditional or competing values. Everything about life in such a world is technological.

Closely related is the theory of technological *determinism*, the idea that technology drives the course of history. Devices and machines rather than people are the primary engines of change. The strong version of technological determinism maintains that there is a fixed sequence of technological development and, therefore, a necessary path of social change. Technology *imposes* specific social-political consequences. Society responds more to technology than technology to society. For example, we say that the atomic bomb ended World War II, automation caused a loss of jobs, and the Internet has changed the way we do business. We are all familiar with the well-worn theories about the printing press and the Reformation, and the cotton gin and the Civil War. In these cases, the technology is the primary agent of change, not humans.

The weak version of technological determinism states that technology *influences* social relations. It helps to shape and pattern history, but this imposition is not so strong as to determine the course of technological progress and social evolution. Technology mediates and steers a society, but it does not quite drive it; it exerts influence without strictly causing specific effects.

Technological constructivism

Finally, the *social construction* of technology is the idea that society simultaneously shapes technology as technology shapes society. Humanity and technology are situated in a circular relationship, each influencing the other. Social constructivists maintain that when we actually consider the diversity of things we find *technologies* (plural), no singular essence that applies in every instance. Humans make, use, and assign meaning to things in a variety of ways, in relation to a variety of social contexts. Far from being applied science, technology, on this model, is more like *embodied humanity*. Technologies are part human, part material, and always social. The advantage of viewing technology in this way is that it calls attention to the way that humanity, technology, and the environment are bound up together in a relationship of mutual constitution. Humans, things, and contexts all fit together like pieces of a puzzle.

From the perspective of constructivism, the theories of technological neutrality, determinism, and autonomy all suffer from the same weaknesses. They each treat technology as if it were something radically different from humanity; they take the technical qualities of things to be their most important characteristics; and they overlook the obvious fact that if a technology is made and used by a person, then it cannot help but reflect human ends, values, and ideas. Constructivists insist that technology cannot be value-neutral because people are not value-neutral; technology cannot determine history because it never is so independent from society to be in a position to cause it; and technology cannot be an autonomous force because technology is a human affair, not a mere technical matter.

The social construction approach tries to show how technologies are inextricably bound to human interests, social practices, physical laws, and a very long list of other constitutive factors. Above all, technologies are flexible and responsive to our intentions and desires. We can design whatever purposes and values we like into our things.

Technology and food production

That food production depends on technologies is uncontroversial, but we get a very different picture of how man-made things relate to our food according to which theory of technology we adopt. If technology is seen as neutral, then so is its relation to food production. The nature of the products, not the nature of production, is what matters. On the other hand, if technology is seen as autonomous, then the entire system of production – including the forms of life related to it – reflects technical imperatives. Or if technology is seen as a social construction, then its role in food production is subject to contingent social choices. In other words, there is no simple answer to questions about how technology relates or should relate to food. It depends on how one fundamentally understands what man-made things are.

To illustrate the point, let's consider three kinds of technology-intensive forms of food production – industrial agriculture, factory-farmed animals, and highly processed convenience foods – each understood in light of different theories of technology.

Neutrality and food production

On a neutrality model, food production is evaluated in terms of its consequences. The concern is about the product, not the technology – with the ends not the means. The means themselves are neutral, even separable from the ends. Granted, there might be trade-offs that might weigh for or against a technology/system, but the machinery itself is indifferent to the outcome. The only choice is to take it or leave it; adopt a set of technologies or reject them; or set a boundary around them and limit how far they should extend. But transforming or reforming the technologies is not an option on this model, because there is nothing to reform if technology is applied science.

Industrial agriculture would not be possible were it not for several key technologies and technological systems. These include systematic plant breeding, monoculture crops, fossil-fuel energy, farm machinery, synthetic-nitrogen fertilizers, pesticides and herbicides, irrigation, processing, and long-distance transportation of both bulk raw and processed foods. The benefits of Green Revolution agricultural technologies are efficiency, higher yields, increased productivity, greater availability, improved distribution, economic development, and lower prices. The costs include a litany of harms: energy use, pollution, and climate change; wasted drinking water; chemical wastes in soil and water; deforestation and desertification; soil erosion and loss of biodiversity.

The industrialized production of livestock, poultry, and fish has many of the same benefits and harms associated with intensive farming. The benefits of factory farming animals for food include efficiency, high yields, widespread availability, low prices, and contributions to local and national economies. Among the harms are the abuse of animals, environmental hazards, health risks to farmworkers, and food-safety problems. Industrial livestock production uses vast amounts of water, fossil fuels, inorganic fertilizers, and field machinery. The environment surrounding factory farms is often heavily polluted by animal wastes and offal that foul the air and seep into groundwater and surface waters.

Food processing is a vast category that includes pasteurizing, canning, freezing, irradiating, artificially sweetening, and in vitro techniques; use of food additives and artificial ingredients designed to help prevent spoilage and contamination or to make food look and taste better; and the inclusion of dietary supplements with nutritional properties, such as vitamins, minerals, proteins, herbs, or enzymes. We find a similar litany of costs and benefits in processed foods as we do in other industrialized food production. Among the benefits of food processing are improved preservation, increased distribution potential, fortification, consumer choice, and convenience. Among the harms and risks often associated with processed food are reduced nutritional value, adverse health effects, pollution, and an increased amount of energy expended in processing.

On a neutrality model, the technologies of factory farming and food processing are typically not questioned. They are either accepted or rejected wholesale in favor of extensive (sustainable) production methods, humanely pastured animals, or whole and natural foods. Either way the focus of discussion – if one truly maintains a consistent theory of technological neutrality – is on the consequences of use, not the devices themselves. We find an implicit theory of neutrality in the discourses of risk assessments, cost–benefit analyses, and environmental impact assessments.

Autonomy and food production

On the model of autonomous technology, food production is seen as an example of "technological rationality": a mindset that takes a detached, objective, and overly scientific view of the world. According to this approach, the problem with food production is that it is part of a worldview that treats everything as nothing more than mere objects to be controlled. The detached objectivity of technological rationality is at best limited, at worse alienating. It disconnects us from the world and from each other. While this rationality may be useful for dealing with legitimate technical matters, food production has historically been more than a mere set of technical problems with technical solutions. The more we rely on technology for food production, the more alienated we become from the land and from each other.

The theory of technological autonomy evokes Romantic themes of man versus nature, life out of balance, and the desire to restore lost harmony with nature. On this reckoning, connection with nature is good and alienation from it is bad. When it comes to food production, the technology only makes things worse. We find this take on technology in the local food movement and in much of the organic food literatures, as well as in other calls to eschew industrial agriculture and processed food in favor of sustainable living and traditional cooking and farming methods (Petrini 2006).

We also find this grim view of technology in the agrarian literature. Agrarianism stresses the role of farming and ranching in the formation of moral character and in preserving culture and traditions. By living a rural lifestyle connected to the climate and soil, we acquire a sense of identity and place that can only come about by direct contact with the land. Agrarianism was an early-20th-century response to the social and environmental costs of industrialization and urbanization, premised on the conviction that social life, food production, and the health of the land are inseparably related. That is to say, communities and the environment thrive only when farming is done properly; both suffer when farming is done poorly. The agrarian narrative celebrates the virtues of an agricultural lifestyle, such as care for the land, animals, and each other, and calls for them to be recovered to mitigate the social and economic blight, pollution, and destruction of traditions brought about by large-scale industrial agriculture (Freyfogle 2001; Wirzba 2004).

This agrarian narrative often animates the discourses that criticize new technologies, such as genetically modified food, in vitro meat, nanotechnology, and other technical solutions to social and environmental problems. The problems we face, according to agrarianism, are due to increasingly complex technical systems that are geared toward efficiency, higher yields, profit, and convenience. Farming is made worse by industrialization; factory farming is even worse because it treats animals, not just natural environments, as mere things to be managed and manipulated; and highly processed foods represent the full fruition of technologically mediated food production. Industrialized farming, animal, and food production are bad not because of the consequences but rather because they involve too much alienating technology. The solution is, of course, to try to live more wholesome, natural, and simple lives free from artifacts and chemicals. Farming should be more extensive and traditional, animal husbandry more humane, and food should be recognizably food. However, the only choices on this model are either to accept or reject the technologies, never to modify them in such a way as to make the related practices and lifestyles more desirable.

Social construction and food production

The constructivist model treats technology as a social construction that interacts with other social forces rather than as a neutral tool or autonomous entity with its unique rationality. Technology is now seen as *inter*dependent in relation to society rather than independent of it. Food production on this account is inseparably related both to its technologies and to its social-political use context – or political economy, to put it in Marxist terms. The best way to understand the relationship between food and technology is to examine the conditions that lead to the development of a food-production enterprise and the conditions under which it functions. There we typically find a standard set of agents and circumstances: economic imperatives, political realities, and environmental and technological constraints. Predictable capitalist forces drive and pattern food production – yet it is also shot through with contingencies that frustrate attempts to find unchanging rules.

The technologies used in industrialized agriculture should be understood as a series of countless yet related choices. Major choices of things like agricultural machinery for planting, fertilizing, and irrigating typically require compatible machinery for harvesting, sorting, and loading. Related technologies of transportation, distribution, and infrastructure must also be compatible. The choices are not based entirely on concern for cost and efficiency; nor are they completely arbitrary. Instead, machinery reflects a range of preferences specific for a particular farm, farmer, and product. They have to all fit together. That said, the range of choices is always limited by a few constants, above all the national, often international, political economy. Profit motives, expanding markets, and business models are relative constants, as are the typically competing interests of workers and owners. This conjunction of agriculture, technology, and political economy holds for large-scale industrial, small-scale sustainable, and for both advanced and developing nations.

Animal production is no different. One cannot make sense of the design of a confined animal feeding operation or slaughterhouse apart from the political economy and contingent social contexts in which it operations. On a constructivist understanding of technology, things are designed with ends, purposes, and interests. That means things can be designed differently with different values built into them. For example, the humane or harmful character of a factory farm is literally built into its design. It is not a matter of merely using the confinement operation or gestation crate for good or bad purposes. Although a humane gestation crate might be a stretch (and more of an example of something to be accepted or rejected outright) humane living conditions are not. The design features of a livestock facility are what largely (but not entirely) promote animal welfare. It is a necessary but not sufficient condition. The technologies that make up the facility minimally should be spacious, safe, heated, ventilated, sufficiently lit, and stimulating among other design features. Yet if the facility caretakers act irresponsibly or without compassion then the animals will still not live in humane conditions, no matter how well designed the building is. Technologies on a constructivist model do not determine events; but, they play an important role.

The production of heavily processed junk foods is similar. The mass production and distribution of convenience foods with long shelf lives would not be possible without 20th-century advances in manufacturing, packaging, and food science. In many ways, this class of foods is an entirely technological product. The ingredients themselves typically come from places that bear no resemblance whatsoever to the natural world. Yet even the most artificial processed food is shaped by social considerations, market forces, and regulations. As a result, the relationship is complicated and more than a matter of simply embracing or rejecting this class of food, which includes defensible things like pasteurized milk, canned beans, and emergency meals distributed to refugees and victims of natural disasters.

There is nothing intrinsically good or bad about the technological character of highly processed foods. Yet these food are intrinsically technological, so any modification of a food item to make it better in some way that benefits the public good (tastier, healthier, safer) will inevitably require some kinds of changes in the technological character of its production, i.e., design change. The social ends and technological means are linked on a constructivist model.

Food consumption and technology

Consumption raises a unique set of questions concerning the relationship between food and technology. Namely, food is eaten, and we tend to treat edible things somewhat differently than we do inedible things. Most of us are wary about what we put into our mouths. We tend to be conservative about strange and unusual foods. Yet our food is often filled with artificial ingredients and processed in ways most of us would find unappetizing. Most of us would prefer to eat wholesome, natural foods to high-tech foods filled with additives. Surveys show that both American and European consumers are overwhelmingly willing to pay more for healthy foods, particularly those grown on farms that care for the land (*Eurobarometer* 2014; *W. K. Kellogg Foundation* 2012). People value foods that are natural, clean, and traditional; we are skeptical about certain kinds of technological processes and additives. The question is, which technologies and additives, and for what reasons are we skeptical?

Neutrality and food consumption

On a neutrality model, the salient issue is the consequence of ingesting technologies along with our food. Let's take artificial ingredients to be the test case – particularly the long list of unpronounceable additives found in highly processed convenience foods. There are a number of good reasons why artificial ingredients are good to put into food. Most of them are practical and technical issues food manufacturers and distributors have to contend with, such as preservatives to prevent spoilage, or replacement vitamins and minerals lost in processing. The consequentialist arguments claim that the benefits of artificial ingredients outweigh whatever other harms they might pose. In other words, the technological element in food is neither intrinsically good nor bad. It depends on what its effects are.

Artificial ingredients can make food safer, better looking, and better tasting. They can add sweetness without adding calories, give reduced-fat foods the texture and mouth-feel we have come to expect, offset color loss due to storage conditions, and prevent crystallization in food products. In other words, they can make food more enjoyable to eat. They can also be beneficial. For example, *Plumpy'Nut*, a nutrient-enriched peanut butter used to treat severe acute malnutrition, has made famine relief far more effective than it has ever been. Food with additives can also be fortified to be more nutritious. *Enov Nutributter* is a nutritional supplement intended to fortify the diets of children after they stop breastfeeding. It provides missing nutrients in children ages 6 to 24 months to aid in their motor and cognitive development.

The vast majority of artificial ingredients are safe to eat. Regulatory agencies, such as the FDA and UK Food Standards Agency, study, monitor, and regulate all food additives to ensure their safety. In the US a food manufacturer must seek FDA approval to make a new food or color additive and provide evidence that a substance is safe. From a consequentialist perspective, artificial ingredients either improve our food or do no harm.

Then again, there might be occasions when artificial ingredients either pose risks or have some other adverse effects that outweigh their benefits. For example, the consensus among nutritionists is that highly processed foods – the kinds of convenience foods that only exist because of artificial ingredients – should be avoided (Nestle 2007). These foods are high in saturated fats, sodium, and sugar, and they provide little nutritional value. Most processed convenience foods contain additives that should either be avoided or eaten in moderation (Center for Science in the Public Interest 2015). Some additives, particularly food colorings, pose risks to children. The UK Food Standards Agency recommends that parents eliminate food colorings from the diet of children with Attention Deficit Hyperactivity Disorder. The European Food Safety Authority (EFSA) maintains a list of food additives and colors that pose risks for infants and very young children (EFSA 2015). Recently, the European Commission requested that all authorized food additives be systematically evaluated by the EFSA. There are legitimate concerns about the safety of many food ingredients, particularly for infants and children.

Autonomy and food consumption

On a model of technological autonomy, the conjunction of food and technology is never a good thing. Artificial ingredients are seen as impurities that endanger our health and erode our well-being. These impurities are bad in themselves, not because of any consequences. It is simply better to be as natural and pure as possible. The more natural foods we eat, the more healthy and balanced our lives will be. Food, according to this Romantic ideal, should have organic origins and be free from additives and excessive processing. People, food, and the environment are all connected in the act of eating, provided we eat the right foods in the right way. Artificial foods, with artificial ingredients produced by industrial facilities, disconnect us from our food and from each other. The closer we are to our food sources, the more in touch we are with a vital part of our health and our communities. The further we are from our food sources, the more alienated we are. At the risk of over-simplifying: connection is good, disconnection is bad. It is better to be connected to than cut off from our food. Technology gets in the way.

Michael Pollan's food writing relies on a Romantic theory of technological autonomy. He makes a strong distinction between wholesome natural foods (tied to a traditional diet) and unwholesome processed foods (tied to industrialized production). The reason that traditional diets are healthier and better for the environment is because they treat food as more than its chemical parts. It is always a part of a diet and a lifestyle. His oft repeated mantra is to "eat food, not too much, mostly plants" – to eat the kinds of things our grandparents might have grown up eating and to avoid new developments in agriculture and food processing. Food is culture, not science. For Pollan, a broad, holistic view of food is good, and a narrow, reductivist view is bad (Pollan 2009). This is another version of a critique of technological autonomy.

Social construction and food consumption

On a constructivist model, the good and bad, beneficial and harmful character of highly processed food is a function of several different factors, not merely the presence or effects of food additives. Whether it is better not to consume foods laden with technologies will be relative to circumstance. It depends what the artificial ingredients are, what purpose they serve, how often consumed, what other technologies and practices are related, and if the food manufacturer deserves to be supported. Answers to these questions can help explain what it is that makes *Plumpy'Nut* so much more justifiable than some cool-ranch, bacon-flavored snack food.

Consider a simple point: not all artificial food ingredients are the same. The FDA's main classes include preservatives, sweeteners, color additives, flavors and spices, fat replacers, nutrients, emulsifiers, stabilizers and thickeners, pH control agents, leavening agents, anti-caking agents, humectants, yeast nutrients, dough strengthener and conditioners, firming agents, enzyme preparations, and gases (FDA 2010). Is it the case that all of these are problematic simply because they have chemical-sounding names, or are some more problematic than others? The intrinsic arguments (of technological autonomy) against artificial ingredients hinge on their man-made, artificial character, which inherently worsens food. The extrinsic arguments (of technological neutrality) hinge on the consequences of eating them. Presumably, if the bad consequences could be lessened or removed there would be no reason to avoid artificial ingredients. Of this class of ingredients that are extrinsically bad, some seem to be worse than others. Preservatives, food dyes, sweeteners, fat substitutes, and artificial flavors tend to be the ones we have qualms with, either because they have health risks or are part of deceptive schemes to make food appear better. Emulsifiers, thickeners, nutrients, anti-caking agents, and the rest are less controversial.

Yet the moral valence of food technologies depends on how informed consumers are and how accurately food is labeled. Each of us is responsible for what we purchase and eat, provided we have choices. If food ingredients are labeled accurately, then it is the consumer's responsibility to make informed choices whether or not to consume foods with additives. However, if the best available science can establish long-term harms to the habitual consumption of legal food ingredients, then producers bear some responsibility, as well. Children, of course, need special protection since they are unable to make informed decisions about their well-being.

But adults need special protection, as well, from ingredients whose effects we cannot reasonably be expected to understand. Although adults *should* know the effects of eating too much fat, sugar, and salt, we cannot be expected to know that certain combinations of these ingredients are addictive, as mounting evidence seems to indicate (Parker-Pope 2012). Nor can we be expected to know that certain artificial flavors are designed to entice us to eat more than we would with a naturally occurring, non-synthesized flavor. Addictive foods and ingredients should be labeled. They are part of deceptive schemes to which people can never in principle consent.

Finally, because artificial ingredients are produced by the food industry in large-scale industrial complexes, it is reasonable to questions whether their use deserves your support, or if should be eschewed in favor of more ethical alternatives. This is an industry that very aggressively creates a favorable sales environment for its products. It does so by lobbying political representatives to eliminate or not enforce unfavorable regulations; by co-opting nutrition experts by supporting favorable research; and by marketing and advertising, often to children who are unable to read ads critically (Nestle 2003: 95–136). Sometimes the food industry succeeds in producing and publicizing goods that people actually want and need; other times its means are less honest and serve to deceive people into thinking they want and need things they really do not. The success of the food industry is due less to consumer demand than to its own efforts, even force. The deck is stacked in their favor. Or to put it another way, foods made by mom-and-pop producers typically do not have artificial ingredients in them; foods made by multinational food companies do. That may be reason enough to avoid their products on ethical grounds.

Some artificial ingredients, in conjunction with various market and political forces, play a key role in the health-related problems associated with a high-fat, high-sugar diet. Without artificial flavors, colors, sweeteners, and preservatives, unhealthy Western-style convenience foods would likely be consumed far less. According to the World Health Organization (WHO), 35% of adults are overweight, 11% obese. Sixty-five percent of the world's population lives in countries where being overweight and obese cause more deaths than being underweight (WHO 2015). The causes appear to be urbanization, sedentary forms of work, and a diet of energy-dense foods high in fat. Food technologies make unhealthy foods available and thus enable unhealthy lifestyles. On a model of autonomous technology, the artificial ingredients are responsible for making our diets worse. The product itself is the problem. On a constructivist model, these technologies are simply one, albeit vital, part of a vast web of actors, things, and events that make up food production and consumption.

Conclusion

We've seen how the models of technological neutrality and autonomy fail to do justice to the contingent, flexible, socially embedded character of man-made things. A constructivist model is a better way of understanding what technologies are and how they relate to food production and food consumption. To say technologies are constructed realities moves us away from scientific and technical considerations into the mangle of social life and political economy. It lets us see the relationships between food and technologies as contingent, open-ended, and flexible. If things were designed in a particular way, they can be designed differently. Farms, livestock facilities, and food-manufacturing plants large and small involve countless man-made things. Most of these things are neither problematic nor crucial; most are innocuous parts of a larger whole.

The key to an insightful analysis of their relationship is to identify precisely which technology networks are essential for what particular kind of food production, and how the technological component can be changed for the better. Granted, technological modification alone is not going to reverse climate change or bring about perpetual peace, but at least it is something that is reasonably within our control. Any designs we might collectively have to improve global food and agricultural systems will have to be designed into production. It is a daunting task but it can be made easier the sooner we reject the idea that technologies are either neutral or autonomous and recognize the social dimensions of our technical choices.

References

Center for Science in the Public Interest. "Chemical Cuisine," viewed 15 July 2015, http://www.cspinet. org/reports/chemcuisine.htm.

Eurobarometer. (2014) "Europeans, Agriculture, and the Common Agricultural Policy," *Eurobarometer* 80(2), viewed 26 May 2016, http://ec.europa.eu/public_opinion/archives/ebs/ebs_410_en.pdf.

European Food Safety Authority. (2015) "Food Safety: From the Farm to the Fork," viewed 15 July 2015, http://ec.europa.eu/food/fs/sc/oldcomm7/out06_en.html.

Food and Drug Administration. (2010) "Overview of Food Ingredients, Additives, and Colors," viewed 15 July 2015, www.fda.gov/Food/IngredientsPackagingLabeling/FoodAdditivesIngredients/.

Freyfogle, E. T. (ed.) (2001) *The New Agrarianism: Land, Culture and the Community of Life*, Washington, DC: Island Press.

Nestle, M. (2003) *Food Politics: How the Food Industry Influences Nutrition and Health*, Berkeley: University of California Press.

Nestle, M. (2007) *What to Eat*, New York: North Point Press.

Parker-Pope, T. (2012) "Craving an Ice Cream Fix," *New York Times*, 20 September, viewed 15 July 2015, http://well.blogs.nytimes.com/2012/09/20/craving-an-ice-cream-fix/.

Petrini, C. (2006) *Slow Food Revolution: A New Culture for Eating and Living*, Rome: Rizzoli.

Pollan, M. (2009) *In Defense of Food: An Eater's Manifesto*, New York: Penguin.

Wirzba, N. (ed.) (2004) *The Essential Agrarian Reader: The Future of Culture, Community, and Land*, Berkeley: Counterpoint.

W. K. Kellogg Foundation. (2012) "Perceptions of the U.S. Food System: What and How Americans Think about their Food," viewed 15 July 2015, http://www.wkkf.org/resource-directory/resource/2005/09/perceptions-of-the-us-food-system-what-and-how-americans-think-about-their-food.

World Health Organization. (2015) "Obesity and Overweight: Fact Sheet No. 311," viewed 15 July 2015, http://www.who.int/mediacentre/fs311/en.

5

THE ETHICS OF EATING AS A HUMAN ORGANISM

Caleb Ward

Introduction

Every ethical engagement with the question of eating other organisms depends on presuppositions, often unexamined, about the nature of the human being. Traditional accounts of the ethics of eating – particularly those grounded in an idea of rights extended to animals – often rely on a thoroughgoing exceptionalism with respect to human responsibilities. These draw a sharp distinction between humans and non-human animals on account of the human rational faculty or another feature that entails our unique need to justify eating other organisms. When ethical theories are unreflectively built on this perspective, they risk losing sight of the fact that humans are not only free to choose whether or not to destroy organisms and ecosystems, but we are at the same time participants in natural processes that exceed our agency. In contrast, approaches that seek to jettison human exceptionalism entirely – such as the "paleo diet" heuristic – often err toward the other extreme, naturalizing human behaviors and thereby undermining the possibility of critique. In this chapter I provide an approach to ethical inquiry that seeks to navigate between these two poles. Drawing on the philosophy of Henri Bergson (1990 [1896], 1998 [1907]), I consider the ethics of human food production from the starting point of the human as an organism and human practices as organic activity. By situating human life – and, therefore, morality – within nature, yet not subsuming it therein, this inquiry takes up a perspective more commensurable to food as an object of inquiry that is overdetermined by both nature and culture.

All organisms interact with their environments to create the necessary conditions for life: nourishment, habitat, and so forth. While every organism is structured to pursue a different approach to this project, there are tendencies that emerge: most animals address needs through active mobility, for example, while most plants tend toward more passive strategies. The human animal tends to pursue its objects by relying heavily on the *intellect*, the capacity to analyze matter before dismantling and reassembling it into the appropriate configurations to satisfy our needs.

In the case of nutritive activities, all animals extract nourishment from ingested organic matter through largely unconscious processes of digestion and absorption, and those processes are for the most part determined by the bodily structure of each species. Organisms vary widely, however, as they pursue their food prior to the moment of ingestion. While non-human animals for the most part cognize their meals without recourse to science or intellectual knowledge, the human's success is dependent on practices such as agriculture, animal husbandry, and cooking.

We feed ourselves by these technological operations of intellect, and thus we seem to approach the production of food in much the same way that we engage in our other activities of fabrication: we organize our activities to impart form onto matter.

While intellect is well suited to the task of shaping inert matter into objects of service to the human organism, Bergson argues that the intellect's approach comes up against a limitation when we apply it to living things. When the intellect turns itself toward knowing and acting on other organisms as its objects, Bergson suggests that it misrecognizes what is living and treats organisms as if they were mere material. This is the source of the sometimes-disastrous ethical and environmental results of human activities. Bergson contrasts the dispassionate, external knowledge that subtends human activity with an organic *sympathy* – an instinctual knowledge from the inside – that has primacy among other species, enabling more synergistic approaches to their nutritive projects. While the intellect typically overpowers this sympathetic instinct in human activities, it seems to be possible for sympathy to reemerge in the form of human *intuition*, which can perhaps bring intellect into attunement with the nature of living things.

In the conventional practices of industrial beef production, the human's clumsy, external approach to other organisms is tragically on display. Yet, the industry has recently begun to shift away from the assembly-line model; contemporary technologies, such as those designed by animal scientist Temple Grandin, have begun to incorporate a form of sympathy into the process of food production. This chapter elaborates on the framework sketched above and uses it to pursue as a case study a critical examination of Grandin's adaptive designs for moving cattle. Drawing on Grandin's own words about her connection to the inner life of cattle, I explore how her designs seem to express that her fabricating intellect is informed by an intuition for life. Yet, Grandin's approach remains embedded within the industry of meat production, which supplies the overarching logic to her technologies in the shape of an indifferent, intellect-driven structure of productivity. Acknowledging that there is some form of organic sympathy present in all acts of eating, I argue that the misrecognition of life that persists even in Grandin's designs is not symptomatic of all acts of turning animals into food, but it is instead a product of turning organisms into commodities, which are only incidentally connected to the human's project of feeding itself. With this example, I hope to show how the expansive organic view of human activity can offer a novel vantage point for critique of our misrecognition of life.

Organisms in action

In *Matter and Memory* (1990 [1896]), Bergson describes how life is organized according to the relationship between perception and action. By means of perception, all organisms identify particular relevant aspects of their surroundings, and, through the mobilization of consciousness, they respond to their perceptions by acting appropriately. In the simplest forms of life, such as amoebas, the moment of perception automatically incites a mechanism of action; the organism is limited by its structure to simply receive stimuli and reflect them into external mobility. In complex organisms, however, there is a hesitation between perception and action, as a result of an inner life that is not present in the amoeba. Organisms with central nervous systems interpret the perceptual experience, formulating external actions in response only to those perceptions recognized as being of vital interest to the organism. For these complex organisms, the mobilization of the body never responds to the full content of perception: some perceptions are not reflected outward into action, but rather are absorbed into consciousness. This produces affections that take the form of sensations, emotions, or even knowledge in the inner life of the organism. In short, as the organism inhabits its environment, every perceptual encounter produces some combination of internal affections and outward-facing action in the physical world.[1]

In *Creative Evolution* (1998 [1907]), Bergson proposes two broad tendencies – instinct and intellect – that shape the work of selecting actions in response to perception. These two tendencies always coexist in an organism, but they differ in priority from one species to the next. Both provide the resources an organism needs to select and respond appropriately to the perceptions that bear upon its survival. Most non-human animals are characterized by instinct; they select actions for the most part unreflectively, in direct response to the environmental processes that stand out as relevant in the foreground of their perceptions. In these animals' responses to other living things – to potential food, to predators, and so forth – there can be seen a kind of *sympathy*: a responsiveness among organisms that share a vital interest in one another's lives.[2]

Bergson illustrates organic sympathy by describing the behavior of several genera of wasps that obtain nutriment through a particular form of predation (Bergson 1998 [1907]: 171–175). These wasps organize their activities around the need to secure living prey on which to feed their larvae, and each genus accomplishes this end by administering a series of paralytic stings to a particular type of victim. To strike the delicate balance of immobilizing without killing, each genus uses a procedure that befits the physical organic structure of the intended prey. So, the sphex that feeds on a certain cricket stings at each of the three primary nerve centers controlling the cricket's legs, while the sand wasp that feeds on a caterpillar stings at nine nerve centers. Even from the perspective of contemporary science, the surgical precision of these paralytic wasps is difficult to explain. According to Bergson, this is because science understands knowledge always according to the paradigm of intellect, in which an observer gathers information from the outside and then formulates actions accordingly. On this view, it seems impossible for the wasp to know how to direct its actions without undergoing a process of trial and error. Yet, as Bergson notes, research shows[3] that the wasp has no process of scientific deduction that precedes its behaviors. Rather, in the urgent matter of life or death for these wasps, instinct alone enables success. As the organisms work to establish the conditions for life befitting their structure, their activities are directed by an innate form of consciousness, different from our own. Rather than gather knowledge through extrinsic observation, these wasps do not properly know at all; their accuracy arises from the sympathy they share with the organisms they take as prey. Thus, the wasps do not interpret the activities of the living organisms they need for their survival; rather, the wasps participate directly in those activities.

Like these wasps, human beings continually undertake activities to further the survival of the organism. In contrast with the wasps' vital participation led by instinct, however, such human activities are for the most part directed by a reigning intellect. The human consciousness is structured to reflect on that which it perceives, and the human organism generally puts its thoughts into action strategically to generate effective results. With only a few exceptions – such as the newborn reaching for its mother's breast (Bergson 1998 [1907]: 162–163) – even the most necessary activities for human sustenance are regulated according to this reflective faculty; in the case of food, the intellect is the means by which we cultivate or capture other organisms and prepare them to meet our needs, before we ingest them into the body and subject them to the unreflective processes of digestion, absorption, and redistribution of nutrients.

In all such efforts to sustain its life, the human animal succeeds by planning efficient procedures and fabricating effective tools. Bergson attributes the prosperity of the human to the intellect's native ability to grasp abstract relations, even as the intellect cannot understand directly – that is, without investigation – the objects it encounters.[4] The intellect's talent for abstraction makes it possible for us to recognize that our tools for life are made more effective when they are produced using other tools; through this logic the intellect expands human activities of fabrication to ever-higher levels of instrumentality. This approach reaches its apotheosis in the methods of science, which seek through analytic knowledge to put at the disposal of the human being the whole of the material world. The human organism maximizes its mobility, captures its nutriment, and evades its predators through the amazing, refined efficiency of technologies based on scientific knowledge, which has been deduced from observation and then codified in language for transmission across generations.

The intellect's misrecognition of life

While the intellect's abstraction makes possible the remarkable success of the human organism, this same mode of thought leads, according to Bergson, to many of our shortcomings in attempting to manipulate living matter. Bergson writes:

> We see that the intellect, so skillful in dealing with the inert, is awkward the moment it touches the living. Whether it wants to treat the life of the body or the life of the mind, it proceeds with the rigor, the stiffness and the brutality of an instrument not designed for such use. The history of hygiene or of pedagogy teaches us much in this matter. [...] [In these practices] we are amazed at the stupidity and especially at the persistence of errors. We may easily find their origin in the natural obstinacy with which we treat the living like the lifeless and think all reality, however fluid, under the form of the sharply defined solid. We are at ease only in the discontinuous, in the immobile, in the dead.
>
> (Bergson 1998 [1907]: 165)

Bergson's examples above, health and pedagogy, both continue today to exceed the precision of intellectual inquiry, and to those two I would also add psychology, child development, and, crucially for this volume, nutrition.

Because the intellect is structurally wedded to the work of fabricating instruments for action, Bergson argues, science is doomed to misunderstand the portion of matter that is organic, dynamic, and capable itself of generating novelty. When the intellect deals with living creatures, it reduces them to constitutive parts, naming their components and looking to the possibilities for disassembling and reassembling them for use. Built upon this foundation, science will always reduce the essential motion and novelty of organic life to stasis and mechanical automatism, or at best, as we see in neuroscience and some contemporary biology, to a correlative and probabilistic approximation.

In the technologies through which humans deal with life, there appears a native tendency toward these errors of intellect. As the disciplines of systematized knowledge mobilize human action according to their blueprints, the dynamism of life is invariably suppressed to maximize the pliability of matter in the service of prescribed ends. This has become particularly salient as humans have developed activities that make possible the large-scale production of food for the species; here, the technological fabrication supervised by the intellect is thoroughly designed as if the living were no more than inert.

Sympathetic innovation in raising cattle

Modern practices of animal agriculture, in particular the process of raising large numbers of cattle for food, seem to epitomize the indifference to life that Bergson diagnoses in the fabricating intellect. From the activities of birthing, growing, and finishing to those of slaughter, processing, and distribution, humans manipulate these organisms as the raw material for a larger process of fabrication. The living potential for action present in the cattle is addressed as a problem to be solved; it is a mere attribute of the material, an attribute whose effects must be managed and minimized for the industry to proceed efficiently.

Consider, for example, the feedlot in which beef cattle are "finished" or fattened over the last several months of their lives. As cattle arrive at the feedlot by truck, they must be dipped in a sanitizing bath, vaccinated, and inspected for medical conditions or injuries. To achieve these tasks, handlers move cattle one by one through an enclosure, called a cattle alley (or cattle chute), into a structure in which veterinarians can administer treatments. After medical treatment, in most modern facilities, cattle are tagged and entered into a computer system to record medical history, age, weight, and other biodata useful for assessing monetary value and ensuring appropriate categorization as they progress through the pipeline.

It is clear from this process that the principles that govern the typical cattle feedlot present only a slight variation on industrial conventions for maintaining any inventory. However, the mistake that the intellect makes in this assumption – that living organisms are akin to inert matter – becomes clear by examining more closely the case of the cattle alley.

In the conventional cattle alley, handlers separate cattle and prod them forward through a straight, fenced-in enclosure, marshaling them one by one through the dipping pool. The animals present a challenge to their handlers by becoming unruly, by refusing to keep moving, and by gathering in crowds that block the flow of traffic. It is tempting to consider these difficulties as akin to the challenge the industrial blacksmith faces taming molten iron; from the perspective of the cattle handlers working the alley, the animals seem essentially to be a difficult and dangerous material to manipulate. Such a fabricating view identifies technology as the mediating term between human will and the matter it seeks to shape, as if the right means of separation between the two can enable the human being to overcome the difficulty presented by the material. Yet, Bergson would argue that the difficulty faced when moving cattle is actually a product of the presuppositions of the intellect – the same presuppositions that give rise to the inadequate analogy between cattle handling and smithing. The handler strains against the cattle not because of an archetypal struggle between matter and will, but because the entire technology of producing these animals is designed according to the misrecognition of living organisms as mere inert matter. In fact, the problem of moving cattle is not an extension of the problem of moving any other material object; cattle are actually consciously perceptive organisms that are inclined, as most animals are, to self-locomotion.

While it appears from Bergson's account of intellect that this misrecognition may be inevitable in human manufacturing, recent innovations in the cattle-moving industry suggest that organic sympathy may come to play a greater role. Temple Grandin is an autistic woman who has made significant industrial design interventions into the cattle industry over the past 30 years. Among her first inventions to gain widespread use was a more adaptive design for the cattle alley. Grandin's design transforms the cattle alley into a space that resonates more closely with the organic structure of cattle consciousness, suppressing perceptual cues that might inspire fear or hesitation and enabling cattle to follow their instinctual tendencies.[5]

Drawing on her awareness that cattle like to stay together in herds and move in circles, Grandin's cattle alley begins with a wide pathway into a crowd pen that is open and semicircular. After cattle move along this curved pen, they enter an area of the alley that narrows into a long arc. According to Grandin, this design allows the animals to see far enough ahead to know that the alley is not a dead end – which, Grandin says, they would resist entering – but it prevents them from seeing so far as to become frightened by the human activity at the other end (Grandin 1989).

Grandin further controls the cattle's perceptual experience by replacing the fences typical of conventional designs with solid walls that better hide handlers and other traffic from view. She emphasizes the importance of eliminating all extraneous visible objects such as stray flags or dangling chains that might distract cattle and encourage balking behavior or hesitation. She even specifies the level of light in a structure – not too dark, since cattle will not move into a dark space – and works with ranchers to reduce shadows that might be perceived as menacing (Grandin 2011 [1998]).

In an industry that has been defined in recent decades by its massive, impersonal scale, Grandin's work stands out as a recalibration that brings into focus the perspective of the individual animal. I do not mean that she treats each cattle as a unique being with its own attributes and identity; this is not the purpose of Grandin's work, which is often implemented on feedlots that process tens of thousands head of cattle at a time. Rather, I mean that Grandin's designs take seriously the singular organism as a consciousness with its own view of the world, albeit a view that is circumscribed by the possibilities entailed by the species' organic structure. By operating at the level of the perceptions of cattle as they move through the alley, Grandin recognizes that life is experienced always at the scale of the individual. This attention to scale is a hallmark of sympathy: the organism is grasped as a particular organism, not conceptualized in the abstract as essentially a mere instance of a larger genus of interest for some task. Even in the efficiency of the sphex stinging the cricket, the outcome is made possible by the vital interest the sphex has in the encounter with the organism it takes as its prey. It is only through an intellectual knowledge that science can say that the sphex is interested in a genus of crickets and not in the particular cricket – with its particular salient features – that is recognized in the moment of predation.

Recall that, according to Bergson, the life of an organism is bifurcated into the affections absorbed and the mobility that is reflected outward in the form of physical expression and action. Contrary to typical intellectual innovation, Grandin's interest in cattle did not set out from a search for more effective means of dealing with the external animal mobility or the efficiency of the production line. Rather, it is clear from the accounts she gives in interviews (see Grandin 2010b; Sutton 2006) that the initial motivation for her work was an interest in the experiences internal to cattle life: how perceptual input leads to the inner affections of cattle – the actual pain and fear that their surroundings inspire in the cattle mind.

She says that, in the wild eyes and incessant lowing of the cattle on the feedlot, she recognized expressions of an emotional state that was familiar to her own experience as an autistic person in neurotypical society (Sutton 2006). Rather than approach cattle as a problem of matter to be mastered, which would be typical of the human intellect, Grandin responds to this insight by working to adjust the perceptions of the animals to improve their qualitative affective experience. While the stirring of empathy that motivates this work is recognizable as a particularly human emotional phenomenon, it structurally resembles the sympathetic discernment that takes place in the instincts of other organisms. This is an example of the human intuition that can arise when the human's organic sympathy with life is heard alongside the voice of intellect. By way of intuition, Grandin recognizes that she and the cattle are implicated in the same organic processes – that they are relevant to one another because of their conscious organic structures. Unlike the purely instinctual wasp, however, Grandin is able to use the considerable power of human consciousness to contemplate her insight and turn her actions toward ends that she formulates. The sympathetic form of her designs, even as they operate on the scale of mass industry, exhibits these intuitive origins.

I have emphasized the role played by something akin to sympathy in Grandin's work to highlight the way in which her innovations depart from the conventional human approach, i.e., to conceptualize organic matter through the intellect. I make no claim, however, that intuition is the dominant force in her work. Intellect and scientific inquiry play an important function in Grandin's design process. To produce viable new designs for cattle management, her original intuition – that she and the cattle experience similar emotions – had to be intensified through an intellectual process of scientific study. After the initial recognition of kinship, she began research, taking cattle as her object, to deduce causal relationships between animal perceptions and particular behaviors. In this scientific stage, superior attention to detail – something she attributes to her autism (Grandin 2010a: 9:30) – allowed her to get to know cattle behaviors in a way that was increasingly accurate in its predictions, and therefore more useful for fabricating a technological intervention. Through this process of observation and rational deduction, Grandin gathered the knowledge that enabled her to act on her intuited interest in minimizing cattle distress, with the byproduct of encouraging predictably calm cattle movements. Thus, Grandin was capable of producing sympathetic designs adapted to the structure of cattle consciousness only through an activity that was intellectual in process, but intuitive in motivation.

The industry has embraced Grandin's work because her intervention, though targeted toward the absorptive side of cattle consciousness, reverberates outward in changed behavior, maximizing cattle's active mobility through the system and minimizing interruptions caused by balking or rearing. Grandin's designs draw out productivity from the inner experience of the cattle, encouraging their organic activity to align with the human project of fabrication. This goes well beyond simply exerting the human will from the outside, like yoking oxen to pull a plow. Just as the wasp's paralyzed prey continues to metabolize and maintain its flesh as food for the larva, the cattle in Grandin's system mobilize themselves in support of the human technology that will ultimately turn them into food. This leads to increased efficiency in terms of both human labor and time, thus dovetailing perfectly with the goals of the fabricating science of beef production.

Moving from phenomenology to critique: the slaughterhouse and the ethics of food

By making the meat industry more efficient, Grandin's sympathetic designs facilitate increases in both volume and profit. The industry in the US continues to slaughter around 33 million cattle per year – a number that has remained stable for the past ten years and is down slightly from the ten-year period prior to that (USDA 2014) – but the growth of the production of beef globally during that same period has raised serious nutritional, ecological, and climatological problems. In addition to these human and environmental questions, the flourishing of the industry intensifies a challenging situation for animal ethics, one to which Grandin, despite her interest in the inner lives of cattle, provides responses that are unsatisfying from a philosophical standpoint. When asked the ethical question of why it should be acceptable to kill cattle for food, Grandin often responds, "The cattle would have never been born if we hadn't raised them" (Sutton 2006: 19:00). It is likely self-evident to a philosophical reader that this response represents a fallacy: existence cannot be judged as more or less valuable than non-existence, because existence is the condition of possibility of all value, whether positive or negative. In light of this, I consider Grandin's unreflective response to actually be consistent with the logic of her relationship with other organisms. Because her attention is focused on the inner affections – emotions and sensations – of cattle, philosophical questions of existence and justification are outside the scope of her interest. She goes on: "I feel very strongly we've got to give the animals a decent life. And of all the meat animals, beef cattle when they are done right probably have the best life" (Sutton 2006: 19:05).

Part of the process of making sure cattle are "done right" is the final stage in the life of the animal, "processing" at the slaughterhouse. Before Grandin's rise to prominence, cattle workers often attributed the unruliness of cattle at the entrance to the slaughterhouse to the animals' sense that death awaited. Through her sensitivity to the individual scale of cattle affections, however, Grandin had the insight that cattle in the slaughterhouse do not know that they are in mortal danger. Lacking the intellect's capacity for abstraction, cattle can discern no structural meaning for the exercises through which they are driven every day, nor for the particular cattle alley that leads to the final blow of the stunner. Grandin observed that cattle became distressed in response to the same types of visual cues at the slaughterhouse as in the feedlot. Her response to this recognition was to devise a new, sympathetic design, nicknamed the "Stairway to Heaven," for moving cattle through the slaughterhouse in a manner that minimizes fear and pain experienced along the way. The resulting product is now used to process half the cattle raised for beef in North America (Phifer n.d.), and it has been widely lauded by animal welfarists for reducing suffering as cattle participate in the final stages of the beef production pipeline.

Thus, it seems that Grandin's model treats living things as living up until the decisive moment when they are treated as things – that is, when they are killed and turned into steaks and other beef products to circulate in the global market. As we see with the "Stairway to Heaven," Grandin remains consistent in her approach even in the most intimate engagement with the ultimate fabricating purpose of the beef industry. She seems to consider the broader purpose and structure of the meat industry to be static, but she mobilizes organic sympathy to redesign the variables that govern how the cattle are conducted through that structure.[6] In response to her intuition of cattle affections, she designs technologies that minimize the disturbance to the inside consciousness, while manipulating the outside of the animal in the way prescribed by the industry's goals. It could be said that Grandin treats a living thing accordingly as living in the means, but the end is still to render that living thing inert. This reflects the fact that the process of commercial beef production is guided by a logic that assumes the living to be indistinguishable from other raw material, even as Grandin shows a kind of sympathy toward the animal in fulfilling that telos.

Yet, perhaps this interpretation is guilty of an overly simplistic assumption about the phenomenon of food. It is unsatisfactory to say that the inherent character of technologies that raise animals for food is to treat the living as lifeless. Rather, it is a fundamental characteristic of nutriment – across nearly all organisms – that what is absorbed into the body as food is made up of organized matter. We eat from the realm of matter that at some point has lived, although in the process of doing so we render matter no longer living.[7] In a sense, instrumentality is a part of the natural shape of food: there is a nutritive necessity, universal among organisms, that requires us to destroy living matter to achieve our own survival. The material we take into our bodies as food is only desirable because another organism has rearranged it into molecular forms – proteins, carbohydrates, lipids – that are indispensible for human survival. When an organism eats another, its body biologically discerns and benefits from the work done by the living thing that is no longer living. The organic generativity that was actual in the organism that is destroyed – the eaten – is extinguished and appropriated to maintain the novel potentiality of the eater. Thus, a sympathetic relationship – a proper recognition of life as life – exists between eater and eaten, prior to the interpretive mediation of intellect.

When organisms kill to create the nutritive conditions for survival and for surviving well, they do not render the living inert as a part of the endless chain of fabrication that Bergson critiques. Thus, while intellect suppresses novelty by treating the living as matter that can be fabricated into instruments for further purposes, there is some form of sympathy that subtends the relationship with food for all animals. This nutritive sympathy does not suppress the novelty expressed by living things in pursuing its ends; rather, it recognizes the generative power of the living organism as what makes the organism potentially food.

In light of this structure of organic life, I argue that the misrecognition of the living takes place not insofar as an animal is rendered food, but insofar as that food is itself reduced to being a mere *thing*. So, when cattle is made into steak, that steak can actualize its organic value if it is eaten by another organism that seeks to reintegrate its once-living tissue into new possibilities for life. However, from the perspective of the commercial meat industry, the steak is only incidentally food; primarily, it is a commodity that fulfills its purpose merely by being converted into money –

the most abstract intellectual instrument of fabrication – regardless of whether it is ultimately eaten. Thus, in the science of beef production, the living organism is treated as inert because its ultimate purpose is to be processed into a form that can be efficiently exchanged – to become absorbed into the intellectual genericism of a commodity. When the industry achieves this outcome, the organic activity of the animal that has become the food disappears. The living cattle is objectified as if it were merely inert material to be harnessed for an end (namely, profit), and the same is true of the human organic activity – i.e., labor – that is objectified in the commodity foods that are produced. This remains the case even with the use of sympathetic technologies, such as Grandin's, that are more appropriate to the organism's structure. As long as it is not truly engaged in the project of feeding the human organism, animal agriculture is guilty of the tragic mistake of the intellect: destroying the novelty of living things by misrecognizing life as mere material usable for some further end.

Conclusion: the need for critique of the human organism

My account of food and its attendant technologies in this chapter has descended from an understanding of the human need to eat that is shared with all organisms, to the fabricating methods of human food production that treat animals as mere matter, to Grandin's sympathetic interventions that are ultimately reabsorbed into the service of the commercial telos of the meat industry. In response to the ethical inadequacy of Grandin's approach, I examined how the organic activity of turning living things into food does not in itself replicate the intellect's error; I argued instead that only insofar as food production takes on a commoditized structure does it misunderstand life as inert matter.

Temple Grandin's remarkable interventions show how the use of a kind of sympathy does not divest the fabricating intellect of its tendency to instrumentalize life, even as the technologies of human food production approach the level of intuitive sophistication comparable to the paralytic wasp. Wasp and human share a vital interest to create out of organic matter the conditions for their lives as organisms, but the human overlays on this interest the intellect's desire that potential food, like all matter, serve an instrumental purpose for further fabricating activity. By destroying organisms for the purpose of profit rather than of food, we allow this instrumentalizing intellect to define our relationship with life.

In areas of human activity interested in life, today's technological innovations are increasingly developing integrated, dynamic approaches to fabrication, built upon adaptive models that mold themselves to the shape of the living things they seek to control. In addition to the work of Temple Grandin and of other animal welfarists, we can discern this movement in medicine as psychiatric medications make increasingly sophisticated interventions into brain chemicals, in agricultural technology as plants are engineered to generate pesticides from the inside, and in warfare as so-called enhanced interrogation techniques become increasingly tailored to the particular psyches of the humans they target. In each of these cases, sympathy is achieved not by relaxing the intellectual drive, but by applying an intensified scientific knowledge refined through increasingly exacting measurements, calculations, and manipulations.

Bergson provides an account of the structure of life that helps us situate such practices in perspective within the dynamic, self-expanding whole of organic activity. However, his rigorous descriptive account must be supplemented with a radical ethical approach to pursue the fact that at stake in this failure of intellect – to treat the living as inert – are actual lives that place immediate moral claims on humans. These include both the lives of the non-human animals that are turned into food-commodities and the lives of the humans that are treated as mechanistic assembly-line workers for this process.[8] Thus, while food ethics requires that we recognize that the human is an organism inherently implicated in relations with other organisms, we must also augment this expansive perspective with additional political notions. Only from critical analysis both of the political dimension of humans' fabricating pursuits and of the organic dimension of our participation in the novel movement of life can we make ethical demands that are appropriate to our role in the organic totality of Earth.

Acknowledgments

I would like to thank Megan Craig, Michael Kryluk, and Michèle Leaman for their insightful feedback on the ideas presented in this chapter.

Notes

1 Despite its appearances, Bergson's account – and by extension my own – is not a thoroughgoing inside–outside/mind–body dualism. The processes of affection and action inform one another and interpenetrate within the organism at all times. Further, action is of course not merely external. Together as a unified whole, action and affection make up the process of what it is to be an organism.
2 Note that the term "sympathy" in this discourse lacks the human emotional connotations of the conventional usage. This will become important to keep in mind as the term is applied to animal welfare efforts.
3 While the research Bergson cites is today over a century old, his larger point still stands.
4 Bergson writes, "The new-born child, so far as intelligent, knows neither definite objects nor a definite property of any object; but when, a little later on, he will hear an epithet being applied to a substantive, he will immediately understand what it means" (Bergson 1998 [1907]: 163). Bergson claims that the child also innately comes to understand the relationships of cause and effect, of like with like, and others. The ease with which humans grasp these abstractions is evidence of the power of the intellect.
5 For images showing the organic shape of Grandin's designs, see <http://www.grandinlivestockhandling systems.com/ranch.html>.
6 This troubling epistemic blind spot is acutely discernible in a series of videos created by the American Meat Institute, in which Grandin gives tours of various slaughtering facilities. In one video of a turkey slaughterhouse, Grandin walks the viewer through the process of stunning, in which each bird hangs upside down by metal foot restraints with its head submerged in water. The water is then electrified so a current runs the length of the bird's body. The stunning is done ostensibly to ensure that the bird does not have consciousness as its throat is slit (and, more plausibly, to keep the bird immobile so the cutting machine can operate at a higher level of accuracy and efficiency). On behalf of the affections experienced by the turkey, Grandin gives the ameliorative advice that slaughterhouse workers should ensure that the birds are not blinking after they are stunned, since that is evidence that they may still be conscious of pain. She shows no sign, however, of acknowledging the deeper question of whether or not such a practice can be justified in principle (*Video Tour of a Turkey Farm and Processing Plant Featuring Temple Grandin* 2013).
7 An exception could perhaps be identified in the case of certain active cultures that continue to live in the gut.
8 This dehumanization operates across multiple intersecting dimensions, including race, colonialism, and socioeconomic class. In 2003, 38% of production and sanitation workers in the US meat and poultry processing industry were foreign-born noncitizens. Across the industry, 42% of workers were Hispanic, and an additional 20% were black. The annual mean wage for these workers was about $26,500 (US Government Accountability Office 2005: 16).

References

Bergson, H. (1990 [1896]) *Matter and Memory*, trans. N. M. Paul and W. S. Palmer, New York: Zone Books.
——. (1998 [1907]) *Creative Evolution*, trans. A. Mitchell, Mineola, NY: Dover.
Grandin, T. (1989) "Behavioral Principles of Livestock Handling," *Livestock Behaviour, Design of Facilities and Humane Slaughter*, updated 2015, viewed 20 May 2015, http://www.grandin.com/references/new.corral.html.

——. (2010a) "The World Needs All Kinds of Minds," *TED Video*, viewed 20 May 2015, http://www.ted.com/talks/temple_grandin_the_world_needs_all_kinds_of_minds.

——. (2010b) Interview by Carrie Gracie, *The Interview*, BBC World Service, viewed 20 May 2015, http://www.bbc.co.uk/programmes/p006zvn7.

——. (2011 [1998]) "Directions for Laying Out Curved Cattle Handling Facilities for Ranches, Feedlots, and Properties," *Livestock Behaviour, Design of Facilities and Humane Slaughter*, viewed 20 May 2015, http://www.grandin.com/design/curved.handling.facilities.html.

Phifer, T. (n.d.) "CSU's One of a Kind Mind: Temple Grandin's Amazing Life with Autism," *Colorado State University*, viewed 19 May 2015, http://source.colostate.edu/temple-grandin/.

Sutton, E., dir. (2006) "The Woman Who Thinks Like a Cow," *BBC Horizon*, Season 42, Episode 17.

USDA National Agricultural Statistics Service. (2014) Cited in "Farm Animals Statistics: Slaughter Totals," *The Humane Society of the United States*, viewed 20 May 2015, http://www.humanesociety.org/news/resources/research/stats_slaughter_totals.html.

US Government Accountability Office. (2005) "Workplace Safety and Health: Safety in the Meat and Poultry Industry, while Improving, Could Be Further Strengthened," Report to the Ranking Minority Member, Committee on Health, Education, Labor, and Pensions, US Senate, viewed 20 May 2015, http://www.gao.gov/new.items/d0596.pdf.

Video Tour of a Turkey Farm and Processing Plant Featuring Temple Grandin. (2013) Washington, DC: National Turkey Federation with The American Meat Institute, viewed 20 May 2015, http://www.animalhandling.org/ht/d/sp/i/80622/pid/80622.

PART II
Gender and food

6

WOMEN'S WORK

Ethics, home cooking, and the sexual politics of food

Mary C. Rawlinson

How is it that at the precise historical moment when Americans were abandoning the kitchen, handing over the preparation of most of our meals to the food industry, we began spending so much of our time thinking about food and watching other people cook it on television? . . . We live in an age when professional cooks are household names, some of them as famous as athletes or movie stars. . . . This is peculiar. After all, we're not watching shows or reading books about sewing or darning socks or changing the oil in our car, three other domestic chores that we have been only too happy to outsource – and then promptly drop from conscious awareness. But cooking somehow feels different. The work, or the process, retains an emotional or psychological power we can't quite shake, or don't want to. And in fact it was after a long hour of watching cooking programs on television that I began to wonder if this activity I had always taken for granted might be worth taking a little more seriously.

—Michael Pollan, *Cooked: A Natural History of Transformations* 2013

A woman, like Mr. Pollan's own mother, who has spent decades in the kitchen preparing meals for her family, can only laugh at the great food maven's belated discovery that cooking is "one of the most interesting and worthwhile things we humans do" (Pollan 2013: 11). For most of his career, Pollan focused on food production and distribution and "gave little thought to cooking" (Pollan 2013: 2–3). With the publication of *Cooked: A Natural History of Transformations* in 2013, Pollan announces his realization that cooking meals at home based on whole foods and fresh ingredients would be more effective than any other intervention in addressing the social, political, and environmental urgencies that he has diagnosed under the current infrastructures of global food.[1]

It was not cooking in general that Mr. Pollan "took for granted," but *his mother's* cooking:

Cooking has always been a part of my life, but more like the furniture than an object of scrutiny, much less a passion. I counted myself lucky to have a parent – my mother – who loved to cook and almost every night made us a delicious meal. By the time I had a place of my own, I could find my way around a kitchen well enough, the result of nothing more purposeful than all those hours spent hanging around the kitchen while my mother fixed dinner.

(Pollan 2013: 2)

His mother's cooking was part of the atmosphere or ambience of his life, an element of his feeling "at home," as stable and reliable as the furniture.[2] Her work differs from that of the celebrity chefs, not only because it is invisible and unpaid, but also because of its *everydayness*. The domestic chores that are marked masculine – changing the oil, cleaning out the gutters – tend to be seasonal rather than routine. The daily chores of providing meals and childcare continue to fall overwhelmingly to women.[3] Even those who love to cook will find the unrelenting routine of feeding a family tiring at times. Pollan's mother was a fulltime homemaker and had the time to cook. Working mothers find it more difficult to find that time, a circumstance ruthlessly exploited by the fast-food industry, as Pollan notes (see Pollan 2013: 186–189). Pollan also rightly quotes the probable link between the rise in obesity in the US and the decline in home cooking (Pollan 2013: 191), as well as the environmental crises precipitated by the turn to global food. Yet, Pollan's work is symptomatic of writers on food and food ethics in *taking for granted* the knowledge and practices embedded in women's long history of feeding their families and communities. His book is less about home cooking than about the masculine arts of barbequing, brewing, and commercial baking. In this way, although his book is intended as a corrective to the overlooked role of cooking, it epitomizes the failure in discussions of food ethics to attend to the continuing history of women's labor in the kitchen.

Philosophers and food writers fail to tarry with women's labor long enough to notice that home cooking provides a rich field for the discovery of figures and principles in ethics. The public health issue of obesity or the environmental effects of global food's commodity crops and CAFOs cannot be addressed without reconfiguring the gender division of labor and the antithesis between work and family, so that humans may eat differently. Food justice and ethical eating will require changes in *everydayness*, in the organization of space and time, the integration of work and family, the distribution of work, and the respect for domestic labor.

Everydayness: on being at home through food

Though philosophers and ethicists have rarely paid attention to food, anthropologists have long recognized its importance as an infrastructure of culture and identity.[4] The domestic feast, with its more-or-less rigorous rules about what must be eaten, marks tribal and familial identities, just as the diversity of restaurants in even a modest-sized town in the US – Chinese, Korean, Thai, Indian, Mexican, Italian, French, German – marks a nation's cosmopolitanism and the omnivorous American appetite for every type of cuisine. The curry house in every English village is a testament to Britain's imperialist past, just as the prevalence of couscous restaurants in certain *quartiers* of Paris evokes France's colonial adventures in northern Africa. Everyday home cooking, however, represents something quite different than either the feast or the worldliness of a postcolonial catholic taste.

Imagine for a moment what is not the case: imagine that women have the option of cooking for their families on a daily basis without undermining their ability to participate in the public spheres of science, politics, or business. If cooking at home would do more than any other intervention to address the social, environmental, and public health crises associated with the way humans eat under agribusiness and the processed-food industry, then reflection needs to be directed not to Pollan's "Homeric" barbecues or brotherly brews, but toward (his mother's) everyday home cooking, something he dwells on only briefly. To appreciate this labor, food ethics requires a phenomenology of domestic cooking as an essential element of homemaking, the knowledges and practices that actually sustain intergenerational communities in places of their own.[5] As anthropologists and historians have demonstrated, it is first and foremost through food that a member of a community is made to feel at home. Both the familiarity of the foods and the regularity of the meals contribute to his sense of security and solidarity with others, as well as to his own singularity. What are the essential routines of the domestic cook by which she creates a home for herself and others?[6]

Planning

Most domestic cooks think both seasonally and weekly, maximizing their use of ingredients when they are in season and establishing a rhythm within the week to accommodate the other tides of family life and the punctuation of minor feasts like a Saturday or Sunday dinner. In their planning, these cooks will rely on a repertoire of recipes often accumulated and transmitted over generations, just as their cooking will serve multiple generations. Their culinary thinking reflects their desire to produce a "delicious meal," nourishing, appetizing, and satisfying, within the bounds of what is accessible and affordable. *This daily act of anticipating the needs of others and aiming, by maximizing one's talents and capacities, to satisfy them in pleasurable and effective ways provides a model of ethical agency.* This planning embodies intergenerational solidarities and focuses on promoting the pleasure and health of both the cook and those for whom she cooks.

Procurement or shopping

While the US market has been almost entirely conquered by global agribusiness, in France, for example, small farmers, grocers, and cheesemongers still thrive. Like most urbanites, Parisians are distinctly parochial, attached with fierce pride each to her own *quartier*. Everyone insists that his market or *boulangerie* or café is the best. The argument of the *quartiers* is always about food. You do not need to live in Paris for long, nor to possess more than a modest amount of French, to find yourself becoming attached to the man who so thoughtfully chooses your melon to be ripe at the right time or the *fromager*, who patiently takes you on a little tour of France, visiting, cheese by cheese, the flora and soil of every region. At first, the *boucher* seems faintly displeased at the thought of selling his meat to an American, who will no doubt overcook it, but he is won over by my persistent respect and the pictures of my Christmas lamb. These relationships form a social infrastructure that sustains both singularity and community. Instead of taking food for granted, the shopping cook respects the knowledge of those who labor to produce and deliver wholesome foods. Traditional markets in Asia and Latin America that have not yet been globalized provide a similar sort of social infrastructure, as well as vibrant informal economies, largely run by women.

In contrast, global supermarket chains encourage a weekly shopping trip that ends in a large cart piled high with processed foods. One US megastore is much like any other, whether you are in Boston or Bakersfield. The space is homogenous and anonymous; they purvey the same brands of processed foods, meat, and produce, and there is little interaction among staff and customers. The organizing principle of such spaces is not the food, but managing the customer to maximize profit.[7]

Local markets in France, Asia, or Latin America encourage a different kind of temporality, spatiality, and sociality. These venues encourage daily shopping, reducing waste, maximizing freshness, and enriching the social infrastructure.[8]

Procurement or shopping in these scenarios is not the alienating and unpleasant experience of the US megastore, but an inspiriting excursion with knowledgeable advisors among wholesome and delectable foods that engage all the senses to provoke distinction, deliberation, and decision. These are occasions to be delighted by the profusion of the market: vivid oranges and greens of fruit, pungent odors of cheese, wands and *boules* of bread, great pyramids of spices that assault the nose with sharpness or sweetness, briny sea creatures like rugged stones arrayed on beds of ice, the dreamy perfume of a perfectly ripe melon. Food feasts the eyes, from the brilliant abundance of the farmers' market to the cook's careful arrangements of color and texture on plate and platter. Taste, smell, and texture provide constant knowledge and pleasure from procurement to presentation. Food appeals to every sense: it is by *hearing* the melon respond to his tapping that the *verger* will select the right one. A market in Cartagena or Yogyakarta offers equally dazzling displays, purveyed by equally sociable and knowledgeable farmers and shopkeepers, but any visitor to those markets would know one from the other, and that she was most definitely not in Paris – not only by the marvelous, sensuous differences among the foodstuffs, but also by the dramatically different styles of persiflage.

Cooks that rely on their own gardens, hens, and cows enjoy a different aesthetic experience, more closely tuned to the rhythms of the seasons and the temporality of other animals' lives. As long as they are not subject to violence or climate disaster, small farmers enjoy both food security and fresh food, however "cash poor" they might be.[9] There is no comparison between the taste of a just-picked tomato and one from the grocery shelf. The cream and buttermilk at the supermarket bear only a vague resemblance to the substances I enjoyed as a small child on my grandmother's farm. When we picked wild blackberries, I would be allowed to skim off the top of the milk chilling in its metal can some of the scrumptious, slightly pink, almost foamy cream that had settled in a thick layer. At once airy and unctuous, the cream bathed the tart berries in a hint of sweetness and a rich, fat texture. A wooden churn stood in the corner of my grandmother's kitchen, with which she produced her own deliciously sour buttermilk, a slightly thin yellowish liquid full of gnarly chunks of butter. A glass of cornbread and buttermilk was a favorite treat of my mother: *Take a tall glass. Crumble a corn muffin in it. Pour in buttermilk. Eat with a long iced tea spoon.* Under global agribusiness, foods are homogenized and freshness drastically reduced, resulting in the elimination of so much flavor that it is just not possible to achieve this degree of pleasure, however simple, with the ingredients available to most US shoppers. Any gardener knows the pleasant shock of the first summer tomato after a winter of eating store bought.

The aesthetic element provides not merely pleasure, but the occasion for serious consideration and decision-making, as the cook must elect the herb that will flavor the stew, decide how ripe the cheese should be, or determine which flavors and dishes will marry well with one another to provide a healthy and delicious meal. The domestic cook may rely on her network of providers for advice and counsel, but in the end she herself must be the cook and develop her own judgment on how, week after week, to put together a week of nourishing meals.

The respect that the cook shows both for her purveyors and for her ingredients acknowledges her dependence on them. Like the cook, ethical thinking discovers itself to be always already indebted to what has been eaten and to those by whom the thinker has been fed. Philosophy has preferred to characterize humans as perceivers and knowers and to base ethics in speculative principles of reason, but a phenomenology of food reveals how the ethical thinker is always already claimed by the right, prior to any argument of reason, in virtue of the respect that is due the food that sustains him and the labor embodied in it. The claim of the ethical is established not by reason, but by life itself. As a condition both of singularity and of solidarity, this invisible domestic labor, unpaid and uncounted in the productivity scales of global capital, commands respect [*respectare*: looking back]. His experience of eating claims the thinker to look back at his food, at the sacrifice and labor it embodies as conditions of his own life, so that he finds himself as a node in a network, where the claim of the right has preceded him. Reflecting philosophically on food and cooking reveals that the necessity of ethical claims derives from these relationships, not from the law of non-contradiction, nor from theories of virtue and human nature.[10]

Preparation and cooking

Prior to the hegemony of the nuclear family in Anglo-European culture after World War II, women worked together to prepare meals for an extended family, as they still do in many parts of the world and in many communities and households. Children love to be involved in preparation, washing vegetables, picking herbs, or stripping an ear of corn. They enjoy measuring and mixing and stirring. They marvel at the miraculous transubstantiations of flour and water – first into dough, then into bread – or of a liquid batter into a sturdy cake. *With the decline in home cooking comes the loss of the kitchen as a social space of intergenerational collaboration, though it is this very figure of intergenerational solidarity that is required to address contemporary urgencies such as climate disaster or the obesity epidemic.*

Some foods require much preparation and little cooking; some require little preparation and long cooking; and some require both substantial preparation and significant cooking time; but all good food takes time. Nothing more undermines the practice of home cooking than a lack of time, which takes the form of hungry children and nothing ready to feed them. Women working two jobs or irregular hours haven't the luxury of watching a pot, while professional women often can serve home cooking only by relying on another woman to do the work – and that other woman's own family then lacks home cooking.[11] The gender division of labor and its correlative distinction between work and family install spatialities and temporalities that make homemaking, including home cooking, virtually impossible.[12] If home cooking would be the most effective intervention into the environmental and public health crises linked to agribusiness and processed food, then the culture of possibilities that determines gender, labor, and food will need to be reconfigured.

A phenomenology of cooking and food reveals that, beyond its link to public health and environmental crises, the decline of home cooking also reshapes identity and social relations. It not only constitutes the loss of an essential intergenerational space, but also signals an increasing emphasis on speed that threatens to collapse the temporal differences in which self-consciousness exists. *Without the deferral and delay of a watched pot, self-consciousness lapses into the indistinction and distraction of the instantaneous and loses the distances and differences of an expansive self, as well as the deferral to the temporality of the other that ethical thinking requires.*[13] A phenomenology of home cooking confirms the situation of the philosopher or ethicist in a network of relationships that precede him and from which he can never entirely extricate himself. It reveals how the practices of the home cook inculcate and embody as essential elements of ethics an asymmetrical reciprocity and an attunement across time to the claim of the right.

In "Water," the only section of *Cooked* actually devoted to home cooking, Pollan marvels at the way in which the whole world of braises and stews, of almost everything cooked in a pot, begins with sweating onions, to which will be added just two or three other ingredients to make the base of the dish: celery and carrots in butter for a *mirepoix* or sweated in olive oil for a *soffrito* or garlic and tomato in oil for a *sofrito* or spices and ghee for a *tarka* (Pollan 2013: 127).[14] Yet, his reaction to this labor contrasts sharply with his descriptions of barbequing, baking, and brewing, all activities that involved an initiation into a masculine cult.[15] During his apprenticeship to the "pitmasters," Pollan enjoys every stage of the preparations for the "Homeric feast" and its "Apollonian clarity," from the butchering of the hog to the camaraderie of the cookfire. His first impulse after his successful barbeque is to call one of his male tutors or "pitmasters" to "boast." The whole experience leaves him "the very proudest." This chapter does not interrogate and appreciate home cooking; rather, it celebrates Man's mythical triumph over fire, as Pollan's frequent references to Homer and to Bachelard's psychoanalysis of fire confirm (see, e.g., Pollan 2013: 109–111).

Similarly, the section on air focuses on commercial bakers and the science of baking as well as the production of wheat, rather than on baking at home, which Pollan admits he does only occasionally.[16] Still, baking reinforces lessons he has learned from gardening. Baking, like gardening, requires a patient attentiveness to others and to the environment, as well as an active interest in discerning what is needed to insure that the garden or bread flourishes. The home cook is often a gardener: she is claimed by the bread, as she is by the garden, because both are alive and depend on her, at the same time that they sustain her and those for whom she cooks. Pollan focuses on his mastery of the chemistry of bread baking and his pride in his loaf.

Like most writers on food and food ethics, Pollan does not tarry long enough with the home cook to see in her relations – to her animals and plants, to her purveyors, to the climate and environment, and to those she feeds – a paradigm of just the sort of intergenerational and inter-species collaborations necessary, not only to health and environmental justice, but also to ethics. A phenomenology of home cooking reveals how ethical claims arrive as a call to attend with discernment to the complex networks that sustain both singularity and solidarity. To be claimed by the right is to find one's self among the differences and distinction of other singularities and to collaborate in the solidarities that sustain each and all.

From the beginning, the labor involved in actually feeding his family multiple times a week appears to Pollan as "drudgery," a word, he notes, that is never heard among the "pitmasters" around the cookfire (Pollan 2013: 127). Against the bright light of the ceremonial "Homeric" feast or the alchemical magic of the baker or the poetic intoxications of the brewer, the humble pot of the home cook seems "prosaic," dull and tiresome. Unlike in barbequing, brewing, and baking, in braising his tutor is a woman, and she presses on him the "three p's," patience, presence, and practice, but he confesses that these habits "did not come easily" to him, as he tends toward impatience, multitasking, and theory. "Watching onions sweat? The work just isn't demanding enough to fully occupy consciousness . . ." (Pollan 2013: 142). In fact, Pollan proves wrong both practically and theoretically. A good *mirepoix*, as he learns by experience, takes multiple skills and capacities for judgment. It calls, above all, for patient respect for the time the onion requires for its reliable transubstantiation from crunchy, opaque, and eye-watering to a lovely, soft, translucent sweetness. Theoretically, the claim of the onion on the cook, to tarry with it and respect the time it takes to come into its own, provides a figure of ethical life: the other takes time to disclose and to make her ethical claim, requiring attention and patience from the thinker, just as the onion required it from the cook, if the thinker is to promote the other's singularity. In contrast to the boastful masters of barbecuing and brewing, the home cook practices an everyday attunement to the network of relations in which she is situated – attitudes and habits that are reinforced, perhaps even inculcated by, the patient, precise knowledge of her practice, as well as by the respect for her ingredients and collaborators that infuses all good home cooking. *The temporality of the other regulates the ethical relation. Attunement to the other takes time.*

The knife, as the primary tool of the domestic chef, separates the apprentice from the accomplished cook. Pollan seems surprised and somewhat miffed when his tutor finds his knife technique inadequate, but the taste of food is often determined by how it has been cut. A certain mathematical precision is required in the thinness of the potato slices for a *galette* or to properly shred beef for a Szechuan dish. Thinness, thickness, grain; cube, slice, dice, shred, chop, mince: these all represent both technical skill and a set of decisions about the taste and texture desired. Sometimes the onions are minced to melt away into no more than a flavor. Sometimes they are diced into chunks to retain some texture and crunch and a stronger, sharper taste. Any home cook will attest that the food processor, however convenient, cannot replace the attentive skill of the knife, which takes its own time both to acquire and to deploy.

Though he glorifies the barbeque and announces himself "most deeply engaged" by fermentation, of the techniques he learned during his year's education in cooking, Pollan admits that "the most sustainable and sustaining" was braising. In a single paragraph, he acknowledges that his ability to make a good braise or stew has changed the way he and his family eat, so as to promote not only their pleasure and health, but also their relationships and identity as a family. He concedes that the practices of the knife and the braise encourage the habits of precision, patience, and attentive presence – habits of mind that are essential to ethical life.

Pollan insists that he remembers very little of his mother's kitchen, yet in a few paragraphs, starting with her turquoise casserole, he unfolds the core idea of food ethics or any ethics. He describes his mother, night after night, presenting to the family some fragrant and satisfying stew or soup from the bright blue pot. However, Pollan fails to tarry with his mother's attentive labor, knowledge, and skill. Impatient for theory and mastery, he moves on quickly to a more general discussion of the pot as a repository of memories and a gathering force, especially for the family. Pollan so quickly imposes both his theory of elemental transformation and the experience of professional cooks that only in these few pages on his mother does the voice of the home cook actually begin to be heard. Few writers on food and food ethics have lingered long enough in the kitchen with the home cook to learn what is embedded in her knowledge and practice. Fewer have treated home cooking as an activity worthy of philosophical reflection and ripe with ethical implications far beyond the scope of "food ethics," insofar as the latter limits its focus to individual choice or state policy.[17]

Cooking his braises and stews, Pollan found his family naturally collecting around him. His teenage son would come down to the kitchen table to do his homework. His wife would wander in, led by the fragrant aromas of the simmering stew. Eating together from the same pot provides the opportunity for the attentiveness to the other on which ethical life depends. Amidst the distractions and speed of life under global capital, the kitchen of a home cook provides the place and time for the conversations that produce and sustain both singularity and intergenerational solidarity.

A phenomenology of home cooking yields new figures and principles for ethics that are not anticipated by the law of property and sexual propriety, nor by the rights of Man, nor by the fraternal myth of mastery over nature and human nature:

- *Everyday home cooking, the daily act of anticipating the needs of others and aiming to satisfy them in pleasurable and effective ways, provides a model of the ethical reciprocity[18] that sustains both health and happiness, as well as a just relation to nature and other animals. The justice of these relationships depends on each one enjoying the opportunity to realize her talents and capacities in the promotion of singularity and solidarity.*
- *The respect that the cook shows both for her purveyors and for her ingredients presents an essential principle for ethics: what sustains life deserves respect.*
- *The cook's own labor and skill claim respect. Justice requires that her labor no longer be taken for granted.*
- *With the decline in home cooking comes the loss of the kitchen as a social space of intergenerational collaboration, yet it is that very figure of intergenerational solidarity that is required to address contemporary urgencies such as climate disaster or the obesity epidemic.*
- *Without the deferral and delay of a watched pot, self-consciousness lapses into the indistinction and distraction of the instantaneous and loses the distances and differences of an expansive self, as well as the capacity for detachment and attunement to the other that ethical thinking requires.*
- *The temporality of the other regulates the ethical relation. Attunement to the other takes time.*

Philosophers rarely pay attention to food. Those that do so focus either on the ethics of food choice or on public policy. By tarrying with the home cook in a phenomenology of her practice, the philosopher discovers ethical figures and principles that do not depend on speculations or abstractions. These figures and principles emerge in the network of relationships in which each is situated and where each is claimed by the right.

The privilege of being served: a seat at the table

Pollan enjoyed the privilege of being served, while his mother was regularly the last to sit and eat. As the historian Massimo Montanari argues, "If the table is a metaphor for life, it represents in a direct and exacting way both membership in a group and the relationships defined within that group" (2006 [2004]: 95). Montanari demonstrates how social and political power is always reflected, not only in what people eat, but also in the spatiality and temporality of dining, and most especially in the disposition of diners around the table. Just as the lord or chieftain sat at the center of the banquet table, with the power of others measured by their proximity to or distance from him, so too the patriarchal power that each member of the fraternal order exerts in his own family is represented in his position at the head of the table, where he is served first, reserving to himself only the task of ceremonially carving the roasted meats. Women, as Montanari notes, traditionally eat after men and often in a different, less public space.

The ladies I met in Rajasthan, who spend almost all day each day gathering firewood for cooking, hauling fresh water, and preparing food for their families, while caring for their children, would find Pollan's sudden discovery of the importance of cooking hilariously obtuse: he could take cooking to be like the furniture because he had *the privilege of being served*. Women have been feeding men and their children for millennia, often without a seat at the table or a fair share of food for themselves. Pollan refers to a "parent" that provided his daily meals, as if the fact that the cook was his mother were accidental, rather than a reflection of the infrastructures of gender and race that persist today in determining what and how humans eat. Paying attention to the history of what and how humans eat reveals the regular determination of women's bodies and labor as the property of men, to be exchanged among men.[19] At the same time, thinking through the history of culinary practices forces a confrontation with racism and imperialism. Whole genres of Indian food exist only in relation to the British occupation of the subcontinent. The food of the Deep South in the US exposes a history of cultural appropriation and subjection, in which whites appropriated African-American foods as their own, while relegating African Americans to subservient roles and denying them a seat at the table. Food justice requires a critique of who enjoys *the privilege of being served*, as well as an account of the respect that is due to the labor represented by each day's (or night's) "delicious meal." It requires a critique of the racial, gender, and class injustices that are reflected in who produces, prepares, and serves food and in who, on the other hand, is served.

Having finally noticed his mother among the furniture and having finally realized that the single most important intervention in current practices – both for health and the environment – would be for Americans to start cooking whole foods and fresh ingredients at home, eschewing fast food and prepared meals, Pollan announces that cooking is "*too important to be left to one gender*" (2013: 10). For Pollan, his discovery of the importance of cooking implies that it can no longer be left to women – not that women and women's labor should be made visible and appreciated for the knowledge and ethical thinking that they have always embodied. Indeed, Pollan chooses not to learn about home cooking from home cooks, and among his many tutors, only one is a woman with whom he actually cooks at home. As a result, he lacks the experience from which a robust phenomenology of food might emerge.[20]

Irigaray repeatedly warns against any reliance on a concept of equality that merely extends the rights of Man to women.[21] Based on this conceptual gesture, women in developed countries now regularly hold two fulltime jobs, as primary domestic caregivers and wage earners. This fiction of equality – for it is a fiction on every economic indicator and in every realm of power – also implies that the experience of women, those millennia feeding their families, does not constitute an appropriate field for the discovery of new universals and concepts for ethics. No doubt, Pollan's dawning realization that feeding his teenage son might be a way of bonding with him was a knowledge his own mother already possessed and actualized a generation before. The proclamation of abstract rights of equality by global agencies matters little to the women who are bought and sold in marriage, or scarred by acid for going to school, or driven out of the working poor into prostitution in an effort to feed their families, but respect for women's agency, knowledge, and practice, and a readiness to learn from a home cook might.

Philosophical reflection on women's experience as domestic cooks will require not only a new respect for noncapitalized labor, but also a new recognition of homemaking, and particularly of the table, as a key element in the formation of identity, citizenship, and political life, as well as in public health. Solidarities arise from the universal need to eat. Food combines this universalism with the most intense regionalism, and cooking invites the transplantations and cross-pollinations of cosmopolitanism. Perhaps, the solution to the task of building a community capable of sustaining collective action, while preserving the singularity of each and all, may be found by making visible the long history of women's labor in binding generations and making alliances through food.[22]

Notes

1 By "global food," I refer to the food produced by agribusiness and the processed-foods industry. These industries aim at (1) standardization and the production of uniform foodstuffs and tastes globally, (2) vertical integration or control over every phase of the food process from production to ingestion, and (3) maximizing the degree of processing and increasing the distance between whole foods and consumers in order to maximize profit. Pollan's *The Omnivore's Dilemma* (2007) reports extensively on the unsustainability of global agribusiness, given its environmental costs. It pays less attention to the way in which the spread of global agribusiness undermines local cultures and threatens the social relations on which singularity and solidarity depend. See Rawlinson (2016), chapter six.

2 Homelessness, whether that of a working mother in the US whose low-wage fast-food or supermarket job is inadequate to sustain her family or of a refugee fleeing civil violence or war, always precipitates food insecurity, just as the regularity of meals is an essential part of the experience of feeling secure and "at home."

3 See, e.g., the summary of articles by the journal *Gender and Society* that confirm this inequality, at <http://gas.sagepub.com/site/misc/Index/Classroom/Division_of_Household_Labor.xhtml>.

4 The primary text on the culture of food or food as culture remains Lévi-Strauss' four-volume series *Introduction to a Science of Mythology* (1964–1971).

5 The gendered practice of home cooking is almost invisible in discussions of the ethics of sourcing food, or of what foods should be consumed, or of how hunger and nutrition are distributed globally, or in debates about who has agency in the consumption of food.

6 Do not be too quick, dear reader, to criticize my pronouns. I do not mean to prescribe cooking as an obligation for women, but to recognize women's knowledge and women's practices as essential to ethical and political life. Nor do I mean to limit this homemaking to the nuclear family. Indeed, this homemaking may reveal figures that should inform not just food ethics, but all ethics and politics.

7 Hans Taparia, an assistant professor at the New York University Stern School of Business and an organic food entrepreneur, and Pamela Koch, director of the Laurie M. Tisch Center for Food Education and Policy at Columbia University, predict that agribusiness and global food will not survive unless companies like Nestlé and McDonald's morph into enterprises that purvey whole foods in local markets (2015).

8 The American food writer Patricia Wells, who lives in Paris, recounts the not uncommon sight of an elderly Frenchwoman buying *one* apple or *one* lamb chop or a single macaroon. In these markets every purchase, however small, is considered worthy of respect.

9 My father and grandmother actually used the term "land poor" to describe our family. We ate well from the land but had no cash. For example, when my father was growing up, shoes were a major issue.

10 Here I repeat Hegel's arguments from the *Phenomenology of Spirit* (1977 [1807]) regarding the moral "insolence" of reason in asserting that the right is contingent on reason's own test, rather than imposed as a necessity by the irreducibility of social relationships in human identity. The thinker has always already been claimed by the other. See paragraph 434.

11 These relationships are regularly marked by racial and economic inequities, as well as by inequities between citizens and insecurely documented persons.

12 A voluminous literature exists on the possibility/impossibility of women enjoying both their generativity as homemakers and their generativity as agents in public life. In 2015 the US President's Council of Economic Advisors reported that among developed nations the US had fallen to 20th in percentage of women in the workplace, a decline that appears to be linked to the impossibility of pursuing two fulltime endeavors at once. Current infrastructures of work make little accommodation for family in the US, particularly below the level of the management/professional class. Current arrangements deny to women the opportunity to thrive in both domains of their generativity, both as mothers and homemakers and as workers with talents and capacities that matter to sustaining solidarities and collaborative projects.

13 Baudrillard (2010: 48–50) links the "liquidation" of reality and the capacity for self-representation to the liquidation of differentiated values under the homogeneity of global capital and to instantaneous flows of capital and information that make the self-consciousness of historical narrative impossible.

14 Pollan focuses on braises, but a braise and a stew are variations on the same technique. A braise usually includes a large piece of meat that will be cooked slowly until it shreds. A stew usually includes small cubes of meat. Except for this difference, stews and braises follow the same recipe: Sear the meat on all sides. In the case of stews, do not add too much meat to the pot at once or it will not brown properly. Remove the meat from the pot, scraping up the browned bits. Sweat some onions in oil or butter along with two or three other vegetables and preferred spices. Return the meat to the pot and cover the meat and vegetables with water or broth. Simmer until meat is tender, 1½–2½ hours. There are infinite variations, not only in the vegetables and spices chosen for the base, but also in technique. Deglaze the pot with wine before sweating the onions, and add the reduction to the cooking liquid. For a *blanquette*, allow neither the meat nor the *mirepoix* to brown while cooking. For *tablones*, sauté cumin, cinnamon, and chilies with the onions, and use beer and beef broth for the cooking liquid; but, when the meat is done, remove it from the pot and boil the liquid down. Add tomato paste to make a thick sauce, spoon it over the meat, and serve.

15 In his masculine preference for fire, Pollan unequivocally reflects the ancient gender division of labor. As the historian Massimo Montanari observes, "The dialectic of roasting and boiling is also implicitly one of gender. The pot boiling on the domestic hearth enters into the arena of female competence. Stoking the fires to roast meat is more often than not a 'man's' specialty, actually better expressed as virile or masculine, which calls up images of brutal simplicity as well as mastery over natural forces" (2006 [2004]: 49).

16 In the section on earth, Pollan celebrates fermenting, pickling, and brewing. He cites Nietzsche and Coleridge, among others, on the importance of "intoxication" to poetry and philosophy. He revels in becoming a "maker" by brewing his own beer. Pollan ends the section with what he "likes to think" is a demonstration of the beneficial effects of modest intoxication on literary performance.

17 In the US literature on food, cooks who appreciate its social and political implications seem to emerge from the South. See, e.g., Edna Lewis' simple but magisterial evocation of the role of food in the joy and pleasure of life in Freetown, Virginia, among the descendants of emancipated slaves (2015 [1976]). Food played an important role in forging solidarity while preserving singularity.

18 The reciprocity between the cook and the served is asymmetrical, as is the reciprocity between mother and child, teacher and student, boss and worker, or law and citizen. Perhaps, contrary to the model of a contract among equals, ethical relationships are always asymmetrical.

19 See Rawlinson (2016), chapter two, on the continuing commodification of women's bodies under global capital.

20 Sister Noella, his second female tutor, is not a home cook, but the head of her religious order's cheese-making operation. She appears in the section on air, but her element is just as much liquid. See where he quotes Bachelard's *Water and Dreams*: "all water is a kind of milk … every joyful drink is mother's milk" (Pollan 2013: 177). His two female tutors are both associated with fluidity, patience, and a responsibility to their ingredients, as opposed to the mastery of fire or the chemical processes of fermentation.

21 See, e.g., Irigaray (2000), pp. 90–91, 132–133.

22 The author would like to thank Caleb Ward for his very helpful comments on an earlier version of this paper.

References

Baudrillard, J. (2010) *The Agony of Power*, trans. by A. Hodges, Los Angeles: Semiotexte.

Hegel, G. W. F. (1977 [1807]) *Phenomenology of Spirit*, trans. by A.V. Miller, Oxford: Oxford University Press.

Irigaray, L. (2000) *Democracy Begins between Two*, trans. by K. Anderson, London: The Athlone Press.

Lévi-Strauss, C. (1969–1981 [1964–1971]) *Introduction to a Science of Mythology*, vols. 1–4, trans. by J. Weightman and D. Weightman, New York: Harper Colophon.

Lewis, E. (2015 [1976]) *The Taste of Country Cooking*, New York: Knopf.

Montanari, M. (2006 [2004]) *Food Is Culture*, trans. by A. Sonnenfeld, New York: Columbia University Press.

Pollan, M. (2007) *The Omnivore's Dilemma*, New York: Penguin Books.

——. (2013) *Cooked: A Natural History of Transformations*, New York: Penguin.

Rawlinson, M. C. (2016) *Just Life: Bioethics and the Future of Sexual Difference*, New York: Columbia University Press.

Taparia, H. and P. Koch. (2015) "Real Food Challenges the Food Industry," *The New York Times*, 8 November, op-ed.

7

MEAT AND THE CRISIS OF MASCULINITY

Thomas E. Randall

Introduction

Global demand for ruminant meat is projected to double by 2050 based on 2006 levels (Steinfeld et al. 2006). This phenomenon is mostly due to an increase of meat-based diets in some of the fastest-growing economies and populations in the world. A rise in personal consumer income in countries such as Brazil, China, Indonesia, and Mexico has progressively made meat consumption an affordable and popular choice (Myers and Kent 2004). Accordingly, the global livestock sector is experiencing unremitting growth. However, this trend is contributing towards much environmental detriment and carbon release. The livestock industry alone produces 14.5 percent of total anthropogenic greenhouse gases (Gerber et al. 2013), with its expansion causing extensive deforestation to cultivate animal-feed crops (McAlpine et al. 2009). In turn, biosequestration is declining alongside global biodiversity (Ripple 2014). A tension thus manifests between worldwide consumer demand for meat and the sustainability of this dietary preference.

For these reasons, numerous reports have called for a reduction (or complete removal) of meat from our diets (de Bakker and Dagevos 2012; Ripple 2014; Steinfeld et al. 2006). This article examines how the gender identity *hegemonic masculinity* forms a significant socio-psychological barrier, which prevents some demographics from ameliorating their carnivorous food habits. Hegemonic masculinity creates and reinforces the gender expectation (for men in particular) to engage in carnivorous behavior (Adams 2010; Schoesler et al. 2015). However, identifying one's gender with hegemonic masculinity is becoming ever more precarious, with many contemporary social movements challenging its influence (inadvertently or otherwise). This has caused a crisis in masculinity. Yet paradoxically this crisis seems to have only buttressed the requirement of meat consumption for those who conform to this gender identity.

In what follows, I explore why this crisis of masculinity has unfolded and what it means for the reduction of meat-based diets. First, I delineate what is meant by hegemonic masculinity and how this gender identity forms a symbolic alliance with meat. Then I examine how a crisis of masculinity has transpired through four major social movements that have sought to undermine hegemonic masculinity, and why this crisis has buttressed meat consumption for those who continue to identify with this gender. Finally, I explore the innovative notion of a plurality of masculinities, demonstrating potential ways the crisis of masculinity could be resolved. The conclusion aims to show that one can still identify as masculine, while simultaneously reducing carnivorous food habits and improving environmental sustainability.

Meat and hegemonic masculinity

Hegemonic masculinity is a socially constructed gender identity, which has dominated the archetypal perception of how men ought to act and behave. This model sets particular expectations as to what traits, persona, and actions men should adopt and carry out if they wish to identify as masculine. These expectations are numerous, but traditionally cover the following qualities: virility, strength, and robustness (Meah 2014), alongside an association with "sporting, military and mythopoetic images" (Gelfer 2013: 78). Historically, these qualities and associations have become so strongly attached to men they are often portrayed as essential to a man's very being. The frequently presented, and patently romanticized, "man the hunter" illustration (Sobal 2005) aims to demonstrate that a man's virility is entwined with their evolutionary pathway – in other words, the image celebrates "a primitive masculinity [. . .] normalizing aggressive characteristics by tying them to male, gendered ('natural'), behaviors" (Calvert 2014: 19). Thus, normatively speaking, displays of power and belligerence ought not only be expected but also accepted because they are innate to male human behavior.

This initial account pinpoints what is exactly *hegemonic* about this type of masculinity. Situating the concept of hegemonic masculinity within a cultural-theoretical framework, we can gainfully draw from the thought of Antonio Gramsci. "Hegemony" refers to where an ideology, belief, or specific cultural custom of a particular group gains public legitimacy from "the entire society" (Gramsci 1971: 248).[1] That is to say that a certain idea becomes hegemonic when it *dominates* all other relevant belief-systems through its institutional acceptance as the norm. This in itself neither implies nor discounts any violent ascendancy to domination; control can also be achieved "through culture, institutions, and persuasion" (Connell and Messerschmidt 2005: 832). While this description hints towards an overt acceptance of a belief-system, this is not the critical point Gramsci wished to make. What is more important to emphasize is the subliminal character of hegemonic belief: more often than not, a hegemonic belief retains dominance through a society's inadvertent continuation of the belief's proposed standards. This belief, seen to be the "natural" way of life, is thus reinforced within the population's mindset, generating social pressure to conform from a variety of angles (Lears 1985: 572). The type of masculinity outlined above is hegemonic, then, due to its widespread institutional acceptance: to be a "real man" these masculine expectations and qualities must be satisfied. As Steve Craig comments, "traditional characteristics of masculinity are made to seem so correct and natural that men find [domination] not just expected, but actually demanded" (Craig 1992: 3).

Significantly, the normalization of these gender expectations denotes a deeper concern regarding power struggle and historical male dominance over women and femininity. While "man the hunter" sought to kill for food and lead and protect his tribe, "women were gatherers, carers and servers" (Meah 2014: 191). This widely portrayed image has substantial temporal connections to the more contemporary idea of the "male breadwinner" and "female housewife." What these representations reveal is the construction and establishment of patriarchy, and the longstanding social subordination of women in favor of male economic and social supremacy. Hegemonic masculinity has simultaneously systematized and encouraged the subjection of women – and even of effeminately perceived men – with its focus on displaying control, power, and strength. Indeed, Richard Rogers asserts, "Hegemonic masculinity is predicated on domination and exploitation of others" (2008: 282).

Domination over women and femininity is not where the final line is drawn for hegemonic masculinity; it is here that the symbolic alliance between hegemonic masculinity and meat-eating is made. Food consumption is "frequently linked to identity and to who we are as individuals" (Calvert 2014: 18). Unsurprisingly then, the dominance exhibited by "man the hunter" spills over to an anthropocentric worldview of controlling "other species in nature, acting as carnivores who engage in aggressive acts to bring home food" (Sobal 2005: 137). Hunting for meat not only reveals masculine traits of strength and virility, but also the desire for dominion over the surrounding environment. Over time, the intrinsic act of eating meat itself – regardless of whether the animal was hunted by the consumer – has become synonymous with these same masculine qualities. This especially regards the consumption of red meat due to this robust association with predation. Moreover, with modern-day nutritional science connecting animal protein consumption with increased strength and muscle gain, the meat product has come to represent the framework of hegemonic masculinity.

Consistent with the nature of hegemonic belief, this connection has been bolstered by a multitude of popular cultural outlets. For instance, in an attempt to draw more men back into their religious communities, churches in Australia have set about creating "masculine spaces," involving hunting and camping trips (Gelfer 2013: 78). Men's fitness magazines routinely encourage the consumption of extensive amounts of animal protein to build muscle (Parasecoli 2005). Even from an early age, various nursery rhymes and children's stories institute expected food-gender roles. Consider the nursery rhyme "Sing a Song of Sixpence": here, the king is presented with a pie of blackbirds (presence of meat), while the queen is eating bread and honey (absence of meat) (Adams 2010: 27). It is perhaps no accident that in this nursery rhyme, the king (a male symbol of wealth and power) receives the meat, while the queen, even though holding considerable wealth and power, receives none.

Indeed, in its historical connection to human dominance over nature, meat came to be aligned with male economic and social clout as well. Meat became "closely associated with power and privilege," especially throughout medieval Europe – "a staple for the gentry and a rare treat for the peasants" (Ruby and Heine 2011: 448). The consumption of animal flesh symbolized the standard of an upper-class meal – a power association that still persists in Anglo-American society as "class privilege" (Rogers 2008: 297). This symbolism is a likely explanation for the rise of meat-based diets in developing countries, as a way of showcasing increased wealth (Myers and Kent 2004).

The link between meat and (male) coveting of economic and social power can once more indicate the patriarchal nature of hegemonic masculinity. Fast-food advertisement makes for an intriguing study of meat's relation to the subjugation of women. Many fast-food companies rely on, and amplify, "the beliefs and perceptions that drive the meat binge" (Boyle 2012: 158). Their advertisements seek to underpin the connection between hegemonic masculinity and meat to boost sales. Rogers' analysis of Burger King's "Manthem" advertisement classically demonstrates this male–meat association fast-food companies are intent to strengthen (2008: 293–296). However, it is the sexual politics of these advertisements that reinforce hegemonic masculinity's demand for dominance over both women and nature. A now-infamous 2005 advertisement from Carl's Jr. featuring Paris Hilton, a Bentley, and an oversized burger is exemplary to this end. That the burger is oversized alludes to the overconsumption of animal protein, taking from nature more than is necessary to enforce the hunter's supremacy. Hilton is sexually objectified and consumed visually by the onlooker. The Bentley represents high economic status and power. All this ties into the narrative of hegemonic masculinity subordinating women (in this case, reducing women to a sexual object for the onlooker's pleasure), the desire for economic and social clout (the Bentley), and enhancing physical strength (consuming considerable amounts of animal protein). Sexism and patriarchy, but also class discrimination and anthropocentrism, are thus all interlinked through this association of meat consumption and hegemonic masculinity.

This point is made clearer through Carol Adams' concept of the *absent referent*. It is no coincidence, Adams notes, that many similes and metaphors within the English language subtly link sexual violence, environmental exploitation, and meat-eating – all three displaying varying forms of brutality. The labeling of meat products (for instance, sausage and bacon) serves to "erase the animal, its treatment, and the systems of production that transformed it into meat" (Rogers 2008: 284). Without reference to the actual killing of animals, meat products become free-floating images (Adams 2010: 48). The animal's butchering becomes an absent referent, objectifying the animal purely as food. This absent referent then finds intersection with descriptions of sexual violence, in which we appropriate "the experience of animals to interpret our own violation" (Adams 2010: 46). "Treated like a piece of meat" is one such referent in which our objectification of animals as food is used to describe sexual objectification. "The rape of the land" is a similar metaphorical statement, one that uses sexual violence as the absent referent to analyze the objectification of nature as a resource. Through this referent, Adams contends, "patriarchal values become institutionalized" (2010: 42) by way of language, in which the (male) dominator objectifies animals, women, and nature. This appropriately echoes Gramsci's contention that "every language contains the elements of a conception of the world" (1971: 325).

As hinted within the "Sing a Song of Sixpence" nursery rhyme, this association between meat and hegemonic masculinity is so prevalent that dietary preferences that include the complete absence and/or rejection of meat have become closely aligned with femininity. Adams has influentially argued that "because meat eating is a measure of a virile culture and individual, our society equates vegetarianism with emasculation or femininity" (Adams 2010: 15) – a statement that has since been substantially reinforced by multiple psychological studies. Paul Rozin et al. (2012) were some of the first to empirically test the legitimacy of Adams' feminist-vegetarian critique of the sexual politics of meat. The study confirmed the theoretical link between meat (especially red meat) and hegemonic masculinity, stating: "the male–meat link is actually a meat–strength/power–male link" (Rozin et al. 2012: 641). This was corroborated by Hank Rothgerber's study, which offers a more telling remark: "The relative lack of male enthusiasm for animal rights and vegetarianism may best be understood as an outgrowth of the construction of masculinity itself" (2013: 364). With regards to the link between vegetarianism and femininity, Matthew Ruby and Steven Heine (2011) have shown how omnivorous men view vegetarian men as more effeminate. While it is true that these studies took place in North America, the same findings have been replicated across the world: from Finland and the Baltic States (Prättälä et al. 2007) to even India (Roy 2002). These studies thus support the claim that meat and hegemonic masculinity are entwined in an emblematic social construction.

The crisis of masculinity

With the link between meat and hegemonic masculinity established, it is now possible to explore how hegemonic masculinity has formed a socio-psychological barrier to reducing meat consumption. Given the comments in the previous section, it at first seems obvious why those who identify with hegemonic masculinity would not want to reduce their carnivorous food habits. This deduction, however, is too reductive. There is a more substantial reason as to why identification with hegemonic masculinity has led to a solidifying link with meat consumption. To examine this reason, a fuller understanding of Gramscian thought on the concept of hegemony is required. This will then necessitate a brief historical treatment of four major social movements beginning near the close of the 20th century, to provide a much richer explanation of the barrier hegemonic masculinity presents to reducing meat consumption.

In the previous section, I examined how a certain belief can reach and maintain hegemonic status. For the sake of brevity, one key point was overlooked in this overview of Gramscian thought: the fall from dominance of various hegemonies. This can now be explicated. Hegemonic belief relies on institutionalized acceptance to retain dominance. This ultimately depends on how successful those defending this belief are in claiming "at least some plausibility that their particular interests are those of society at large" (Lears 1985: 571). This suggests hegemonic belief is not a static affair, but is open to attack or subversion whenever subordinated groups make their voices heard and convince others of their plight. Walter Adamson has written that given the massive scale required for a hegemonic belief to appeal to all groups in society, it is "bound to be uneven in the degree of legitimacy in command and to leave some room for antagonistic cultural expressions to develop" (1980: 174). Indeed, significant social movements, in many ways related, which took place from the 1950s to present day (especially in Western societies) have called into question the legitimacy of hegemonic masculinity. Notably, the following four social movements (broadly conceived) have formed multiple counter-hegemonic alternatives: the women's labor movement, the civil and gay rights movements, the antiwar movement, and the animal liberation and environmental movements.

The challenge of the women's labor movement can be best outlined first. After the Second World War, multiple developments in the global composition of labor challenged male privilege in the workplace. Consequently, the traditional identity of man displaying power and control through economic and social clout as the "breadwinner" became subject to scrutiny. Western economies began moving closer to financial- and service-based markets, signaling a decline in blue-collar work and increased accessibility for women into a traditionally male-dominated workplace. "The rise of pink collar work, and the perceived feminization of white collar work" began blurring the "established gender configurations" hegemonic masculinity demanded to remain distinct (Rogers 2008: 286–287). Even in developing countries this blurring is bearing out. Climate change has resulted in opportunities for women to enhance their social and economic positions through the value of their local knowledge in community adaptation programs. From the Philippines (Tatlonghari and Paris 2013) to Peru (Godden 2013), climate change has allowed many women to enter at various points in a previously inaccessible workplace.[2] These advancements directly undermine male economic supremacy.

Second, civil and gay rights movements have sought to unveil the racist and homophobic attitudes hegemonic masculinity endorses. The historical "prestige of (white) men" in holding economic and social power has been openly objected to through numerous civil rights movements across the globe (Rogers 2008: 287). Public segregation and vocational discrimination have seen considerable reductions since the conception of these movements, though many challenges still remain. The gay rights movement, with similar success, has attacked the casting stereotype of homosexual men as "unnatural" and effeminate to be subordinated by "natural" heterosexual masculine men. This perspective of homosexuality, as a condition to be brought under masculine control, has lost broad societal consensus. Rising worldwide support for legalized same-sex marriage vividly illustrates the declining authority of hegemonic masculinity in this regard.

Third, antiwar movements have overtly contested hegemonic masculinity's association with military endeavors showcasing (male) strength and belligerence (Calvert 2014). Strong opposition to the Vietnam War in the 1960s, and more recently against the invasion of Iraq and Afghanistan throughout the 2000s, argued against the inevitability of war. Displays of aggression and power were criticized as obstacles to diplomatic concord. This trend against brutality and violence was matched in the animal liberation and environmental movements of the 1960s and '70s. The demand for greater transparency in the operations of slaughtering animals for meat, fur, and other animal products, was of signal importance for the global animal welfare movement. Veg(etari)-anism directly defies a meat-based culture, and thus the masculine associations with it. Moreover, the growth in environmental science from the 1960s onward has repeatedly disproved humans' perceived dominance over nature. Rachel Carson's *Silent Spring*, fears of nuclear destruction, and various broadcasted oil spillages helped generate widespread anxiety about how vulnerable humankind actually is in the face of nature.

These counter-hegemonic alternatives continue into the present, allied in their subversion of the demands and expectations of a racist and heterosexist hegemonic masculinity. However, these efforts have not been without a response from those who still identify with this hegemonic discourse. In an attempt to cling to dominance, many have sought to reinforce the legitimacy of hegemonic masculinity against this current of public outcry. But, owing to poor argumentation, these responses have been lackluster at best. An example is the hegemonic masculine reaction to the animal liberation movement. Annie Potts and Jovian Parry (2010) have documented in New Zealand how reactions to "vegansexuality" (where vegans choose to have sexual relations and partnerships exclusively with other vegans) have been broadly hostile, stemming from a largely omnivorous, heterosexual male community. Vegansexuals were construed as "(sexual) losers, cowards, deviants, failures and bigots" (Potts and Parry 2010). Male vegans were especially hounded as effeminate and "gay." Recall that it is demanded and expected of men to eat meat to gain muscle strength, remain virile, and stay true to their "hunter" evolutionary roots. Unless men are following this "natural" course of life, they are not truly men and become linked with the perceived "non-masculine unnaturalness" of homosexuality, regardless of their actual sexual preference. In fact, attempts to undermine vegansexuality were almost all *ad hominem* attacks, aiming to subvert this dietary and sexual preference through ridicule.[3] Unsurprisingly, this response has failed to gain public legitimacy.

Following this brief overview, it is now possible to summarize the wide-ranging and serious labels that these above four movements perceive hegemonic masculinity to represent: anthropocentrism, class discrimination, homophobia, patriarchy, racism, and sexism. It is an understatement to say that these attitudes are not advantageous to retaining hegemonic dominance, especially within contemporary liberal democracies. As exemplified by the *ad hominem* remarks reported in Potts and Parry's (2010) study, efforts to retain hegemonic masculinity as the dominant belief-system have become desperate in their clinging to power. So strong are these counter-hegemonic alternatives, and so weak are the responses to them, that hegemonic masculinity appears mostly on the back foot. Yet hegemonic masculinity, through its claim to traditionalism, still permeates modern society. A vast majority of men still come to identify with this gender through major social influences (from senior familial relations to men's fitness magazines). But with traditional masculine traits of strength, virility, and power being marginalized as negative social behaviors, many men are suffering from a crisis of masculinity given their very gender identity is being subverted.

It is here where the symbolic importance of meat takes the foreground. While many men cannot pursue these primitive masculine qualities to their full extent, these associations are still fulfilled symbolically through the consumption of meat. This action alone, signifying male dominance in all its forms, satisfies the expectations hegemonic masculinity demands. There is no need to actually go out and assert dominance over others when this dominance is figuratively locked into the eating of meat itself. Meat becomes a palpable reminder of the "systems of power structured around the dualisms of race, ethnicity, class, sexuality, and nature/culture" (Rogers 2008: 297). Indeed, Rogers writes that meat has become "coded as a means of restoring hegemonic masculinity in the face of threats to its continued dominance" (2008: 282). Rothgerber echoes this view: it is believed that "compromised masculinity can be regained through meat consumption" (2013: 364). Meat consumption thus becomes a definitive way for men to still feel "masculine" despite the fall from dominance of hegemonic masculinity.

One might ask why the animal liberation movement has not been influential to those who identify with hegemonic masculinity. In a psychological study conducted by Rothgerber (2013), various men were asked to justify their carnivorous behavior. What Rothgerber found was a pervasive denial of animal suffering, "congruent with male norms of stoicism, toughness, and emotional restriction. Masculine men are not supposed to relate to the less fortunate, to display sensitivity or empathy, or to discuss their feelings" (2013: 365). As Jeffery Sobal has articulated, "Western men are often characterized by their suppression of emotions [. . .] which is a useful attribute for the hunting, killing, butchering, and eating of animals" (2005: 137). Believing they are expected to maintain emotionless reactions to the harshness of meat production, men are not as easily swayed by many good arguments in favor of improving animal welfare – even if they have the resources to adopt meatless diets (Gal and Wilkie 2010). Adams has succinctly summed this up:

> while [experts] think that all that is necessary to make converts to vegetarianism is to point out the numerous problems meat-eating causes – ill health, death of animals, ecological spoilage – they do not perceive that in a meat-eating culture none of this really matters.
>
> (2010: 15)

We are left, then, with the question of how to convince hegemonic-masculine men to lower their consumption of meat. The last section of this article aims to provide possible solutions to this problem.

A plurality of masculinities

Two major points have been argued thus far. First, meat and hegemonic masculinity are symbolically associated. Second, threats to hegemonic masculinity have reinforced meat consumption. These connections form part of a social narrative. That is, there is nothing endemic to meat's symbolic connection to masculinity. Rather, this connection is due to the perpetual reinforcement of meat's representative role in safeguarding traditional male identity. Certainly, due to the long-standing pervasion of hegemonic masculinity, it has been assumed by a large proportion of society that there are no other substantial ways of portraying one's masculinity. Mark Newcombe et al.'s study highlights this point: "The dominant form of socially constructed masculinity, hegemonic masculinity, tends to subordinate femininity and *other forms* of masculinity" (2012: 392; emphasis added). However, the assault on hegemonic masculinity is opening greater negotiating space for what it means to be masculine. Meat consumption could be reduced, or even stopped, by revealing a whole host of non-hegemonic masculinities one could identify with.

In fact, one of the more promising directions of new social research consists in formulating and empirically documenting a plurality of masculinities. R.W. Connell and James Messerschmidt laid important groundwork in acknowledging that a homogeneous masculinity contradicts ethnographers' recordings of the "unique trajectories of men's lives [with] every structural analysis [defining] new intersections of race, class, gender and generation" (2005: 845). Importantly, even within Western societies where hegemonic masculinity has been dominant, a growth in recent academic scholarship has "increasingly emphasized the multiple, fluid, dynamic, and contested nature of masculinities" (Meah 2014: 193), in which "divergent versions of masculinity can coexist within a social context" (Sumpter 2015: 104). In other words, through experiencing the various contexts in which a plethora of masculinities can reside simultaneously, it is left to the agency of the individual to interpret and present their own masculine identity to themselves and others.

This does not necessitate a radical overhaul of how masculinity has been traditionally interpreted. Perhaps all that is needed to begin is a creative reinterpretation of certain masculine traits, one that sloughs off their domineering past. Examples of this can be found among veg(etari)an bodybuilders and athletes (Rothgerber 2013: 371). As seen in the second section of this article, the act of building muscle archetypically revolves around the overconsumption of animal protein. This in turn represents an anthropocentric dominance over nature. However, much greater publicity has begun to center on how animal protein is unnecessary to gain muscle – overthrowing the stereotypical image of the thin, weak veg(etari)an through exhibiting muscle gain and veg(etari)-anism as not mutually exclusive. Notably, it is the *visible* demonstration of veg(etari)an bodybuilders that provides an immediate, tangible, and persuasive argument to onlookers, rather than simply taking for granted the theoretical background to this end. The same goes for veg(etari)an athletes, showcasing performances of strength and endurance without the need to pander to the "man the hunter" illustration. As role models to many men for how to behave and act in a masculine way, veg(etari)an athletes leave a positive impression of reduced meat consumption.

These images of veg(etari)an bodybuilders and athletes contribute towards reconceptualizing men's relationship with nature. Their emphasis is centered on the sustainable pursuit of bodily wellbeing, rather than on seeking mastery over the environment. With animal protein no longer vital to muscle growth, "practices of self-control [. . .] may contribute to more healthy food preferences with respect to meat" (Schoesler et al. 2015). Furthermore, how *power* is understood within this context also plays a major role. Having the power to protect the environment, rather than to dominate it, still establishes a traditional masculine attribute, but without the accompanying negative social connotations. Indeed, as Rothgerber speculates, masculinity might be framed in such a way that it is "a man's responsibility to protect animals from harm – that real men protect those that are dependent on them" (2013: 372). To be masculine in these ways can be seen as encouraging environmental sustainability, rather than being antagonistic to it.

This is a start. Yet further studies have highlighted the plurality of masculinities that already exist in social spheres conventionally unassociated with hegemonic masculinity. Angela Meah (2014) has shown how men's involvement in preparing food within the domestic sphere challenges the viewpoint that this kind of household participation entails emasculation. In part due to the rapidly changing social and structural conditions in the workplace, "for some men, the domestic sphere can represent an opportunity to retreat from the everyday pressures and expectation of work-based identities" (Meah 2014: 199). Indeed, this kind of gender fluidity enhances a man's freedom to take control, not over others, but over his own identity within different social contexts. With hegemonic masculinity losing its legitimacy, an opportunity arises for men to liberate themselves from various social pressures by recognizing that masculinity can be flexibly understood in more ways than one. Significantly, Meah (2014) also shows how subverting the feminine portrayal of the domestic sphere contributes to the overcoming of patriarchy and the objectification of women as merely housekeepers.

Meah's (2014) study further indicates how a plurality of masculinities can lower meat consumption. Sobal (2005) has written that the complexity of multiple masculinities "provides opportunities for marital partners to negotiate about gender and food choices" (148). This new negotiating space within the household mitigates just how much meat is consumed in the domestic sphere, with food decisions made between marital partners leveling out the extremes of meat-based diets. As a result, a greater variety of food choices are becoming mainstream, with flexitarian diets (predominantly plant-based with occasional meat product) growing in popularity. Recent findings by Erik de Bakker and Hans Dagevos (2012) have actually documented a growth in flexitarianism, particularly in the Netherlands. In fact, a continuation of positive flexitarian promotion could help remove the stress on the nutritional importance of meat, thereby endorsing "the normalization and familiarity of meatless or meat-limited food products" (de Bakker and Dagevos 2012: 884). In these ways, the possibility of a plurality of masculinities has great potential for moderating and lessening meat-based diets.

There is not enough space here to exhaustively describe how a plurality of masculinities could help overcome every negative association with hegemonic masculinity. Indeed, research to this end is ongoing. While I touched upon how patriarchy, sexism, and anthropocentrism could be addressed, I hope to have made clear my primary concern in this article: how the recognition of a plurality of masculinities can lead to a reduction in meat consumption for those that previously identified with hegemonic masculinity. This is to say that one's masculine self-identity can be perfectly congruent with not having to eat meat through the possibility of having access to various masculine models, with the above examples showing just how this might work. Ultimately, this means men "have greater freedom and control in their food choices, and are less tightly bound by singular or hegemonic cultural prescriptions to consume meat" (Sobal 2005: 149). This is not to say meat-based diets will be reduced immediately – modifying an aspect of one's gender identity is a complex matter that takes time. But visible demonstrations of how masculinity can still be displayed without the need for meat's representation (like showcasing veg(etari)an athletes) will go some way to ending this symbolic relationship. I conclude, therefore, that the notion of a plurality of masculinities offers the prospect for one to still identify as masculine, while simultaneously reducing carnivorous food habits and improving environmental sustainability.

Notes

1 Regarding hegemony, Gramsci was of course referring to the capitalist system. His thought, though, can be fruitfully applied to gender studies for demonstrating how certain gender identities permeate throughout society to a greater extent than others.
2 This is not to make a normative point about climate change. I am merely describing the fact that the changing climate has led to an increased opportunity for women to enter the workplace.
3 As a side note, this example also proves just how interrelated these four movements are against hegemonic masculinity – in this instance, the animal liberation and gay rights movements.

References

Adams, C. (2010) *The Sexual Politics of Meat*, 20th Anniv. ed., New York: Continuum.
Adamson, W. L. (1980) *Hegemony and Revolution: A Study of Antonio Gramsci's Political and Cultural Theory*, Berkeley: University of California Press.
Boyle, E. (2012) *High Steaks: Why and How to Eat Less Meat*, Gabriola Island, Canada: New Society Publishers.
Calvert, A. (2014) "You Are What You (M)eat: Explorations of Meat-Eating, Masculinity and Masquerade," *Journal of International Women's Studies* 16(1): 18–33.
Connell, R. W. and J. W. Messerschmidt. (2005) "Hegemonic Masculinity: Rethinking the Concept," *Gender and Society* 19(6): 829–859.
Craig, S. (1992) *Men, Masculinity and the Media*, London: Sage.
de Bakker, E. and H. Dagevos. (2012) "Reducing Meat Consumption in Today's Consumer Society: Questioning the Citizen–Consumer Gap," *Journal of Agricultural and Environmental Ethics* 25(6): 877–894.
Gal, D. and J. Wilkie. (2010) "Real Men Don't Eat Quiche: Regulation of Gender-Expressive Choices by Men," *Social Psychological and Personality Science* 1(4): 291–301.
Gelfer, J. (2013) "Meat and Masculinity in Men's Ministries," *The Journal of Men's Studies* 21(1): 78–91.
Gerber, P. J., H. Steinfeld, B. Henderson, A. Mottet, C. Opio, J. Dijkman, A. Falcucci and G. Tempio. (2013) *Tackling Climate Change Through Livestock – A Global Assessment of Emissions and Mitigation Opportunities*, Rome: Food and Agriculture Organization of the United Nations.
Godden, N. (2013) "Gender and Declining Fisheries in Lobitos, Peru: Beyond Pescador and Ama De Casa," in M. Alston and K. Whittenbury (eds.), *Research, Action and Policy: Addressing the Gendered Impacts of Climate Change*, New York: Springer, pp. 251–263.

Gramsci, A. (1971) *Selections from the Prison Notebooks of Antonio Gramsci*, trans. and ed. by Q. Hoare and G. N. Smith, London: Lawrence & Wishart.

Lears, T. J. J. (1985) "The Concept of Cultural Hegemony: Problems and Possibilities," *The American Historical Review* 90(3): 567–593.

McAlpine, C. A., A. Etter, P. M. Fearnside, L. Seabrook and W. F. Laurance (2009) "Increasing World Consumption of Beef as a Driver of Regional and Global Change: A Call for Policy Action Based on Evidence from Queensland (Australia), Colombia and Brazil," *Global Environmental Change* 9: 21–33.

Meah, A. (2014) "Reconceptualizing 'Masculinity' Through Men's Contributions to Domestic Foodwork," in A. Gorman-Murray and P. Hopkins (eds.), *Masculinities and Place*, London: Ashgate Publishing Limited, pp. 191–208.

Myers, N. and J. Kent. (2004) *The New Consumers: The Influence of Affluence on the Environment*, Washington, DC: Island Press.

Newcombe, M. A., M.B. McCarthy, J.M. Cronin and S.N. McCarthy. (2012) "'Eat Like a Man': A Social Constructionist Analysis of the Role of Food in Men's Lives," *Appetite* 59: 391–398.

Parasecoli, F. (2005) "Feeding Hard Bodies: Food and Masculinities in Men's Fitness Magazines," *Food and Foodways* 13: 17–37.

Potts, A. and J. Parry. (2010) "Vegan Sexuality: Challenging Heteronormative Masculinity Through Meat-free Sex," *Feminism and Psychology* 20(53): 53–72.

Prättälä, R., L. Paalanen, D. Grinberga, V. Helasoja, A. Kasmel and J. Petkeviciene. (2007) "Gender Differences in the Consumption of Meat, Fruit and Vegetables are Similar in Finland and the Baltic Countries," *European Journal of Public Health* 17(5): 520–525.

Ripple, W. J. (2014) "Ruminants, Climate Change and Policy," *Nature Climate Change* 4: 2–5.

Rogers, R. A. (2008) "Beasts, Burgers, and Hummers: Meat and the Crisis of Masculinity in Contemporary Television Advertisements," *Environmental Communication* 2(3): 281–301.

Rothgerber, H. (2013) "Real Men Don't Eat (Vegetable) Quiche: Masculinity and the Justification of Meat Consumption," *Psychology of Men and Masculinity* 14(4): 363–375.

Rozin, P., J.M. Hormes, M.S. Faith and B. Wansink. (2012) "Is Meat Male? A Quantitative Multimethod Framework to Establish Metaphoric Relationships," *Journal of Consumer Research* 39(3): 629–643.

Roy, P. (2002) "Meat-eating, Masculinity, and Renunciation in India: A Ghandian Grammar of Diet," *Gender and History* 14(1): 62–91.

Ruby, M. B. and S. J. Heine. (2011) "Meat, Morals, and Masculinity," *Appetite* 56: 447–450.

Schoesler, H., J. de Boer, J.J. Boersema and H. Aiking H. (2015) "Meat and Masculinity Among Young Chinese, Turkish and Dutch Adults in the Netherlands," *Appetite* 89: 152–159.

Sobal, J. (2005) "Men, Meat, and Marriage: Models of Masculinity," *Food and Foodways* 13: 135–158.

Steinfeld, H., P. Gerber, T. Wassenaar, V. Castel, M. Rosales and C. de Haan. (2006) *Livestock's Long Shadow: Environmental Issues and Options*, Rome: Food and Agriculture Organization of the United Nations.

Sumpter, K. C. (2015) "Masculinity and Meat Consumption: An Analysis Through the Theoretical Lens of Hegemonic Masculinity and Alternative Masculinity Theories," *Sociology Compass* 9(2): 104–114.

Tatlonghari, G. and T. Paris. (2013) "Gendered Adaptations to Climate Change: A Case Study from the Philippines," in M. Alston and K. Whittenbury (eds.), *Research, Action and Policy: Addressing the Gendered Impacts of Climate Change*, New York: Springer, pp. 237–250.

Further Reading

C. Adams, *The Sexual Politics of Meat*, 20th Anniv. ed. (New York: Continuum, 2010) is the definitive feminist-vegetarian critique on the link between meat consumption and patriarchy. A. Gorman-Murray and P. Hopkins (eds.), *Masculinities and Place* (London: Ashgate Publishing Limited, 2014) is a wide-ranging volume that documents a plurality of masculinities within various geographical and cultural contexts. G. L. Mosse, *The Image of Man* (Oxford: Oxford University Press, 1996) is an in-depth analysis of the historical events that culminated to form a crisis of masculinity.

8

UNDERSTANDING ANOREXIA AT THE CROSSROADS OF PHENOMENOLOGY AND FEMINISM

Corine Pelluchon
Translated by Eva Boodman

Introduction

Anorexia is included in the behavioral and eating disorders listed in the American Psychiatric Association's *Diagnostic and Statistical Manual of Mental Disorders* (APA 2000). It appears with depression, bipolar disorder, schizophrenia, and bulimia, the major clinical disorders, with the last associated with anorexia as if it were simply the other facet of the same addictive pathology. Beyond the critique that this pairing does not allow for an analysis of each of them in its specific expression of food deprivation, it also is necessary to discuss the reduction of anorexia to a pathology. This is not to say that we are ignorant of the dramatic consequences of undernutrition. Nor are we rejecting the ways that psychiatry and psychoanalysis can help individuals trace the genesis of their disorder and untangle the threads of a story that might have led them to find satisfaction [*jouissance*] in restricting their food intake and instituting weight loss as a way of existing. However, the hypothesis I defend in this article is that the medicalization of anorexia will not provide a full understanding of it. Medicalizing anorexia does not allow us to understand why there is a fixation on food or how we might support the anorexic person or guide her to find a form of self-expression other than self-imposed deprivation.

This hypothesis – that the facts seem to confirm, if we judge by the number of relapses after hospitalization in spite of many years of psychoanalysis – leads us to approach anorexia as a way of being or "style," in the sense of the phenomenologist Henri Maldiney (2012 [1973]): "A behavior, a conduct, an utterance, all constitute a certain way of being in the world, a certain way of inhabiting.... Its meaning is disclosed in the why" (137). The style tells "why" and reveals the way a person inhabits the world and her own body. Rather than focusing on the symptoms suffered and urging the anorexic person to regain a "normal" weight – where "normal" is, for them, too heavy, and as with all other injunctions to be normal, disgusts them – phenomenology takes as its starting point a person's way of existing, of being themselves *(Eigenwelt)*, of being present in the world *(Umwelt)*, and of being-with-others *(Mitwelt)* (Binswanger 1971). What happens when we apply the forms of *Daseinsanalyse* developed by Ludwig Binswanger to anorexia?

To highlight the ways that the phenomenological approach contributes to our understanding both of anorexia and of strategies of support for those affected by anorexia, I will analyze Kafka's "A Hunger Artist" to illustrate my claim. More than all the theoretical works seeking a psychiatric explanation of anorexia, and even more than narratives that tell the story of a person who engages in voluntary self-control in order to lose weight and must deprive herself of food to do so, this short story brings to light the drama that plays out in anorexia. It is a battle for autonomy, which is to say that we are dealing with a subject who, in order to exist and be recognized, needs to deprive herself in ways that lead to extreme weight loss (Pelluchon 2015: 180–200). It will also be a matter of showing that, in spite of appearances that seem to bear witness to the great fragility of anorexic people and to their faculty of denial, "the hunger artist" in Kafka's story claims a certain superiority over others and refuses, contrary to people with bulimia, to bend to social norms.

Instead of slipping into norms linked to socially constructed roles, suffocating under the weight of the injunction of the other, and "cracking" by having a bulimic crisis, the restrictive anorexic person that we recognize in the traits of the hunger artist has a power of refusal that is proportional to her desire to be a subject. Moreover, she holds herself to an ideal that is very lofty: it is linked to the aestheticizing of existence and the need for a kind of nourishment less trivial than what suits most mortals, as we see with the mystical anorexics of the Middle Ages. Clearly it would be misguided and restrictive to ask of anorexics, who are beholden to their symptom (extreme thinness) as an expression of identity, to gain weight. These examples show that, beyond her symptom, the anorexic person has a formidable will to live that can be harnessed to help her find modes of self-expression other than dietary restriction. An approach that ties identity to symptoms supposes too that in analyzing the person's relationship to her body, we think of her representations of eating in terms of incorporation.

But when one bears witness not to the exteriority of things but to our receptivity to them, eating becomes infinitely more than a nutritional function. Its symbolic, affective, and social dimensions are essential. Eating is moreover a challenge to the dualisms of mind/body, interior/exterior, individual/society, reason/affect. Is anorexia itself a battle for autonomy, the backdrop to what is the mind/body dualism so often denounced by feminist philosophers? Does this explain an anorexic's focus on the act of eating (to her, an unacceptable and disgusting metabolic process and one that motivates her to master her emotions and impulses) while food deprivation is a manifestation of spirit over body, the "I" over the world and others (even over life) for which biological mechanisms are denied?

I will then synthesize these elements of analysis that shine new light on anorexia by insisting on the fact that, most of the time, it is girls and women who suffer from this problem. What is the contribution of a gender-oriented approach to anorexia? And, more generally, what contribution is made by feminism's inquiry into the conditions for the emancipation of women, who still encounter obstacles to their will to be recognized as subjects, and whose bodies are privileged as places of self-expression?

"A Hunger Artist" and anorexia as a battle for autonomy

To misname things, according to Camus in *L'homme révolté*, adds to the suffering of this world, as we see with the word "anorexia." This word, the etymology of which is "absence of appetite," is misleading because there is no certainty that this is literally or figuratively the case for anorexics. Hunger is tamed or denied, but anorexics are in no way lacking in the energy needed to live, as their hyperactivity attests: their desire to live is evident, even if it appears in a paradoxical form. On the contrary, if we focus on the anorexic's experience – as Binswanger does when he invites his patients to reflect on the way they make themselves present to things and communicate with others – we understand that eating disorders are an expression of painful orality [*oralité douloureuse*] that engages the totality of an individual's relationship to themselves and the world. Moreover, even if this self-expression has morbid consequences, it must be seen as part of a style – that is, part of the perspective a person brings to bear on the world. It is a question of an aesthetic and its associated value judgments, which express themselves in oppositions like hard/soft, firm/flaccid, empty/full, and in the ideals of transparency, purity, self-mastery, and other impulses that present-day anorexics share with the mystics of the Middle Ages.

Kafka's "A Hunger Artist" allows us to understand that what is at stake in anorexia is autonomy and not primarily or necessarily the desire to be thin. In this short story we see clearly that food deprivation brings satisfaction that is sought for its own sake and not (as with political or religious fasting) with the aim of obtaining the grace of God or to exert pressure on the populace or those in power (as in the case of Gandhi). As with anorexics for whom extreme thinness cannot be explained by the desire to look like models, the hunger artist's deprivation – a rebellion against the laws of the body – is sought after beyond the state of thinness as a way of obtaining satisfaction [*jouissance*]. The fact of starving oneself is, for Kafka's character, an art.

Because he must stay in a cage and starve himself for forty days, the artist of hunger cannot do otherwise than deprive himself of food. He transcends himself "to the point of inconceivability, because he feels no limit to his capacity to starve himself" and cannot bring himself to feed himself by the end of the forty days. He is "too fanatically obedient to hunger" and cannot make anyone understand the art of hunger (Kafka 1990: 173–174). This is because his deprivation and his abnegation are an art and an occupation. He has a need for the other men to admire the spectacle of his emaciated body emptied of its substance. The praise that he receives at the beginning of his career ravishes him, and he suffers a feeling of injustice and despair when the crowd, abandoning him, runs towards other performances and forgets to notice the number of days that he has gone without eating – to the extent that "no one, not even the hunger artist himself, knows what he accomplished" (Kafka, 1990: 228–229).

Talking about food deprivation as an art helps us to understand what the stakes are for the anorexic person's food deprivation. The restrictions the anorexic imposes express most of all her claim to originality. In a certain way, the desire she has to be thin is an accessory. Not only is it the case that not all dieting women become anorexic; in anorexia, there is a claim to originality in the affirmation of the anorexic's capacity to defy the laws of nature and to conquer their urges. When we do not understand that anorexia, particularly in its restrictive form, is a person's way of existing and a way of shaping her life into a spectacle or an object of contemplation, we sidestep its philosophical significance.

The anorexic, in her obsession with mastery and all-powerfulness, does not want to acknowledge that she is in danger of dying and that the complications to which she exposes herself will result in her encountering more and more obstacles to her projects. What started as a kind of freedom becomes a necessity that subjects the hunger artist as forcefully as a drug addiction. There are no limits to this art, the mastery of which, Kafka writes, does not diminish as one ages. In this sense, the analogy with drug addiction is pertinent: it suggests that the anorexic person cannot escape the cycle on her own. However, this analogy – namely that it is just as hard for an anorexic to stop their food deprivation as it is for an addict to stop consuming heroin – has two drawbacks.

The first is that it is silent on the fact that anorexia distinguishes itself from other addictions (drugs, alcohol, gambling, or sex) where the person is dependent on a product or an activity. Anorexia is certainly an addiction, but the anorexic is dependent on deprivation itself. Moreover, the difference between anorexics and drug addicts or people who drive themselves into ruin from gambling is that the anorexic is proud of their addiction (Kestemberg et al. 1972: 231–232). This is why she presents herself as an artist of hunger and wants to be recognized in that way.

In the same way that drug addicts can think only of getting their dose, the anorexic organizes her life around food. However, she resists food and will not succumb to any dish. Her obsession is to deprive herself. Very often, she will cook for others and worry about what they are eating. Her pride and identity are tied to deprivation. Not only does she not have to demean herself to prevent herself from eating, contrary to drug addicts who steal or prostitute themselves; she also derives satisfaction from her deprivation.

This characteristic distinguishes anorexics from bulimics, who can steal money to procure astronomical quantities of food in order to ingest it and, in certain cases, vomit it out. Bulimia presents a structure closer to drug addiction than does anorexia. The restrictive anorexic is a person who seeks to dominate her body in order to exist in the eyes of others. If there is a family drama behind this story that leads someone to abstain from almost all food in order to affirm herself as a subject – a drama that has to do with identity and is tied to the struggle to feel recognized in her singularity – this is still not enough to explain the persistence of anorexic symptoms at least since the Middle Ages.

Anorexia is a pathology of control, attached to the violence felt by someone unable to attain self-acceptance. In the first place, she struggles to live up to expectations, and then she has the feeling of losing herself, of no longer knowing who she is. The model of the wise child, of the good student who does everything that is expected of her and does well in school, is common among anorexics. It is in this sense that we can talk, in their regard, of a *faux self* (Brusset 2008: 176–177). They have done everything to live up to what was expected of them, often without originality or passion, but then they lose themselves and "crack" by violently opposing the injunctions of their loved ones and society. The refusal to eat is an attack against parents and against one's expectations of oneself, and it is the expression of a will to live that cannot find a positive expression other than as a cry of pain or opposition. The emaciated appearance of the body is enough for this opposition to manifest and enough to retake control from others who have sought to subject the anorexic or who have made her disappear under the weight of injunctions and norms.

Anorexia is a rebellion against a *faux self* that the anorexic has assumed but that does not suit her. But it is also a revolt against those who did not listen to what she had to offer or say. This battle for autonomy and recognition includes the anorexic's reflecting back on her loved ones the guilt-inducing spectacle of her emaciated body as a violent form of revenge against the dependence that has suffocated her. She has suffered from being ignored; she has had the feeling of being silenced and found that she was good at that game, but she has had enough: no food will enter her gagged mouth.

This interpretation, which takes anorexia to be an illness of control, is shared by many of the best specialists of the eating disorder. However, when an effort is made to look past the symptoms, and when an anorexic's formidable will to live is brought to light, it is clear that what is at stake philosophically in anorexia is autonomy. It is not a matter of saying that the anorexic subject lacked autonomy or did not succeed in affirming her autonomy, but quite the opposite: she claims it. The anorexic is unwilling to abide by the standard of living that is presented to her as the norm.

Healing will not be sustainable if we don't recognize that an anorexic is beholden to a symptom that allows her to affirm herself as a subject. Instead of imposing a norm, which will be interpreted by the anorexic as a rejection of her autonomy, the goal of support must be to give her the means to affirm herself otherwise. The goal is not even "healing," if we take that to mean attaining a normal weight, but to insure that her life and freedom are not threatened by the consequences of undernutrition.

By thinking of anorexia as a style, we are not encouraging the anorexic person to attach herself to her symptom. Rather, this approach seeks to allow for a change in the expression of the self and, most importantly, to combat the anorexic's resistance to change. This is because one of the characteristics of anorexics is their tendency to lock themselves into habits and constraining frameworks for daily life, with rituals that are reassuring to them but are also a manifestation of their fear of change. Change, which is the essence of life and which is at work in our body's nutrition, is unacceptable for the anorexic. The body is fixed for them, as if change, beginning with the body's metabolism, were synonymous with losses that mark the subject's failure and powerlessness. Instead of counting the calories that the patient should ingest and treating only her symptoms, it is most important to listen to her.

It is not uncommon for someone who demonstrates painful orality to feel misunderstood by others. The anorexic person often lacks confidence in herself and others: she will not trust enough to let anything enter her mouth; she is afraid to fill herself or else devour food to fill a void. This is why the anorexic feels brutalized by anyone who enforces her obedience to a norm; this affirms her idea of the world, others, and herself, and isolates her even more. Rather than asking an anorexic to gain weight and to respect an intake of 2000 calories a day – to adhere to a norm to which she is averse – it seems more pertinent to focus our work on the obstacles to reducing weight loss (Lalau 2012).

Thus, painful orality is a way of being in the world and to be in relation with oneself and others, where the relationship to eating is an expression of the affective register of this mode of being. A person's lived experience of her relationship to eating and to her body – particularly to her stomach – is the point of departure for this way of being that makes orality the paradigm of both vulnerability and the capacity for enjoyment and action. The difficulty for the anorexic subject is to accept both of the latter without guilt. Next, it is a matter of seeing how our representations of eating allow us not only to eat better but also to live better.

A gendered approach to the problem

The stubbornness and struggle for autonomy that characterize anorexia are common to both mystical anorexics and those of today, who do not necessarily believe in God. The refusal to abide by norms, which is an expression of the refusal to resemble others and to have their shape, is also a refusal of the functions assigned to women, like maternity. The approach to this problem is necessarily gendered, since the social norms of wife and mother determine a woman's identity as a function of the husband she marries and the children she bears. This approach explains that the rejection of this model – of normative gender roles – assumes the form of a rejection of womanly shape and a will to thinness that escape the formulaic destiny of femininity.

The will of the subject to be autonomous can easily be seen in the embodied expression of women whose roles and status depend on their bodily appearance and their age. In this regard, anorexia illustrates the failure of the subject to find a form of self-expression that goes beyond the body's physical power. In her obsession with thinness, the anorexic is riveted to her body, as if she cannot extricate herself from a framework that assimilates women to matter and the body and men to the will and the mind. We will revisit the mind/body dualism that can also explain an anorexic's disgust with food.

Thinness can equally be understood as an expression of an anorexic's difficulty in making her voice heard; in finding a path of self-affirmation within society when she feels she belongs to two worlds; or in being subjected to the social norms imposed by others while she is seeking an original existence and self-expression that break with the corporeal destiny of women. Sing Lee suggests that we should stop reducing anorexia to the obsessive desire to lose weight (Katzman and Lee 1997: 385–394). Lee analyzes this phenomenon in societies where the norm of thinness does not exist, but where a subject's exile or belonging to two cultures isolates her from the cultural framework that would give meaning to her personal distress. Confronted with the disappearance of her cultural frame of reference along with the valorization of autonomy and competition, she cannot find a way to affirm herself and to negotiate the disconnect that she endures.

We find this refusal to abide by social roles and classic norms of feminine modesty in Catherine de Sienne, who died of cachexia in 1380. She fought against the bourgeois matrimonial strategy of the family of merchants she belonged to. Born frail, she was fed, whereas her twin sister Giovanna was put in a nursery and died shortly thereafter. Giovanna was, after her death, dispossessed shortly before the birth of a third sister, Nanna, who became (as her name suggests), the replacement for the deceased twin. In this way, Catherine "found herself to be, from early childhood, in the position of quasi-deceased" (Maître 2000). Catherine spends her entire life oscillating between life and death. She decides at the age of twelve never to get married. Several years later, she attempts to escape the conjugal life imposed on her by her mother – a life that would alter her sense of herself as a woman – by refusing care when she contracts smallpox and abstaining from all cooked foods, with the exception of bread, until she loses half her weight.

These kinds of self-deprivation that lead Catherine de Sienne towards death are clearly related to crises in her family relations and with "the claim to absolute self-conquest," as we see in her letter-testament to Raymond de Capoue, where she writes that her soul has become separated from her body and can now breathe. In this text, food metaphors abound, in particular when she discusses the relationship with God, which is a body-to-body relationship, the prototype of which is breastfeeding. Like Kafka's hunger artist, the anorexic's search for food deprivation becomes a way to affirm domination, purity, and abnegation, which expresses itself too in the desire for other foods: "I wasn't able to find food that I like. If I had found it, believe me, I wouldn't be at all remarkable; I would have filled my belly like you and the others," the hunger artist tells the inspector, before he is replaced by a young panther to attract the attention of the spectators (Kafka 1990 [1922]: 202).

Mind–body dualism and the rejection of the metabolic process

The hunger artist's response can be interpreted as a mark of his contempt for earthly food and as a testament to his rejection of the body. The external domination that he exerts on his body reflects a dualist framework, as in the text written by another anorexic patient we have seen:

> My brain, which should decode and express the signals emitted by my body through hunger and thirst, has inverted the process. It is the authoritarian dictator of what my body needs without consulting it. As if it weren't a part of my body. This dictatorship gives it the illusion of controlling this body, even though in thinking this it has fallen into its own trap. . . . The ideal, for me, would be to be a mind with no bodily container. I feel like a prisoner of this body, even though my prison is actually just my way of thinking. Even in knowing all of this, I feel divided. . . . My brain seems invincible while my body becomes more and more fragile. . . . As soon as my body fills itself with food, . . . my brain immediately blames it and insults it. My mind is separated from my body and must take command over it.
>
> (Lalau 2012: 229–230)

A dualism that makes the mind a tyrant and the body a burdensome hunk of matter also explains why food is the object of this sort of refusal (Bordo 1993). Combustion, which is a synonym of life, gives way to slow-burning self-destruction, little by little. This is because food is paradigmatic of what is substantial about the body. Food mixes itself into the body and this is repugnant for the patient who sees her body as an idealized and immaculate vessel. The anorexic could only *psychically* digest what food is by getting past the dualisms of body/mind, interior/exterior, and sensation/brain.

An anorexic's idealized image of an evanescent body and obsessive fear of food intake – that is, of fattening – is a natural companion to an anorexic's refusal to accept change and the dynamic process by which metabolism transforms food into energy. The focus on food as the enemy comes from the rejection of a body made of fluids – a substantial body – that represents all that is dirty, limp, shameful. The body must obey the mind, which is the locus of identity. Mind–body dualism is not responsible for anorexia. However, conceptual frameworks that encourage rigid representations of eating reassure the anorexic person and feed her ambition: to make the body disappear in order to exist and to affirm her rebellion against the injunctions of others, especially the mother. This rebellion subjugates the body that her mother bore and connected to the basic functions of life to ensure her survival. Anorexia is a cry demanding a response to an originary call that was not heard.

Another way to interpret the hunger artist's claim that he cannot find any food to his liking is to move our focus away from his self-deprivation and the will to mastery and rebellion they express, and to focus instead on the secret aspirations they conceal. Here we are revisiting the fact that anorexia is a style, linked to an aesthetic and to value judgments attached to representations. Everything limp, fat, or flabby manifests a lack of control, a vulgarity, a baseness to which the hunger artist opposes a lofty ideal made from asceticism and purity. The search for food that can satisfy the anorexic's ethos – particularly her hunger for beauty, elevation, and originality – can be a constructive way to support her. Aside from responding by looking for foods that the hunger artist will like, it is imperative to destroy mistaken representations that lead him to think that foods are enemies. These mistaken representations can be corrected by information that can give anorexic people a better understanding of food and can give them – in keeping with the etymological origins that associate knowledge *(savoir)* with savor *(saveur)* – the taste for eating.

The constructive and deconstructive components of the phenomenological approach, when they are linked to the work of psychiatrists and nutritionists, allow the anorexic person to relearn how to eat; that is, to stop fearing the otherness of foods that are good for us and that we share with others. The idea here is to give the anorexic person the means to begin affirming her identity without asking her to be like everyone else by attaining a normal weight. That standard will always be too much for her, because what she sees in the mirror is different from what we see.

Phenomenology of non-constitution and feminism

The dualisms of mind/body, interior/exterior, reason/affect, man/woman are not the cause of anorexia, but they can still serve to explain why anorexics have so much trouble experiencing calm in their relationships towards food. Moreover, the "dictatorship" that the anorexic makes her body endure illustrates the real force of the dualist schema and of the paradigm of domination so often denounced by feminists, who are interested in man's relationships to nature, the body, and even to animals (Adams and Donovan 1995; Plumwood 1991). In contradistinction, the path towards a more harmonious relationship to one's body and to others requires us to reflect on the corporeality of the subject.

Corporeality does not merely refer to the fact of having a body and being mortal; it is a matter of contesting the privileged status of consciousness to give meaning to everything, as Levinas writes in *Totality and Infinity* (1994 [1961]). This kind of phenomenology is a phenomenology of non-constitution; it is the companion to the rehabilitation of sense in its pathic dimension, as the expression of the interaction between me and the world and as a being-with-the-world-and-with-others (Maldiney 2012 [1973]: 188–190). According to this framework, eating is erected as a paradigm because it rejects all the dualisms mentioned above and takes existence seriously in its materiality (Pelluchon 2015).

Vulnerability, morality, and birth are no longer interpreted as limits to our power, as they are for philosophies of liberty that affirm the originary character of dereliction and life as being-towards-death (Pelluchon 2015: 37–52, 64–78). In Heidegger's *Being and Time* (2008 [1927]), for instance, only a "thrown resoluteness" and the decision to give existence to what is important for me can tear me out of facticity and the degradation of the "they." Contrary to Heidegger's view, we are led to adopt a more relational conception of the subject from the moment we recognize that we are never truly independent, but rather that intersubjectivity is installed at the heart of the subject (which we can see in the event of birth). Furthermore, my vulnerable lived experience does not subjugate me but feeds my existence, in the sense that the fact of living has an originary relationship to pleasure (Pelluchon 2015: 42–43). Put differently, the alterity of food is no longer menacing, and we no longer consider our needs in terms of privation, as if we needed to fill a void. We can now think of needs as a reference to enjoyment [*jouissance*], which, according to Levinas, "explodes the elemental structure of things" and highlights my sensible immersion in the world.

This dimension is manifest in the pleasure we take in certain foods. And yet, those with eating disorders completely sidestep this dimension of pleasure that not only refers to hedonism, but describes (just like any philosophy of taste) a structure of existence – an *existential* – that highlights the depth of connection between myself and the world, the body and the mind, interior and exterior, the private and the social. We find this same crisis of taste in the tendency to reduce food to nutritional intake, like when we do not make the time to eat or when we snack. The lack of respect for oneself, the force of the framework of mental domination over the body, man over woman, persists in our eating habits. This is what we see in all eating disorders – in anorexia, bulimia, and obesity – but also in the overconsumption of meat that creates a life of misery for animals raised as livestock.

Conclusion

Transcending the dualisms of mind/body, nature/culture, and man/woman and prioritizing the subject's corporeality are both essential contributions that feminism has made to thought. In this way, these contributions have spurred a renewal of ontology and political theory, and they can cast new light on the phenomena – like anorexia and eating disorders in general – that express the totality of a person's relationship with the world and with others. It is also for this reason that feminist theories are consonant with the approaches of some French phenomenologists who are trying – following Levinas or Maldiney – to substitute Heidegger's ontology of care for a more material understanding of being-there, which is always a being-with-things-and-with-others (Pelluchon 2015).

If we are to understand anorexia and support those who suffer from it to affirm themselves in ways other than self-deprivation, it is important to shift our focus away from symptoms and towards their way of being, existing, and relating to their body, to the world, and to others. It is also a matter of situating this expression of painful orality within a social context, where a pervasive network of meanings explains that some people, notably women, can only express their autonomy by mistreating their bodies. The pacified relationship with food and with themselves illustrates, through the idea of incorporation or absorption, the way that exterior becomes interior to constitute me. In order to grasp this battle for autonomy that has mind/body dualism as its backdrop, it can be helpful to analyze it at the crossroads of feminism and phenomenology.

References

Adams, C. J. and J. Donovan (eds.) (1995) *Animals and Women: Feminist Theoretical Explorations*, Durham and London: Duke University Press.

American Psychiatric Association. (2000) *Diagnostic and Statistical Manual of Mental Disorders*, 4th ed., text revision (DSM-IV-TR), Arlington, VA: American Psychiatric Association.

Binswanger, L. (1971) *Introduction à l'analyse existentielle*, trans. by J. Verdeaux and R. Kuhn, Paris: Minuit.

Bordo, S. (1993) *Unbearable Weight: Feminism, Western Culture, and the Body*, Berkeley: University of California Press.

Brusset, B. (2008) *Psychopathologie de l'anorexie mentale*, Paris: Dunod.

Heidegger, M. (2008 [1927]) *Being and Time*, trans. by J. Macquarrie and E. Robinson, New York: HarperCollins.

Kafka, F. (1990 [1922]) *Un artiste de la faim et autres récits*, trans. by C. David, Paris: Gallimard–Folio Classique.

Katzman, M. A., and S. Lee (1997) "Beyond Body Image: The Integration of Feminist and Transcultural Theories in the Understanding of Self Starvation," *International Journal of Eating Disorders* 22: 385–394.

Kestemberg, E., J. Kestemberg, and S. Dacobert. (1972) *La Faim et le corps. Une étude psychanalytique de l'anorexie mentale*, Paris: PUF.

Lalau, J. (2012) *En finir avec les régimes: Vers une alliance du corps et de l'esprit*, Paris: F. Bourin.

Levinas, E. (1994 [1961]) *Totalité et Infini: Essai sur l'extériorité*, Paris: LGF, Biblio Essais.

Maître, J. (2000) *Anorexies religieuses, anorexie mentale: Essai de psychanalyse sociohistorique (de Marie de l'incarnation à Simone Weil)*, Paris: Le Cerf.

Maldiney, H. (2012 [1973]) *Regard, parole, espace*, Paris: Le Cerf.

Pelluchon, C. (2015) *Les Nourritures. Philosophie du corps politique*, Paris: Le Seuil.

Plumwood, V. (1991) "Nature, Self and Gender: Feminism, Environmental Philosophy, and the Critique of Rationalism," *Ecological Feminism* 6(1): 3–27.

PART III
Food and cultural diversity

9

THE CHALLENGES OF DIETARY PLURALISM*

Emanuela Ceva, Chiara Testino, and Federico Zuolo

Introduction

The existence of diverse and often competing food standards is one of the most ordinary and yet theoretically underexplored facts of contemporary societies. Such standards concern what is permissible to eat and how food should be produced and prepared. Vegetarianism illustrates the former, religious ritual animal slaughter exemplifies the latter. The normative implications of this sort of pluralism – call it "dietary pluralism" (henceforth DP) – have rarely been the subject of philosophical discussion. This is quite surprising given the centrality of certain dietary claims to a person's integrity. Eating is, arguably, one of the most ordinary and yet intimate actions, in relation to which individual evaluative standards, cultural habits, and legal regulations are very often inextricably interwoven in constituting a person's sense of her own self.

By referring to illustrative cases of ritual slaughter and the request for a vegetarian option in public canteens, in this chapter we aim to show the philosophical importance of DP by identifying its main features (Section 1) and the challenges it raises for political institutions (Sections 2 and 3). We do that from the perspective of liberal political philosophy. This decision is motivated in consideration of the many studies of different kinds of pluralism in this area (e.g., concerning language, religion, or ethics), which make the absence of a full-fledged treatment of DP all the more puzzling and, therefore, worthy of some attention.

What is dietary pluralism?

DP is a complex phenomenon that consists in the diffusion on a global scale of different food-related habits and practices. DP does not only concern the kinds of food that different people eat but also, for example, its preparation and consumption, its symbolic and/or ritual meaning, as well as the different moral, religious, or scientific beliefs that motivate the adoption of dietary habits and practices by certain individuals or groups.

Understood in this way, DP may easily be seen to derive from a series of adaptive responses, which became necessary – or at least sufficient – to allow the first communities of human beings to survive. The process of differentiation of dietary habits and practices is characterized by an interaction between human beings and their environment in which they are not merely passive beings – entirely determined by their biological necessities or by contingent events out of their control – but also active agents in the transformation of the surrounding world according to their needs, choices, and cultural, scientific, social, and economic knowledge. DP is, therefore, a complex phenomenon dependent on environmental, historical, and cultural variables and on the co-presence of necessities related to human needs for self-sufficiency, survival, and the choices of individuals and groups. The study of the history of food (Toussaint-Samat 2009) suggests a major influence of cultural factors on the variability of human dietary habits and practices (Montanari 2006). Knowledge of how to recognize what is edible and how to provide it, as well as the development of increasingly sophisticated and efficient techniques regarding how to control food sources and preserve them, soon became the determining factor in ensuring human survival and flourishing.

Agriculture and the domestication of plants and non-human animals have been, as is well known, both the effects and causes of several changes during human evolution. Through more or less successful attempts at domestication, humans have achieved more secure and abundant food sources – but they have also radically changed their environment, lifestyles, and food habits.

Codified dietary rules emerged in human communities in ancient times. Even when expressed through moral and religious precepts, such rules have typically been instruments of social control and political and economic power (see Harris 1977). Dietary prescriptions and prohibitions, codified in contexts where religion was not primarily a question of conscience but a social, cultural, and political tool, lend themselves to be interpreted as aiming at ensuring the survival of the population and, at times, of hierarchical relations of power. Dietary rules consist, for example, in hygienic norms concerning food preparation and consumption, or restrictions on the kinds of food permitted and the frequency of its consumption. Think, for instance, of the rules for hunting and fishing or the prohibition of eating some animals considered sacred. It is easy to see that such rules were instrumental to the preservation of food, in general, and to ensure that the food destined for the elite would not run out. Traces of these rules remain in the form of precepts in a majority of religions practiced to date and contribute to DP.

There are also more recent facts that have influenced human nutrition and contributed to DP at a global level (see Scrinis 2013). These concern, in the first place, the industrialization of food production. The application of the most advanced scientific and technological knowledge to the industrial production of food has made processed food increasingly available. Improved ability to manipulate nutrients has led to a radical transformation of, so to speak, traditional foods or to the creation of new foods – such as functional foods – or to the pharmaceutization of others. The value of such innovations is disputed; some emphasize their role in improving living conditions and in extending the life expectancy of large segments of the population, whereas others stress the dangers in introducing certain foods into the human diet – this is the case of "junk food" as well as food containing additives which, if not associated with correct dietary practices, could threaten consumers' health.

A similarly controversial status applies to the diffusion of nutritionism as a science. Nutritionism undoubtedly has remote origins, but it is only in the contemporary age that it seems to have reached its full development and acquired a social and political role. Theories on human nutrition are often controversial as they aim to direct human dietary choices either towards or away from the consumption of certain kinds of food – think, for instance, of the vegetarian/vegan diet, the paleo diet, and nutrigenomics. The empirical bases of such diets are quite controversial given the scientific disagreement on their relative potential benefits or harm to human health. What is more, when nutritionism is used as a ground for motivating public policies, it raises intricate issues concerning the justification of state paternalism and the dietary autonomy of individuals (see Bonotti 2016).

Lastly, the expansion and globalization of the food market seem to have had controversial effects. From an empirical point of view, it might look obvious that such phenomena have increased consumers' opportunities for choice by making available to them a variety of foods that were once considered exotic and hard to obtain. However, according to some, this risks seriously restricting people's dietary opportunities in the long run because of the negative impact that the policies of multinational food corporations are expected to have on biodiversity (see Paarlberg 2010 and Schanbacher 2010). In a straightforward sense, large food companies are gradually monopolizing the global market, with possible negative effects on access to food for certain people – who do not have access to privileged channels of food distribution – and on the quality of food itself. Such considerations have inspired, for example, such movements as Slow Food, which are committed to promoting biodiversity and local products.

These are only some of the factors that historically have contributed to DP, and it is not clear whether they will lead, in the long run, to the enhancement or, in fact, the impoverishment of this condition. By referring to such factors we have aimed at explaining the occurrence of DP and accounting for its multifaceted connotation. In the next section, we discuss what implications can be drawn from such considerations with regard to the normative importance of DP.

The normative importance of dietary pluralism

Knowledge of the history of human nutrition and the mechanisms that have influenced it may provide the basis for offering some normative considerations regarding DP and its importance. In the first place, as suggested above, such knowledge helps us to understand the origin and nature of some dietary rules, as well as to see their overall variability across cultures and groups, and their symbolic function as regards the social and political aspects of food. This is important in order to bring out, for example, the significance of certain dietary prescriptions and taboos whose emergence has typically been associated with certain religious or cultural practices although, as we have already seen, they may also serve nutritional and social functions.

Second, understanding the historical determinants of DP makes it possible to illuminate the reciprocal influence between different food cultures and environmental, political, and economic phenomena. This may offer the basis for drawing out the normative implications of different dietary habits and practices in these domains for the design of food policies. In particular, understanding the depth and breadth of the influence of human nutrition on how human beings see themselves and their social environment may provide a better grasp of the reasons why food-related habits and practices are morally relevant. Nutrition matters to people for their health and general well-being, and it is the basis of many social exchanges. This consideration is crucial and will be revisited in order to understand the relation between a person's dietary habits and her integrity.

A third interesting aspect that emerges when looking at the historical evolution of nutrition is the difficulty, if not the impossibility, of answering such questions as those regarding the most appropriate diet for humans: Should human beings be carnivores? Vegetarians? Omnivores? On issues of this sort, strong disagreement persists and casts doubts on the very possibility of drawing normative conclusions from premises about humanity. To acknowledge the variety of diets that human beings have followed over history calls for a certain caution in seeking general criteria of edibility as, historically, humans seem to have eaten almost anything. These considerations raise important normative questions: Are there dietary practices that are really necessary for survival? Why should we preserve and justify current dietary practices rather than propose radically new and morally superior ones? Are there moral limits to what human beings could consider as food?[1]

We do not aim to answer these questions here, nor are we committed to the view that a conclusive answer to them is even possible. What we would like to emphasize is that, once we understand the changing nature and origin of DP along the historical lines we have suggested, such questions and, most importantly, the answers that different people have given to them over time appear *reasonable*. This is the case because at the root of such answers lies, as shown, a complexity of political, economic, and cultural reasons, and, given such complexities, it is implausible to envisage normative dietary criteria as having universal validity.

Interestingly, the characterization we have proposed makes DP an instance of what John Rawls (1993) has famously called "reasonable pluralism." DP can be explained in the majority of cases as a result of the so-called "burdens of judgment" (Rawls 1993: 54–58) that are the many hazards which people may incur while they exercise their practical reason in their political life. Among other things, the burdens of judgment include the complexity of evidence and the difficulty of evaluating it; the differently perceived relative weight of different considerations; the vagueness of many concepts relevant for moral and political judgment; and the impact of personal experience on the way in which different people regard certain facts and values. So long as judgments are made through reason, the burdens affecting them are not merely mistakes of which we should be rid, but are somehow essential to the normal intellectual activities of reasonable people. From the discussion above, it seems that these burdens apply to many humans' judgments concerning food and its regulation. DP is reasonable to the extent that, as history shows, it is the result of a correct and diligent exercise of human reason aiming at solving the extremely complicated problem – which is at once individual and collective – of how to satisfy the basic human need to secure adequate nutrition.

In sum, we propose to characterize DP, as a normatively relevant notion, as follows:

> *Dietary pluralism* (DP): The coexistence in the same political community under common institutions of a plurality of dietary habits and practices responsive to individual diversities (e.g., health conditions), and social, religious, and cultural standards (e.g., standards of edibility, quality, and adequacy of food) – which, albeit reasonable, may differ quite radically as to what is considered food and what are adequate criteria of food production, consumption, and commercialization.

That DP is an instance of reasonable pluralism does not imply that elements such as personal taste or aesthetic standards have no influence on individual dietary practices; nor does it entail that, given their common nature, any dietary request should receive the same institutional response. It rather corroborates the idea that DP is no mere transient feature of contemporary societies, but a persistent human condition with epistemological roots. This condition is normatively important for its implications in three domains. First, it has axiological implications: as a result of the burdens of judgment, different people develop different standards of what a good diet is. Second, it has anthropological implications: a plurality of reasonable views about food and its regulation inform different forms of human life. Third, and most importantly for our purposes, it has political implications: standards of reasonableness should apply to the public justification of food policies developed in response to the different reasonable demands for accommodation put forward by the holders of different dietary views.[2]

It is our aim to specify these political implications in the remainder of the chapter. For the time being, suffice it to notice that the characterization of DP as reasonable pluralism calls for institutional consideration of the demands for accommodation of different dietary needs. Such demands may not be briskly brushed aside as merely the expression of people's "expensive tastes" or more or less transient idiosyncrasies. Our analysis thus far has shown that there is at least a prima facie case for considering the demands of DP as deeply entrenched in people's conceptions of the good and, therefore, part and parcel of the standards by which people assess the acceptability of social and political rules in the light of their congruence with their integrity.

By integrity we mean someone's inner coherence with her own conscientiously held moral and ethical standards. Integrity, so understood, is a content-independent notion (in the sense that it does not demand any specific substantive action per se) and a second-order moral value that demands compliance with someone's substantive moral and ethical standards, whatever they may be. In this sense, integrity is a property of a person's sense of her own self. Violations of integrity imply the violation of the demands of one's own conscience, which is the locus of one's deepest values and personal convictions (Childress 1979). These may derive from individual moral and ethical beliefs, as well as from someone's religious or cultural commitments. Failure to live with integrity does not merely entail thwarting some more or less idiosyncratic preference, but undermining one's own moral standards, the violation of which would result in feelings of regret, shame, and loss of one's identity and self-respect.

Respect for this kind of integrity poses constraints on the state's legitimate action. We want to suggest that such constraints are particularly stringent for liberal institutions in virtue of their commitment to treating all citizens as equally capable of self-legislation: a person's capacity to form and pursue a life plan articulated through rules of which she can regard herself as both the author and the addressee (see Bird 1996; Boettcher 2007; Larmore 2008). To treat people in accordance with this capacity means that any constraint on the exercise of their capacity for legislation should be justified to them and made congruent with their moral standards so that action in accordance with such constraints does not impinge on their integrity (Ceva 2011).

The importance of this requirement may be seen as an entailment of the very nature of the liberal project of public justification. According to the liberal canon (Waldron 1987), the rationale of the public order consists in the establishment of a stable framework within which individuals can jointly pursue their possibly diverging life plans. The public order is, therefore, justified as a limit to the arbitrary power of individuals and to secure cooperation between them, as free and equal persons, in the pursuit of their life plans on terms that they can all accept on moral grounds. All participants in the scheme of cooperation, thus established, hold a moral claim against the institutions constitutive of the public order that all collective decisions be justified to them. Now, given the centrality of dietary habits and practices to people's life plans, it is apparent that food-related constraints should bear the burden of public justification and that institutional action may not disregard people's reasonable demands in this domain.

To be sure, some may think that when it comes to food, the most pressing normative issues do not concern the accommodation of DP but, more fundamentally, the demands of distributive justice to ensure adequate access to nutrition for everyone globally. However, even if that were the case, our analysis has shown that in order to understand what such demands of distributive justice amount to, consideration of DP is inescapable. As shown above, the standards of what counts as "adequate" nutrition are not immune to DP as they vary across time, space, individuals, and cultures. Therefore, besides its centrality in the liberal project of public justification, there is also a non-trivial sense in which DP is central for institutions to discharge their duties of distributive justice concerning the satisfaction of such a fundamental human need as nutrition. We devote the remainder of the chapter to illustrating and specifying these general considerations.

Two illustrative cases of dietary pluralism

In this section, we discuss two prominent cases of DP to illustrate instances that have a clear normative relevance for public institutions: the case of ritual animal slaughter and that concerning the presence of a vegetarian option in public canteens. These are interesting cases because they exemplify circumstances under which (1) state action is required to enforce a dietary standard, and (2) some such standards are in conflict with some minority dietary habits as a result of reasonable DP.

Let us start with the case of ritual animal slaughter. The majority of contemporary western rulings on animal slaughter establish that animals should be stunned before being slaughtered in order to minimize suffering. Jewish and Muslim ritual methods of slaughtering, instead, provide that animals be slaughtered with a knife without previous stunning. Disagreement on this issue is an instance of DP concerning food production and consumption. Many western countries have granted an exemption from the obligation to stun animals to accommodate ritual slaughter in accordance with Muslims' and Jews' right to religious freedom (Haupt 2007).[3] This scenario suggests a clash of principles between the commitment to minimizing animal suffering and that to protecting people's right to religious freedom.

Interestingly, both principles are generally and widely accepted; are they necessarily in tension with each other when applied to the case of ritual slaughter? This seems disputable. If we take the principle of the minimization of animal suffering seriously, concerns about ritual slaughter do not follow as a matter of course. One may argue that, although we always have a duty to avoid unnecessary pain, we should focus on the overall pain that animals experience throughout their lives rather than primarily on that experienced at the time of their death. After all – the argument goes – what is so special about death if we compare it to months or years of suffering in the often painful conditions of industrial farming (Zuolo 2015)? This point is particularly important when considering the claim that, in fact, ritual practices of animal slaughter were designed and adopted to minimize animal suffering at the time of death (Lerner and Rabello 2006/2007). Seen in this light, rather than a clash between two irreconcilable principles, DP in this case concerns two clashing interpretations of the same principle (that which requires the minimization of animal suffering during slaughter – see Zuolo 2014).[4]

This characterization allows the interpretation of this case as an instance of reasonable DP because it instantiates a clash between two interpretations of a principle concerning the standards of food production and consumption that can be explained by appealing to the burdens of judgment. In our suggested interpretation, neither approach to the regulation of animal slaughter may be seen as stemming merely from an idiosyncratic matter of taste. Both may, in fact, be seen as the results of a "diligent exercise of human reason" – aiming at solving the issue of how to ensure adequate human nutrition in a way that is consistent with abidance by the moral commitment to minimizing the pain of animals during slaughter.[5]

What is more, the case points to an issue of reasonable DP that has clear normative relevance for institutional action. The general commitment to minimizing pain requires that such a commitment be realized through institutional action whenever relevant. This is certainly the case with the regulation of animal slaughter, which is part and parcel of the state's action to secure adequate nutrition (in compliance with general health and safety standards). As seen, relevant challenges of DP arise when such regulations clash with the dietary prescriptions of certain minority groups that demand accommodation for their practices. Such demands must be given consideration, on the basis of our argument in the previous section, because rules concerning animal slaughter have, over history, acquired particular importance for certain religious and cultural groups and may, therefore, be seen as an integral part of their conceptions of the good. This makes abidance by these rules for the members of such groups a component of the sense of their own selves, and failure to comply – as seen – would result in an infringement of their integrity. Insofar as the liberal project of public justification, as characterized above, requires that public rules be justified to the members of society on morally acceptable grounds, it follows that such demands of accommodation of DP should occupy a secure space in the political agendas of the societies within which they emerge.

The second illustrative case concerns the request for a vegetarian option in public canteens on the basis of moral and/or religious convictions. For the sake of simplicity, we offer a normative analysis of the case of food in prison canteens but, with some moderate tweaks, the same considerations apply to such other public contexts as schools and hospitals.

The freedom of individuals detained in jails is justifiably restricted as a consequence of the violation of others' rights or in view of the prevention of further crimes. However, in a liberal framework, even if lacking personal liberty, the fundamental rights of an individual in jail must be granted. These rights include, we can plausibly assume, that of freedom of conscience/religion and that to adequate nutrition. Taken together, the satisfaction of these rights requires that appropriate meals be provided to inmates and that the standard of appropriateness include respect for the inmates' conscientious/religious beliefs.

Can we take this seemingly straightforward conclusion at face value? Not quite. Albeit plausible, this conclusion becomes problematic in circumstances of DP, when different dietary standards demand accommodation. In the first place, although such requests for accommodation may be reasonable (in the interpretation offered above), their joint realization might be problematic in circumstances of scarce resources: who ought to bear the costs of catering to inmates' different dietary requirements? A general commitment to individual well-being makes the demand that the collectivity pay to cater for inmates' dietary needs seemingly acceptable in the presence of health conditions. But can the same logic be extended to demands based on someone's cultural or religious habits? Secondly, the case points at the problem that the accommodation of DP may imply a violation of the principle of state neutrality. This is a specific problem with which liberal institutions are faced: if liberal institutions must remain neutral with respect to alternative conceptions of the good (including religious ones), why should they grant a special accommodation to claims based on some such specific conceptions?

An interesting case in point to exemplify these concerns is the legal case *(Jakóbski v. Poland)* of a Polish citizen who, during his detention in jail, put forward the request for a vegetarian menu in compliance with his Buddhist religious requirements. According to Mahayana Buddhism, to which the claimant adhered, people ought to avoid meat in virtue of the principle of compassion for all living beings. The prison management and Polish authorities never met the claimant's request on the ground that it was insufficiently motivated (no health-related reason was in fact adduced). Eventually, the European Court of Human Rights recognized that the claimant's right to religious freedom had been violated (Application no. 18429/06).

This case is interesting from the perspective of DP because, although we may presume that the prison authorities had no wish to deny the claimant's right to religious freedom, they deemed that this right could not entail the provision of a special menu given the practical impossibility of meeting each and every prisoner's dietary needs and the necessity for a public institution to provide healthy and decent food for all its subjects at a sustainable cost. It was not the individual demand that was deemed unjustified; the problem was, rather, its satisfaction in the joint circumstances of DP and scarcity of resources.

This point is directly related to the first problem singled out above: are the costs of the accommodation of DP ever justified? An answer to this question necessarily seems to depend on the content of the request for which accommodation is sought. While it seems indisputable that the prison authority should not be held accountable to catering for the inmates' requests for luxury food, it seems equally plausible to think that our argument in the previous section grounds a prima facie case for the accommodation of requests that either do not require any sophisticated preparation or for which compliance is central to the claimant's integrity. Both conditions are easily met in the case under scrutiny, as the ECHR's judgment recognized.

As to the second problem regarding state neutrality, critics of the accommodation may argue that, in circumstances of DP, institutional actions, to be generally acceptable, must be grounded in non-controversial principles. This requires in turn that dietary provisions be as independent as possible of controversial conceptions of the good but be based on such generally held facts as those deriving from scientific knowledge about nutrition. On this basis, prison management may justify the dietary options they make available only on the ground that they are nutritionally correct. However, as seen above, nutritionism is not immune to DP both as a general scientific approach to food and in virtue of cross-cultural variations of dietary standards of adequacy concerning food production and consumption. Science can certainly establish the average amount of nutritional needs for human beings, but how such needs should be satisfied can plausibly vary depending on whether, say, the necessary proteins are of animal origin or not. The corollary of this general statement is that there is no neutral standpoint in this domain because the standard dietary set of options is usually determined by a majority, which is in its turn a cultural majority bearing dietary standards that are the object of DP. In western countries, the majority has traditionally been omnivore. But DP suggests that there is nothing necessary or unavoidable in this option. In these circumstances, lack of consideration of minority claims is not an entailment of neutrality, but a benchmark of oppression and discrimination (see Galeotti 2002).

One may protest that precisely in view of the impossibility of being neutral, the regulation of dietary options can never be the object of justified institutional action. Institutions should, rather, leave the issue to individual freedom of choice. Certainly, this is a viable solution in many circumstances, for example as concerns the legitimacy of certain institutional campaigns that "nudge" people into buying certain kinds of food and not others – usually on health-related grounds. But the state may not so easily refrain from regulating access to food in such self-enclosed contexts as prisons, or – in fact – public hospitals and schools. Leaving it to individuals to cater for their own dietary needs would imply that the state surrenders the task of taking care of people's health and well-being in these self-enclosed contexts, in which the regulation of life falls squarely under the state's responsibility. This is questionable both in itself and for the implications it might have in terms of generating inequalities in people's access to decent and adequate food (that would become dependent on individuals' variable resources). In such cases where public institutions cannot abstain from acting in circumstances of DP, there is a prima facie case for the accommodation of minority claims or, at any rate, a duty to justify publicly the set of dietary options that is on offer.[6]

Before closing, we should like to emphasize that nothing in our argument implies or requires the special status of religious beliefs in justifying consideration of certain demands of DP. The right to religious freedom, reference to which was made in the discussion of both cases in this section, may in fact be seen as a specific instantiation of the more general right to freedom of thought and conscience. Religious belief is one of the paramount expressions of someone's conscience as the locus of moral and existential claims, but it is by no means the only one. Therefore, nothing we have argued in the chapter grants religion any special status as the source of dietary claims that are eligible for accommodation.[7] What assimilates religion to other grounds for normatively relevant claims of accommodation in circumstances of DP is its being the source of demands with which compliance may plausibly be taken as central to people's integrity, that is to the sense of their own selves. This applies to any conscientious demand, regardless of whether it originates from religion, culture, or individual ethical beliefs.

Conclusion

Our main aim in this chapter has been to argue for the normative importance of DP for a theory of the state's action, in general, and to show the specific challenges it raises for the liberal project of public justification in particular. To be sure, there is more to be said about the challenges of DP in different accounts of the public order and on the criteria to establish what specific dietary claims ought to be accommodated within them.

Nevertheless, we hope our analysis has hit two important targets. First, we have offered a historically informed normative discussion of why DP should be taken into serious consideration, as an instance of reasonable pluralism, within any theory of the state's action. Second, we have made a prima facie case for the accommodation of dietary claims that may not be brushed aside as idiosyncratic preferences insofar as they contribute to people's sense of their own selves, compliance with which is a mark of integrity. Taken together, these two claims circumscribe the domain of DP as an important source of normatively relevant challenges with which contemporary societies must grapple.

Notes

* Research for this chapter was carried out within the framework of the FIRB Research Project "Feeding Respect," funded by the Italian Ministry of Education, University and Research, and it is part of the University of Pavia strategic theme, "Towards a governance model for international migration: an interdisciplinary and diachronic perspective" (MIGRAT-IN-G). One of the authors, Federico Zuolo, has carried out the research for this paper also with the support of an Alexander von Humboldt Foundation Senior Research Fellowship (Project "Politics and Animals"). The authors have contributed equally to the chapter.

1 From this perspective, one of the most debated issues is whether eating other sentient beings is morally permissible for humans. This controversy depends by and large on the different approaches to the rights of non-human animals and their moral status – see, among others, Singer (1993), Singer and Mason (2006), Francione (2008), Donaldson and Kymlicka (2011); for a controversial theory about the symbiotic nature of domestication, see Pollan (2006).

2 For a general discussion of these dimensions of pluralism, see Kekes (2000).

3 For a discussion of different provisions, see Ferrari and Bottoni (2010).

4 It goes almost without saying that these considerations are insufficient to defend ritual animal slaughter, which remains a controversial practice. For a case against religion-based claims for accommodations that harm non-human animals, see Casal (2003).

5 Whether or not current specific regulations concerning the treatment of non-human animals are all things considered consistent with the principle of the minimization of animal suffering is a further controversial issue, engagement with which goes beyond the aims of the present work. For a critical discussion, see Singer and Mason (2006).

6 Two contrasting positions concerning the general plausibility of this view may be found in Caney (2002) and Ceva (2011).

7 For a recent discussion of this claim in the debate on religious toleration, see Leiter (2013).

References

Bird, C. (1996) "Mutual Respect and Neutral Justification," *Ethics* 107: 62–96.

Boettcher, J. (2007) "Respect, Recognition and Public Reason," *Social Theory and Practice* 33: 223–239.

Bonotti, M. (2016) "Food Policy, Nutritionism and Public Justification," *Journal of Social Philosophy* 46(4): 402–417.

Caney, S. (2002) "Equal treatment, exceptions and cultural diversity." In P. Kelly (ed.), *Multiculturalism Reconsidered*, Cambridge: Polity, pp. 81–101.

Casal, P. (2003) "Is Multiculturalism Bad for Animals?," *The Journal of Political Philosophy* 11: 1–22.

Ceva, E. (2011) "Self-Legislation, Respect, and the Reconciliation of Minority Claims," *Journal of Applied Philosophy* 28(1): 14–28.

Childress, J. F. (1979) "Appeals to Conscience," *Ethics* 89(4): 315–335.

Donaldson, S., & Kymlicka, W. (2011) *Zoopolis: A Political Theory of Animal Rights*, Oxford: Oxford University Press.

Ferrari, S., & Bottoni, R. (2010) "Legislation Regarding Religious Slaughter in the EU Member, Candidate, and Associated Countries," DIALREL Project Report 2010, viewed July 2015, http://www.dialrel.eu/images/report-legislation.pdf.

Francione, G. L. (2008) *Animals As Persons: Essays on the Abolition of Animal Exploitation*, New York: Columbia University Press.

Galeotti, A. E. (2002) *Toleration as Recognition*, Cambridge: Cambridge University Press.

Harris, M. (1977) *Cannibals and Kings*, New York and Toronto: Random House.

Haupt, C. (2007) "Free Exercise of Religion and Animal Protection: A Comparative Perspective on Ritual Slaughter," *George Washington International Law Review* 39: 839–886.

Kekes, J. (2000) *Pluralism in Philosophy: Changing the Subject*, Ithaca and London: Cornell University Press.

Larmore, C. (2008) *The Autonomy of Morality*, Cambridge: Cambridge University Press.

Leiter, B. (2013) *Why Tolerate Religion?* Princeton: Princeton University Press.

Lerner, P., & Rabello, A.M. (2006/7) "The Prohibition of Ritual Slaughtering (Kosher Shechita and Halal) and Freedom of Religious Minorities," *Journal of Law and Religion* 22: 1–62.

Montanari, M. (2006) *Food is Culture*, New York: Columbia University Press.

Paarlberg, R. L. (2010) *Food Politics: What Everyone Needs to Know*, Oxford: Oxford University Press.

Pollan, M. (2006) *The Omnivore's Dilemma: A Natural History of Four Meals*, New York: The Penguin Press.

Rawls, J. (1993) *Political Liberalism*, New York: Columbia University Press.

Schanbacher, W. D. (2010) *The Politics of Food: Global Conflict Between Food Security and Food Sovereignty*, Santa Barbara, CA: Prager.

Scrinis, G. (2013) *Nutritionism. The Science and Politics of Dietary Advice*, New York: Columbia University Press.

Singer, P. (1993) *Practical Ethics*, Cambridge: Cambridge University Press.

Singer, P., & Mason, J. (2006) *The Ethics of What We Eat: Why Our Food Choices Matter*, New York: Rodale.

Toussaint-Samat, M. (2009) *A History of Food*, Chichester: Wiley-Blackwell.

Waldron, J. (1987) "Theoretical Foundations of Liberalism," *The Philosophical Quarterly* 37: 127–150.

Zuolo, F. (2014) "The Priority of Suffering Over Life: How to Accommodate Animal Welfare and Religious Slaughter," *The Ethics Forum / Les Atelier de l'Ethique* 9: 162–183.

——. (2015) "Equality among Animals and Ritual Slaughter," *Historical Social Research* 40(4): 110–127.

10

FOOD SECURITY AT RISK

A matter of dignity and self-respect*

Elena Irrera

Introduction

Food security represents a phenomenon that encompasses a rich array of interrelated problems, goals, and strategies. Since the mid-1970s, it has gained increasing attention within the broad panorama of studies on food-related issues, qualifying itself not only as a practical need to be met, but also as the object of cross-cutting theoretical concerns and fields of inquiry amenable to synergistic collaborations (such as nutritional and health-care science and education, agricultural research and technology, political theory, legal, and environmental studies). Theorists and policy-makers who, over the last two decades, have attempted to address the problem widely accept the definition of *food security* proposed by FAO at the 1996 World Food Summit held in Rome:

> [Food security can be defined as] a condition where all people, at all times, have physical and economic access to sufficient, safe and nutritious food to meet their dietary needs and food preferences for an active and healthy life.
>
> (FAO 1996; cf. 2004: 5; 2013: 16–17)

As might be suggested, such a definition – and, more pointedly, the connotations of the word "security" itself – implicitly recalls the idea that a number of risks and threats might hamper the full-fledged realization of the concept at stake in practical life (Kent 2005: 22–23). The most urgent challenges faced by feeding policies and interventions in fields like health, hygiene, agriculture, water supply, and education revolve around the spectrum of hunger and the various forms of physical disease related to such a condition. FAO regards hunger as synonymous with chronic undernourishment, the latter being described as a condition of inadequate dietary energy intake that might develop along with malnutrition (a condition resulting when a person's diet does not provide an adequate supply of nutrients like calories, proteins, carbohydrates, vitamins, and minerals) (FAO 2015; 2008).

Public attempts to reduce and eradicate undernourishment and malnutrition are premised on a view of food security and adequate food in which nutritional aspects and dietary needs outstrip specific food preferences, and the nature of the contribution played by food preferences in the actualization of food security appears to be a relatively unexplored issue in food studies. In this essay I shall attempt to provide an account of food security and food adequacy in light of the role played by food in the development of individual identity and in the cultivation of the dignity and self-respect that appear to stem from implementing autonomously chosen paths of life. My discussion unfolds into three sections. In the first one, I offer a short description of the concept of food security and stress some of its normative implications, with particular reference to the so-called "right to adequate food." In the second, I outline a sketchy philosophical background for the notions of dignity and self-respect, which I will present as underlying explanations of the cultural aspect of food security. In the last section I analyze the condition of minority members in pluralistic societies allegedly inspired by liberal principles. I suggest that the societies in question offer an eminently suitable standpoint from which to view the cultural as well as nutritional threats to global food security.

The multi-dimensional nature of food security and food adequacy

Any attempt to reflectively engage with the polyvocal nature of food security, and the corresponding variety of methods – scientific, technical, political, and legislative – required to bring it to fruition, requires not only a descriptive approach, but also a normative characterization. If examined from a purely descriptive standpoint, food security can be qualified as a *condition* in which all people, at all times, are enabled to pursue safe and nutritious food, so as to successfully meet their dietary needs and food preferences in view of a healthy and active life (FAO 2009: 1). Here the definition provided in FAO (1996) is reasserted, with the specification that the nutritional dimension is integral to food security. There are four main conceptual pillars of such a condition:

1) *Food availability:* availability of sufficient quantities of food of appropriate quality.
2) *Food access:* access by individuals to adequate commodities (material resources and/or rights such as access to common resources) for the acquisition of foods enabling the pursuit of a nutritious diet.
3) *Utilization of food:* proper digestion and absorption of nutrients in food through adequate diet, clean water, sanitation, and health care.
4) *Stability:* a population, household, or individual must have access to adequate food at all times, avoiding the risk of losing access to food as a consequence of sudden shocks like an economic or climatic crisis, or cyclical events (FAO 2006; for a more articulated discussion of these pillars cf. Rosier 2011: 1–2).

Failure to meet at least one such requirement risks engendering a condition that is generally named *food insecurity*.

It is worth noting that neither the description of food security provided above nor a specification of its four dimensions make any explicit reference to the idea of an *adequate* food, i.e., a food whose unavailability might engender a condition of insecurity. A different definitory approach, instead, is registered in the following attempt to address the concept of food security from a community-centered perspective. A phenomenon known as *community food security* (CFS) is for instance defined as a situation in which all community residents obtain a safe, culturally acceptable, nutritionally adequate diet through a sustainable food system that maximizes community self-reliance and social justice (Hamm and Bellows 2003: 37).[1]

Remarkably, cultural acceptability is introduced in the above definition as a conceptually distinct property from adequacy; in other words, the former is not thought to contribute to a more articulated theoretical elaboration of the latter. Only in recent years have official meeting documents, technical reports, and scholarly publications begun to stress the need to provide a more far-ranging account of food security and food adequacy, testifying to a change in official policy thinking (FAO 2006; cf. Clay 2002). As a target to be reached or simply approached, food security can be envisaged as a prescriptive ideal (see Hospes and Hadiprayitno 2010: 22), that is, as one that inspires the elaboration and implementation of governmental policies at local, regional, national, and international levels, as well as the development of programs by nongovernmental organizations (e.g., for-profit and non-profit foundations, or advocacy and special interest groups).

The correct approach to the problem of food security involves both the coexistence and interaction of two distinct types of commitment: first, the formulation of recommended actions, which *can* lead to (without necessarily resulting in) the production of legally binding frameworks for food security problems; second, a conceptual clarification of existing provisions, as a propaedeutic step to a full implementation of rights and obligations. A document that incorporates both kinds of commitment is the one entitled *Voluntary Guidelines to Support the Progressive Realization of the Right to Adequate Food in the Context of National Food Security* (FAO 2004). The document, drafted by an intergovernmental working group established in 2002 on the occasion of the 123rd Session of the FAO Council, proposes in the first place to fulfill Objective 7.4 of the *World Food Summit Plan of Action* reported in the *Rome Declaration on Food Security*, which established the task "to clarify the content of the right to adequate food and the fundamental right of everyone to be free from hunger," as well as the need "to give particular attention to implementation and full and progressive realization of this right as a means of achieving food security for all" (FAO 1996).

Although the above-mentioned document does not provide legally binding recommendations (this is explicitly claimed in *Voluntary Guideline* 2.9 of FAO 2004: 1), it is reasonable to suppose that the normative provisions it contains, by offering workable avenues for the implementation of the right to food and for the identification of right-holders, duty bearers, and accountable agents, ultimately point in the direction of a more strictly legal approach (see, for instance, van der Meulen 2010: 97). An exhaustive treatment of all the national and international law documents pertaining to the right to food and its most relevant legal expression, i.e., the right to *adequate* food, is beyond the scope of this essay.[2] I will therefore confine myself to pointing out that the right to food, generically stated, is mentioned in article 25, paragraph 1, of the *Universal Declaration of Human Rights* (adopted by the United Nations General Assembly in 1948) as integral to the right to an adequate standard of living:

> Everyone has the right to a standard of living adequate for the health and well-being of himself and of his family, including food, clothing, housing and medical care and necessary social services . . .
>
> (UNHR 1948)

The same right was reaffirmed and codified as the right of everyone to "an adequate standard of living for himself and his family, including adequate food" in article 11, paragraph 1, of the *International Covenant on Economic, Social and Cultural Rights* (formulated in 1966, but entered into force in 1976; UNHR 1966).

The issue of the cultural acceptability of food is brought into prominence only in official documents elaborated in view of a better definition of the right to adequate food, such as the General Comment No. 12, adopted by the UN Economic and Social Council at the Twentieth Session of the Committee on Economic, Social and Cultural Rights, on 12 May 1999 (CESCR 1999). The comment, specifically referring to the above-mentioned article 11, frames the idea of cultural acceptability in the context of a critical discussion of the meaning of "adequacy." After pointing out that the "precise meaning of 'adequacy' is to a large extent determined by prevailing social, economic, cultural, climatic, ecological and other conditions," it presents cultural acceptability as one of the many conceptual aspects inherent to the right to adequate food:

> The Committee considers that the core content of the right to adequate food implies: The availability of food in a quantity and quality sufficient to satisfy the dietary needs of individuals, free from adverse substances, and acceptable within a given culture.
>
> (CESCR 1999)

Remarkably, in the comment under examination, frequent reference to populations vulnerable to the threat of food inadequacy is not supported by an in-depth reflection on the role often played by food in the protection of individual identity, dignity, and self-respect. More to the point, difficulties related to the procurement of a culturally adequate food are not singled out as relevant threats to food security. Significant progress in this direction has been made in the new millennium, partly due to the creation by the UN Commission on Human Rights of the post of *Special Rapporteur on the Right to Food*, whose task is to examine and issue reports on the status and implementation of the relevant right in specific national and international situations. As the UN Human Rights Council states,

> For the Special Rapporteur, the right to food is the right to have regular, permanent and unrestricted access, either directly or by means of financial purchases, to quantitatively and qualitatively adequate and sufficient food corresponding to the cultural traditions of the people to which the consumer belongs, and which ensure a physical and mental, individual and collective, fulfilling and dignified life free of fear.
>
> (UNHR 1996–2015: c)

The idea of a food that is expressive of one's cultural tradition goes beyond the idea that certain food practices are not rejectable in light of one's relevant values and convictions. In line with such a view of food adequacy and cultural acceptability, jurist and politician Stefano Rodotà emphasizes the possibility that food adequacy implicitly recalls the value of human dignity. In his own words,

> "Adequacy" means to rise above a minimalist (although fundamental) approach on freedom from hunger. What one nourishes through the right to food security is not only one's body, but also the dignity of the person. This implies that adequacy is not simply a quantitative concept, but also a qualitative one.
>
> (Rodotà 2011)

Such statements gesture at the idea we are defending, that a significant area of human vulnerability and threat to food security is represented by the unavailability and/or failed access to a food that expresses the distinctive identity of those individuals who pursue it. Food consumption, in other words, may strongly rely on the need experienced by individuals to abide by practices entrenched either in their original culture or in a set of values critically chosen, revisable, and not necessarily anchored in one's native culture. Viewed under such a light, food habits represent a viable path not only for the individual development and consolidation of a specific identity, but also for the acquisition of values like personal dignity and self-respect.

The quest for dignity and self-respect: underlying reasons of food security?

The need for a right-based approach towards issues of food security expressed in officially recognized documents points to the inherent limits of interventions inspired by the principle of charity.[3] On this view, what the latter fail to preserve is the capacity of individuals to autonomously elaborate their food preferences and acquire the food that they regard as representative of their life values and plans. It is not by chance that, in the above-mentioned Comment No. 12 (point 15), the right to adequate food is qualified as one that, like any other human right, imposes three levels of obligations on the states: to *respect*, to *protect*, and to *fulfill* (encompassing the obligations to *facilitate* and to *provide*). As it has been suggested (Hospes and Hadiprayitno 2010: 97), none of these obligations involve a direct distribution of the required food. For the obligation to respect is to be understood as mere non-interference, and the one to protect simply refers to possible threats of interference by third parties. Notably, not even the obligation to facilitate amounts to an invasive intervention of institutions on individual food habits and needs, and the one to fulfill seems to apply only to cases of emergency.

As it might plausibly be hypothesized, the underlying rationale of such obligations is a concern for the capacity for self-determination of individuals. This concern coheres neatly with the fact that the right to adequate food is presented as one to which *each and every* individual, and not "all people" (see the FAO definition of food security), has the legitimate authority to lay claim (Hospes and Hadiprayitno 2010: 20). The aspects of human nature that the right to adequate food brings to surface are not simply a shared striving for sheer material survival or a condition of bodily and mental integrity, but also the capacity of individuals to shape through their food habits specific dimensions of their identity (e.g., religious and/or ethical) and, if desired, to make them amenable to revision.

Individual identity, then, may encompass not simply inherited and unquestioned traditions of thought and life, but also a plurality of chosen values that – as liberal thinkers such as John Stuart Mill (1982 [1859]: 122), Ronald Dworkin (1983), and John Rawls (1980: 544) have maintained, can be either confirmed or dismissed in the course of one's personal experiences. The individual's capacity to formulate life-plans and to subscribe to specific practices develops along with the creation of personal meanings and value attributions. In this respect, the adequacy of the chosen object is not integral to the object itself, but resides in the individual attachment to the object at stake (Raz 2001: 38).

The argument of adequacy may well apply to the case of food, which, being treated as the object of a distinctively human right, cannot be defined as adequate irrespectively of individual experiences and values. We might wonder, then, which values are the ones that consumption of culturally adequate food is designed to protect and cultivate. In the documents we have examined thus far, a central place seems to be held by dignity. In the preamble of the *Universal Declaration of Human Rights*, dignity is mentioned as a value that, recognized along with human rights, supplies the foundation of freedom, justice, and peace in the world. Also, as we read in the preamble, it is with regard to dignity and human rights that human beings can be judged as free and equal by birth. Such values, together with the "worth of the human person," inspire the search for social progress and better standards of life in larger freedom. Elsewhere in the declaration, however, dignity is presented as a more foundational value in relation to human rights, being the *end* that human rights themselves are meant to promote, along with the free development of each individual's personality (article 22). Also, in the preamble of the aforementioned *International Covenant on Economic, Social and Cultural Rights*, it is mentioned as a *normative source* from which human rights themselves can be derived.

Regardless of its possible roles, dignity emerges as a value worth protecting, given that it ideally outlines a zone of inviolability, which ought not to be crossed if one wants to preserve the very meaning of what it is to be a person (Walsh 2013: 246). This concept therefore has Kantian resonances. In Kant's *Groundwork of the Metaphysics of Morals* (1998 [1785]), dignity is described as a property attached to what "is raised above all price and therefore admits of no equivalent" (4: 434) and, more specifically, as one "the *existence of which in itself* has an absolute worth" (4: 428). Dignity sets human beings apart from other beings and confers them a special status (Dillon 1995: 14), acting as the ground of laws that, given their moral nature, can be followed only by beings in possession of rationality. The foundational moral law, which Kant names the *categorical imperative*, is formulated as follows: "So act that you use humanity, whether in your own person or in the person of any other, always at the same time as an end, never merely as a means" (4: 429).

Dignity is a value that, once recognized, commands respect. This is for instance what can be inferred from a reading of *Metaphysics of Morals* (1991 [1897]: 6: 434–435), where Kant declares,

> [But] man regarded as a *person*, that is, as the subject of a morally practical reason, is exalted above any price; for as a person *(homonoumenon)* he is not to be valued merely as a means to the ends of others or even to his own ends, but as an end in himself, that is, he possesses a *dignity* (an absolute inner worth) by which he exacts *respect* for himself from all other rational beings in the world. He can measure himself with every other being of this kind and value himself on a footing of equality with them.

Notably, it is not clear where the respect that persons equally owe to each other stems from. For Kant often seems to suggest that dignity resides in (a) humanity in itself (see for instance *Groundwork* 4: 439–440, where Kant speaks of the "dignity of humanity as rational nature"), (b) the humanity *inherent* in every person/rational being (see *Metaphysics of Morals* 6: 420, 429; *Critique of Practical Reason* 5: 161), or even in the moral law which human beings have the capacity to follow (e.g., *Groundwork* 4: 425, 440; *Critique of Practical Reason* 5: 82, 87).

Nevertheless, in all these cases dignity appears as a value grounded in the individual's capacity to determine their own agency on the basis of rationally established principles (Hill 2013: 321). Viewed in this sense, the value of dignity invoked in the *Universal Declaration* as a proper foundation for human rights reveals that the juridical status of individuals is not necessarily an irreducible one, but hinges on the possession of specific human properties, such as rational self-determination and normative agency. On the other hand, the value of human dignity might be thought to incorporate aspects that go over and above mere rationality, such as a capacity to cultivate desires compatibly with respect for other people (Tasioulas 2013: 305).

One of the human experiences through which a universal value like dignity finds expression is the sense of one's own worth. Such an experience, which is generally thematized by philosophers, sociologists, and psychologists in terms of self-respect, represents a powerful motivational source in that it encourages individuals to pursue specific beliefs, ambitions, and life-plans, i.e., the same that contribute to shaping their specific human identity. The principle of self-respect, just like the value of dignity, has been widely invoked by political philosophers and policy-makers as a good that well-ordered societies should seek to achieve. A notable formulation of the principle at stake has been proposed by the liberal philosopher John Rawls. Both in *A Theory of Justice* (1971) and in *Political Liberalism* (1993), Rawls treats political societies as systems of cooperation for mutual advantage that ought to be informed by a unanimously accepted and institutionally implemented public conception of justice. On his view, a public conception of justice ought to be established with a view to bringing into full-fledged actualization two moral powers that persons (or citizens, understood as free and equal persons) distinctively possess: (a) a sense of justice, i.e., "the capacity to understand, to apply, and to act from the public conception of justice which characterizes the fair terms of social cooperation"; and (b) a capacity for a conception of the good, i.e., "the capacity to form, to revise, and rationally to pursue a conception of one's rational advantage or good" (Rawls 1996: 19). Provided that a sense of one's own worth is a necessary precondition for the pursuit of one's projects and, more generally, for the actualization of both capacities, an authentically well-ordered society will be one equipped with an institutional setting designed to promote such a good. It is not by chance that, in paragraph 29 of *A Theory of Justice*, self-respect is introduced as a value which, if successfully and constantly promoted by certain societies, testifies to the superiority of their underlying principles of distributive justice over competing conceptions of justice (Rawls 1971: 178). For the public recognition of Rawls' principles of justice "gives greater support to men's self-respect, and this in turn increases the effectiveness of social cooperation" (Rawls 1971: 178).

With particular reference to the capacity for a conception of the good, the author states,

> [I]t is clearly rational for men to secure their self-respect. A sense of their own worth is necessary if they are to pursue their conception of the good with zest and to delight in its fulfillment.
>
> (Rawls 1971: 178)

Self-respect, tantamount to the sense that one's plan is worth carrying out, is regarded by Rawls as a *primary good*, that is, as one that every rational man supposedly wants (Rawls 1971: 62, 214) and, more specifically, as one of a social nature, given that, alongside rights, liberties, income, and wealth, it ought to be equally distributed in societies (unless, as Rawls explains in his work, an unequal distribution of such goods is to the advantage of the least favored) (Rawls 1971: 303).

It is worth noting that Rawls believes that self-respect is "perhaps the most important primary good." Some reasons for his contention can be found in paragraph 67 of *A Theory of Justice*, where he treats self-respect as a value endowed with two distinctive aspects: on the one hand, "it includes a person's sense of his own value, his secure conviction that his conception of his good, his plan of life, is worth carrying out"; on the other:

> [S]elf-respect implies a confidence in one's ability, so far as it is within one's power, to fulfill one's intentions. When we feel that our plans are of little value, we cannot pursue them with pleasure or take delight in their execution.
>
> (Rawls 1971: 440)

Without self-respect, then, no possession of money or awareness of rights would be a successful guarantee for a continuative pursuit of one's life-plans, and it is in this sense that it can be regarded as a more relevant good than others (Rawls 1996: 318). Given that self-respect is an individual experience and cannot be an object of distributive policies, what really count as primary goods in Rawls' theory of justice are the so-called "social bases of self-respect," i.e., "aspects of political institutions that are essential preconditions for a society that successfully enables citizens to develop and cultivate a sense of self-respect" (Rawls 1999: 366). In liberal societies, such preconditions are meant to promote a sense of self-respect that can be achieved only when every individual is recognized as equal in dignity to the other members of the political community. A society informed by a conception of justice that fails to support these values and the capacity for individual self-determination in which they ultimately reside risks engendering conditions of insecurity, as happens with concern for food habits.

Elena Irrera

The case of minority subjects in multicultural societies: some possible threats to food security

Liberally oriented multicultural societies, committed to a defense of dignity and self-respect, are an eminently suitable backdrop for the consideration of some of the threats facing food security. The societies at issue can be described as *pluralistic* insofar as they encompass a multiplicity of (and, often, a range of interactions between) identities and paths in search of equal recognition and valorization. Within the framework of pluralistic societies, it is possible to identify peculiar situations of difficulty, which, more than others, bring out the conceptual and normative premises of a condition of food insecurity, i.e., some difficulties faced by minorities with regard to access to (1) culturally and/or nutritionally adequate food, and (2) nutrition information.

By *minority* I mean a group that does not enjoy a well-grounded stability and/or public recognition within a certain context, being equipped with scant power and low social status in relation to the majority. Under such a light, the most prominent qualifying traits of a minority are limited access to material and/or non-material resources, a recent entrance in a certain society (e.g., in the case of immigrants), ethnic and/or religious peculiarities whose maintenance is threatened, a possible history of discrimination (Butera and Levine 2009: 2), and lack of adequate participation to the political process. Minorities, then, can be seen as individuals who claim specific forms of recognition of their authority as moral agents, i.e., as human beings who deserve to pursue their chosen life-plans on an equal footing with others.[4]

Minority groups that appear to be particularly vulnerable to threats to food security are those constituted by migrants uprooted from their native life context and forced to confront themselves with various practices of the new host countries. A first threat to the food security of such minority subjects is represented by the possible insurgence of psychophysical diseases engendered by their contact with a new culture. Such diseases can be the consequence of a particular phenomenon, which many studies of intercultural psychology have named *acculturation*, a word that, although originally referring to reciprocal interaction between the members of different cultures and the subsequent changes in their original patterns (Redfield et al. 1936: 149), has been often used with reference to the tendency of minorities to be affected by the cultural paradigms of the dominant culture. As Berry explains, the apprehension of new cultural codes by migrant individuals implies some degree of dispersion of the ones already interiorized. Such a process, which Berry names "culture shedding," can be accompanied by some tension between the new assimilated codes and those that are doomed to dispersion, i.e., a tension that may range from minimal levels of conflict up to peaks of "acculturative shock" (1992).

The outcomes of such tension generally vary depending upon the subjective propensity of minorities to show flexibility or rigidity towards the new cultural codes; in some cases, the conflict between the original and the newly acquired patterns of behavior may seriously affect individual health. However, even the most flexible subjects seem to encounter difficulties in their search for adequate nutrition and accurate informational guidance, the latter needed to remove a number of impediments to health. A widely diffused tendency among migrants is the one relative to the acquisition of a diet that might be described as *hybrid* in virtue of the coexistence of aspects of original food habits and of new nutritional practices.[5] Such a change in food habits can take two different directions. On the one hand, minority subjects might experience an improvement of their health condition, for instance thanks to a greater availability of highly nutritious food in their new environment, or in virtue of an individual attitude of openness towards the reasons and information conveyed by health-care professionals and/or written guidelines. More frequent, unfortunately, is the occurrence of negative changes in nutritional matters, which often reveal themselves in an increased consumption of a food excessively high in calories and of minimal nutritional value (Ghaddar et al. 2010).

The main determinants of such negative changes are not only of an economic kind, but also of a social nature. Difficulties related to access to health-care information, for example, may be responsible for nutritionally inadequate choices, alongside undue exposure of immigrants to marketing messages that compel them to identify low-cost food with minimal nutritional value. What is more, even those minorities equipped with sufficient economic resources and predisposed to engaging in a dialogue with health-care professionals might find impediments to receiving the correct information. This might happen because of frequent foreign language miscommunications, or even because of lack of adequate training for nutritional experts in matters concerning aspects of the migrants' native cultures.

The difficulties listed so far may contribute to providing a more articulated view of the possible threats to a condition of food security. For food security, as well as food insecurity, prove themselves to be phenomena whose underlying reasons include lack of adequate information on the nutritional properties of the consumed food, insufficient competence of health-care professionals about nutritional problems related to cultural diversity, and impediments to the pursuit of food habits that seem largely inextricable from the convictions and values constitutive of individual identity. Such habits, as we have seen, might qualify the distinctive dignity of human beings and provide them with a solid sense of self-respect, i.e., the value which, when possessed, enables each individual to consider her plans of life worth pursuing. As a phenomenon endowed with cultural implications, food security appears to depend not only on the availability, access, and utilization of food, but also on appropriate satisfaction of the quest for an equal recognition of individual dignity by governments and organizations. It is such a quest that policies conducted both at a national and at the cross-national level ought to address.

Notes

* Research for this chapter was carried out within the framework of the FIRB Research Project "Feeding Respect," funded by the Italian Ministry of Education, University and Research and directed by Dr. Emanuela Ceva (University of Pavia).
1 The term "safety" here refers to the quality of a food free of disease organisms or toxins, and it ought not be taken as a synonym of "security."
2 For extensive discussions of this topic, see Hospes and Hadiprayitno (2010: 43–78) and Kent (2005: 45–62).
3 For an extensive treatment of the differences between the concepts of "food charity" and "right to food," see Riches and Silvasti (2014).
4 For a detailed account of such an authority, see Darwall (2006).
5 For a more detailed treatment of such issues, see Irrera and Sartini (2014).

References

Berry, J. W. (1992) "Acculturation and Adaptation in a New Society," *International Migration* 30: 69–85.
Butera, F. and Levine, J. M. (eds.) (2009) *Coping with Minority Status: Responses to Exclusion and Inclusion*, Cambridge: Cambridge University Press.
CESCR. (1999) General Comment No. 12: The Right to Adequate Food (Art. 11) (contained in Document E/C.12/1999/5), viewed 29 March 2015, http://www1.umn.edu/humanrts/gencomm/escgencom12.htm.
Clay, E. (2002) *Food Security: Concepts and Measurement*, paper published in Rome: FAO, 2003, viewed 11 July 2015, ftp://ftp.fao.org/docrep/fao/005/y4671e/y4671e00.pdf.
Darwall, S. (2006) *The Second-Person Standpoint: Morality, Respect, and Accountability*, Cambridge, MA and London: Harvard University Press.
Dillon, R. S. (ed.) (1995) *Dignity, Character and Self-Respect*, New York and London: Routledge.
Dworkin, R. (1983) "In Defense of Equality," *Social Philosophy and Policy* 1: 24–40.
FAO. (1996) *Rome Declaration on World Food Security*, viewed 11 July 2015, http://www.fao.org/docrep/003/w3613e/w3613e00.HTM.

——. (2004) Voluntary Guidelines to Support the Progressive Realisation of the Right to Adequate Food in the Context of National Food Security, viewed 11 July 2015, ftp://ftp.fao.org/docrep/fao/009/y7937e/y7937e00.pdf.

——. (2006) "Food Security," *Policy Brief*, Issue 2, viewed 11 July 2015, http://www.fao.org/forestry/13128–0e6f36f27e0091055bec28ebe830f46b3.pdf.

——. (2008) *An Introduction to the Basic Concepts of Food Security*, viewed 11 July 2015, http://www.fao.org/docrep/013/al936e/al936e00.pdf.

——. (2009) *Declaration of the 2009 World Summit on Food Security*, viewed 11 July 2015, http://www.fao.org/fileadmin/templates/wsfs/Summit/Docs/Final_Declaration/WSFS09_Declaration.pdf.

——. (2013) *The State of Food Insecurity in the World 2013: The Multiple Dimensions of Food Security*, viewed 11 July 2015, http://www.fao.org/docrep/013/al936e/al936e00.pdf.

——. (2015) *The FAO Hunger Map 2015*, viewed 11 July 2015, http://www.fao.org/hunger/en.

Ghaddar, S., Brown, C.J., Pagán, J.A. and Díaz, V. (2010) "Acculturation and Healthy Life Style Habits among Hispanics in the United States-Mexico Border Communities," *Revista Panamericana de Salud Pública* 28(3): 190–7.

Hamm, M. W. and Bellows, A. C. (2003) "Community Food Security and Nutrition Educators," *Journal of Nutrition Education and Behavior* 35: 37–43.

Hill, T. E. (2013) "In Defence of Human Dignity: Comments on Kant and Rosen," in McCrudden, C. (ed.), *Understanding Human Dignity*, Oxford: Oxford University Press, pp. 313–26.

Hospes, O. and Hadiprayitno, I. (eds.) (2010) *Governing Food Security: Law, Politics and the Right to Food*, Wageningen: Wageningen Academic Publishers.

Irrera, E. and Sartini, B. (2014) "Rispetto, Sicurezza e Pluralismo Alimentare. Tensioni Concettuali e Prospettive di Conciliazione," *Notizie di Politeia* 114: 94–108.

Kant, I. (1991 [1797]) *The Metaphysics of Morals*, M. Gregor (ed.), Cambridge: Cambridge University Press.

——. (1997 [1788]) *Critique of Practical Reason*, M. Gregor (ed.), Cambridge: Cambridge University Press.

——. (1998 [1785]) *Groundwork of the Metaphysics of Morals*, 2nd ed., M. Gregor (ed.), Cambridge: Cambridge University Press.

Kent, G. (2005) *Freedom from Want: The Human Right to Adequate Food*, Washington, DC: Georgetown University Press.

Mill, J. S. (1982 [1859]) On Liberty, Harmondsworth: Penguin.

Rawls, J. (1971) *A Theory of Justice*, Cambridge, MA and London: Harvard University Press.

——. (1980) "Kantian Constructivism in Moral Theory," *Journal of Philosophy* 77(9): 515–72.

——. (1996) *Political Liberalism*, 2nd ed., New York: Columbia University Press.

——. (1999) "Social Unity and the Primary Goods," in Freeman, S. (ed.), *Collected Papers of John Rawls*, Cambridge: Harvard University Press, pp. 159–86.

Raz, J. (2001) *Value, Respect and Attachment*, Cambridge: Cambridge University Press.

Redfield, R., Linton, R. and Herskovits, M.J. (1936) "Memorandum for the Study of Acculturation," *American Anthropologist* 38: 149–52.

Riches, G. and Silvasti, T. (eds.) (2014) *First World Hunger Revisited: Food Charity or the Right to Food?*, 2nd ed., New York: Palgrave Macmillan.

Rodotà, S. (2011) *Il Diritto al Cibo*, viewed 11 July 2015, http://saperedemocratico.it/stefano-rodota-il-diritto-al-cibo.

Rosier, K. (2011) "Food Insecurity in Australia: What is it, Who Experiences it and How can Child and Family Services Support Families Experiencing it?," viewed 11 July 2015, https://aifs.gov.au/cfca/publications/food-insecurity-australia-what-it-who-experiences-it.

Tasioulas, J. (2013) "Human Dignity and the Foundation of Human Rights," in McCrudden, C. (ed.), *Understanding Human Dignity*, Oxford: Oxford University Press, pp. 291–312.

UNHR. (1948) *Universal Declaration of Human Rights*, viewed 11 July 2015, http://www.ohchr.org/EN/UDHR/Documents/UDHR_Translations/eng.pdf.

——. (1966) *International Covenant on Economic, Social and Cultural Rights*, viewed 11 July 2015, http://www.ohchr.org/Documents/ProfessionalInterest/cescr.pdf.

——. (1996–2015) *Special Rapporteur on the Right to Food*, viewed 11 July 2015, http://www.ohchr.org/EN/Issues/Food/Pages/FoodIndex.aspx.

van der Meulen, B. (2010) "The Freedom to Feed Oneself: Food in the Struggle for Paradigms in Human Rights Law," in Hospes, O. and Hadiprayitno, I. (eds.), *Governing Food Security: Law, Politics and the Right to Food*, Wageningen: Wageningen Academic Publishers, pp. 81–103.

Walsh, D. (2013) "Dignity as an Eschatological Concept," in McCrudden, C. (ed.), *Understanding Human Dignity*, Oxford: Oxford University Press, pp. 245–58.

11

INDIGENOUS PEOPLES, FOOD, AND THE ENVIRONMENT IN NORTHEAST INDIA

Sandra Albert

Introduction

The northeast region of India covers 8% of the geographical area of the country and is home to 3.1% of the population, or approximately 40 million persons (Census 2011). Within this confined area of mountains, hills, and river valleys is a rich array of ethnic communities who live in one of the lushest biodiversity hotspots on earth. Because it is a natural land bridge between the subcontinent and the rest of East Asia, numerous migrations have occurred through the millennia, and the resultant mix of populations makes this region a fascinating locale for social study. Some of the tribes have populated this region since ancient times and have preserved social customs such as matriliny. This paper presents a brief overview of the region and its people, drawing together aspects of environment, biodiversity, food, and nutrition and uses a few illustrative examples from Meghalaya State in northeast India.

Indigenous peoples and northeast India

India has a population of 104.3 million indigenous or tribal people who form 8.6% of the country's total population as per Census (2011). The term indigenous is somewhat contested in India, and instead tribal is the most commonly used term, particularly in the northeast region (Karlsson and Subba 2006). Groups that were enumerated as tribes during British rule came to be reclassified as Scheduled Tribes (ST) after the Constitution was adopted in 1950 (Xaxa Committee 2014). Article 342 of the Constitution provides for the listing of tribes into the "Schedule" so as to extend certain administrative and political concessions. In overall numbers tribals are a minority in the country, but they are present in most states. In places where they are relatively numerically dominant, two distinct administrative arrangements, the Fifth and the Sixth Schedules, have been provided for them in the Constitution. These are aimed at providing protection to the tribal populations through the enactment of separate laws for the Scheduled Areas (Xaxa Committee 2014). Broadly the STs inhabit two distinct geographical areas: a large segment inhabits nine contiguous central states (Madhya Pradesh, Chhattisgarh, Jharkhand, Telangana, Andhra Pradesh, Maharashtra, Orissa, Gujarat, and Rajasthan), and many others live in the distinct area of the northeast region, comprising eight states (Assam, Nagaland, Mizoram, Manipur, Meghalaya, Tripura, Sikkim, and Arunachal Pradesh) (Ministry of Tribal Affairs 2013).

India's indigenous people have largely agrarian economies, and the vast majority (90%) live in rural areas (Ministry of Tribal Affairs 2013). Despite the special provisions made for the betterment of tribals, they remain among the poorest and marginalized sections of society. The Xaxa Committee (2014) notes that while the state has emphasized development, it has done "little to enhance the protections provided in the Constitution through the everyday practice of statecraft," and the committee argues that this is a key reason for the continued marginal status of tribals.

The northeast region covers an area of 262,179 sq. km., which, as mentioned above, forms about 8% of the country's geographical area. Two-thirds of the area is hilly terrain, and about 52% is covered with forests. While the region is rich in natural resources, it became land-locked in 1947 after the country's partition, and the region was pushed into economic dependence and underdevelopment (North East Council 2008). While the northeast is often referred to as a singular entity, the region is highly diverse with over 200 tribes and sub-tribal communities, each with its own language, culture, and political structures (Xaxa Committee 2014).

There are four major linguistic groups within the Indian subcontinent: Austro-Asiatic, Dravidian, Indo-European, and Tibeto-Burman (Kumar et al. 2007). The Austro-Asiatic is considered to be the oldest of the linguistic groups and consists of three sub-families: Mundari, Mon-Khmer, and Khasi-Khmuic. Most of the tribes of the northeast region belong to the Tibeto-Burman group, while the Khasi tribe of Meghalaya alone belongs to the Austro-Asiatic group, specifically the Khasi-Khmuic sub-family (Kumar et al. 2007; Reddy et al. 2007). Archaeological evidence, based on stone tools from the Garo hills of Meghalaya, suggests that this region was inhabited as early as the Paleolithic period. Northeast India forms the only land bridge between the Indian subcontinent and Southeast Asia. Genetic evidence from mt-DNA and Y-chromosome studies suggests that northeast India could have been a major ancient human migratory corridor for the initial peopling of East and Southeast Asia (Reddy et al. 2007).

Meghalaya state in northeast India has a predominantly indigenous population (86%), with the matrilineal Khasi-Jaintia and Garo being the main tribes (Registrar General & Census Commissioner 2013). The Khasis are among the oldest inhabitants of the subcontinent; recent genetic studies demonstrate the time to the most recent common ancestor to be around 57,000 years (Kumar et al. 2007). Khasis comprise more than half of Meghalaya's population of 3 million. They are one of the 15 most populous tribes of India (Xaxa Committee 2014).

Biodiversity and biodiversity hotspots in northeast India

Biological diversity is the totality of genes, species, and ecosystems (United Nations 1992). Loss of biodiversity disrupts the balance in ecosystems, making them more vulnerable to destruction by natural events such as floods. Ecosystems with flourishing biodiversity are capable of providing goods and services to humans that aid and enhance their survival (Sahai 2014). Biodiversity hotspots are locations in which an unusually rich concentration of local biological diversity is found (Myers et al. 2000). To qualify as a hotspot, two quantitative criteria are applied: a region has to contain at least 1,500 vascular plants as endemics (>0.5% of the world's total), and it has to have 30% or less of its original vegetation (Mittermeier et al. 2011). Over the years the number of biodiversity hotspots identified has increased to 35 across the world (Williams et al. 2011). These regions are estimated to be endemic to at least 50% of vascular plants and 42% of terrestrial vertebrates, in habitat totaling just 2.3% of the world's land area (Mittermeier et al. 2011). One of the threats contributing to habitat loss is population growth in the hotspots. Population in these hotspots has continued to grow faster than the global average, and it is estimated that there are now about 1.5 billion people, or 21% of the human population, living in these areas (Williams 2011).

Much of northeast India falls under the Indo-Burma and the Himalayan biodiversity hotspots (Mittermeier et al. 2011). The region has a broad altitudinal range and thus offers diverse habitats that have a wealth of avifauna. The biodiversity hotspots in northeast India are considered to be the center of origin of several species. The northeast has been described as a treasure house of citrus germplasm with its 23 species, one subspecies, and 68 varieties of citrus (Malik et al. 2006). In what is perhaps one of the earliest ethnographic records of the region, Gurdon (1914), quoting from the "First letter book of the East India Company," refers to the orange and lemon of Sikkim and Khasia as having been carried by Arab traders into Syria, "whence the Crusaders helped to gradually propagate them throughout Southern Europe."

The Food and Agriculture Organization of the United Nations (FAO) estimates that about 10,000 of the total 300,000 plant species globally have been used for food since the beginning of agriculture. Of these only about 200 species have been cultivated commercially. Thirty crops are estimated to provide 90% of humanity's caloric intake, and 50% is supplied by four crops: rice, wheat, maize, and potatoes (Hunter and Fanzo 2013).

Agricultural biodiversity or agrobiodiversity includes the different categories of biological resources associated with agriculture. Aside from agriculturally relevant crops and livestock, it includes many other organisms, such as soil fauna, weeds, pollinators, pests, and predators that have indirect effects on agriculture (Fanzo et al. 2013). It results from the interactions between the environment, genetic resources, management systems, and cultural practices. Indigenous peoples often possess knowledge that is developed over several generations from their experience and their interaction with the environment (Sahai 2014). These knowledge systems are often dynamic rather than static (Balasubramanian 2006; Sahai 2014). Local knowledge, for instance knowledge about the local varieties of plants that are best adapted to local conditions, is an integral part of agrobiodiversity.

Nutritional challenges, food systems, and sustainable diets

Considerable progress has been made around the world in addressing nutritional insecurity, since the formulation of the first millennium development goal to reduce suffering from hunger by half. But millions of people still suffer from hunger and poor nutrition – globally about 795 million people are undernourished (FAO et al. 2015). The global nutrition report states that although many countries are making good progress, the world is currently not on course to meet the global nutrition targets set by the World Health Assembly (IFPRI 2014).

In low- and middle-income countries, maternal and child malnutrition incudes the spectrum of undernutrition, being overweight, and obesity (Black et al. 2013). In 2014, 39% of adults aged 18 years – more than 1.9 billion adults – were overweight. Of these over 600 million were obese (WHO 2015). Although overweight and obesity is of growing concern, undernutrition continues to be a larger burden than overweight and obesity in the developing world (FAO 2013). India has the second-highest estimated number of undernourished people in the world (FAO et al. 2015).

In addition to protein-energy malnutrition, the developing world is afflicted with what has been referred to as "hidden hunger" or micronutrient deficiencies (Burchi et al. 2011). It is estimated that micronutrient deficiencies undermine the growth, development, health, and productivity of over 2 billion people (Hunter and Fanzo 2013). There is strong biological probability for a causal link between maternal iron deficiency anaemia and adverse birth outcomes (Black et al. 2013). It is estimated that 45% of under-five mortality is attributable to undernutrition, while it accounts for over 50% of years lived with disability in children less than 4 years old (IFPRI 2014). The social and economic costs of malnutrition are estimated to be about $3.5 trillion per year or $500 per person globally (FAO 2013).

Globally, agricultural systems have the potential to produce sufficient food, particularly the staple grains, but providing access to affordable and nutritious food continues to be a challenge (FAO 2015). In developing countries, overreliance on a few staple grains and processed oils and sugars has resulted in diets that lack micronutrients (Hunter and Fanzo 2013). While the green revolution in Asia alleviated hunger, the change in agricultural production from diversified cropping systems to cereals and monoculture may have contributed to poor dietary diversity, micronutrient deficiencies, and malnutrition (DeClerck et al. 2011).

Nutrition interventions in developing countries have been described as piecemeal, fragmented, and single-nutrient oriented (Frison et al. 2006). Increasingly researchers are documenting the immense variety of food species that can contribute to sustainable diets and address nutritional deficiencies effectively, but which are often ignored by the prevailing food production systems (Fanzo et al. 2013). Thus interventions that are food based and involve dietary diversification are proposed as better alternatives.

Within public health systems, food fortification is widely promoted as the most effective solution to address micronutrient deficiencies. But food fortification is not as harmless as was previously assumed. For instance, iron supplementation has been associated with an increase in diarrheal diseases, and iron fortification produces a more pathogenic gut microbiota profile, associated with increased gut inflammation (Zimmermann et al. 2010). Thus although food supplements can address specific dietary deficiencies, a nutritious diet is perhaps the best approach to combat all forms of malnutrition (FAO 2013).

The first International Scientific Symposium on Biodiversity and Sustainable Diets, held at FAO headquarters in 2010, defined sustainable diets as:

> Those diets with low environmental impacts which contribute to food and nutrition security and to healthy life for present and future generations. Sustainable diets are protective and respectful of biodiversity and ecosystems, culturally acceptable, accessible, economically fair and affordable; nutritionally adequate, safe and healthy; while optimizing natural and human resources.
>
> (Burlingame and Dernini 2012)

Vinceti et al. (2013) in their background paper make a case for exploring the largely untapped potential of forest to contribute to food security, nutrition, and sustainable diets. Globally forests and tree-based agricultural systems contribute to the livelihoods of an estimated one billion people. The role of forests in supporting human food security and nutrition remains largely under-researched and poorly understood (Sunderland et al. 2013).

Nutritional deficiencies among indigenous peoples

In general, nutritional deficiencies are currently more prevalent among tribal than among non-tribal communities in India. The National Nutrition Monitoring Bureau's survey, assessing diet and nutritional status of the tribal population in nine states (the northeast region was not sampled), reported nutrient intake to be below the recommended levels, particularly for micronutrients such as vitamin A, iron, and riboflavin (National Nutrition Monitoring Bureau 2009). The median intakes of all the nutrients were below the Recommended Dietary Allowance among pregnant and lactating women. The prevalence of malnutrition was high among school-age children and adolescents. The prevalence of chronic energy deficiency was 40% and 49% among adult tribal men and women, respectively, while the prevalence of overweight and obesity was 2.6% and 3.2%, respectively.

Meghalaya state has some of the worst nutritional indices in the northeast region. The district-level family health survey reports high prevalence of anaemia in the following subgroups: children (6–59 months) 70.7%, adolescents (15–19 years) 42.3%, women (15–49 years) 53.9%, and pregnant women (15–49 years) 63.9% (DLHS-4 2013). Studies on Khasi women have reported inadequate consumption of important nutrients such as calcium, vitamin A, and iron. Both height and weight were below reference values among young girls, and average protein, energy, iron, and carotene consumption was significantly lower than the recommended dietary allowance (Agrahar-Murugkar 2005). A recent study assessing prevalence of vitamin A deficiency (VAD) in Meghalaya found 2.5% children (0–5 years) and 5.9% of 5- to 15-year-olds to have clinical VAD. The overall prevalence among children under 15 years was 4.5%, while overall 9.1% of children between 0 to 15 years had a history of night blindness (Nongrum and Kharkongor 2015).

But the Khasis of Meghalaya were healthier in times past. In early anthropology records Gurdon (1914) describes the Khasis as a short-statured but well-nourished tribe, with muscular men, buxom women, and remarkably pretty children. They eat simple diets of rice, millets, sago palm, pork, beef, and other wild produce of the forests (Blah and Joshi 2013; Gurdon 1914). The negative change in their health and wellbeing is perhaps a function of historical, socio-political, and developmental influences. Over the years consumption patterns have changed, as have cooking processes; of note is Gurdon's observation that Khasis used pots made of iron for cooking vegetables. The use of iron vessels in the past is not surprising, as iron smelting in the area was a thriving industry dating back 2,000 years (Prokop and Suliga 2013). In the present day, iron vessels have largely been replaced by the ubiquitous aluminum vessels that Khasi women take pride in keeping ashine. We can find a clue to the relevance of this fact in the low incidence of iron, folate, and vitamin B12 deficiency observed among *!Kung Bushmen* who use iron cooking vessels, when compared with more economically advanced populations (Metz et al. 1971). The absence of anaemia in this tribe has been attributed to the dietary iron intake being supplemented through iron derived from their cooking pots.

Conservation of biodiversity among indigenous societies

Indigenous peoples have been described as "the custodians of our environment and its medicines for thousands of years" (Nettleton et al. 2007). They often rely on the biodiversity around them for food and traditional medicines (Albert et al. 2015; Nettleton et al. 2007). One example of the traditional biodiversity conservation practices of indigenous communities is the concept of "sacred groves." These tracts of virgin forest that are protected by local people through cultural and religious beliefs and taboos (Khan et al. 2008). The sacred groves are living repositories of a rich biodiversity of flora and fauna. In India, sacred groves are found mainly in tribal-dominated areas in the northeast region, in central India, and in the Western Ghats in southern India. They are referred to by indigenous terms in the local languages, for instance *law kyntang, law lyngdoh,* and *law niam* in the Khasi language. About 98 sacred groves have been identified in Meghalaya (Samati and Gogoi 2007), varying in size from one to 550 hectares (Jeeva et al. 2006). But religious transformation, particularly Christianization, has caused an erosion of traditional mores that once protected the sacred groves of Meghalaya (Samati and Gogoi 2007).

Meghalaya's indigenous people have other forms of community forests, such as *law a dong* – whose products are used to support livelihoods (ADC 1958) – and *law sumar.* The *law sumar,* or protected land, is also used for religious ceremonies, but it is different from *law kyntang* (sacred groves), as the felling of trees is permitted every five to six years with permission from the local traditional governance authorities for use by the community (Kharpuri 2012). Mining is forbidden in the *law sumar* forest areas due to their protected nature, especially if they are used for performing rituals of the indigenous religion (Kharpuri 2012).

There are several ecological threats to biodiversity, particularly from mining and industrialization. India's major mineral reserves lie under the same areas that hold most of its forests and water systems. Often these lands are also inhabited by the nation's poorest and marginalized: the tribals. If India's mineral map, tribal habitation, forests, and watershed areas were to be mapped together, they would superimpose over each other (CSE 2008). Three states with major tribal belts – Orissa, Chhattisgarh, and Jharkhand – together account for 70% of India's coal reserves, 80% of high-grade iron ore, 60% of bauxite, and much of its chromite reserves. The forest cover in these states are higher than the national average (CSE 2008).

Meghalaya has over 90% of the total reserve of limestone in northeast India. Limestone occurs in an extensive belt approximately 200 kilometers long, along the southern border of Meghalaya. Mining activity is usually accompanied by degradation of land, soil, and natural vegetation, contributing to deforestation and damage to biodiversity. Limestone mining in Meghalaya has been characterized by an almost complete absence of rehabilitation measures to address environmental hazards (Kharpuri 2012). Likewise coal mining has caused considerable damage to the environment in Meghalaya (Sarma 2005; Swer and Singh 2003).

A study assessing the effect of limestone quarrying on the soil and vegetation in Mawsmai, East Khasi Hills, demonstrated deleterious effects on water-holding capacity of the soil, pH level, organic carbon content, and biodiversity of plant species. The physical and chemical characteristics of the mined soil were significantly altered in comparison to the control sites (*law sumar* community-protected forests). The pH of the young quarry sites (0- to 2-year-old spoils) was found to be highly alkaline, unlike the soil in the control site, in which pH tended to be neutral. And the loss of vegetation cover and top-soil layer on account of mining contributed to depletion of nutrients and organic carbon in the mine spoils. Forested land where mining is carried out has witnessed large-scale deforestation and a transition from forest to grasslands (Kharpuri 2012).

Northeast India is home to a large number of indigenous rice varieties (Ngachan et al. n.d.), but these are rapidly being lost due to changes in land use and agricultural policy, which generally favor certain high-yield varieties (Choudhury et al. 2013). Currently the agrarian economy of the northeast region produces only about half the food-grain requirement of the region; the rest is sourced through imports from other regions of India (Mohapatra 2006). A rapidly growing population places high demands on the public distribution system. Meghalaya has a high decadal growth, and one of the highest fertility rates in the country, combined with one of the highest levels of unmet need for contraception (Oosterhoff et al. 2015). Despite the extensive presence of indigenous varieties of rice, the public distribution system relies on importing hybrid varieties from other regions of India. From the policymakers' perspective, subsidized imports are required to bridge the deficits and to meet the needs of a growing population. But an unintended consequence of the availability of low-cost subsidized rice is ostensibly a lack of interest in growing indigenous varieties among local farmers (Roy 2015). Another example is that of millets, which once contributed significantly to food security in India, but have now been supplanted by rice as a staple (Bergamini et al. 2013).

Role of wild edibles and traditional foods in health

Wild food plants have sustained humanity through the ages, but the agricultural revolution and modernizing influences led to a shift in preferences and possibly less dietary diversity (Grivetti and Ogle 2000). Wild edibles have the potential to supply both macro- and micronutrients to human diets, and they provide an additional source of dietary supplements in tribal communities in India (Agrahar-Murugkar 2006; Mahapatra and Panda 2012). One ethnobotanical study in Meghalaya identified 110 different wild edible plants whose roots, tubers, stems, leaves, flowers, fruits, and seeds were used by the indigenous peoples (Kayang 2007). An inventory of wild edibles in Meghalaya, identified 249 species belonging to 153 genera and 82 families (Sawian et al. 2007). These comprised over 13% of the total vascular plant species identified in Meghalaya. Five percent of the wild edibles identified were also cultivated (Sawian et al. 2007).

Effective use of wild edibles for improving diets is a function of several converging factors, such as knowledge, availability, affordability, and access. A case–control study evaluating knowledge of vitamin-A-rich foods among mothers with children who had clinical VAD found knowledge in this group to be less than among the control group (Nongrum and Kharkongor 2015). Mothers with poor knowledge were 2.5 times more likely to have a child deficient in vitamin A. An important factor that influenced the consumption of vitamin-A-rich food was maternal education. A mother with no formal school education was 9.3 times more likely to have a child with VAD. Another significant factor was family size; households with more than two children had higher odds (0.28) of having a child with VAD. The Khasis refer to night blindness, a symptom of VAD, by the local term *matiar* (literally meaning "hen eyes") or its variations *matir* and *matiew*. The traditional remedy for this condition is reportedly consumption of beef liver in raw, boiled, or roasted form. Most members in these communities (87%) were dependent on markets for food; thus, affordability of vitamin-A-rich foods was also raised by mothers as a concern (Nongrum and Kharkongor 2015).

While there is doubtless potential for wild edibles to supplement macro- and micronutrients in human diets, the practicalities of collection and use requires that knowledge of benefits must be prevalent within the community. However, there has been a progressive loss of knowledge and interest in wild food and medicinal plants among indigenous populations. An intergenerational study done in Meghalaya on knowledge and consumption of wild food plants demonstrated both variables decreasing across the generations (Ellena 2013).

Engaging local knowledge to build a sustainable way forward

Women have long been custodians of valuable indigenous knowledge related to the preservation and management of natural resources, including forests and their products (IFAD n.d.). Women have played a pivotal role in the preservation of agrobiodiversity. In the northeast, seed selection, seed preservation, plant breeding, and cultivation of rice varieties has traditionally been in the domain of women's knowledge (Krishna 2005). But with the introduction of cash crops and market forces in the agriculture sector, women's knowledge and roles in agriculture are being progressively undermined (Mukhim 2005). Policy approaches that are geared to improving productivity and cash incomes, rather than to preserving biodiversity, demonstrate low appreciation of the complex diversity of the region's landscapes, peoples, and farming systems. Thus agricultural policies often advance new forms of patriarchy in these communities (Krishna 2005).

Maintaining diversity within agricultural systems is practiced by many smallholder farmers globally (Sunderland 2011). Local farmers rarely maintain records, nor are they aware of the biodiversity that they preserve. To cite one example, documented by the North East Slow Food and Agrobiodiversity Society (NESFAS) in Meghalaya, Kong Redian Syiem of Khweng village said she grew about 12 varieties of plants, but a closer look by the NESFAS team revealed that she actually grew 70–80 varieties of food plants in her little farm, including 20 varieties of yam. Her family of 11 subsists entirely on what they grow and is known as the healthiest family in the village (NESFAS 2014).

According to the NESFAS team a key reason for traditional foods falling out of favor within communities is the perceived "better taste" of the newer foods. An intergenerational study noted that children did not seem to value the tastes of wild food plants and tended to prefer the "food from the market" over the "food from the forest" (Ellena 2013). To address this issue, NESFAS, through their cook's alliance, is engaging in flavor development while using traditional ingredients to promote innovations in local cuisines (NESFAS 2014). More sustained efforts to raise consciousness and improve nutritional awareness is required.

The recent global nutrition report makes a case for more high-quality research to understand nutritional challenges in different settings (IFPRI 2014). There are ongoing nutritional transitions taking place within indigenous communities in northeast India, but there is little documentation of the changes and their effects. Although small initiatives have begun, such as the NESFAS movement, much more can and must be done to find local solutions to meet the nutritional needs of the region.

Some final words, as stated by Florence Egal (Fanzo et al. 2013):

> It is urgent to remind policy makers that agriculture is primarily about using natural resources to feed people. Sustainable development will only happen if we manage such resources in a sustainable way, building on local cultures, protecting and strengthening livelihoods, and ensuring good nutrition and health.

Acknowledgements

I thank the NESFAS team in Shillong for sharing data, community experiences, and scientific material during the preparation of this manuscript.

References

ADC. (1958) "United Khasi-Jaintia Hills ADC Management of Forests Act," Meghalaya: KHADC, viewed 13 July 2015, http://khadc.nic.in/acts_rules_regulations%20_n%20_bills/Acts%20n%20Rules-arranged/19A.&%2024A.%20Forest%20Act,%201958%20&%20Rules%201960.pdf.

Agrahar-Murugkar, D. (2005) "Nutritional Status of Khasi Schoolgirls in Meghalaya," *Nutrition* 21: 425–431.

——. (2006) "Interventions Using Wild Edibles to Improve the Nutritional Status of Khasi Tribal Women," *Human Ecology Special Issue* 14: 83–88.

Albert, S., Nongrum, M., Webb, E. L., Porter, J. D. & Kharkongor, G. C. (2015) "Medical Pluralism Among Indigenous Peoples in Northeast India – Implications for Health Policy," *Tropical Medicine & International Health* 20: 952–960.

Balasubramanian, A. (2006) "Is There an Indian Way of Doing Science?" in Balasubramanian, A. & Devi, T. N. (eds.), *Traditional Knowledge Systems of India and Sri Lanka*, Chennai, India: Centre for Indian Knowledge Systems, pp. 183–192.

Bergamini, N., Padulosi, S., Ravi, S. B. & Yenagi, N. (2013) "Minor Millets in India: A Neglected Crop Goes Mainstream," in Fanzo, J., Hunter, D., Borelli, T. & Mattei, F. (eds.), *Diversifying Food and Diets: Using Agricultural Biodiversity to Improve Nutrition and Health*, London: Routledge, pp. 313–325.

Black, R. E., Victora, C. G., Walker, S. P., Bhutta, Z. A., Christian, P., De Onis, M., Ezzati, M., Grantham-McGregor, S., Katz, J., Martorell, R. & Uauy, R. (2013) "Maternal and Child Undernutrition and Overweight in Low-Income and Middle-Income Countries," *The Lancet* 382: 427–451.

Blah, M. M. & Joshi, S. R. (2013) "Nutritional Content Evaluation of Traditional Recipes Consumed by Ethnic Communities of Meghalaya, India," *Indian Journal of Traditional Knowledge* 12: 498–505.

Burchi, F., Fanzo, J. & Frison, E. (2011) "The Role of Food and Nutrition System Approaches in Tackling Hidden Hunger," *International Journal of Environmental Research and Public Health* 8: 358–373.

Burlingame, B. A. & Dernini, S. (2012) "Sustainable Diets and Biodiversity," proceedings of the International Scientific Symposium Biodiversity and Sustainable Diets United Against Hunger (2010), FAO, Rome, Italy.

Census of India. (2011) *Census of India 2011*, New Delhi, India: Office of the Registrar General & Census Commissioner, GoI, Ministry of Home Affairs, http://censusindia.gov.in/.

Choudhury, B., Khan, M. L. & Dayanandan, S. (2013) "Genetic Structure and Diversity of Indigenous Rice (Oryza Sativa) Varieties in the Eastern Himalayan Region of Northeast India," *SpringerPlus* 2: 228.

CSE. (2008) *Rich Lands Poor People: Is 'Sustainable' Mining Possible?*, New Delhi: Centre for Science and Environment.

Declerck, F. A., Fanzo, J., Palm, C. & Remans, R. (2011) "Ecological Approaches to Human Nutrition," *Food & Nutrition Bulletin* 32: 41S–50S.

DLHS-4. (2013) *District Level Household and Facility Survey – 4: State Fact Sheet Meghalaya (2012–13)*, India: Ministry of Health & Family Welfare, viewed 13 July 2015, https://nrhm-mis.nic.in/DLHS4/Meghalaya/ Meghalaya.pdf.

Ellena, R. (2013) "Ethnobotanical Knowledge, Consumption and Values of Wild Food Plants: A Comparative Study Among Different Generations and Gender in Tyrna, Khasi Hills, Meghalaya, India," Thesis, MSc Ethnobotany, University of Kent at Canterbury.

Fanzo, J., Hunter, D., Borelli, T. & Mattei, F. (2013) *Diversifying Food and Diets: Using Agricultural Biodiversity to Improve Nutrition and Health*, London: Routledge.

Food and Agriculture Organization of the United Nations [FAO]. (2013) *The State of Food and Agriculture: Food Systems for Better Nutrition*, Rome: Food and Agriculture Organization of the United Nations.

——. (2015) *Regional Overview of Food Insecurity: Asia and the Pacific: Towards a Food Secure Asia and the Pacific*, Bangkok: FAO.

FAO, IFAD [International Fund for Agricultural Development] & WFP. (2015) "The State of Food Insecurity in the World 2015—Meeting the 2015 International Hunger Targets: Taking Stock of Uneven Progress," Rome: FAO.

Frison, E. A., Smith, I. F., Johns, T., Cherfas, J. & Eyzaguirre, P. B. (2006) "Agricultural Biodiversity, Nutrition, and Health: Making a Difference to Hunger and Nutrition in the Developing World," *Food & Nutrition Bulletin* 27: 167–179.

Grivetti, L. E. & Ogle, B. M. (2000) "Value of Traditional Foods in Meeting Macro- and Micronutrient Needs: The Wild Plant Connection," *Nutrition Research Reviews* 13: 31–31.

Gurdon, P. R. T. (1914) *The Khasis*, London: Macmillan and Co., Ltd.

Hunter, D. & Fanzo, J. (2013) "Agricultural Biodiversity, Diverse Diets and Improving Nutrition," in Fanzo, J., Hunter, D., Borelli, T. & Mattei, F. (eds.), *Diversifying Food and Diets: Using Agricultural Biodiversity to Improve Nutrition and Health*, London: Routledge, pp. 1–13.

IFAD [International Fund for Agricultural Development]. (n.d.) "Enhancing the Role of Indigenous Women in Sustainable Development: IFAD Experience with Indigenous Women in Latin America and Asia," viewed 16 July 2015, http://www.ifad.org/english/indigenous/pub/documents/indigenouswom enReport.pdf.

IFPRI [International Food Policy Research Institute]. (2014) "Global Nutrition Report: Actions and Accountability to Accelerate the World's Progress on Nutrition," Washington: International Food Policy Research Institute, pp. 7–8.

Jeeva, S., Mishra, B. P., Venugopal, N., Kharlukhi, L. & Laloo, R. C. (2006) "Traditional Knowledge and Biodiversity Conservation in the Sacred Groves of Meghalaya," *Indian Journal of Traditional Knowledge* 5: 563–568.

Karlsson, B. G. & Subba, T. B. (2006) "Introduction," in Karlsson, B. G. & Subba, T. B. (eds.) *Indigeneity in India*, London: Kegan Paul Ltd, pp. 1–17.

Kayang, H. (2007) "Tribal Knowledge on Wild Edible Plants of Meghalaya, Northeast India," *Indian Journal of Traditional Knowledge* 6: 177–181.

Khan, M., Khumbongmayum, A. D. & Tripathi, R. (2008) "The Sacred Groves and their Significance in Conserving Biodiversity an Overview," *International Journal of Ecology and Environmental Sciences* 34: 277–291.

Kharpuri, L. (2012) "Edaphic and Phytosociological Study in a Limestone Mining area at Mawsmai, Meghalaya," PhD Thesis, Martin Luther Christian University, Shillong.

Krishna, S. (2005) "Gendered Price of Rice in North-Eastern India," *Economic and Political Weekly* 40: 2555–2562.

Kumar, V., Reddy, A. N., Babu, J. P., Rao, T. N., Langstieh, B. T., Thangaraj, K., Reddy, A. G., Singh, L. & Reddy, B. M. (2007) "Y-chromosome Evidence Suggests a Common Paternal Heritage of Austro-Asiatic Populations," *BMC Evolutionary Biology* 7: 47.

Mahapatra, A. K. & Panda, P. C. (2012) "Wild Edible Fruit Diversity and its Significance in the Livelihood of Indigenous Tribals: Evidence from Eastern India," *Food Security* 4: 219–234.

Malik, S., Chaudhury, R., Dhariwal, O. & Kalia, R. K. (2006) "Collection and Characterization of Citrus Indica Tanaka and C. Macroptera Montr.: Wild Endangered Species of Northeastern India," *Genetic Resources and Crop Evolution* 53: 1485–1493.

Metz, J., Hart, D. & Harpending, H. (1971) "Iron, Folate, and Vitamin B12 Nutrition in a Hunter-gatherer People: A Study of the !Kung Bushmen," *The American Journal of Clinical Nutrition* 24: 229–242.

Ministry of Tribal Affairs. (2013) *Statistical Profile of Scheduled Tribes in India*, 2nd ed., India: Ministry of Tribal Affairs Statistics Division.

Mittermeier, R. A., Turner, W. R., Larsen, F. W., Brooks, T. M. & Gascon, C. (2011) "Global Biodiversity Conservation: The Critical Role of Hotspots," in Zachos, F. E. & Habel, J. C. (eds.), *Biodiversity Hotspots*, New York: Springer, pp. 3–22.

Mohapatra, A. C. (2006) "Agrarian Developments and Food Security in the North-East Region," in Basu, D., Francis Kulirani, B. & Ray, B. D. (eds.), *Agriculture, Food Security, Nutrition and Health in North-East India*, New Delhi: Mittal Publications, pp. 13–20.

Mukhim, P. (2005) Gender Concerns and Food Security in Rice Farming Systems of North east India, *Dialogue* 7(1), viewed 18 November 2015, http://www.asthabharati.org/Dia_Jul%2005/pat.htm.

Myers, N., Mittermeier, R. A., Mittermeier, C. G., Da Fonseca, G. A. & Kent, J. (2000) "Biodiversity Hotspots for Conservation Priorities," *Nature* 403: 853–858.

National Nutrition Monitoring Bureau. (2009) "Diet and Nutritional Status of Tribal Population and Prevalence of Hypertension among Adults – Report on Second Repeat Survey," Hyderabad, India: National Institute of Nutrition, Indian Council of Medical Research, viewed 8 June 2015, http://nnmbindia.org/NNMBTribalReport.pdf.

NESFAS. (2014) "Annual Report 2013–2014," Shillong, Meghalaya, India

Nettleton, C., Stephens, C., Bristow, F., Claro, S., Hart, T., McCausland, C. & Mijlof, I. (2007) "Utz Wachil: Findings from an International Study of Indigenous Perspectives on Health and Environment," *Ecohealth* 4: 461–471.

Ngachan, S. V., Mohanty, A. K. & Pattanayak, A. (n.d.) "Status Paper on Rice in North East India," India: Rice Knowledge Management Portal (RKMP), Directorate of Rice Research, Hyderabad, viewed 15 July 2015, http://www.rkmp.co.in/sites/default/files/ris/rice-state-wise/Status%20Paper%20on%20Rice%20in%20North%20East%20India.pdf.

Nongrum, M. S. & Kharkongor, G. C. (2015) "High prevalence of vitamin A deficiency among children in Meghalaya and the underlying social factors," *Indian Journal of Child Health* 2(2): 59–63.

North East Council. (2008) "North Eastern Region Vision 2020: General Strategies for the Region. Peace, Progress and Prosperity in the North Eastern Region: General Strategies for the Region," Ministry of Development of North Eastern Region, Government of India.

Oosterhoff, P., Dkhar, B. & Albert, S. (2015) "Understanding Unmet Contraceptive Needs Among Rural Khasi Men and Women in Meghalaya," *Culture, Health & Sexuality* 17(9): 1105–1118.

Prokop, P. & Suliga, I. (2013) "Two Thousand Years of Iron Smelting in the Khasi Hills, Meghalaya, North East India," *Current Science* 104: 761–767.

Reddy, B. M., Langstieh, B., Kumar, V., Nagaraja, T., Reddy, A., Meka, A., Reddy, A., Thangaraj, K. & Singh, L. (2007) "Austro-Asiatic Tribes of Northeast India Provide Hitherto Missing Genetic Link Between South and Southeast Asia," *PLoS One* 2: e1141.

Registrar General & Census Commissioner. (2013) "Scheduled Tribes in India," Ministry of Home Affairs, India, viewed 14 March 2014, http://tribal.nic.in/WriteReadData/CMS/Documents/census.pdf.

Roy, P. (2015) Personal Communication with Chairman, North East Slow Food & Agrobiodiversity Society (NESFAS).

Sahai, S. (2014) *Biodiversity Matters*, New Delhi, India: Gene Campaign.

Samati, H. & Gogoi, R. (2007) "Sacred Groves in Meghalaya," *Current Science* 93: 1338–1339.

Sarma, K. (2005) "Impact of Coal Mining on Vegetation: A Case Study in Jaintia Hills District of Meghalaya, India," Thesis, International Institute for Geo-information Science and Earth Observation, Netherlands, viewed on 18 November 2015, https://www.itc.nl/library/Papers_2005/msc/ereg/sarma.pdf.

Sawian, J. T., Jeeva, S., Lyndem, F. G., Mishra, B. P. & Laloo, R. C. (2007) "Wild Edible Plants of Meghalaya, North-east India," *Natural Product Radiance* 6: 410–426.

Sunderland, T. (2011) "Food Security: Why is Biodiversity Important?," *International Forestry Review* 13: 265–274.

Sunderland, T. C. H., Powell, B., Ickowitz, A., Foli, S., Pinedo-Vasquez, M., Nasi, R. & Padoch, C. (2013) *Food Security and Nutrition: The Role of Forests*, Bogor, Indonesia: Center for International Forestry Research (CIFOR).

Swer, S. & Singh, O. (2003) "Coal Mining Impacting Water Quality and Aquatic Biodiversity in Jaintia Hills District of Meghalaya," *Himalayan Ecology* 11: 29.

United Nations. (1992) "United Nations Convention on Biological Diversity," United Nations, viewed 22 June 2015, https://www.cbd.int/doc/legal/cbd-en.pdf.

Vinceti, B., Ickowitz, A., Powell, B., Kehlenbeck, K., Termote, C., Cogill, B. & Hunter, D. (2013) "The Contribution of Forests to Sustainable Diets," Rome: FAO, viewed 18 November 2015, http://www.fao.org/forestry/37132–051da8e87e54f379de4d7411aa3a3c32a.pdf.

WHO [World Health Organization]. (2015) "Obesity and Overweight: Fact Sheet No. 311," Geneva: World Health Organization, viewed 2 July 2015, http://www.who.int/mediacentre/factsheets/fs311/en/.

Williams, J. N. (2011) "Human Population and the Hotspots Revisited: A 2010 Assessment," in Zachos, F.E. & Habel, J.C. (eds.), *Biodiversity Hotspots*, New York: Springer, pp. 61–81.

Williams, K. J., Ford, A., Rosauer, D. F., de Silva, N., Mittermeier, R., Bruce, C., Larsen, F. W. & Margules, C. (2011) "Forests of East Australia: the 35th Biodiversity Hotspot," in Zachos, F.E. & Habel, J.C. (eds.), *Biodiversity Hotspots*, New York: Springer, pp. 295–310.

Xaxa Committee. (2014) "Report of the High-level Committee on Socio-Economic, Health and Educational Status of the Tribals of India," Ministry of Tribal Affairs, Government of India.

Zimmermann, M. B., Chassard, C., Rohner, F., N'goran, E. K., Nindjin, C., Dostal, A., Utzinger, J., Ghattas, H., Lacroix, C. & Hurrell, R. F. (2010) "The Effects of Iron Fortification on the Gut Microbiota in African Children: A Randomized Controlled Trial in Côte d'Ivoire," *The American Journal of Clinical Nutrition* 92: 1406–1415.

PART IV
Liberty, choice, and food policy

12

FOOD LABELING AND FREE SPEECH

Matteo Bonotti

Introduction

In contemporary political theory, there is a growing interest in the normative dimensions of food governance. Some of this literature is concerned with issues of state paternalism (i.e., the interference of the state with a person's freedom in order to promote her own good, against that person's will). The discussion in this area has especially focused on the question whether the state can permissibly coerce people not to consume certain unhealthy foods through the use of food bans and food taxes (Conly 2013a; Conly 2013b; Resnik 2014), or less drastically, guide them towards the consumption of healthier foods through the use of "nudges" (Thaler and Sunstein 2008). Other authors have focused on the normative implications of ethical and cultural diversity for food governance (Ceva 2014), the moral status of non-human animals in relation to food consumption and production (Lomasky 2013; Milligan 2010), and issues of international and environmental justice (Navin 2014; Peterson 2013). A further area of research concerns those aspects of food governance that are in different ways – though not always explicitly – related to freedom of speech. The first concerns food advertising (Marks 2013), the second addresses weight stigma (Voigt et al. 2014: 94–108), and the third, on which I focus in this chapter, relates to food labels.

More specifically, three kinds of labels have received special attention in the recent literature. The first category includes nutrition labels. Contrary to the common view that information always contributes to the exercise of individual autonomy, Bonotti (2014) and Loi (2014) have argued that nutrition food labeling ought to respect the legitimate interests of two categories of consumers: those who want to know everything about their food in order to make informed dietary choices, and those who would rather remain ignorant about the specific contents and effects of their food in order to elude the costs (e.g., emotional, psychological, or, more simply, hedonic) that may result from obtaining that information. According to both Bonotti and Loi, the right to avoid certain information can contribute to, rather than hinder, autonomous agency – and certain labels fail to respect such a right. These include the "traffic light" labels currently adopted on a voluntary basis in the UK, which provide information about the percentages of fat, saturated fat, salt, sugar, and calories of each food and classify them using red, amber, or green colors based on the level of each nutrient, and proposed labels containing pictures of diet-related health conditions akin to those already used for cigarette packaging in some countries (Stephens 2014).

The second category of food labels receiving recent attention concerns genetically modified (GM) foods. Kirsten Hansen (2004) has argued that voluntary negative labeling of non-GM foods is sufficient to respect the autonomy of consumers since those who would like to avoid GM foods – a small number of consumers, according to Hansen – could simply assume that non-labeled foods contain GM ingredients. However, in response to Hansen's argument, Alan Rubel and Robel Streiffer (2005) have claimed that the group of consumers who demand information about GM ingredients is in fact quite large, and negative labels would not be sufficient to respect their autonomy since most people assume that non-labeled foods are GM-free. According to Rubel and Streiffer, generic positive labeling stating that that food "may contain" (Rubel and Streiffer 2005: 82) GM ingredients would be both cost-effective and better than negative labels at promoting consumers' autonomous agency. Rubel and Streiffer also point out that respect for consumers' autonomy is especially important when GM foods may contain genes the consumption of which may conflict with consumers' religious or cultural beliefs, or with their ethical views concerning animal welfare (Rubel and Streiffer 2005: 80). This aspect is also emphasized by Assya Pascalev, who stresses the importance of GM food labels for guaranteeing consumers' integrity, i.e., "[their] . . . ability to be true to . . . [their] fundamental values and deepest commitments, to achieve a coherent integration of the various aspects of the self and to maintain self-identity" (Pascalev 2003: 586). Helena Siipi and Susanne Uusitalo (2008) also highlight this aspect and advocate the need for comprehensive information campaigns about GM foods alongside the use of labels.

A third category of labels discussed in the recent literature includes labels conveying information about the social and environmental impact of foods. Authors working in this area have highlighted the importance of food labeling for guaranteeing the "ethical traceability" of foods (Beekman 2008), and for ensuring that citizens can "use their [food] preferences as an expression of social agency" (De Tavernier 2012). Similarly, Lorenzo Del Savio and Bettina Schmietow (2013) have pointed out that the duty to provide consumers with information through food labels is grounded in the view that "consumers have an interest in their being moral agents, that is, they have an interest in making choices according to their own moral principles" (Del Savio and Schmietow 2013: 790).

Having provided this brief overview of the recent literature, in this chapter I intend to assess in what ways different theories of free speech can contribute in justifying the duty of food producers to disclose information using food labels. In the first section I examine the argument from truth, and I claim that, while it justifies the permissibility of food labels (except when such labels are misleading), it does not seem sufficient to justify a mandatory duty for food producers to provide information. In the second section I analyze the argument from autonomy and self-fulfillment, and I argue that while this argument provides the rationale for mandatory food labels, it should be reinterpreted in terms of John Rawls' idea of the "second moral power," i.e., "the capacity to form, to revise, and rationally to pursue a conception of one's rational advantage or good" (Rawls 2005: 19). In the third and final section I consider the argument from democracy, and I claim that while this argument justifies imposing disclosure requirements upon food producers, it also needs to be accompanied by an examination of the structural and environmental context within which consumers receive and assess the information conveyed by food labels. Consideration of structural factors may justify imposing limits on the kind of information that food labels may convey.

Before proceeding with my analysis, I would like to offer a slightly different categorization of food labels from the ones previously illustrated. According to this classification, food labels can be divided into three main categories: factual, judgmental, and social labels. *Factual* labels are those that provide factual information about foods, which may include ingredients, nutritional contents, and country of origin. *Judgmental* labels are those that present factual information in a way that also involves a value judgment regarding the desirability (or lack thereof) of a certain food for the consumer. Examples of this include the abovementioned traffic light labels. The judgment these labels convey concerns the implications of eating certain foods *for the consumers themselves*, rather than for third parties. Finally, *social* labels are those that contain information that would enable consumers to fulfill certain moral and political duties. These may include fair trade labels, environmental labels, and animal welfare labels. I believe that this classification is more helpful for assessing the relevance of different theories of free speech for food labeling.

Food labels, free speech, and the argument from truth

The first theory of free speech that I intend to assess is the argument from truth, sometimes also called the "marketplace of ideas" defense of free speech – as famously defended by John Stuart Mill, for whom the absence of state censorship would enable the truth to emerge from the free exchange of ideas (Mill 2006). According to Mill, we should not silence an opinion, because, if that opinion is true, to do so may prevent us from abandoning our mistaken views. Alternatively, even if our opinion is obviously true, it may become a dead dogma if it is not challenged by other opinions, and it may be unable to promote action. In other cases, different opinions may be partially true, and only freedom of speech could allow the whole truth to emerge (Mill 2006: 22–63).

Mill's rationale for this argument is grounded in the idea that, by contributing to the discovery of the truth, freedom of speech also contributes "to the mental well-being of mankind (on which all their other well-being depends)" (Mill 2006: 60). "The truth of an opinion," Mill argues, "is part of its utility" (Mill 2006: 29), and the latter should be considered as "the ultimate appeal on all ethical questions; but it must be utility in the largest sense, grounded on the permanent interests of man as a progressive being" (Mill 2006: 17). The truth that freedom of speech enables people to discover therefore contributes to their flourishing as autonomous, rational, and self-determining individuals.

What implications, then, does this argument have for food labels? Clearly, factual labels can provide a contribution to the discovery of the truth and the advancement of consumers' knowledge. Nutrition labels, for example, provide information about the nutritional content of foods, which can enable consumers to acquire knowledge (i.e., justified true belief) about what they eat. Judgmental and social labels can also provide this contribution. For example, a traffic light label may convey the message that, because a food contains 25% saturated fats (factual claim), it is "bad" for you (judgmental claim conveyed through the color-coded element of the label). Similarly, animal welfare labels (see, e.g., Tonsor and Wolf 2011) convey both factual information about the conditions in which animals have been reared, transported, and slaughtered (factual information) and the message that such conditions meet (or do not meet) certain morally desirable standards (judgmental claim). All three kinds of labels, therefore, deserve free speech protection based on the argument from truth.

It is also important to point out that Mill's apparent emphasis on the cognitive content of the kind of expression that deserves protection does not imply that factual food labels should deserve greater protection than judgmental and social labels. On the contrary, the latter are especially relevant to his analysis. His argument, indeed, is "particularly applicable to types of expression [e.g., moral, political, social, etc.], which can only rarely, if ever, establish truths with the same degree of assurance that obtains in mathematics or the natural sciences" (Barendt 2005: 10). This is because, as Mill claims:

> As mankind improves, the number of doctrines which are no longer disputed or doubted will be constantly on the increase: and the wellbeing of mankind may almost be measured by the number and gravity of the truths which have reached the point of being uncontested.
>
> (Mill 2006: 51)

It is with regard to moral and political speech – and, therefore, of judgmental and social labels – that the argument from truth is especially relevant.

However, while it is true that the information conveyed by food labels can normally contribute to truth discovery and to consumers' knowledge, this may not always be the case – it could sometimes be misleading and actually prevent truth discovery and knowledge. For example, labels conveying factually false information or, more subtly, labels conveying misleading information, such as the abovementioned traffic light labels, may fall into this category. Indeed the Italian government recently condemned the UK's traffic light labeling system for unduly damaging some traditional Italian foods such as mozzarella, Parma ham, and Parmesan cheese. While many Italian foods do indeed contain high percentages of fat or salt (e.g., cured meats and cheeses), and are therefore labeled as "red," the Italian government pointed out that such foods should be judged as parts of the balanced Italian diet, which also involves a high level of consumption of fruits and vegetables (Davies 2013). Following Italy's complaint, the European Commission recognized the excessively simplistic and misleading nature of UK traffic light labeling and sent a "letter of formal notice" to the UK government, demanding a response to Italy's concerns (Squires and Waterfield 2014).

This example suggests that while the argument from truth justifies producers using food labels of their choice, it cannot justify allowing them to convey information in ways that may be misleading and therefore prevent the realization of the very goal (i.e., truth) that justifies that freedom in the first instance. This therefore in principle justifies restrictions on traffic light labels or on the proposed labels containing pictures of diseases and health conditions resulting from unhealthy eating. The latter, too, may be considered misleading as they unduly associate specific health conditions with the consumption of certain foods, thus decontextualizing the latter from overall diets and lifestyles. These restrictions would not run afoul of the truth argument for free speech. Instead, they would comply with something akin to what Alexander Brown, in his recent analysis of hate speech, calls the "Nuanced Principle of Truth" (Brown 2015: 113) and the "Nuanced Principle of Knowledge" (Brown 2015: 119). Such principles justify restrictions on uses of hate speech that prevent rather than promote truth discovery and knowledge. The same argument can be made regarding misleading food labels.

It is important to stress that considering certain labels as misleading does not rely on endorsing a controversial conception of the good, e.g., one according to which food should only be judged in the holistic way illustrated by the Italian government. Instead, my criticism relies on the idea that given that some people endorse a holistic approach to food, whereas others prefer an analytic/nutritionist approach (which assesses the healthiness of individual nutrients and foods independently from overall diets), food labels should convey information in a way that respects both positions. Traffic light labels fail to do so. As well as relying on a nutritionist approach, they also exploit non-rational psychological processes and imperfections in the decision-making capacities of consumers (e.g., by using color-coding) in order to affect their choices (Magnusson 2010: 7; The Co-operative Group 2013).

Furthermore, it should be noted that while the argument from truth supports the view that "ideas, as well as information, should be freely communicable in order to discover the truth" (Barendt 2005: 25), it does not seem to justify a mandatory duty for food producers to provide information. The argument, at least as Mill presents it, implies that the state should not prevent food producers from providing (and consumers from receiving) certain information through food labels, except in those cases where food labels undermine truth discovery. However, it does not seem to provide a rationale for imposing a duty on food producers to provide food labels on their products. One could, of course, claim that given the importance of truth discovery for people's wellbeing, food producers (and anyone who holds information) should be forced to speak.

However, that is not the way in which Mill presents the argument. In order for the duty to disclose information to be fully justified, it is therefore necessary to refer to a second major argument for free speech, i.e., the one grounded in the ideas of individual autonomy and self-fulfillment.

Food labels, free speech, and the argument from autonomy and self-fulfillment

According to the argument from individual autonomy and self-fulfillment:

> Restrictions on what we are allowed to say and write, or (on some formulations of the theory) to hear and read, inhibit our personality and its growth. A right to express beliefs and political attitudes instantiates or reflects what it is to be human.
>
> (Barendt 2005: 13)

Some versions of the argument stress the right of speakers as autonomous beings (Dworkin 1981). Other versions of the argument, however, focus more on the audience's rights. According to Thomas Scanlon, for example, "the powers of a state are limited to those that citizens could recognize while still regarding themselves as equal, autonomous, rational agents" (Scanlon 1972: 215). Therefore, "[a]n autonomous person cannot accept without independent consideration the judgment of others as to what he should believe or what he should do" (Scanlon 1972: 216).

Based on this line of argument, it can be claimed that consumers' interest in autonomy demands the disclosure of information through food labels. The idea that there is a link between free speech, individual autonomy, and food labels is indeed not new. As Eric Barendt points out, "[d]rug manufacturers and food producers . . . are commonly obliged to disclose the chemical ingredients or dietary qualities of their products and (in the case of the former) warn of any risks from taking the medicine" (Barendt 2005: 412). This obligation is grounded in the "interests of consumers in finding out attributes of the goods and services they want to buy, rather than speakers' rights" (Barendt 2005: 412). And those interests, I believe, can be traced back to the idea of autonomous agency.

However, as in the case of the argument from truth, misleading labels (such as traffic light labels) may not be permissible on the basis of the argument from autonomy. Such labels may exercise "undue influences" (Brown 2015: 60) on consumers' autonomy since they tend to "manipulate the mind or decision-making processes of . . . [their] . . . targets" (Brown 2015: 61). In this sense, they are akin to nudges, which have been criticized based on the view that "[s]ystematically exploiting non-rational factors that influence human decision-making, whether on the part of the government or other agents, threatens liberty, broadly conceived" (Hausman and Welch 2010: 136; see also Glaeser 2006). This criticism can be accommodated within the autonomy-based theory of free speech, especially if we consider Scanlon's revised version of the argument, according to which "these interests [the audience's interest in autonomy] might in some cases be better advanced if we could shield ourselves from some influences" (Scanlon 1979: 534). Similarly, David Partlett points out, "speech may be constrained when it invades the basic value it [i.e., freedom of speech] was designed to protect" (Partlett 1989: 453).

At this point it might be pointed out that I have overemphasized the distinction between the arguments from truth and from autonomy. Indeed, we have seen that for Mill the discovery of the truth is not valuable in itself but only in so far as it contributes "to the mental well-being of mankind (on which all their other well-being depends)" (Mill 2006: 60). This is "utility in the largest sense, grounded on the permanent interests of man as a progressive being" (Mill 2006: 17). This suggests that the argument from truth, once reinterpreted as a subset of the argument from autonomy and self-fulfillment, may also be employed as a justification for disclosure requirements. Disclosure of information through food labels, that is, can be imposed upon food producers in order to enable consumers to make informed (i.e., truth-based) and autonomous choices about their foods. This kind of obligation, as we have seen, is already recognized in various jurisdictions with regard to medicines, particular foods, or cigarettes (Barendt 2005: 412). The argument from autonomy and the argument from truth should therefore be considered as complementary rather than mutually exclusive.

The argument from autonomy, however, faces two important challenges. First of all, the idea that human beings should constantly pursue self-development and intellectual growth through the free expression of (and unconstrained access to) different beliefs, information, and opinions, is far from being an uncontroversial view. For example, this view is not endorsed by those who "are likely to be satisfied with other freedoms, or prefer the security or intellectual anaesthesia that accompanies rigid controls on expression" (Schauer 1982: 49). However, this problem can be circumvented by appealing to a slightly different version of the argument, i.e., what Scanlon calls "the Principle of Limited Authority" (Scanlon 1973: 1042). By drawing on Rawls' argument in *A Theory of Justice* (Rawls 1999), Scanlon claims that freedom of speech is justified because the deliberating parties in the Original Position would not give governments "the authority to decide matters of moral, religious or philosophic doctrine (or of scientific truth) and . . . to restrict certain activities on the grounds that they promulgate false or corrupting doctrines" (Scanlon 1973: 1042). Elsewhere, he claims that "freedom of expression . . . seeks to protect . . . our interest in deciding for ourselves how to conduct our private lives" (Scanlon 2011: 545). This version of the argument seems to be purified of the thick Millian conception of human flourishing that underlies the standard version.

The duty of food producers to provide labels on their products, therefore, can be justified by appealing to the second of what John Rawls calls the "two moral powers" (Rawls 2005: 19), i.e., "the capacity to form, to revise, and rationally to pursue a conception of one's rational advantage or good" (Rawls 2005: 19). This implies that even though the state, according to Rawls, should not endorse any conception of the good (including one grounded in a Millian conception of individual autonomy), it should ensure that citizens are able to pursue *their* conceptions of the good (e.g., religious, philosophical, ethical, etc.). This demands that foods be labeled. Failing to do so would infringe upon consumers' liberty of conscience, which according to Rawls, "is among the social conditions necessary for the development and exercise of this power" (Rawls 2005: 313).

An argument on similar lines has been put forward, for example, by Del Savio and Schmietow (2013). According to them, the duty to provide consumers with information through food labels is grounded in the view that "consumers have an *interest* in their being moral agents, that is, they have an interest in making choices according to their own moral principles" (Del Savio and Schmietow 2013: 790, original emphasis). Preventing consumers from having access to morally relevant information, therefore, would act against that interest. There are two elements that are particularly useful in Del Savio and Schmietow's account. First, they explicitly appeal to a Rawlsian framework and aim to justify the duty to label on uncontroversial neutral grounds, i.e., the idea that the failure to inform would violate consumers' "moral integrity" (Del Savio and Schmietow 2013: 793). In my version of the argument, failure to label would undermine consumers' ability to cultivate and exercise their second moral power. Second, even though they only apply their argument to labels providing information about the environmental footprints of foods, Del Savio and Schmietow acknowledge that it would also be applicable to labels providing other morally relevant information, including the conditions of farmers and workers employed in food production or the welfare of animals.

However, and crucially, they point out that there is reasonable moral disagreement among people on these and similar issues. For example, they claim:

> whilst for environmental impact there are non-question-begging ways of publishing information (e.g., x kg CO2 per y kg product), the specification of features that are relevant for global justice and animal welfare requires a selection of topics that is open to challenge; notice, for instance, that existing supererogatory labels on these issues are formulated in normative terms (e.g., *fair* trade').
>
> (Del Savio and Schmietow 2013: 794, original emphasis)

This, however, seems to stretch their argument too far. While labels informing consumers that food producers respect animals'"welfare" or treat workers "fairly" (thus using normatively loaded terms) might admittedly look controversial (e.g., What does animal "welfare" involve? What does it mean to treat workers "fairly"?), this does not preclude the use of labels which would only provide factual information about the conditions of animals or workers.

The idea would be to decouple uncontroversial and controversial information, and only provide the former on food labels. After all, even Del Savio and Schmietow claim that while factual information about environmental footprints is uncontroversial (and therefore should be provided on food labels), the idea of "environmental sustainability" often associated with it is not (Del Savio and Schmietow 2013: 788). Yet this solution might face insurmountable practical problems. While it may be easy, for example, to provide nutritional or environmental impact information succinctly on food packaging, it might be much more difficult to do the same with regard to the factual information concerning the treatment of workers or animals involved in the production and distribution of foods.

An alternative, therefore, might be in such cases to still allow existing labels (e.g., animal welfare labels or fair trade labels) to be used, with the proviso that consumers should be duly informed about the meaning currently attributed to such labels, e.g., the criteria that foods need to meet in order to be labeled as "animal welfare" or "fair trade" certified. This could be accomplished through information campaigns, such as those proposed by Siipi and Uusitalo with regard to GM food labeling and involving "[f]ree leaflets . . . visible posters containing relevant information in the stores . . . [or printing] on the packets of GMF products an address of a website where relevant information is available" (Siipi and Uusitalo 2008: 361; see also Bonotti 2014 and Jackson 2000). Furthermore, such a system would still allow citizens to deliberate about, and possibly revise, existing labeling criteria.

This solution may also help to overcome the second major challenge that the argument from autonomy faces. Alongside the potential disagreement regarding the value of individual autonomy which, we have seen, can be resolved by appealing to Rawls' second moral power, fulfilling the latter's demands may also give rise to a conflict between disclosure requirements and the liberty of conscience of food producers. Indeed it is true that "negative freedom of speech covers a right not to be forced to subscribe to opinions one does not hold, not a right to withhold information" (Barendt 2005: 412). However, we have seen that many food labels, especially those conveying moral and political messages, may be contentious. Imposing on food producers a duty to label their products as "fair trade" or "animal welfare" certified, may risk forcing them to convey opinions and views they do not hold – i.e., if they do not agree with the currently-agreed-upon criteria for these certifications. Therefore ensuring that mandatory labels are accompanied by comprehensive campaigns explaining to consumers that certifications such as "fair trade" and "animal welfare" do not necessarily reflect the views of all food producers, but only the current dominant (and contestable) understandings of such terms, would offer a reasonable compromise between the duty to inform consumers and the liberty of conscience of producers.

Food labels, free speech, and the argument from democracy

The third major argument for free speech is the one from democracy, mainly defended by Alexander Meiklejohn (1961; 1979), for whom freedom of speech contributes to citizens' understanding of political affairs and is therefore crucial for their ability to exercise democratic self-government. According to Meiklejohn:

> The First Amendment does not protect a "freedom to speak." It protects the freedom of those activities of thought and communication by which we "govern." It is concerned, not with a private right, but with a public power, a governmental responsibility.
>
> (Meiklejohn 1961: 255)

"Self-government," according to Meiklejohn, "can exist only insofar as the voters acquire the intelligence, integrity, sensitivity, and generous devotion to the general welfare that, in theory, casting a ballot is assumed to express" (Meiklejohn 1961: 255). Like the argument from autonomy, this argument focuses on the interests of the audience over the interests of the speakers.

It is clear, from these brief considerations, that the argument from democracy has implications for food labeling, and that it imposes disclosure requirements upon food producers. Cass R. Sunstein, for example, advances the following argument:

> Suppose that we wanted to increase the democratic character of contemporary government by promoting citizen participation in and control over governmental processes. A good initial step would be for government to provide enough information for people to make knowledgeable judgments. Government itself might supply information or require disclosure by private citizens and companies.
>
> (Sunstein 1993: 657)

The argument from democracy is possibly the least controversial and most inclusive of the existing arguments for free speech, since, unlike at least some versions of the arguments from truth and autonomy, it is not grounded in any contentious conception of the good (Bonotti 2015). However, its inclusiveness also gives rise to some problems. More specifically, it seems that the argument from democracy would justify the use of food labels to convey misleading information (see Post 2000: 35ff), something that the argument from autonomy, we have seen, would rule out. Indeed, according to Meiklejohn:

> When men govern themselves, it is they – and no one else – who must pass judgment upon unwisdom and unfairness and danger. And that means that unwise ideas must have a hearing as well as wise ones, unfair as well as fair, dangerous as well as safe, un-American as well as American. Just so far as, at any point, the citizens who are to decide an issue are denied acquaintance with information or opinion or doubt or disbelief or criticism which is relevant to that issue, just so far the result must be ill-considered, ill-balanced planning for the general good.
>
> (Meiklejohn 1979: 27)

This contrasts with the *Central Hudson* test adopted by the US Supreme Court, according to which commercial speech can receive First Amendment protection only if it does not relate to unlawful activity and is not misleading (Post 2000: 34). However, as Post points out, the apparent contradiction between Meiklejohn's argument and the *Central Hudson* test can be overcome "by redefining the misleading requirement to focus [not on the content of commercial speech but] on the specific conditions that might be understood to render consumers dependent and vulnerable" (Post 2000: 41) rather than free and equal agents capable of rational and reflective judgment. This argument would thus rule out misleading food labels (e.g., traffic light labels) while also providing the rationale for considering the importance of structural and environmental factors (e.g., education, socio-economic conditions, etc.) when assessing food labeling regimes.

Conclusion

Due to the controversy often spurred by governments' attempt to interfere with people's dietary choices through coercive measures (e.g., food taxes and food bans), the use of food labels to inform consumers and (non-coercively) encourage them to adopt certain dietary habits is likely to become increasingly prominent in the policy agendas of western liberal democracies. This correspondingly demands a greater degree of philosophical engagement with the normative issues surrounding food labeling. In this chapter I have offered a brief overview of the current literature in the area, and I have illustrated how different theories of free speech may both justify requiring food producers to adopt certain food labels and impose restrictions on the kind of information such labels can permissibly convey.

Acknowledgments

I am very grateful to Josh Milburn for his comments on an earlier draft of this chapter.

References

Barendt, E. M. (2005) *Freedom of Speech*, 2nd ed., Oxford: Oxford University Press.

Bonotti, M. (2014) "Food Labels, Autonomy and the Right (Not) to Know," *Kennedy Institute of Ethics Journal* 24: 301–21.

Bonotti, M. (2015) "Political Liberalism, Free Speech and Public Reason," *European Journal of Political Theory* 14: 180–208.

Brown, A. (2015) *Hate Speech Law: A Philosophical Examination*, New York and Abingdon: Routledge.

Ceva, E. (ed.) (2014) *Pluralismo Alimentare: Giustizia, Tolleranza e Diritti*, special issue of *Notizie di Politeia*, Anno XXX, N. 114.

Conly, S. (2013a) "Coercive Paternalism in Health Care: Against Freedom of Choice," *Public Health Ethics* 6: 241–5.

Conly, S. (2013b) *Against Autonomy: Justifying Coercive Paternalism*, New York: Cambridge University Press.

The Co-operative Group. (2013) "A Healthy Relationship Can Be Bad for Women's Health," viewed 30 October 2015, http://www.co-operative.coop/corporate/Press/Press-releases/Food/A-healthy-relationship-can-be-bad-for-womens-health/.

Davies, L. (2013) "Italy Claims 'Traffic-Light' Labelling Unfair on Mediterranean Food," *The Guardian*, 21 October, viewed 30 October 2015, http://www.theguardian.com/world/2013/oct/21/italy-traffic-light-food-labels-unfair.

Del Savio, L. and Schmietow, B. (2013) "Environmental Footprint of Foods: The Duty to Inform," *Journal of Agricultural and Environmental Ethics* 26: 787–96.

De Tavernier, J. (2012) "Food Citizenship: Is There a Duty for Responsible Consumption?," *Journal of Agricultural and Environmental Ethics* 25: 895–907.

Dworkin, R. (1981) "Is There a Right to Pornography?," *Oxford Journal of Legal Studies* 1: 177–212.

Hansen, K. (2004) "Does Autonomy Count in Favor of Labeling Genetically Modified Food?," *Journal of Agricultural and Environmental Ethics* 17: 67–76.

Hausman, D. M. and Welch, W. (2010) "Debate: To Nudge or Not to Nudge," *The Journal of Political Philosophy* 18: 123–36.

Glaeser, E. L. (2006) "Paternalism and Psychology," *The University of Chicago Law Review* 73: 133–56.

Jackson, D. (2000) "Labeling Products of Biotechnology: Towards Communication and Consent," *Journal of Agricultural and Environmental Ethics* 12: 319–30.

Loi, M. (2014) "Food Labels, Genetic Information, and the Right Not to Know," *Kennedy Institute of Ethics Journal* 24: 323–44.

Lomasky, L. (2013) "Is It Wrong to Eat Animals?," *Social Philosophy and Policy* 30: 177–200.

Magnusson, R. S. (2010) "Obesity Prevention and Personal Responsibility: The Case of Front-of-Pack Food Labelling in Australia," *BMC Public Health* 10: 1–16.

Meiklejohn, A. (1961) "The First Amendment Is an Absolute," *Supreme Court Review* 1961: 245–66.

Meiklejohn, A. (1979) *Political Freedom: The Constitutional Powers of the People*, Westport, CT: Greenwood Press.

Mill, J. S. (2006) *On Liberty and the Subjection of Women*, London: Penguin Books.

Milligan, T. (2010) *Beyond Animal Rights: Food, Pets and Ethics*, London and New York: Continuum.

Navin, M. (2014) "Local Food and International Ethics," *Journal of Agricultural and Environmental Ethics* 27: 349–68.

Partlett, D. (1989) "From Red Lion Square to Skokie to the Fatal Shore: Racial Defamation and Freedom of Speech," *Vanderbilt Journal of Transnational Law* 22: 431–90.

Pascalev, A. (2003) "You Are What You Eat: Genetically Modified Foods, Integrity, and Society," *Journal of Agricultural and Environmental Ethics* 16: 583–94.

Peterson, G. R. (2013) "Is Eating Locally a Moral Obligation?," *Journal of Agricultural and Environmental Ethics* 26: 421–37.

Post, R. (2000) "The Constitutional Status of Commercial Speech," *University of California Law Review* 48: 1–57.

Rawls, J. (1999) *A Theory of Justice* (revised edition), Oxford: Oxford University Press.

Rawls, J. (2005) *Political Liberalism* (expanded edition), New York: Columbia University Press.

Resnik, D. B. (2014) "Paternalistic Food and Beverage Policies: A Response to Conly," *Public Health Ethics* 7: 170–7.

Rubel, A. and Streiffer, R. (2005) "Respecting the Autonomy of European and American Consumers: Defending Positive Labels on GM Foods," *Journal of Agricultural and Environmental Ethics* 18: 75–84.

Scanlon, T. M. (1972) "A Theory of Freedom of Expression," *Philosophy and Public Affairs* 1: 204–26.

Scanlon, T. M. (1973) "Rawls's Theory of Justice," *University of Pennsylvania Law Review* 121: 1020–69.

Scanlon, T. M. (1979) "Freedom of Expression and Categories of Expression," *University of Pittsburgh Law Review* 40: 519–50.

Scanlon, T. M. (2011) "Why Not Base Free Speech on Autonomy or Democracy?," *Virginia Law Review* 97: 541–48.

Schauer, F. (1982) *Free Speech: A Philosophical Enquiry*, Cambridge: Cambridge University Press.

Siipi, H. and Uusitalo, S. (2008) "Consumer Autonomy and Sufficiency of GMF Labeling," *Journal of Agricultural and Environmental Ethics* 21: 353–69.

Squires, N. and Waterfield, B. (2014) "Italy Wins Ruling on 'Simplistic' UK Health Warnings against Salami, Prosciutto and Cheeses," *The Daily Telegraph*, 2 October, viewed 30 October 2015, http://www.telegraph.co.uk/news/worldnews/europe/italy/11136715/Italy-wins-ruling-on-simplistic-UK-health-warnings-against-salami-prosciutto-and-cheeses.html.

Stephens, P. (2014) "Food Should be Regulated Like Tobacco, Say Campaigners," *BBC News*, 19 May, viewed 30 October 2015, http://www.bbc.co.uk/news/health-27446958.

Sunstein, C. R. (1993) "Informing America: Risk, Disclosure, and the First Amendment," *Florida State University Law Review* 20: 653–77.

Thaler, R. H. and Sunstein, C. R. (2008) *Nudge: Improving Decisions about Health, Wealth, and Happiness*, New Haven: Yale University Press.

Tonsor, G. T. and Wolf, C. A. (2011) "On Mandatory Labeling of Animal Welfare Attributes," *Food Policy* 36: 430–37.

Voigt, K., Nicholls, S. G. and Williams, G. (2014) *Childhood Obesity: Ethical and Policy Issues*, New York: Oxford University Press.

Further Reading

E. Golan, F. Kuchler, and L. Mitchell, with contributions by C. Green and A. Jessup, "Economics of Food Labeling," *Journal of Consumer Policy* 24(2001): 117–184, offers an excellent overview of the issues surrounding food labeling from the perspective of economic theory. R. A. Shiner, *Freedom of Commercial Expression* (Oxford: Oxford University Press, 2003) provides the most comprehensive overview of the legal and philosophical issues concerning commercial speech. C. E. Baker, "Commercial Speech: A Problem in the Theory of Freedom," *Iowa Law Review* 62(1976–1977): 1–56, is another useful source.

Related topics

Animal Welfare; The Challenges of Dietary Pluralism; Food and Environmental Justice; Ethical Consumerism: A Defense; Obesity and Coercion.

13

FOOD ETHICS IN AN INTERGENERATIONAL PERSPECTIVE

Michele Loi

Introduction

The dominant controversy in food policy arguably revolves around an ideological conflict between supporters and opponents of state interference with individual liberty in the realm of food choices. According to public health scholars, effective policies against obesity involve obesity monitoring and extensive political interference with market freedom in the food sector. The all-encompassing scope of nutrition as a social and economic issue affects such different sectors as trade, agriculture, transport, urban planning, and economic development, all amenable to regulation aimed at obesity prevention and control (Gortmaker et al. 2011). This raises the specter of state paternalism, i.e., government-backed interference for the sake of promoting the good of the individuals interfered with. A widely shared belief among liberals is that the paternalistic public policy cannot be justified from the moral point of view (Dworkin 2010; Mill 1859).

The aim of this chapter is to review some recent arguments that attempt to justify interfering with individual food choices without appealing to a paternalist rationale. In these arguments, individual choices are interfered with for the sake of *preventing harm to (or disadvantage in) future generations*. Since paternalistic policies are defined by their *intention* or *rationale*, these policies are not paternalistic even if, as a collateral effect of preventing harm or disadvantage in others, they promote a healthier lifestyle that is also good for the persons whose liberty is interfered with.

This essay comprises five sub-sections. The first examines epidemiological and social-science rejoinders to the anti-paternalist liberal argument. Following Del Savio (2015), I will highlight weaknesses in these counter-objections. The second deals with the evidence from social epidemiology of connections between nutrition in parents and susceptibility to adult disease in their children and grandchildren. The third one reviews recent findings on the molecular correlates of these processes, that is to say, epigenetic phenomena. The fourth presents two non-paternalistic arguments for state interference with food choices, based, respectively, on social justice and intergenerational justice. The fifth considers the potential objection that such arguments shift the burden of responsibility and moral blame disproportionally on pregnant mothers, or on citizens of low socio-economic status (SES).

Principled anti-paternalism and empirical anti-anti-paternalism

As Del Savio (2015) argues, anti-paternalist arguments come in two broad species: utilitarian (more broadly, consequentialist) and principled/deontological. According to utilitarian anti-paternalism, the argument against paternalistic interventions is that they tend to be self-defeating. The ground for this claim is epistemic: since individuals are more closely concerned with their own good than third parties ("wisdom of individuals"), they tend to have better knowledge than third parties concerning what is, or is not, good for them ("ignorance of third parties"). It may be noticed that both claims of "wisdom of individuals" and "ignorance of third parties" are (empirically falsifiable) descriptive premises. This makes utilitarian anti-paternalism objectionable: by showing that individuals are not wise and third parties are not always ignorant, the anti-anti-paternalist can reject the (epistemic) rationale of utilitarian anti-paternalism.

An alternative consequentialist argument, that Del Savio mentions but does not examine in detail, relies on the premise that individual good is constituted in such a way that it requires individual agency and self-determination to be achieved. This contrasts with a purely epistemic account of the utilitarian anti-paternalism, since in this case the relation between first-personal choice and well-being is *essential:* true happiness is something that agents can only achieve if they engage their faculty of deliberation, take responsibility for it, and activate their cognitive and conative abilities in the pursuit of their goals. If so, there is a sense in which the state, by reducing the realm of exercise of such capacity of self-governance, undermines the conditions of achieve-ment of the highest, truest, or most authentic forms of human happiness.[1] This argument also relies on a claim – that true happiness essentially requires a significant degree of agential control and autonomy – which could turn out to be false, a posteriori.

By contrast, the principled (or deontological) liberty-based justification appeals to an idea of sovereignty over oneself that is valid a priori and establishes a right against external interference, irrespective of the outcomes of its exercise. As Feinberg writes:

> The life that a person threatens by his own rashness is after all his life; it belongs to him and to no one else. For that reason alone, he must be the one to decide – for better or worse – what is to be done with it in that private realm where the interests of others are not directly involved.
>
> (Feinberg 1984: 59)

Del Savio (2015) analyzes several actual or potential critiques of such a "principled libertarian" variety of anti-paternalism. Anti-anti-paternalist arguments, as I shall call them, rely on descriptive premises, i.e., empirical findings from natural or social science, to show that many food choices of persons who are low-SES individuals are not authentic "choices," or exercises of free agency, in the sense required for the liberty-based anti-paternalist argument to go through. These empirical arguments allege that powerful cognitive biases, social, and motivational influences undermine descriptive claims of human choice, freedom, and responsibility.

Del Savio's list of considerations often adduced in the public health ethics debate include: the obesogenic environment (White 2007); framing effects in canteens and restaurants (Sunstein and Thaler 2008), including serving size and the tidiness of serving tables (Wansink and Cheney 2005). Other rejoinders against principled anti-paternalism are that persons control their choices *within* their opportunity set, but have higher-order preferences concerning the opportunity sets themselves, which are not satisfied by exercising freedom of choice within options offered by markets (Anand and Gray 2009); that the neural correlates of feeding behavior, such as poor activation of the pre-frontal cortex in obese subjects with normal blood-sugar levels, show that people are not really free when choosing energy-dense food, but in a state similar to addiction (Page et al. 2011); the mismatch between evolutionary-wired eating habits and the food plenti-tude of some modern societies (Skipper 2012); mindless eating; the contagion effect – namely the fact that how much and what kind of food people eat is affected by choices of the persons in their social network (Christakis and Fowler 2007); the hyperbolic discount rate of future health gains compared to present enjoyment (Pampel et al. 2010); adaptive preferences (Sen 1997); budget constraints and poor information (Pampel et al. 2010).

The soft-paternalist arguments claim that such arbitrary, irrational factors and framing effects curtail our autonomy (Skipper 2012). In response, Del Savio (2015) argues that the soft-paternalist argument proves *too much:* it is problematic because the empirical conditions that undermine human agency generalize widely.[2] People rarely have control over their opportunity sets, often activate neural networks shaped by their past habits, and are often influenced by framing effects as well as by the choices of their friends and relatives; persons normally try to realize hard-wired urges and desires, which are suboptimal in a post-Pleistocene environment. If these criteria are used to exclude human volitions from the realm of authentic human choices, there are very few instances of authentic exercises of human agency and freedom – a more problematic conclusion (both phenomenologically and ethically) than the paternalism the arguments aim to avoid. Skep-ticism about agency in the realm of food choice generalizes and leads to a generalized skepticism about human agency as such.

Anti- (principled) anti-paternalists often remark that a socio-economic patterning of food access, due to transformations in retail geography, is among the causes of inequality in obesity and food-related disease distribution, although the evidence for such a claim has been disputed (White 2007). Even if empirically correct, this claim does not show that the habits of low-SES individuals are irrational or non-autonomous, since shopping in the nearest shop (which may contain only a few healthy options) may be the most rational thing to do in light of a trade-off between free time and healthier food, given that free time is a scarce resource.

Finally, as Del Savio (2015) points out, the claim that the budget constraints people face are the outcome of unjust or inequitable social systems does not *in itself* demonstrate that the choices of low-SES individuals are less rational and autonomous than those of high-SES individuals, who have a lot of money to spend on food. Low-SES individuals with tight budgets may be as rational (or irrational) in their choice of food, given their budget or time constraints, as high-SES individuals with more money to spend on healthier food. Empirical arguments showing that the preference for more caloric food is influenced by all kinds of biases do not show that high-SES individuals with more money to spend are freer from cognitive biases, framing effects, hard-wired environmentally suboptimal drives, and other forms of heteronomy. The choices of low-SES individuals are as worthy of respect, *qua* instances of autonomous human agency, as those of high-SES individuals, even when they lead to worse health expectations. Even if there is an injustice in unequal access to adequate nutrition across different SES groups, it does not make persons from lower SES less capable of rational or autonomous choice.

The DOHaD theory: how adult health is programmed in utero and is affected by diet in previous generations

According to the boldest defenders of anti-paternalism, such as John Stuart Mill, interference with individual choices may be justified *for the sake of preventing harm to others*. Notice that I have written "may be" and not "are always" justified. According to the most plausible interpretation of Mill's *harm principle, harm to others* is only a *necessary condition* for the legitimacy of state interfer-ence. Whether such interference is justified *all things considered* depends on a complex balancing of the expected result of the policy, i.e., whether the utility deriving from prohibiting or regulating a certain conduct is greater than the utility lost as a result (Bonotti 2013).

A few recent seminal papers (Del Savio et al. 2015; Dupras et al. 2014; Hedlund 2012; Kollar and Loi 2015; Landecker 2011; Loi et al. 2013; Niculescu 2011; Rothstein et al. 2009; Stapleton et al. 2013) have explored the ethical, legal, sociological, and political implications of theories concerning the *developmental origin of health and disease* (DOHaD), also known as the "Barker Hypothesis" (Barker 1995). According to DOHaD theories, the health of children (F1 generation) is affected by events in the life course of mothers and possibly fathers (F0). The strongest evidence exists for the influence of *in utero* developmental effects on adult health outcomes. According to the Barker hypothesis, fetal development adapts to the *in utero* environment, which leads to maladaptation when a mismatch between the *in utero* and *post-natal* environment occurs. For example, the (F1) (children) generation of mothers (F0) who were pregnant with them during the Dutch Hunger Winter (a famine induced by a Nazi embargo in WW2) have a higher propensity to cardiovascular disease (Barker 1995; Langley-Evans 2009). Overeating has been tested in animal models, by feeding pregnant mice with a high-fat diet, leading to insulin resistance, abnormal cholesterol metabolism, higher blood pressure, increased adiposity, decreased muscle mass, reduced loco-motor activity, and accelerated puberty in the offspring. There is also evidence that overnutrition during prenatal life alters the appetite- and energy-regulating neural network of the hypothalamus (K. A. Lillycrop and Burdge 2011). Further intergenerational effects involving the F2 and F3 generations have been detected in animal models, involving transmission through both male and female lines (Drake and Liu 2010). For example, maternal low-protein diet (F0) affects the F1 generation *in utero* and until weaning; the breeding of females with control males generates a F3 generation in which altered metabolism is detectable.

Controlled experiments such as those needed to establish intergenerational effects on multiple generations are not feasible for humans, but epidemiological evidence indicates that food availability during the grandparents' childhood (F0 generation) influences the cardiovascular disease and diabetes risk in the F2 grand-offspring (Kaati et al. 2002). The apparent contradiction of those findings (grandchildren are negatively affected by *too much* food during their grandparents' childhood, while children are negatively affected by *too little* food during maternal gestation) can be reconciled in the DOHaD paradigm: it suggests that "fetal growth retardation followed by rapid 'catch-up growth' in childhood is a major risk factor for disease" (Langley-Evans 2009: 38).

The transgenerational etiology of non-communicable diseases has obvious implications for public health and social policy in obesity prevention (Niculescu 2011). The potential social implications are not limited to attention to maternal nutrition during gestation. It is remarkable that the "rapid catch-up growth in F0 leads to negative health impact in F2" causal link describes a *male-line* nutrition-related mechanism, i.e., one from grandfather nutrition to grandchildren disease susceptibility. Other cases of male-line-related transgenerational effects involve paternal mid-childhood tobacco smoking (linked to early growth in sons) and paternal betel nut chewing (influencing early onset of the metabolic syndrome) (Kaati et al. 2007).

Epigenetics as a molecular mechanism for DOHaD

The shifting interest of molecular biology and biostatistics from merely genetics to *epigenetics* is partially responsible for a resurgence of interest in DOHaD and the intergenerational transmission of acquired traits. Epigenetics refers to molecular mechanisms such as RNA sequencing, histone modification, and methylation analysis, that influence the *expression* of DNA information, i.e., the processes determining which proteins are produced and when. Gene expression is crucial for the molecular understanding of health and disease. The limits of a narrowly genetic understanding of disease and health have been revealed by technical progress in the sequencing of the entire human genome. With a huge amount of genetic information already generated and analyzed, it has finally become clear that genomics cannot contribute substantially to advances in diagnostics and therapy, unless it will be coupled with a more thorough understanding of "gene x environment" interactions. Epigenetics – the science that deals with gene expression – is naturally seen as the nexus of a major shift from reductionist accounts of genetics to system thinking in biology. Thus, progresses in epigenetics are believed by many to overcome the nature/nurture divide and clear the path for convergence between social epidemiology (and social science) and molecular approaches in biomedicine (Landecker and Panofsky 2013).

Unsurprisingly, publications connecting epigenetics and DOHaD are steadily growing, and an entire new field of "epigenetic epidemiology" has emerged (Ebrahim 2012). Animal studies are used to provide "proof of concept" of epigenetic mechanisms involved in the intergenerational transmission of acquired susceptibilities. For example, some studies show that maternal dietary protein restriction during pregnancy leads specifically to a decrease in the methylation status of specific genes in the liver of the offspring after weaning (Lillycrop et al. 2005). One hypothesized epigenetic mechanism for DOHaD is the acquisition of early, lineage-specific methylation during early prenatal development, affecting gene expression and therefore metabolic capacity until adulthood. In order to explain the transmission of acquired susceptibilities to subsequent generations, one hypothesized molecular mechanism is that conditions affecting the maternal environment (F0) or post-natal events in the offspring (F1) create patterns of DNA methylation in the sperm cells or oocytes of the offspring (F1) that are transmitted to the grandchild (F2) if they are not "erased" upon fertilization (Drake and Liu 2010; Lillycrop and Burdge 2011). Both mechanisms can lead to increased susceptibility to obesity in the offspring or grand-offspring of both malnourished and obese parents (Lillycrop and Burdge 2011).

Animal studies have detected differential methylation in genes affecting fetal and offspring development, leading to characteristic phenotypes affected by differences in the maternal intake of nutrients. The exemplary case is the agouti mice, where different nutrients in maternal diet induce differences in the coat color of the offspring, an effect that is associated with varying degrees of methylation in genes affecting pigmentation. In humans, some methylation differences have been detected in the blood of individuals who were exposed to famine *in utero* during the Dutch Winter, compared to same-sex siblings who were not exposed (Kaati et al. 2007).

This growing body of scientific findings suggests the emergence of a new biological paradigm that challenges the standard picture of heredity established during the twentieth century. The relative intergenerational stability of the genome, in the Mendelian picture, derives from the physiological isolation of the germ-line, preventing direct causality from the environment to the genotype. In this paradigm, biological inheritance is not unaffected by the natural and social environment experienced by the parents. In the neo-Darwinian synthesis, adaptation to changing circumstances is achieved through Darwinian selection of the fittest. Apart from the population-level variation in relative frequencies of different alleles, environmental events do not shape the biological components of heredity, with only the exception of events, such as nuclear explosions and other kinds of heavy pollution, that favor an abnormal rate of genetic mutations. After the new-Darwinian synthesis, the capacity of social institutions to *biologically* shape the destiny of future generations was regarded to be insignificant, since the germ-line does not carry information reflecting the experience of previous generations, with the liberating result that every generation – in a sense – starts anew. By contrast, the label of "soft inheritance" – inheritance affected by the environment or phenotype of the parents – is often used to group together (once discredited) Lamarckian and neo-Lamarckian modes of inheritance (Jablonka and Lamb 2005; Lock 2013; Meloni 2015). Future generations also inherit an epigenome that bears traces of the adaptation of their parents to a specific environment, and these traces are liable to be further affected (improved or worsened) by virtue of interacting with new environments.

With the possibility of intergenerational DOHaD and the epigenetic heredity of acquired traits, the scope for human responsibility in influencing hereditary features is significantly enlarged, at the individual as well as the social level (Hedlund 2012). What each one of us transmits to his or her child, and what we as a society transmit collectively, is affected by our everyday habits, which are influenced by political and economic choices, including those concerning our fundamental social institutions, shaping our circumstances.

"The biological is political": implications of the new biology for the paternalism/anti-paternalism debate

What this emerging body of science illustrates is the possibility that what we eat today affects the health of our children tomorrow. What are the potential moral and political implications of this fascinating scientific possibility?

On the one hand, this biological picture undermines the idea that obesity (and other food-behavior-related risk factors) is entirely a matter of individual responsibility. What appear to be outcomes of "personal" lifestyle choices may, in more than one way, have been influenced prenatally or even pre-conceptionally. At the same time, *additional* responsibilities for pregnant mothers, and more generally parents, potential parents, and social institutions, emerge (Chadwick and O'Connor 2013; Hedlund 2012). The argument that "right or wrong, it's my body" can no longer be maintained, because what happens *to* and *in* one's body can induce harmful predispositions in the body of one's offspring.

The possibilities of DOHaD and epigenetic epidemiology may ground, as the evidence accumulates, a non-paternalist argument for interfering with "individual" food choices. Discoveries in DOHaD and epigenetics may in the near future justify public health interventions, as well as policy interventions in different areas of social work (Combs-Orme 2013) that are not premised on a paternalist justification, because they aim to avoid the inheritance of disadvantageous epigenetic traits. In a manner reminiscent of the taxation of inheritance, policy may be justified as aiming at a reduction of inherited inequalities in the susceptibility to non-communicable diseases. Its goal would be to prevent the intergenerational transmission of inequality, which would derive – because of intergenerational DOHaD and epigenetics – from present inequalities in parental diets.

More analytically, at least two (non-paternalist) "arguments from future benefits" (Del Savio et al. 2015: 3) can be distinguished. The first argument relies on two premises: (1) the state should strive to *achieve equality of opportunity* among citizens in the same generation; and (2) *equality of opportunity* in one generation (F1) is affected by the distribution of *outcomes* in the previous (F0) generation. One may refer to this as the "social justice" argument.

This argument can be formulated by appealing to more than one specific conception of equality of opportunity. Luck-egalitarian equality of opportunity requires similar welfare outcomes (among the similarly prudent) for members of the F1 generation irrespective of their epigenetic or DOHaD-related brute luck. If welfare in F1 is influenced by the food choices of F0, some people in F1 suffer opportunity disadvantage as a result of F0 food choices, through no fault of their own. This violates the luck-egalitarian principle of equality of opportunity (Loi et al. 2013). Rawlsian equality of opportunity requires similar opportunities of success irrespective of initial social class of origin. Since obesity and other food choices are socially patterned, the children of low-SES parents in F1 who inherit unfavorable susceptibilities suffer opportunity disadvantage *reflecting their initial social class of origin*. This violates Rawlsian equality of opportunity (Kollar and Loi 2015; Loi et al. 2013; Stapleton et al. 2013). More generally, an argument can be made that, if equality of opportunity (in F1) ought morally to be achieved, interfering with the dietary choices of persons F0 is justified, as a means to preventing the transmission of disadvantageous susceptibilities to members of the next generation (F1). The refusal to interfere with parental dietary freedom would permit unequal opportunities between the offspring of more well-off and less well-off children.

Summing up, the *social justice* argument is grounded in the moral/political imperative to achieve equality of opportunity between persons in the *same* generation. It focuses on inequalities that have an intergenerational cause, those due to different food choices by individuals in the previous generation (which may have a socio-structural cause). DOHaD and epigenetic theories provide a possible explanation of the biological mechanisms contributing to the inheritance of these inequalities.

The second argument, by contrast, is grounded in the moral/political imperative to achieve some kind of equality among individuals in *different generations.* Let us call this the "intergenerational justice" argument. It focuses on average individuals in different *generations* (or birth cohorts), and asks whether they all have different expectations of well-being, or opportunities for welfare, through no fault of their own.

Suppose that the average individual in F0 has comparably healthier food habits than an average individual in F1. F1 is the first generation where consumption of energy-dense, nutritionally poor food becomes widespread. As a result, the average individual in F1 transmits unfavorable susceptibilities to her F2 child. The average F2 individual begins her life with a kind of "epigenetic handicap," meaning that, other things being equal, average individuals of F2 are more likely to suffer from cardiovascular diseases, hypertension, obesity, etc., than their F1 parents were. Since F1 owe their better health prospects to the healthier habits of their parents (F0), such inequality appears undeserved and unjust. It is as if the F1 generation passes an "epigenetic debt" to future generations: by departing from the normal, healthier, epigenome inherited by F0, as an effect of its malnutrition, F1 does not give F2 (inheriting an altered epigenome) an equal opportunity to reach equally good health outcomes. Such (underserved) inequalities – i.e., the fact that the average individual of F2 has worse health expectations than the average member of F1 through no fault of her own – arguably constitute an instance of intergenerational injustice (Del Savio et al. 2015).

The feminist rejoinder: will pregnant women be oppressed by DOHaD theories and epigenetics?

In a recent *Nature* comment (Richardson et al. 2014), Sarah S. Richardson and colleagues warn against the tendency to popularize findings in DOHaD and epigenetics that lend support to moralizing the behavior of pregnant mothers. They argue that science communication should avoid attitudes that might be stigmatizing against low-SES women for what are perceived as imprudent choices during gestation. That attitude fails to track the root causes of the problem – i.e., unequal social structures – and end up blaming the victim. Do the arguments developed in section 2 and 3 present us with the same risk? Clearly, they do. That means that a reasonable policy response to the injustice created by virtue of DOHaD and epigenetic effects must carefully avoid creating worse injustices (e.g., inequalities between men and women) than those it aims to prevent. How does this problem relate to the overall debate on public health and obesity?

First, caution is needed in science communication to avoid misunderstanding about the *severity* of the consequences imputed to the maternal and paternal food choices. The current evidence on epigenetic mechanisms of DOHaD and "Lamarckian" heredity is mainly supported by findings in animal models, while the evidence for humans is sparse but still not strong. So clearly the tendency by media outlets to over-emphasize those findings should be countenanced by a proper appreciation of the *degree* of risk involved and of the *strength* of the evidence for it.

The arguments of intragenerational and intergenerational justice offer a *pro tanto* reason for justice to interfere with the food-related lifestyle of pregnant women (or potentially, all prospective reproducers, since findings about male-line intergenerational transmission of epigenetic programming due to dietary factors are beginning to emerge). Interfering with the food choices of pregnant women and reproducers in this perspective is *not* paternalistic. But it may be objectionable for other reasons, for instance because these narratives *express* a view of women as "fetal containers" (Annas 1986). The criminalization of unhealthy parental food behavior – which would clearly be a disproportionate response to DOHaD findings – can also be counter-productive in terms of public health, for instance because it may keep low-SES women away from clinical care (Loi and Nobile 2015).

Conclusions

These findings and arguments can be used to respond to liberal (anti-paternalistic) arguments according to which individual food choices are outside of the scope of governmental action. The point of these arguments is not to criminalize or blame low-SES parents for whom it may be (prudentially) rational to eat in a certain way – but instead to support the reform of those social and economic circumstances that *make it* rational for low-SES parents, for example, to buy ready-made, calorie-rich, but poorly nutritious food in the first place. According to transgenerational DOHaD and epigenetic theories, these reforms are owed to future generations.

Admittedly, self- or other-imposed healthy diets and lifestyles can be suboptimal in overall utility terms for some people (because they are perceived as oppressive, or because a healthier and longer life could be for some persons worse overall than a shorter life with plenty of episodes of immediate gratification). If individuals were the only persons affected by *their own* diets, this could well justify an anti-paternalist complaint against state interference. However, if the hypothesis of intergenerational transmission of adult disease risk is correct, there is a rejoinder to this objection, namely that the state owes to future generations that they inherit a more beneficial and equal epigenome, and that they avoid inheriting risk factors for adult diseases. Achieving this aim may justify interfering with the liberty in food choices of individuals who already exist. Public interference with eating habits in a population is, in other words, a matter of other-regarding, not of paternalist, moral obligation.

In conclusion, food ethics in an intergenerational perspective avoids the problem of paternalism altogether, but it may turn out to be problematic in different ways, for instance because it may turn out to be very difficult to assess findings of DOHaD and epigenetics in humans, to the point necessary for evidence-based policy. Moreover, it may lead – if couched in unsuitable narratives – to a disproportionate restriction of the freedom of pregnant mothers, or, if the rationale of such policy is misunderstood, to blaming low-SES individuals for the worse health prospects of their children. Public health personalities, ethicists, sociologists, and political scientists developing such arguments should proceed with caution.

Notes

1 According to John Stuart Mill, higher pleasures and the interests of man "as a progressive being" (Mill 1859) engage human agential capacities more fully than pleasure as a passive state, the ultimate constituent of happiness as previous utilitarians, such as Bentham or James Mill, had conceived it.

2 It is also problematic because, on the other hand, it concedes the crucial principled libertarian premise against paternalism.

References

Anand, P., & Gray, A. (2009) "Obesity as Market Failure: Could a 'Deliberative Economy' Overcome the Problems of Paternalism?," *Kyklos* 62(2): 182–190.

Annas, G. J. (1986) "Pregnant Women as Fetal Containers," *Hastings Center Report* 16(6): 13–14.

Barker, D. J. (1995) "Fetal Origins of Coronary Heart Disease," *BMJ (Clinical Research Ed.)* 311(6998): 171–174.

Bonotti, M. (2013) "Legislating about Unhealthy Food: A Millian Approach," *Ethical Perspectives* 20(4): 555–589.

Chadwick, R., & O'Connor, A. (2013) "Epigenetics and Personalized Medicine: Prospects and Ethical Issues," *Personalized Medicine* 10(5): 463–471.

Christakis, N. A., & Fowler, J. H. (2007) "The Spread of Obesity in a Large Social Network over 32 Years," *New England Journal of Medicine* 357(4): 370–379.

Combs-Orme, T. (2013) "Epigenetics and the Social Work Imperative," *Social Work* 58(1): 23–30.

Del Savio, L. (2015) "Determinants of Food Choices as Justifications for Public Health Interventions," in T. Schramme (Ed.), *New Perspectives on Paternalism and Health Care*, Dordrecht: Springer International Publishing, pp. 247–262.

Del Savio, L., Loi, M., & Stupka, E. (2015) "Epigenetics and Future Generations," *Bioethics* 29(8): 580–587.

Drake, A. J., & Liu, L. (2010) "Intergenerational Transmission of Programmed Effects: Public Health Consequences," *Trends in Endocrinology & Metabolism* 21(4): 206–213.

Dupras, C., Ravitsky, V., & Williams-Jones, B. (2014) "Epigenetics and the Environment in Bioethics," *Bioethics* 28(7): 327–334.

Dworkin, G. (2010) "Paternalism," in *The Stanford Encyclopedia of Philosophy*, viewed 15 November 2015, http://plato.stanford.edu/archives/sum2010/entries/paternalism/.

Ebrahim, S. (2012) "Epigenetics: The Next Big Thing," *International Journal of Epidemiology* 41: 1–3.

Feinberg, J. (1984) *The Moral Limits of the Criminal Law*, New York: Oxford University Press.

Gortmaker, S. L., Swinburn, B., Levy, D., Carter, R., Mabry, P. L., Finegood, D., Huang, T., Marsh, T., & Moodie, M.L. (2011) "Changing the Future of Obesity: Science, Policy and Action," *Lancet* 378(9793): 838–847.

Hedlund, M. (2012) "Epigenetic Responsibility," *Medicine Studies* 3(3): 171–183.

Jablonka, E., & Lamb, M. J. (2005) *Evolution in Four Dimensions: Genetic, Epigenetic, Behavioral, and Symbolic Variation in the History of Life*, Cambridge, MA: MIT Press.

Kaati, G., Bygren, L. O., & Edvinsson, S. (2002) "Cardiovascular and Diabetes Mortality Determined by Nutrition During Parents' and Grandparents' Slow Growth Period," *European Journal of Human Genetics* 10(11): 682–688.

Kaati, G., Bygren, L. O., Pembrey, M., & Sjöström, M. (2007) "Transgenerational Response to Nutrition, Early Life Circumstances and Longevity," *European Journal of Human Genetics* 15(7): 784–790.

Kollar, E., & Loi, M. (2015) "Prenatal Equality of Opportunity," *Journal of Applied Philosophy* 32(1): 35–49.

Landecker, H. (2011) "Food as Exposure: Nutritional Epigenetics and the New Metabolism," *BioSocieties* 6(2): 167–194.

Landecker, H., & Panofsky, A. (2013) "From Social Structure to Gene Regulation, and Back: A Critical Introduction to Environmental Epigenetics for Sociology," *Annual Review of Sociology* 39(1): 333–357.

Langley-Evans, S. C. (2009) "Nutritional Programming of Disease: Unravelling the Mechanism," *Journal of Anatomy* 215(1): 36–51.

Lillycrop, K. A., & Burdge, G. C. (2011) "Epigenetic Changes in Early Life and Future Risk of Obesity," *International Journal of Obesity* 35(1): 72–83.

Lillycrop, K. A., Phillips, E. S., Jackson, A. A., Hanson, M. A., & Burdge, G. C. (2005) "Dietary Protein Restriction of Pregnant Rats Induces and Folic Acid Supplementation Prevents Epigenetic Modification of Hepatic Gene Expression in the Offspring," *The Journal of Nutrition* 135(6): 1382–1386.

Lock, M. (2013) "The Epigenome and Nature/Nurture Reunification: A Challenge for Anthropology," *Medical Anthropology* 32(4): 291–308.

Loi, M., Del Savio, L., & Stupka, E. (2013) "Social Epigenetics and Equality of Opportunity," *Public Health Ethics* 6(2): 142–153.

Loi, M., & Nobile, M. (2015) "The Moral and Legal Relevance of DOHaD Effects for Pregnant Mothers," in C. S. Rosenfeld (Ed.), *The Epigenome and Developmental Origins of Health and Disease*, Amsterdam: Elsevier Science Ltd, pp. 463–481.

Meloni, M. (2015) "Heredity 2.0: The Epigenetics Effect," *New Genetics and Society* 34(2): 117–124.

Mill, J. S. (1859) *On Liberty*, London: Penguin Classics.

Niculescu, M. (2011) "Epigenetic Transgenerational Inheritance: Should Obesity-prevention Policies be Reconsidered?," *Synesis: A Journal of Science, Technology, Ethics, and Policy* 2(1): G18–G26.

Page, K. A., Seo, D., Belfort-DeAguiar, R., Lacadie, C., Dzuira, J., Naik, S., Amarnath, S., Constable, R.T., Sherwin, R.S., & Sinha, R. (2011) "Circulating Glucose Levels Modulate Neural Control of Desire for High-Calorie Foods in Humans," *The Journal of Clinical Investigation* 121(10): 4161–4169.

Pampel, F. C., Krueger, P.M., & Denney, J. T. (2010) "Socioeconomic Disparities in Health Behaviors," *Annual Review of Sociology* 36: 349.

Richardson, S. S., Daniels, C. R., Gillman, M. W., Golden, J., Kukla, R., Kuzawa, C., & Rich-Edwards, J. (2014) "Society: Don't Blame the Mothers," *Nature* 512(7513): 131–132.

Rothstein, M. A., Cai, Y., & Marchant, G. E. (2009) "The Ghost in Our Genes: Legal and Ethical Implications of Epigenetics," *Health Matrix* 19(1): 1–62.

Sen, A. K. (1997) *Choice, Welfare and Measurement*, Cambridge, MA: Harvard University Press.

Skipper, R. A. (2012) "Obesity: Towards a System of Libertarian Paternalistic Public Health Interventions," *Public Health Ethics* 5(2): 181–191.

Stapleton, G., Schröder-Bäck, P., & Townend, D. (2013) "Equity in Public Health: An Epigenetic Perspective," *Public Health Genomics* 16(4): 135–144.

Sunstein, C. R., & Thaler, R. R. (2008) *Nudge: Improving Decisions About Health, Wealth, and Happiness* (1st ed.), New Haven, CT: Yale University Press.

Wansink, B., & Cheney, M. M. (2005) "Super Bowls: Serving Bowl Size and Food Consumption," *JAMA* 293(14): 1723–1728.

White, M. (2007) "Food Access and Obesity," *Obesity Reviews* 8: 99–107.

14

HEALTH LABELING

Morten Ebbe Juul Nielsen[1]

Introduction

This paper focuses on a particular, and important, aspect of food labeling, namely what is termed health labeling (henceforth HL). HL can take the form of a positive health claim ("this product is very healthy"), but it might also be a warning ("overconsumption of this product is unhealthy"). Furthermore, HL can take the form of a claim about the process or production of a given product ("organic," "non-GMO," etc.), associated rightly or wrongly with health effects. HL raises many different concerns, but the focus here is on two: (1) epistemic and empirical problems concerning, mainly, which features to pick out as relevant for a "health impact" assessment of food products; and (2) more general normative problems with HL.

At first blush, given some level of optimism about the trustworthiness of producers or state agencies issuing the health claims, HL might seem quite innocuous and uncontroversial. After all, since the objective is to make the consumer's choice easier – to make the healthy choice the easy choice, as the slogan goes – and given that no one is actually forcing consumers to follow the easy choice, how could HL ever give rise to serious problems?

To get a taste, as it were, of the challenges, consider the following. Almost any food product on the market is not unhealthy if consumed in moderation or if its consumption goes hand in hand with a balanced diet and some amount of physical exercise.[2] Hence, very few – if any – food products are unhealthy *per se*. Some products that many take to be less than healthy might have surprising health benefits if consumed in the right proportion, or for specific people (e.g., alcohol). And all products, including those that are commonly associated with healthy living, turn out to be quite unhealthy if consumed in large enough doses. Moreover, for most of the commonly accepted health indicators, e.g., fat or salt, risk cannot plausibly be said to be linked to the consumption of a *specific* product (say, dried meat, which is normally quite high in salt) but depends on one's overall diet, or pattern of consumption.

This article attempts to argue that HL is far from uncontroversial, epistemically or normatively. We normally assume that companies (whether they are producers or retailers) have at least a qualified right of free speech. Hence, unless one can point to obvious countervailing normative considerations – the right of the consumer not to be misled, health safety concerns, etc. – it would seem that companies have a right to label their products as they see fit, including a right to "health label" their products. This necessarily involves a very large grey zone. Of course there will be examples where health labeling is uncontroversially morally innocent (e.g., labeling water as "calorie neutral") or uncontroversially morally wrong (e.g., labeling bacon with "cures cancer"). Other cases will be less clear. Yet there are studies that indicate that HL can be beneficial for the consumer (see, e.g., Evans et al. 2008), and it would be a mistake not to take that possibility into consideration. If not otherwise stated, I take promotion of health/prevention (or alleviation) of disease to be not only a prudential, but also a morally desirable goal, at least *ceteris paribus*. However, all things are not always equal: health is not the only moral desideratum, nor the moral baseline, and other values might conflict with the health promotion/disease prevention goals associated with HL. This issue is discussed in section 3 below.

Some final remarks: while the literature on health labeling is sparse, there has been a lot of work done on branding and the normative concerns associated with it. Branding is a broader concept, that of establishing or trying to establish a clear and stable connection between a company or a specific product and some special value(s), differentiating the company or the product from others. *Health branding* accordingly refers to branding that attempts to link some product or company with health or health benefits. HL is obviously one of the most direct ways of trying to build a brand reputation for a company or a product, establishing such a link in the minds and preferences of consumers. Branding is a much-discussed topic in business ethics and in the literature of Corporate Social Responsibility, and it opens up a wider range of normative concerns than HL. For instance, what if a company whose brand, widely and justifiably associated with low-calorie products, launches a very energy-rich chocolate bar without clearly stating that this product is qualitatively different from the rest of their products? Moreover, branding can take a variety of forms, some of them raising issues of discrimination (e.g., using only slender, young, white female models in campaigns), "stealth marketing" such as the use of subtle smells and sounds to encourage consumption, and so on that are mostly beyond the scope of this essay. Nevertheless, one should not draw too sharp a line between HL and health branding, precisely because HL is a key component in health branding. Many of the issues raised in the following are thus as relevant for health branding as they are for HL.

What is health labeling?

As mentioned above, HL is a subpart of health branding, which can be seen as a part of a company's broader marketing effort. Marketing is often the subject of criticism in the literature, and food marketing is far from an exception. To wit,

> Food marketing has a negative impact on the nation's diet and hence health. . . . Marketing is relentless, is overwhelming in amount, is carried out in many new forms referred to by the industry as 'stealth' approaches . . . and hence erodes the nation's goal of fostering healthier living.
>
> (Brownell et al. 2010)

HL is obviously a part of the marketing strategy of many food companies. But while many aspects of marketing and branding are discussed and often criticized in business ethics and related academic fields, HL has not drawn much attention. One reason for this might be that HL can be seen as an antidote to some of those features of food marketing that are common objects of critique, above all that food marketing is manipulative, makes us eat too much and eat "unhealthy," "industrial," "unnecessary" food. HL seems, almost by definition, to promote a healthier pattern of consumption.

What is health labeling, more precisely? Following Anker et al. (2011),[3] one can distinguish three components of the more general health-branding concept, namely *functional* claims, *process* claims, and *symbolic* content. Functional claims state or imply a connection between some properties of the product and physical or mental health. "Omega-3 is good for your heart" would be a positive such claim; "reduced salt" a negative. Process claims pertain to the production of the product, where it again is stated or implied that the process itself means that the product has certain health-conducive properties, or at least that they are healthier than some relevant counterpart. For instance, "organic" implies a certain method of production that many consumers think is inherently healthy. Naturally, functional and process claims often overlap. A given product, say organic vegetables, can be construed as healthy both because of its intrinsic properties and because of its method of manufacturing. Lastly, and slightly more complex, is the symbolic content. Often, marketing of "healthy" foods is heavily laden with symbolism easily associated by consumers with a "healthy lifestyle." Note the almost complete absence of overweight or (unimaginable!) obese models in the promotion of "healthy" foods and drinks, for instance. Other examples would be the use of sports stars as promoters, or the use of certain (hard to specify, but easily recognizable) romanticized, rural, "calm" sceneries or settings in commercials, conveying not only a message about health, but a complete lifestyle associated with the product.

Case study: the Nordic "keyhole mark" food label system

The Nordic "keyhole" (Danish: "Nøglehulsmærket") label has been operating in Denmark since 2007, and for some years more in Norway and Sweden. The label is trademarked and owned by the Swedish National Food Agency (Livsmedelsverket), a government-run institution. Experts of that institution assess, when prompted by producers, whether a given product can be labeled with the keyhole mark. The label is put on food products selected according to strict criteria. They should, as compared to similar products within the relevant category, either contain more dietary fibers or whole grains, or contain less or healthier fat, or contain either less salt or sugar; meeting just one of these criteria is sufficient. A string of products that are deemed non-healthy cannot be labeled with the keyhole mark (e.g., fizzy drinks and candy). As of 2015 around 2,000 products on the Danish market are labeled with the keyhole mark. The system is optional for producers, and the system does not itself screen products unless prompted by producers.[4]

Some of the criticisms leveled against this program are instructive. First, since the system is optional, a "better" product that is not included in the system might be placed beside an inferior product with the label, but the label will lead most consumers to believe that the one with the label is healthier. Given market mechanisms, this should not be a major worry, since producers can be assumed to be keen to get the label on their products if possible. Still, small or new companies, as well as foreign producers, might be at a disadvantage here. Second, it might serve as an obstacle to improvements (such as salt reduction, etc.) to products that won't be able to achieve keyhole status anyway, because they cannot "win" in comparison to other products. Third, a very different form of critique raised primarily outside academic circles accuses the products marked with the keyhole mark for being of low gustatory quality.

The label is recognized as a health mark by a majority of consumers, while it is uncertain how many consumers know that the mark signifies not "healthy as such" but "healthier by one criterion as compared to similar products." No surveys have been made to establish whether consumers trust the state-agency-run label more than health labels/health branding made by private companies, but it is likely that this is the case.

Epistemic and empirical complexities

In the above, one of the complexities of HL was spelled out. The most basic empirical challenge concerns the assumption that must underlie any health label claim: that we can say that consumption of this product really *is* healthy. However, we will recall that in practice, no (legal) product is healthy or unhealthy in itself; rather, it is one's pattern of consumption that is healthy or unhealthy, in combination with other factors such as physical exercise. What we called *functional* claims are, in the views of most specialists, highly dubious (see, e.g., Cowburn and Stockley 2005; Grunert and Wills 2007). Note that there are two problems at play here. On the one hand, it is hard to claim that a product is healthy (or unhealthy) in itself, and this seems to undermine the justifiability of using HL. On the other hand, since almost all products can be healthy if consumed in moderation and as part of an overall healthy diet, one might say that almost *all* products could be labeled as healthy – which wouldn't be very helpful for the consumer. How to carve out a definition of healthy products that steers a course between these extremes is not immediately clear.

Anker et al. (2011) agree on the point that no single food product is healthy or unhealthy in itself (or, at the very least, that such claims are extremely dubious), but they argue that we need to distinguish between narrow functional claims (roughly, "*this* product will improve your health") and broad functional claims, where the latter is a claim that "intentionally conveys that a food product, consumed as a part of a specific type of lifestyle, can promote health" (Anker et al. 2011). In other words, if a functional health claim somehow drives the consumer towards a more healthy pattern of consumption overall (i.e., it goes hand in hand with other, healthier choices), or consolidates an already healthy pattern of consumption, then a given (broad) functional claim is not spurious.

At first blush, the distinction seems sound. Given that healthy eating concerns one's overall diet rather than specific products, a focus on the former makes more sense than the latter. And it is not unimaginable that picking up one healthy item might trigger a chain of effects where one becomes more likely to pick up another. However, the reverse might also be true: by buying one "healthy" product, you are "allowed" to pick up another, less healthy one. Another concern is whether the distinction, or at least the definition of broad functional claims, is really helpful. The definition might be overly inclusive in the following sense: if it suffices for a product to be labeled as healthy if it somehow drives or consolidates a healthy pattern of consumption, then almost all products *could* be labeled as healthy. Alcohol, for instance, seems to be slightly beneficial if consumed in moderation (see di Castelnuovo 2006). Moving from total non-consumption to light to moderate is, then, a drive towards a healthier diet! But intuitively, few would find it plausible to label beer and wine as healthy. (Those of us that have this conviction might of course be wrong about that.) On the other hand, the definition might be under-inclusive if it excludes products that *could* be part of a healthy diet but fail, for whatever reason, to contribute to promoting or sustaining a healthy diet generally. It might then be contended that what is central to the definition of broad functional claims is the *intention* of producers or retailers. If they sincerely believe that a product would contribute to consumers' health by fostering a better pattern of consumption, then it would not be morally wrong to label the product as healthy. However, since we have no clear way of establishing the intentions of producers and retailers (and which agents with intentions are we talking about more specifically – Company executives? Shareholders? Someone else?), basing public policies and moral judgment on these intentions seem risky at best.

A specific epistemic problem with normative implications is whether or not HL in the form of functional claims will help undermine efforts to inform and educate the public about nutrition, cooking, and healthy lifestyles (Nestle 2002). The reasoning here is that by reducing the (perceived) need to learn nutritional facts, consumers are likely to become "nutritionally illiterate."

Hence, consumers will overall be worse off in terms of their ability to actually pursue a healthy lifestyle. HL could in some cases be held to undermine sound heuristics such as "prefer darker bread to lighter" if a particular type of white bread was labeled as healthy because it is, in fact, nutritionally better than other white breads (Anker et al. 2011). While this is a worry that should not be dismissed out of hand, it is not clear why this dynamic should *necessarily* take place. Public education about nutrition could act as a safeguard – for instance, by providing clear and reliable information about why a product is labeled unhealthy.

Process claims raise other problems. It is for instance not clear why organic production necessarily should lead to healthier products, even though many consumers seem to believe so.[5] This is of course a highly controversial issue, but quite a few papers and meta-analyses conclude that there are no or only very few demonstrable positive health effects of organic food (Dangour et al. 2009; Smith-Spangler et al. 2012). Clearly, in the absence of solid scientific evidence for the health qualities of certain processes, it is ethically dubious to claim or imply that those processes are healthy. And since it is at least an open question whether, e.g., organic or "non-GMO" processes *are* healthier than conventional production or products that contain GMOs, there is some reason to be skeptic about the justifiability of the (quite widespread and consciously orchestrated) association of organic/non-GMO and health.

There are at least two normative concerns that arise here. Most obvious is the classic issue of deceit or manipulation. The consumer should not be led to form beliefs about health properties that are epistemically unsound or downright false (this of course goes for both process and functional claims). Another problem, also relevant for both kinds of claims, concerns *market fairness*. It is probably safe to say that companies can gain a competitive edge when their products are viewed as healthy. A *zeitgeist* of "the somatic ethics" (Rose 2001) privileges health concerns almost over any other; hence, at least a substantial proportion of consumers are prone to prefer what they see as healthier products over less healthy. But if the process claim of organic products is empirically dubious, the market advantage gained by the association between "health" and "organic" is unfair to conventional producers.

General normative problems of HL

Having set out some of the key issues associated with HL due to the epistemic or empirical uncertainty of health functional and process claims, we can turn to other normative concerns.

Medicalization and the creation of undue concerns

Medicalization is the process whereby some element of everyday life not previously thought of as a health issue becomes subsumed under a medical discourse and treated as a health problem (Conrad 1992). A key example in the present context is obesity. While it is an overstatement to say that previously no one conceived obesity as a medical problem, surely there has been an explosion of concern over weight as a key indicator of health and especially obesity as a health problem. This can be seen from the discourse of the "obesity epidemic" arising in the early 2000s, where obesity has simply come to be labeled a disease by the American Medical Association.[6] But more generally, the very process of *eating* could be said to be medicalized. Consumers search the internet for advice on "super foods" that promise to protect us against cancers, lead to a longer life, etc., and certain ingredients or components of food are suddenly revealed as major killers. And obviously, the market for diet food remains enormous.

In itself, medicalization is not necessarily a problem. For instance, gastric bypass patients must eat according to a very strict diet regime, and diabetics can often increase well-being and alleviate symptoms by avoiding certain foods, following a diet, etc. However, companies can capitalize on our more general concern about food and health in various ways. The clear perceived association between slimness and health makes slimness one of the top markers of healthy food (see Anker et al. 2011). However, overweight (and obesity) are not necessarily indicators of bad health, and conversely, slimness is not a guarantee of good health. More generally, medicalization seems to go hand in hand with a more troubling issue, namely the creation of undue concerns about one's health, and HL could plausibly be one factor in this. By drawing attention to the health-related aspects of food products, the consumer is constantly reminded of the issue of health.

We need to ask the question: why are a substantial proportion of consumers so concerned about "healthy food"? Clearly, we are concerned about our health – let us set aside the complex cluster of questions about identity- or status-driven consumption that probably play a role here as well – so fostering already existing health concerns, or even creating new concerns, is a tempting strategy for companies that want to gain advantages in the marketplace (recall the discussion of unfair market advantage above.) Here, HL can work in two ways: it can signify that a given product is (part of) the solution, or more subtly, HL can signify that there is something to be worried about in the first place. By pointing to a potential "health problem" by indicating alleged health-promoting or -protecting properties, it can remind the consumer, or create the impression, that there is a health problem in the first place. A related problem is that concern can affect individuals negatively: feelings of worry and anxiety over the health status of oneself and/or one's family would count as a negative on any plausible account of well-being. This negative assessment of course needs to be balanced by positive contributions to the health of individuals that could be gained by HL (Hastings et al. 2008). Some worries, while in themselves negative, are proportionate to the behavioral changes they induce and the beneficial effects thereof. But not all worries are proportionate, and in any event, all effects need to be included in an all-things-considered assessment of HL. This includes the very many consumers who really have nothing to worry about, but who might be "pathologized" into believing that they are really at the risk of disease and need to eat healthier.[7]

This places HL in the public health ethics discussion of collateral damage and the prevention paradox (Rose 1985). For many public health interventions, it is ineffective to try to pinpoint high-risk individuals and focus on them while not involving the majority of the population. If we want an effect, we need to involve the mass of medium- and low-risk individuals, most of whom will not benefit at all from the intervention. To illustrate, imagine that we can prevent, postpone or alleviate some heart diseases affecting 0.5% of the population if we roll out health labels warning about "bad fats" on all products that contain certain forms of fat and/or "good fat" labels on the products that contain more beneficial forms of fat. For the vast majority, there is no benefit from such an intervention – but some of the non-affected will be harmed by undue concerns and worries. And since there really is no such thing as a free lunch – someone (the consumer) needs to pay for the intervention – everyone is actually harmed economically, albeit only very little.[8] This needs to be weighed against the probability of affecting someone (some proportion of the 0.5% at risk) positively. The question in these cases is always whether or to what extent we can justify harm to someone in order to save others from disease or premature death.

Healthism

In the above, some of the more specific concerns arising in conjunction with our medicalized discourse about food included medicalization *per se*, the creation of undue worries, and the exploitation of such concerns. This section deals with a broader subject, namely the privileging of health over other relevant components of the good (including, *inter alia*, personal preferences, gustatory qualities, and social and cultural meanings associated with food), and their relationship to HL.

The basic premise of (justifiable) HL must be that it can affect not just health, but more generally individual *well-being* in a positive way, at least *ceteris paribus*. Health is but one, albeit in many cases an important, instrumental aspect of well-being. Likewise, health is but one instrumental aspect of food. For example, food can be an expression of one's identity. Choosing what to eat, and thus expressing one's identity or, more prosaically, one's preferences, can be viewed as intrinsically valuable over and above its nutritional value. As J.S. Mill proffered, "If a person possesses any tolerable amount of common sense and experience, his own mode of laying out his existence is the best, not because it is the best in itself, but because it is his own mode" (Mill 1988: 135). Food is a source of pleasure, including (for some) even what might be called aesthetic pleasure, not incomparable to the pleasure derived from experiencing great art. And there are important social or cultural aspects of food. Sharing food – literally "breaking bread" – is probably one of the most deeply rooted social events or actions. Food and meals associated with important life events or rites of passage take on meanings that are not reducible to whether or not they are healthy. Cultural groups express their identity in their choices of foods and meals,[9] and if we are to show at least a modicum of respect for cultural groups, we need to accept – at least sometimes – that persons do not rank health above their culturally embedded preferences. Hence, an all-things-considered assessment is inadequate if it stops with health. Well-being needs to be included, and, depending on which palette of values one thinks is reasonable, such values as autonomy, self-expression, and respect for cultural values might also need to be included.

The HL-related concern here is that the focus on health implicit in HL drives consumers towards healthism and crowds out these other values associated with food. To take the simplest case where other values are set aside, if the justification of HL is promotion of well-being, then it is not sufficient to show that health is promoted. If the focus on health means that other sources of well-being (the ones just mentioned) are diminished or even cut off, then it might be the case that health is promoted, but well-being is diminished, all things taken into consideration. However, "healthism" is a rather vague term. Healthism denotes an undue individual and/or societal obsession with health, where health becomes the goal of a host of other activities that previously (and plausibly) were seen as goals in themselves. For example, sports in such a paradigm are not enjoyed for their playful aspects or for the spirit of fair play and friendly competition, but because they are healthy; one should have sex because it is good for cardiovascular health, and so on.[10] In the context of HL, by focusing on the health aspects of food, we forget the other values connected with food, and hence we risk losing important sources of well-being. Moreover, since health is not a goal in itself,[11] healthism in a certain way puts the cart before the horse. It might be the case that some individuals really do identify with the values of the somatic ethics and live their lives in order to be healthy. However, most individuals entertain a host of other projects – have other conceptions of the good, as it is said in political philosophy – and some individuals would prefer a little less health (or longevity) to a little more pleasure. By (contributing to) privileging health over any other concern, HL is, in a metaphorical sense at least, unfair to those individuals. More concretely, a critique of healthism can point to the health obsession that proves directly harmful to some individuals: eating disorders like anorexia (or the obsession with "eating right," termed orthorexia (see Bratman 1997)) could be linked to HL, since HL can be seen as a part of a culture fixating on health rather than other values.

How seriously should we take the concerns regarding healthism? It might be said that in itself, HL cannot create the obsession with health in question; since HL does not create the problem (if or to the extent it exists), HL is morally innocuous. The empirical premise is probably sound, yet the worry is that HL capitalizes on, or further accelerates, the general societal trend of healthism. This of course needs to be balanced against the potentially beneficial aspects of HL, an assessment beyond the scope of this article.

Summary and suggestions for practice

In this brief sketch of the most relevant ethical concerns regarding HL, the following stands out:

Health labeling is a form of health branding. HL is a subset of wider health branding practices. We can view HL as consisting of three aspects: functional claims about the health properties of products; process claims concerning the production of the products; and symbolic health claims, linking the product with ideals and images of "healthy living."

Healthy patterns of consumption, not healthy products. Few, if any, legal food products are healthy or unhealthy in themselves. Rather, what is or can be healthy are overall diets, or patterns of consumption, along with and in relation to other factors such as level of physical exercise, etc. The notion of "broad product claims" tries to take this into consideration; however, the distinction between narrow and broad functional claims is not entirely clear or unproblematic.

Process claims. While in principle it is easy to empirically confirm or disconfirm whether or not a product is, e.g., organic or GMO-free, the connection between these process claims and healthy properties is tenuous. However, many consumers simply equate these claims. This can be misleading, and it can lead to unfair market advantage.

Undermining sound heuristics. Some worry that HL leads to an undermining of sound heuristics of consumption and nutritional knowledge. However, it is not entirely clear that this process will take place, or that it could not be countervailed by, e.g., clearer information about the labeling itself.

Medicalization. HL can be seen as a part of an undesirable move towards subsuming more and more of our lives under a medicalized discourse. This can be misleading, and it can create undue worries about non-existing health problems.

Healthism. In terms not dissimilar to medicalization, HL can be seen as a part of an undesirable social trend towards an obsession with health, imperializing aspects of our lives previously enjoyed for their own sake. This could lead to a crowding out of other important aspects of food such as pleasure, aesthetic enjoyment, and the social and cultural values associated with food and the meal.

If both producers and consumers are to benefit from health labeling, then these issues need to be further analyzed and appropriate action taken. Especially important is the public's trust in the health claims made by food producers. This is complicated since the public's patterns of consumption are in effect a part of the answer as to whether a specific product *is* healthy. On the other hand, this should not be an excuse for producers or retailers for labeling just about anything as healthy. As some studies have indicated, there is a potential for good health effects (which hopefully cashes out as promotion of well-being) in health labeling. If producers free ride or manipulate by making spurious health claims, we risk undermining that potential. Therefore, some degree of conservatism and a quite high bar for when a product could rightfully be called "healthy" is probably called for.

Notes

1 Morten Ebbe Juul Nielsen is grateful for the support from Copenhagen University's 2016 fund-programs, GO—*Governing Obesity* and *Global Genes – Local Concerns.*
2 The terms "healthy" and "unhealthy" are generally meant to mean "probabilistically healthy" (or unhealthy). This is easiest to explain for the unhealthy category: a food product is probabilistically unhealthy if its consumption at some not unreasonable level and above leads to an increase in risk for increased mortality or morbidity.
3 See also Keller et al. (2008).

4 For an overview, see http://www.noeglehullet.dk/services/English/forside.htm, accessed 13 March 2015.
5 A recent Danish survey indicated that fully or predominantly organic *diets* or patterns of consumption *are* healthier, not because of any intrinsic qualities of organic foods, but because the overall pattern of consumption chosen by those who prefer organic products is healthier. See Denver and Christensen (2015).
6 See http://www.ama-assn.org/ama/pub/news/news/2013/2013–06–18-new-ama-policies-annual-meeting.page, accessed 23 June 2015.
7 As one of my colleagues – a very healthy, very fit woman of some age – said when we discussed health labeling: "I am fed up with seeing almost all the things in the grocery labeled as 'healthy' or 'fat-free' or whatever. It is this constant reminder that I should worry more about my own health that really bugs me."
8 Of course, *some* forms of health labeling might be quite costly in their effects for particular consumers. For instance, if a consumer is led to believe that organic food is healthier than conventional and wants to swap a 100% conventional diet for a similar 100% organic diet, then the average rise in cost is estimated to be 47%. See http://www.consumerreports.org/cro/news/2015/03/cost-of-organic-food/index.htm, accessed 28 June 2015.
9 I do not want to get embroiled in the discussion over whether we are sometimes justified in treating groups as "moral entities" or not. Suffice it to say that nothing important here hinges on whether one views groups as mere aggregations of individuals or not.
10 Clearly, healthism is closely connected to medicalization, but the core of the latter is problematizing something as unhealthy, whereas healthism more concerns (good) health as a goal in itself.
11 This is a complicated discussion. However, it can be averred that on most plausible theories of the (intrinsic) good, good health is merely a means (as indicated in the above, often an important means) to getting what is good in itself. For example, on a hedonistic theory of intrinsic value, only pleasure is enjoyable. Often, being in good health is a prerequisite for many pleasures. But that means that good health is an instrumental good, not an intrinsic one. Things are slightly more complicated for preferentialist theories of the good, for it might plausibly be said that we want – have a preference for – good health, at least *ceteris paribus*. However, on "objective" preferentialist theories, it seems that the reasoning just made about the value of health according to hedonist theories holds true as well. It is irrational to want good health merely for its own sake, but often rational to want it as a means to satisfying other preferences.

References

Anker, T. B., Sandøe, P., Kamin, T., & Kappel, K. (2011) "Health Branding Ethics," *Journal of Business Ethics* 104(1): 33–45.
Bratman, S. (1997) "Health Food Junkie," *Yoga Journal* September/October: 42–50.
Brownell, K. D., Kersh, R., Ludwig, D. S., Post, R. C., Puhl, R. M., Schwartz, M. B., & Willett, W. C. (2010) "Personal Responsibility and Obesity: A Constructive Approach to a Controversial Issue," *Health Affairs* 29(3): 379–387.
Conrad, P. (1992) "Medicalization and Social Control," *Annual Review of Sociology* 18: 209–232.
Cowburn, G., & Stockley, L. (2005) "Consumer Understanding and Use of Nutrition Labelling: A Systematic Review," *Public Health Nutrition* 8(01): 21–28.
Dangour, A. D., Dodhia, S. K., Hayter, A., Allen, E., Lock, K., & Uauy, R. (2009) "Nutritional Quality of Organic Foods: A Systematic Review, TL-90," *The American Journal of Clinical Nutrition* 90(3): 680–685.
Denver, S., & Christensen, T. (2015) "Organic Food and Health Concerns: A Dietary Approach Using Observed Data," NJAS—Wageningen Journal of Life Sciences 74(75): 9–15.
di Castelnuovo, A. (2006) "Alcohol Dosing and Total Mortality in Men and Women," *Archives of Internal Medicine* 166(22): 2437.
Evans, W. D., Blitstein, J., Hersey, J. C., Renaud, J., & Yarock, A. L. (2008) "Systematic Review of Public Health Branding," *Journal of Health Communication* 13(8): 721–741.
Grunert, K. G., & Wills, J. M. (2007) "A Review of European Research on Consumer Response to Nutrition Information on Food Labels," *Journal of Public Health* 15(5): 385–399.
Hastings G., Freeman J., Spackova R., & Siquier, P. (2008) "HELP: A European public health brand in the making," in Evans, D. W. and Hastings, G. (Eds.), *Public Health Branding: Applying Marketing for Social Change*, Oxford: Oxford University Press, pp. 93–107.
Keller, K. L., Apéria, T., & Georgson, M. (2008) *Strategic Brand Management: A European Perspective*, Upper Saddle River, NJ: Prentice Hall.

Mill, J. S. (1988) *Utilitarianism, On Liberty and Considerations on Representative Government*, edited by H. B. Acton, London: Dent.

Nestle, M. (2002) *Food Politics: How The Food Industry Influences Nutrition and Health*, Berkeley: University of California Press.

Rose, G. (1985) "Sick Individuals and Sick Populations," *International Journal of Epidemiology* 14(1): 32–38.

Rose, N. (2001) "The Politics of Life Itself," *Theory, Culture & Society* 18(6): 1–30.

Smith-Spangler, C., Brandeau, M. L., Hunter, G. E., Bavinger, J. C., Pearson, M., Eschbach, P.J., Sundaram,V., Liu, H., Schirmer, P., Stave, S., Olkin, I., & Bravata, D. M. (2012) "Are Organic Foods Safer or Healthier than Conventional Alternatives?: A Systematic Review," *Annals of Internal Medicine* 157(5): 348–366.

15

THE GOVERNANCE OF FOOD

Institutions and policies

Michiel Korthals

Introduction

Governance of food is confronted with huge challenges, like the fact that currently nearly one billion people are hungry, and more than two billion undernourished, malnourished, or over-nourished (obese). Moreover, the future prospects for food supply are grim: nine billion people will inhabit the earth in 2050, and climate change will in particular affect large agricultural areas, especially in the poor but populous South; so, food security will become an even bigger problem. Add to these the adverse effects of modern agricultural practices on the environment due inter alia to high levels of (chemical) inputs, increasing urbanization and the risks of food safety and public health effects of unhealthy and tasteless food supplies (Caraher and Coveney 2004).

The aims of food governance, whether international or national, are covered for the most part by these issues. A second aspect is important to consider when thinking about food governance, namely, who are the actors involved, and what are their responsibilities? Candidates are states, market parties, civil society organizations (NGOs), and international agencies. Thirdly, what ethical values are leading in establishing a strategy of food governance? Often, values like profits and shareholder value are recognized, but more ethical acceptable values are justice, participation, and the right to adequate food. The United Nations Declarations of Human Rights (UNDHR) underscores the right to adequate food, which includes the right of citizen-consumers to choose their own food. Moreover, the declaration mentions justice and freedom to live the life that citizen-consumers prefer, which guarantee them informed food choice in accord with their own perception of quality. Fourthly, food governance decides upon what policy instruments are used and their ethical status.

In this chapter we will discuss these four issues one by one. These four issues can be characterized by four main dilemmas of food governance that will be thematized here. First, small (food-supply oriented) or broad (food-demand oriented) aims of food governance; second, actor positions that are oriented toward the state, market, science, or civil society; third, food governance that is profit-oriented and top-down (be it from international or national organizations or local and regional) or works from below, taking into account justice and participation; and finally, whether the implementation should be legally compulsory, voluntary, manipulative, or a combination of these. In this article, these issues and dilemmas will be discussed from an ethical point of view.

In the last decade, food ethics has emerged as a new branch of inquiry into the intricacies of the agri-food sector (Have 2016; Herring 2014; Thompson 2014). Confronted with the challenges of food production and consumption, the current governance structure is, according to many, insufficient to tackle these problems; they are limited by the power and intangibility of large international corporations, increasing poverty for rural populations, and ideologies that often deny the seriousness of these problems and put responsibilities on the powerless (consumers). However, there are alternatives for a more democratic governance structure.

The aims of food governance: small or broad

One of the main ethical dilemmas of food policy is the range of objectives that this kind of policy should embrace: small, which means exclusively focusing on food production and consumption, or broad, oriented towards health, sustainability, animal welfare, and taste (quality). All these objectives have different, controversial definitions. A healthy food item for example can be interpreted as not "poisonous" and not causing a fever attack; but it can also be interpreted as not causing a chronic disease that appears after ten or more years (when taken all these times). The small objective is mostly called food security, which the United Nations defines as the "availability at all times of adequate world supplies of basic food-stuffs . . . to sustain a steady expansion of food consumption . . . and to offset fluctuations in production and prices" (United Nations 1975). However, food production can produce lots of food without the guarantee of access to food, in particular for the poor. Access and entitlement on the individual level are as important as supply. This statement is instructive, from the FAO Director General in 1982: "The ultimate objective of world food security should be to ensure that all people at all times have both physical and economic access to the basic food they need" (FAO, quoted in Shaw 2007: 241–242). Moreover, the dietary needs and preferences of people differ enormously. To address this, the United Nations introduced the Right to Food as a human right in 1966 at the International Covenant on Economic, Social and Cultural Rights (article 11), which encompasses the right to available, accessible, and adequate food. Adequate here meant "culturally acceptable." A FAO definition of 2001 reflects this so-defined Right to Food: "Food security [is] a situation that exists when all people, at all times, have physical, social and economic access to sufficient, safe and nutritious food that meets their dietary needs and food preferences for an active and healthy life" (FAO 2002). Finally, people should be able to prepare their food for consumption, and food systems should improve the capabilities that support these capacities. Many people of lower economic status (LES) do not have the skills required to prepare and cook healthy food, at least not those skills suitable to the dynamics and unhealthy effects (of highly processed food) of the current industrial food supply. This is convincingly demonstrated by the director of a Canadian food bank, Nick Saul, in his book about ways to overcome food poverty (Saul and Curtis 2013). Food poverty, not only in the sense of lack of money but also of skills, leads to obesity and its concurrent chronic diseases (Moss 2013; Roberts 2008).

These three additions to the small definition of food security should, according to many, be combined with other aims. The range of objectives can be more broadly defined than the implementation of this Right to Food, to include the environment, health, animal welfare, and quality or taste of food. Because food production and food consumption is at the crossroads of so many important public and private issues, it seems unwise to restrict the aims of food policy to the small definition.

Nevertheless, many international and national organizations still keep to the small definition of the aims of food governance. Article 1 of the statutes of the Codex Alimentarius, the United Nations organization of food law, declares that the Commission aims at protecting the health of consumers (in general not interpreted as free from chronic diseases) and ensuring fair practices in food trade. However, the codes for production, processing, manufacturing, transport, and storage practices of foods focus exclusively on food hygiene and food safety. Fair trade is scantily paid attention to. The World Trade Organization underlines food safety as well as its main aims when the protection of humans and animals is at stake (food safety). The Dutch government has the same opinion: food policy should not cover "vague" issues like the quality and taste of food; it "excluded the values of taste, convenience and pleasure from the start" (LNV 2005). It argues that the consumer has the responsibility to take care of taste and convenience of food. The government has the responsibility to regulate and monitor food safety, the environmental impact of food, and the healthiness of food (again, interpreted in a very limited sense); occasionally animal welfare and fair trade are also mentioned.

There are philosophical/ethical positions that agree with these exclusions of broader and "vague" aims like quality and taste, on the basis of the idea that food is a resource that enables people to live their own life (good life) and to live a life in peace with others (justice). Food belongs to the standard needs and endowments of every human being. Resourcism, as this position is called, has as its main proponent John Rawls. He conceptualizes resources in terms of the social primary goods, including basic rights, liberties, decent educational and employment opportunities, and wealth and income. Every rational person would want these goods, although people can differ in everything else (Rawls 1971: 92, and 1993: 181). The goods provide the "all-purpose means" (Rawls 1993: 76). Some, like Pogge, do not doubt that this definition of primary goods as resources can "take full account of the full range of diverse human needs and endowments" (2010: 31). Even from a very different ethical position, Singer (2006) argues in favor of the same: we need a neutral definition of food.

Others disagree, in particular Amartya Sen (2009). Sen argues that values, opinions, attitudes differ, and that universal principles should be broken down to context specific measures enabling flourishing of individuals. This context focusing is in line with what Pragmatists argue, namely that food is an essential aspect of livelihoods and individual flourishing (Korthals 2004). Food is an identity-achieving factor for humans, and it contributes to their quality of life. The values people connect to food items can differ enormously, and so can their definitions of good food. The context-laden meaning of food is not a barrier but a source of diversity (including biodiversity, because it stimulates the cultivation of very different plants) and of opportunities to taste the varieties of life. Food enables people to develop skills like cooking that they can be proud of. But more importantly, the social aspect of food is nearly always a rally point for being together, either in preparing and cooking, or in enjoying the meal. Food as meal encourages informal ties, without which no society can endure. Family ties and friendships develop during meals, in particular when people have the idea that they come together to enjoy a quality meal and that the food producer and the cook have made an effort to let them enjoy (even or better in particular in routinely daily meals). Quality and taste play an important role in every meal, and their definitions differ contextually.

There is good evidence that the "objective" taste of food is declining, because of the decrease, in industrialized fruit and vegetable production, of the (objective) micronutrients like phytonutrients responsible for a rich and varied taste (Estabrook 2012). The multiple qualities and tastes of food should therefore also be one of the main aspects of food governance. The social context of food supply and food governance should enable people sufficient opportunities to obtain food, assist people in making their own food choices, and enable people to learn and sustain skills for food consumption. The test for food governance and food policies is whether they can contribute to a productive, safe, sustainable, animal-friendly, healthy, tasteful, and equitable food system.

Social actors and institutions of food governance

In the western world, broadly speaking, at least four social actors contribute to food governance and its institutions: governments, private market parties, international organizations like Codex or FAO, and civil society organizations. Governments are mostly concerned with food security and food safety. Some governments indeed take into account the access and opportunities of their populations, but not all. The governance of food safety is a second task of governments, and it often implies that a food-safety institution is established, and that certification and labeling programs are supported. In line with the neoliberal ideology of the last decades, the producers of food often have quite some influence on these policies and institutions, which determines the range of issues targeted in food-safety programs. In the Netherlands, food safety is mostly interpreted as safety from microbiological contamination and from pollution. Food safety in the long-term, like protection of consumers against chronic diseases (obesity, type 2 diabetes, cardiovascular diseases, cancer) due to too much salt, sugar, and satiable fat is not targeted (Moss 2013; Nestle 2002). Moreover, responsibility structures for past and future problems are not clearly defined, which means that diseases that are direct consequences of food production, like Q-fever (life threatening with nearly 4000 severe cases), are largely neglected. New tasks of government (and others) of the developed countries are dealing with climate change and curbing the impact of meat production (Singer 2006) – but only hesitantly are these issues taken into account.

An important new issue in which public food governance is involved is the current nearly global regime of Intellectual Property Rights (IPR) and its problems (Tansey 2008). Intellectual Property Rights are property rights that give the inventor of, for example, genetic information of plants – i.e., their DNA sequences – the exclusive access to that information. Inventors can charge what they like, and for medicine and seeds the final price is often much higher than the material costs. The argument that these higher costs are necessary to continue the invention is flawed, because at least one-third of the budget of, for example, the largest seed company, Monsanto, goes to their lawyers to chase so-called illegal use of their seeds. For many small enterprises, like the majority of Dutch seed companies, but also for researchers, such exclusivity prevents cooperation. These seed companies make use of breeders' rights, which allow the continuing improvement of seeds without the necessity to pay for royalties – their inventions belong to a kind of common pool. Now some governments are in favor of breeders' rights, others are against it and in favor of IPR. There are some mixtures, but in general IPR with respect to seeds and medicine can make them very expensive and unavailable for poor farmers – who still number 2 billion with 500 million households. IPR also steers research into new inventions toward profitable drugs, not to drugs for poor people. (Recall that most severe and widespread diseases are among poor people, the majority of the human population.) The result is that pharma and seed companies invest more into research and development of drugs to address relatively rich people's diseases (like baldness) and seeds (like seeds for fodder), as compared to research addressing chronic diseases and food for the global poor. Justice would require more commercial and scientific-technological attention to the needs of poor farmers, traders, and consumers (Timmermann 2013).

Globally, countries differ enormously in their emphases on certain aspects of food governance, and this is reflected more or less in the power balances between international regulations and agencies. In the twentieth century the "Washington consensus," a neoliberal policy to establish as much market and to dismantle governmental regulations, was a dominant force coming from the US. However, in the last decades new international blocs of countries have risen to power, like the BRIC countries (Brazil, Russia, India, China), and geopolitical troubles have caused food hypes and market failures. Farmers and traders working locally, independent of world markets, have a better chance to survive than others.

Secondly, there are private or market parties – the large ones coordinate their actions in labeling and certifications systems. These actors are retail companies like Carrefour or Ahold, transport companies, food processing industries like Cargill, farmers and their associations, marketing and advertising companies (which can spend more than $400 billion annually), and banks and insurance companies that have a financial stake in agri-food companies. Together they strive for transparency of food chains for the participants (not necessarily for consumers), for example by certification schemes. Barling and Duncan (2015) remark about these systems:

> The explosion in the number and variety of food and beverage product certification schemes has been a feature of governance trends in the food sector, moving rapidly beyond food safety assurance to embrace sustainability criteria from fair trade to natural resource protection, such as the catch from sustainable fisheries or sustainable palm oil production. Global consumption–production networks are linking developed world consumers with developing world producers, led by the work of development and environmental NGOs, sometimes in tandem with industry (e.g., Marine Stewardship Council), and widening the range of actors involved in private governance.

Nevertheless, the transparency is often limited to the next and the previous links in the chain – which means for example that measures taken in link number three and not identified in number four can have considerable influence in link five and further, which can be unnoticed until consumers feel the effect. The Dutch scandal about horsemeat sold as beef is a case in point, as is the appearance of certain zoonosis.

Interaction between public and private governance institutions happens quite systematically, and the large multinational agri-food and retail companies like Monsanto, Syngenta, Kraft, Unilever, and Carrefour often bypass particular (small) governments to directly lobby with international organizations, be it the EU, WHO, FAO, or WTO. Because of the weak position of (inter) national governments and agencies vis-à-vis large, international corporations, they often give corporations the task to target certain political objectives, like the reduction of salt in food, via self-regulation. However, this type of informal strategy to reach certain policy ends often doesn't succeed. Nevertheless, slowly steps are being made by some larger corporations – for example in the direction of sustainability. They can be encouraged by international agencies like UNEP (2012) that outline programs of corporate social responsibility.

Civil society groups like NGOs concerned with food production are growing in number and influence. Social media like Twitter, Facebook, and the Internet in general contribute to their increasing power positions. NGOs have a very relevant task to open new information resources, to give members of the public opportunities to come into contact with each other, and to find out the intricacies of the food system and its alternatives. Many consumers connect via the Internet and find out what they really want and what the positive and negative advantages are of their purchases. Sometimes NGOs can cooperate with governments and corporate actors in setting standards. Until now professional organizations, like food toxicologists, food and nutrition scientists, and other food professionals, have not been very active – often they followed the organizations that employed or financed them. This is a problem of integrity.

Finally, international agencies like Codex Alimentarius contribute to the governance of food by setting standards of safe and sometimes healthy food. As mentioned earlier, safety is in most cases defined in the narrow sense of microbiological safety. In Europe the institutions of the European Food Law, like European Food Safety Authority (EFSA), have some influence, for example in regulating health claims, genetic modified crops, and novel foods (Meulen and Velde 2008).

The various actors have, in principle, different responsibilities and accountabilities over past and future developments in the agri-food system. However, the unclear relationship between public and private actors makes it quite easy for both sectors to postpone necessary measures and to continue unsafe, unhealthy, and unsustainable situations. Very often the least powerful, the consumers, are held responsible for acting as conscious citizens in decreasing waste, making healthy choices, or animal-friendly food choices. However, the sheer complexity and incoherencies of the system make it impossible for a normal consumer to find out the ethical problems of, for example, the meat or milk chain (Coff et al. 2009).

From an ethical point of view, a less complex system with an emphasis on food sovereignty (Desmarais et al. 2010) would be more acceptable with the focus of more subnational and local governance and with clear participation and involvement of consumers (Korthals 2004). The challenges that the current agri-food system is now confronted with, like climate change, waste, lack of quality, and unhealthy food, are the products of its quasi-global and national fragmentation and opaqueness, where democratic control is lacking. Alternative food systems with more democratic forms of governance are growing in influence, and many consumers make it clear that they want more influence in the food chains, rather than only at the end as buyers.

Different strategies of implementation of policies

The different actors can use different strategies in implementation of food policies. Governments have strong instruments like laws and fiscal regulations. Governments can also take informal strategies, like giving advice and creating default contexts of food production and consumption. For example, in the case of the disastrous consequences of climate change and the contribution of meat production to this process, governments could perhaps bring themselves to implement laws against meat production and eating, to implement taxation on meat, or to implement the requirements that all catering and restaurants would offer primarily vegetarian meals. (This would be a case of nudging in the sense of changing the default.) Private actors do not have legal instruments, but have quite effective informal ones, like marketing, advertising, manipulation, and nudging. Nudging is not manipulation; while it never completely eliminates alternatives, manipulation does. Manipulation often leads to misleading actions, which officially are prohibited and also ethically unacceptable. However, manipulation often takes place because marketers are looking for all kinds of holes in the existing legal requirements.

Table 15.1 Various strategies of implementation by actors of food governance (partly from House of Lords 2011).

	Mechanism	Degree of freedom	Examples
Formal: laws, governments	Obligations, prohibitions	No freedom	Fines, prison
Formal: fiscal regulations, governments	Punishments	Limited freedom	Taxation on unhealthy food items
Informal: via information and advices, governments, and others	Communication	Free choice	Health and Food Information center
Informal: default context, government, and others	Facilitation	Free choice	Subsidies for self-organization, web-platform, etc.
Informal: nudging, government, and others	Context framing	Free choice	Descriptive norms for fair trade buying
Manipulation, private partners	Misleading consumers, threats	No freedom	Many health claims, ads targeting children

From an ethical point of view, laws, taxation, and advice are acceptable, but manipulation and marketing directed towards children are not. Children are not able to make a reasonable choice about what is good for them, so in particular, the young ones should not be bombarded with all kinds of food that are unhealthy, like alcohol and fast food. Misleading marketing is as a matter of fact ethically not acceptable. Nudging and marketing are acceptable under certain conditions, like transparency and accountability of the producers of these messages. Producers should adhere to values of care, responsibility, and integrity to work accordingly.

Can current food governance cope with the challenges?

As mentioned in the introduction, current global and national food governance is confronted with severe challenges: not enough food for nearly one billion hungry people; inadequate food for more than two billion undernourished, malnourished, or over-nourished (obese); the need to increase agricultural production to take into account that more than nine billion people will inhabit the earth in 2050, balanced by the need for severe cuts in chemical inputs. Climate change will in particular affect large agricultural areas of the poor but populous Global South (Schutter 2014). Also troublesome is the focus of the rich and nearly rich countries on meat, which means nowadays that approximately 60% of agrarian areas are cultivated for fodder. Further, the risks of food safety and health effects will increase due to longer chains and unhealthy and tasteless food supplies. The current governance structure seems to be insufficient to tackle these problems; it cannot live up to the test for good food governance and food policies, and it cannot contribute to a productive, safe, sustainable, animal-friendly, healthy, tasteful, and equitable food system. The powerful large international corporations and (neoliberal) ideologies often deny the seriousness of these problems, and they put the responsibilities of increasing poverty of rural populations on the powerless (consumers).

Nevertheless, seen exclusively from the standpoint of food security, the current (unsustainable) food system should be able to feed 15 billion people, however with enormous costs; but, probably most countries and citizens are not willing to bear these costs (De Schutter 2014; Lang et al. 2009).

So, the question is, what to change in the current food governance? What new institutions and agencies does the current and future population of the earth need for an ethically acceptable food supply? First, food and agricultural policies should target more often the complex interplay of food security, food safety, health, environment, animal welfare, and quality of food. Yes, even food quality should be an objective of food policies, because quality of food (as a matter of fact in the plural, culturally dependent sense) enhances the quality of life of citizens, both because better tastes make people better motivated to acquire and maintain their cooking skills, but also because the search for and improvement of good tastes enables people to feel more respected and encouraged to act as citizens. This type of food policy should refrain from imposing one type of food agriculture, but respect the variety and pluralism in food production and consumption.

This implies, secondly, that priority should be given to the transformation of the food system from supply driven to demand driven, i.e., citizen–consumer driven. Science and technologies to improve the quality of food should always be accompanied by consumer participation about the complexities of new food technologies. Technologies should be incorporated within social strategies, not outside them. Thirdly, the trend of modernization to functional differentiation of different societal needs should be counteracted by establishing "bridges" and intermediaries between the different functional sections; health, for example, should not be concentrated in the medical sectors, but in the food sector as well. Fourthly, global, international organizations should more than ever establish balances between global and local initiatives, according to the idea of subsidiarity (to place solutions where there are problems). They should also cooperate with international corporations to improve the food system. Because food is central to the identity of citizen-consumers, indeed for each in a different way, deliberation and recognition of conflicts and disagreements on values, and food and farming styles should be in the middle of these various aspects food policies (Korthals 2004). Fifthly, agricultural policies should take into account the important role of sustainable farming practices, like Agroecology (Tittonell 2013) and Community Agricultural practices; urban farming, with a growing population living in cities, should have highest priority. Sixthly, from a justice perspective, the majority of the world population consists of small-scale farmers or traders. They have a right to be supported by governance policies as small farmers and traders; from a livelihood perspective it is unwise to chase them out of their land to the cities, because life in the urban areas is mostly "nasty, brutish and short" (De Schutter 2014; Desmarais et al. 2010; IAASTD 2009). Quality agriculture with respect for farmers is a good policy alternative here.

Conclusion

This essay started by mentioning challenges of the current food governance system. Then we gave an overview of four issues of food governance, which can be described in terms of four dilemmas: broad or small range of aims; governance as oriented toward state, market, science, or civil society, or a combination of these; governance from the top down or from below (be it from international or national organizations or local and regional ones) and based on food supply or food demand; and, finally, governance that is obligatory or voluntary. We discussed first the aims of food governance, be it international or national. The broad range of topics that are intrinsically connected with food, like health, environment, climate change, biodiversity, fair trade, quality of food, and convenience are mostly narrowed down to one or two very specific topics such as food safety and health in a quite small sense (not covering chronic diseases). Secondly, we discussed the role and responsibilities of the actors involved. Candidates such as states, market parties, civil society organizations (NGOs), and international agencies do play a role, but currently the role of international corporations together with powerful governmental lobbies are quite dominant in making food policy decisions, while structures of responsibility and accountability are weak. Thirdly, we analyzed the ethical values leading to establishing a strategy of food governance, referring to the United Nations Declaration of Human Rights (UNDHR), which underscores the right to adequate food, including the right to choose your own food. Moreover, the declaration mentions justice and freedom to live your own life, according to quality of food and informed food choice. Fourthly, food policy decides upon which instruments are used and their ethical status. Laws, taxation, advice, and non-manipulative technologies like nudging are ethically acceptable, but manipulation and marketing to children are not. Finally, we offered some considerations concerning the status of the current food governance structure and its potentials to address the challenges ahead.

References

Barling, D. and J. Duncan. (2015) "The Dynamics of the Contemporary Governance of the World's Food Supply and the Challenges of Policy Redirection," *Food Security* 7(2): 415–424.

Caraher, M. and J. Coveney. (2004) "Public Health Nutrition and Food Policy," *Public Health Nutrition* 7(5): 591–598.

Coff, C., D. Barling, and M. Korthals (eds.) (2009) *Ethical Traceability in Communicating Food*, Dordrecht: Springer.

Desmarais, A., N. Wiebe, and H. Wittman. (2010) *Food Sovereignty: Reconnecting Food, Nature and Community*, London: Food First Books.

Estabrook, B. (2012) *Tomatoland: How Modern Industrial Agriculture Destroyed Our Most Alluring Fruit*, London: Andrews McMeel Publishing.

FAO. (2002) *The State of Food Insecurity in the World 2001*, Rome: FAO.

Have, H. T. (ed.) (2016) *Encyclopedia of Global Bioethics*, Dordrecht: Springer.

Herring, R. J. (ed.) (2014) *Handbook on Food, Politics and Society*, Oxford: Oxford University Press.

House of Lords. (2011) *Behavior Change*, HL paper 179, London: Stationery Office.

International Assessment of Agricultural Knowledge, Science and Technology for Development (IAASTD). (2009) "Agriculture at a Crossroads," viewed 11 October 2015, http://www.agassessment-watch.org/.

Korthals, M. (2004) *Before Dinner*, Dordrecht: Springer.

Lang, T., D. Barling, and M. Caraher. (2009) *Food Policy: Integrating Health, Environment and Society*, London: Earthscan.

LNV. (2005) Strategische Dialoog Voedselkwaliteit, viewed 11 October 2015, http://www.archief.verant woordeveehouderij.nl/producten/Verwaarding/Dierenwelzijnsindex.pdf.

Meulen, B. v. d. and M. v. d. Velde. (2008) *European Food Law Handbook*, Wageningen: Wageningen Academic Publishers.

Moss, M. (2013) *Salt, Sugar, Fat*, London: Allen.

Nestle, M. (2002) *Food Politics*, Berkeley: University of California Press.

Pogge, T. (2010) "A Critique of the Capability Approach," in H. Brighouse and I. Robeyns (eds.), *Measuring Justice, Primary Goods and Capabilities*, Cambridge: University Press, pp. 17–61.

Rawls, J. (1971) *A Theory of Justice*, Boston: Cambridge University Press.

———. (1993) *Political Liberalism*, New York: Columbia Press.

Roberts, P. (2008) *The End of Food*, London: Bloomsbury.

Saul, N. and A. Curtis. (2013) *The Stop: How the Fight for Good Food Transformed a Community and Inspired a Movement*, New York: Melville.

Schutter, O. de. (2014) *Final Report: The Transformative Potential of The Right to Food*, New York: UN.

Sen, A. (2009) *The Concept of Justice*, London: Lane.

Singer, P. and J. Mason. (2006) *The Way We Eat*. New York: Rodale.

Tansey, G. (2008) *The Future Control of Food: A Guide to International Negotiations and Rules on Intellectual Property, Biodiversity and Food Security*, London: Earthscan.

Thompson, P. and D. Kaplan (eds.) (2014) *Encyclopaedia of Food and Agricultural Ethics*, Dordrecht: Springer.

Timmermann, C. (2013) *Life Sciences, Intellectual Property Regimes and Global Justice*, Wageningen: Diss.

Tittonell, P. (2013) *Farming Systems Ecology: Towards Ecological Intensification of World Agriculture*, Wageningen: WU.

UNEP. (2012) *Avoiding Future Famines: Strengthening the Ecological Foundation of Food Security through Sustainable Food Systems*, Nairobi: United Nations Environment Programme.

United Nations. (1975) *Report of the World Food Conference, Rome 5–16 November 1974*. New York: UN.

16

FOOD AT THE NEXUS OF BIOETHICS AND BIOPOLITICS

Christopher Mayes

Introduction

Food has become an area of fascination and concern in Western consumer societies. Craft beer, organic coffee, free-range meats, artisanal markets, community gardens, and the rise in food media are all expressions of this fascination. These aesthetic interests are mirrored by concerns over nutritional value, genetic modification, obesity, food deserts, and the sustainability of industrial agriculture. These trends have co-evolved and reinforce one another. The belief that industrial agriculture and chain supermarkets produce food that undermines human and environmental health contributes to the belief that organic agriculture and farmers' markets will enhance human health and the environment. These beliefs and practices have produced a wide literature including journalistic investigations in mainstream newspapers, activist polemics, and academic research. Although each varies according to genre, most of these accounts celebrate alternative food practices and warn against the status quo of industrial agriculture. Much of this discourse appeals to a notion of ethical food practices.

For over a hundred years there have been calls for greater attention to the political and moral dimensions of food production, distribution, and consumption. The novels of John Steinbeck and Upton Sinclair, and the social analyses of Karl Marx and Max Weber, all highlight significant questions of justice and the political economy of agriculture. However, these broader perspectives only gain purchase among a wider audience to the extent that they relate to consumers. In *The Jungle*, Sinclair documented the dangerous and brutal conditions of the workers in Chicago's meatpacking industry. His US audience, however, were more horrified by the sanitary conditions, which resulted in the Pure Food and Drug Act (1906) (Kantor 1976). This led Sinclair to quip, "I aimed for the public's heart, and by accident hit it in the stomach." Likewise today, much of the discussion surrounding the ethics of food focuses on consumer practices. Organic food and shopping at farmers' markets is promoted not only for being tastier or healthier, but more ethical. The dominance of the consumer perspective is not only present in journalistic and popular accounts of ethics in relation to food, but also more sophisticated academic analyses. These analyses tend to be associated with the field of bioethics.

In some respects the growth of food ethics within or alongside bioethics is a natural fit. Bioethics is a field of inquiry that rapidly grew and was institutionalized in universities to address concerns over developments in the life sciences. The establishment of bioethics research centers in the

1970s coincided with concerns over the impacts of the industrial food system and agricultural biotechnologies on health, the environment, and society. Although there were attempts to create a distinct food and agricultural ethics, this never received the same financial or institutional support as bioethics (Thompson 2015a). As such, bioethics became the dominant interdisciplinary field that inquired into biotechnology and the manipulation of molecular life. However, bioethics arguably reinforces a narrowed perspective of food ethics that focuses on issues pertaining to the consumer rather than broader issues throughout the food system. Thus wider considerations of the ethical features of the production and distribution of food tend to be neglected in favor of consumer-oriented concerns.

Bioethics has been criticized within and without for over-emphasizing individual autonomy to choose and the associated responsibilities and obligations associated with that choice (Dawson 2010; Mann 2010). This chapter suggests that food ethics is in danger of being drawn into the orbit of bioethics and its narrowed perspective. Clearly there are important ethical obligations and responsibilities associated with what is eaten. And there has been some important work done to identify and articulate these obligations and responsibilities (Irvine 2013; Pence 2002; Pollan 2006; Singer and Mason 2006). However, this chapter draws attention to the fact that food is not only a (bio)ethical concern, but also a biopolitical concern.

In the first part of this chapter I outline the limitations of bioethical discourses of choice and responsibility surrounding food and health. In the second part I argue that much of the bioethical discourse ignores the biopolitical dimension of food systems and directives encouraging individuals and populations to make healthy food choices. I do not argue that bioethical analyses are redundant or should be ignored. Rather, I conclude this chapter by suggesting that the inclusion of a biopolitical perspective is a crucial corrective for bioethics to critically respond to concerns surrounding food, and that together a substantial political and ethical analysis of food is possible.

Food as a bioethical problem

Since the 1970s applied ethics journals, societies, and centers have proliferated. The main areas of research include: medical ethics, clinical ethics, nursing ethics, agricultural ethics, animal ethics, and environmental ethics. Food ethics is a relative latecomer to this group. However, it is rapidly catching up. Despite the diversity of these fields of inquiry, they are commonly placed under the umbrella of bioethics. This is partly due to a shared focus on normative questions associated with developments in the life sciences. It is also due to the "success" of bioethics in becoming established in universities, hospitals, and government institutions. The recognition of bioethics as a field capable of responding to advancements in the life sciences, particularly biotechnology, resulted in institutional and financial support for research centers and academic positions. While sub-fields such as agricultural ethics try to remain distinct from bioethics, they have never received the institutional support or commercial interest that bioethics receives. As such, much of the ethical research on the life sciences, be it nutrition, veterinary, or agricultural science, seeks to strategically fit within the scope of bioethics.

In some respects the inclusion of diverse sub-fields into bioethics research centers, journals, and societies could be viewed as mutually beneficial. However, a large part of the reason why bioethics has so successfully attracted institutional support is that it focuses on the ethical issues of the life sciences as they pertain to individual human health. The focus on human individuals and use of concepts such as autonomy and personhood has been criticized for being too narrow and limits the capacity for researchers to fully address the broad concerns, such as the environment, non-human animals, public health, or agriculture (Dawson 2010; Irvine et al. 2013; Thompson 2015a). While bioethics can lend some of its institutional support to related applied ethics fields, there is the danger of those fields implicitly or explicitly adopting a research agenda shaped by concern of individual autonomy and human health.

In the case of food, it is clear that autonomy and human health are important ethical considerations. The growing interest in food ethics has led to a raft of popular books as well as academic monographs, journal articles, and courses. Many of these deal with the individual as a consumer who has ethical obligations to others or is owed ethical respect. Paul Thompson (2015a) observes that phrases like "'food ethics' tend to be associated with personal conduct and eating ethically." As will be argued below, the narrowing of food ethics to fit with a bioethical preoccupation with individual autonomy and human health results in the exclusion of key issues. However, before making that argument it is necessary to outline the important work that does treat food as an object of bioethical concern. This work can be divided into two broad areas: consumer autonomy and ethical consumption. The former deals with the duties and obligations consumers are owed by manufacturers and governments. The latter deals with the duties and obligations that consumers owe others.

A significant reason for the rise in ethical thinking about food is the belief that consumers are alienated from their food. Processes of reformulation, genetic modification, a globalized food system, perennial availability of seasonal foods, industrial agriculture, disconnection of rural and urban communities, and the competing messages regarding healthy diet all contribute to a belief that we consumers don't know what is in our food, where it comes from, or the conditions under which it is produced (Brom and Gremmen 2000; Guthman 2011; Ristovski-Slijepcevic et al. 2010; Scrinis 2013). These epistemological concerns compound fears about potential consequences for individual and population health. That is, if consumers do not know what is in their food or where it came from, then they cannot make informed decisions about their own health. This has led some commentators to argue that the autonomy of consumers has been undermined and that they are dependent on producers and retailers.

Autonomy is a central value in liberal moral philosophy and it is this tradition that dominates much of Anglo-American bioethics (Callahan 2012; Charlesworth 1993). Closely tied to autonomy is the idea of consumer choice, a central value in neoliberal economics. These two values combine to establish rhetorically powerful arguments for the need to respect and enable consumer autonomy in relation to food choice. Frans Brom writes that respect for consumer autonomy:

> implies that they have the prima facie right to live their life according to their own value system. Their right to live according to their own life plan implies that they ought to have the choice for products that fit in with their view of life.
>
> (Brom 2000: 131)

However, due to the many stages involved in producing and distributing modern food items, there is concern that consumer autonomy can be manipulated, thereby undermining the right for individuals to live their lives according their own value systems.

The manipulation of food choice, for instance, is a concern for bioethicists who believe that food choices not only affect the health of the individual, but burden the rest of society due to health costs associated with obesity (Callahan 2013; Singer 2012). Further, public health advocates argue that large food corporations manipulate food choice through advertising so-called "junk foods" to children (Henderson et al. 2009; Reeve 2013). There is also extensive concern that these corporations mislead consumers through promoting foods for possessing specific health-promoting or disease-preventive qualities (Brownell and Warner 2009; Gilmore et al. 2011; Marks 2013; Outram and Stewart 2015). These concerns are heightened by widespread anxiety over diet-related diseases such diabetes or conditions such as obesity. Thus it is argued that activities such as advertising undermine parents' autonomy to decide what is best for their children, while also undermining and manipulating the capacity for people to make informed decisions about food products that may or may not affect their health.

In addition to diet-related diseases and conditions, bioethicists argue that food safety is also an issue of consumer autonomy (Gostin 2010; McGee 2007; Resnik 2010; Siipi and Uusitalo 2008). Outbreaks of mad cow disease and *e. coli*, as well as anxieties about trans fats and genetically modified foods, reinforce suspicion about industrialized food systems and lead to calls for consumer autonomy to be respected through the establishment of various regulatory practices and organizations (Beekman 2008; Brom 2000; Draper and Green 2002; Jensen and Sandøe 2002; Loureiro and Umberger 2007).

The issue of consumer autonomy, whether related to advertising or food safety, is often dealt with via food labels. The food label has come to be understood as a small but powerful apparatus that delivers and secures consumer autonomy from manipulation and harm. This is due to the belief that the label addresses the epistemological gap between consumption and production. Whether it is a nutrition label, GM-free label, or an organic label, the purpose is to provide the individual with the appropriate knowledge that enables the consumer to act autonomously and choose his or her own course of action. Whether these labels *actually* allow individuals to act autonomously is contentious (Emanuel 2012; Frohlich 2010; Mayes 2014). However, it is undeniable that many public health researchers, consumer advocates, and ethicists consider them crucial for individual health and autonomous decision-making (Blewett et al. 2011; Campos et al. 2011; Silverglade and Heller 2010; Singer and Mason 2006).

Hub Zwart has written a (very) short history of food ethics. Zwart traces the ethical concern with food from the ancient world (Greek, Hebrew, and Christian) to the modern preoccupation with food labels (Zwart 2000). While in the ancient world there was concern about whether eating certain foods altered one's relationship with gods, the law, or community, in modernity there is greater emphasis on knowledge and individual choice. It is here that the label becomes crucial. Zwart concludes his history of food ethics by arguing that the acceptance or rejection of food labels allows the consumer to "develop a moral Self, to live a morally examined life and to take sides in the political conflicts of the present" (Zwart 2000: 125). This role of the label in allowing an individual to fashion a moral or ethical self via their choices is important for the second feature of food as an object of bioethical concern: ethical consumption.

Ethical consumption is the idea that individuals have a responsibility towards others in the way they consume. In a special issue of the *Journal of Bioethical Inquiry* on food ethics, Rob Irvine states that "ethical consumption may mean buying different products and boycotting others" (Irvine 2013: 146). Peter Singer, arguably one of the most well-known bioethicists, has argued for a long time that individuals have a responsibility to spend their money and consume in ways that do not harm others, particularly animals and vulnerable people (Singer 1972; 1977). In 2006, Singer co-authored *The Way We Eat: Why Our Food Choices Matter* with Jim Mason.

As with consumer autonomy, the food label is central for ethical consumption. Information becomes the key for consumers to act ethically towards others and to also develop an ethical self by knowing what it is that they are eating. For instance, there are numerous ethical shopping apps that assist consumers (who own smartphones) to know whether a certain item is cruelty-free, vegan, fair-trade, contains GMOs, or aligns with particular political views. Ethical food labels and apps purport to give individual consumers the knowledge that they need to make choices that are responsible and that respect others. However, ethical food labels cannot always be trusted (Irvine 2013; Parker et al. 2013). Parker, Scrinis, and others have argued that ethical labels can be used in descriptive ways to further the interests of food corporations (Mayes 2014; Parker and Scrinis 2014).

Ethical consumption is an avenue into raising awareness about important issues. These practices should not simply be dismissed as irrelevant. However, there is a strong tendency for these (bio) ethical analyses to focus on the individual consumer (Ashby and Rich 2013), which narrows the perspective to market economies and liberal moral philosophy. However, it was not always this way. Early proponents such as Fritz Jahr, Van Rensselaer Potter, and Hans Jonas had a wider vision for bioethics (Potter 1971; Sass 2007; Vogel 2006). Yet the process of institutionalization stunted attempts for bioethics to focus on the biosphere rather than reduced to biomedicine and human biological health (Thompson 2015a).

There needs to be a wider understanding of food ethics that questions the wider political economy of food systems that condition individual choices. Of course, there are critiques of the food system (Patel 2009). Thompson suggests a broader definition of food ethics that "might include not only making better choices yourself but also designing menus, public policies, or even cities to encourage better food choices by everyone" (Thompson 2015b: 5). This is a useful broadening of food ethics, yet it is still oriented towards the choices of a consumer as the ultimate point of reference. Thompson recognizes this when he identifies "the 'fundamental problem' in food ethics [as] the enduring tension between the interests of poor farmers in the developing world and the hungry masses of growing urban centers" (Thompson 2015b: 7). That is, a tension between producers and consumers. Thompson places this tension in the morally and politically heightened context of the developing world and concerns of food security. However, this tension persists within developed industrial counties and between those countries and the developing world. Thompson focuses his analysis through the lens of food security. My contention, however, is that a food ethics tied to bioethics is incapable of adequately analyzing these concerns. I suggest that the theoretical and analytic resources of bioethics need to be tempered through the adoption of a biopolitical lens.

Food as a biopolitical problem

First comes a full stomach, then comes ethics.

—Bertolt Brecht

The provision of food for hungry people is perhaps one of the most fundamental ethical acts. Food and hunger are underexplored themes in the work of Bertolt Brecht. For example, in the *Three-penny Opera* Brecht writes his famous line about the priority of a full stomach over ethics. In *Mother Courage and Her Children* food is entwined with the family's survival through bartering and selling provisions. Brecht shows that concern for others is very difficult, if not impossible, without a full stomach and the satisfaction of one's physical needs. Henry Shue, a prominent human rights philosopher, makes a similar point by arguing that a right to food precedes other rights and other ethical ideals (Shue 1996). In considering the ethics of food, it is necessary to be aware of the prior need of having a full stomach. However, importantly, there are earlier questions still: Whose stomachs will be filled? Whose food will they eat? And, why are they hungry in the first place? These questions are political in nature and precede the consumer and questions of individual ethics. This section focuses on the political dimension of food, or what I will argue is the biopolitical dimension.

Biopolitics is closely associated with the work of the philosopher Michel Foucault. According to Foucault, the development of the life sciences in the eighteenth century served to legitimate modern political power to take charge of individual bodies and manage the life of the population (Foucault 1998: 143). For example, knowledge derived from epidemiology and population statistics enabled governments to identify a normal distribution of disease within a population, which led to various strategies of disease prevention and health promotion. Foucault summarized the dual objective of biopolitics as: to "*foster* life or *disallow* it to the point of death" (Foucault 1998: 138). Those whose lives were disallowed are placed outside of the polis. The most violent and crude expression of biopolitics was the scientific racism of Nazi Germany.

Today, however, the lives of refugees, the mentally ill, prisoners, migrant workers, non-human animals, and others are often placed outside and have their existence questioned by the polis. Foucault and others argue that subtle uses of life sciences have been mobilized to govern populations in post-war liberal democracies (Donzelot 1980; Foucault 1980). Public health sanitary practices, surveillance of children's nutritional intake, and social workers monitoring maternal practices, insurance schemes, and social security, are some of the expressions of biopolitics that seek to govern the bodies of individuals and the life of the population (Lemke 2011). According to Foucault, these biopolitical strategies were "without question an indispensable element in the development of capitalism" (Foucault 1998: 140–141).

With the foregoing in mind, I contend that food is a biopolitical problem. Food is a biopolitical problem rather than simply a political problem for at least three reasons: food itself is biological, food sustains biological life, and food is tied to the economic and physical strength of populations. These features see food intimately entwined with the management of populations and programs of economic growth. In viewing food through a biopolitical lens, it is possible to address some of the questions mentioned above that precede the ethics of consumption. There are many avenues through which to explore the biopolitics of food and agriculture: non-human animals, agricultural biotechnology, nutritional guidance, biodiversity, and others (Ferreira et al. 2015; Nally 2011; Smith 2011). An extensive analysis of food as a biopolitical problem is not possible in this short section. However, I will briefly address food security and associated successful failures of the market.

Writing in response to famines occurring the 1970s, Peter Singer famously argued in his paper "Famine, Affluence, and Morality," that if it is in our power to prevent something very bad from happening, without thereby sacrificing anything else morally significant, we ought, morally, to do it (Singer 1972: 231). Singer leaves open what is morally significant and emphasizes that many individuals have excess wealth with which they purchase expensive consumer items. Singer argues that most people would recognize that shoes, televisions, or a cup of coffee are far less significant than a human life. Yet, most people buy these items without considering the lives that could be saved if the money was donated to aid organizations responding to famine. Singer argues that individuals with excess wealth have a moral duty to use it to save lives via famine relief. Singer reaches this conclusion largely due to his Benthamite utilitarianism, but also due to his diagnosis of the problem. For Singer, the problem of famine is a lack of food among poor populations. The solution is to provide food, either via monetary donations to purchase food, or through donations of food. Despite its intuitive sense, food security scholars do not believe this to be an accurate account of the problem (McDonald 2011; Moseley et al. 2010).

As Thompson notes (2015b: 108–109), the work of Amartya Sen led to a reframing of the problem of famine from a lack of food to a breakdown in the distribution of food (Sen 1981). According to Sen, famine was not due to the scarcity of food in a specific region, but disruptions in distribution resulting from complex economic, social, and political breakdowns (Sen 1981). As such, the influx of food via food aid programs into a food insecure region would not address the structural problems, and may in fact exacerbate them. Hungry people would be fed, especially in urban areas. However, smallholder farmers and local agriculture would suffer, as the price for food would dramatically decrease. That is, food aid undermines the capacity for smallholder farmers to produce food for themselves and others, leading to a dependence on aid and erosion of local agriculture. According to Thompson, "that *is* the fundamental problem in food ethics" (Thompson 2015b: 114).

It is worth pausing to consider in what sense food security is the fundamental problem of food ethics. Is it the problem that food ethics *must address*? Or is it the problem *with* food ethics because it is tied to unequal relations that result in the security of some and insecurity of others? The answer is both. Food ethics needs to address food security, but a food ethics that is focused on individual consumer rights and issues of autonomy is part of the problem. This can lead to a preoccupation with the ethical obligations we may have to people who are hungry without addressing the way our ethical analyses do not allow for light to be shone on some of the fundamental issues. Food spikes, migrant labor, land grabs, structural adjustment programs, free-trade deals, and a host of other factors that are part of the global food system produce the conditions where the insecurity of the most vulnerable corresponds to the continued security and benefit of the privileged. This occurs not only between developed and developing nations, but also within nations. For example, the exploitation of migrant and undocumented laborers in Europe and the US benefits the commercial agricultural producers and consumers (Munshi 2003; Patel 2009; Rye and Andrzejewska 2010). As Julie Guthman notes, "the market cannot simultaneously keep farmers in business and provide good food for workers; paying food workers and farm workers living wages would make food prohibitively expensive" (2011: 139).

Thompson concludes his analysis of food security by claiming: "Our first responsibility in a globalizing world is to see this *as* a problem that has not gone away with modernization" (Thompson 2015b: 129). This statement reveals a tension between positivist bioethical perspectives that consider modernity and processes of modernization as largely beneficent, and the critical perspective of biopolitics that considers modernity and processes of modernization as dangerous and problematic. That is, a biopolitics perspective does not expect food insecurity to disappear with modernity, but that the political and economic set-up of modernity uses the insecurity of some for the security of others.

The idea that the security of the few is tied to the insecurity of the many – or in biopolitical terms, to foster the life of some while disallowing the life of others – can be seen in the role of global agricultural markets and free-trade agreements. These breakdowns can occur within a country or through external factors such as food spikes on commodity markets. During his time as the United Nations Special Rapporteur on the Right to Food, Olivier De Schutter argued that "the right to adequate food should be placed at the center of the efforts of the international community" (De Schutter 2008: 2). According to De Schutter, the right to food should not only come into consideration during emergency situations or natural disasters, but also in consideration of "the soaring prices of food" that result from speculation on commodity markets (De Schutter 2008: 2). De Schutter's analysis points to the biopolitical problem of food. Food is a commodity essential to trade and economics (Department of Foreign Affairs and Trade 2008; Enterprise and Industry 2012; Office of Health and Consumer Goods 2012), yet it is also a substance intrinsic to life – cultural, social, and biological. The dual role of food as utility-value for life and commodity for financial investment can be understood through a biopolitical framework.

In *Security, Territory, Population*, Michel Foucault examines the problem of food scarcity in the eighteenth century. In that context the economic and political concern over food had to do with preventing the "scourge of scarcity," which risked food riots and political unrest (Foucault 2007: 29–30). In the neoliberal context, grain scarcity has proved to be profitable to traders in agricultural commodities on derivatives markets. However, the speculation on agricultural commodities has also led to food spikes, fluctuating markets, and political unrest in sub-Saharan Africa, parts of the Middle East, and India (Kennedy 2012). De Schutter and others argue that food should not be treated like other commodities due to its essential role in sustaining life (utility-value) and the way speculation of these markets negatively affect smallholder farmers in the developing world. Despite recognition of the social and political unrest caused by speculation on agricultural commodities, there is little political will to regulate such markets. This could be due to the fact that in contrast to the "scourge of scarcity" in eighteenth-century Europe, where food riots would occur in France or England and could threaten the privileged and powerful, unrest in India or sub-Saharan Africa does not affect those in New York, London, or Sydney (Taylor 1996).

It could be argued that the speculation on agriculture commodities and free-trade agreements that open up small markets to large producers are permitted so long as there is an excess of the utility-value of food for the life of populations of dominant trading partners. That is, so long as there is enough food to fill the stomachs of the populations influencing and controlling political and economic trends, then speculation and free trade are permitted. This is not to suggest that the reluctance to regulate speculation on agriculture commodities or to protect local markets from free-trade agreements, which threaten the lives of many in developing nations and of the working poor in industrial nations, is reducible to corporate greed or lack of humanitarian concern. Rather these trends are part of Western governments' strategies of security.

For example, the biopolitics of food security is evident in Australian agricultural policy. Australia is a net exporter of food. In 2009–10, Australia exported $24.3 billion worth of food and imported $10.1 billion (Spencer and Kneebone 2012). Yet, food security has become a key part of Australian agricultural policy rhetoric. Food security is not a direct, but an indirect concern in Australia. It is used to justify opening up new markets for Australian food producers to guarantee Australia's economic and national security. Food security is also used as a humanitarian response to current food insecurity among Australia's regional neighbors, but this is also tied to developing future markets for agricultural exports (Kaldor and Mayes 2014).

The biopolitics of food can bring into perspective the way food trade and production practices are entwined with strategies of security and management of population life. In shifting the focus from individual autonomy to population security, a biopolitics of food is able to reveal the conditions that influence and precede consumer choice. As mentioned, there is more than food security that can be addressed through this lens. However, the objective of this section has been to emphasize the way the global food system is set up such that the security of some is conditioned by the insecurity of others.

Concluding remarks

The purpose of this chapter has not been to argue that food ethics is redundant or that researchers engaged in this area are unaware of food security or injustices in the global food system. This is clearly not true. Rather the argument has been that food is at the nexus of bioethics and biopolitics. However, the institutional lure of bioethics, particularly the emphasis on autonomy and human health, can result in a narrowing of the lens to issues pertaining only to the consumer. Clearly, there are important ethical issues regarding ethical consumption. However, there are also biopolitical concerns that precede the consumer's choice, such as economic trade, national security, and population health.

The widespread interest in food mentioned in the introduction provides an opportunity to draw on that interest and explore broader issues. Julie Guthman concludes her book *Weighing In* suggesting that "we need to harness this exploding interest in food and use the power of public politics to change food systems" (Guthman 2011: 195). This is a possibility. However, this chapter also shares Guthman's concern that "when food itself becomes the locus of social change, it tends to erase from consideration the countless ways in which the food system has gone awry socially and environmentally, especially for those who labor in the food industry" (Guthman 2011: 161). This chapter has argued that the biopolitics that frames the bioethics of food can help to ensure that the desires of the consumer do not overshadow the lives and security of the producers.

References

Ashby, M. A. and L. E. Rich. (2013) "Eating People Is Wrong . . . or How We Decide Morally What to Eat," *Journal of Bioethical Inquiry* 10(2): 129–131.

Beekman, V. (2008) "Consumer Rights to Informed Choice on the Food Market," *Ethical Theory and Moral Practice* 11(1): 61–72.

Blewett, N., N. Goddard, S. Pettigrew, C. Reynolds, and H. Yeatman. (2011) *Labelling Logic: Review of Food Labelling Law and Policy*, Canberra: Commonwealth of Australia.

Brom, F. W. (2000) "Food, Consumer Concerns, and Trust: Food Ethics for a Globalizing Market," *Journal of Agricultural and Environmental Ethics* 12(2): 127–139.

Brom, F. W. and B. Gremmen. (2000) "From the Guest Editors Food Ethics and Consumer Concerns," *Journal of Agricultural and Environmental Ethics* 12(2): 111–112.

Brownell, K. D. and K. E. Warner. (2009) "The Perils of Ignoring History: Big Tobacco Played Dirty and Millions Died. How Similar Is Big Food?," *The Milbank Quarterly* 87(1): 259–294.

Callahan, D. (2012) *The Roots of Bioethics: Health, Progress, Technology, Death*, New York: Oxford University Press.

———. (2013) "Obesity: Chasing an Elusive Epidemic," *Hastings Center Report* 43(1): 34–40.

Campos, S., J. Doxey, and D. Hammond. (2011) "Nutrition Labels on Pre-Packaged Foods: a Systematic Review," *Public Health Nutrition* 14(8): 1496.

Charlesworth, M. (1993) *Bioethics in a Liberal Society*, Cambridge: Cambridge University Press.

Dawson, A. (2010) "The Future of Bioethics: Three Dogmas and a Cup of Hemlock," *Bioethics* 24(5): 218–225.

Department of Foreign Affairs and Trade. (2008) *About Australia – Food Industry*, viewed 12 January 2012, http://www.dfat.gov.au/facts/foodindustry.html.

De Schutter, O. (2008) Address by the UN Special Rapporteur on the Right to Food, Paper Read at High-Level Conference on World Food Security: The Challenges of Climate Change and Bioenergy, Rome.

Donzelot, J. (1980) *The Policing of Families*, London: Hutchinson of London.

Draper, A. and J. Green. (2002) "Food Safety and Consumers: Constructions of Choice and Risk," *Social Policy & Administration* 36(6): 610–625.

Emanuel, E. J. (2012) "Healthy Labels, Not Stealthy Labels," *New York Times*, viewed 5 March 2012, http://opinionator.blogs.nytimes.com/2012/03/05/healthy-labels-not-stealthy-labels/.

Enterprise and Industry. (2012) *E.U. Food Market Overview*. European Commission, viewed 14 December 2012, http://ec.europa.eu/enterprise/sectors/food/eu-market/index_en.htm.

Ferreira, F. R., S. D. Prado, M. C. D.V. S. Carvalho, and F. B. Kraemer. (2015) "Biopower and Biopolitics in the Field of Food and Nutrition," *Revista de Nutrição* 28(1): 109–119.

Foucault, M. (1980) "The Politics of Health in the Eighteenth Century," in Colin Gordon (ed.), *Power/Knowledge: Selected Interviews and Other Writings 1972–1977*, New York: Pantheon Books, pp. 166–182.

———. (1998) *The Will to Knowledge: The History of Sexuality Volume 1*, trans. by Robert Hurley, England: Penguin Books.

———. (2007) *Security, Territory, Population: Lectures at the Collège de France 1977–78*, trans. by Graham Burchell, Arnold I. Davidson (eds.), New York: Palgrave Macmillan.

Frohlich, X. (2010) "Buyer Be-aware: the Ethics of Food Labelling Reform and 'Mobilising the Consumer'," in Romeo Casabona, L. Escajedo San Epifanio, and A. Emaldi Cirión (eds.), *Global Food Security: Ethical and Legal Challenges*, Wageningen, the Netherlands: Wageningen Academic Publishers, pp. 221–227.

Gilmore, A. B., E. Savell, and J. Collin. (2011) "Public Health, Corporations and the New Responsibility Deal: Promoting Partnerships with Vectors of Disease?," *Journal of Public Health* 33(1): 2–4.

Gostin, L. O. (2010) "Trans Fat Bans and the Human Freedom: A Refutation," *The American Journal of Bioethics* 10(3): 33–34.

Guthman, J. (2011) *Weighing In: Obesity, Food Justice, and the Limits of Capitalism*, Berkeley, CA: University of California Press.

Henderson, J., J. Coveney, P. Ward, and A. Taylor. (2009) "Governing Childhood Obesity: Framing Regulation of Fast Food Advertising in the Australian Print Media," *Social Science & Medicine* 69(9): 1402–1408.

Irvine, R. (2013) "Food Ethics: Issues of Consumption and Production," *Journal of Bioethical Inquiry* 10(2): 145–148.

Irvine, R., C. Degeling, and I. Kerridge. (2013) "Bioethics and Nonhuman Animals," *Journal of Bioethical Inquiry* 10(4): 435–440.

Jensen, K. and P. Sandøe. (2002) "Food Safety and Ethics: The Interplay between Science and Values," *Journal of Agricultural and Environmental Ethics* 15(3): 245–253.

Kaldor, J. and C. Mayes. (2014) "What We Talk about When We Talk about Food Security: The Mobilization of Food Security in Australian Food and Agricultural Policy Discourse," *Agri-Food XXI Conference*, Sydney, NSW.

Kantor, A. F. (1976) "Upton Sinclair and the Pure Food and Drugs Act of 1906," *American Journal of Public Health* 66(12): 1202–1205.

Kennedy, R. (2012) "Betting the Farm on Hunger," *Al Jazeera*, viewed 28 September 2012, http://www.aljazeera.com/indepth/features/2012/09/2012911125854157194.html.

Lemke, T. (2011) *Biopolitics: An Advanced Introduction*, New York: New York University Press.

Loureiro, M. L. and W. J. Umberger. (2007) "A Choice Experiment Model for Beef: What US Consumer Responses Tell Us About Relative Preferences for Food Safety, Country-of-Origin Labeling and Traceability," *Food Policy* 32(4): 496–514.

Mann, S. (2010) *Bioethics in Perspective: Corporate Power, Public Health and Political Economy*, Cambridge: Cambridge University Press.

Marks, J. H. (2013) "Objects Closer Than They Appear: Regulating Health-Based Advertising of Food," *The American Journal of Bioethics* 13(5): 23–25.

Mayes, C. (2014) "Governing Through Choice: Food Labels and the Confluence of Food Industry and Public Health to Create 'Healthy Consumers'," *Social Theory and Health* 12(4): 376–395.

McDonald, B. L. (2011) *Food Security*, Cambridge, UK: Polity.

McGee, G. (2007) "A Clean Well Lighted Place: In Search of Food Ethics in the 21st Century Grocery Store," *The American Journal of Bioethics* 7(10): 1–2.

Moseley, W. G., J. Carney, and L. Becker. (2010) "Neoliberal Policy, Rural Livelihoods, and Urban Food Security in West Africa: A Comparative Study of The Gambia, Côte d'Ivoire, and Mali," *Proceedings of the National Academy of Sciences* 107(13): 5774–5779.

Munshi, K. (2003) "Networks in the Modern Economy: Mexican Migrants in the US Labor Market," *The Quarterly Journal of Economics* 118(2): 549–599.

Nally, D. (2011) "The Biopolitics of Food Provisioning," *Transactions of the Institute of British Geographers* 36(1): 37–53.

Office of Health and Consumer Goods. (2012) *Processed Foods Index Page*, US Department of Commerce 2012, viewed 14 December 2012, http://trade.gov/td/ocg/food.htm.

Outram, S. M. and B. Stewart. (2015) "Should Nutritional Supplements and Sports Drinks Companies Sponsor Sport? A Short Review of the Ethical Concerns," *Journal of Medical Ethics* 41(6): 447–450.

Parker, C., C. Brunswick, and J. Kotey. (2013) "The Happy Hen on Your Supermarket Shelf," *Journal of Bioethical Inquiry* 10(2): 165–186.

Parker, C. and G. Scrinis. (2014) "Out of the Cage and into the Barn: Supermarket Power Food System Governance and the Regulation of Free Range Eggs," *Griffith Law Review* 23(2): 318–347.

Patel, R. (2009) *Stuffed and Starved: Markets, Power and the Hidden Battle for the World Food System*, Collingwood, VIC: Black Inc.

Pence, G. E. (2002) *The Ethics of Food: A Reader for the Twenty-first Century*, London: Rowman & Littlefield.

Pollan, M. (2006) *The Omnivore's Dilemma: A Natural History of Four Meals*, New York: Penguin Group.

Potter, V. R. (1971) *Bioethics: Bridge to the Future*, New Jersey: Prentice-Hall.

Reeve, B. (2013) "Private Governance, Public Purpose? Assessing Transparency and Accountability in Self-Regulation of Food Advertising to Children," *Journal of Bioethical Inquiry* 10(2): 149–163.

Resnik, D. (2010) "Trans Fat Bans and Human Freedom," *The American Journal of Bioethics* 10(3): 27–32.

Ristovski-Slijepcevic, S., G. E. Chapman, and B. L. Beagan. (2010) "Being a 'Good Mother': Dietary Governmentality in the Family Food Practices of Three Ethnocultural Groups in Canada," *Health* 14(5): 467–483.

Rye, J. F. and J. Andrzejewska. (2010) "The Structural Disempowerment of Eastern European Migrant Farm Workers in Norwegian Agriculture," *Journal of Rural Studies* 26(1): 41–51.

Sass, H.-M. (2007) "Fritz Jahr's 1927 Concept of Bioethics," *Kennedy Institute of Ethics Journal* 17(4): 279–295.

Scrinis, G. (2013) *Nutritionism: The Science and Politics of Dietary Advice*, New York: Columbia University Press.

Sen, A. (1981) *Poverty and Famines: An Essay on Entitlement and Deprivation*, Oxford: Oxford University Press.

Shue, H. (1996) *Basic Rights: Subsistence, Affluence, and U.S. Foreign Policy*, New Jersey: Princeton University Press.

Siipi, H. and S. Uusitalo. (2008) "Consumer Autonomy and Sufficiency of GMF Labeling," *Journal of Agricultural and Environmental Ethics* 21(4): 353–369.

Silverglade, B. and I. R. Heller. (2010) *Food Labeling Chaos: the Case for Reform*, Washington, DC: Center for Science in the Public Interest.

Singer, P. (1972) "Famine, Affluence, and Morality," *Philosophy & Public Affairs* 1(3): 229–243.

——. (1977) *Animal Liberation: Towards an End to Man's Inhumanity to Animals*, London: Granada Publishing Ltd.

——. (2012) "Weigh More, Pay More," *Project Syndicate: A World of Ideas*, viewed 28 August 2012, http://www.project-syndicate.org/commentary/weigh-more—pay-more.

—— and J. Mason. (2006) *The Way We Eat: Why our Food Choices Matter*, Emmaus, PA: Rodale.

Smith, M. (2011) *Against Ecological Sovereignty: Ethics, Biopolitics, and Saving the Natural World*, Minneapolis: University of Minnesota Press.

Spencer, S. and M. Kneebone. (2012) *FOODmap: An Analysis of the Australian Food Supply Chain*. Canberra: Department of Agriculture, Fisheries and Forestry.

Taylor, L. (1996) "Food Riots Revisited," *Journal of Social History* 30(2): 483–496.

Thompson, P. B. (2015a) "Agricultural Ethics: Then and Now," *Agriculture and Human Values* 32(1): 77–85.

Thompson, P. B. (2015b) *From Field to Fork: Food Ethics for Everyone*, Oxford: Oxford University Press.

Vogel, L. (2006) "The Genesis of Bioethics in Hans Jonas, Leo Strauss, and Leon Kass," *Hastings Center Report* 36(3): 32–44.

Zwart, H. (2000) "A Short History of Food Ethics," *Journal of Agricultural and Environmental Ethics* 12(2): 113–126.

17

OBESITY AND COERCION

Clement Loo and Robert A. Skipper, Jr.

Introduction

This chapter explores the role of deliberate choice in consumer feeding behavior and its connection to obesity. In the West, especially in North America, many people, including health professionals, believe that obese people are stereotypically unhealthy eaters who lack self-control and are not motivated to be physically active (Salas et al. 2014). In general, medical treatment for the overweight or obese patient reflects the stereotype of the obese person: Eat healthy, control your portions through "will power," cognitive behavioral therapy, or pharmacotherapy, and, lastly, exercise (Steelman and Westman 2010).[1] In other words, medical interventions send the message that the obese patient should learn to make better lifestyle choices.

At least in the US, the same stereotype is reflected in public health initiatives to combat the obesity epidemic. The recommendations of the FDA, USDA, American College of Sports Medicine (ACSM), Academy of Nutrition and Dietetics (AND), and the Patient Protection and Affordable Care Act (ACA) each endorse interventions designed to inform consumers about healthy diets. Such interventions include programs intended to educate children and adults about caloric energy balance (ACSM, AND); *MyPlate*, the Obama administration's illustration of a healthy dinner plate (USDA, FDA); and mandatory calorie counts on vending-machine food items and in fast-food restaurants (ACA), among others. The guiding assumption of each of these initiatives is that providing information about the nutritional composition of food items and guidelines for a diet that will maintain a healthy weight will enable consumers to make better dietary choices (Manore et al. 2014). Overweight and obesity is, after all, a matter of choice, the logic goes, and those who continue to make bad choices are lazy, indiscriminate, and impulsive people.

But is the situation so simple? We think not. In fact, the stereotype of the obese person does not hold up to scrutiny: The differences between the nutritional contents of diets, amount of exercise, and capacity for restraint and dis-inhibition between non-obese and obese people are marginal at best (Salas et al. 2014). Indeed, obesity experts now know that the condition has multiple interacting causes, including ones that are genetic, metabolic, psychological, sociocultural, and environmental (e.g., Finegood 2011). Intervention strategies, alas, have not caught up with this scientific knowledge. In this paper, we focus on the role of choice, and we argue that on a particular but reasonable conception of consent, people may not have much choice in being overweight or obese. It may be instead that they are coerced into their condition.

Choice and consent

When we consider "choice" in this chapter, we do not mean choice in the sense of having more than one option available to achieve some concrete end. In such a case, one could have choices available and yet be recognizably constrained in one's deliberative autonomy. This point is often illustrated through appeal to a class of instances in which individuals must perform some action under duress, e.g., signing a contract under threat of blackmail, confessing to a crime due to police badgering, and so on. In such instances the individual has options available, but only in a very weak sense. That is, there is nothing physically preventing such an individual from choosing the threatened harm rather than performing the action that is encouraged by the other party. Yet, one might argue that because such a person is under threat, the person has no substantive choice to make.

Substantive choices are the sorts of choices we are interested in here; these are choices that, at a minimum, require consent. Following Elliott (2006), our notion of consent requires that individuals be able to actively identify which behaviors or activities are most likely to achieve self-held objectives and then actively choose to perform those behaviors or activities. Consent, in turn, has four conditions that must be satisfied: (1) disclosure, (2) understanding, (3) competence, and (4) voluntariness (Elliott 2006).

The first three of these conditions (i.e., disclosure, understanding, and competence) are essential because, as noted by Faden et al. (1986), consent requires intentionality. For an individual to consent to or decide, act, or effect, that individual must have as her purpose that particular decision, act, or effect. If an individual were merely to passively assent to some request without any intention or thought regarding the content of that request, then they could not be properly understood as giving consent (Faden et al. 1986).

Intent, and the planning associated with it, requires that an individual have adequate knowledge of the likely consequences of the choice she faces and the effects of their consequences vis-à-vis the individual's values, needs, and wants. Without such knowledge, one will not be able to determine how her choices might relate to various outcomes; she would thus be unable to plan.

For an individual to gain sufficient information to act intentionally requires the following. First, adequate information must be available to the individual. Second, information must be presented in an accessible manner. And third, the individual must have the capacity to use that information to make decisions based on her self-interest. These three requirements are captured in Elliott's (2006) disclosure, understanding, and competence conditions.

For the disclosure criterion to be met, the decision-maker must have available to her adequate information about potential consequences, both positive and negative, of available alternative actions. Such information should address potential risks and benefits of the options that are the most salient for the chooser and make clear how opting for different available alternatives would affect the likelihood of obtaining those risks and benefits.

To satisfy the understanding requirement, information must be available in a format that promotes the decision-maker's ability to identify likely consequences of choices and to determine how those consequences relate to her objectives. Information must be in a language, dialect, and vocabulary that is accessible to the chooser. And, finally, the information should be presented in media that are readily accessible to the decision-maker.

The competence condition requires that the decision-maker have the faculties to adequately understand how the predictable consequences of available choices presented to them are likely to satisfy or frustrate the decision-maker's needs, interests, and preferences. Put more concretely, for someone to be competent to make a decision, she must have the cognitive, emotional, psychological, cultural, and biological toolkit available to be able to recognize how each of the likely outcomes of the options presented to her may contribute to the achievement of values or disvalues important to her.

The final condition, voluntariness, is central for autonomous action. This condition requires that the relevant choices are not made under duress and reflect primarily the intent and wishes of the decision-maker. To meet the voluntariness condition, the decision-maker must be free from either coercion or manipulation. The condition of the decision-maker must not constrain her choice of alternatives in such a way that she cannot base her decisions on satisfying her interests, desires, and needs. An individual should be able to choose free from threat of harm and from mis-information.[2] In what follows, we understand choices about diet to require consent as outlined above.

Obesity and consent: disclosure and the problem of labeling

The nutrition facts labels found on the back of packaged foods (in the US) are one way nutrition information is made available to consumers (see Figure 17.1 on the following page).[3] The Food and Agriculture Organization of the United Nations (FAO) and the World Health Organization (WHO) convened a conference in 1962 and developed what is known as *Codex Alimentarius. Codex* is a collection of standards and best practices intended to promote consumer health and welfare through the regulation of international food trade. In the 340 or so individual standards within *Codex*, all of those relating to the provision of nutritional and food information to consumers address food labeling.

In spite of *Codex*, labeling standards differ substantially between countries. Some countries, like the US, require labeling of packaged foods; other countries make labeling voluntary; still other countries have no requirements for labels at all. Indeed, Hawkes' (2004; 2006) review of labeling regulations found that, within the 74 reviewed countries, only 10 had mandatory labeling requirements; 45 countries had voluntary labeling, and 19 countries had no policy. Given this considerable variation in food labeling regulations, it is not at all clear that consumers are getting enough information about the nutritional characteristics of their food.

It is unclear whether consumers receive adequate information even in countries where labeling is mandatory. This is true for two reasons: First, countries that require labeling differ in the kind of information that must be included on labels. Some follow *Codex* guidelines, while others have adopted their own standards, such as Mexico's *Norma Oficial Mexicana*. Such varying standards between nations with mandatory food labeling laws make it hard to know whether consumers are getting the information necessary to make informed choices about what they eat. Second, even if countries consistently employed the most robust labeling schemes, it is unclear whether labeling provides the right kinds of information to promote healthy eating. Consider the following: Within the US, which follows *Codex* labeling guidelines and has one of the most robust labeling systems, food labels are formatted in terms of recommended daily values, or %DV (see Figure 17.1). Labels report on product content in terms of absolute amount in grams, the total amounts of fat, carbohydrates, and protein (in both grams and %DV), the percent of recommended daily intake of select nutrients, such as vitamins A, C, etc., and total calories of the item. The FDA recommends that the average American, understood to be between the age of 4 to adulthood and consuming 2,000 calories per day, should consume 65g of fat, 300g of carbohydrates, 50g of protein, 2.4g of sodium, 3.5g of potassium, 25g of fiber, and smaller amounts of a number of other micronutrients and minerals (FDA 2013).

But there is a problem with this approach to labeling. For the sake of simplicity and ease of use, the %DV set by the FDA make some abstractions about the so-called "average American," and those abstractions can undermine the usefulness of %DV for individuals who wish to use them as a guide to healthy eating. By setting the %DV equal to the mean nutritional requirements of all Americans from the age of 4 to adulthood, the %DV grossly underestimate the nutritional needs of some populations, while grossly overestimating those needs for others.

Nutrition Facts

Serving Size 1 cup (228g)
Servings Per Container about 2

Amount Per Serving

Calories 250   Calories from Fat 110

% Daily Value*

Total Fat 12g	**18%**
Saturated Fat 3g	**15%**
Trans Fat 3g	
Cholesterol 30mg	**10%**
Sodium 470mg	**20%**
Total Carbohydrate 31g	**10%**
Dietary Fiber 0g	**0%**
Sugars 5g	
Proteins 5g	

Vitamin A	4%
Vitamin C	2%
Calcium	20%
Iron	4%

* Percent Daily Values are based on a 2,000 calorie diet. Your Daily Values may be higher or lower depending on your calorie needs:

	Calories:	2,000	2,500
Total Fat	Less than	65g	80g
Saturated Fat	Less than	20g	25g
Cholesterol	Less than	300mg	300mg
Sodium	Less than	2,400mg	2,400mg
Total Carbohydrate		300g	375g
Dietary Fiber		25g	30g

For educational purposes only. This label does not meet the labeling requirements described in 21 CFR 101.9.

Figure 17.1   Generic food label prescribed by Codex and the FDA.[4]

As Yates (2006) notes, required daily allowances of various nutrients vary dramatically between different age and gender groups. Premenopausal adult females require greater amounts of iron in their diets than other demographic groups, for example (Yates 2006). Similarly, the elderly require far more vitamin B6 than their younger counterparts (Yates 2006). The upshot is that normalizing %DV across the entire population for a broad age range misrepresents the nutritional needs of a variety of groups, particularly vulnerable groups such as children and the elderly. By following %DV on food labels rigorously, members of these groups could find themselves experiencing nutritional deficiencies or excesses.

According to Elliott's (2006) disclosure condition for consent, consumers must have adequate information about the potential positive and negative consequences of making particular choices. When information is not available, especially systematically, as is the case with variance among food labeling laws across country borders, consumers do not get adequate information. Moreover, when information is presented abstractly, as in the case of food labels in the US, it is apparent that some consumers get incorrect information. Thus, despite the efforts of food labeling, the disclosure condition for consent is not clearly met. Thus, consumers are not in a good position to make substantive choices about what they eat.[5]

Obesity and consent: understanding and the New York labeling law

Above we suggest that nutritional labeling is often inadequate for disclosing nutritional information about food to equip consumers to make informed decisions. However, evidence suggests that, even when labels provide adequate information, individuals may have difficulties understanding and using that information to improve their diets. Below, we consider Elbel's work on whether calorie labeling in fast-food restaurants increases the chances that consumers make better food choices (Elbel 2011; Elbel et al. 2009).

In 2009 New York City enacted legislation requiring all food-service establishments to post the caloric content of their products on all menus and menu boards. This law was intended to provide consumers with the information necessary for them to reduce their calorie intake as a way to respond to the obesity epidemic. However, the labels may have had the opposite effect.

Elbel and his team (2009) collected receipts and surveyed fast-food patrons in a predominantly low-income, African-American area in New York City and compared those data with data collected from a demographically similar area in Newark, New Jersey, where no calorie counts had yet been posted. Elbel et al. (2009) found that, though more than half of patrons surveyed (approximately 55%) reported that they noticed the newly presented calorie information and the majority of those individuals (approximately 60%) reported that the information influenced their meal choices, the mandated labeling had no effect on purchasing and eating behavior. Elbel (2011) followed up on this study to determine why the mandated labeling failed to improve eating behavior despite reports by consumers that the presented information was influential to meal choices.

In this second study Elbel (2011) surveyed customers at fast-food restaurants to determine whether they were (1) aware of the number of calories one should consume to maintain a healthy weight and (2) able to estimate the number of calories for the meal they just consumed. The design of the study is similar to that in Elbel et al. (2009), but it takes account of responses given pre- and post-labeling in both New York City and Newark. Both before and after labeling, Elbel found that ~30% of those surveyed in each city answered that the recommended calorie intake to maintain a healthy weight is 1,500–2,000 calories (Elbel 2011). Strikingly, ~40% of those surveyed in New York and Newark pre-labeling reported that a diet intended to maintain a healthy weight consisted of fewer than 1,000 calories; post-labeling found that these estimates were ~10% lower in each city (Elbel 2011). Both pre- and post-labeling, fewer than 10% of those surveyed reported that a healthy weight could be maintained by consuming 3,000 calories or more (Elbel 2011). An additional ~10% did not know or did not answer. Additionally, Elbel found that patrons in New York and Newark underestimated the calorie counts of their purchased meal by ~25%; there was a ~5% improvement in these estimates post-labeling.

Elbel concludes from both studies that mandatory labeling has at best a negligible effect on calorie consumption in fast-food restaurants; he further calls for research that explores new ways of conveying nutritional information to consumers (Elbel 2011; Elbel et al. 2009). We agree, and we further suggest that mandatory labeling of food in restaurants and retail outlets fails the understanding condition for consent: Relevant information must be in a format that promotes a decision-maker's ability to use it. Calorie counts may be a bad way to convey information about how to make meal choices that contribute to a healthy weight. After all, consumers demonstrate that they can go quite wrong estimating the calorie counts of their meals and not use or not understand the recommended calorie range for maintaining a healthy weight.

Obesity and consent: competence and mindless eating

So far, we have examined whether adequate information presented in a useable form helps consumers make healthy food choices. Here, we suggest that even if good, useable information is provided to consumers, they still may be unable to make substantive choices. Consider the phenomenon of "mindless eating" (Wansink 2007; discussed in a public health context in Skipper 2012).

In one study, Wansink and Cheney demonstrated that serving bowl size influences the amount of food a consumer serves and eats (2005). At a contrived Super Bowl party two buffet tables on opposite sides of a room held identical, energy-dense snack foods. Students invited to the party, but blind to the experiment, were alternately led to a table and asked whether they would like any snacks. At one table, students served themselves from two large, 4-liter serving bowls; at the other table, the serving bowls contained the same amount of food in two smaller, 2-liter bowls. Students used a 1-cup scoop to serve themselves on 10-inch plates. Beverages were made available after food was served. An hour later, food plates were taken away and each student's waste food was recorded and subtracted from the amount taken. All students were similar in BMI, weight, time since previous meal, age, education, and sex.

Students who served themselves from the large bowls took 53% more and ate 56% more than those who served themselves from the smaller bowls. In terms of actual calories, 146 more calories were served and 142 more calories were eaten on average for these students as compared to those who served themselves from the smaller bowls. The effect was greater in men; for women the size of the serving bowl did not have a statistically significant effect on consumption. That the minor environmental cue of bowl size affected consumption suggests that packaging can lead to unintended overeating.

Wansink and Payne performed a similar study to determine whether environmental cues cause decreases in consumption, as well (Wansink and Payne 2007). They contrived another Super Bowl party at a public sports bar. Groups of students were encouraged to serve themselves chicken wings from a buffet table. Wansink determined that 11 tables (31 students) would be bussed of waste food (bones) continuously, and 10 tables (21 students) would not. Waste food was measured after the party. However, all of the tables would be regularly encouraged to serve themselves more wings. Not surprisingly, according to Wansink and Payne, students at the bussed tables consumed on average more than those at unbussed tables: 27.3% (or 2.5 wings per person) more. The effect of the cue (waste food at the unbussed tables) was stronger in men than in women. Environmental cues caused a reduction in consumption, suggesting that the students who saw how much they had eaten were better able to track their total consumption, or that the sight of the bones remaining on the table suppressed their appetites, or that the unbussed tables caused embarrassment at just how much was consumed, or some other, similar explanation. What is important here is not so much the explanation of *how* the cues influenced the students, but rather *that* the cues had influence at all.

The upshot of Wansink's studies (and others like them) is that we are not good at judging portion size or tracking our consumption in distracting environments without lurid external cues. Moreover, our bodies are bad at telling us when we are physiologically sated. Further, it so happens that it does not matter if the taste of the food is less than good. Wansink and Park showed that the serving size cue is influential even if consumers perceive that the taste of the food is not good (Wansink and Park 2001). Managing our consumption of food is not firmly in our control. The competence condition requires that individuals be able to use appropriate information to make decisions that serve their interests, concerns, and needs. If Wansink and his collaborators are correct, our environment affects our ability to use information to make decisions about eating.

Obesity and consent: voluntariness, food deserts, and market capture

Finally, we consider whether consumers' food choices satisfy the voluntariness condition for consent. Here, recall, decision-makers must be free to make decisions that reflect self-interest; critically, the decision-maker must be free from either coercion or manipulation. We argue that there are populations in which consumers' food choices do not meet the voluntariness condition.

In the US, rates of obesity and its negative impacts on health are higher in impoverished, racial/ethnic minority neighborhoods than they are in more affluent and predominantly White neighborhoods (Cubbin et al. 2001). This disparity can be and has been explained by the lack of access to supermarkets that offer whole foods and the excess of and relatively easy access to convenience stores and fast-food restaurants that offer processed foods (Walker et al. 2010). Such neighborhoods are called "food deserts" (Cummins and Macintyre 2002). According to Walker et al. (2010), there are four main features of food deserts. First is poor access to supermarkets. Walker and his colleagues found that, nationally, the lowest-income areas have ~30% fewer supermarkets than the highest-income neighborhoods. This disparity is made worse by problems accessing transportation, severe work schedules, increased responsibilities of being a single parent, and the lack of time to cook that results from these. Second, African-American neighborhoods typically have fewer supermarkets relative to predominantly White neighborhoods: indeed, Walker found fewer than half the number of chain supermarkets in predominantly African-American as compared to White neighborhoods. Third, there is a larger number of small, local convenience stores in low-income neighborhoods relative to more affluent areas. These stores, more accessible than supermarkets, lack variety and stock poor-quality food items. Fourth, there are fewer chain supermarkets as compared to independent supermarkets in impoverished neighborhoods. Because of economies of scale, chain supermarkets are able to offer food and other goods at lower prices than independent stores, making it more difficult for members of impoverished neighborhoods to purchase whole foods and, especially, dry goods at reasonable prices.

Arguably, these features of food deserts constrain choices for those who reside in them. While food deserts are often considered to be a problem in the US and not in other parts of the world (Walker et al. 2010), constrained food choices are not unique to the US. In the last couple of decades, as trade barriers between nations have fallen, transnational corporations based in the US and Europe substantially increased investment and sales in low- and middle-income countries (LMICs). US companies that produce packaged goods, such as PepsiCo, Coca-Cola, Kraft, and General Mills, have exported as much as $30 billion of packaged foods (e.g., carbonated beverages, breakfast cereals, savory snacks) per year to a variety of countries, including Mexico, Thailand, and countries in South America (that is, the Mercosur) (Wilkinson 2004). European corporations, such as Danone, Diageo, and Nestlé, have average annual exports of more than $60 billion to countries in Southeast Asia (ASEAN nations), but also to countries in the Mercosur (Wilkinson 2004).

Traditionally, the foundation of LMIC food systems is local agriculture and independent food retailers (Wilkinson 2010). But lifestyle changes driven in part by increased urbanization in LMICS has helped US and European corporations experience considerable growth across markets. That growth has been combined with consolidation of production. The consequence is that US and EU corporations have captured production from domestic farmers and retail markets from independent domestic retailers. We are convinced that the effect of the change in foundation of the LMIC food system has constrained consumer choice (Loo and Skipper 2015).

The voluntariness condition requires that the alternatives available to an individual be sufficiently unconstrained to allow her to make decisions based on self-interest. In both food deserts and LMICs individuals have limited access to whole foods in particular. As a result, they are unable to choose health-promoting diets, and rates of obesity are higher when compared to populations who live in locations with greater access to fresh foods (Gottlieb and Joshi 2010; Ornelas 2010). When it comes to obesity and food choices, it seems that, for many, the voluntariness condition is not met.

Conclusion

With respect to dietary choice, Elliott's (2006) conditions for consent, that is, disclosure, competence, understanding, and voluntariness, are not met in certain segments of the global population. Indeed, the cases we discuss suggest that those who have their choices most constrained are disadvantaged with respect to their socioeconomic status. Is there a role for government in mitigating this apparent inequality?

If overweight and obesity are simply a matter of making bad choices, then government should not intervene. Consider New York Court of Appeals Judge Eugene F. Pigott's opinion in New York Statewide Coalition of Hispanic Chambers of Commerce v. The New York City Department of Health and Mental Hygiene, in which he reversed New York's statute limiting the serving size of sugary drinks:

> By restricting portions, the Board necessarily chose between ends, including public health, the economic consequences associated with restricting profits by beverage companies and vendors, tax implications for small business owners, and personal autonomy with respect to the choices of New York City residents concerning what they consume.
>
> (New York Statewide Coalition of Hispanic Chambers of Commerce v. The New York City Department of Health and Mental Hygiene 2014)

Pigott's view follows that of a number of liberal and libertarian political philosophers who argue that personal autonomy is a fundamental good necessary for the flourishing of individuals (Kymlicka 1989). They suggest that autonomy is a necessary precondition for allowing individuals to pursue their interest, commitments, and goals in order to pursue their life plan (Kymlicka 1989). On this view, liberal democratic governments must protect the autonomy of their citizens (Kernohan 1999; Kymlicka 1989; Young 1990) with the exception of when such autonomy results in direct harm to others (Nozick 1974).

However, we have offered reasons to suspect that our dietary choices, particularly for members of disadvantaged populations, are severely constrained if not in some cases altogether removed. And, given the apparently limited ability for individuals to effectively choose to eat healthier diets, traditional approaches – interventions that provide information to educate individuals so that they make better choices – are doomed to fail.

There is a clear need for a new conversation about how to address obesity (see, e.g., Finegood 2011; Skipper 2012). Such a conversation needs to be one that does not treat obesity as a matter of personal choice but instead recognizes that it is a matter of context and environment. In this conversation attention must shift from interventions aimed at shifting personal behavior to attention to interventions that address obesity through structural changes to the food system.

Notes

1 The super-obese patient is eligible for gastric bypass surgery to divide the stomach into a small upper chamber and a larger, remnant pouch. This is offered in addition to diet, therapy, drugs, and exercise (Steelman and Westman 2010).
2 "Threat of harm" here is broadly defined as direct threats of immediate harm as well as indirect threats such as concerns regarding future employment, risk of economic loss, or social alienation.
3 Other labeling requirements (in the US) include restrictions on front-of-package labeling, calorie labeling in restaurants and at retail outlets, and calorie labeling on vending-machine food items (FDA 2014).
4 This image and other sample food labels are available for educational use through the FDA at <http://www.fda.gov/Food/IngredientsPackagingLabeling/LabelingNutrition/ucm114155.htm>.
5 To be sure, consumers may go to the FDA website (www.fda.gov) to learn how to read food labels. However, the sheer volume of information provided is likely to paralyze consumers (Kahneman 2013).

References

Cubbin, C., Hadden, W., & Winkleby, M. (2001) "Neighborhood Context and Cardiovascular Disease Risk Factors: The Contribution of Material Deprivation," *Ethnicity and Disease* 11: 687–700.

Cummins, S., & Macintyre, S. (2002) "Food Deserts – Evidence and Assumption in Health Policy Making," *British Medical Journal* 325: 36–438.

Elbel, B. (2011) "Consumer Estimation of Recommended and Actual Calories at Fast Food Restaurants," *Obesity* 19: 1971–1978.

Elbel, B., Kersh, R., Brescoli, V., & Dixon, L. (2009) "Calorie Labeling and Food Choices: A First Look at the Effects On Low-Income People in New York City," *Health Affairs* 28: w1110–w1121.

Elliott, K. (2006) "An Ethics of Expertise Based on Informed Consent," *Science and Engineering Ethics* 12: 637–661.

Faden, R. R., Beauchamp, T. L., & King, N. M. P. (1986) *A History and Theory of Informed Consent*, Oxford: Oxford University Press.

FDA (Food and Drug Administration). (2013) "Guidance for Industry: A Food Labeling Guide," viewed 19 September 2015, http://www.fda.gov/Food/GuidanceRegulation/GuidanceDocumentsRegulatory Information/LabelingNutrition/ucm064928.htm

———. (2014) "Food Labeling: Nutrition Labeling of Standard Menu Items in Restaurants and Similar Retail Food Establishments Final Regulatory Impact Analysis FDA–2011–F–0172." Washington: Government Printing Office, viewed 19 September 2015, http://www.fda.gov/Food/IngredientsPackagingLabeling/LabelingNutrition/ucm114155.htm.

Finegood, D. (2011) "The Complex Systems Science of Obesity," in Cawley, J. (ed.) *The Oxford Handbook of the Social Science of Obesity*, New York: Oxford University Press, pp. 208–236.

Gottlieb, R., & Joshi, A. (2010) *Food Justice*, Cambridge, MA: MIT Press.

Hawkes, C. (2004) "Nutrition Labels and Health Claims: The Global Regulatory Environment," *World Health Organization Publications*, viewed 26 August 2014, http://www.who.int/publications/en/.

Hawkes, C. (2006) "Uneven Dietary Development: Linking the Policies and Processes of Globalization with the Nutrition Transition, Obesity and Diet-Related Chronic Diseases," *Globalization and Health* 2: 1–18.

Kahneman, D. (2013) *Thinking, Fast and Slow*, New York: Farrar, Strauss, and Giroux.

Kernohan, A. (1999) *Liberalism, Equality, and Cultural Oppression*, New York: Cambridge University Press.

Kymlicka, W. (1989) *Liberalism, Community and Culture*, Oxford: Clarendon.

Loo, C., & Skipper, R. (2015) "Obesity, Coercion, and Development: Food Justice and the Globalization of Processed Foods," in Rawlinson, M., and Ward, C. (eds.) *Global Food, Global Justice: Essays on Eating Under Globalization*, New Castle Upon Tyne, UK: Cambridge Scholars Press, pp. 72–91.

Manore, M. M., Brown, K., Houtkooper, L., Jakcic, J., Peters, J. C., Edge, M. S., Steiber, A., Going, S., Gable, L. G., & Krautheim, A.M. (2014) "Energy Balance at the Crossroads: Translating Science into Action," *Medicine & Science in Sports & Exercise* 46: 1466–1473.

New York Statewide Coalition of Hispanic Chambers of Commerce v. The New York City Department of Health and Mental Hygiene, 16 N.E.3d 538 (N.Y. 2014).

Nozick, R. (1974) *Anarchy, State, and Utopia*, New York: Basic Books.

Ornelas, L. (2010) "Shining a Light on the Valley of Heart's Delight: Taking a Look at Access to Healthy Foods in Santa Clara County's Communities of Color and Low-Income Communities," *Food Empowerment Project*, San Jose, CA.

Salas, X., Forhan, M., & Sharma, A. (2014) "Diffusing Obesity Myths," *Clinical Obesity* 4: 189–196.

Skipper, R. (2012) "Obesity: Towards a Libertarian Paternalistic System of Public Health Interventions," *Public Health Ethics* 5: 181–191.

Steelman, G., & Westman E. (eds.) (2010) *Obesity: Evaluation and Treatment Essentials*, London: Informa Healthcare.

Walker, R. E., Kaene, C. R., & Burke, J. G. (2010) "Disparities and Access to Healthy Food in the United States: A Review of Food Deserts Literature," *Health & Place* 16: 876–884.

Wansink, B. (2007) *Mindless Eating: Why We Eat More Than We Think*, New York: Bantam.

Wansink, B., & Cheney, M. (2005) "Super Bowls: Serving Bowl Size and Food Consumption," *JAMA* 294: 1727–1728.

Wansink, B., & Park, S.B. (2001) "At the Movies: How External Cues and Perceived Taste Impact Consumption Volume," *Food Quality and Preference* 12: 69–74.

Wansink, B., & Payne, C.R. (2007) "Internal and External Cues of Meal Cessation: The French Paradox Redux?" *Obesity* 15: 2920–2924.

Wilkinson, J. (2004) "The Food Processing Industry, Globalization and Developing Countries," *e-Journal of Agricultural and Development Economics* 1: 184–201.

——. (2010) "The Globalization of Agribusiness and Developing World Systems," *Monthly Review* 61: 38–49.

Yates, A. A. (2006) "Which Dietary Reference Intake is Best Suited to Serve as the Basis for Nutrition Labeling for Daily Values?" *The Journal of Nutrition* 136: 2457–2462.

Young, I. M. (1990) *Justice and the Politics of Difference*, Princeton: Princeton University Press.

18

ETHICAL CONSUMERISM

A defense

Sabine Hohl

The harms occurring in our current system of food production are numerous and well known. Animal-based agriculture has been identified as one of the largest contributors to climate change (Goodland and Anhang 2009; Steinfeld et al. 2006).[1] Billions of animals are raised under the atrocious conditions of factory farming, suffering miserable lives and often cruel and untimely deaths. Industrialized food production is closely tied to diverse environmental problems such as soil degradation, water shortage, and deforestation (Steinfeld et al. 2006). Moreover, many of those who work in food production – farmers, field workers, and slaughterhouse workers – do not enjoy adequate working conditions, nor do they receive fair compensation for their efforts in many cases.[2]

In light of these facts, it is not surprising that food is currently one of the most active areas of ethical consumerism. Movements that promote vegetarian and vegan diets, local production, fairer trade relations, and the protection of workers' rights have gained an increasing amount of attention in recent decades. But what role can ethical consumerism play in the prevention of the harms mentioned above? Is it to be recommended as a morally valuable practice and as an important contributor to improvements at the collective level? Or is there, in fact, reason to be skeptical of ethical consumerism?

With ethical consumerism on the rise, criticism of the practice has also increased in recent times. One of the common objections against ethical consumerism states that it is a feel-good movement that actually subverts or prevents meaningful change in collective food politics by effectively lulling people into complacency. Having made what is presented as an ethical choice at the supermarket, critics suppose, consumers will then lack the awareness necessary to take part in political activism. There is also a worry that ethical consumerism is an elitist and exclusionary movement, and that it ultimately fosters the very consumerist values that contribute to the harms in food production. A further criticism states that attempts to change the system of food production through ethical consumerism are simply ineffective – the efforts made by a few consumers will be like a drop in the ocean. To this we can add the objection that at least some forms of ethical consumerism might represent a type of "vigilantism" (Hussain 2012).

The objective of this article is to present and assess these criticisms, and to ultimately defend food-related ethical consumerism against them. I will argue that the ineffectiveness objection fails, as consumers contribute to the harm that is caused in the food sector even though they might not always be able to individually make a difference for the relevant outcomes. Furthermore, ethical consumerism need not be elitist; it does not necessarily reaffirm consumerist values; and it complements and fosters attempts at collective change rather than standing in opposition to them. Finally, I will also address the worry that some forms of ethical consumerism might constitute a form of vigilantism. I will defend the claim that, under current non-ideal conditions, it is justified to take action as a consumer since the interests at stake are important enough to outweigh concerns about procedural requirements of the democratic process.

Preliminaries

Ethical consumerism is the practice of basing one's consumption choices in ethical considerations, at least partially (Hussain 2012: 112). These can include concerns regarding workers' rights, the fairness of trade relations, the environment, or the well-being of animals. Consumers are faced with the task of taking into account a variety of ways in which their purchasing choices might contribute to harm and injustice – making the "right choice" can therefore seem like a complicated matter (Lichtenberg 2010). For example, should one focus on vegetarian and vegan products, or is it more important to consider locally sourced products? For reasons of space, I cannot address the complexity involved in balancing diverse ethical considerations under conditions of limited information in this article, and I will proceed under the assumption that consumers can make educated guesses regarding which consumption choices are more ethical than others. In reality, this condition will obviously not always be met.

The term ethical consumerism covers a broad range of actions, from individual purchases motivated by ethical considerations to collectively organized activism, such as large-scale boycotts of specific manufacturers or the development of "green" and "fair trade" labels. A distinction is often drawn between a type of ethical consumerism that is entirely private and a type of politically motivated ethical consumerism that aims to raise awareness and to influence other agents' behavior. A consumer who engages in private ethical consumerism merely wants to avoid being personally implicated in the harms associated with a certain product, while a consumer participating in the second type of ethical consumerism intends to influence the behavior of others. Hussain calls this latter type "social change ethical consumerism" (2012: 112).

As an instance of private ethical consumerism, consider the following example: Lisa goes vegan because she no longer wants to contribute to the animal suffering caused by the meat and dairy industries. Compare this to the following case: Carl boycotts Coca-Cola because of the company's alleged working rights violations in Colombia. He hopes that Coca-Cola will come under pressure due to lower sales numbers and improve their policies regarding workers' rights in response. This latter example falls under social change ethical consumerism, as Carl intends to influence other agents' (in this case Coca-Cola's) behavior. Note that the distinction does not refer to the degree to which ethical consumerism is collectively organized – another important respect in which different actions that fall under ethical consumerism can differ from each other – but rather to the motive that drives the action. Individual actions (or omissions) and collective efforts both can count as instances of social change ethical consumerism.

In practice, we often find a mixture of the two motives. A consumer interested in supporting social change may at the same time also want to avoid being personally implicated in a harmful practice, and vice versa. If we consider the case of Lisa, for example, it seems unlikely that she would exclusively care about detaching from the wrongs of animal agriculture and not give any thought to potential political reform in this area. Moreover, the action of buying or boycotting certain products for ethical reasons almost always has a social dimension, as other people are likely to notice these efforts. In this article, I will discuss both private and social change ethical consumerism, and I will point out whenever objections only apply to one type or the other.

The case of food is arguably special in several respects. Eating is intimately linked to our physical and psychological well-being, and it is closely related to traditions, identities, and ways of life. This identity aspect of food raises the stakes of ethical consumerism. Jonathan Safran Foer captures this in a passage of his book *Eating Animals*, where he describes his emotional reaction to the prospect of his young son never getting the chance to eat his grandmother's signature dish (carrots and chicken) due to his and his wife's choice to raise him on a vegetarian diet (Safran Foer 2010: 15). Moreover, moral criticism of the way animals are used in food production tends to lead to the conclusion that one should abstain from buying a wide array of products.

For these reasons, food can be considered an especially fraught area for ethical consumerism. Some of the objections to ethical consumerism in general seem to have a special bite when applied to food, such as concerns about elitism. In what follows, I will discuss these objections in a general manner and use the case of food-related ethical consumerism to illustrate them.

Ineffectiveness

Picture a consumer in a supermarket, faced with a myriad of food choices. She picks up a steak, and then puts it down again – its production must have involved cruelty to animals and a wasteful amount of water. But is her choice really going to matter? Surely her decision is not going to affect meat production, she tells herself. The ineffectiveness objection states that individual consumers cannot make a difference for the harms occurring in or resulting from our current system of food production, and that therefore there is no moral reason to abstain from buying products that are linked to such harms – or conversely, to purchase more ethically produced goods.[3]

The ineffectiveness objection is especially convincing when we consider individual consumption choices in isolation. Some instances of social change ethical consumerism are less vulnerable to the objection because they include an effort to communicate with others and influence their behavior. For example, Carl may not only personally boycott Coca-Cola, but he may also encourage others to join him. Once the focus is widened to include effects on other consumers, it seems obvious that individual consumers' actions can have an impact (see Schwartz 2010: 61–62).

However, it is still important to address the ineffectiveness objection because consumers might wonder whether their personal purchasing choices themselves matter from a moral perspective, or if they might in fact as well just *pretend* to consume ethically. Carl might tell himself that when no one witnesses it, it is morally unproblematic for him to buy Coca-Cola products. Assuming that worries about being perceived as hypocritical can be put aside, and that the ineffectiveness objection is successful with regard to individual consumption choices, this would appear to be the right conclusion. It therefore makes a big difference – theoretically and practically – if the moral relevance of consumption choices lies only in their indirect effects on other consumers, or if they can be considered direct contributions to harm.

According to the "individual difference principle" invoked in the ineffectiveness objection (for a discussion of this principle, see Kutz 2000: 116), an individual can only have a moral reason to omit an action if there is a positive likelihood that this will prevent harm from occurring. With regard to much of the harm caused in the production of food, this condition does not appear to be met. There are two ways of refuting the ineffectiveness charge. The first is to argue that individual actions can in fact make a difference, even though it does not seem so at first sight. The second is to attack the principle itself: having the power to make a difference to an outcome might not in fact be necessary to give people reason to adapt their behavior in face of it.

Consequentialist theorists have developed sophisticated versions of the so-called "threshold argument," attempting to show that buying products associated with harm often does have a negative expected value, despite initial appearances to the contrary (Almassi 2011; Kagan 2011;

Matheny 2002).The core idea of the argument is that there is a small, but non-negligible chance that any given purchase will be necessary to cross a production threshold. For example, a certain number of purchases is needed to trigger increased steak orders by the supermarket or the establishment of an additional production unit, which would cause more animals to suffer. Although the effects in question may be very small or improbable, they still cannot be discounted from the moral perspective. According to the threshold argument, the suggested answer to the consumer who is considering whether or not to buy a steak and doubting her personal impact is that her perception that the purchase cannot make any difference to the outcome is in fact a mistaken one.[4]

This answer is convincing in many cases. Effects of individual actions tend to be discounted easily due to "size illusions" (Glover 1975: 175). In other words, we encounter psychological trouble acknowledging the moral significance of small improvements or deteriorations in large-scale harms. For example, the suffering of one cow more or less may seem insignificant when billions of animals are suffering.The same difficulty occurs with regard to small probabilities of causing or preventing harm.The threshold argument is helpful as a reminder that we should be careful not to succumb to size illusions.

That being said, there are some cases in which this answer to the ineffectiveness charge does not work. In some contexts, the harm being caused is in fact over-determined, meaning that no individual contribution is necessary for the harm (or a certain level of harm) to occur. However, some theorists argue that even when an individual consumer's action cannot unilaterally change the outcome, as in the case of over-determined harm, there can still be a causal connection between the action and the harmful outcome that is sufficient to generate moral reasons against performing the action (Braham and van Hees 2012; Hohl 2014).This strategy seeks to show that the individual difference principle needs to be rejected and replaced by another principle: what is needed is not the power to prevent an outcome, but the power to avoid making a causal contribution to it (Braham and van Hees 2012).The intuitive idea is that, as long as a consumer has the option of detaching from an over-determined harm, there is moral reason to do so – even if this does not change the outcome.

Let us consider the following example to illustrate this intuition. Alex proposes to his six friends that he will go hunting for boar if at least four of them are willing to eat some of the meat at a barbecue. If only three or fewer people place an order, he will not go hunting and instead serve seitan burgers. Each of the friends has the option to agree to consume some of the meat or to refrain from doing so. An individual friend's decision only makes a difference to the outcome if exactly three other friends decide to eat some boar. In that case, his or her decision to eat meat will be necessary for Alex to actually go hunting. Now let us assume that five of the seven friends decide to eat some boar. Everyone is informed of this fact and knows what the others have decided.They then report to Alex, and he goes hunting and kills a boar. Since one more person than necessary agreed to eat meat at the barbecue, none of their individual orders were necessary for Alex to go hunting. Berta is one of the friends who agreed to eat boar meat. Did she not have any reason to tell Alex she would prefer a wheat burger, simply because her decision could not have changed the outcome? This seems to be an implausible conclusion.

The same reasoning can be applied to large-scale harms: whether or not the threshold for additional steak orders by the supermarket is hit exactly should not be considered morally relevant information. Even if the placement of an additional order by the supermarket is over-determined, in the sense that it would have happened independently of any individual consumer's behavior, those who bought steaks can still be identified as contributors to that additional order, and they therefore had reason to omit that action.[5]

In conclusion, the individual difference principle should be rejected, despite its common-sense appeal. In addition, it can be pointed out – for those who remain unmoved by the argument put forward in the last few paragraphs – that the individual difference condition is in fact fulfilled in many cases, as shown by the threshold argument. In combination, these two arguments should convince many consumers that their individual purchasing choices constitute morally relevant contributions to collective outcomes.

Consumerism

A second worry about ethical consumerism is that it reaffirms harmful consumerist patterns by sending the message that consuming can be a morally valuable act. This worry about the consumerist tendencies of ethical consumerism has several aspects.[6] One fear is that presenting some consumption choices as ethical tends to obscure the fact that we are consuming too much overall. But especially where environmentalist concerns are relevant, consuming *less* is a large part of the solution.

It is certainly an accurate observation that talk of ethical consumption often makes it seem that the choice is between consuming products that are more ethical or less, not between consuming more or less overall. A good example is Johnson's (2008: 249–250) description of how the organic food store chain Whole Foods rather successfully presents the goals of achieving pleasure and of acting ethically as always in harmony. Corporations who market "ethical" products have an interest to promote the message that buying ethically does not require any reduction of consumption or other sacrifice. If consumers buy into this framing, then they are indeed likely to be misled.

There are however several ways of addressing this issue without giving up on ethical consumerism. One important strategy is to avoid casting consumer ethics as a sphere separate from ethics in general. In other words, actions that involve consumption should be assessed from the point of view of morality just as any other action. This makes it easier to raise awareness of the fact that sometimes the best choice is to avoid buying anything at all. Moreover, the importance of the overall level of consumption and its environmental impact should be discussed prominently as a central part of consumer ethics. Ethical consumerism should also involve a critical assessment of the actions of corporations that are active in the sector.

This last point leads us to the related second fear: namely, that ethical consumerism might be co-opted by consumerist values and thereby lose its grounding in morality. Ethics-based labels, such as "fair trade" labels, are often used as marketing devices. Once it becomes fashionable to buy these labels, there is a risk that consumers start caring more about the labels themselves and the lifestyle promises they make than about the ethical concerns behind them. As a response to this problem, it is worth pointing out that the fact that some consumers might end up being motivated to buy more ethically not for moral reasons, but because they view it as fashionable, is not a purely negative phenomenon. The positive side lies in the fact that additional consumers can be "won over" this way. When we consider the consequences of promoting ethical consumerism, the danger of ethical concerns being put in the background due to a focus on what is fashionable has to be weighed against the potentially significant gains resulting from this same process.

The relationship between ethical consumerism and the market economy is a two-way street: ethical consumerism introduces ethics to the market sphere, but it also makes ethics vulnerable to being co-opted by market logic. The question is whether this means that, on balance, it would be better to avoid ethical consumerism altogether. To arrive at the conclusion that ethical consumerism should not be recommended at all because of its consumerist tendencies, we would have to assume that the detrimental effects outweigh the benefits, and that promoting ethical consumerism is harmful overall. This is unlikely to be the case. The weaker claim that ethical consumerism can be co-opted by consumerist tendencies seems plausible, but the implication of accepting that claim is that we should draw attention to this danger and combat it wherever it leads to harmful results, not that ethical consumerism should be rejected entirely because of it.

Wrong focus

Probably one of the most common complaints about ethical consumerism is that it receives too much attention compared to political activism within democratic institutions: rather than adopting a green lifestyle, people should instead vote green (see, for example, Sinnott-Armstrong 2010). I will call this the "wrong focus" critique. The objection states that the focus should be on supporting collective solutions rather than on the individual lifestyle changes that typically receive center stage in ethical consumerism. This rejection of ethical consumerism as overly focused on individuals is often motivated by the idea that the problems that ethical consumerism aims to tackle are fundamentally systemic problems that require political solutions, to be implemented by governmental institutions. This objection applies with particular force to forms of ethical consumerism that do not include a strong element of collective organization.

While calling for political solutions is indeed important, it is not immediately obvious how an argument against ethical consumerism could be deduced from this. There appears to be no trade-off between attempts to promote collective solutions and ethical consumerism. The two strategies simply operate on different levels and through different channels; they do not stand in competition with each other. Whoever chooses to adopt a greener lifestyle can still vote green or even become a green activist or politician, making "go green or vote green" a false contrast (see also Hohl 2014: chapter 7). Individual lifestyle changes are unlikely to detract from efforts at promoting collective changes, and they might even support the latter in some ways.

However, the idea that ethical consumerism might compete with activism in the formal political system could be supported with the following argument: ethical consumerism might create a false comfortableness, an illusion that one's hands are clean, even when they are not. In this way, it could make individuals less likely to support political solutions, because they may have become convinced that the problems in question have already been adequately addressed through market mechanisms. In response, it seems implausible that a significant number of individuals will in fact reach this conclusion. Ethical consumerism is typically promoted as a reaction to the perception of serious harms occurring, and unless major improvements can be seen with regard to them, those who are committed to being more ethical consumers will not suddenly believe that all problems have been solved.

A last aspect of the "wrong focus" critique is the claim that ethical consumerism wrongly puts the responsibility to address harm in food production on individuals, thereby suggesting that what we are confronted with is not a political problem, but rather a matter of private morality. However, this argument itself relies on a distinction between the political and the private sphere that should not be taken for granted. In a sense the rejection of individual responsibility for consumption choices is itself apolitical, for it assumes that consumption is a "politics-free" sphere. Ethical consumerism can in fact be highly political when it involves taking up responsibility for collective problems at the individual level.

Elitism

Ethical consumerism is sometimes criticized as elitist and exclusionary. This criticism is raised with regard to the promotion of ethical diets, such as vegetarianism and veganism, as well as the promotion of fair trade and local production. The basis of this criticism is that buying ethically is typically more expensive, so that socioeconomically disadvantaged people enjoy fewer options of doing so. Because of this lack of access and affordability, it might be elitist to promote ethical consumerism.

There is indeed a risk that people with restricted access to more ethical food options are implicitly blamed by the proponents of ethical consumerism. Some disadvantaged individuals live in "food deserts" and simply cannot access more ethical food options, and some of the more privileged proponents of ethical consumerism might not be sufficiently aware of this fact or might be unable to imagine the degree to which others are forced to pinch pennies. It is important to be aware of these issues of access and affordability in ethical consumerism.

Having the time and energy to consider the ethical implications of one's food choices is often a mark of social and economic privilege. For those who *do* enjoy such privilege it would be objectionable not to make use of it. Iris Marion Young's theorizing on agents' positions in structural processes is useful in this context: depending on their power, privilege, interest, and collective ability, different agents have different opportunities to partake in social activism (Young 2006: 126–130). Consumers in socioeconomically advantaged positions enjoy the privilege to be able to pay more for ethically sourced products. In addition, they have more power simply in virtue of their greater purchasing power. Therefore their responsibility is much greater compared to socioeconomically disadvantaged consumers.

However, the harms that occur in industrialized food production are often being perpetrated against individuals who are even worse off than socioeconomically disadvantaged consumers in Western countries, namely farmers and workers in developing countries, and of course animals. Moreover, today's children and the not-yet-born, mostly in the Global South, will feel the harmful effects of future environmental damage caused by the food industry. This makes it difficult to let anyone, even socioeconomically disadvantaged consumers, off the hook entirely. Socioeconomically disadvantaged consumers are right to protest against undeserved criticism by more advantaged groups, and against any insensitive peddling of expensive ethical diets. At the same time, farmers in developing countries are probably justified in making some demands even of disadvantaged consumers in Western countries.

As a final point, practices that start out as fairly elitist ones – in the sense of only being accessible to a minority of well-off consumers – can sometimes help to increase access and affordability for everyone over time. In the beginning, there is often only a niche market for new products that expands later on, with the products in question becoming more accessible and affordable in the process. For example, supermarket chains take note if some products are increasingly in demand in smaller niche stores and might then offer similar products at a lower price. Similarly to the consumerism objection discussed above, the elitism critique raises an important point, but does not establish the conclusion that ethical consumerism should be rejected. Rather, certain real-world manifestations of it are sometimes deficient because they ignore social class as an important factor, but they can be improved.

Vigilantism

Let me now turn to a final issue, namely the permissibility of ethical consumerism. Hussain (2012) recently argued that social change ethical consumerism is subject to certain restrictions that can be deduced from the importance of respecting democratic values, particularly procedural requirements. As he points out, individuals use their economic power as a means to influence others when they partake in social change ethical consumerism (2012: 112). But unlike within formal democratic institutions, there is no way to ensure that citizens can participate equally in the practice, or that a deliberative and inclusive decision-making process takes place. In other words, ethical consumerism has an "anarchistic" side.

Hussain argues that social change ethical consumerism must conform to certain requirements in order to be permissible, namely requirements that follow from the importance of upholding democratic values. As he puts it, "(. . .) citizens are authorized to use their market powers to advance a social agenda when they treat their buying choices as part of the wider democratic process, a kind of ongoing, informal prologue to formal democratic lawmaking" (2012: 125). He calls this view the "proto-legislative account" of ethical consumerism, contrasting it with a view he dubs "common good anarchism," which in principle grants individuals an unrestricted authority to privately pursue the common good via the market mechanism. Important requirements to be imposed on ethical consumerism listed by Hussain concern the protection of basic liberties and an appropriately representative exercise of bargaining power. He also mentions that ethical consumerism should respect the formal democratic process by not taking up issues that the former has already addressed (2012: 126).

I believe that the proto-legislative account as proposed by Hussain restricts the permissibility of ethical consumerism too severely. A first problem lies with the conditions under which the proto-legislative view is supposed to apply. These differ significantly enough from our current conditions to put the applicability of the view into question. Hussain explicitly restricts his argument to situations in which "(. . .) political morality actually directs citizens to treat the formal democratic process as authoritative" (Hussain 2012: 134). That is, the democratic process itself needs to conform to certain standards in order to be authoritative, and the restrictions on ethical consumerism can and should be relaxed when severe injustice is present. Common good anarchism can then be justifiable if the good is important enough and the democratic system fails to protect it.

Hussain however assumes that the restrictions of his account do in fact apply in current liberal democracies, implying that the harms we are currently facing are not serious enough to override worries about procedural requirements (2012: 135). If the formal political system were open for the concerns that currently drive ethical consumerism, and if the issues in question were taken as seriously as they should be, then activists could simply promote their agenda through the channels of the democratic system. But this assumption is too optimistic. For example, the seriousness of the wrongs committed against animals is not appropriately reflected in current public discourse. Animal-based agriculture is simply far too entrenched and too strongly protected by an influential lobby for meaningful political change to happen in the short to mid term.

In light of this, we can identify our current conditions as non-ideal: democratic political systems are currently unlikely to adequately respond to concerns about harms occurring in food production. Given that the harms in question are serious, ethical consumerism in this area should not be considered an objectionable form of vigilantism. Particularly in the case of food politics, where the producer side such as the dairy and meat industry exerts significant power within formal political institutions as well as through the market, it is justified to apply pressure on these agents through ethical consumerism.

Secondly, the market mechanism generally is not democratic and does not guarantee everyone an equal amount of influence. It is unclear why this should be considered problematic particularly with regard to ethically motivated consumption choices, but not with regard to "standard" consumption choices. Hussain (2012: 135–138) defends this claim by arguing that the market mechanism creates huge benefits for all participants by allowing Pareto improvements, and that this outweighs its procedural defects. The market is a very beneficial institution overall, and therefore consumers do not need to justify their purchasing decisions as long as the latter are based on price–quality consideration, which is central to the market's mode of functioning.

But why should we not view ethical considerations as a type of quality consideration, too? The market mechanism works regardless of *why* consumers show a specific preference, as long as producers can detect why certain products are in demand. If a vegan buys ice cream made from soy that is more expensive than ice cream made from dairy, he is expressing his preference, and the market mechanism works by making it possible for him to buy the product he prefers, and by benefiting the supplier of the product, who will almost certainly be aware that his ice cream is often bought by vegans. As with any other market transaction, both sides benefit, and no third party seems to be harmed.[7] The benefits of the market mechanism that Hussain cites therefore apply to ethical consumerism as well – in fact, the latter only exists *because* using the market for ethical purposes can work. Hussain therefore fails to show why ethically motivated consumption choices should be considered any more problematic than "standard" consumption choices.

Conclusion

In this article, I defended ethical consumerism against several objections. I argued that ethical consumerism can exert an impact on the harms occurring in food production, and that it does not stand in opposition to political action but rather complements and supports it. Concerns about elitism and consumerism fostered by ethical consumerism are to be taken seriously, but they do not undermine the moral and political value of ethical consumerism at a fundamental level. In conclusion, a type of well-informed and self-aware ethical consumerism can help to combat the harms occurring in food production, and it can prepare the ground for future collective reform in this area.

Notes

1 The two reports come to different results, with Goodland and Anhang (2009) attributing a higher share of anthropogenic greenhouse gas emissions (over 50%) to animal-based agriculture. The lower estimation by the FAO still cites an 18% contribution by livestock activities to total anthropogenic greenhouse gas emissions (Steinfeld et al. 2006: 112).
2 Although the problem of atrocious working conditions is not specific to the food sector or to animal agriculture, slaughterhouse work is worth mentioning as an especially egregious case. This work is physically dangerous because of the use of sharp instruments in a fast-paced work environment, and many workers appear to be traumatized by it (Dillard 2008).
3 This objection is discussed at length by Christopher Kutz (2000: chapters 4.2 and 4.3), and by David Schwartz (2010: chapter 3). It applies not only to consumption choices, but also to any action that seems to contribute to collectively caused harm (see, for example, Sinnott-Armstrong 2010 for a discussion regarding individual contributions to climate change).
4 Of course these proposed solutions to the problem of ineffectiveness have been subject to objections, and debate about them is ongoing (see, for example, Chartier 2006).
5 For a more detailed account of the principle of individual contribution, see Braham and van Hees (2012) and Hohl (2014: chapter 5).
6 Josee Johnston (2008) provides a discussion of this worry from a sociological perspective.
7 Of course suppliers of dairy-based ice cream may experience a reduction in sales, but this is not different from any other case of market competition.

References

Almassi, B. (2011) "The Consequences of Individual Consumption: A Defence of Threshold Arguments for Vegetarianism and Consumer Ethics," *Journal of Applied Philosophy* 28(4): 396–411.
Braham, M. and van Hees, M. (2012) "An Anatomy of Moral Responsibility," *Mind* 121(483): 601–634.
Chartier, G. (2006) "On the Threshold Argument against Consumer Meat Purchases," *Journal of Social Philosophy* 37(2): 233–249.
Dillard, J. (2008) "Slaughterhouse Nightmare: Psychological Harm Suffered by Slaughterhouse Employees and the Possibility of Redress through Legal Reform," *Georgetown Journal on Poverty Law & Policy* 15(2): 391–419.

Glover, J. (1975) "It Makes No Difference Whether or Not I Do It," *Proceedings of the Aristotelian Society, Supplementary Volumes* 49: 171–209.

Goodland, R. and Anhang, J. (2009) "Livestock and Climate Change," *Worldwatch Magazine* 22(6): 10–19.

Hohl, S. (2014) *Individuelle Verantwortung für kollektiv verursachte Übel*, Universität Zürich: Unpublished PhD thesis.

Hussain, W. (2012) "Is Ethical Consumerism an Impermissible Form of Vigilantism?," *Philosophy & Public Affairs* 40(2): 111–143.

Johnston, J. (2008) "The Citizen–Consumer Hybrid: Ideological Tensions and the Case of Whole Foods Market," *Theory and Society* 37(3): 229–270.

Kagan, S. (2011) "Do I Make a Difference?" *Philosophy & Public Affairs* 39(2): 105–141.

Kutz, C. (2000) *Complicity: Ethics and Law for a Collective Age*, Cambridge: Cambridge University Press.

Lichtenberg, J. (2010) "Negative Duties, Positive Duties, and the 'New Harms,'" *Ethics* 120(3): 557–578.

Matheny, G. (2002) "Expected Utility, Contributory Causation, and Vegetarianism," *Journal of Applied Philosophy* 19(3): 293–297.

Safran Foer, J. (2010) *Eating Animals*, London: Penguin Books.

Schwartz, D. T. (2010) *Consuming Choices: Ethics in a Global Consumer Age*, Lanham, MD: Rowman & Littlefield.

Sinnott-Armstrong, W. (2010) "Its Not My Fault: Global Warming and Individual Moral Obligations," in Gardiner, S. M. (ed.), *Climate Ethics: Essential Readings*, New York: Oxford University Press: 332–364.

Steinfeld, H., Gerber, P., Wassenaar T., Castel, V., Rosales, M., and de Haan, C. (2006) *Livestock's Long Shadow*, Rome: Food and Agriculture Organization.

Young, I. M. (2006) "Responsibility and Global Justice: A Social Connection Model," *Social Philosophy & Policy* 23(1): 102–130.

PART V
Food and the environment

19

HUNGRY BECAUSE OF CHANGE

Food, vulnerability, and climate

Alison Reiheld

Introduction: the problem

While many still seek to prevent or mitigate anthropogenic climate change, others focus on adaptation to the consequences of climate change. One much-discussed consequence of climate change is sea level rise. It has become the subject of many an article, editorial, and speculative fiction novel, including Paolo Bacigalupi's books *The Drowned Cities* and the award-winning *Ship Breaker*, both of which are set in a future US where the coastal areas are much changed and a civil war grips areas which did not take adaptive measures. More serious still are the impacts climate change is likely to have not only on the production of food but on the global supply chains of food on which so many now depend impacts which render people vulnerable and give rise to moral obligations to reduce that vulnerability.

These impacts are already visible. In California, drought has afflicted farmers 11 of the last 14 years. More than $2 billion in agricultural losses in California were due to drought in 2014 (Fischetti 2015). In recent years, US growing zones were shifted north by the USDA. David Wolfe, professor of plant and soil ecology at Cornell University, argues that "this revision of the hardiness zone map gives us a clear picture of the 'new normal'" (Samenow 2012). While monitoring agencies note large-scale changes, laypersons in some areas are beginning to viscerally feel the initial effects of what *may* be global climate change, but is certainly a change in local climate.

Indeed, farmers across the world have been noticing shifts in climate that affect their food production. In Peru, farmers and community members in Sullucuyoc Village have observed an increase in minimum temperatures ("It is warmer in the evenings") and changes in rainfall patterns such as heavier rainy seasons and increased erosion and landslides. Scientific climate projections suggest this will only worsen, as more rain comes in the rainy season and, during the dry season, rains decrease by up to 40% along with continued temperature increases of entire degrees Celsius (CARE 2011). Community members in Sullucuyoc Village identified the following food-related impacts of these climate change hazards: lower productivity of coffee, passion fruit, and avocado; loss of food crops such as manioc and vegetables; new pests and diseases in plants and animals; and loss of biodiversity through the disappearance of plant species (CARE 2011). Alone, such local data indicate nothing about climate change. A hot summer in St. Louis, Missouri, doesn't prove global warming; neither does a bitterly cold winter prove it is not happening, despite the pithy sarcasm in the common wintry remark "so much for global warming." It is large-scale data which show that such local phenomena are not isolated but rather part of a larger pattern. The Intergovernmental Panel on Climate Change (IPCC) claims that we will see more such shifts in rain and drought and temperature in the future, perhaps with drought, flooding, hunger, diseases, and stunted economic growth beginning sooner than previously estimated (Fischetti 2014). Shifts in rain, drought, and temperature are features of the environment that, along with soil, are major determinants of food production and are contributors to both hunger and thirst. Arid regions require more irrigation, making access to water of even greater importance. We see this in the increasingly tense battles over water rights in California and Colorado as drought affects farmers and those seeking drinking water in regions that, when first settled, were too arid to support the large-scale agriculture which now dominates local economies and feeds the US. NASA climate research scientist Benjamin Cook points out that, "Even where rain may not change much, greater evaporation will dry out the soils" as temperatures rise (Fischetti 2015).

In addition, many nations' food consumption has shifted away from traditional foods produced locally to more processed foods produced abroad. Such nations are particularly subject to disruptions in global food production and chains of sale. They include the various nations known collectively by the UN as the Pacific Islands, such as American Samoa, Fiji, New Caledonia, and the Cook Islands. These patterns of food production and consumption are well-established. Indeed,

> the foods that are most commonly consumed in Pacific communities have changed significantly. In particular, people have shifted away from traditional foodstuffs toward westernized, high-fat foods. . . . Corresponding with a fall in local food production, imported foods comprise between 30 and 90 percent of all foods eaten in the Pacific.
> (World Health Organization 2002)

Such patterns are the case even in developed nations, which also import significant portions of their food. In the US, winter fruits and vegetables can come from as far away as Chile or Argentina, and most food is produced hundreds of miles away from where it is consumed. Saudi Arabia imports 80% of its food, much from East Africa. Mozambique has become a banana exporter as a result of corporate farms that have pushed local farmers off of their subsistence farming lands, such that food grown there no longer stays in the country. In Liberia, land which once grew food for local markets has been converted to growing oil palms for Malaysian palm oil giants such as Sime Darby. In Europe, as in Saudi Arabia, many food items come from the "African breadbasket" where commercial farms with the aim of exporting crops and selling only some to local markets continue to displace farms growing food for local distribution and consumption (Bourne 2014). While the conversion to corporate farming in many regions of Africa has value for locals who find that wages on commercial farms are more dependable than their own enterprises, it increases the proportion of the world's population which depends on global food supply chains for their food and on globalized markets for their pay, even as local water supplies are used up.

In such a situation, it is easy to lose sight of the fact that not only do we need to maintain food production and distribution in the face of climate change, we need to increase it: by 2050, we must be able to feed 2 billion more people than the over 7 billion people we are already attempting to feed. And it is around this time that we expect to begin feeling the most severe impacts of climate change (Fischetti 2015) on freshwater, temperature, and other features of the environment which affect crops.

This complicated system of agricultural production and distribution has already made some people vulnerable and, when disrupted by climate change, may exacerbate existing vulnerabilities and create new ones. Such vulnerability creates an ethical demand, the enormity of which might seem impossible to address given how widely it expands our moral community. However, an adequate conception of vulnerability coupled with an adequate conception of obligation can make it possible to address even this most transnational and cosmopolitan of demands.

Vulnerability

Vulnerability is a notion many people deploy without adequate reflection. There is a tendency to formulate it primarily in terms of vulnerability to exploitation, in which case it is conceived of as vulnerability *to coercion*, due either to diminished autonomy or constrained circumstances. This conception of vulnerability appears in medical ethics with respect to patients' ability or inability to give autonomous, informed consent. Ruth Faden and Tom Beauchamp famously delineate an institutional or legal sense of informed consent from a philosophical sense of informed consent as autonomous authorization. When informed consent as autonomous authorization has taken place, the patient (1) has substantial understanding of the risks and benefits of the recommended treatment, (2) *is not being coerced by outside forces*, and (3) autonomously authorizes the treatment in question (Faden and Beauchamp 1986, my emphasis). As established in guidelines for research on human subjects, vulnerability can also be presented in a related way as a compromised ability to advocate for oneself. Indeed, on at least one view, "vulnerable persons are those with reduced capacity, power, or control to protect their interests relative to other agents" (Mackenzie et al. 2014: 6).

In this sense, we are all vulnerable to climate change because of the global food supply chain. But this conception of vulnerability, alone, will not suffice. Mackenzie, Rogers, and Dodds propose a *taxonomy of vulnerability*, outlining three different sources of vulnerability (inherent, situational, and pathogenic) and two different states of vulnerability. Vulnerability can exist in two states: dispositional or occurrent, a distinction which "refers to the states of potential versus actual vulnerability" (Mackenzie et al. 2014: 8). A generalized universal vulnerability to climate change because of the global food supply chain would be dispositional for all but occurrent for some. But despite its universality, I contend that this vulnerability would *not* be what Mackenzie et al. call *inherent* vulnerability, which "refers to sources of vulnerability that are intrinsic to the human condition" (2014: 6). So, while all patients who participate in biomedical research are vulnerable to coercion and manipulation, and this is an inherent universal, this is not the case with universal vulnerability to climate change's effects on the global food supply chain: that vulnerability is based not in the human condition per se, but rather in the economic context of food production and distribution. Such context-specific vulnerability – despite the universality of the context – is what Mackenzie et al. refer to as *situational* vulnerability. Such vulnerability "may be caused or exacerbated by the personal, social, political, economic, or environmental situations of individuals or social groups" and may be "short term, intermittent, or enduring" (Mackenzie et al. 2014). Particularly ethically troubling are *pathogenic* vulnerabilities, which can be generated by a variety of sources (including abusive or dysfunctional interpersonal relationships, but also sociopolitical oppression or injustice), and can even occur when a response intended to ameliorate vulnerability paradoxically exacerbates other vulnerabilities or creates new ones (Mackenzie et al. 2014: 9). With a sufficiently large scale of causation, I suspect even pathogenic vulnerabilities could be universal. However, Florencia Luna (2009) argues that such universal notions of vulnerability, while perhaps true in some sense, provide little or no traction for anyone seeking to explain how some people seem to be more vulnerable than others to the threats they may face in common. This would be the case whether the universality is inherent, situational, or pathogenic. To fail to attend to differences in vulnerability between groups is to ignore ethically salient factors of the world as it is.

And yet, labeling particular populations as vulnerable is not the right way to address this problem, either. Luna (2009) contends that labeling particular populations as vulnerable risks eliding real differences in vulnerability. CARE international also addresses this concern when it argues that the United Nations Framework Convention on Climate Change (UNFCCC) negotiations look at vulnerability at the wrong level by comparing nation-states' relative vulnerability to change, as though vulnerability were universal within each country. Indeed, CARE says, "Rarely does the UNFCCC process consider the critical issue of differential vulnerability within countries and communities based on socio-economic and political factors such as age, gender and social or political marginalization" (CARE 2011).

Such a granular approach is entirely consistent with Luna's analytic approach to vulnerability. Luna (2009) advocates attention to *layers of vulnerability* which allow us to see how vulnerability is cumulative and affects some folks more than others, even within the same households or subpopulations, and even when there are global food networks that might seem to affect all equally. Such layers of vulnerability can be quite particular. As CARE (2011) notes, women are less educated and less mobile, tied as they are to families of birth and of marriage in many cultures. This reduced mobility makes many women even more vulnerable than men in their families, men who may in fact be expected to move away to work and send money home. Of course, such expectations for men can create vulnerabilities for certain men, as evidenced by the large numbers of Bangladeshi and other Asian men who work dangerous, fast construction jobs in the sparkling cities of Malaysia and of Abu Dhabi, Saudi Arabia, and Arab Gulf states more generally (labor rules in host and donor nations often forbid women to perform contract migratory labor) (Kibria 2011).

Let us now consider further Luna's layers of vulnerability. Luna argues that vulnerability should be understood "dynamically and relationally" rather than as a series of too-rigid necessary and sufficient conditions:

> ... there might be different vulnerabilities, different layers operating. These layers may overlap: some of them may be related to problems with informed consent, others to social circumstances. The idea of layers of vulnerability gives flexibility to the concept of vulnerability. For example, if the situation of women is considered, it can be said that being a woman does not, in itself, imply that a person is vulnerable. A woman living in a country that does not recognize, or is intolerant of *reproductive rights* acquires a layer of vulnerability.... In turn, an educated and resourceful woman in that same country can overcome some of the consequences of the intolerance of reproductive rights; however, a *poor woman* living in a country intolerant of reproductive rights acquires another layer of vulnerability.... Moreover, an *illiterate* poor woman in a country intolerant of reproductive rights acquires still another layer. And if she is migrant and does not have her documentation in order or she belongs to an aboriginal group, she will acquire more and more layers of vulnerabilities. She will suffer these overlapping layers.... Another way of understanding this proposal is not by thinking that someone *is* [essentially or inherently] vulnerable, but by considering a particular situation that *makes or renders* someone vulnerable. If the situation changes, the person may no longer be considered vulnerable.

(2009: 128–129)

This is the great practical strength of Luna's conception of vulnerability. The conditions that give rise to a situational or pathogenic vulnerability can be changed as well as responded to, while an inherent vulnerability can only be responded to. The granularity of Luna's conception allows us to look at the specifics of situations and ask, *how can we remove at least some of these layers of vulnerability?* Or as Luna herself puts it, "After we identify different layers of vulnerability . . . we can think of various ways of avoiding or minimizing those layers" (2009: 131). Luna wisely acknowledges that in some cases, it may not be possible to minimize the layers of vulnerability identified. What of climate change, and hunger and thirst? Can these be mitigated? Or are we stuck with all the layers of vulnerability implied by climate-change-related shifting factors in access to food and water? I think not.

One of the keys to reducing vulnerability to climate change is to attempt to strip away layers where possible. Let us consider this with a particular layer of vulnerability, namely, dependence on global agricultural markets for pay and for food. For farmers in Mozambique or Liberia, it is essential to retain control over their land rather than giving it to foreign corporations. Consider the story of 45-year-old Chirime, who farmed her land in Mozambique, land which had fed her and her five children for years. Farming is a respectable form of work for a woman to undertake to provide for her family, and comparable options may be very limited for women in patriarchal societies. And yet, this livelihood was taken from Chirime. As Joel Bourne (2014) writes for *National Geographic:*

> She never saw the big tractor coming. First it plowed up her banana trees. Then her corn. Then her beans, sweet potatoes, cassava. Within a few, dusty minutes, the plot . . . was consumed by a Chinese corporation building a 50,000-acre farm. . . . 'No one even talked to me. . . . Just one day I found the tractor in my field plowing up everything. No one who lost their *machamba* has been compensated!' Local civil society groups say thousands lost their land and livelihoods to the Wanbao Africa Agricultural Development Company – all with the blessing of the Mozambican government, which has a history of neglecting local farmers' rights to land in favor of large investments.

While Chirime's story is not a story of climate change yet, it is a story of how individuals are made or rendered vulnerable by power structures around them and by global food distribution systems and economic globalization.

As climate change advances, it is unclear whether nations such as Mozambique will have the water necessary to support continued corporate involvement. Indeed, corporate involvement in large-scale oil palm plantations can have its own negative environmental impact on local water quality and hydrology (Carlson et al. 2014; Jordan 2014). If this structure collapses due to climate change to any degree, people who once farmed their own land and were able to make use of low-tech irrigation techniques will now have neither land nor skills nor outside pay. Without the land and the skills to farm it, they cannot grow their own food. Without pay, they cannot import it. The threats posed by large-scale oil palm plantations to local citizens in need of food and water are compounded by the "significantly eroded water quality" in hydrological systems around these plantations, freshwater systems which local people depend on for drinking water and food (Jordan 2014). Worse still, according to Lisa Curran of the Stanford Woods Institute for the Environment, a drought could combine with these existing effects to cause local collapse of freshwater ecosystems (Jordan 2014). This situational and pathogenic vulnerability is dispositional and serious. As Bourne (2014) notes,

> the thorniest question is, who will do the farming in Africa's future? Will it be poor farmers like Chirime working one-acre plots, who make up roughly 70 percent of the continent's labor force? Or will it be giant corporations like Wanbao, operating industrial farms modeled on those of the American Midwest?

USAID's Gregory Myers says that the key to making such projects benefit locals is "protecting the land rights of the people" (Bourne 2014). We may not be able at this point to alter the effects of climate change on temperature and access to freshwater, and the layers of vulnerability these will impose, but we can address property rights so as to strip away other layers of vulnerability. We can also mitigate harm done by large-scale oil palm plantations to freshwater systems by ensuring that natural vegetative cover near streams and rivers is not cleared, that dense road networks used to move and process palm crops do not intersect directly with waterways (Jordan 2014), and that other means of reducing layers of vulnerability are undertaken.

Another layer of vulnerability, as mentioned above, is lack of mobility. Adaptation to climate change will require that people be able to move away from regions no longer habitable at all, or no longer habitable in the same numbers. It will be tempting for nations with broad food production capacities, especially ones which may not be hard hit by climate change, to close their borders. Yet this adds a layer of vulnerability for others. The prospect of a massive influx of people from, say, North Africa into Europe or into the African Breadbasket nations is a legitimate concern. But to attempt to prevent it altogether is to render vulnerable populations even more vulnerable.

Who should address these ethical demands to reduce vulnerability? Neither the UN nor any single nation – not even the US – is in a position to singlehandedly remove layers of vulnerability produced by global food supply chains, transnational corporations, and global climate change. How are we to determine *which* moral agents, whether individual or collective, should both consider themselves responsible and be held accountable by others?

Obligations regarding vulnerability to hunger

Thomas Pogge describes an agreement between 186 nations, at the 1996 World Food Summit in Rome, that there is a human right to be free from hunger. Yet, he notes, the US government under then-President Bill Clinton went out of its way to claim that the attainment of any such right "is a goal or aspiration to be realized progressively that does not give rise to any international obligations" (Pogge 2001: 2). A nation which is arguably one of the most powerful agents for change in the world acknowledged a universal moral claim and then stated that *this universal moral claim implies no universal obligation*. How, then, to handle claims of obligation arising from vulnerability to hunger and thirst? Mackenzie et al. rightly contend that both inherent and situational vulnerability can "give rise to specific moral political obligations: to support and provide assistance to those who are occurrently vulnerable and to reduce the risks of dispositional vulnerabilities becoming occurrent" (2014: 8). But who should be held responsible? To consider the assignment of responsibility and accountability, we should consider twin grounds for doing so: culpability and capability. One of these grounds, capability, can be found in the work of Onora O'Neill, whose work on assigning agency lies within the realm of justice and ethics.

O'Neill (2001) focuses on the connection between moral claims and moral obligations. With complex or sweeping claims, such as those of global justice – her focus – or the vulnerabilities which are our topic, O'Neill suggests that it is problematic to assign obligations. In a sense, Clinton was correct. There cannot *be* universal obligations that every potential agent must meet because the moral claims in question are positive claims which not everyone can fulfill: hunger cannot be alleviated without exertion of effort to reform systematic problems with food distribution, as O'Neill herself notes. A universal obligation in response to a universal demand would require that every agent must put forth positive effort, not just negative restraint, and not all agents are capable of doing so. Meeting these kinds of demands is hard: "don't tread on me" – negative responsibility – is a lot easier to accomplish than "tread over here while doing x and over there while doing y" – positive responsibility. Yet the latter is certainly the sort of response required to meet the ethical demands of vulnerability: not just refraining from action, but taking action. Who, then, should act, if not all can fairly be asked to do so? As O'Neill sees it, if everyone has the capability to fulfill the remedy (as they do with "don't tread on me"), then they have the obligation to fulfill the remedy (O'Neill 2001: 184–185). However, she takes it further, acknowledging that some positive claims are too big. The issue now becomes not whether every agent can fulfill the remedy, but whether *any agent* can fulfill the remedy in whole or in part. Anyone who does have that capability, even in part, will have a share in the obligation.

O'Neill goes on to describe two major kinds of agent with respect to large-scale social problems such as justice and injustice or, for our purposes, vulnerability to food and water shortages due to the effects of climate change on a globalized food distribution system. These two major kinds of agents are *primary* agents and *secondary* agents. Primary agents have the capacity to determine how principles of justice and ethics are to be institutionalized within a certain domain. They also have the ability to construct other agents or agencies with specific competencies regarding that institutionalization. With respect to hunger, primary agents which are member-states of the United Nations have constructed agencies such as the World Health Organization (WHO) and World Food Programme (WFP), in addition to agencies within their own nation-states such as the US Food and Drug Administration and the Temporary Aid to Needy Families program. Primary agents typically have some means of coercion. Secondary agents, on the other hand, are typically thought of as contributing to justice by meeting the demands of primary agents (O'Neill 2001: 181). Primary agents could be a well-organized body like a legislature, one without a formal structure like a loosely organized town meeting, or an individual like a monarch or head of state. Either way, contends O'Neill, *it is the primary agent that must be convinced certain principles of justice and ethics apply, for without the primary agent, nothing will change.* I am not sure she is correct in this, but certainly change will be slower and cultural rather than rapid and institutional without the work of a primary agent.

Hints of this approach with respect to food ethics can be found in the work of Amartya Sen. Sen established the importance of access to food, versus mere availability, as critical to food security (Drèze and Sen 1989) and food security as critical to human freedom (Sen 1981; 1987) and thus to ethics. Sen recounts Bertolt Brecht's aphorism, "Grub first, then ethics," before famously arguing that in fact food is a central issue in general social ethics. Why? "Since so much in human life does depend on the ability to find enough to eat" (Sen 1987: 1–2). For this reason, vulnerability in the area of food security has a profound and cascading effect on the quality of human lives. In the Sir John Crawford Memorial Lecture, Sen notes that effective public policy "to combat hunger and starvation . . . may depend on the existence and efficiency of political pressure groups to induce governments to act" in order to get food to "vulnerable groups" (1987: 2). In O'Neill's language, these would be secondary agents acting to persuade the primary agent to render aid by pressing the primary to develop a "public distribution system geared to the needs of the vulnerable sections of the community" to "bring the essentials of livelihood within easy reach of people whose lives may remain otherwise relatively untouched by the progress of real national income" (Sen 1987: 8). But this presumes a strong central government, and seems also to presume limited forces above and beyond governments. Such forces do indeed exist and have great power, such as globalized economies operating largely without regulation, based in some nations such as China but operating in others with impunity such as Mozambique. I suspect the overarching transnational structure of agencies like WHO and WFP may call over-reliance on primary agents of justice into question, or even change our conception of what a primary agent can be.

O'Neill acknowledges that many theories of obligation concerning large social issues, like hunger and access to clean water, end up being highly statist. For instance, John Rawls' framework of obligation in his major political works – including *Theory of Justice* and *Law of Peoples* – is deeply statist. Although Rawls occasionally claims otherwise, O'Neill's justification for this claim is that for Rawls, the state is always the primary agent. O'Neill is well aware that all too often states have been agents of *in*justice and *im*morality. Furthermore, even when their ends are just, they may be weak. Thus O'Neill delineates two kinds of states: rogue states, whose ends are not those of justice; and weak states, whose ends may be just but which lack the power to implement them (O'Neill 2001: 182). In the case of a weak state, those who might otherwise be secondary agents are reduced to powerlessness because they cannot rely on an impartially enforced legal code, may have to engage in bribery or nepotism to go about their daily business, or buy protection and make corrupt deals (O'Neill 2001: 182–183). In looking back on the case of palm oil plantations in Mozambique, where the government has made deals with transnational corporations like Wanbao at the expense of its citizens' property rights, we can see evidence for a failed state, or at least a state that has failed in these kinds of cases.

While O'Neill has doubts about the ability of states as agents in some specific cases, Andrew Kuper argues more forcefully that "where there are transnational bodies such as the World Trade Organization, the World Court, and the World Bank," we should do everything in our power to "encourage the entry of players other than nation-states." Kuper calls for an "end [to] the dominance of what David Luban has called 'the romance of the nation-state' and to discern principles for a more complex and promising global institutional configuration" (Kuper 2000: 665–667). UN entities like the WHO and WFP can, and do, serve as secondary agents in an advisory and policy-making capacity. But these groups can also fulfill obligations and, insofar as they have enforcement or implementation powers or can bring compelling pressure to bear, may be able to serve as primary agents. And because they have the capability to act, they must. In addition, primary agents such as Mozambique or the governments of various Pacific Island nations also have an obligation to act because they have the capability to effect regulation of food imports, encourage local production, protect watersheds, and undertake other related tasks. Other primary agents, such as the government of China, may have to balance the desire to encourage economic development with their very real capability-based obligations to remove layers of vulnerability pathogenically caused by their own companies' unrestrained actions.

We have already begun to put this capability-based view of determining which agents are responsible together with a layered analysis of food and water vulnerability due to climate change. We need such a sprawling notion of how to assign obligation and responsibility, for the complexity of moral claims about global justice and the ethical demands of vulnerability with which we are working may have remedies so complicated that *no single agent has the capability to meet them, not even the romantic nation-state.* Thus, *no single agent may be able to remove vulnerability.* However, each layer of vulnerability may carry with it a set of agents who are capable of answering the ethical demands of that layer. And this capability engenders obligation. According to O'Neill, the obligations any particular agent has are determined by assessing that agent's capabilities in light of the overall task of achieving justice and eliminating injustice. Correspondingly and for our purpose, *the obligations any particular agent has are determined by assessing that agent's capabilities in light of the overall task of eliminating layers of vulnerability.*

In some cases, those who are capable of remedy are also culpable. Culpability would stem from having created the very situations that give rise to situational vulnerability, even if those situations are not obviously wrong in and of themselves, or from being the source of pathogenic vulnerability which is more directly and predictably dispositional for vulnerability. As Thomas Pogge (2002) has famously argued, our obligations to those we have harmed can take precedence over our obligations to compatriots, even when those we have harmed are distant strangers. The strength of this cosmopolitan obligation depends not on nation-state associations, but rather on the directness of our causal responsibility and on how avoidable the harm was. In certain situations, such as the case of Wanbao's bulldozing of private farmland to establish a palm oil plantation, avoidability is high and so culpability is clear and resulting obligations are strong.

Both capability to remedy vulnerability and culpability in rendering persons vulnerable provide grounds for assigning obligation. Non-governmental organizations, whether local, national, or transnational, have capabilities that can contribute to addressing the ethical demands of vulnerability to hunger and lack of water from climate change. A few may also be culpable, thereby enhancing their responsibility. Nation-states and for-profit corporations may have a similar balance of capability, culpability, and the corresponding level of responsibility. Even individual moral agents may be culpable or have some capacity-based obligations, which may be met either through grass roots organizing or through their own individual contributions to food and water security for themselves and their neighbors. Indeed, most agents will have capabilities that work for some layers of vulnerability but not others. At the governmental, institutional, and personal levels, agents are responsible for the layers of vulnerability which they can remedy, and especially for the subset of these to which they have contributed.

Conclusion

I have mounted a case for vulnerability as a firm ground for obligations and responsibilities with respect to shortages in food and water, and to explain how we might assign such obligations and responsibilities. Climate change stands to exacerbate underlying vulnerabilities, and this framework implies that even agents who did not cause climate change must stand ready to intervene in climate-change-induced hunger and thirst. I urge the reader to think carefully about how moral agents would effectively reduce layered vulnerability to hunger and thirst. These will be agents who can not only refrain from wrong actions but also undertake positive remedies that render layers of vulnerability progressively weaker, eliminating them where possible. Where vulnerability cannot be removed entirely, agents with the capacity to remove layers can still do what they can to answer its ethical demands. The burden weighs more heavily on those whose actions have rendered persons situationally or pathogenically vulnerable.

Focusing on vulnerability to climate change's effects on food leads us to consider how people are made vulnerable, and in particular how global food supply chains and globalized agribusiness render some people more vulnerable than others. This vulnerability leads to ethical demands which are more cosmopolitan in nature than we might expect, for the chains of cause and effect involved in rendering people vulnerable to climate change's effects on food and water cross national and regional boundaries.

And yet, by refusing to treat the problem of vulnerability as inherent, or as requiring a total solution, we see that it is possible to address these ethical demands. It is not the case that vulnerability is endemic to certain populations and thus impossible to address. Nor is it true that vulnerability is binary and must be resolved in its entirety or not at all. Despite the size of the globalized food production system that is threatened by climate change, we can make an ethically significant difference one layer at a time. Some people will become hungry because of climate change. It is up to us to determine how many, and how hungry, by addressing layers of vulnerability where we are capable and where we are culpable.

References

Bourne, J. K., Jr. (2014) "The Next Breadbasket: Can Africa's Fertile Farmland Feed the Planet?," *National Geographic Magazine*, July, viewed 13 May 2016, http://www.nationalgeographic.com/foodfeatures/land-grab/.

CARE. (2011) "Understanding Vulnerability to Climate Change: Insights from Application of CARE's Climate Vulnerability and Capacity (CVCA) Methodology," *CARE Climate Change Information Centre*, viewed 20 November 2015, http://www.careclimatechange.org/files/adaptation/CARE_Understanding_Vulnerability.pdf.

Carlson, K. M., L. M. Curran, A. G. Ponette-González, D. Ratnasari, Ruspita, N. Lisnawati, Y. Purwanto, K. A. Brauman, and P. A. Raymond. (2014) "Influence of Watershed-Climate Interactions on Stream Temperature, Sediment Yield, and Metabolism Along a Land Use Intensity Gradient in Indonesian Borneo," *Journal of Geophysical Research* 119(6): 1110–1128.

Drèze, J. and A. Sen. (1989) *Hunger and Public Action*, Oxford: Clarendon Press.

Faden, R. and T. Beauchamp. (1986) *A History and Theory of Informed Consent*, New York: Oxford University Press.

Fischetti, M. (2014) "Big Climate Danger Could Arrive as Soon as 2036," *Scientific American*, 27 March, http://blogs.scientificamerican.com/observations/2014/03/27/big-climate-danger-could-arrive-as-soon-as-2036/.

Fischetti, M. (2015) "U.S. Droughts Will Be the Worst in 1,000 Years," *Scientific American*, 12 February, http://www.scientificamerican.com/article/u-s-droughts-will-be-the-worst-in-1-000-years1/.

Jordan, R. (2014) "Oil Palm Plantations Threaten Water Quality, Stanford Scientists Say," *Stanford News Service*, 30 June, viewed 7 July 2015 http://news.stanford.edu/pr/2014/pr-palm-oil-water-062614.html.

Kibria, N. (2011) "Working Hard for the Money: Bangladesh Faces Challenges of Large-Scale Labor Migration," *Migration Policy Institute*, 9 August, viewed 19 February 2015, http://www.migrationpolicy.org/article/working-hard-money-bangladesh-faces-challenges-large-scale-labor-migration.

Kuper, A. (2000) "Rawlsian Global Justice: Beyond the Law of Peoples to a Cosmopolitan Law of Persons," *Political Theory* 28(5): 640–774.

Luna, F. (2009) "Elucidating the Concept of Vulnerability: Layers Not Labels," *International Journal of Feminist Approaches to Bioethics* 2(1): 121–139.

Mackenzie, C., W. Rogers, and S. Dodds. (2014) "Introduction: What is Vulnerability, and Why Does It Matter for Moral Theory?," in C. Mackenzie, W. Rogers, and S. Dodds (eds.), *Vulnerability: New Essays in Ethics and Feminist Philosophy*, New York: Oxford University Press, pp. 1–29.

O'Neill, O. (2001) "Agents of Justice," *Metaphilosophy* 32(1/2): 180–195.

Pogge, T. (2001) "Introduction: Global Justice," *Metaphilosophy* 32(1/2): 1–5.

——. (2002) "Responsibilities for Poverty-related Ill Health," *Ethics & International Affairs* 16(2): 71–79.

Samenow, J. (2012) "New USDA Plant Zones Clearly Show Climate Change," *The Washington Post Capital Weather Gang Blog*, 27 January, viewed 13 February 2015, http://www.washingtonpost.com/blogs/capital-weather-gang/post/new-usda-plant-zones-clearly-show-climate-change/2012/01/27/gIQA7Vz2VQ_blog.html.

Sen, A. (1981) *Poverty and Famines: An Essay on Entitlement and Deprivation*, Oxford: Oxford University Press.

——. (1987) "Food and Freedom," Sir John Crawford Memorial Lecture, *World Public Health Nutrition Association*, 29 October, viewed 6 July 2015, http://wphna.org/wp-content/uploads/2015/02/1985-Sen-Food-and-freedom.pdf.

World Health Organization. (2002) "Obesity in the Pacific: Too big to ignore," *Secretariat of the Pacific Community*, viewed 2 February 2015, http://www.wpro.who.int/publications/docs/obesityinthepacific.pdf?ua=1.

20

BIODIVERSITY AND DEVELOPMENT

John Vandermeer

Recent human history and deep biological history have converged onto a nettlesome conundrum. The world's main store of biological diversity exists in tropical areas of the planet, a consequence of some complicated evolutionary processes. The world's heaviest concentration of poverty exists in tropical areas of the planet, a consequence of some complicated human historical processes. Since generalized development agendas are appropriately concentrated in underdeveloped parts of the world, and since most of that world is concentrated in tropical climates, the interlacing of biodiversity and development is a reality that perhaps deserves more attention that it normally receives. Since agricultural development is normally thought of as part and parcel of general development schemes, the two issues of food and biodiversity are organically linked in contemporary culture.

There are a variety of specific problems that may muddle the more general issue. First, there is sometimes confusion as to what is meant by biodiversity. Second, the focus of attention on biodiversity preservation is frequently, and naively, divorced from the related issue of agriculture as a landscape modification. Third, recommendations for development are sometimes framed in a way that prioritizes socioeconomic factors over biological processes of biodiversity maintenance, frequently a result of ignorance of those biological processes on the part of development initiative architects. I examine these three issues in turn.

What is biodiversity?

It is important to distinguish between two forms of biodiversity when talking about agriculture and development. Many farmers, as well as academics who directly study agriculture, think of the diversity of crops and the varieties that the farmer plants, frequently referred to as "agrobiodiversity." Since the farmer plans this part of the ecosystem, it is convenient to refer to this as the *planned biodiversity* (Perfecto and Vandermeer 2008). Certainly the planned biodiversity has much to do with the provisioning of ecosystem services (e.g., food, fiber, fuel, wood for construction, etc.) and is an important subject for detailed analysis, but in most cases it actually represents only a small fraction of the biodiversity that is actually present in the agroecosystem. A plethora of other organisms, like birds, bats, insects, wild plants, and microorganisms, appear on the farm, whether or not the farmer desires them. This is what is referred to as the *associated biodiversity* (Perfecto and Vandermeer 2008; Perfecto et al. 2009; Vandermeer and Perfecto 2005). When examining questions of biodiversity conservation and its relationship to agriculture, the associated biodiversity is the main subject of interest.

Associated biodiversity is normally thought of when conservation issues are discussed, and it is closely associated with several topics of interest to pure ecological and evolutionary theory. In these more esoteric disciplines, the various components of biodiversity (e.g., species richness, species evenness, phylogenetic structuring, and others) enter in important ways to academic debates. This paper, however, focuses on the peculiar relationship between biodiversity and development; as such, these subjects are not especially relevant. Thus, for the purposes of this exploration, it is best to think of biodiversity as simply the number of types of organisms present. And, to reiterate, the vast majority of types of organisms occur in tropical regions of the world, precisely where most development programs are currently located.

Biodiversity response to landscape intensification

Under the usual assumptions of development, the intensification of agriculture is regarded as a key component. Biodiversity conservationists typically assume that the fraction of land converted from natural vegetation to agriculture is directly and negatively correlated with biodiversity. However, available data suggest that this assumption – that biodiversity is reduced in proportion to the amount of natural areas converted to agriculture – is only partly true. The early conservation movement perceived agriculture as a complete enemy of biodiversity, and many mobilized around a central assumption that the slightest turn toward agriculture meant a dramatic decline in biodiversity. This consolidated into what some have referred to as the "preservationist" position: no amount of agriculture is allowed if we are to truly preserve biodiversity in its purest form.

A simple example and thought experiment is useful to explore this idea. Consider the example of the Huaorani indigenous group in the upper Amazon. Mainly a hunting and gathering group, the Huaorani also practice some "agriculture," especially planting the pejibaye (peach) palm *(Bactris gasipaes)*. Establishing a small clearing in the forest, the Huaorani use this as a central location from which they venture into the forest to hunt monkeys, their main protein source. In that clearing they may plant some cassava, but it seems that they always plant one or more pejibaye palms. The clearing lasts only a short period of time, and the pejibaye does not grow to a size to bear fruit within that time frame. When the extended family moves on to another part of the forest, they repeat the action, planting one or more pejibaye palms. The result seems to be that the extended family builds a geographical memory of the locations of past clearings, and, when the fruit-bearing season of the pejibaye palms arrives, they move through the forest revisiting prior clearings to harvest the fruits of the pejibaye trees they (or their parents or grandparents) had planted. While it appears to an outsider that they are just gathering fruits in the forest, it turns out that they are harvesting some of the fruits from trees that they have planted (Rival 2002).

With regard to biodiversity, one could hardly argue that the Huaorani's "agriculture" has much of an effect on biodiversity. Indeed, whether we are considering plants or parrots, ants or anteaters, this sort of activity could not have more than a trivial effect on biodiversity. (It is even possible to argue that such a practice is positive for biodiversity, but that argument is beyond the scope of this report [see Huston (1979) or Connell (1978) for a discussion of the intermediate disturbance hypothesis]). We can conclude that, at the level of this very "extensive" agricultural system, there is no reduction in biodiversity.

The Huaorani provide a simple example demonstrating how changes in the associated biodiversity can be trivial as the forest changes from "without people" to "with people," even though those people are doing "agriculture" (i.e., planting pejibaye trees). But what happens as agriculture becomes more intensive? At the extreme of the industrial system (the highest level of intensity), we already know that biodiversity is almost completely eliminated (indeed, such elimination is one of the goals of the modern industrial system, which is almost exclusively monocultural). So, we can fix two points: extensive agriculture yields hardly any change in biodiversity from the pre-agricultural state, whereas intensive agriculture yields almost zero biodiversity. The shape of the curve that connects those two points would seem to be an interesting scientific question. Nevertheless, perhaps due to the conservative nature of the traditional conservation movement, only recently has serious study focused on this question (e.g., Cunningham et al. 2013; Daily et al. 2001; Perfecto and Vandermeer 2010; Tscharntke et al. 2012).

Given the evident structures described here, we can say that several patterns are possible (Perfecto and Vandermeer 2008). We show four of those potential patterns in Figure 20.1. When dealing with a sensitive group of species, we expect the pattern to be more or less what the classical conservationist expects: a dramatic decline in biodiversity with intensification. However, the alternate situation, labeled "resilient species pool" in Figure 20.1, shows how the major decline in biodiversity might very well occur at a higher threshold level of intensification. A variety of intermediate situations are also possible, two of which are illustrated as dashed curves in Figure 20.1.

There has not been a great deal of research aimed at distinguishing these hypotheses from one another, but it can be said that for those systems that have been studied, the hypothesis of a resilient species pool seems most correct. That is, it is not until the agricultural system becomes extremely intensified that biodiversity declines dramatically (Perfecto and Vandermeer 2010). This is a potentially important aspect of the subject, something that requires a great deal more research.

Nevertheless, the conclusion that we need to convert current ecologically diverse forms of agriculture, frequently as practiced by small-scale traditional agriculturalists, to intense industrial forms if we seek conservation of biodiversity, as articulated in the so-called "land sparing" argument, is wrong on several counts. First, as noted above, further study is needed to determine exactly the effect of agricultural intensification on biodiversity. Second, and more importantly, conservation of biodiversity is (or should be) a long-term prospect, and we understand less than

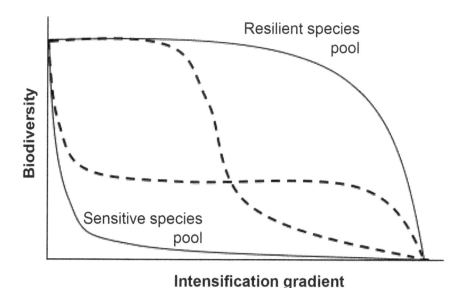

Figure 20.1   Four hypotheses concerning the response of biodiversity to intensification of agriculture (Vandermeer and Perfecto 2005).

we need to about the way associated biodiversity is either maintained or eroded over time, in any form of agriculture. Third, questions about biodiversity within the agroecological system are frequently misplaced, since biodiversity dynamics play out at the level of the landscape (Perfecto and Vandermeer, 2008; 2010; Perfecto et al. 2009).

There is already a body of accepted ecological theory that can be applied to educate the intuition about long-term survival of species. Two theoretical formulations are relevant – metapopulation theory and the equilibrium theory of island biogeography. As has been argued elsewhere (Perfecto and Vandermeer 2010; 2011), some fundamental ecological theory, not at all controversial, is relevant to the question of how land set aside for intensive agriculture might affect the long-term persistence (or not) of biodiversity. This theory is generally dynamic, which is to say, it takes into account the long-term nature of properly constituted conservation goals.

Metapopulations

The first theoretical framework, discussed most in this context, is the idea of a metapopulation. Briefly, many if not most populations in nature exist as metapopulations. Rather than the idealized population distributed over a geographical range, in which every individual can interbreed with every other individual in that range (this ideal is referred to as a panmictic population), most populations exist in some sort of spatial structure. Within that structure, the population is subdivided into subunits, wherein individuals interbreed with one another and then migrate among the subunits. Each subunit is subject to a probability or rate of extinction. Each subunit is also subject to a probability or rate of recolonization (from the collection of other subunits). The easiest way to conceptualize the long-term dynamics of a metapopulation is as a balance between the rate of colonization and the rate of extinction. The classical equation for this formulation (Levins 1969) is:

$$\frac{dp}{dt} = mp(1 - p) - ep$$

Here p is the proportion of potential habitats occupied, m is the migration rate (exchange of individuals among subunits), and e is the extinction rate (probability that the population in a subunit will go extinct). The equilibrium condition is:

$$p^\star = 1 - \frac{e}{m}$$

From this equation it is evident that if m is very large, the ratio e/m is very small, and $p^\star$ is close to 1.0, meaning that almost all the habitats are occupied. If m becomes smaller, the ratio e/m becomes larger and, in the limit as m approaches the value of e, $p^\star$ approaches the value of 0, which means the metapopulation – the collection of subpopulations – becomes extinct.

At the most abstract level this theory of metapopulations can be regarded as the most fundamental theory of landscape structure. If we suppose that the subunits of the metapopulation are the populations of a particular species, then $p^\star$ is the proportion of those subunits in which the species exists. The static approach to the problem, as described in the previous section, simply looks at the value of p at a particular time and assesses the value of e, with the programmatic objective of minimizing e. In contrast, the dynamic approach analyzes both m and e and asks what will be the long-term trend of the population. Most importantly, the dynamic approach seeks to maximize the value of m as well as minimize the value of e. Focusing on the maximization of m requires attention to the factors that determine the size of m. Generally the nature of the agriculture in the matrix will determine the size of m, with a high-quality matrix generating a high value of m, and a low-quality matrix generating a low value of m. Agriculture that results in high matrix quality is generally agriculture that uses mixed cropping, little or no pesticides, organic fertilizer, and, where appropriate, trees – what has come to be called agroecological techniques (Perfecto et al. 2009).

The practical side of this issue is easy to see. As a way of talking about landscapes, let us suppose that they are composed of natural vegetation patches embedded in a matrix of agriculture. Thus we might have patches of rain forest embedded in either a matrix of genetically modified soybeans, or of shaded coffee farms. It is well known that extinction at a local level occurs without human intervention and is unavoidable over the long haul, and that the smaller the fragment within which the population occurs, the higher the extinction rate. Indeed, natural processes of resource overexploitation, predation pressure, or disease outbreaks ensure that local extinctions will occur, and there is largely nothing that can be done about that. To be sure, some populations will resist this seeming inevitability, but, for the vast majority of species on earth, each given subpopulation will eventually become extinct.

In the normal operation of a metapopulation, subpopulations go extinct regularly, but they are normally replaced by migrations of individuals from other subpopulations. The dynamical rules of how those extinctions are balanced by the migrations are given by the equations 1 and 2. Since there is little that one can do to change extinction rates at a local level, it is evident that one should focus on the migration rate in pursuit of any intervention strategy. And the migration rate is determined by the "quality of the matrix" (Perfecto and Vandermeer 2009; 2010), which is most easily constructed through the encouragement of agroecological techniques. The seemingly inevitable conclusion is that development programs that encourage expansion of small-scale agroecological farms are the programs most likely to preserve the maximum biodiversity.

Island biogeography

A second body of ecological theory relevant to this question is the theory of island biogeography (MacArthur and Wilson 1967). This theory is best illustrated with a simple graph, as shown in Figure 20.2.

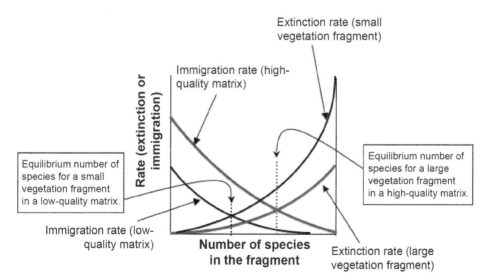

Figure 20.2 Equilibrium theory of island biogeography as applied to the situation of fragments of natural vegetation in a matrix of agriculture.

Referring to that figure, we begin with the horizontal axis recording the number of species at any given time in the fragment of concern. For a given number of species we expect the arrival of new species (that is, species that are not already in the fragment) and we call that the immigration rate. Note that the immigration rate declines with number of species – if there are zero species in the fragment, then every species that arrives is a new one, and the immigration rate will be highest, while if there are the maximum number of species in the fragment, none of the arriving species will be new, since all species are already there. Also, for a given number of species, we expect that a certain number will go extinct for a variety of reasons. That number will be highest when there are the most species already present – if there are no species, none can go extinct, and the most can go extinct when there is a large number. These two rates balance where they cross – when immigration is precisely equal to extinction – creating an "equilibrium" number of species.

Figure 20.2 is the basic figure normally used to describe island biogeography, and it has been adapted here to apply to vegetation fragments (sort of like islands) in an agricultural matrix (sort of like the ocean). It reveals a result that is effectively identical to the result from metapopulation theory. As the quality of the matrix increases, the immigration rate increases, and the expected number of species at long-term equilibrium in the fragment will tend to increase. It is also the case that creating smaller and smaller vegetation fragments will have the effect of reducing the number of species at equilibrium, suggesting that it is indeed good for conservation to preserve as many fragments as possible and fragments that are as large as possible. However, it is equally, if not more important, to ensure a high-quality matrix, as suggested by the general migration curves.

Development and biodiversity

The above consideration of these two well-known ecological theories, metapopulation theory and island biogeography theory, indicates that developmental programs that take seriously conservation must focus on the quality of the matrix rather than on the conventional strategy of protected areas. As landscapes continue to become fragmented – a process that, unfortunately, seems to go on unabated – it is of course a priority for biodiversity conservation that some pieces of natural habitat be preserved. A long-term view of conservation suggests that we ideally should seek to structure landscapes such that as many as possible and as large as possible fragments remain, as landscapes become transformed by the agricultural programs embedded in developmental programs. Indeed the contemporary world is already quite fragmented, especially in the tropics – where, as we have noted, the most biodiversity is located. That fragmentation, as explained above, has set in place a process that will ultimately lead to massive extinctions if a functioning metapopulation structure is not put into place. This imperative means that the matrix in which the fragments are located must be of the highest "quality" possible, a conclusion that derives from elementary ecological theory. This result is sometimes regarded as counterintuitive. If we are concerned with preserving biodiversity, should we not concentrate on those areas where biodiversity is richest? The answer is no. It is precisely the areas between the biodiversity-rich fragments that must be the target of intervention; the matrix through which migrations must take place to maintain metapopulations must be made as high quality as possible. It is also the case that these are the areas most aggressively targeted by developmental programs.

Almost by definition, developmental activity in the matrix determines the matrix quality, whether that activity is directed or proceeds informally. If the developmental activity includes the creation of large industrial monocultures of soybean (or oil palm, or pineapple, or bananas, or maize), the quality of the matrix will be low. Yet, many development programs are aimed in just that direction, largely misguided by the assumption that increased production results from such agricultural systems. If the important parameter determining the quality of the matrix is the ability of organisms to migrate through it, an approximate measure of that parameter would be the degree to which both the biodiversity of concern and the agricultural systems in the matrix approximate the pattern labeled "resilient species pool" in Figure 20.1. If this is the case, promotion of that sort of agriculture is promotion of a high-quality matrix.

There is considerable debate about the actual nature of the agriculture performed by small-scale agriculturalists, but the bulk of evidence suggests that the majority are involved in something approaching agroecological production. There seems to be a dynamic tension between the forces of pseudo-modernization and ecology. On the one hand there is a tendency to consolidate farms, creating large estates that then tend to move to highly intensive and industrial forms of production. This is a tendency that has been in operation for 500 years. On the other hand, there is a tendency to break up the largest farming operations through various political movements, generally referred to as agrarian reform (Vandermeer and Perfecto 2012), generating socio-politico-ecological structures that have strong historical precedent (Van der Ploeg 2009).

A recent trend within the small-farming sector has been to move to more ecologically oriented agriculture, promoted by a combination of concerns ranging from the health of producers (farmers and farmworkers), to the health of consumers, to the health of the environment, to the sustainability of the farming operation. Large-scale operations tend to focus on short-term profits, while smaller operations tend to view a farm as more of an investment in the future. Consequently the literature on relationships among environmental health, human health, and styles of farming has spread rapidly among small farmers worldwide. Of most importance is the tendency to promote farmer-to-farmer education (Holt-Giménez et al. 1999). Furthermore, the promulgation of the ideology of food sovereignty as a development strategy (Rosset 2008; Wittman 2011) has brought with it a focus on agroecological techniques, which inevitably act to create a matrix that is of higher quality than that produced by the industrial system. Indeed, it has been argued (Perfecto and Vandermeer 2010; 2011; Vandermeer and Perfecto 2008) that support for the small-farming sector could be a most important focus for those concerned with biodiversity conservation.

However well we have established that landscape processes determine biodiversity conservation, the expected synergy between farming and natural areas remains poorly studied. That synergy stems from the general idea that farms provide ecosystem services for natural areas, and, reciprocally, natural areas provide ecosystem services for farms. This is an issue that has not been explored systematically, although it is supported by considerable literature from isolated studies (Power 2010). Given the frameworks suggested in this essay, whatever landscape principles should be guiding development decisions, it seems they should apply across the whole spectrum of landscape categories. Presently, the most common situation in the tropical world is the existence of fragments of natural habitat embedded in a matrix of agriculture. The overall planning framework thus should be one of asking questions about ecosystem services provided to the natural habitat by agriculture (in this case we argue that creating a high-quality matrix is a crucial, if poorly acknowledged, aspect of biodiversity conservation), but also questions about ecosystem services provided by natural habitat to agriculture. A vast literature, beyond the intended scope of these notes, exists with regard to pollination services, pest control services, nutrient cycling services, and probably others.

We can envision the overall structure of landscapes along a gradient that converts a matrix of forest to a matrix of agriculture. There are some conceivable developmental situations in which a master planner could ask the question, where along this gradient does one want to be? Most often, however, the landscape begins with, on the one hand, some set of natural remnants, or fragments, in a matrix of agriculture, and, on the other hand, those areas that are fragments of agriculture in a matrix of natural habitat. The latter areas are thought to represent the beginnings of further conversion of natural habitat to agriculture as development proceeds. How to stabilize the system, which is to say, how to maintain the system as is, without further conversion of natural habitat to agriculture, is sometimes the subject of serious study (e.g., Tscharntke et al. 2007), but sometimes, unfortunately, is riddled with political polemic. For questions of biodiversity preservation, the various complications associated with perceptions of what biodiversity consists of, coupled with its long-term dynamics in a landscape composed of natural vegetation situated in a matrix of agriculture, is clearly influenced, both directly and indirectly, by decisions about development programs.

References

Connell, J. H. (1978) "Diversity in Tropical Rain Forests and Coral Reefs," *Science* 199: 259–267.

Cunningham, S., S. J. Attwood, K. S. Bawa, T. G. Benton, L. M. Broadhurst, R. K. Didham, S. McIntyre, I. Perfecto, M. J. Samways, T. Tscharntke, J. Vandermeer, M. Villard, A. G. Young, and D. B. Lindenmayer. (2013) "To Close the Yield-Gap While Saving Biodiversity Will Require Multiple Locally Relevant Strategies," *Agriculture, Ecosystems and Environment* 173: 20–27.

Daily, G. C., P. R. Ehrlich, and G. A. Sanchez-Azofeifa. (2001) "Countryside Biogeography: Use of Human-Dominated Habitats by the Svifauna of Southern Costa Rica," *Ecological Applications* 11(1): 1–13.

Holt-Giménez, E., G. Sain, M. A. Altieri, A. B. Yurjevic, I. Scoones, J. Thompson, and A. Saravia. (1999) *Campesino a Campesino: Voices from Latin America's Farmer-to-Farmer Movement for Sustainable Agriculture*, (No. E11 34), CIMMYT, México, DF (México); IICA, San José (Costa Rica).

Huston, M. (1979) "A General Hypothesis of Species Diversity," *American Naturalist* 113: 81–101.

Levins, R. (1969) "Some Demographic and Genetic Consequences of Environmental Heterogeneity for Biological Control," *Bulletin of the Entomological Society of America* 15(3): 237–240.

MacArthur, R. H. and E. O. Wilson. (1967) *The Theory of Island Biogeography*, Princeton: Princeton University Press, pp. 3–203.

Perfecto, I. and J. Vandermeer. (2008) "Biodiversity Conservation in Tropical Agroecosystems," *Annals of the New York Academy of Sciences* 1134(1): 173–200.

——. (2010) "The Agroecological Matrix as Alternative to the Land-Sparing/Agriculture Intensification Model," *PNAS* 107: 5786–5791.

Perfecto, I., J. Vandermeer, and A. Wright. (2009) *Nature's Matrix: Linking Agriculture, Conservation and Food Sovereignty*, London: Earthscan.

Power, A. G. (2010) "Ecosystem Services and Agriculture: Tradeoffs and Synergies," *Philosophical Transactions of the Royal Society B: Biological Sciences* 365(1554): 2959–2971.

Rival, L. (2002) *Trekking through History: The Huaorani of Amazonian Ecuador*, New York: Columbia University Press.

Rosset, P. (2008) "Food Sovereignty and the Contemporary Food Crisis," *Development* 51(4): 460–463.

Tscharntke, T., C. Leuschner, M. Zeller, E. Guhardja, and A. Bidin. (2007) "The Stability of Tropical Rainforest Margins: Linking Ecological, Economic and Social Constraints of Land Use and Conservation – An Introduction," in T. Tscharntke, C. Leuschner, M. Zeller, E. Guhardja, and A. Bidin (eds.), *The Stability of Tropical Rainforest Margins: Linking Ecological, Economic and Social Constraints of Land Use and Conservation*, Berlin: Springer, pp. 1–8.

Tscharntke, T., Y. Clough, L. Jackson, I. Motzke, I. Perfecto, J. Vandermeer, T. C. Wanger, and A. Whitbread. (2012) "Global Food Security, Biodiversity Conservation and the Future of Agricultural Intensification," *Biological Conservation* 151(1): 53–59.

Vandermeer, J. and I. Perfecto. (2005) *A Breakfast of Biodiversity: The True Causes of Rain Forest Destruction*, 2nd ed., Institute for Food and Development Policy.

——. (2012) "Syndromes of Production in Agriculture: Prospects for Socioecological Regime Change," *Ecology and Society* 17: 39.

Van der Ploeg, J. D. (2009) *The New Peasantries: Struggles for Autonomy and Sustainability in an Era of Empire and Globalization*, London: Routledge.

Wittman, H. (ed.) (2011) *Food Sovereignty: Reconnecting Food, Nature & Community*, Oxford: Pambazuka Press.

21

SUSTAINABILITY

Paul B. Thompson

As the 20th century came to a close, the interplay of word and context came to be increasingly acknowledged in both Continental and analytic traditions of philosophy. George Steiner's *Grammars of Creation* (2000) begins with a meditation on the palpable sense that European culture has entered its endgame. He goes on to link this theme to a loss of confidence in the generative powers of art, in general, and of writing, in particular. Although Steiner does not discuss sustainability, his study of the interplay of language, technology, and cultural confidence is suggestive for any philosophical treatment of the concept. For many, the idea of sustainability has replaced the way that progress and creative advance once animated thought and linked humanistic endeavor to the sciences. The discourse on sustainability has neglected such larger ontological or eschatological themes, however. This essay will hold close to themes actively advanced under the banner of sustainability and will leave more speculative metaphysical connections to the imagination of the reader.

There is clearly a dominant discourse of sustainability. Its genealogy can be traced to the 1987 report of the World Commission on Environment and Development (henceforth "the Brundtland report"), which called for "development that meets the needs of current generations without compromising the ability of future generations to meet their own needs." The Brundtland report's definition of *sustainable development* spawned a decade of debate among specialists about how this terse and provocative phrase would receive more specificity in the policy and programming of international organizations (such as the World Bank or the Organization for Economic Cooperation and Development [OECD]). By century's end, this discourse morphed into a discussion of more general social goals articulated through metaphors such as the "three pillars" of sustainability or "the triple bottom line": environment, economy, and society.

The most widely known philosophical discussion of sustainability occurs in the writings of Bryan Norton, who uses the word "sustainability" as a name for his comprehensive environmental philosophy. Yet, as influential as it has been in some quarters, Norton's approach to sustainability does not begin to capture the breadth of topics either within the dominant discourse of sustainability, or within alternatives that challenge it. This chapter's overview of sustainability will begin with a discussion of Norton's work, followed by a synopsis that classifies the discourse according to two overlapping but nonetheless distinguishable philosophies of sustainability. The relevance of the sustainability discourse to food ethics will not be directly thematized but will, nonetheless, be obvious.

Norton's sustainability

Following pathbreaking work on biodiversity and a failed attempt to forge consensus among environmental philosophers, Bryan Norton has devoted the last 25 years of his career to the theme of sustainability. His 2005 book, *Sustainability: A Philosophy of Adaptive Ecosystem Management*, argues that the environmental crisis is, in large part, a failure to integrate diverse strands of knowledge *about* ecosystems (ecology, toxicology, systems biology, and the diverse fields we have come to call "climate science"), but also a failure to recognize the inevitability of value judgments and a corresponding incapacity to discuss or negotiate value conflicts in planning, policy, and environmental management. The examples discussed in the book reflect Norton's long-running interest in conservation biology, the protection of habitat for threatened species, and the challenges to these goals posed by urbanization and human incursion on the ecosystems that support all forms of life on Earth. A succinct statement of Norton's prescription for change is that humanity must learn how to discuss these problems: environmental science cannot be expected to save the day. Sustainability is, in this respect, a project in building collective communicative capacity around the various environmental challenges that human beings face on a worldwide basis.

In effect, Norton's sustainability is an expansion and replacement of the "convergence hypothesis" advanced in his 1991 book, *Toward Unity among Environmentalists*. Norton was there reacting to the way that anthropocentrically justified environmental programs were being attacked on philosophical grounds by those who advocated direct moral status for non-human animals, in some cases for all living organisms (biocentrism), or for seemingly abstract entities such as ecosystems or species (ecocentrism). Norton argued that as one expands one's horizons both spatially and temporally, the implications of taking these alternative philosophical positions converge on one and the same prescriptions. Thus as the scope of the anthropocentrist's concern comes to recognize humanity's dependence on global ecosystems and extends to future generations, defense of non-humans, conservation of species, and protection of ecosystems are easily defended on anthropocentric grounds. In his shift to sustainability, Norton maintained his interest in unifying diverse and seemingly antagonistic philosophical commitments around a common set of social goals and policy prescriptions. Much of the effort in his most recent book, *Sustainable Values, Sustainable Change* (2015), is devoted to developing a decision-oriented account of how consensus on action-oriented policies can be achieved.

In the course of making this more comprehensive argument, Norton devoted just a few chapters in *Sustainability* (2005) to the contemporary debate over sustainability occurring among non-philosophers. He took the distinction between weak and strong sustainability to be the centerpiece of that debate. As noted, the discourse of the 1990s was shaped by the Brundtland Commission's formulation of a definition of sustainable development. Economists of the time measured development through indicators, such as Gross Domestic Product (GDP), strongly associated with total capital accumulation. Herman Daly, who had criticized the fixation on GDP, argued that fixed amounts of natural resources constrain the future potential for economic growth on a global basis (1990). These natural resources – including the Earth's ability to supply renewable resources such as clean air and water or fertile soils – were referred to as "natural capital." Daly and other advocates of *strong sustainability* argued that meeting the Brundtland goal of not compromising future generations' ability to meet their own needs would require strict conservation of natural capital. The opposing view began with the observation that strict conservation of natural capital was incompatible with the Brundtland commitment to improving human well-being in less-developed countries, and it went on to argue that there is a fair amount of intersubstitutivity among the various forms of capital, including manufactured capital (factories and technology), human capital (knowledge), and social capital (collective abilities for cooperative activity). This view advocated *weak sustainability*: commitment to conservation of *total* capital, while recognizing that technological advances and increases in human or social capital would be needed to replace dwindling natural capital.

It should be noted that the dichotomy between weak and strong sustainability leaves room for many intermediate positions. For example, one can admit that advances in technology or social cooperation could, for example, reduce the amount of water wasted by replacing inefficient irrigation systems, on the one hand, or by convincing people to take shorter showers, on the other. One might also admit that getting to a situation where these efficiencies and social practices are possible will require expenditure of natural capital over the short run. Yet such an admission need not also compel one to permit any and all declines of natural capital on the grounds that some unimagined new future technology will permit our children's grandchildren to manufacture water out of thin air. Norton's new book recapitulates the strong vs. weak sustainability debate by explicitly advocating for this kind of middle-ground position. While, in *Sustainability*, Norton admitted that his approach is effectively a form of weak sustainability, in *Sustainable Values, Sustainable Change* he claims that maintaining some forms of natural capital is an absolute necessity. The problem is knowing *which* natural capital must be preserved: Is it natural habitats, the systems that render ecosystem services for clean air and water, climate regulation, or even some stock of minerals? Consistent with the position he has argued since *Toward Unity*, Norton denies that putatively "value-free" environmental sciences can answer this question. Some process for the elicitation and construction of a community value consensus is essential (Norton 2015).

Although Norton's argument is focused on political and managerial processes in developed industrial states, it is consistent with an approach to sustainability that emphasizes distributive justice. While people in extreme poverty may consume fewer resources than those who enjoy a higher standard of living, they also have far less ability to adjust their activity under changed conditions. This holds whether change is broadly positive or negative. When technological advances do become available, the poor have a limited ability to take advantage of them, hence damaging practices persist. When conditions take a turn for the worse, as is currently taking place due to climate change, the poor shoulder a disproportionate share of the harm. Thus the philosophical position Norton advocates condones temporary use of natural capital (such as fossil fuels) in the hope that it will limit present-day overfishing, scavenging for food in forests, and the destruction of ecosystems. Yet at the same time, Norton recognizes that continued sustainability will require the development of less destructive forms of total consumption (including energy) in the future (Norton 2005). In short, although Norton's contribution has been to argue for a procedural understanding of sustainability as adaptive management, he does not contest the underlying problematic put forward by the Brundtland Commission in 1987.

The broader sustainability discourse

As noted above, much of the public discourse on sustainability is propelled by heuristic devices, such as the ubiquitous "three circle" and "three pillar" diagrams that indicate that sustainability must be sought in environmental, economic, and social dimensions. The use of such metaphors in the business community may in part account for some philosophers' tendency to presume that there couldn't be much of importance associated with them. Slavoj Žižek has pilloried the way that profit-oriented firms and their spokespeople have embraced "fair trade" and other labels in the name of sustainability (Žižek 2009). But even in this highly superficial discourse there are points to notice. Foremost is the relationship between the adjectival and the noun form. Starting with Brundtland's focus on sustainable development, the discourse has celebrated numerous forms of "sustainable X": sustainable energy use, sustainable building materials, sustainable coffee, sustainable design. In each case, the X in question is a practice or process, and the implicit problem of sustainability resides in the manner in which this practice might be made "more sustainable." As Aiden Davison has noted, the tendency to focus so intently on the practice at hand means that the question of sustainability as such is sublimated entirely within the prior discourse that has framed the practice or process in question (Davison 2001).

With respect to the business community, there has been a tendency to presume that economic sustainability can be equated with profitability, while environmental sustainability is improved by adopting business practices that conserve natural resources, reduce pollution, and limit the waste stream of a company's production process. Companies such as Walmart have discovered that these two goals may complement one another, as when recycling cardboard shipping containers removes waste from landfills while generating significant new sources of revenue. The "social" piece of sustainability has been more difficult to reconcile with the business perspective. Some have drawn on a previous literature in "corporate social responsibility" to interpret social sustainability in terms of supply chains that recognize fair trade or monitor the labor practices of suppliers. Others emphasize "social permission to operate," noting that companies cannot expect to conduct operations that are viewed as offensive or unethical without incurring costs in the form of protest, negative publicity, and lawsuits.

It should be noted at the outset that equating economic sustainability with business profitability leads to a substantially different conception of sustainability than the macroeconomic debate over economic growth and the substitutivity of capitals discussed above. Both are focused on economic phenomena, but an economy consisting of profitable businesses may not be sustainable in a macroeconomic sense (as Schumpeter's [1950] theory of "creative destruction" and business cycles also attests). Gaining fluency in the sustainability debate thus requires an ability to translate across multiple domains and discourse communities, and this capability points to one way in which understanding sustainability requires a certain amount of philosophical sophistication. Given the complexity of cross-cutting and intersecting discourse communities, it is useful to develop broad (and thus relatively abstract) conceptual approaches to the key goals and imperatives of sustainability, even if they do not fully circumscribe the debate. This is arguably something that Norton's approach to sustainability does not even attempt to do.

In *The Agrarian Vision* (2010) I offered a diagnostic approach in terms of two broad ways of conceptualizing sustainability. *Resource sufficiency* is attained (or advanced) to the extent that the inputs needed to carry on a practice or process are foreseeably available. In contrast, *functional integrity* is improved by strengthening the internal elements and organization of a system so that it is less vulnerable to self-destruction and collapse. The Brundtland emphasis on the *process* of development implicitly aligns this conception of sustainability with the resource-sufficiency approach. Close inspection of the literature on sustainable development shows that debate has centered on the foreseeable availability of various forms of capital as reflected in the strong sustainability/weak sustainability debate. Theorists focused on the integrity of ecosystems have grown increasingly frustrated by the continuing dominance of this Brundtland fascination with capital, and some have recently advocated the abandonment of sustainability in favor of resilience. There are thus clearly two competing paradigms. In the analysis that follows I will continue to use the phrases "resource sufficiency" and "functional integrity," but in deference to the emerging usage I will speak of the "Brundtland paradigm" and "the resilience paradigm." Understanding what matters philosophically about sustainability remains, I argue, a problem that can best be approached by analyzing the differences between these paradigms.

The Brundtland paradigm

The discussion of weak and strong sustainability above reflects how the goal of "development that meets the needs of the present without compromising the ability of future generations to meet their needs" became embroiled in debates over the way that different types of resources – natural, manufactured, human, and social – have the potential to be constraining or facilitative. The Brundtland Commission was convened to consider how longstanding inequality in the standard of living in industrialized economies and less-industrialized countries (often former colonies of European powers) could be addressed, especially given the growing recognition that resource depletion and pollution were only making the task more difficult. Since 1987, the challenge of climate change has made this larger task even more challenging. There is thus a deep sense in which the Brundtland approach analyzes sustainability in terms of the foreseeable availability of those resources (again, natural, manufactured, human, *and* social) needed to equalize the standard of living on a global basis.

This analysis had roots in 1960s and 1970s debates over human population growth and "neo-Malthusianism." The enormously influential book, *The Population Bomb* (1968), by Paul and Anne Ehrlich (Anne was denied authorship credit) made basic principles of population ecology and biological carrying capacity accessible to a broad audience. As with Malthus' original formulations in the early 1800s, the argument is made primarily in terms of a mismatch between the natural rate of growth in population and the ability of that population's habits to produce enough for every individual to eat. In natural ecosystems this balance is upheld by predator–prey relationships, but as humans have eliminated their natural predators (including disease organisms), the total human population has grown at the exponential rates that Malthus estimated. The Ehrlichs predicted an era of increasing famine and food shortage, accompanied by warfare over control of the land, water, and energy that are the essential resource-inputs for food production (Ehrlich and Ehrlich 2009). In many respects, the post-Brundtland debate over strong and weak sustainability only generalizes the food and famine orientation of population ecology, reformulating it in the more abstract terms of capital and economic growth.

There is also a longstanding ethical dimension to the debate focused on inequalities in the distribution of control over resources such as land, water, and energy, and the role of political and economic power in the future allocation of goods – especially food – produced through the use of these resources. In an obvious sense, then, the debate being conducted in response to the Brundtland Commission's definition of sustainable development replicated a centuries-long philosophical dispute over distributive justice. In what sense are those who *do* control these resources obligated to ensure the welfare of those who do not have them? Is redistribution of resources required by ethics or the theory of justice? Are those who lack the resources needed for their very survival justified in violent or other extreme actions needed to ensure their future? Given an approach to development formulated in terms of resource sufficiency, these *are* the philosophical questions of sustainability.

However, Davison (2001) argues that the Brundtland report's fixation on development defeats the philosophical task of understanding sustainability itself. "Development" has been subjected to a withering critical discourse during the last several decades. Beginning in earnest with the independence movements that led to the collapse of European colonial empires following World War II, development theory enjoyed a period when Marxists and neo-liberals carried on a lively debate. By the 1970s left-leaning theorists had become convinced that neither centralized planning nor market-driven capital investment were leading to improvements in former colonial states. Dependency theorists argued that technical and managerial expertise were being denied to developing economies, while world-system theories were identifying how the very mobility of capital that had been intended to foster development in both centralized and market models was in fact simply replicating the de-skilling and exploitation of labor seen during the early phases of the industrial revolution, only now at a global scale (Davison 2001). The problem, in other words, was *development*, and the Brundtland focus on environmental limits only served to obscure flaws in a fundamental process that needed to be totally re-organized, rather than made "more sustainable."

Language was working its ways here, and Davison's criticism can be broadened. Whether or not one endorses the critique of development, we should notice how the grammar of "sustainable X" can be rapidly turned toward making X "more sustainable." Such a turn of phrase places a barrier to questioning whether the process or practice in question is worth sustaining in the first place. One frequent trope in the discourse is to question whether sustainability is "a journey or a destination." In its best sense the opaque metaphor is intended to note the difference between an ameliorative conception of sustainability where there are always opportunities for further improvement, and a conception that implies a future state where all the criteria for sustainability have been fully satisfied. But the best sense need not be the one that prevails in a non-ideal discourse. Too often the effect has been to steer efforts being put forward under the banner of sustainability toward the traditional technocratic norm of increasing the efficiency of the practice or process in question. A practice X is made "more sustainable" by making technical changes that allow one to get more of what one wants with lower inputs. In the context of food, this has generally meant the type of increase in agricultural yields that we associate with industrial agriculture.

But Davison's perceptive criticisms notwithstanding, some good things occurred in the sustainability era. Clark Miller has argued that while sustainability has had negligible to disappointing impact on debates in social and political theory, it has allowed a number of neglected issues to gain purchase in "street-level" decision-making (2005). Where sustainability has entered the discourse for local politics at the city, county, or regional level, it has proven to be not only an effective way to get a number of resource conservation and environmental protection initiatives into the mix, it has allowed questions of social equity, and racial, gender, and ethnic exclusion to be included along with the usual concerns over job creation and taxes. As noted already, this aspect of the sustainability discourse inherits much from prior debates over socially responsible business practices. Nevertheless, it is also quite compatible with classic philosophical discussions of distributive justice that can be readily linked to resource sufficiency. Miller is arguing that through the cunning of history, the sustainability debate allowed *less-powerful* actors to raise basic questions of distributive justice in a new and potentially more effective political forum. The turn to sustainability has given a centuries-old philosophical debate over distributive justice new salience in urban and regional politics (Davison 2005).

The resilience paradigm

Yet even before the Brundtland report was released in 1987, a philosophically distinct conceptualization of sustainability was being promulgated. The most influential voices promoting this alternative vision came from the science of ecology, and some of its earliest articulations came in connection with sustainable agriculture. This paradigm is grounded in the concepts of general systems theory, specifically in the recognition that *some* configurations of systemically integrated stocks and flows reproduce their overall structure and pattern over time, while others inevitably become unstable, leading to overshoot, oscillation, and collapse. One key insight of general systems theory was the abstract or mathematical nature of system structure. Uniform structure and behavior relationships could be deduced from the organization of stocks, flows, and feedback, irrespective of the kind or type of thing that was systemically organized: information, energy, financial capital, physical goods (such as water and food), or populations of organisms. Thus, a form of system organization that would exhibit fluctuation, instability, and collapse when observed in any one setting could be expected to perform similarly when replicated in another. Systemic organization can also be seen to cohere in hierarchical relationships: within a single cell, at the multi-cellular level of an organism, at the level of a herd, group, or population, and finally at the super-organismal level of a species or a regional or even planetary ecosystem. Depending on linkages, failure at a low level in the hierarchy could have negligible effects at other levels, or alternatively it could bring the entire structure down in a heap.

What is more, many systems – and not just living systems – can be observed to have an adaptive capacity that permits significant change in response to stresses and threats arising within the system's functional environment. Most living organisms exhibit some degree of adaptive capacity, and the diversity of alleles within an interbreeding population of organisms avails the potential for dramatic shifts in organismal phenotypes over time. Sustainability is exhibited in three ways. A *robust* system can resist destabilizing and disruptive threats that impinge on key functions or feedback from without. For example, roadways built from concrete will resist impact of flooding more successfully than unpaved footpaths. *Resilience* indicates the system's ability to recover functionality following a perturbation: a resilient electric grid will come back on line quickly even when one or more substations fail. Finally, a system is *adaptive* to the extent that it is able to make adjustments within its own organizational components that allow it to withstand significant (and often permanent) change in its external environment. In other writings, I have called this the "functional integrity" view of sustainability, but in light of considerable influence exerted by the Stockholm Resilience Institute, it is now more widely associated simply with the word "resilience" (Orr 2014; Rockström et al. 2009).

In fact, associating resilience with farming systems may be an idea as old as agriculture itself. Its contours can be recognized clearly in the writings of Arthur Young (1741–1820) and in the French physiocrats. Historian Stephen Stoll recounts debates occurring contemporaneously with the American Revolution between "skimmers" – farmers who raped fertile lands for short-term profit only to move on to new, virgin soils after a decade or less – and those who called for more careful manuring and maintenance of soil nutrients. The concern here was less for the land itself than for the sustainability of towns and counties that depended on a stable farming population in order to support a permanent civil society. The skimmers' abandonment of lands depleted the population needed to sustain viable churches, schools, and government offices, not to mention the commercial enterprises emerging on many a local Main Street (Stoll 2002).

By the early 1900s Liberty Hyde Bailey (1858–1954) campaigned for "permanent agriculture" as a form of farming that would base its conservation of soil fertility and clean water on scientific principles. Bailey was the founding dean of Cornell University's agricultural college, and arguably the most famous agricultural scientist of his era. No one used the word "sustainability" in connection to food and farming until comparatively recent times, but permanent agriculture was clearly a progenitor. On the one hand, Bailey based his vision on humanity's obligations to "the Holy Earth," and he argued that it was time for people to recognize the land itself as ontologically capable of being the object to which a moral obligation might be owed. On the other hand, his work with Theodore Roosevelt's Country Life Commission stressed the civic and social side of sustainability with respect to the reproduction of institutions crucial for rural quality of life (Thompson 2010).

The agricultural examples are especially cogent for illustrating the underlying ethical and political commitments of the resilience paradigm. Bailey's "Holy Earth" and "Country Life" specify systemically organized autopoetic entities that are adaptively reproduced over time. His position requires that we view these systems themselves as having a kind of moral value or status akin to that with which we regard other human beings. This claim is not especially novel with respect to Bailey's concern for rural communities. The continuation and reproduction of the polis has been a subject for grounding moral and political obligations since antiquity. Bailey is calling attention to the rural component of the socio-political system we know as the polis, and it is a prescient call given the extent to which urbanity has erased the city's link to the biophysical systems on which it depends (Anonymous 1917). In arguing that this biophysical system *itself* can be the subject of moral regard, Bailey made an early statement of a claim that has been central for contemporary environmental philosophy: it is time to move beyond a philosophy that exhausts the moral significance of land through concepts of property and to recognize instead the sense in which land *is* a system with elements of robustness, resilience, and adaptation. Correlative to these, there are profound ways in which the biophysical systems on which human social life depends can exhibit vulnerabilities that call for a moral response (Bailey 1915).

Thus the resilience paradigm appears to invest the system itself with a form of value that calls for moral consideration and respect. Alternatively, one might deny that the sustainability of a system is itself of any enduring value and insist that the continued function of systemic relationships has value only insofar as the system produces other goods – energy, food, finance – that human beings want. This *is*, in effect, to insist upon a resource-sufficiency view. In this manner, the debate between sustainability construed alternately in terms of resource sufficiency and functional integrity tracks the now well-trodden paths of anthropocentrism and ecocentrism in environmental ethics. The resource-sufficiency viewpoint demands that systems be viewed in purely instrumental terms, while the resilience paradigm presumes that *some* systems, at least, deserve protection from human-caused destruction purely on their own merits.

The strength of the Brundtland paradigm may reside in the clarity with which it can be linked to classical questions in distributive justice. Correlatively, the resilience paradigm's emphasis on systems can function as a retreat from normativity, a quasi-positivist intellectual move that allows scientists and other systems analysts to probe the structure of key systems without bothering to articulate why they matter. Yet the systems perspective of the resilience paradigm does have normative commitments of its own. They arise primarily in the way that one construes the boundedness of the system at hand. Are human beings part of the system, or are they exogenous "drivers" that can only affect it from without? Are human institutions analyzed within the system, and if so, are they institutions that we would actually *want* to sustain? Institutions of religious intolerance and structural racism appear to be quite resilient, and even in an era where human slavery has had no legal sanction anywhere for nearly a century, those engaged in human trafficking have found ways to adapt. These weaknesses notwithstanding, attention to system hierarchy and integration can reveal questions of deep ethical significance that more conventional ethical approaches simply do not broach. Aldo Leopold's recognition that he must learn to "think like a mountain" may yet be a prominent case in point (Leopold 1948).

Conclusion: sustainability in agriculture and food systems

By 1980, agricultural scientists were conducting a debate over sustainability that prefigured the larger contrast between the Brundtland and resilience paradigms. Advocates of efficiency-increasing chemical, mechanical, and biological technologies were citing Malthus and defining sustainable agriculture in terms of the technical feasibility of producing enough food to feed a growing global population. They saw agriculture as a technology crucial to the sustainability of continued population growth. In contrast, a rump group of agronomists were focused on the farm as an ecosystem, questioning whether new technologies were disrupting feedbacks crucial to the subsystem of microorganisms that reproduces fertile soils. A similarly minded group of social scientists were noticing the rapid transformation to a few large farms in industrially oriented regions and wondering whether the banks, schools, and other institutions of rural areas could be sustained as those areas became depleted of farmers (Thompson 2010). Thus within food and farming the contours of a larger debate between resource sufficiency and functional integrity have been visible for some time.

In 2015, a report from the US National Research Council and the Institute of Medicine frames agriculture, food processing, and their related industries in terms of a comprehensive food system, and it utilizes insights from systems theory to argue that health outcomes, environmental impacts, and socio-economic effects can be derived from system structure and linkages. The report recognized significant adaptive capacity within the system, though it noted that adaptation might take the form of maintaining inequalities and power relationships, as much as improving system performance with respect to food security and environmental sustainability. It criticized much of the existing literature on food, nutrition, and environmental impacts of food production for failing to reflect systemic iterations, and it emphasized how US food and agricultural policy-making has taken a piecemeal approach that fails to take account of the way that changes in one element of the food system stimulate adaptive responses that can have adverse consequences in other system components. The report questions whether future improvements in the performance of the food system can be achieved simply through technological advance. Significant attempts to reconfigure the organization of the food system may be needed to improve resilience and to achieve distributive justice (Nesheim et al. 2015).

Although the report does not frame its findings explicitly in the discourse of sustainability, the system orientation of its authors is especially suggestive for scholars who wish to do future work on sustainability within the context of agriculture and food production. The systems orientation will be especially relevant for those who understand sustainability to include elements of social and economic organization and the distribution of health or nutritional impacts on disempowered or marginalized populations. From a values perspective, the report also exemplifies the challenges posed by the binary of paradigmatic approaches discussed above. For the most part, the report suggests that the food system derives its ethical significance in virtue of its human health, environmental, economic, and social impacts. This is consistent with the Brundtland paradigm's assumption that sustainability can be understood in terms of continued and more effective means to deliver beneficial outcomes. Given this orientation, the reason for developing a systems model or framework is to anticipate where constraints on that ability reside and to plan for types of capital substitution (often in the form of more research) that can compensate for them. However, the report's frequent references to ways in which the current food system is dysfunctional and vulnerable to continued instabilities suggests a critique formulated in the type of thinking more characteristic of the resilience paradigm. Here, the system itself is what must be valued (though this perspective does not exclude recognition that evidence for dysfunctionality may be found in adverse or harmful outcomes). From the systems perspective, power can be analyzed in terms of the ability to affect existing linkages and feedback relationships. Human beings, food animals, and ecosystem components that have little power in this sense cannot affect system organization in an adaptive way except through impacts that resonate throughout the larger system. This feedback can lead to a catastrophic collapse of the system when the weak links (human or non-human) become utterly incapable of bearing the stress to which they are being subjected in the status quo. There is thus a profound sense in which marginalized groups represent threats to the functional integrity of the system, even as the effects they experience can be interpreted as uncompensated and unjust harms from the perspective of distributive justice.

For the time being, the philosophical challenge of sustainability consists in the way that each of these paradigmatic approaches induces complementary forms of value blindness. The value that is placed on system integrity in the resilience perspective may obscure ways in which a highly resilient or sustainable system reproduces gender inequalities or structural racism. Such a focus on system adaptation may make people insensitive to the way that highly resilient systems can fail to deliver an adequate or fair share of goods and services to powerless groups and marginalized individuals. Those who view the food system in purely instrumental terms, on the other hand, may overlook ways in which well-intentioned policy reforms induce system adjustments that are geographically or conceptually distant and presumptively unrelated to the immediate goals of an intervention. They may neglect system linkages and, in the worst case, allow threats to system integration to escalate beyond any easy point of recovery. Although a full discussion cannot be undertaken here, financial crises that are becoming commonplace in recent years may exemplify this particular form of blindness to systemic structures.

The larger eschatological themes with which this chapter began remain intriguing, however. For the most part, participants in the discourse of sustainability remain existentially committed to an active posture, to undertaking intellectual and political efforts that will rescue civilization from the abyss, even if as individuals many of them are less than optimistic. As the 21st century has worn on, the specter of global climate change dwarfs a discourse obsessed with minor adjustments in industrial food systems, or substitution of human ingenuity and technological advance for dwindling natural capital. The retreat from progress to sustainability may eventually give way to resignation. At that point, philosophy may resort to the more conciliatory discourses characteristic of the ancient Stoics, who fully expected prosperity to give way eventually to chaos. For now, at least, the discourse of sustainability continues to draw upon forward-looking political and moral ideals. It seeks to mutually engage the dichotomous orientations of resource sufficiency and functional integrity in a dialectical synthesis with truly adaptive potential. Would that be progress, or merely sustainability?

References

Anonymous. (1917) *The Report of the Commission on Country Life*, New York: Sturgis and Walton Co.

Bailey, L. H. (1915) *The Holy Earth*, New York: Charles Scribner's Sons.

Daly, H. E. (1990) "Toward Some Operational Principles for Sustainable Development," *Ecological Economics* 2: 1–6.

Davison, A. (2001) *Technology and the Contested Meanings of Sustainability*, Albany, NY: SUNY Press.

Ehrlich, P. R. (1968) *The Population Bomb*, New York: Ballantine Books.

Ehrlich, P. R. and A. H. Ehrlich. (2009) "The Population Bomb Revisited," *The Electronic Journal of Sustainable Development* 1(3): 63–71.

Leopold, A. (1948) *A Sand County Almanac and Sketches Here and There*, New York: Oxford University Press.

Miller, C. A. (2005) "New Civic Epistemologies of Quantification: Making Sense of Indicators of Local and Global Sustainability," *Science, Technology & Human Values* 30: 403–432.

Nesheim, M. C., K. Clancy, J. K. Hammett, R. A. Hammond, D. L. Haver, D. Jackson-Smith, R. S. Johnson, J. D. Kinsey, S. M. Krebs-Smith, M. Liebman, F. Mitloehner, K. M. Pollack, P. J. Stover, K. M. J. Swanson, and S. M. Swinton. (2015) *A Framework for Assessing Effects of the Food System*, Washington, DC: National Academies Press.

Norton, B. (1991) *Toward Unity among Environmentalists*, New York: Oxford University Press.

——. (2005) *Sustainability: A Philosophy of Adaptive Ecosystem Management*, Chicago: University of Chicago Press.

——. (2015) *Sustainable Values, Sustainable Change*, Chicago: University of Chicago Press.

Orr, D. W. (2014) "Living and Breathing in a Black Swan World," *Solutions* 5(5): 33–39.

Rockström, J., W. Steffen, K. Noone, Å. Persson, F. S. Chapin III, E. F. Lambin, T. M. Lenton, M. Scheffer, C. Folke, H. J. Schellnhuber, B. Nykvist, C. A. de Wit, T. Hughes, S. van der Leeuw, H. Rodhe, S. Sörlin, P. K. Snyder, R. Costanza, U. Svedin, M. Falkenmark, L. Karlberg, R. W. Corell, V. J. Fabry, J. Hansen, B. H. Walker, D. Liverman, K. Richardson, P. Crutzen, and J. A. Foley. (2009) "A Safe Operating Space for Humanity," *Nature* 461: 472–475.

Schumpeter, J. (1950) *Capitalism, Socialism and Democracy*, New York: Harper.

Steiner, G. (2000) *Grammars of Creation*, New Haven: Yale University Press.

Stoll, S. (2002) *Larding the Lean Earth: Soil and Society in 19th-Century America*, New York: Hill and Wang.

Thompson, P. B. (2010) *The Agrarian Vision: Sustainability and Environmental Ethics*, Lexington: University Press of Kentucky.

World Commission on Environment and Development. (1987) *Our Common Future*, Oxford: Oxford University Press

Žižek, S. (2009) *First as Tragedy, Then as Farce*, London: Verso.

Further Reading

G. K. Douglas, *Agricultural Sustainability in a Changing World Order* (Boulder, CO: Westview Press, 1984) is an overlooked work of particular relevance to scholars of food ethics and food systems. H. E. Daly, J. B. Cobb, and C. W. Cobb, *For the Common Good: Redirecting the Economy toward Community, the Environment, and a Sustainable Future* (Boston: Beacon Press, 1994[1989]) is a work by an economist and a process theologian that was a deeply influential analysis of sustainability, which continues to hold philosophical interest. A. Holland, "Sustainability," in *A Companion to Environmental Philosophy*, D. Jamieson (ed.), pp. 390–401 (Oxford: Blackwell, 2001) provides a snapshot of what philosophers were saying about sustainability at the dawn of the 21st century. S. Dresner, *The Principles of Sustainability*, 2nd Ed. (London: Earthscan, 2008) links the debate that ensued in the wake of the World Commission on Environment and Development to classic themes in liberal political theory, distributive justice, and the philosophy of economics. M. H. Benson and R. K. Craig, "The End of Sustainability," *Society and Natural Resources* 27(2014): 777–782 argues for the resilience paradigm and claims that the sustainability debate of the 1990s and early 21st century has reached a dead end.

22

FOOD AND ENVIRONMENTAL JUSTICE

Graeme Sherriff

Introduction

Environmental justice is a notion that has received increasing attention in policy, politics, and academic research. It can be understood to stem from concerns not only that environmental resources are being unfairly distributed, but also that mainstream environmentalism places insufficient emphasis on justice for communities, in the Global North and South. It can be seen as a call for stronger consideration of social justice in environmentalism.

Food is an environmental resource and is essential for human survival. Shortages of food can therefore be the root of a strong sense of injustice. More than being a physiological requirement, however, food is something that is bound up with our practices and cultures and can also have a profound effect on our psychological wellbeing. It is this relationship with food that makes it more than simply an issue of distribution and access – as much quality as quantity. Moreover, our consumption and, for those who have them, dietary choices, can impact upon others through global supply chains and environmental concerns such as climate change and deforestation.

This chapter explores the relationship between food and environmental justice. It starts by outlining environmental justice and tracing the history of this concept, and it then considers why food is of particular interest from an environmental justice perspective. It then looks at four issues relating to food and environmental justice: the accessibility of food where people live; climate change and its relationship with the production, distribution, and consumption of food; justice issues in the supply chains that provide for our towns and cities; and scale and the notion of localism.

What is environmental justice?

The environmental justice movement is understood to have originated in 1970s North America with roots in the civil rights and anti-toxics movements, and it is from these beginnings that the concept has developed. Protests about the location of toxic disposal sites, for example, raised concerns about disproportionate impacts upon particular demographic groups, particularly in terms of race and ethnicity. Agyeman saw this movement as representing a "grass-roots (re)definition of environmental issues, not (only) as wildlife, recreational or resource issues, but as issues of justice, equity and rights" (Agyeman 2000). The environment, it was argued, was, or should be, as much about having a safe and healthy environment "where we live, work and play" (Novotny 1995) as it was about rainforests and endangered wildlife.

Gottlieb and Joshi (2010) introduce food justice as "where, what, and how we eat." It is, they argue, about ensuring a fair distribution of the benefits and risks of where, what, and how food is grown and produced, transported, distributed, accessed and eaten (Gottlieb and Joshi 2010). The concept of food democracy builds on another central tenet of environmental justice, that of procedural justice, in which fair and inclusive procedures are in place to address injustices and tackle systemic issues (Agyeman 2003).

Before further unpacking the ways in which environmental justice is pertinent in debates on food and agricultural production, it is useful to understand the ways in which the idea of environmental justice has developed and been conceptualized in different contexts. Recent research has identified campaigns on potential injustices experienced due to age, gender, indigenous status, disability, and income. The scope of environmental justice can be seen to have broadened from a focus on "environmental bads" to encompass "goods," i.e., the provision of environmental resources, such as transportation and greenspace, alongside protection from air pollution and toxic waste.

Agyeman posits just sustainability as a concept that brings together environmental justice with more conventional environmental campaigns towards a "sustainable society, locally, nationally and internationally, both within and between generations and between species" (Agyeman 2003: 323). In his exploration of justice and the environment, Dobson (1998) compared these two agendas to the circles of a Venn diagram: they have areas of common concern, but they do not wholly map onto one another. *Just sustainability*, then, is arguably the overlapping area of Dobson's Venn diagram.

Oxfam's donut of a "Safe and Just Space for Humanity" (Raworth 2012) is useful in illustrating the relationship between conventional environmental concerns, such as habitat destruction and resource use, and justice concerns, such as access to resources. It puts forward a *social foundation*, below which the ability of people to survive and thrive is threatened, and an *environmental ceiling*, above which environmental limits are threatened. The safe and just space is therefore in between these lower and upper limits.

Approaches to environmental justice have varied as the idea has been adopted in different geographical contexts. In the UK there has been no direct equivalent of the environmental movement in the USA. It is still the case that it can be seen as an emergent policy principle rather than a direct focus of grassroots anger (Agyeman 2000), and there has been much more of a focus on income than on race and ethnicity. In contrast to the grassroots origins of environmental justice in North America, work in the UK was initiated by established environmental NGOs such as Friends of the Earth (Walker 2012).

Environmental justice in South Africa drew many parallels with North America, making connections between the civil rights movement and anti-apartheid struggles, sharing a focus on toxic and polluting activities, and also highlighting contrasts between these concerns and more traditional colonial and post-colonial ideologies relating to wilderness and nature conservation (Walker 2012). In Central and Eastern Europe, the Transatlantic Initiative on Environmental Justice (Steger 2007) networked with North American contacts to work on regional issues, with a focus on the discrimination against Roma.

Mainstream environmental campaigns and policies are, arguably, increasingly recognizing social justice elements of environmental issues; a campaign need not self-identify as environmental justice to reflect social justice concerns. Climate change, for example, is presented as an international justice issue. This discussion of environmental justice and its relevance to food, then, is not limited to activity that refers to itself as environmental justice *per se*. Rather, it explores issues of fairness and justice that permeate discourses around how and what we eat.

Food as an environmental justice issue

Amongst the plethora of issues that concern environmental justice – including transport, air pollution, waste, and housing – food brings its own uniqueness and complexity to the table. In an increasingly urbanized and global society, our food is generally produced, processed, and packaged as part of a globalized supply chain, with attendant impacts around the world. In this sense, it is like any consumer product, but there are a number of reasons to think that it would be a mistake to treat food like any other consumer item – televisions, mobile phones, or clothes, for example.

Food presents a special challenge, not least because it is a physiological requirement, and one that we need to consume often: at its most basic level, it is not substitutable. Having access to satellite television does not make up for a lack of access to food. In comparison to shortages of other consumer goods, lack of food provokes a very strong sense of injustice.

Moreover, what we consume impacts upon our wellbeing. This means it is not simply the provision of food that should be of concern for environmental justice, but access to a healthy, culturally appropriate diet. Food is bound up in our social and cultural lives, an important part of family life, religious festivals, and rites of passage. To eat well is not the same for everyone, and this cultural sensitivity guards against universalist approaches to food provision. "Studies of food justice," then, "offer an excellent opportunity to bring the environmental justice and just sustainability literature together with contemporary social science approaches to race because food is deeply intertwined with both personal and cultural identities" (Alkon and Agyeman 2011: 10).

The temporality of food is distinctive: we consume food often and make choices about it daily, yet its availability is subject to seasonality. Compared to consumer items such as cars and televisions, about which we make choices much less frequently, food is something we engage with on a daily basis. Although this means in theory that there are opportunities for rapid changes in diets, this potential must be understood within the context of its enduring social and cultural meanings. That is, influencing how and what people eat requires more than the presentation of information about, say, health and environmental impact as a way of influencing rational choices; it involves engaging with habitual behaviors and cultural norms. It is also important to recognize that not everyone has the same food choices available to them: those with limited access and choice have less opportunity to make decisions that benefit their health and reduce their environmental impact.

Finally, food requires a high level of end-user knowledge. We need knowledge and skills to plan our diets, select, store, and prepare meals, and these competencies can be the difference between a healthy relationship with food and an unhealthy one. Access to food is a necessary, rather than sufficient, condition for a healthy diet.

Local food justice: access to food

A well-established issue relating to food and environmental justice is the accessibility of food to disadvantaged populations. This can be observed not only on a global scale, but also within societies in the Global North. A report by Friends of the Earth as part of the ESRC Global Environmental Change Program (Stephens et al. 2001), an early part of the NGO's environmental justice work, found that around 20 percent of the UK population could not afford healthy food, especially where other costs, such as fuel and rent, take priority. Food insecurity in developed countries has been linked to obesity, diabetes, anxiety, depression, loss of dignity, and lower educational attainment and behavioral issues in children (Burns et al. 2010). In the Marmot review of health inequalities and the social determinants of health, food and diet were recognized as part of a group of health issues with "persistent and complex causes and relationships [which are] multi-faceted, between, for instance, early years, education, employment, living environment, income and health" (Marmot et al. 2010).

Numerous studies of cities in the USA have identified links between limited or no fresh food access and health-related disparities associated with race, ethnicity, and income (Gottlieb and Joshi 2010), and inadequate or expensive transport links can accentuate the accessibility issue, illustrating the complex relationship between urban planning and health.

Access to a healthy diet may also be constrained by knowledge and skills, whether meal planning or food preparation. Projects such as the Bentley Bulk local food initiative (Sherriff 2009), Growing Manchester (Kazmierczak et al. 2013), and Incredible Edible Todmorden (Thompson 2012) all incorporate elements of education and awareness raising. Such an understanding demands a nuanced conceptualization of food security, an example being that "all community residents obtain a safe, culturally acceptable, nutritionally adequate diet through a sustainable food system that maximizes self-reliance and social justice" (Hamm and Bellows 2003: 37).

Access to appropriate healthy food can be particularly difficult in times of economic difficulties, and the period of austerity in the UK and much of Europe has prompted concerns about the adequacy of government services to ameliorate such food poverty. Dowler et al. (2011) note that in 2006 Defra started to use the term food security as a measure of the sustainability and reliability of food supply chains in the UK, rather than conceptualizing it as a global issue. In times of austerity, with job insecurity and cuts in social support, food banks and other charitable activities are filling the gaps for those who cannot afford to, or otherwise cannot access, the food they need. This has meant, Tsilimpounidi et al. (2014) argue, that third-sector and charitable organizations face the challenge of allocating resources on an ongoing basis rather than fulfilling their established role as emergency provision. This is difficult, since the organizations are not set up to challenge the underlying systemic issues that perpetuate food poverty: "The evidence highlights that short-term food provision can relieve symptoms of emergency need but (necessarily, given the aims and capacity of such initiatives) does not address the underlying causes of that need" (Lambie-Mumford and Dowler 2014: 1420). Tsilimpounidi et al. (2014) refer to the growing number of food banks in the country and the rising number of enquiries about food banks to the Citizens Advice service as evidence of growing reliance on food aid. Lambie-Mumford and Dowler find that "there is no sign that increasing uptake of food aid is abating" (2014: 1422).

One way to improve food access is to promote local growing projects at the individual, household, or community level. These form part of urban agricultural practice (Hardman and Larkham 2014a). An example is Real Food Wythenshawe, the lottery-funded venture designed to tackle issues around food security and healthy eating in Wythenshawe, an area of Manchester in North West England, which hopes to use urban agriculture, amongst other activities, to have a positive impact on the area, facilitate access to fresh fruit and vegetables, and to encourage the population to eat more healthily (Hardman and Larkham 2014a). In a broader context, Manchester City Council's Growing Manchester program sought to support a wide range of community food-growing projects, with environment, health, and food access among their drivers (Kazmierczak et al. 2013). Incredible Edible Todmorden began as a small unplanned community initiative and gathered significant momentum around the guerrilla planting of herbs, fruit trees, and vegetables in the Yorkshire town, with public sector organizations and private businesses coming on board, and the local schools getting involved and, research suggests, arguably giving the town a new identity and placing healthy eating higher on the agenda of many residents (Thompson 2012).

Such initiatives, then, create opportunities for individuals and communities to be involved in food growing and therefore to learn more about the constituents of a healthy diet and gain access to produce, a set of capacities that might be termed *social productivity* (Viljoen and Bohn 2014). Involvement itself can have wider social benefits: Germany's Interkulturelle Gärten, for

Graeme Sherriff

example, are aimed at helping integration in a "migration society" by bringing together people from myriad backgrounds with food and outdoor activity as a focus (Sherriff 2009). Urban food growing can also provide a "unique and distinctively effective means of retaining and transmitting collective memories of how to grow food" (Barthel et al. 2013: 5).

However, there are questions of justice that are raised by a reliance on such urban agriculture approaches. One is that such initiatives often rely on volunteer energy, and we should "be cautious of designing solutions that rely on volunteer energy, because the long-term sustainability of such initiatives is questionable and, just as importantly, because there is a question of justice at stake" (Sherriff 2009), with the implication that some communities should spend time growing food whilst others have ample provision of affordable produce nearby. The availability of green spaces is also an issue (Walker 2012), as not all communities will have land available on which to grow food and not all will want to use this land for food growing when other activities such as community sport may be seen to be just as important. This is not to underestimate the wealth of other benefits from involvement in food growing, including physical exercise, improving the local environment, and access to produce, but to point out that there may be justice concerns relating to expecting disadvantaged communities to rely on it as a strategy for addressing food insecurity.

Global food justice: a changing climate

Climate change is recognized as one of the most pressing and all-encompassing environmental issues. This is the change experienced in climate as a result of rising global mean temperatures due to an accentuation of the naturally occurring greenhouse effect, a process commonly referred to as global warming. Food, at production, distribution, and consumption stages, impacts upon climate change, contributing 31 percent of all consumption-related greenhouse gas emissions, with the UK figure estimated at 19 percent (Sustainable Development Commission 2008).

Climate change is an issue of international and intergenerational justice. "With climate change," argues Walker (2012: 179),

> we are confronted with evidence of patterns of inequality and claims of environmental justice that span the globe, that permeate daily life and which pose threats to the current and future health and well-being of some of the poorest and most vulnerable people around the world.

Climate change is a manifestation of *inter*generational (in)justice, since current emissions are expected to cause climate change impacts in coming decades, therefore affecting future generations. It is also an example *intra*generational (in)justice: whilst the greatest proportion of greenhouse gas emissions come from the Global North, the most affluent and economically developed countries, the world's poorest and most vulnerable will be hit hardest by climate change, and this applies at the global scale as well as within countries in the Global North (Marmot et al. 2010). Efforts to reduce carbon emissions can result in complex ethical decisions that balance the needs of current and future generations: "The rights as well as the short-term interests of ourselves and our children may conflict with the needs of many future generations or the survival of other species" (Lever-Tracy 2014: 264).

The vulnerability of agriculture to changes in climate reflects a vicious circle in which food production affects climate and changes in climate impact in turn upon agriculture. There is a need for policy makers to balance uncertainty and risk: whilst outcomes of climatic changes may be very uncertain, they could carry a high risk of causing major damage. The emerging

234

consensus is that higher latitude regions such as North America and Northern Europe may benefit from longer periods of warm weather that may increase yields, but that water shortages may constrain production. In the low latitude regions such as Africa, parts of Asia, South America, and Australasia, negative impacts are arguably already being seen. Extreme weather could affect transport and storage infrastructure, fertilizer plants, and manufacturing sites, and could put the rural poor, who rely in a direct way on getting to market to both buy and sell, in a particularly vulnerable position. Such fluctuations could threaten the security of world food supply and bring increased volatility to food prices, again affecting poor consumers the most. Lever-Tracy (2014) reports on modeling research that indicates that, with global temperature rising by one degree Celsius by 2050, yields in developing countries would decline for important crops, including irrigated crops in South Asia. This would affect the price of rice, wheat, maize, and soybeans, in turn affecting the price of meat. Calorie availability would decline, the researchers argue, with the potential effect of increasing child malnutrition by 20 percent.

The human face of food production

One justice dimension of food is the concern about the impact of industrialized and globalized agriculture and associated industries. Protests within the global neoliberal economy can be seen as "a call for recognition and preservation of diverse cultures, identities, economies and ways of knowing" (Schlosberg 2004: 524). People's movements exist with the aim of "conserving livestock diversity and protecting the basis of sustainable agriculture" as a reaction to the pressure to produce meat for export (Shiva 1999: 59).

   In Brazil, for example, large areas of land are used to grow soya beans for consumption by farm animals in Europe, the equivalent of 5.6 million acres of land in 2004 (Lang and Heasman 2004). These *ghost acres* highlight equity concerns and hint at justice implications: as land is used to grow food for export, it becomes unavailable to the poor to grow staples to meet basic needs. This process fuels displacement to urban areas, adding to overcrowding and creating new challenges of feeding rapidly urbanizing populations. Between 1979 and 1999, for example, when Kenya almost doubled the proportion of its vegetables being grown for export, vegetable consumption in the country decreased by 39 percent (Jones 2001). Brown and Getz (2011: 122) give the example of small-scale farmers in Mexico being forced off their land as a result of "neoliberal domestic policies and international trade regimes"; many of those farmers then find themselves working as wage laborers on the USA side of the border, "within the same agrifood regime that rendered it impossible for them to sustain their families through small-scale farming in Mexico" (2011: 123). The authors argue that the "devaluation of farm labor has been, at least in part, achieved because of the invisibility of farmworkers within the material and ideological landscapes shaping California's political economy" (2011: 123).

   An example of these global impacts through the corporate food regime is the *palm oil industrial complex* (Pye 2010). The non-profit, industry-led Roundtable on Sustainable Palm Oil has been created to promote the production and use of sustainable palm oil (Laurance et al. 2010), following concerns about the ecological and humanitarian impacts of its rapid spread across tropical regions, especially Malaysia and Indonesia. Environmental justice campaigners allied themselves with indigenous peoples, whose lifestyles, such as farming smallholdings, were seen as exemplars of sustainable resource management. International NGOs have campaigned on this issue, not only from the angle of more conventional environmental concerns, such as deforestation and the plight of the orangutan, but also from the point of view of the displacement of, and health impacts experienced by, the indigenous peoples.

Well-known standards like Fair Trade offer a way to try to ensure higher labor and exchange standards and wages; but some argue that this does not bring fundamental systemic change but is only "a way for farmers, hanging on by their fingernails, to be able to hang on a little longer" (Patel 2013: 317). It is argued, for example, that under-representation of farmers on the certification bodies, in comparison to that of distributors and retailers, means prices are still relatively low, and pressure to grow monocultures continues. Again, the point is not to dismiss these efforts to improve trading standards and working conditions, but rather to show that these have been subject to claims of (in)justice.

Challenging localism

In some ways, then, environmental justice can be seen as a critique of mainstream environmentalism and just sustainability as a way to find common ground. The notion of *local food* has been favored in mainstream environmentalism, but has received criticism from both environmental and social justice angles. Consuming food that has been produced close to home and therefore with reduced *food miles*, it is argued, is more efficient in terms of transport, storage and, often, packaging. An environmental criticism of this focus has been that sometimes produce can be more efficiently produced in warmer climates without the need for greenhouses, and that this can offset the transport costs. That is, the food-miles metric may be too simplistic and fails to take into account the complexities of transportation, production, and seasonality, since the impact of where food is produced may vary throughout the year (Hardman and Larkham 2014a: 27). Born and Purcell (2006) refer to the *local trap*, arguing that it cannot be assumed that local food systems are more sustainable or socially just than other scales.

Environmental justice commentators build on these concerns. The notion of local food, it is argued, risks a focus on one ideal solution resulting in tensions between a good life and inclusivity and tolerance towards different cultural viewpoints. Agyeman raises the question of what happens when diverse local populations want to buy locally grown and culturally appropriate foods "which are not what should be grown locally according to the predominantly ecological focused local food movement" (2013: 68). Examples would be produce and packaged products from around the world that connect people with family and home countries. This is compounded, he argues, by the tendency for local food movements to be dominated by what are perceived to be middle class interests like family farms and restaurants. Guthman et al. (2011: 264) refer to the "Unbearable Whiteness of Alternative Food," questioning how inclusive such movements are. At a more global level, Agyeman (2013) questions the implications for farmers of a focus on the local, asking if it is appropriate to, in effect, deny export markets to farmers in developing countries and if local farmers will struggle to sell only to their locality.

Another aspect of localism is bringing decision-making about issues relating to food to the city or city-region scale through mechanisms that include food partnerships, councils, and other strategies. One example is the Brighton and Hove Food Partnership, created in 2003, reflecting the priorities of civil society groups, health promotion staff in the Primary Care Trust, and the city council's Sustainability Commission (Morgan 2014). Another is the Bristol Food Policy Council formed in 2011. Toronto has become a key exemplar of urban agriculture in the Global North, and Hardman and Larkham (2014b: 400) observe that the city's food charter, which aims to ensure that "residents [have] access to an adequate supply of nutritious, affordable and culturally-appropriate food," has been "a significant part of this success story."

Agyeman argues that the local is sometimes constructed as "discrete, homogenous, and static," yet there is a need for recognition of the possibility that "deeply unequal power relations exist within any given locality" (Agyeman 2013: 64). The extent to which food policies and councils are able to reflect the needs and aspirations of diverse communities is therefore an important consideration. He makes the distinction between being at the table and setting the table, arguing that even when local communities are able to give input to discussions, the agenda does not necessarily reflect their priorities. He highlights the importance of factors that may help to make such decision-making inclusive, such as structure of meetings and organizations, reliance on people giving up their free time, the need for financial resources, cultural and language barriers, meeting times and locations, the physical limitations placed by the numbers of seats in comparison to the potential diversity of the community, and the challenges of engaging people in policy, as opposed to standalone projects (Agyeman 2013).

DuPuis et al. (2011) echo this concern about exclusionary politics and local elite control, giving the example of California's devolved pesticide regulatory structure, which is supposed to prioritize local needs but has historically addressed goals defined solely in terms of crop production rather than the protection of agricultural workers. They argue that those most vulnerable in the equation tend not to have a say: "the associated regulatory abandonment of ecology and human health concerns is particularly easy when agricultural regions are populated largely by politically disenfranchised immigrant farm-worker communities" (2011: 294).

The point is not to condemn notions of localism and efforts to develop food strategies that closely involve communities, particularly as a degree of localism is seen as a central tenet of sustainability, but rather to point out that policies do not necessarily reflect the needs and aspirations of diverse communities simply by virtue of being local. An alternative may be the *reflexive localism* that DuPuis et al. (2011) posit. This, they suggest, would take into account "different visions of justice, community, and good food" (2011: 297).

Summary

Environmental justice has developed from its roots in 1970s North America into a movement, policy perspective, and area of research that has international reach and a range of conceptualizations and local resonances. To an extent it is a critique of mainstream environmentalism, which some felt to be too focused on conventional environmental issues (such as rainforest destruction and endangered species) that seemed a long way from the more immediate issues affecting communities, such as pollution and toxic waste. Contemporary environmental justice commentators continue to provide this critical eye, highlighting the social justice dimensions of approaches to environmental issues, including food accessibility, localism, and climate change. Just sustainability, introduced by Agyeman (2003), sought to bridge environmental justice and more mainstream environmentalism, emphasizing the social justice elements implicit in sustainability to find common ground.

Food production and consumption are intimately related to human health and also have profound implications for local and global environmental issues, such as air and water pollution, rainforest destruction, and climate change. At a local level, issues of food accessibility, together with knowledge and skills related to dietary choice and food preparation, imply disparities in the extent to which different communities have a healthy, or unhealthy, relationship with food. Globally, supply chains that bring food to towns and cities have international reach and ramifications for communities, whether those laboring on agricultural lands, those displaced to make way for industrial agriculture, or those in low-lying countries suffering the impact of sea-level rise as a result of climate change. Food is therefore an issue with substantial social justice implications, many of which are mediated through the effects of its production, distribution, and consumption on local and global environments.

As an environmental justice issue food is distinctive. At the most basic level, it is a physiological requirement: it is not substitutable by other resources. We have an ongoing relationship with it and make decisions about it on a daily basis, yet it is bound up in our habitual behaviors and cultural norms. It is an important part of our social, religious, and cultural lives. Our relationship with food depends on a high degree of end-user knowledge in terms of the ability to choose and prepare meals. Whilst there is much discussion of dietary choices and about taking responsibility for the health and environmental impacts of our diet, an environmental justice perspective reminds us that levels of access to food, extent of dietary choice, richness of skills and knowledge, and ability to influence what is available in one's locality, vary between and within communities.

References

Agyeman, J. (2000) "Environmental Justice: From the Margins to the Mainstream?," Town and Country Planning Association, 'Tomorrow Series' Paper 7, London: Town and Country Planning Association.

——. (2003) *Just Sustainabilities: Development in an Unequal World*, Cambridge, MA: MIT Press.

——. (2013) *Introducing Just Sustainabilities: Policy, Planning and Practice*, London & New York: Zed Books.

Alkon, A. H. and J. Agyeman. (2011) "Introduction: The Food Movement as Polyculture," in A. H. Alkon and J. Agyeman (eds.), *Cultivating Food Justice: Race, Class, and Sustainability*, Cambridge: MIT Press, pp. 1–20.

Barthel, S., J. Parker, and H. Ernstson. (2013) "Food and Green Space in Cities: A Resilience Lens on Gardens and Urban Environmental Movements," *Urban Studies* 50(January): 1–19.

Born, B. and M. Purcell. (2006) "Avoiding the Local Trap: Scale and Food Systems in Planning Research," *Journal of Planning Education and Research* 26: 195–207

Brown, S. and C. Getz. (2011) "Farmworker Food Insecurity and the Production of Hunger in California," in A. H. Alkon and J. Agyeman (eds.), *Cultivating Food Justice: Race, Class, and Sustainability*, Cambridge: MIT Press, pp. 121–146.

Burns, C., B. Kristjansson, G. Harris, R. Armstrong, S. Cummins, A. Black, and M. Lawrence. (2010) *Community Level Interventions to Improve Food Security in Developed Countries*, Hoboken, NJ: John Wiley & Sons, Ltd.

Dobson, A. (1998) *Justice and the Environment: Conceptions of Environmental Sustainability and Theories of Distributive Justice*, Oxford: Oxford University Press.

Dowler, E., M. Kneafsey, H. Lambie, A. Inman, and R. Collier. (2011) "Thinking about 'Food Security': Engaging with UK Consumers," *Critical Public Health* 21(4): 403–416.

Dupuis, E. M., J. L. Harrison, and D. Goodman. (2011) "Just Food?," in A. H. Alkon and J. Agyeman (eds.), *Cultivating Food Justice: Race, Class, and Sustainability*, Cambridge: MIT Press, pp. 283–308.

Gottlieb, R. and A. Joshi. (2010) *Food Justice*, Cambridge: MIT Press.

Guthman, J., J. Agyeman, and A. H. Alkon. (2011) "If They Only Knew: The Unbearable Whiteness of Alternative Food," in A. H. Alkon and J. Agyeman (eds.), *Cultivating Food Justice: Race, Class, and Sustainability*, Cambridge: MIT Press, pp. 263–282.

Hamm, M.W., and A.C. Bellows. (2003) "Community Food Security: Background and Future Directions," *Journal of Nutrition Education and Behavior* 35(1): 37–43.

Hardman, M. and P. J. Larkham. (2014a) *Informal Urban Agriculture: The Secret Lives of Guerrilla Gardeners*, London: Springer.

——. (2014b) "The Rise of the "Food Charter": A Mechanism to Increase Urban Agriculture," *Land Use Policy* 39: 400–402.

Jones, A. (2001) *Eating Oil: Food Supply in a Changing Climate*, London: Sustain – The Alliance for Better Food and Farming.

Kazmierczak, A., A. Connelly, and G. Sherriff. (2013) "Growing Manchester Programme: Final Evaluation Report," viewed 8 October 2015, http://www.foodfutures.info/www/images/stories/pdf/UoM-Food-Futures-GrowManc_FINAL.pdf.

Lambie-Mumford, H. and E. Dowler. (2014) "Rising Use of 'Food Aid' in the United Kingdom," *British Food Journal* 116(9): 1418–1425.

Lang, T. and M. Heasman. (2004) *Food Wars: The Global Battle for Mouths, Minds and Markets*, London: Earthscan/James & James.

Laurance, W. F., L. P. Koh, R. Butler, N. S. Sodhi, C. J. A. Bradshaw, J. D. Neidel, H. Consunji, and J. M. Vega. (2010) "Improving the Performance of the Roundtable on Sustainable Palm Oil for Nature Conservation," *Conservation Biology* 24(2): 377–381.

Lever-Tracy, C. (2014) "Climate Change, Ethics and Food Production," in P. B. Thompson and D. M. Kaplan (eds.), *Encyclopedia of Food and Agricultural Ethics*, London: Springer, pp. 364–371.

Marmot, M. G., J. Allen, P. Goldblatt, T. Boyce, D. McNeish, M. Grady, and I. Geddes. (2010) "Fair Society, Healthy Lives: Strategic Review of Health Inequalities in England Post-2010," The Marmot Review, viewed 11 November 2015, www.ucl.ac.uk/marmotreview.

Morgan, K. (2014) "The New Urban Foodscape: Planning, Politics and Power," in A. Viljoen and K. Bohn (eds.), *Second Nature Urban Agriculture: Designing Productive Cities*, London: Routledge, pp. 18–23.

Novotny, P. (1995) "Where We Live, Work and Play: Reframing the Cultural Landscape of Environmentalism in the Environmental Justice Movement," *New Political Science* 16(1): 61–79.

Patel, R. (2013) *Stuffed And Starved: From Farm to Fork: The Hidden Battle For The World Food System*, London: Portobello Books.

Pye, O. (2010) "The Biofuel Connection – Transnational Activism and the Palm Oil Boom," *Journal of Peasant Studies* 37(4): 851–874.

Raworth, K. (2012) "A Safe and Just Space for Humanity: Can We Live within the Doughnut?," *Oxfam Discussion Papers*.

Schlosberg, D. (2004) "Reconceiving Environmental Justice: Global Movements and Political Theories," *Environmental Politics* 13(3): 517–540.

Sherriff, G. (2009) "Towards Healthy Local Food: Issues in Achieving Just Sustainability," *Local Environment* 14(1): 74–92.

Shiva, V. (1999) "Ecological Balance in an Era of Globalization," in Nicholas Low (ed.), *Global Ethics and Environment*, London: Routledge, pp. 47–69.

Steger, T. (ed.) (2007) "Making the Case for Environmental Justice in Central and Eastern Europe," report produced by Center for Environmental Policy and Law, The Health and Environment Alliance, and The Coalition for Environmental Justice, viewed 8 October 2015, http://www.env-health.org/IMG/pdf/ceu_teljes_pdf.pdf.

Stephens, C., S. Bullock, and A. Scott. (2001) "Environmental Justice: Rights and Means to a Healthy Environment for All," viewed 11 November 2015, http://www.foe.co.uk/sites/default/files/downloads/environmental_justice.pdf.

Sustainable Development Commission. (2008) "Green, Healthy and Fair," viewed 11 November 2015, http://www.sd-commission.org.uk/publications.php?id=692.

Thompson, J. (2012) "Incredible Edible – Social and Environmental Entrepreneurship in the Era of the 'Big Society,'" *Social Enterprise Journal* 8(3): 237–250.

Tsilimpounidi, M., A. Sampson, and A. Voela. (2014) "Food Banks in East London: Growth by Stealth and Marginalisation by the State," Centre for Social Justice and Change, Research Report 3, London: University of East London.

Viljoen, A. and K. Bohn. (2014) "Utilitarian Dreams: Productive Life in the City," in A. Viljoen and K. Bohn (eds.), *Second Nature Urban Agriculture: Designing Productive Cities*, London: Routledge, pp. 40–47.

Walker, G. (2012) *Environmental Justice: Concepts, Evidence and Politics*, Abingdon: Routledge.

PART VI
Farming and eating other animals

23

THE ETHICS OF HUMANE ANIMAL AGRICULTURE

James McWilliams

Like many books that have had a lasting influence, the impact of *Animal Liberation* (1975) was largely unintended. Peter Singer's utilitarian argument for avoiding animal suffering remains a brilliant if incomplete justification for not eating animals. Specifically, it never effectively addresses the *reductio ad absurdum* conclusion that, according to Singer's logic, would make it morally defensible to also kill, say, impaired infants (Leiter 2015). But, if Singer's philosophy hasn't been completely convincing, the graphic means through which he captured animal suffering on factory farms certainly has. More than any single source, it has immeasurably influenced the way we think about farm animals, turning a topic that very few consumers once thought about – animal welfare – into a matter of mainstream concern and debate. Today, nearly 95 percent of Americans say they are "very concerned" about the welfare of farm animals (Animal Welfare Institute 2015). *Animal Liberation*, whether it meant to or not, has had everything to do with that.

The ongoing emphasis on the humane treatment of farm animals has been enhanced and sustained by a steady output of subsequent books, documentaries, and media reports, all of which emulate the muckraking tenor of Singer's seminal volume. Beginning with the abattoir, writers have uncovered illicit aspects of slaughter that consumers had never before considered – or even thought to consider – thereby popularizing the rank corruption and callous amorality endemic to slaughter plants. In spite of the Humane Slaughter Act of 1978, investigators have all-too-easily documented cases of abuse so egregious that meat eaters began to take notice and demand changes in the way animals were treated. In some cases, consumers became vegetarians, in other cases, vegan. More often than not, though, they demanded that the structure of animal agriculture undergo meaningful changes to accommodate the welfare of animals. These competing responses – reforming or rejecting meat production – sparked an important debate about the ethics of humane animal agriculture.

As for the findings themselves, they can be difficult to swallow. In her book *Slaughterhouse*, Gail A. Eisnitz reported instances of animals being skinned alive: "A lot of times the skinner finds out the animal is still conscious when he slices the side of its head and it starts kicking wildly," a worker told her (Eisnitz 2006: 29). Timothy Pachirat, in his book *Every Twelve Seconds*, recalled the routine and tragic imprecision of the stun gun in the knocker box – something he witnessed repeatedly as an undercover worker at a Nebraska slaughterhouse. "Sometimes the power, angle, or location of the steel bolt shot is insufficient to render the cow unconscious," he writes, "and it will bleed profusely and thrash about wildly while the knocker tries to shoot it again" (Pachirat

2012: 54). In *The Chain* (2014), journalist Ted Genoways attributes the horrible mishaps of the abattoir to the rapid pace of work, which management constantly accelerates. "The speed of work," one Hormel employee told Genoways, "is causing an epidemic of quietly crippling injuries." As for the pigs being slaughtered by those workers, another explained, "gotta do what you gotta do to push those fucking pigs" (Genoways 2014: 37). These discoveries made an ongoing impression on a generation of consumers who were inspired by Singer to look deeper into the food system and ethically evaluate its inner mechanisms.

Conditions further down the chain of production turn out to be no better than the slaughterhouse. The billions of farm animals being raised for food in the United States live radically truncated lives marked by acute suffering before they are even loaded into a trailer bound for the slaughterhouse. With the rise of industrial agriculture after World War Two, and its rapid intensification in the 1970s (a time when Earl Butz, Secretary of Agriculture, was telling farmers to "get big or get out"), economic and political pressures incentivized farmers to pack animals into increasingly tighter and tighter spaces and scale up. Scores, if not hundreds, of journalists have shocked readers with frank descriptions of this welfare-averse race to the bottom (or the top?). It is now common knowledge that industrial animal agriculture is cynically engineered to foster corporate profit at the expense of animal welfare.

Today CAFOs – concentrated animal feeding operations – account for nearly 99 percent of the meat we eat. Before the rise of industrial agriculture, most farm animals lived outdoors and were granted at least a limited opportunity to engage in natural behaviors. Today, animals have been completely objectified and stored like cargo units in shipping containers. Farrowing and gestation crates hold sows in confinement so restrictive they cannot turn around, much less move; veal crates do the same for male calves; chickens are crammed into battery cages – often eight birds per tiny cage – or artificially lit barns; dairy cows are parked in tight milking stations, their udders hooked to mechanical pumps like fire hoses to a hydrant; beef cattle – the only factory-farmed animal that gets to be outside for a spate of time – are eventually situated in front of a trough on a manure-saturated feedlot that stretches as far the eye can see. Reflecting on these conditions, the *New York Times* food writer and columnist Mark Bittman excoriated the industry for its "infuriating disregard for the welfare of its animals" (Bittman 2010).

Confinement, moreover, spawns its own set of unsavory practices – all of which increase production while further detracting from the basic welfare of farm animals. When animals are confined into ever-tighter spaces, their natural demeanor yields to more aggressive, perseverating behaviors. Chickens vying for inches of space will inevitably peck their sharp beaks into each other, often with fatal consequences; frustrated pigs will bite each other's tails; angry cattle will bore into each other with sharply edged horns. To mitigate this confinement-induced aggression, factory farmers alter the animals' bodies to accommodate the burdens of crowding. Chickens have their beaks clipped, pigs lose their tails, cattle are dehorned and branded. These choices are not done to foster animal welfare – say, to keep animals from harming each other for the animals' sake – but rather to maximize production in a consolidating industry increasingly depended on marginal gains from maximized output (Unferth 2011).

Confinement similarly distorts the natural reproductive behavior of farm animals, making it effectively impossible for them to breed according to natural seasonal and biological schedules. Dairy cows offer an especially troublesome example of industrially controlled reproduction. Mother cows are artificially impregnated; their calves are removed within two days – and often within moments – of their birth (an emotionally traumatic experience for both animals) before being shunted to either the dairy or veal industries; serial impregnation and hormone-induced milk production leads to disease and lameness at alarming rates for dairy cows. According to the USDA, a million cows per year are slaughtered prematurely as a result of complications arising from artificial impregnation and milking mishaps. Dairy cows that live out the entirety of their reproductive years typically are slaughtered for hamburger meat. A leading animal rights philosopher has, with good reason, declared, "there's more suffering in a glass of milk than a pound of steak" (Unferth 2011). Recall that impregnated sows live in a tight cage, and that male chicks born in hatcheries are legally disposed of by being tossed alive into a grinder, and it quickly becomes clear that milk cows are not the only animals suffering the cruel reproductive repressions of the factory farm.

It is not only billions of domesticated animals that suffer the ravages of factory confinement. While the harm done to animals within the confines of factory farming are both significant and chilling, it is important to understand the impact of industrial animal agriculture on sentient life beyond CAFOs. There are fewer threats more serious to wildlife than animal agriculture. Humanity's appetite for animal products has led to unprecedented rates of desertification, deforestation, ocean acidification, dead zones, and destruction of grasslands (Bland 2012). Land dedicated to grazing accounts for 26 percent of the earth's terrestrial surface. A third of the earth's arable land is wasted on crops grown to feed animals kept in confinement. Almost 40 percent of all pesticides used today are sprayed on corn and soy grown for animal feed. Between 14 and 18 percent of all greenhouse gases result from animal agriculture (Bland 2012). Animal agriculture's degradation of the earth's most precious natural resources accounts for what the environmental writer Elizabeth Kolbert calls "the sixth extinction," an event for which human behavior is the leading cause. It is for good reason that many environmental critics have started asking if it is ever possible to be a meat-eating environmentalist (Barclay 2014).

Given the widespread public opposition to factory farming – assisted in no small part by popular books such as Michael Pollan's *The Omnivore's Dilemma* – it stands to reason that various groups have mobilized against the industrialization of animal products. These mobilizations represent a broad spectrum of tactics, but in general, the opposition breaks down into two camps. One camp argues that humans can morally justify eating animals so long as those animals are raised under conditions more humane than those on standard factory farms. A vaguely defined but powerful "Food Movement," in addition to organizations such as the Humane Society of the United States (HSUS), have been the most vocal and influential supporters of this humane animal agriculture position. Some refer to this position as "welfarist."

Second, another position – mostly supported by animal advocates, and informed by academic philosophers – argues that the only morally consistent response to industrial animal agriculture is to stop eating animal products altogether. These proponents seek, in varying degrees, to abolish animal agriculture and, in extreme cases, all forms of animal exploitation. Accordingly, they are often referred to as abolitionists. The clash between welfarists and abolitionists, as we will see, has generated one of the more consequential discussions in the realm of food ethics.

"Humane animal agriculture" is a vague concept that's open to interpretation. HSUS and other animal welfare organizations have their own working idea of what it means. It should be noted that these welfare-oriented groups by no means explicitly encourage the consumption of animal products. In fact, most employees of these organizations are vegan. But at the same time they also work closely with factory farms to improve conditions within existing industrial systems, an approach that can, intentionally or not, make factory farms appear to be humane, especially when they are praised by welfare groups for their welfare-oriented concessions. In some sense, at least according to much HSUS rhetoric, "improvement" equals "more humane," and "more humane" equals "a victory for animals." Thus, more often than not, HSUS and like-minded organizations define the ethical choice as the better choice, making this assessment based primarily on the adaptation of incremental improvements within the preexisting structure of industrial agriculture.

Over the past two decades, HSUS has successfully deployed a two-pronged approach to achieving their goals. First, they launch undercover investigations into industrial suppliers (including Tyson Foods and Smithfield Foods), capturing stark cases of animal abuse (Humane Society 2010). Next, they strategically exploit the horrific imagery they uncover to promote reforms that incrementally mitigate such terrible conditions. HSUS has used this strategy to lobby hard against battery cages, gestation crates, foie gras production, and tail dockings, no doubt improving the lives of millions of animals. In many cases, they have won critical legislative victories while convincing large corporations to change tactics and ban products raised under conditions of radical confinement and systemic animal mutilation (Humane Society 2012).

Although HSUS diligently pursues these reforms (much to the industry's chagrin), it is critical to note that HSUS never conspicuously promotes the ending of industrial agriculture per se – only its reformation. It therefore seems safe to suggest that, in so far as HSUS takes an ethical stance on eating animals, it would support eating animals from reformed factory farms rather than unreformed ones. Put differently, the message delivered by HSUS goes essentially like this: if you're going to eat meat, it is better to eat less of it and to buy it from sources that HSUS has identified as improved and reformed. More often than not, for the nation's most powerful animal welfare organization, the ethical buck stops there.

A different approach to confronting the evils of factory farming comes from the Food Movement. The Food Movement arose as a countercultural response to the food system's increasing expansion and homogenization (Pollan 2010). Galvanized to a large extent by the publication of Michael Pollan's *The Omnivore's Dilemma*, it seeks not so much to reform industrial animal agriculture from within, as HSUS and others attempt to do, but to provide unique sustainable and humane alternatives to it. More often than not, these alternatives are expected to rely on small farms, farmers' markets, seasonal food, "slow food," local food, and farm-to-table supply chains – all aspects of a foodshed notable for its non-industrial scale and scope. Much of this movement harkens back to an era when food was supposedly simpler and purer, produced non-industrially and without extensive processing. A common mantra defining the movement is "don't eat anything that your grandmother would not have recognized as food" (Pollan 2010).

The Food Movement actively promotes the consumption of animals. Those animals just have to be raised "humanely" – that vague term – on alternative, preferably local farms. The Food Movement also has a specific idea of what "humane" entails. Recall that there are no official federal guidelines for the definition of "humane." And further note that numerous independent "humane" certifiers offer standards that dramatically differ from one another (some allow tail docking, some do not; some ban castration without anesthesia, some do not) (McWilliams 2012). Still, almost all advocates of the alternative "humane" approach to raising animals agree that it includes, at the least, providing animals outdoor access, feeding animals a natural diet rather than a diet of industrial feed, and maybe even allowing animals to enjoy some reproductive freedom. The Food Movement generally avoids discussing the ethics of eating animals in absolute terms – after all, a principled interpretation of "humane" might negate consuming animals altogether – but it implicitly suggests that eating animals raised more humanely than factory-farmed animals is, by comparison, an ethically superior choice, certainly more ethical than purchasing meat from a factory farm.

HSUS and Food Movement approaches to reforming factory farming might seem fundamentally different, but in fact they share important commonalities. Both groups routinely support each other's measures. HSUS has lent moral support to small farms raising animals in a non-industrial manner. The Food Movement lobbies for many of HSUS's political initiatives, such as battery-cage bans. Most notably, both groups advance their agendas on the basis of ethical relativism – at least when it comes to the question of eating animals. The humane choice for these reformers is the choice that is "better" than what standard factory farms currently practice. In terms of the ethics of humane animal agriculture, both camps, in this respect, allow consumers to have their meat and eat it too, all the while drawing attention to the plight of farm animals before they are killed and commodified. When it comes to the killing itself, they tend to either remain silent, or declare that, as it is often said, "death is just one bad day."

Animal rights advocates – comprised of activists and academics alike – take issue with the very notion of humane animal agriculture, judging it to be an oxymoron. Their arguments assume several forms, but they tend to be based on absolute principles rather than relative comparisons. In this sense, their arguments also tend to be more abstract, less grounded in the tangible reality of the food system as it operates in the world, and thus harder to garner media attention. There are numerous philosophical traditions that advocates rely on to make the case against eating animals – utilitarian and rights-based traditions are the most common – but objections to the exploitation of farm animals on "humane" farms originate in a deceptively simple question: on what basis can one treat animals well (by, say, providing them open space and a natural diet) and then, when they reach a certain weight, slaughter and eat them? What, in other words, accounts for the shift in treatment from the day before slaughter to the day of slaughter? What principle justifies death for an animal whose very existence insisted upon humane treatment? These questions comprise (as I have called it in another context) "the omnivore's contradiction" (McWilliams 2014).

Unless farmers are killing animals as a hobby (an absurd prospect), humane farmers do their work to fulfill the popular demand for animal products (which, in a basic sense, makes them no different from factory farmers). It is on this point – the production of animals for human pleasure rather than human need – where the ethics of humane animal agriculture become most vulnerable. A natural preference for any habitual act – such as eating meat – cannot be an ipso facto justification for that act. Recall that even the most humane form of animal agriculture eventually involves the infliction of unnecessary suffering on a sentient being; even the most loving treatment of farm animals ends in a violent and unnecessary death. Although there are powerful cultural forces encouraging us to believe otherwise, there remains in our discussions of food and agriculture a need to justify – rather than excuse – that violence. Producers and consumers of animal products are no more exonerated from their behavior on the basis of convention, desire, or precedent than were slave owners or the perpetrators of ethnic genocide. Those who can avoid eating animal products but do not thus face an ethical dilemma, one upon which the suffering of billions of animals is at stake. Highlighting the omnivore's contradiction – and pushing for an answer to it – is an attempt to start the process of seeking a deeper justification for the prospect of humane animal agriculture.

Unfortunately, supporters of eating humanely raised animals have studiously avoided the hard ethical conundrum at the core of our decision to eat animals. Michael Pollan, the guru of the Food Movement, gave the movement a pass when it came to animal ethics, explaining, "what's wrong with animal agriculture – with eating animals – is the practice, not the principle" (Pollan 2002). This is a stunning remark. After all, if animal suffering has moral relevance (and, if you want farms to be humane, then you believe that it does), then Pollan's comment is no different than saying that owning a slave is only about how you treat that slave rather than the ethics of slavery per se. It is within this conveniently pragmatic framework – one that's shared by the Food Movement and the HSUS/welfarist camp – that the argument for eating animals from humane sources is advanced as an ethically superior option to eating animals from standard and unreformed factory farms. It is within this framework, in other words, that relativism on the issue of animal ethics prevails among supporters of humane animal agriculture.

But, we might rightly ask, so what? If non-industrial farms, in addition to factory farms that adopt HSUS-type reforms, lead to meaningful improvements in the lives of animals, then what is the problem? On the face of things, there is no question that these reforms improve animal lives. A chicken that can spread her wings, a pig with access to the outdoors, and a cow roaming native grasses are animals undeniably happier than their counterparts who are prisoners crunched into radical confinement and fed industrial feed spiked with antibiotics and growth hormones. In this way, pragmatism, it seems, leads to less suffering and, insofar as less suffering is understood to be "more humane," then "more humane" is understood to be ethically superior. Conclusion: you should eat animals from humane farms. This is largely where the ethical discussion of eating animals, at least in the mainstream media, now stands.

And this argument works – as far as it goes. But it may not go all that far. There are two ways to evaluate these pragmatic welfare claims. The first is on their stated merits and promises; the second is on the principled objections that its proponents refuse to engage. As for the first, one might reasonably ask to what extent the reality of humane animal agriculture conforms to its rhetoric. Put differently, what are the limits to "humane" when one is domesticating sentient animals for food? This question is rarely asked, but here is why it matters: there is a quiet, but dangerous, assumption in animal welfare that if an alternative farm is an improvement on the standard industrial arrangement, then it is ipso facto a humane choice. And this is, of course, a logically invalid assumption. We are left with this question: is "better than factory farming" the same as "humane"?

Considerable evidence suggests that the answer is "not necessarily." Reformed factory farms, as well as the vast majority of non-industrial farms, transport animals to large USDA approved slaughterhouses, places that, as we have seen, are riddled with violent abuses. Likewise, while it is hard to quantify these measures, there is much to suggest that small, non-industrial farms engage in a number of actions not typically considered to be humane. They castrate animals without anesthesia, subject animals to alarming rates of predation, and, when attempting to slaughter on their own (for personal consumption or to sell locally), botch the task with terrible consequences for the animals' welfare. Animals raised outdoors might be momentarily happier critters but, in addition to high rates of predation (especially for chickens), they need to be nose-ringed if they are pigs (otherwise they tear up pastures), they are more susceptible to certain diseases because they are outdoors (especially with chickens), and, again with pigs, they will roll over and accidentally kill and sometimes eat their offspring (something a farrowing crate, however cruel, prevents). The fact is that, to some degree, raising an animal for food automatically entails abuse.[8]

"Humane" agriculture can also have serious environmental consequences that bear directly on the welfare of wild animals. Raising animals on pasture requires more land – land that, if left in its natural state, would foster wildlife populations otherwise diminished when that land is turned over to pasture. Brazilian and Argentinian planters clearing rainforests to produce grass-fed beef provide a glaring example of how supposedly humane agriculture can cause dire ecological damage to wildlife habitats. Further consider the well-documented connection between grass-fed cattle and methane output. Grass-fed cows produce three to four times more methane than their grain-fed counterparts, a critical statistic given that methane is a greenhouse gas that is 23 times more potent than carbon dioxide. Add to this the fact that the rangeland damaged by livestock harms both native plants and animal populations, and the impact of humane animal agriculture on wildlife seems to belie the "sustainable" reputation it enjoys.[9]

We rarely hear about these well-documented problems in the media. The idea of humane animal agriculture is buttressed by the popular media's selective attention to the bucolic aesthetics of non-industrial agriculture. The same media that has so carefully exposed the horrors of factory farming has less carefully presented alternative animal agriculture as an idyllic Eden, where the purest form of animal happiness prevails. The result of this agrarian aestheticism is that consumers end up making moral choices that are sharply biased by unreasonably bucolic images rather than informed by a closer understanding of what it is actually required to turn an animal into an object. Snapshots of agricultural life are just that – snapshots – and they should play a highly qualified role in shaping our larger ethical assessments of the systems we are evaluating. After all, a snapshot of a chicken being jammed into a cone and having its neck slit open by a humane farmer is just as representative a snapshot of humane animal agriculture as is a picture of that same bird enjoying pasture time on a sunny day. But we never see the cone shot. Because so much of the consumer's opinion is shaped by the way these topics are presented in the popular media, the aesthetic presentation of humane animal agriculture needs to be better scrutinized as a measure of the underlying reality.

There is also an inherent economic limitation to humane animal agriculture. In their book *Compassion by the Pound* (2010), Jayson Lusk and F. Bailey Norwood empirically demonstrate how humane measures come at precise costs. Consumers who support humane animal agriculture by purchasing animal products from non-industrial venues experience this fact in the form of sticker shock. Subsidies notwithstanding, it pays to industrialize food. It pays to consolidate animals and take advantage of scale economies through a corporate scale of production. It pays to vertically integrate and rationalize the messiness of animal agriculture. Factory farms did not form because they were incentivized to do so by governmental subsidies (although they have undoubtedly benefitted). They formed because it was a more efficient way to meet demand in a profitable manner. They formed because they worked. The only cost was animal welfare. And now humane farmers are trying to buy back that welfare and pass the costs on to the consumer (Lusk and Norwood 2010).

This economic reality is a stubborn – one might say even impossible – reality for the alternative systems to ignore. It relies ultimately on a wildly improbable expectation: that the vast majority of consumers who eat animals will voluntarily spend more money to support more humane alternatives. This sounds like a wonderful proposition, but it turns out to be quixotic. In the history of the market economy, there has yet to be a single case of consumers collectively choosing to pay more money to support a more humane option *of anything*. Advocates of humane animal agriculture have yet to confront this issue head on, but, given the hurdle presented by the economics of animal agriculture, it seems incumbent upon them to do so. Otherwise, it is hard not to dismiss the humane alternatives as a more ethical response to animal agriculture that, due to its expense, can only be practiced by the socioeconomic elite. And what is the worth of a reform that is only limited to a privileged few?

One can perhaps best exemplify this economic hurdle with a quick thought experiment. Imagine if industrial systems, with the wave of a wand, were totally eliminated, and that all animals were placed on small, non-industrial, meaningfully humane farms. What would happen then? In a relatively open economic environment (call it, with caution, a "free market"), it would not be long before one farm began to seek market share from another. Competition would set in. This would happen the moment that an enterprising farmer instituted a slightly higher level of confinement – a decision that, as Lusk and Norwood show, pays off in terms of efficiency. With that move, the race toward consolidation would be on, with farms scrambling to consolidate in order to edge each other out of market share. In time, farmers would have replicated, in a short period of time, the long history of animal agriculture in the United States, which has been driven by an economically rational march toward growing more animals in less space. If there is an axiom to take from this example, it might be that the promise of humane animal agriculture is contingent on economic regulations that would stymie basic market forces. To put it as bluntly as possible, humane animal agriculture might very well require socialism in order to survive.

If these critiques of humane animal agriculture are correct, if both reformed factory farming and non-industrial alternatives fail to live up to their promises, where does this leave ethically inclined consumers who are worried about the welfare of farm animals they eat? According to the animal advocates who oppose welfarism on principled grounds, it leaves them, for starters, without animal products on their plate. No matter how humane the farm, the omnivore's contradiction remains unresolved, still awaiting an answer, an explanation. The responses provided by the Food Movement have been more like excuses – "it lived a good life" – all of them centering on the *relatively* more humane treatment of animals while avoiding the deeper moral conundrum of granting an animal moral consideration one day and killing that animal the next. We have seen how the pragmatic prospects of humane animal agriculture have serious flaws. But abolitionists want to do more than highlight those flaws. They want to take the campaign against animal exploitation to its logical conclusion, one that, they claim, insists that eating animals (when other choices are available) is unethical and, as such, should be abolished.

Two related concepts are essential to understanding the vegan project: sentience and speciesism. Sentience denotes a level of consciousness that affords animals moral worth. There are myriad ways to designate sentience. For our purposes, it is enough to rely on the philosopher Tom Regan's assessment that any creature that could be considered "the subject of a life" qualifies as sentient (Regan 1985). At the least, these animals are self-aware in a morally meaningful way, insofar as they can feel pleasure and pain, experience an emotional life, and form a sense of individual continuity over time. All farm animals almost certainly fall into this category. Speciesism happens when humans treat a sentient species with a different set of standards than their own species. Speciesism involves giving one species selective moral consideration on the basis of species membership alone. Combine the two concepts – sentience and speciesism – and it is possible to make strong ethical cases against eating animals – cases that have the potential to render the relativistic arguments advanced by the Food Movement and HSUS less persuasive.

Philosophers have made many such cases, but two dominate: utilitarianism and rights theory. Utilitarianism, which locates its modern origins in the work of Jeremy Bentham, is a consequentialist approach to animal ethics, which is exemplified in the contemporary work of Peter Singer. Utilitarians believe that, because animals can suffer, humans owe them equal moral consideration based on that shared ability to suffer. The moral choice, according to utilitarians, is the choice producing the most good – "the greatest good for the greatest number." When applied to eating animals, the conventional utilitarian argues that the suffering experienced by a slaughtered animal almost always outweighs whatever pleasure humans derive from eating its flesh. Note that, in order to avoid speciesism, one cannot justify eating animals on the sole basis of being human, but rather he must concede that if it is somehow moral to eat animals on the basis of a utilitarian calculation, it would also have to be moral to kill and eat humans (if one's tastes leaned in that direction). Naturally (and thankfully), most people would find a utilitarian justification for violent cannibalism to be absurd.

The conventional rights-based approach, as primarily defined by the philosopher Tom Regan, is something quite different. Still, it reaches the same principled conclusion that it is unethical to eat animals if acceptable options are available. According to animal rights theory, a sentient animal has an inherent claim against being harmed by humans because, as with humans, it is "a subject of a life." As Regan and other rights-theorists see it, what matters when it comes to our treatment of animals are not the interests of the animals per se, but rather the individual who has those interests – an individual with rights. To really understand how this perspective differs from Singer's utilitarianism, note that, under the rights-based approach, the harm caused to an animal would still be unethical if it produced more happiness than suffering. The determining factor here is that the harmful act violated that animal's right to bodily autonomy. No calculation is necessary. If animals can be said to have rights, and supporters of humane animal agriculture indicate by virtue of their welfare improvements that they do have rights, then killing them would seem to be the most egregious violation of those rights.

These principled objections to eating animals have dominated philosophical discussions over the last 40 years. As indicated, welfarists and the leaders of the Food Movement have avoided them, preferring to evaluate the idea of humane animal agriculture on purely pragmatic, relative grounds. In light of the most powerful utilitarian and rights-based claims, one can see why welfarists adhere to their pragmatism. It is easy to decide that one form of agriculture is better for animals than another – doing so requires little thought or effort. It is, by contrast, much harder to justify killing and eating animals in terms consistent with utilitarian or rights-based objections. To the extent that the leading voices of the Food Movement have even bothered to confront these principled claims, they have come up empty. One of the most careful and thoughtful writers covering agricultural issues – *Grist*'s Nathanael Johnson – surveyed the ethical arguments for eating animals and candidly reported: "my enquiries did not turn up any sophisticated defense of meat" (Johnson 2015).

But inconsistent positions die hard. After noting just how impractical it was for his readers to give up eating animals, Johnson, who, again, could find no philosophical justification for eating animals, nonetheless concluded, "let's focus on giving farm animals a life worth living" (Johnson 2015). And so, while the popularity of eating humanely raised animals continues to grow, the omnivore's contradiction – *how does one grant moral worth to animal welfare and then kill the animal?* – persists. Thus the concept of humane meat remains an unrealized ideal at best and, at worst, something of a small hoax.

Despite decades of enthusiasm, the prospect of ethical meat from domesticated animals is stuck in an ethical bind. The Food Movement and other advocates of ethical meat agree that there is no moral justification for factory farms. HSUS agrees, too, but it works to nudge factory farms toward the practices of more humane farms. While condemning industrial confinement as a cruel affront to an animal's welfare, these proponents of humane animal agriculture, as we have seen, still face a contradiction – how can you honor an animal's welfare one day and kill that animal the next? Rather than confront this objection, they have instead hidden behind the relativist stance that humane farms, slaughter notwithstanding, are better off than factory farms, resting the case there. And it is true: they are.

But better is not always right. Principled objections from utilitarians and animal rights theorists have presented strong arguments against all forms of farmed-animal exploitation, up to and including slaughtering a well-treated animal for food we do not need. Supporters of humane animal agriculture have yet to offer a viable counter argument. As such, they pursue an action that stands in opposition to widely accepted moral principles. Further, they have yet to defend what they claim to be virtuous. As a result, this debate rages on.

Notes

1 These practices are outlined in McWilliams (2015).
2 These problems are outlined in Kemmerer (2014).

References

Animal Welfare Institute. (2015) "Consumer Perceptions of Farm Animal Welfare," viewed 14 November 2015, https://awionline.org/sites/default/files/uploads/documents/fa-consumer_perceptionsoffarmwelfare_-112511.pdf.

Barclay, E. (2014) "Can You Call Yourself an Environmentalist and Still Eat Meat?," *NPR.org*, viewed 14 November 2015, http://www.npr.org/sections/thesalt/2014/06/11/320776028/can-you-call-yourself-an-environmentalist-and-still-eat-meat.

Bittman, M. (2010) "Is Factory Farming Worse than We Know?" *markbittman.com*, viewed 24 November 2015, http://markbittman.com/horrific-animal-abuses-uncovered-at-smithfiel/.

Bland, A. (2012) "Is Livestock Destroying the Planet?" *Smithsonian.com*, viewed 24 November 2015, http://www.smithsonianmag.com/travel/is-the-livestock-industry-destroying-the-planet-11308007/?no-ist.

Eisnitz, G. (2006) *Slaughterhouse*, New York: Prometheus Books.

Genoways, T. (2014) *The Chain*, New York: Harper Collins.

The Humane Society of the United States. (2010) "HSUS Exposes Inhumane Treatment of Pigs at Smithfield," viewed 24 November 2015, http://www.humanesociety.org/news/press_releases/2010/12/smithfield_pigs_121510.html.

——. (2012) "McDonalds Takes Action Toward Ending Gestation Stall Use," viewed 24 November 2015, http://www.humanesociety.org/news/press_releases/2012/02/mcdonalds_takes_action_02132012.html.

Johnson, N. (2015) "Is there a Moral Case for Meat?," *Grist.com*, viewed 24 November 2015, http://grist.org/food/is-there-a-moral-case-for-meat/.

Kemmerer, L. (2014) *Eating Earth*, New York and London: Oxford University Press.

Leiter, B. (2015) "Should Our Circle of Moral Concern Expand to Include Non-human Animals as Full Members?," *Aeon*, viewed 24 November 2015, https://aeon.co/conversations/should-our-circle-of-moral-concern-expand-to-include-non-human-animals-as-full-members-and-will-it-one-day-2#response_1808.

Lusk, J. and F. B. Norwood. (2010) *Compassion by the Pound*, New York and London: Oxford University Press.

McWilliams, J. (2012) "Nature's Perfect Package," *Harper's*, August, http://james-mcwilliams.com/wp-content/uploads/2012/07/Harpers_Aug_2012-2McW.pdf.

——. (2014) "The Omnivore's Contradiction," *The American Scholar*, viewed 24 November 2015, https://theamericanscholar.org/loving-animals-to-death/.

——. (2015) *The Modern Savage*, New York: Thomas Dunne Books.

Pachirat, T. (2012) *Every Twelve Seconds*, New Haven: Yale University Press.

Pollan, M. (2002) "An Animal's Place," *New York Times*, viewed 24 November 2015, http://faculty.smu.edu/jkazez/animal%20rights/an%20animal's%20place.html.

——. (2010) "The Food Movement, Rising," *The New York Review of Books*, viewed 24 November 2015, file:///Users/jamesmcwilliams/Downloads/USA_nybooks.com_21-05-10.pdf.

Regan, T. (1985) *The Case for Animal Rights*, New York: Basil Blackwell.

Singer, P. (1975) *Animal Liberation*, New York: HarperCollins.

Unferth, D. O. (2011) "Gary Francione: Animal Advocate," *The Believer*, viewed 24 November 2015, http://www.believermag.com/issues/201102/?read=interview_francione.

24

CONFINEMENT AGRICULTURE FROM A MORAL PERSPECTIVE

The Pew Commission Report

Bernard E. Rollin

One of the most momentous social revolutions of the past century was occasioned by the industrialization of animal agriculture. Yet despite its profound effect on all aspects of human life, including demographic distribution of human population, sustainability of the food supply, effects on public health, major modifications on the workforce, environmental despoliation, consolidation of wealth, technological innovation, the quality of life of billions of sentient creatures – this revolution was ignored by scholars in the United States until the first decade of the 21st century. It was only then that Johns Hopkins University, in conjunction with The Pew Charitable Trusts, undertook the first comprehensive critical analysis of the negative effects of intensive, industrialized agriculture.

The Pew Charitable Trusts represent a foundation funded by the family who owned the Sun Oil Company. The projects undertaken by the foundation vary greatly from public health issues to studying the implications of biotechnology to preserving public lands. The Johns Hopkins Bloomberg School of Public Health is the most prominent and well-funded ($1 billion) public health school in the world. One prominent unit in the school is the Center for a Livable Future – their mission statement is as follows:

> To promote research and to develop and communicate information about the complex interrelationships among diet, food production, environment and human health, to advance an ecological perspective in reducing threats to the health of the public and to promote policies that protect health, the global environment and the ability to sustain life for future generations.

The director of the Center, Dr. Robert Lawrence, realized that significant amounts of antibiotics, cutting-edge and otherwise, were being used to keep intensive confinement operations viable, and that no systematic study had ever been done of factory farms or, as they preferred to label themselves, CAFOs, or Confined Animal Feeding Operations, in relation to public health and welfare. Lawrence approached Pew, asking them to fund what would become the first study of such operations, the Independent Commission on Confined Animal Feeding Operations. Pew contributed over 2.5 million dollars to fund this study, which lasted two and a half years and was undertaken by a very select group of experts.

The Chairman of the Commission was former governor of Kansas, John Carlin, notably raised on a dairy farm and a wise politician. The remaining commissioners were acknowledged experts in their fields chosen for their knowledge in areas relevant to Commission concerns. This assured our credibility, which we knew the industry would attack. These areas included rural sociology, running a food catering company, public health, serving in a state legislature, serving as US Secretary of Agriculture, animal welfare, human medicine, Western ranching, sustainable agriculture, nutrition, occupational health, producing humane meat, ethics and animal ethics, infectious disease, corporate agriculture, and law.

The Commission met regularly over more than two years in a variety of venues mostly determined by the presence of CAFOs. Every recommendation that appeared in the final Report required the support of all commissioners, a policy adopted to show a united front, which, given the heterogeneity of members, was essential to be taken seriously.

As a society, Americans have lost touch with agriculture. Those of us who live in cities may well have never seen a farm animal. One hundred years ago, more than half the population lived on farms or had relatives who lived on farms. When I lived in New York City, I recall having an argument with an eight-year-old who insisted that concrete was the natural groundcover all over, with vegetation only occurring by virtue of human intervention. The development of human civilization was directly dependent on the creation of a secure and predictable food supply. Such a food supply freed people from the uncertainties and vagaries of depending on hunting and gathering and enabled the establishment of communities.

Predictability regarding food was assured by the development of both plant and animal agriculture, which operated synergistically. Cultivation of crops and plants secured human ability to depend on (barring catastrophes of weather) foods of plant origin, and on a steady and local source of animal feed. Animal agriculture, starting some 12,000 years ago, in turn provided a source of labor for crop production, as well as a predictable reservoir of animal protein for human consumption. The secure food supply ramified in the ability to develop manufacturing, trade, commerce, and, in Hobbes' felicitous phrase, the "leisure that is the mother of philosophy," construed in the broadest sense as speculative thought, science, technological innovation, art, and culture.

Certain values were necessarily presupposed with the development of traditional agriculture. In the case of animal agriculture, the overriding value was good husbandry, a word derived from the Old Norse meaning "bonded to your household," regularly alluded to in the Old Testament. Indeed, when the psalmist seeks a metaphor for God's ideal relationship to human beings, he can find nothing more appropriate than the iconic good shepherd: "the Lord is my shepherd; I shall not want. He maketh me to lie down in green pastures. He leadeth me beside still waters. He restoreth my soul." So significant is husbandry in the Bible, that people are specifically admonished to help an animal in difficulty even if such help violates the Sabbath. Similarly presupposed in agriculture is sustainability, the commitment to not depleting plant, animal, or other necessary agricultural resources, such as water and topsoil.

As we know from passages in the Old Testament, a lamb on its own would live a miserable, nasty, and short life by virtue of the proliferation of predators – hyenas, raptors, wolves, bears, lions, foxes, jackals, and numerous others. With the care and ministrations of the shepherd, the animal lives well until such time as humans take its life, in the meantime supplying us with milk, wool, and, in the case of some domestic animals, the labor that became indispensable to the working of the land for crops.

The history of Western civilization cannot overestimate the power of this symbiotic image. For thousands of years in Christian iconography Jesus is depicted both as shepherd and as lamb, a duality built into the very foundations of human culture. The pastor, a word harkening back to *pastoral*, tends to his flock; the members of his congregation are his sheep. Moreover, when Plato discusses the ideal political ruler in the *Republic*, he deploys the shepherd–sheep metaphor: the ruler is to his people as a shepherd is to his flock. Qua shepherd, he exists to protect, preserve and improve the sheep; any payment tendered to him is in his capacity as wage earner. So too the ruler again illustrates the power of the concept of husbandry on the psyche.

With these values solidly in place, and with people freed of worrying about where the next meal is coming from, civilization was free to progress in all the modalities mentioned above. In one of the most momentous ironies in the history of civilization, this ancient contract with the animals, as well with the Earth, in terms of sustainability, contained within it the seeds of its own undoing. It was in virtue of a secure and predictable food supply that humans could proceed with trade, manufacturing, invention, and the general flourishing of culture.

By the late 19th century, industrial proliferation and innovation had reached a point where sustainability and good husbandry seemed to be no longer essential presuppositions of civilization. The ancient contract, which we may characterize as husbandry with regard to animals and stewardship with regard to the land, was the presupposed bedrock upon which economics, art, and culture rested. Yet with the profound hubris of an Icarus who challenged inherent human limitations, with blind and abiding faith in the humanly crafted tools, which repeatedly showed themselves as impotent in the face of natural disaster, we thumbed our noses at both morality and prudence. As the ancients crafted the tower of Babel, so we began to overreach the constraints imposed on us by the natural world. In both crop and animal agriculture, the ancient values of sustainability, stewardship, and husbandry inexorably gave way to modernist values of industrialization, productivity, and efficiency. The symbiotic partnership between humans and the Earth and between humans and animals was rapidly transmuted into patent exploitation with no respect or attention to what priceless elements were lost.

One of my students (the son-in-law of an animal science colleague of mine) was raised with the background of Western ranching – one of the few remaining agricultural industries still solidly based in husbandry – and was acutely aware of what had been lost in modern agriculture. The youngest of five siblings, he could not make a living on the family ranch and went to work in a pig factory. One day he noticed that the baby pigs were sick, and he notified the manager. He communicated that although the animals were infected, they could easily be cured with an inexpensive antibiotic. The boss admonished him, stressing the point that they did not treat sick animals but rather kill them, illustrating his point by picking up a baby pig by the back legs and dashing his head against the side of a concrete pen in a procedure called "blunt trauma" in the industry. Unable to accept this, the young man purchased the antibiotic with his own money and came in on his day off to treat the baby pigs. When they were cured, he again notified the boss, who responded by attempting to fire him. His contract precluded that, and he worked there for another six months. Shortly thereafter, he wrote to his father-in-law that he was quitting the job and going back to school to become an electrician. He concluded the letter: "I know you are disappointed that I am leaving agriculture, *but this ain't agriculture!*"

The Pew Commission began its work with a meeting held in Des Moines, Iowa, a central location for the swine industry. The meeting began with various guests expressing their opinions and concerns. One older woman, dressed in "Little House on the Prairie" regalia, expressed concerns about the Commission, notably focusing on the fact that we were not in the main people from agricultural backgrounds. However, she opined, "agricultural producers would be satisfied if everything the commission concluded was based upon 'sound science,'" i.e., research bought and paid for by the swine industry. In an attempt to educate her, I commented that if the Commission were trying to find out *how* to raise pigs in tight confinement, her suggestion would be relevant. But that was not our task. We were asking the societal question of whether we *ought* to raise pigs in confinement, and to that question science had no relevance. Her "Huh?" demostrated that she had missed my point.

Subsequent meetings were held in venues where the CAFOs being examined were located. In addition to Iowa, a central locus for the pork industry, meetings were held in California's Central Valley, where giant mega-dairies are located; North Carolina, where huge swine CAFOs are sited; Arkansas, home of huge poultry operations; and Colorado, where commissioners toured a large feedlot and also observed some family ranches. In the course of those travels, as well as in commission headquarters in Washington DC, commissioners heard over 50 hours of testimony from experts and stakeholders. As mentioned earlier, the issues we focused upon were the various effects of CAFOs on public health, both physical and psychological; environmental effects of CAFOs, including effects on pollution of air and water; the effects of CAFOs on rural communities and the way of life therein; and finally their effects on animal welfare.

The Commission found that many dimensions of public health were adversely affected by the presence of CAFOs. For example, we found in California that the presence of huge dairies, primarily in the Central Valley, was responsible for air pollution so severe that the normal view of nearby mountains was totally obscured. Even more important was the fact that we were told by state health officials that every man, woman, and child living near the dairies was spending approximately $1,500 more for healthcare per capita than if the dairies had not been located where they were.

There are swine barns in Iowa where workers must wear respirators while working in these confined systems. In addition to the human health issues occasioned by particulate matter in the dust, it is worth noting that animals do not wear any protective gear and are thus highly susceptible to respiratory difficulties. When the Commission toured poultry operations, the barn we visited was selected as exemplary by the producers. Nonetheless, because of the high degrees of ammonia present in the barn, the air was very irritant to the commissioners, and many of us left the building within five or ten minutes of our entrance, after experiencing asthma-like symptoms. Commissioner James Merchant and his associates reported a 44% prevalence of asthma among farm children living on swine farms, and a 55.8% prevalence of asthma living on farms that added antibiotics to feed. Other investigators reported that children living within three miles of a CAFO experienced significantly higher rates of physician-diagnosed asthma, used more asthma medication, and had more asthma-related emergency room visits and/or hospitalizations than children living further away (Merchant et al. 2005). A variety of studies serve to evidence the claim that statistically significant increases in asthma result from children residing close to CAFOs (Pew 2008: 17). In addition to children, vulnerable populations such as the elderly or individuals with chronic or acute pulmonary or cardiac disorders are at greater risk when living near polluted CAFOs (Pew 2008).

According to Commission reports, more than 24 odoriferous chemicals are released from CAFOs (Cole et al. 2000). Many of these compounds are toxic to the nervous system and can result in such behavioral problems as depression. In 1995 Schiffman and his colleagues found increased levels of negative mood states such as tension, depression, anger, fatigue, confusion, and reduced vigor among people living near swine CAFOs compared to people not living near such facilities (Schiffman et al. 1995).

Accumulation of hydrogen sulfide in the air resulting from agitation of manure pits housing swine wastes is another documented source of illness. Since these pits are often located underneath confinement buildings, they represent major potential dangers to workers, as well as a diminished quality of life for the animals (Kilburn 1997).

Regarding the psychological effects of living near CAFOs, I have my own theory that is based more in psychology than physiology. Take, for example, a swine operation raising pigs from babyhood. Baby pigs are extraordinarily cute, possessing many similar neonatal traits to puppies. Just as we would expect psychological damage in people euthanizing puppies and kittens, it is reasonable to expect the same thing when one is euthanizing baby pigs or raising them in tight confinement. There is doubtless a great deal of stress in killing any baby animal, or in raising them under impoverished conditions. I would suggest that people working in swine factories or other CAFOs experience what I call "moral stress" (Rollin 1987) as a result of the conditions in which these animals are kept. This in turn can result in psychological pressure regarding one's complicity in raising them that way or in killing them. Thus it is possible, and in my view likely, that such conditions can induce stress and guilt, which predispose individuals to disease. My conjecture is buttressed by many conversations I have had with employees in swine factories or high confinement dairies, who are extremely reticent to discuss their feelings about the animals and often avoid such requests for information. From their body postures and facial expressions, one can deduce their discomfort at having to kill these animals or keep them in appalling conditions, thus possibly augmenting the sense of discomfort at such employment. This, in turn, can lead to psychological problems such as lack of sleep, irritability, feelings of guilt, etc. This should be researched further.

Probably the most frequently discussed health problem associated with CAFOs is the issue of the development of antibiotic resistance by bacteria and resistance to drugs by viruses and parasites. This is a naturally occurring phenomenon, and pathogens regularly develop new mechanisms for creating resistance. In 2000, I was invited to serve on a WHO (World Health Organization) panel charged with setting criteria for "prudent use of antimicrobials" to avoid further accelerating resistance.

One very powerful factor driving antimicrobial resistance since the 1940s has been the proliferation of antibiotic use in animal agriculture. It was discovered in the 1940s that feeding antibiotics to farm animals increases their ability to gain weight of the desirable sort. From the start, warnings were sounded by microbiologists regarding the danger implicit in such a practice; killing off pathogens would allow for the development of colonies of bacteria that are resistant to that antibiotic, creating the possibility of untreatable infections. In addition, low levels of antibiotics are fed to farm animals to help prevent infection. In fact more than half the antibiotics used in the United States are given to farm animals. Resistant bacteria pass to humans largely by way of fecal contamination. The beef industry is diligent about cleaning hides and carcasses at slaughterhouses, largely out of fear of another resistant pathogen, E. coli O157 H7, which can be lethal and is extremely difficult to treat.

All areas of confinement agriculture deploy liberal amounts of antibiotics in the course of raising animals – for example, Johns Hopkins researchers discovered vancomycin in the groundwater near chicken plants in the Delaware–Maryland–Virginia region. After concluding its report, the Pew Commission made numerous recommendations aimed at curtailing antibiotic use in farm animals (Pew 2008: 61–71). However, Congress ignored these recommendations due to the influence of large pharmacy companies, which would lose millions if such prescribing of antibiotics were to be limited.

The sheer number of animals present also increases the risks of CAFOs to human health. Whereas before the rise of confinement agriculture a farmer might deal with a couple of hundred pigs, in today's pig and chicken farms one is working with thousands, tens of thousands, and even hundreds of thousands of animals in small spaces. The likelihood of encountering a sick animal suffering from a zoonotic disease (i.e., a disease transmissible from animals to humans) is hugely increased. In addition, the transfer of pathogens between animals becomes inevitable, and, as these disease organisms mutate and proliferate, the danger of epidemics is also significantly increased. Swine flu and bird flu provide noteworthy examples. There is no question that industrialized operations have increased the amount of animal products available to consumers and have also decreased the price of such products. On the other hand, the health risks detailed above should give one pause before embracing confinement agriculture unequivocally.

The majority of the Commission recommendations dealt with antibiotic resistance. The report detailed 12 such recommendations (Pew 2008: 61–71):

1) Phase out and ban antimicrobials employed for growth promotion. Such a ban would cost the average American $5–10 per year.
2) Clearly define those antimicrobials that are used in human medicine.
3) Improve monitoring and reporting of antimicrobial use in food-animal production.
4) Improve monitoring and surveillance of antimicrobial resistance in the food supply, the environment, and animal and human populations, so as to refine our knowledge of antimicrobial resistance and its impacts on human health.
5) Increase veterinary oversight of all antimicrobial use in food-animal production. Curtail over-the-counter sales of antibiotics.
6) Implement a trace-back system for all food animals that allows 48-hour tracking of sick animals.
7) Increase the level of monitoring for workers who live or work close to CAFOs.
8) Increase research on the public health effects of CAFOs on people who live or work near these operations, and utilize the results to create a new system for siting and regulating these operations.
9) Establish strong relationships between physicians, veterinarians, and public health personnel to manage risks to human health resulting from confined feeding operations.
10) Create a central food-safety administration that combines the responsibilities of the USDA, FDA, and EPA for assuring food safety.
11) Develop a flexible, risk-based system for food safety that allows for different production systems.
12) Spend more research money on eliminating food-safety diseases at the production systems.

Sweden has historically been more sensitive to environmental issues than North America. In the 1960s, Sweden passed a referendum that abolished the use of antimicrobials for farm products. In 1989, Sweden passed another bill essentially abolishing confinement agriculture as it is taken for granted elsewhere in the world. When I was in Geneva, I had lunch with the Swedish Minister of Agriculture who told me the story of the elimination of antibiotics in animal feeds. When the bill passed, Swedish beef farmers were panicked. How can we raise these animals without antibiotics? Farmers frantically sought substitutes, including adding zinc oxide to feeds. Nothing worked. One old farmer remarked that, as a boy, he had worked with his grandfather raising beef. He recalled that the old man had scrupulously cleaned the pens between loads of cattle. When he was done doing that, infection did not strike the cattle, and he eliminated the need for antibiotics. Shortly thereafter, all the beef farmers began the practice of cleaning instead of using antimicrobials. Seemingly miraculously, the cost of beef production dropped precipitously, since millions of dollars were not being spent on harmful and dangerous antibiotics.

In the end, this was a triumph of common sense. After all, beef had been raised for centuries in the absence of antibiotics. And it stood to reason that it could be so raised again. In fact, as a general principle, there is no reason that agriculture could not go back to a more husbandry-based system, except for the desire to produce beyond the limitations of natural capacity. At cattle meetings I regularly attend, producers rant that, absent antibiotics, we cannot feed the world. I always point out that they are really not committed to feeding the world unless the world can pay for it. The fact is that perhaps beef might become more expensive, but producers could make up their loss simply by raising the price. Nowhere is it written, after all, that beef has to be cheap, particularly when the lower price comes at the expense of the animals and their well-being.

Environmental problems

An additional set of moral problems emerging from confinement agriculture is the effect it has on the environment. One of the key features of traditional agriculture was its sustainability. A presupposition to the development of agriculture was the concept of sustainability, i.e., assurance that the conditions and resources necessary were indefinitely renewable. As children, we might have learned about balanced aquariums. If we wished to keep a fish tank where the fish lived and we did not want to keep tinkering with it, we needed to assure that the system in question was as close to "perpetual motion," a system that required little maintenance because all parts worked together. That meant including plants that produced oxygen and consumed carbon dioxide, enough light to nourish the plants, or rather plants that thrived in the available light source, water that was properly constituted chemically, and scavengers to remove wastes. When such a system worked, it required minimal maintenance. If something was out of balance, plants and animals would die and require constant replacement. Such a fish tank aimed at being a balanced ecosystem. Thus, it represents a model of traditional approaches to cultivation of land, wherein one sought to cultivate plants that could be grown with indefinitely available resources. This model conserved and maximized these resources, which would not run out or require constant enrichment. Hence, the beauty of pastoral agriculture is that it is a renewable cycle: pasture nourishes herbivores and herbivores provide us with milk, meat, and leather, and their manure enriches the pastoral land.

Cultivation of land evolved locally with humans. If one did not attend to the constraints imposed by nature on what and how much can grow in a given region, the region would soon cease to yield its bounty, by virtue of salinization, depletion of nutrients, overgrazing, or insect infestation. Thus, over time, humans evolved, as one book put it, to "farm with nature," which became, like animal husbandry, both a rational necessity and an ethical imperative. Local knowledge, accumulated over a long period of trial and error, depicts how much irrigation was too much, what would not grow in given soils, what weeds left standing protected against insects, and where shade and windbreaks were necessary. Thus, accumulated wisdom was passed on – and augmented – from generation to generation, and it was sustainable, i.e., required minimal tweaking or addition of resources. The genius of agriculture was to utilize what was there in a way that would endure. If the land did not thrive, you did not thrive. Traditional agriculture, thus, was inherently sustainable, and through trial and error, over a long period, it evolved into a "balanced aquarium."

Contemporary agriculture thumbs its nose at sustainability, with productivity and profit now serving as the regnant values. "Enough" is no longer enough – we now strive for *more*. Chicken, for example, is no longer a luxury; it is cheap enough to be accessible to all citizens. Of course, *quality* is sacrificed to quantity – compare eggs from free-range hens to factory-farmed eggs. And to achieve plenitude, one needs an indefinite amount of input: vast amounts of fossil fuel, water, chemicals, etc. In addition, whereas animal waste in traditional agriculture served to nourish the land, in contemporary agriculture waste disposal becomes a major environmental problem and a source of pollution, not only of land, but also of rivers and streams and even the ocean, with "algal blooms" killing sea life. In tragicomic newspeak, an excessive amount of shit is called "nutrients." Pesticides and toxic agricultural chemicals further contaminate water and soil. We have already discussed the human health consequences of excess.

As just mentioned, confinement agriculture uses a tremendous amount of water. To cite an example employed in the Pew report (Pew 2008: 27), it takes about 420 gallons of water to produce one pound of grain-fed broiler chicken, which is highly significant considering that we raise more than ten billion broiler chickens per year! In addition, irrigation consumes massive amounts of water. Indeed, irrigation has reduced the Ogallala aquifer by more than half. To stress the magnitude of this issue, the Pew report affirms that,

> because the aquifer's very slow recharge rate is vastly outstripped by irrigation and other human needs, the aquifer is at risk of being fully depleted, threatening not only agriculture but drinking water supplies for a huge area of the United States.
>
> (Pew 2008: 27)

In addition, livestock operations account for 18% of current anthropogenic greenhouse gas emissions, which emissions are alleged to be responsible for global climate change. Also, livestock production is extremely consumptive of energy. Whereas the ratio of fossil-fuel energy inputs per unit of food energy produced averages three to one across all agricultural products, industrially produced meat changes the ratio to as much as 35 to one (Pew 2008: 29).

Environmental recommendations

Commission recommendations fell into four main categories:

1) Improve enforcement of existing federal, state, and local regulations regarding CAFOs and their effects on the environment. According to the Commission report, "funding should be increased to enable federal and state authorities to enforce CAFO regulations in order to reduce the number of large operations negatively impacting the soil, air, and water" (Pew 2008: 74–75).
2) Develop and implement a new system to deal with farm waste to replace the current broken system to protect Americans from the adverse environmental and human health hazards of CAFO waste.
3) Increase and improve monitoring and research on farm waste.
4) Increase research into new ways of managing farm waste.

Rural America

The industrialization of agriculture has had enormous consequences for a rural way of life. Thomas Jefferson warned that nothing is as important to the preservation of American democracy as small family farms. Whoever controls the food supply in essence rules over the rest of us. For this reason, Jefferson envisioned small, local farmers engaged in healthy competition. The idea of one megacorporation producing all the agricultural product of a certain sort was inconceivable to Jefferson. Yet this is almost exactly what has taken place with the rise of corporate industrialized agriculture. From 1989 until the present we have lost over 85% of small pork producers, and five CAFOs now produce 90% of the pork consumed. Given the buying power of large, corporate entities, buying, for example, vast amounts of feed, communities consisting of small pork producers could not compete, and ended up selling their farms at pennies on the dollar; those farms were then acquired by large corporations. Large, corporate entities employ the cheapest labor they can find, usually migratory workers from Mexico and South America, who are willing to work for rock-bottom wages. With no way to earn a living other than to work for the corporation, formerly independent producers will leave the community. And if some people manage to remain, there is invariably significant conflict between native citizens and migratory workers. This in turn further erodes any sense of community that might remain.

Researchers have shown that when citizens try to reappropriate their communities through the political process, they may well be shadowed and intimidated by corporations' security forces, as has occurred in North Carolina. Furthermore, given the vast amounts and high concentration of manure produced by the large factories, odor becomes a major issue, eroding both property values and quality of life.

Whereas one might think that the corporate farms enrich the community by the amount they spend, much of the money in fact is spent outside the immediate area, effectively reducing the "multiplier effect" money has when it stays in the community. And given the lack of power that workers have, sometimes further weakened by their legal status, the services for members of the community, such as social services and public health, are further diminished and weakened. Since any remaining small producers are unable to compete with the corporations, they rapidly price themselves out of the market. In the poultry industry, the birds are generally supplied to the growers by the corporations, who also dictate all of the husbandry protocols, making for a good deal of frustration and bitterness among the growers as prices are totally dictated to them.

Rural community recommendations

1) More attention should be paid by state, local, and federal governments to the siting of CAFOs, with an eye towards preserving quality of life for those who live in the area. These considerations should include setback distances, methods of production, numbers of extant CAFOs, public input, degree of local control, fees to fund inspection and regulation, an environmental impact statement, and a nutrient management plan.
2) Create policies that ensure a competitive marketplace for animal agriculture, and avoid the tendencies toward monopoly that naturally accompany large operations. If fair competition cannot be assured by contemporary legislation, new laws should be considered. Policy should be adopted to prevent large corporations, particularly in the poultry and swine industry, from forcing small growers to take out massive loans so they can supply the corporation.

What most consumers fail to realize is that while foods of animal origin are indeed "inexpensive at the store register," other costs, economic and otherwise, are often ignored. For example, when vast amounts of meat are shipped from processing plants on a daily basis, the damage done to infrastructural presuppositions of such shipping, such as roads and bridges, is enormous, and is invariably borne by the taxpayers. These costs are not evident at the store cash register. Thus the true cost of CAFO production is *externalized*, paid by citizens in general and not exclusively by those who purchase the products.

Animal welfare

Even more concealed from public scrutiny are the costs paid by the animals in the industry's pursuit of "cheap meat." Consider the following example: 50 years ago, one could purchase a Hershey's bar for a nickel – I recall how upset I was when the price was raised to six cents! Today, the same candy bar costs me $1.50 – an increase in price of 30 times! The price of frying chicken, on the other hand, has increased a mere threefold. The way I explain that differential to my students is by pointing out that the cheap price of the chicken is accomplished "on the backs of the animals." The unrelentingly severe conditions under which the animals are raised and how far they are from satisfying their basic needs account for how chicken can be so cheap.

The first time the Commission met as a group, only about three commissioners had any comprehension of the welfare issues; thus, I was asked to do a presentation explaining why animal welfare was a problem. To the great credit of virtually all the commissioners, they grasped the issues immediately and were visibly shaken, many moved to tears, when they first saw confined sows in gestation crates. The indignant response was, "no one would dare keep a dog in anything approximating those conditions."

One cannot comprehend the horrendous dimensions of the lack of animal welfare in confinement agriculture until one has seen it for oneself. For example, a row of small cages housing sows does not sound so bad until one has seen the tiny space provided, the trapped panic evident in the animals' behavior, the patently demented expressions evidenced by the animals. In some dairy herds, where the animals are raised on concrete instead of the soft loam demanded by their natures, up to 40% of the herd can suffer extremely painful lameness, and the cows can suffer metabolic burnout from excessive demand for milk production. Chickens used for egg production are kept in tiny cages allowing them as much space as a piece of printer paper, and a high percentage of the animals suffer bone bruising and fractures. Veal calves tethered in small wooden crates are in a state of borderline anemia, and they must be dragged to the trucks when they are transported to slaughter because their lack of exercise makes them unable to walk.

The patent hypocrisy of the industry has repeatedly been made manifest in advertisements. Perdue, one the largest chicken producers, regularly ran ads affirming that "at Perdue we raise 'happy chickens,'" accompanied by photographs of a spacious barnyard illustrating the traditional mixed farm, housing free-range horses, cows, chickens, and other farm animals. Equally egregious were the infamous "happy cow ads" affirming that "great cheese comes from happy cows, and happy cows come from California." A veterinary school Dean friend of mine reacted to what he called the "damn lie," pointing out that "these animals never see a blade of grass," and are raised on concrete where they are subject to a high degree of lameness and have a working life of only two and a half lactations. Their tails are often amputated surgically or by occluding blood supply to the tail, with no anesthesia or analgesia. Allegedly, the tails serve to promulgate manure, spreading disease. In fact, this theory has been repeatedly debunked. In other confinement systems, animals are likewise surgically mutilated with no use of anesthesia or analgesia.

Recommendations for animal welfare

1) Establish federally mandated rules for proper welfare practices to be audited by independent auditors. (Some businesses, such as Chipotle Mexican Grill, already do this to reassure customers.)
2) Implement better animal husbandry practices. (This recommendation aims at restoring good animal husbandry as traditionally existed in agriculture.)
3) The most remarkable Commission recommendation: Phase out the most intensive and inhumane production practices within a decade to reduce risks to public health and improve animal well-being. The following are listed: gestation crates, farrowing crates, battery cages, tethering of veal calves, forced feeding of veal calves, forced molting by feed removal to extend the hen's laying period.

Many of these recommendations have been enacted in 12 states after the Humane Society of the United States placed them in a ballot initiative referendum. In 2008, I convinced senior management at Smithfield, the world's largest pork producer, to phase out gestation crates by enjoining them to poll their customers. These crates have also been eliminated in Europe. Additionally we must eliminate surgical and other mutilations performed without anesthesia and analgesia, such as castration, dehorning, tail docking, desnooding, and sewing bull penises to the body wall for heat detection.

Conclusion

The Pew Commission Report represents an articulation of animal agriculture severed from the fanatic pursuit of productivity and profit, aimed at restoring sustainability, husbandry, respect for the environment, rural communities, animal welfare, and small agriculture played out in non-monopolistic contexts. It is necessary to stress, as I did at the final commission meeting held at the National Press Club, that those who developed confinement agriculture did not harbor base motives or any desire to hurt nature, the environment, or animals. Confinement agriculture should be viewed as an audacious, noble experiment, but in the end, a failure.

References

Cole D., Todd L., and Wing S. (2000) "Concentrated Swine Feeding Operations and Public Health: A Review of Occupational and Public Health Effects," *Environ Health* 108: 685–99.

Kilburn K. H. (1997) "Exposure to Reduced Sulfur Gas Impairs Neurobehavioral Function," *South Med J* 90: 997–1006.

Merchant, J. A., Naleway A.L., Svendsen E.R., Kelly K.M., Burmeister L.F., Stromquist A.M., Taylor C.D., Thorne P.S., Reynolds S.J., Sanderson W.T., and Chrischilles E.A. (2005) "Asthma and Farm Exposures in a Cohort of Iowa Children," *Environ Health Perspect* 113: 350–6.

Pew Charitable Trusts and Johns Hopkins Bloomberg School of Public Health. (2008) *Putting Meat on the Table: Industrial Farm Animal Production in America.*

Rollin B. E. (1987) "Euthanasia, Moral Stress, and Chronic Illness in Veterinary Medicine," *Veterinary Clinics of N America-Small An Prac* 41(3): 651–9.

Schiffman S. S., Sattely Miller E.A., Suggs M.S., and Graham B.G. (1995) "The Effect of Environmental Odors Emanating from Commercial Swine Operations on the Mood of Nearby Residents," *Environ Health Perspect* 113: 567–76.

Further Reading

G. John Benson and Bernard E. Rollin, *The Well-Being of Farm Animals: Challenges and Solutions* (Ames, Iowa: Blackwell, 2004) is a set of papers by leading experts on many of the issues raised in *Farm Animal Welfare* (below). Bernard E. Rollin, *Farm Animal Welfare: Social, Bioethical, and Research Issues* (Ames, Iowa: Iowa State University Press, 1995) is an objective survey of animal welfare issues occasioned by the rise of industrial agriculture. It grew out of a report commissioned by USDA.

25

ANIMAL WELFARE

David Fraser

Animal welfare is a complex concept, a social movement, and a topic of both philosophical debate and scientific research. It is also an area of increasingly global policy and action where a *practical ethics* approach by philosophers can make important contributions.

Historical context

During the 18th and 19th centuries, at a time when blood sports and blatant acts of cruelty to animals were common and perfectly legal in many parts of Europe, reformers sought to stamp out cruelty to animals as part of a broader program of social progress. This led to the criminalization of deliberate cruelty and the banning of recreations such as bull-baiting and dog-fighting, initially in the United Kingdom and then in many other countries. In line with such concerns, many animal protection organizations that were formed during this time were called societies "for the prevention of cruelty to animals."

During the 20th century, with an increasing trend toward large-scale, institutionalized use of animals in food production and biomedical research, the focus of animal ethics shifted from acts of cruelty to the use of animals for utilitarian purposes in ways that resulted in deprivation and curtailment of their freedom. This concern was increasingly expressed in terms of the "welfare" of animals. The term was used in 1925 with the founding of the organization that became the Universities Federation for Animal Welfare. The process was consolidated during the 1960s when, with increased use of restrictive environments for food-producing animals, many people became concerned that production systems designed along the lines of industrial efficiency would cause animals to have a poor quality of life. With this change in the nature of the concerns, the discourse shifted from one of cruelty to one of animal welfare, and scientists began doing research in order to understand and improve the welfare of animals (Woods 2011).

As these developments unfolded, academic philosophers also began paying substantial attention to animal ethics (Midgley 1983; Regan 1983; Singer 2009 [1975]). While a few focused explicitly on animal welfare, some saw welfare as an inadequate concept and tried to replace it with alternative concepts, such as animal rights (Regan 1983) and feminist approaches to animal ethics (Donovan 1990).

Since the 1990s, animal welfare has increasingly become a globally recognized area of social policy. Beginning in 2001, for example, the World Organisation for Animal Health has been developing global animal welfare standards, and many large corporations and international agencies have included animal welfare in their activities and corporate social responsibility programs. Thus, in less than a century, animal welfare has developed from an unfamiliar and somewhat radical idea to a widely accepted area of action, research, and social policy, and, at the same time, a controversial topic among philosophers and reformers.

Defining animal welfare

In what we might call an *animal welfare approach* to animal issues, the main focus is the quality of life of animals. ("Welfare" and "quality of life" for animals have been used more or less as synonyms in the animal welfare literature since the 1980s, and this usage is followed here.) However, defining what constitutes welfare or quality of life for animals has been a matter of much debate. As this debate has unfolded, it has become clear that people are using the term to capture three main areas of concern (Fraser 2008).

An obvious concern is the subjective well-being of animals, especially the feelings and emotions that animals experience. These include negative emotions such as fear, pain, frustration, and distress, together with unpleasant feelings of hunger, thirst, cold, heat, and illness. Also included are positive states such as comfort, contentment, pleasure, and enjoyment. In the absence of any simple English word, these are commonly called the *affective states* of animals, meaning those feelings and emotions that are experienced as hedonically positive or negative.

A second concern, linked to traditional goals of veterinarians and farmers, is that animals should have good health and functioning of the body – that they should be kept as free as possible from illness, injury, parasites, and similar problems, as might be evidenced by normal levels of vigor, growth, reproduction, and longevity.

A third concern is that animals should be able to lead reasonably "natural" lives. This theme has taken several forms. At the simplest level, some critics want animals to experience reasonably natural environments – for example, to be outdoors in the elements rather than permanently indoors in windowless barns. Critics have also noted that animals have characteristic types of natural behavior, such as foraging and socializing in certain ways, and they want animals to be free to carry out such behavior. As a third variation, Bernard Rollin (1995), in a neo-Aristotelian approach, notes that each animal species has a characteristic *telos* or nature, and he proposes that animal welfare depends on animals being kept in a way that respects this nature. More recent ideas arguably have expanded on this notion. For example, Nussbaum (2004) notes that animals have certain "capabilities," which they should be allowed to develop and exercise; Gjerris et al. (2006) calls for the "integrity" of animals to be protected; and Franks and Higgins (2012) propose that in addition to having what is valuable to them, animals should be able to exercise "truth effectiveness" by employing their curiosity, exploration, learning, and cognitive abilities, and "control effectiveness" by having agency over events in their lives.

These different conceptions of welfare are complementary to a degree, and they are often in agreement. For example, preventing lameness in dairy cattle is good for the animals' welfare according to all three views: it prevents a significant injury (basic health) and a painful condition (an affective state), and it allows the animals to better perform their natural behavior and exercise their inherent nature and capabilities. In other cases, however, the different views of animal welfare can lead to different conclusions. For example, open housing systems for laying hens allow natural behavior that is impossible in small cages, but they also involve greater risk that hens will become infested with a common mite that causes anemia and likely results in great discomfort for the birds. In such cases, attempts to improve animal welfare according to one criterion may worsen animal welfare according to another.

Achieving social policy on animal welfare is complicated by the fact that people disagree on how they prioritize the different views of welfare. The urban public tends to emphasize natural living and thus tends to see outdoor systems as inherently better for animal welfare than indoor systems. Many farmers attach great importance to basic health, and they may see outdoor systems as compromising animal welfare because these offer less ability to exclude disease pathogens and control the animals' environment (Sørensen and Fraser 2010). Given such diversity, for standards and practices to be widely accepted as promoting animal welfare, they need to take the different views of welfare into account.

Animal welfare as an evaluative concept

Some of the complexity arises because animal welfare is an *evaluative concept*. Like "health" or "safety," a greater degree of welfare implies not merely a different state but (other things being equal) a *better* state. Hence, try as we may to assess animal welfare in an objective and scientifically informed way (see below), conclusions about animal welfare are inevitably underlain by people's ideas about what constitutes a good life for animals, and these are inherently value based (Fraser 1995).

In fact, it seems almost inevitable that people will judge the quality of life of animals to some degree through the lens of how they assess quality of life in general, and this involves a debate that has continued for millennia (Appleby and Sandøe 2002). The emphasis on the affective states of animals has obvious roots in a line of thought that we see in the Greek philosopher Epicurus, the English reformer Jeremy Bentham, and the modern ethicist Peter Singer (2009)[1975]. This holds that a good life is a hedonically pleasant life wherein pleasures predominate and pains are at a minimum. The emphasis on natural environments resonates with a line of thought that we see in the rural poetry of Virgil and the reverence for nature of the Romantic poets and painters. According to this view, a good life is one that is lived in harmony with nature and is not constrained or corrupted by the artificiality that pervades human society. The emphasis on normal development and growth is reminiscent of a third line of thought, extending from Aristotle to Amartya Sen, which holds that each person has certain capabilities and potential, and that a good life involves being able to exercise those capabilities and achieve that potential (Fraser 2008).

The confusion created by the different views of animal welfare has led to some philosophical analysis of the term, and to debates about whether any of the views of animal welfare should have primacy over the others. Philosopher Lennart Nordenfelt (2006: 161) has argued that animal welfare is, at its core, about the happiness or the affective states of animals, and that other considerations (e.g., health or naturalness) may be *conditions for* but are not *part of* animal welfare. Scientist Ian Duncan (1993) agrees. He notes that we can speak about the health and functioning of plants, but we are not concerned about the welfare of plants because they do not (we believe) have any subjective experience of their lives; hence, he argues, welfare must be about subjective experience.

Others have proposed competing visions (summarized in Fraser 2008). Some scientists, for example, have proposed that welfare should be defined operationally in terms of basic health, growth, longevity, or evolutionary fitness, because these can be measured with some objectivity, whereas happiness, and even specific affective states such as fear and pain, are more difficult to quantify. Barnard and Hurst (1996) proposed an evolutionary argument. They noted that animals have been shaped by natural selection not to avoid stress and hardship, but to *expend* themselves in certain ways in order to reproduce successfully. Hence, they argue, animal welfare is not about health, long life, and pleasure, but about being able to follow the evolved life strategy of the species.

Although all of these proposals have merit, the term animal welfare is not merely a scientific or philosophical term that needs to be analyzed and defined more precisely; it is also an everyday term that is used by people in real-life debates, policy decisions, regulations, and international agreements. If philosophers and scientists use the term in a specialized or technical way that fails to correspond to its meaning in everyday use, they may fail to contribute to (or even sow confusion in) these practical discussions. Hence, there has been a widespread tendency to accept that animal welfare is a somewhat fuzzy umbrella concept that involves different concerns which different people emphasize to different degrees (Fraser 2008).

An animal welfare approach

The diverse concerns that are captured in the term animal welfare complicate attempts to characterize an "animal welfare approach" to ethical issues. Some philosophers have offered a simple (arguably simplistic) account by equating an animal welfare approach to the utilitarianism of Jeremy Bentham, or by claiming that it implies a ready acceptance of killing animals, or that it is concerned only with "unnecessary" suffering (e.g., Francione 1996). These statements arguably capture certain variants of an animal welfare approach – Gjerris et al. (2006) call this the "narrow" version of animal welfare – but they are not its defining features.

Some clarity can be gained by contrasting an animal welfare approach with the ideas of certain animal rights philosophers. First, with an animal welfare approach, the key issue is the quality of life of animals, whereas for many animal rightists the key issue is human ownership and use of animals (Regan 1983). Thus, an animal welfare approach is generally not opposed to people owning animals as long as the animals have a good quality of life as a result. Second, where many animal rightists are opposed in principle to deliberate killing, an animal welfare approach is generally more concerned about any associated suffering. Thus, for example, some animal welfarists may not oppose slaughter or euthanasia of animals as long as the death is painless and unanticipated, and it leaves no survivors that are harmed by the death. Others, however, see killing as a harm to animal welfare inasmuch as it forecloses future welfare possibilities for the animal's life. Third, with an animal welfare approach, unintended harms to animals (see below) are a cause of concern, whereas at least some animal rightists tend to downplay such harms, apparently because they are not inflicted intentionally (e.g., Lamey 2007). Finally, whereas some animal rights philosophers see rights as an all-or-none issue – an animal is either a rights-holder or it is not – in an animal welfare approach, concerns vary widely depending on the biology, emotions, and mental capacity of the species. Thus, although welfare concerns arise for fish, rats, and gorillas, the different species raise different concerns and require different treatment. Despite these differences between welfare and rights-based approaches, animal welfarists do not necessarily eschew the use of rights-based concepts or language. For example, many would accept, as proposed by Garner (2010), that animals have a right not to suffer at human hands.

Animal welfare science

Beginning in the 1970s, people began to conduct scientific research on animal welfare, partly to address specific welfare concerns and partly because people expected the science to adjudicate among the conflicting views of welfare. Surely, people seemed to reason, if we had an objective, scientific understanding of animal welfare, this would trump any value-based disagreements about what animal welfare entails. In reality, various scientists appeared to tacitly accept the different views of welfare, each of which formed the basis of animal welfare research (details in Fraser 2008).

Given the emphasis on affective states, a major focus of animal welfare research has been on recognizing and preventing states such as pain, fear, separation distress, and frustration. Such research has led (in some countries) to the banning of certain painful procedures, the mandatory use of pain management in certain situations, and the use of handling methods that do not cause fear in animals. Scientists have also focused on positive states such as pleasure, noting especially that certain types of behavior, such as play and exploration, appear to be accompanied by, and provide evidence of, positive affect.

Other research, often linked to traditional veterinary medicine, focuses on the basic health of animals, for example by identifying environmental features that cause injuries or spread disease, diets that predispose animals to digestive problems such as ulcers, and feeding systems that leave some animals undernourished. For example, research by Ragnar Tauson (1998) showed that certain kinds of cages cause feather loss and injuries to laying hens, and this research formed the basis of early animal welfare standards for cage design.

Yet other research focused on natural behavior, especially by identifying elements of natural behavior that animals are strongly motivated to perform. It was shown, for example, that hens are highly motivated to enter a nest box to lay eggs and to roost on a raised perch at night, and on the basis of such research many countries now require that hens have access to these features.

A key aim of animal welfare research has been to understand the animals' own "point of view," especially by studying their motivations and preferences (Dawkins 1990). Such work has led to many useful insights. For example, chickens, being descended from jungle-dwelling ancestors, strongly prefer areas with overhead cover rather than open pasture. This likely explains why many chickens in free-range systems avoid going outdoors unless there are trees overhead (Dawkins et al. 2003). However, studies of animals' preferences have important limitations. We generally expect animals to have natural preferences for features that would allow them to thrive in the environment where the species evolved; but in very different environments, such as modern farms, an animal's preferences may have become uncoupled from its longer-term welfare. In addition, selective breeding of domestic animals for certain traits may have further distorted the connection between preferences and aspects of welfare such as health. Hence, while animals' preferences provide valuable insights into how to improve their welfare, they do not provide a definitive standard that trumps disagreements over what is best for animal welfare.

Animal welfare and real-world engagement

An animal welfare approach is criticized by some philosophers for not offering a sufficiently profound critique of human use of animals. For example, Gary Francione (1996) criticizes animal welfare for failing to call for a ban on human ownership of animals, and Richard Haynes (2011) sees the term animal welfare as being used to justify the continued exploitation of animals in science and food production.

An alternative interpretation is that many who adopt an animal welfare approach are focused on making feasible changes in the real-world rather than debating theoretical ideals. For example, billions of animals are slaughtered for food each year, and all projections are that the number will continue to increase, especially in emerging economies where per-capita meat consumption is increasing steadily. When the Humane Slaughter Association proposes practices and standards that cause less distress to animals during slaughter, this is not to say that their members want to promote the slaughter of animals, but rather that they recognize that slaughter will undoubtedly continue, and they want to improve the lot of the animals involved. Hence, debates between philosophers and practitioners sometimes seem at cross-purposes, with some philosophers proposing theoretical ideals while practitioners seek practical change.

Nonetheless, it is possible that animal welfarists, by acting to reduce animal suffering, may cause some harmful practices to seem less repugnant to the public and thus reduce fundamental opposition that might lead to a practice being banned. This criticism may apply especially in cases where a ban on a practice appears feasible. For example, in countries that might conceivably ban the harpooning of whales or the use of great apes in biomedical research, attempts to make these practices "more humane" might possibly slow more fundamental reform.

Animal welfare as a global issue

Animal welfare (as distinct from traditional religious respect for animals) began largely as a rich-country issue, but is now receiving a degree of global recognition, partly through the engagement of organizations such as the World Organisation for Animal Health and the Food and Agriculture Organization of the United Nations. This geographic expansion has also brought new topics into the ambit of animal welfare research and action. As examples:

1) Nearly a billion people, including many of the world's poorest people, depend on small-scale animal production for their livelihood (FAO 2009), and some international development agencies support such animal production in order to improve human nutrition and food security for the rural poor. Including animal welfare in these programs, especially to improve animal nutrition, handling, and health care, is seen as contributing to both human and animal welfare.
2) Stray dogs likely number in the hundreds of millions worldwide, and lead to many thousands of human deaths by rabies each year. Traditional killing of stray dogs is often inhumane, and it is generally ineffective at controlling numbers and protecting public health. Programs that provide basic health care, vaccination, and neutering for unowned dogs, stimulated largely by concern over the dogs' welfare, appear to be better at controlling dog numbers (Totton et al. 2010), and they may prove better for human health and safety as well.
3) Hundreds of millions of working animals provide labor for crop production and transportation. These animals are critical to the food supply and livelihood of many people, and they replace human labor and dependence on fossil fuel. Efforts to improve the welfare of these animals – especially nutrition, hydration, health care, and harnessing – are thought to benefit the animals, their owners, and the communities they serve (Ramaswamy 1998).

In the industrialized countries, animal welfare is sometimes seen as running contrary to other interests such as production efficiency and cheap food. In the above examples, an animal welfare approach points to alternative ways of solving problems which often lead to better outcomes for the human participants as well.

New challenges for animal welfare

If the principal concern of animal ethics was cruelty in the 18th and 19th centuries, and the institutionalized use of animals in the 20th century, the 21st century seems poised to add a third major problem area involving unintended harms to animals caused by the world's growing human population and its increasingly pervasive effects on the planet.

Some such harms are a fairly direct result of common human activities. Cars are estimated to kill a million vertebrates per day in the United States alone, and they are thought to have surpassed hunting as a cause of death of wild terrestrial vertebrates (Forman and Alexander 1998). Windows are thought to kill billions of birds per year, and to injure roughly one bird for every one that is killed (Klem 2009). Crop-production practices have devastating effects on animals living in agricultural land. In particular, burrowing rodents commonly reach levels of 100 or more per hectare of farmland, and one study found that plowing resulted in the disappearance of virtually all these animals, presumably by injuring some and leaving others without shelter (Jacob 2003). If such numbers can be applied to the 1.4 billion hectares of arable land in the world, then the amount of injury, suffering, and death must be enormous.

Even greater effects may occur indirectly when human activities alter the processes and balances of nature that are essential to the flourishing of other species. Habitat destruction and marine pollution destroy the ecological systems that support untold numbers of animals. Perhaps most severe of all, climate change is predicted to affect wild animals so drastically as to put many species on a course to extinction (Thomas et al. 2004).

To date, animal welfare and environmental conservation have developed as separate concepts, movements, and areas of research. As these examples show, however, the goals of environmental conservation and animal welfare are, in many respects, closely aligned. What is needed is a coherent ethic for both animal welfare and environmental conservation, and a unified program of action (see essays in Fraser 2010). In fact, several philosophers have proposed approaches that include both animal ethics and conservation. For example, Eric Katz (1983) proposes an environmental ethic that values both the preservation of natural systems and "individual natural entities" such as free-living wild animals; Gary Varner (1998) proposes that concern for individuals (human and non-human), and especially their "ground projects," provides a basis for both animal protection and environmental conservation; and Angus Taylor (1996) proposes that recognizing the right of sentient beings to their "vital needs," including "the vital need to have a flourishing natural environment," would provide a basis for animal ethics and environmental protection. However, much more attention and action are needed to address this enormous and growing problem area.

Another emerging challenge involves fish. Aquaculture is expanding rapidly worldwide and currently involves the annual slaughter of tens of billions of individuals – a number that rivals all terrestrial animal production (Mood and Brooke 2012). Moreover, roughly ten times as many are killed by capture fisheries, mostly by methods that fall far short of standards for humane slaughter (Mood 2010). Clearly there is a growing need for standards, practices, research, and public awareness related to the welfare of fish.

A third challenge involves the growing awareness of the effects on animal welfare of human caretakers. To date, much of the attention in farm-animal welfare standards and practices has been focused on the physical environment, for example by replacing barren cages for hens or narrow stalls for sows. However, comparative data show that basic welfare indicators often vary widely among farms even though the farms use the same type of physical environment. The different welfare outcomes appear to be due to large differences in the quality of care, handling, and attention that the animals receive from the caretakers. Hence, an important avenue for improving animal welfare in the future will be a much greater focus on the selection, training, and professional standards of animal keepers (Hemsworth and Coleman 2010).

Animal welfare as practical ethics

In many of the examples given above, an animal welfare approach falls in the realm of *practical ethics*, which tries to provide workable guidance to people making real-life ethical decisions. In other fields of practical ethics, discussion has often moved away from seeking single foundational principles, in favor of developing mid-level guiding principles, which need to be balanced and applied thoughtfully to real-life problems. Medical ethics, for example, commonly uses four guiding principles (beneficence, non-maleficence, justice, and autonomy), which need to be considered and balanced on a case-by-case basis (Beauchamp and Childress 2008).

In fact, some of the earliest guiding principles for animal welfare followed this approach. For half a century the guiding principles for the use of animals in research have been the

"Three Rs": reducing the number of animals to the least number needed for the purpose, refining procedures to minimize negative effects on animal welfare, and replacing animals with non-animal models or animals thought to be less sentient. A somewhat parallel development for the farm animals involves the "five freedoms" or "five domains of animal welfare," which call for attention to the nutrition, environment, health, behavior, and mental state of animals (Mellor et al. 2009).

A more comprehensive set of principles arose from the observation that people affect animals in four basic ways: by caring for animals on farms, in homes, etc.; by deliberate harms such as slaughter and pest control; by unintended harms that occur when people drive cars, plow fields, etc.; and by disturbing the life-sustaining processes and balances of nature, for example by pollution, habitat alteration, and climate change. The four principles, which are intended to deal with these situations respectively, are: to provide good lives for the animals in our care, to treat all suffering with compassion, to be mindful of unintended harms so that we avoid and mitigate them as much as possible, and to protect the processes and balances of nature that are important to the lives of other beings (Fraser 2012).

An even more comprehensive approach is the "ethical matrix" which embeds animal welfare and other considerations in a structured process to inform ethical decisions (Mepham 2006). It sets out three general guiding principles (well-being, autonomy, and justice) as columns in a matrix, and lists the various affected parties as the rows. A possible action is then assessed for how it affects animal well-being, animal autonomy, and just treatment of animals, while using the same criteria to set out effects on (for example) farmers, farm workers, consumers, and others affected by the decision.

Unsolved philosophical problems

With its focus on practice more than theory, an animal welfare approach leaves many ethical issues unresolved and in many cases barely discussed. One issue is how to balance the different elements of animal welfare when they are in conflict. For example, if organic farmers allow animals more freedom and access to natural environments but are also less likely to use medications that help maintain basic health, can we draw any conclusions about their overall impact on animal welfare, or are we only able to outline the pros and cons of the different approaches?

A second issue involves balancing quality of life versus length of life. For example, some practitioners of wildlife rehabilitation readily euthanize badly injured animals to end their suffering, whereas others try to "save" such animals even if substantial suffering is likely to be involved in their recovery (Dubois and Fraser 2003). The former group appears to prioritize suffering, while the latter seems to prioritize maintaining the animals' options for future quality of life. In this and many other cases, a rational and coherent consensus remains to be articulated.

A third issue involves balancing the welfare of animals in human care against the welfare of free-living animals. For example, some people provide excellent care for colonies of unowned cats while making no attempt to prevent the cats from injuring and killing birds. Perhaps these people feel that cats, with their long history of domestication, merit a level of consideration that wild animals do not (Palmer 2011), but there has been little ethical discussion to help resolve such issues.

A fourth issue, which arises in the management of groups of animals, is how to prioritize the welfare of the "average" animal versus the most vulnerable. For example, if changing from individual housing to group housing is better for most of the animals but seriously disadvantages the smallest and least dominant, what criteria can be used to guide these decisions?

Finally, analysis is needed on how to prioritize the kind of unintended harms described above. In human ethics, intention plays an important role in moral judgments; for example, we view deliberate murder as a more serious wrong than negligence that results in death. Perhaps on this basis, some people appear to attach little priority to unintended harms. But is this appropriate when humans routinely cause a vast amount of unintentional harm to animals, and when these harms seem likely to increase unless they receive special attention?

Confronting these issues will require individuals with a robust understanding of the relevant practices combined with skill in ethical reflection and analysis. There is great scope for philosophers to take an interest in these questions and help to work out practical guidance.

References

Appleby, M. C. & Sandøe, P. (2002) "Philosophical debate on the nature of well-being: Implications for animal welfare," *Animal Welfare* 11: 283–294.

Barnard, C. J. & Hurst, J. L. (1996) "Welfare by design: the natural selection of welfare criteria," *Animal Welfare* 5: 405–433.

Beauchamp, T. L. & Childress J. (2008) *Principles of Biomedical Ethics*, 6th edition, Oxford: Oxford University Press.

Dawkins, M. S. (1990) "From an animal's point of view: Motivation, fitness, and animal welfare," *Behavioural and Brain Sciences* 13: 1–9, 54–61.

Dawkins, M. S., Cook, P. A., Whittingham, M. J., Mansell, K. A. & Harper, A. E. (2003) "What makes free-range broiler chickens range? In situ measurement of habitat preference," *Animal Behaviour* 66: 151–160.

Donovan, J. (1990) "Animal rights and feminist theory," *Signs* 15: 350–375.

Dubois, S. & Fraser, D. (2003) "Conversations with stakeholders: 2. Contentious issues in wildlife rehabilitation," *Journal of Wildlife Rehabilitation* 26(2): 8–14.

Duncan, I. J. H. (1993) "Welfare is to do with what animals feel," *Journal of Agricultural and Environmental Ethics* 6 (Supplement 2): 8–14.

FAO. (2009) *State of Food and Agriculture: Livestock in the Balance*, Rome: Food and Agriculture Organization of the United Nations (FAO).

Forman, R. T. T. & Alexander, L. E. (1998) "Roads and their major ecological effects," *Annual Review of Ecology and Systematics* 29: 207–231.

Francione, G. L. (1996) *Rain Without Thunder: The Ideology of the Animal Rights Movement*, Philadelphia: Temple University Press.

Franks, B. & Higgins, E. T. (2012) "Effectiveness in humans and other animals: A common basis for well-being and welfare," *Advances in Experimental Social Psychology* 46: 285–346.

Fraser, D. (1995) "Science, values and animal welfare: Exploring the 'inextricable connection'," *Animal Welfare* 4: 103–117.

Fraser, D. (2008) *Understanding Animal Welfare: The Science in its Cultural Context*, Oxford: Wiley-Blackwell.

Fraser, D., ed. (2010) *Conservation and Animal Welfare Science* (Special issue), *Animal Welfare* 19: 121–192.

Fraser, D. (2012) "A 'practical' ethic for animals," *Journal of Agricultural and Environmental Ethics* 25: 721–746.

Garner, R. (2010) "Animals, ethics and public policy," *The Political Quarterly* 81: 123–130.

Gjerris, M., Olsson, A. & Sandøe, P. (2006). "Animal biotechnology and animal welfare," in *Ethical Eye: Animal Welfare*, Strasbourg: Council of Europe, pp. 89–110.

Haynes, R. P. (2011) "Competing conceptions of animal welfare and their ethical implications for the treatment of non-human animals," *Acta Biotheoretica* 59: 105–120.

Hemsworth, P. H. & Coleman, G. J. (2010) *Human–Livestock Interactions: The Stockperson and the Productivity and Welfare of Intensively Farmed Animals*, second edition, Wallingford: CAB International.

Jacob, J. (2003) "Short-term effects of farming practices on populations of common voles," *Agriculture, Ecosystems and Environment* 95: 321–325.

Katz, E. (1983) "Is there a place for animals in the moral consideration of nature?" *Ethics and Animals* 4: 74–87.

Klem, D., Jr. (2009) "Preventing bird–window collisions," *The Wilson Journal of Ornithology* 121: 314–321.

Lamey, A. (2007) "Food fight! Davis versus Regan on the ethics of eating beef," *Journal of Social Philosophy* 38: 331–348.

Mellor, D. J., Patterson-Kane E. & Stafford K. J. (2009) *The Sciences of Animal Welfare*, Oxford: Wiley-Blackwell.

Mepham, B. (2006) "The ethical matrix as a decision-making tool, with specific reference to animal sentience," in J. Turner & J. d'Silva (eds.), *Animals, Ethics and Trade*, London: Earthscan, pp. 134–145.

Midgley, M. (1983) *Animals and Why They Matter*, Athens: University of Georgia Press.

Mood, A. (2010) *Worse Things Happen at Sea: The Welfare of Wild-Caught Fish, Summary Report*, viewed December 2010, <http://www.fishcount.org.uk/published/standard/fishcountsummaryrptSR.pdf>.

Mood, A. & Brooke, P. (2012) *Estimating the Number of Farmed Fish Killed in Global Aquaculture Each Year*, viewed May 2015, <http://fishcount.org.uk/published/std/fishcountstudy2.pdf>.

Nordenfelt, L. (2006) *Animal and Human Health and Welfare: A Comparative Philosophical Analysis*, Wallingford: CAB International.

Nussbaum, M. C. (2004) "Beyond 'compassion and humanity': Justice for nonhuman animals," in C. R. Sunstein & M. C. Nussbaum (eds.), *Animal Rights: Current Debates and New Directions*, Oxford: Oxford University Press, pp. 299–320.

Palmer, C. (2011) "The moral relevance of the distinction between domesticated and wild animals," in T. Beauchamp & R. G. Frey (eds.), *The Oxford Handbook of Animal Ethics*, Oxford: Oxford University Press, pp. 701–725.

Ramaswamy, N. S. (1998) "Draught animal welfare," *Applied Animal Behaviour Science* 59: 73–84.

Regan, T. (1983) *The Case for Animal Rights*, Berkeley: University of California Press.

Rollin, B. E. (1995) *Farm Animal Welfare: Social, Bioethical, and Research Issues*, Ames: Iowa State University Press.

Singer, P. (2009) [1975] *Animal Liberation: A New Ethics for Our Treatment of Animals*, fourth edition, New York: Random House.

Sørensen, J. T. & Fraser, D. (2010) "On-farm welfare assessment for regulatory purposes: Issues and possible solutions," *Livestock Science* 131: 1–7.

Tauson, R. (1998) "Health and production in improved cage designs," *Poultry Science* 77: 1820–1827.

Totton, S. C., Wandeler, A. I., Zinsstag, J., Bauch, C. T., Ribble, C. S., Rosatte, R. C. & McEwen, S. A. (2010) "Stray dog population demographics in Jodhpur, India following a population control/rabies vaccination program," *Preventive Veterinary Medicine* 97: 51–57.

Taylor, A. (1996) "Animal rights and human needs," *Environmental Ethics* 18: 249–264.

Thomas, C. D., Cameron, A., Green, R. E., Bakkenes, M., Beaumont, L.J., Collingham, Y.C., Erasmus, B.F.N., de Siqueira, M.F., Grainger, A., Hannah, L., Hughes, L., Huntley, B., van Jaarsveld, A.S., Midgley, G.F., Miles, L., Ortega-Huerta, M.A., Peterson, A.T., Phillips, O.L. & Williams, S.E. (2004) "Extinction risk from climate change," *Nature* 427: 145–148.

Varner, G. E. (1998) *In Nature's Interests? Interests, Animal Rights, and Environmental Ethics*, Oxford: Oxford University Press.

Woods, A. (2011) "From cruelty to welfare: the emergence of farm animal welfare in Britain, 1964–71," *Endeavour* 36: 14–22.

Further Reading

Appleby, M. C., Mench, J. A., Olsson, I.A.S. & Hughes, B. O., eds., *Animal Welfare*, Second Edition (Wallingford: CAB International, 2010) is a collection of chapters on animal welfare issues, science, and related topics. D. Fraser, *Understanding Animal Welfare: The Science in its Cultural Context*, Oxford: Wiley-Blackwell, 2008) describes animal welfare science, its cultural context, and its application in policy. L. Nordenfelt, *Animal and Human Health and Welfare: A Comparative Philosophical Analysis* (Wallingford: CAB International, 2006) is a philosopher's analysis of the concepts as applied to both humans and animals.

26

FOOD, WELFARE, AND AGRICULTURE

A complex picture

Simon Jenkins

Introduction

This chapter will provide an overview of some of the ethical issues at play when using a broadly welfarist perspective to approach questions about what individuals should eat, and about how food for human consumption should be cultivated. By "broadly welfarist perspective," I mean that I will consider the ethical ramifications of actions insofar as they affect the welfare of, i.e., make things go better or worse for, morally considerable beings. Given that all food has to come from somewhere, it may be unsurprising that many of the ethical ramifications in this welfare perspective on food ethics are determined by the origins of food, and the farming and agricultural processes that foods undergo so that people can eat them. These processes are supported, at least financially, when certain food choices are made. Questions that I will address in this chapter are therefore "what should people eat?" and "how should food be processed?" The latter term should not be interpreted narrowly, as in so-called "processed" food, but instead broadly, as meaning the entire process and industry of generating food for human consumption, or for consumption by companion animals kept by humans (i.e., pets).

For the purposes of this discussion, I will not make a distinction between "consumption" as eating and "consumption" as purchasing. There may be some cases where there is a distinction between buying-and-eating something and eating something without buying it, but I will leave this discussion to the "freegans" (Shantz 2005), who draw this distinction the most sharply.

Answering the question "what should I eat?" from this welfarist perspective will depend in large part on what counts as welfare, and, relatedly, on who or what is a candidate for such welfare. There are broadly two types of stakeholder involved in such questions: those who are the food themselves, and those who are not destined to be eaten, but whose welfare is nevertheless altered by various food practices. It is when the welfares of different members of these groups conflict that decisions can become difficult. We will see that some of the tensions at play in answering questions about what to eat and how to produce food revolve around myopic accounts of whose welfare matters.

Before we can identify welfare conflicts, we need a conception of which groups even have welfare to begin with. When there is uncertainty about who or what is a candidate for having welfare, identifying and negotiating these conflicts becomes even more complicated. This chapter will begin by describing some of the historical philosophical debates on what kinds of creatures are candidates for moral considerability, and on what basis. Beginning with Descartes and Kant and their view on the importance of rationality and language, I will trace the expanding sphere of moral consideration through Bentham, who argued for the moral value of nonhuman animals, to Singer, who promulgated the popularity of nonhuman animal ethics from a welfare perspective (as opposed to Regan's rights perspective) in the late 20th century.

I will then consider some problems associated with this welfarist perspective, particularly in cases such as invertebrates, and even plants, whose sentience is in doubt but who may nevertheless have a claim on our actions by virtue of being large in number. This will be shown through a discussion of probabilistic moral reasoning and expected utility. The welfare of these beings may have a bearing on our moral obligations, and I will illustrate this with the example of pesticide use in agriculture. Given the emphasis on welfare and numbers, this chapter may reasonably be taken as outlining a consequentialist perspective on these issues.

Criteria for moral consideration

Let us begin by surveying some of the philosophical discussion on candidacy for moral considerability. This will help us to consider whose welfare matters when it comes to our food choices.

Kant's view on the moral status of nonhumans is clear: "Animals are not self-conscious and are there merely as a means to an end. [. . .] Our duties towards animals are merely indirect duties towards humanity" (Kant 1989: 23). Descartes propounds a similar view, arguing that the capacity for rationality possessed by humans is fundamentally different from any kind of rationality that we might perceive in nonhumans, which for him is not actually rationality at all. He remarks of humans that:

> [T]here are none so depraved and stupid, without even excepting idiots, that they cannot arrange different words together, forming of them a statement by which they make known their thoughts. [. . .] On the other hand, men who, being born deaf and dumb, are in the same degree, or even more than the brutes, destitute of the organs which serve the others for talking, are in the habit of themselves inventing certain signs by which they make themselves understood. [. . .] [T]his does not merely show that the brutes have less reason than men, but that they have none at all, since it is clear that very little is required in order to be able to talk.
>
> (Descartes, in Regan and Singer 1989: 14–15)

Descartes takes language ability as an indicator of reason, and states that nonhumans (or "brutes" as he calls them) do not have the capacity for reason because of their lack of language ability. It is contentious whether Descartes really thinks that this is sufficient to exclude nonhuman animals from moral consideration entirely (Harrison 1992). As Harrison notes, however, it is commonly interpreted as such, and so for my purposes here I will consider it as a putative view, though without committing myself to imputing it to Descartes.

One problem with this account is that there may be counterexamples to both of his cases. First, there simply *are* people who are impaired ("depraved and stupid," in Descartes' terms) such that they cannot communicate their thoughts. Such impairment can be either physical or mental. Second, there are potential cases of nonhumans making themselves understood in ways "that are relevant to particular topics without expressing any passion" (Descartes, in Regan and Singer 1989: 16), which is the distinction he makes between the way in which humans communicate, and that in which nonhumans do. Descartes considered this a necessary condition for having a soul, and therefore moral considerability. Yule (2014) relays some cases of attempts to teach language to chimpanzees. These attempts are controversial and may not satisfy Descartes' definition of what it means to use language, but as Yule points out, they illuminate that "using language" is an ill-defined concept. Its use as a yardstick for moral considerability is therefore somewhat troubling. These counterexamples demonstrate that Descartes' guideline for distinguishing between entities *with* a special, reason-demonstrating language capacity, and those without, does not provide clear answers.

Kant and Descartes exclude nonhuman animals from moral considerability, but we can see that this view is problematic. Bentham was one of the first philosophers to include nonhumans in his conception of the sphere of moral considerability. He discusses the putative necessary conditions for considerability, reason and language, which we have seen proposed by Kant and Descartes. He notes that there is a crossover problem in that not *all* humans will be more rational or linguistically competent than all nonhumans, and posits a new criterion for moral significance:

> [A] full-grown horse or dog is beyond comparison a more rational, as well as a more conversable animal, than an infant of a day, or a week, or even a month, old. But suppose the case were otherwise, what would it avail? The question is not, Can they *reason*? nor, Can they *talk*? but, Can they *suffer*?
>
> (Bentham 2007)

Arguments against the infanthood analogy by appeal to the infant's *potential* to be a more rational or conversable animal than a horse or dog can be easily dispelled by replacing the infant with some human who is in a permanent vegetative state and is expected never to recover. Bentham's suggestion that the correct criterion for moral significance is the capacity to suffer will likely widen the sphere of moral significance to entities beyond just those with rationality, and in spite of his interrogative rhetorical style, it is clear that Bentham thought that full-grown horses and dogs do have the capacity to suffer.

Singer agrees with Bentham that this capacity is of moral significance, and that many currently farmed and eaten animals' possession of this capacity renders eating them unjustifiable. I will take it as an extension of Singer's view that eating any animal product is unjustifiable for the same reasons, and henceforth refer to veganism as the alternative to meat-eating. In elaborating on Bentham's approach to the moral standing of nonhuman animals, he mentions some of the troubling cases in which it is not always clear whether suffering is a factor. He notes:

> [A]s we proceed down the evolutionary scale we find that [. . .] the strength of the evidence for a capacity to feel pain diminishes. With birds and mammals the evidence is overwhelming. Reptiles and fish have nervous systems that differ from those of mammals in some important respects but share the basic structure of centrally organized nerve pathways. Fish and reptiles show most of the pain behavior that mammals do. In most species there is even vocalization, although it is not audible to our ears.
>
> (Singer 1995: 171–172)

For my purposes in this chapter, it is convenient that Singer frames his question regarding which creatures have this capacity as the question of which creatures we should eat: "How far down the evolutionary scale shall we go? Shall we eat fish? What about shrimps? Oysters?" (Singer 1995: 171). Singer's notion of an "evolutionary scale" might today be contentious, if it is taken to implicitly suggest a moral hierarchy. Nevertheless, he ultimately concludes that, so as to be sure to avoid causing undue suffering, we should err on the side of caution and refrain from eating these animals:

> [W]hile one cannot with any confidence say that these creatures do feel pain, so one can equally have little confidence in saying that they do not feel pain. [...] Since it is so easy to avoid eating them, I now think it better to do so.
>
> (Singer 1995: 174)

I will return to Singer's treatment of these edge cases later, but for now it is sufficient that for Singer, moral significance rests on having "the capacity to suffer or experience enjoyment or happiness," which he refers to as "sentience."

We have seen how the welfare arguments surrounding nonhuman animals and their sentience, as considered by Bentham, were then taken up by Singer to produce a moral prohibition on eating animal products. The argument seems straightforward: these animals are morally considerable, and it is therefore morally problematic to eat them. This is due to the suffering that this directly causes them, either in the conditions in which they are farmed or in the manner of their death.

Another possible reason that it may be bad to kill such animals is that it would deny them their future – this question of potentiality has been addressed by various authors, with varying conclusions. Marquis (2014) considers potentiality as it bears on the moral status of human fetuses, but his argument is relevant to nonhuman animals too, as he describes abortion as wrong on the basis of its denial of future life. A forward-looking conception about the value of life is also considered by Parfit (1984), Broome (2004), and Mulgan (2006).

I do not need to enter into a discussion of potentiality in this chapter, because it appears, at least so far, that we have sufficient reason against eating animals without invoking potentiality – eating animals causes them suffering. It may be, though, that the potentiality argument is needed when we get to cases where the animals have a positive net utility in their lives, and where their deaths are not painful (i.e., they are stunned so that they feel no pain). This discussion I will leave for another day. For my purposes here, it is sufficient that death often means the deprivation of a future positive life, so it is legitimate to be concerned with death when coming from a welfare perspective.

Whose welfare?

The picture becomes very complicated once we consider the *wider* welfare picture – that is, the welfare of animals *other* than those directly being killed. Perhaps ironically, this has parallels with an oft-cited defense of eating animals: the argument that the meat-eater simply likes the taste. In this case, the meat-eater is appealing to the welfare of someone besides the animals eaten – i.e., their own. Narveson appears to advance a view like this.[1] This is ordinarily viewed as an insufficient line of argument, as it fails to correctly account for the weightings of the relevant pleasures and instances of suffering. It does not seem plausible that the suffering of a factory-farmed animal is outweighed by the pleasure of even the most ardent meat-eater. To arrive at a weighting that would deliver this conclusion would rely on a very low discounting of the hedonic value of these animals – and we have seen from Bentham and Singer that this is very likely to be a mistake. Nevertheless, though this argument is a failure, it paves the way for a raft of other important considerations in the ethics of meat-eating – the welfare of others.

If the meat-eater is wrong to only consider their own welfare, or to place too much weight on the value of that welfare, then the non-meat-eater is similarly wrong to only consider the welfare of the individual animals being killed for food, or to weigh this welfare too heavily. In reality, there are a number of other stakeholders at play in the rearing of livestock.

This is where environmentalist considerations and reasons for being vegan may come in. The environmental reasons for becoming vegan seem to encompass a huge variety of different considerations, but in common discourse, environmentalism seems to be an end in itself and does not require much justification. It is just *assumed* that harming the environment is bad in itself. But there are various ways of describing what this means, or of fleshing out who or what is the entity that stands to be harmed by our environmentally selfish or reckless actions.

Even if one is only interested in humans, there may be environmental reasons to avoid animal products because of the harm caused to humans by climate change. Some organizations have taken early steps to attempt to quantify this harm and come up with numbers of people killed by climate change.[2]

Radical shifts in climatic conditions mean that individual nonhuman animals suffer and die also. Other lines of argument hold species themselves to be valuable – so that it is not the individuals who are what matters, but the continued existence of the species. According to this line of argument, damaging the environment is therefore bad or wrong because it contributes to the extinction of species (Rolston 2002).

There can of course be overlaps between all of these arguments. It could be the case that one is generally worried about the future of all animals, human and nonhuman, if climate change occurs. This could be due to the suffering they will experience, loss of biodiversity, or just the fact that there may be suffering and a lack of the continuation of life – this is related to the potentiality question considered briefly above.

Sagoff (1984) has pointed out that there can be conflicts between these environmental-type arguments against meat-eating and the "narrow" animal-welfare-type reasons against meat-eating. These are described as narrow insofar as they only consider the welfare of those animals being eaten. We can conceive of a more inclusive welfarist picture where *all* animals' welfare is to be taken into account. If we think that (nonhuman) animals will be harmed by climate change, then we have a problem. Another complicating issue is that which Matheny and Chan (2005) and Archer (2011) have considered: the fact that small creatures are killed in certain crop-related agricultural settings in ways animals are not killed by meat-eating.

I will not attempt to solve these issues here. My aim in this section is only to show that not only is it unclear who or what can be considered to be sentient and therefore have welfare, but that even once we have some answers to these questions, there are overlapping and conflicting interests at a variety of levels, including between those creatures that are harmed in order for them to become food and those that are harmed as a result of food production. These conflicts render the moral consequences of our actions very unclear. I will now move on to discuss a particular example that brings these issues together.

Invertebrate suffering: a troubling possibility

The case of invertebrates poses an interesting example that ties together both the issue of the welfare of those *not* being eaten and concerns about who or what is a morally considerable being. While it is true that eating insects, or entomophagy, is a longstanding practice and has garnered some media attention recently (Davies 2014), I will ignore that possibility for the purposes of this discussion and focus instead on those invertebrates that are killed in the process of more common forms of agriculture, namely the cultivation of crops. These invertebrates are not killed to be eaten, but they are killed in their capacity as "pests" because they tend to eat crops intended for human consumption.

The question of whether invertebrates are sentient is contentious (Dunayer 2004; Eisemann et al. 1984; Elwood 2011; Fiorito 1986; Lockwood 1988; Sherwin 2001; Smith 1991; Sneddon et al. 2014; Sømme 2005; Wigglesworth 1980). Presumably, Singer's precautionary principle (PP), as we might describe it, suggests that we should err on the side of not eating these creatures, as we cannot be confident that they are not sentient. This, however, may be *too* cautious a conclusion. After all, perhaps there is some doubt, albeit very small, about whether, say, plants are sentient. Similar arguments exist about inorganic beings (Oderberg 2008; Tomasik 2015a), even such as electrons (Tomasik 2015b). We do not need to delve deeply into the so-called "hard problem" of consciousness and come up with solid conclusions about what constitutes sentience in order for Singer's principle to be invoked, because Singer's principle is precisely one that operates in the absence of solid conclusions. In the presence of sufficient doubt about whether or not a being is sentient, he says, do not eat it.

It is worth noting that Singer himself probably does not espouse the version of the PP that I am considering here. Given his discussion of plant sentience in *Animal Liberation*, it seems that his view is that we can be sufficiently sure that plants are *not* sentient for eating them to be morally unproblematic. Nevertheless, the truly cautious eater may think that the PP requires us to forgo eating plants.

But forgoing eating plants seems like it may come at too great a cost. This echoes Holm and Harris's concern about the PP (Holm and Harris 1999). Their discussion is a criticism of the PP when invoked as a reason to restrict or limit the development of new technology, but the basic thrust of it applies here too. They worry that "the PP will block the development of any technology if there is the slightest theoretical possibility of harm," and they describe this as a "fatal weakness." Similarly, in the face of the slightest theoretical possibility of a creature's sentience, we must be cautious and not eat it. In this case it is not the development of technology that is blocked, but rather the legitimacy of eating *anything* nutritious enough to sustain our lives.

One could bite the bullet and say that humans should lay down their lives in order to avoid the risk of harming potentially sentient plants. This kind of conclusion will strike some as absurd, and possibly as sufficient evidence that there is something wrong with either the use of the PP under discussion here, or with my assessment of the possibility that plants might be sentient. However, even from a welfarist perspective, I do not think that advocating the removal of humanity from the global picture is a bullet that has to be bitten yet. This is because such a PP can be seen to be too cautious and too restrictive even without recourse to the extreme-sounding conclusions to which it apparently leads us. This is because it requires an overemphasis on the possibility of harm without due appreciation of the potential goods that can be gained from eating things.

We must therefore find a better way to negotiate these uncertainties. If we can negotiate uncertainty in a more balanced way, we can factor in the possibility of invertebrate or plant sentience without having a firm answer as to whether it exists, in a way that sufficiently accounts for other goods that we want to promote, like humans' enjoyment of continued existence/sentience.

Probabilistic moral reasoning may offer us this solution. Such reasoning makes invertebrate sentience a highly important consideration, on the basis that even if the probability that invertebrates are sentient is low, their large numbers render their potential suffering very weighty. I will explain what this kind of reasoning will look like when applied to invertebrate suffering, and I then outline some possible policy changes regarding insecticide use. These changes may go some way towards humans discharging their moral obligations towards invertebrates.

There are various ways to reason probabilistically about what we ought to do. For simplicity's sake, we will stick to what is possibly the most straightforward method of probabilistic reasoning in ethics: the "expected utility" formula. This formula combines the two basic ingredients of probabilistic moral reasoning: the probability of each possible outcome's occurring and the value of those outcomes.

A basic expected utility formula works by multiplying the value and probability of each possible outcome. Imagine you are on a game show, and you are offered a choice between two boxes. The host tells you that if you choose box A, you have a 50% chance of winning $100 (and a 50% chance of winning nothing). If you choose box B, you have a 90% chance of winning $50. Which would/should you choose? The expected utility of choosing box A is 0.5 x 100 = $50. The expected utility of choosing box B is 0.9 x 50 = $45. The best option is therefore box A, as it has the highest expected utility. This kind of reasoning is a fairly intuitive way of coming to conclusions about the value of different options, and ultimately reaching a conclusion about which action to take (in this case the best action is "choose box A!").

Pragmatically, using a formula like this may involve a pre-screening process in which obviously low-expected-utility outcomes are ignored. If there are several other boxes, each with a 1% chance of winning less than $10, I might not bother calculating all of those. However, if there is a box Z with a 1% chance of winning $100,000, this might be worth looking into. The expected utility of this is, after all, $1,000.

The value need not be monetary. I do not wish to enter into discussion here about how exactly value is to be conceived – it is sufficient for the argument that I am advancing here that sentience is valuable *to some extent* – that is to say that pleasurable experiences are good and worth pursuing (for oneself and for others), and unpleasant experiences are bad and worth avoiding/reducing. Other commonly posited valuable things, such as the satisfaction of desires, or simply the preservation of life, the planet, or nature, may yield slightly different answers to the specifics of how we should deal with invertebrate suffering. However, I think that most plausible value theories, except for (illegitimate and untenable) anthropocentric ones that exclude the welfare of nonhumans entirely, will yield the same broad, overall conclusion: there is a weighty moral imperative on humans to reduce (their contribution to)[3] invertebrate suffering.

Alongside other issues regarding value theory, it is also not as easy to establish the probability of invertebrate sentience as in the example above; we don't have a helpful game show host to tell us the exact probability of each outcome. Burning a handful of ants under a magnifying glass might cause x amount of suffering, or it might cause y amount of suffering – it is hard to know.

However, even if we think that the probability of invertebrates being able to suffer is quite low, the sheer number of invertebrates means that any amount of their suffering would be very weighty. Importantly, the number of invertebrates that exists might be irrelevant if we cannot do anything about most of them – the discovery of an invertebrate planet beyond our reach with lots of suffering creatures would have no bearing on our obligations to invertebrates here on Earth. However, invertebrate populations are relatively dense, with the effect that our actions will tend to affect invertebrates in far greater numbers than they will other kinds of animal. Numbers, therefore, dominate, making this like the example of box Z above, with its small chance of winning $100,000.

So now that I have argued that invertebrate suffering matters in expectation, let us consider which actions are available to us in terms of doing something about it. A lower-impact activity might be "pest" control in the home – some ways of removing invertebrates from your home may cause more suffering than others. A larger-scale issue, however, is the control of invertebrates in agriculture. Insecticides kill enormous numbers of invertebrates, but so far discussion on this tends to focus on the instrumental effects of killing invertebrates (bees are a popular and important example). Concern only for the instrumental effects is compatible with the anthropocentric view described above, but it is insufficient for us here – I want to consider the welfare, or at least the *possible* welfare, of the invertebrates themselves.

Lockwood (1988; 2014) lays out a rough schema for how different types of invertebrate control may cause different degrees of suffering. These range from measures that displace invertebrates without killing them ("cultural control") to those that kill invertebrates, the most painful being those that involve slow deaths, like the use of pathogens and parasites.[4]

Again, one is not required to commit to the idea that invertebrates can suffer – only that there is a sufficiently large possibility that their welfare weighs on our actions. This suggests that we should consider the welfare of potentially sentient invertebrates when considering policy regarding the use of insecticides.

It could be argued that the above reasoning applies to plants, bacteria, and even other inorganic things as well, such that the move from the PP to a more balanced probabilistic view that accounts for potential benefit as well as risk does not get us away from the possibly absurd conclusion that we should not eat plants. The chances of plants being sentient may be slim. Nevertheless, they are enormously numerous. As long as the chances of plants being sentient are not zero, we must weigh this into our probabilistic calculus. We therefore must take plants into consideration by virtue of the fact that their sheer numbers make their expected utility very weighty indeed.

I appreciate that this is a serious worry for probabilistic reasoning, and it may indeed lead to conclusions that make humans' continued existences hard to justify. Whether the counter-intuitiveness of these conclusions is sufficient to render the notion of probabilistic reasoning absurd, however, is another question. Nevertheless, there is a practical element to these questions that may provide us with useful guidance. It is perhaps easier to make gains by advocating sensitive pesticide use than by advocating human extinction. This at least drives a wedge between the plants question and the insects question when answering the pragmatic question "what should I eat?" – as answering "nothing" will serve to convince very few people. This will no doubt appear theoretically unsatisfactory to some, but the practical aspects of these questions are important if our aim is to consider how we should act, as was my starting point in this chapter.

Conclusion

In this chapter I have surveyed the issue of which creatures are morally considerable and landed on sentience as a criterion for moral considerability, in the footsteps of Bentham and Singer. I then outlined some of the difficulties there are in establishing which creatures actually possess this sentience. I considered some ways of approaching this uncertainty and of factoring potential sentience into decision-making with regard to eating and farming, using the case of invertebrates and pesticides as an example. This example leads us into potentially dangerous territory when the argumentation is taken to its logical extent, however, given the parallel example of plant sentience. I leave it up to the reader to negotiate this conundrum and decide whether we must reach some probabilistic conclusions about plant sentience, or whether there is some flaw in the methodology of using probabilities in this way to reach conclusions about how to act.

I have described how considering the welfare of only those who are to be eaten can yield vastly different conclusions from considering the welfare of other creatures on top of this. This suggests that policies that focus only on the welfare of the animals that are directly being farmed are potentially as dangerously myopic as policies that ignore the welfare of creatures based on species membership.

The purpose of this chapter has not been to provide solid answers to these questions, but rather to illuminate some of the serious difficulties that are present in considering these issues. The simple-looking questions of what to eat and how to get it have complicated ramifications that can take us through philosophical problems of value theory, consciousness and sentience, decision theory and probability, and environmental ethics.

Acknowledgements

Thanks to Brian Tomasik for inspiring this chapter, and for a great deal of interesting and instrumental discussion, insight, and assistance. Thanks also to Josh Milburn and Simon Knutsson for their helpful comments.

Notes

1 See the interview transcript at Gary Francione's "Abolitionist Approach," available at: website: http://www.abolitionistapproach.com/media/pdf/jan-narveson-20090327.pdf (Accessed 17 Jul 2015).
2 See the Global Humanitarian Forum's "Human Impact Report: Climate Change," available at: http://www.ghf-ge.org/human-impact-report.pdf (Accessed 17 Jul 2015); and the World Health Organization's "Climate Change and Health" fact sheet, available at: http://www.who.int/mediacentre/factsheets/fs266/en/ (Accessed 17 Jul 2015).
3 I think that the obligation would exist even in a world where humans were responsible for *none* of this suffering themselves. I will restrict this discussion, however, to negative responsibilities arising from the suffering that is caused to invertebrates by human activity.
4 It might also be worth noting that insecticides may be a net good – it is possible that insect lives contain more suffering on balance than they do pleasure, such that killing them may be of benefit. This is a controversial idea that may lead to some counter-intuitive conclusions in other areas. See Horta (2010) for further discussion.

References

Archer, M. (2011) "Ordering the Vegetarian Meal? There's More Animal Blood on Your Hands," *The Conversation*, viewed 17 July 2015, https://theconversation.com/ordering-the-vegetarian-meal-theres-more-animal-blood-on-your-hands-4659.
Bentham, J. (2007) *An Introduction to the Principles of Morals and Legislation*, New York: Dover.
Broome, J. (2004) *Weighing Lives*, Oxford: Oxford University Press.
Davies, L.J. (2014) "Should Vegetarians Consider Eating Insects?," *Practical Ethics*, University of Oxford, viewed 20 July 2015, http://blog.practicalethics.ox.ac.uk/2014/06/should-vegetarians-consider-eating-insects/.
Dunayer, J. (2004) *Speciesism*, Derwood: Rice Publishing.
Eisemann, C. H., Jorgensen, W. K., Merritt, D. J., Rice, M. J., Cribb, B. W., Webb, P. D., and Zalucki, M. P. (1984) "Do Insects Feel Pain – a Biological View," *Experientia* 40(2): 164–7.
Elwood, R. W. (2011) "Pain and Suffering in Invertebrates?," *ILAR Journal* 52(2): 175–84.
Fiorito, G. (1986) "Is There "Pain" in Invertebrates?," *Behavioural Processes* 12(4): 383–8.
Harrison, P. (1992) "Descartes on Animals," *The Philosophical Quarterly* 42(167): 219–227.
Holm, S. and Harris, J. (1999) "Precautionary Principle Stifles Discovery," *Nature* 400: 398.
Horta, O. (2010) "Debunking the Idyllic View of Natural Processes: Population Dynamics and Suffering in the Wild," *Télos* 17: 73–88.
Kant, I. (1989) "Duties in Regard to Animals," in T. Regan and P. Singer (eds.), *Animal Rights and Human Obligations* (2nd ed.), Englewood Cliffs, N.J.: Prentice Hall, pp. 23–24.
Lockwood, J. (1988) "Not to Harm a Fly: Our Ethical Obligations to Insects," *Between the Species* 4: 3.
———. (2014) cited in Tomasik, B. "Humane Insecticides," viewed 19 August 2015, http://www.utilitarian-essays.com/humane-insecticides.html#relative-painfulness.
Marquis, D. (2014) "An Argument that Abortion is Wrong," in H. LaFollette (ed.), *Ethics in Practice* (4th ed.), Chichester, West Sussex: Wiley, pp. 137–47.
Matheny, G. and Chan, K. (2005) "Human Diets and Animal Welfare: The Illogic of the Larder," *Journal of Agricultural and Environmental Ethics* 18: 579–94.
Mulgan, T. (2006) *Future People*, Oxford: Oxford University Press.
Oderberg, D. (2008) "Teleology: Inorganic and Organic," in A. M. González (ed.), *Contemporary Perspectives on Natural Law*, Aldershot: Ashgate, pp. 259–80.
Parfit, D. (1984) *Reasons and Persons*, Oxford: Oxford University Press.
Regan, T. and Singer, P. (eds.) (1989) *Animal Rights and Human Obligations* (2nd ed.), Englewood Cliffs, N.J.: Prentice Hall.

Rolston, H. (2002) "Why Species Matter," in C. Pierce and D. VanDeVeer (eds.), *The Environmental Ethics and Policy Book* (3rd ed.), Belmont: Thomson/Wadsworth, pp. 476–83.

Sagoff, M. (1984) "Animal Liberation and Environmental Ethics: Bad Marriage, Quick Divorce," *Osgoode Hall Law Journal* 22(2): 297–307.

Shantz, J. (2005) "One Person's Garbage . . . Another Person's Treasure: Dumpster Diving, Freeganism, and Anarchy," *VERB* 3(1): 9–19.

Sherwin, C. M. (2001) "Can Invertebrates Suffer? Or, How Robust Is Argument-by-Analogy?," *Animal Welfare* 10: 103–18.

Singer, P. (1995) *Animal Liberation* (2nd ed.), London: Pimlico.

Smith, J. A. (1991) "A Question of Pain in Invertebrates," *ILAR Journal* 33(1–2): 25–31.

Sneddon, L. U., Elwood, R. W., Adamo, S. A., and Leach, M. C. (2014) "Defining and Assessing Animal Pain," *Animal Behaviour* 97: 201–12.

Sømme, L. (2005) "Sentience and Pain in Invertebrates: Report to Norwegian Scientific Committee for Food Safety," *Norwegian University of Life Sciences*, viewed 20 July 2015, http://www.vkm.no/dav/413af9502e. pdf.

Tomasik, B. (2015a) "Which Computations Do I Care About?," viewed 17 July 2015, http://reducing-suffering.org/which-computations-do-i-care-about/.

——. (2015b) "Is There Suffering in Fundamental Physics?," viewed 17 July 2015, http://reducing-suffering. org/is-there-suffering-in-fundamental-physics/.

Wigglesworth, V. B. (1980) "Do Insects Feel Pain?," *Antenna* 4: 8–9.

Yule, G. (2014) *The Study of Language* (5th ed.), Cambridge: Cambridge University Press.

27

ANIMAL RIGHTS AND FOOD

Beyond Regan, beyond vegan

Josh Milburn

Ethical questions about the status of nonhuman animals (NHAs) entered mainstream philosophical dialogue in the latter half of the 20th century with the publication of works such as the edited collection *Animals, Men, and Morals* (1972) and especially Peter Singer's *Animal Liberation* (1975). Animal rights (AR) philosophy, though there were earlier proponents, gained prominence after the publication of Tom Regan's *The Case for Animal Rights* in 1983. This work offered a deontological alternative to Singer's utilitarian account of the moral status of NHAs, and, excluding *Animal Liberation*, is probably the most important 20th-century work of animal ethics. As it is through food (including meat, eggs, and milk) that many people primarily "interact" with NHAs, animal ethics has long engaged with issues related to food, especially food ethics and food policy. Today, if we accept AR, it should be uncontroversial to say that we have a duty to adopt a vegan diet. However, it is my contention that this is not, or should not be, *all* that an AR approach to food will say. As the philosophy of food becomes more developed, so must AR approaches to food.

In the first part of this chapter, I will indicate that AR philosophy has moved "beyond Regan," in that a prominent strand of AR theory now addresses AR-related questions from a recognizably *political* standpoint. Specifically, I argue that there has been a *political turn* in AR philosophy, and that this is a positive development. In the second part of the chapter, I will show that this political turn allows us to move "beyond vegan" when we talk of the intersection of food ethics (and, more broadly, the philosophy of food) and AR. By this, I do not mean that AR philosophers should stop endorsing veganism – far from it. I mean that we can begin to conceptualize an *animal rights philosophy of food*. AR perspectives, especially AR perspectives after the political turn, can offer much more to food issues than merely a demand for veganism. In the third part of the chapter, I will demonstrate that a suitably subtle AR account may actually allow for certain non-vegan food practices to continue, but that, contrary to what might be expected, this should offer little consolation for those who continue to consume NHA-derived foodstuffs today. Political approaches to AR may offer us a way to conceptualize strong and genuine rights for NHAs while, in theory, allowing certain non-vegan foods. This demonstrates a second way that AR theory can go "beyond vegan," and one that is of paramount interest for the burgeoning field of food ethics.

Beyond Regan

In his 1983 *The Case for Animals Rights* (hereafter, *The Case*), Tom Regan advances a theory of rights grounded in the notion of inherent value. All subjects-of-a-life (including, though not limited to, mammals of a year old or more) have *inherent value*, this inherent value is *equal*, and this inherent value grounds *rights* not to be treated in certain ways. Regan argues that though NHA subjects-of-a-life are not moral agents, they are nonetheless *moral patients*, and there is no non-arbitrary way to ground the rights of moral agents which would not also ground the rights of moral patients; accordingly, the rights of moral agents and moral patients are equally strong. It is important to remember that though *The Case* was written, and read, as a treatise of moral philosophy – some of its finest contributions come in the form of its critique of Singer's moral vision – it is also a work of *political* philosophy. It is difficult to avoid political philosophy when discussing rights or justice, and *The Case* is replete with references to both. As such, it would be unfair to dismiss Regan as a "merely" moral thinker, and it is likely, especially within the context of the political turn in animal ethics, that Regan will more and more be read as a political thinker. Nonetheless, Regan was and is thought of as a moral thinker first, and his work is the epitome of AR philosophy in the 20th century. The "Regan" which we must move beyond is the 20th-century tendency to consider AR, and animal ethics more broadly, a solely *moral* issue, and not Regan's work in particular.

We must move beyond this – and by "moving beyond," I mean supplementing, and neither ignoring nor dismissing – for at least three reasons. First, there is dissatisfaction with the failure of moral thinking to push change sufficiently strongly. Forty years on from *Animal Liberation*, and over 30 on from *The Case*, over 50 billion "land animals" are slaughtered for consumption worldwide per year. This number does not include fish and other NHAs who live in water, and it does not include those NHAs killed *in pursuit* of foodstuffs, such as male chicks from hatcheries killed within hours of birth. Further, though numbers are growing, vegetarians, and especially vegans, represent only a small percentage of the population. Second, there is recognition that there are certain problems that cannot be fixed by individual choice. Take, as a simple example, tax-funded subsidies given to so-called "pastoral farmers." A rise in the number of vegans would not necessarily have any particular impact on such subsidies, which would require political change. Indeed, if a government aims to keep their farmers afloat, it is conceivable that a rise in vegan-ism could result in *greater* subsidies. Third, we must recognize that our obligations to NHAs are not "merely" a moral matter. Liberals recognize the importance of tolerance and pluralism – and thus permitting people to live in accordance with their own moral ideas – but our obligations to NHAs, argue political AR theorists, are not a part of this. Just as we condemn those who eschew their obligations towards children, so we must condemn those who fail to treat NHAs with the respect they warrant.

We might disagree about which texts do or do not belong as a part of this political turn, or about which characteristics best differentiate those thinkers in the turn from those who are not. One way of thinking about the turn is simply that it consists in a shift of *focus*; while animal ethics has always been political, the turn is characterized by a move *away* from questions about individual behavior and moral status, and *towards* questions about the *inclusion* of NHAs in politi-cal structures and *top-down changes* – legal, institutional, educational, and so on (cf. Milligan 2015; Wissenburg and Schlosberg 2014). The majority of work on political theory and NHAs, as is typical with contemporary political theory, has taken place within a liberal paradigm, whether this is relatively "pure" liberalism (Cochrane 2012; Garner 2013), group-differentiated, relational liberalism (Donaldson and Kymlicka 2013; Valentini 2014), perfectionist liberalism (Nussbaum

2006), cosmopolitan liberalism (Cochrane 2013; Cooke 2014), or even, though these discussions are more skeptical, contractarian/contractualist liberalism (Rowlands 2009; Smith 2012; cf. Garner 2012a; Garner 2012b). Though this chapter takes a more-or-less liberal perspective, it is worth noting that liberal approaches do not have a complete monopoly over the literature (cf. Cochrane 2010). For example, there have also been anarcho-Marxist analyses of the use of NHAs (Torres 2007) and progressive uses of right libertarian concepts for thinking about animal ethics (Ebert and Machan 2012; Milburn 2014).

Ultimately, though the political turn has probably only been occurring for around a decade, there are an array of approaches utilized, and a multitude of debates between authors within it. In this sense, the political turn should not be viewed as a unified tradition. Instead, the political turn should be viewed by animal ethicists as a particular way of doing animal ethics, alongside, for example, *legal* approaches, *moral* approaches, and *theological* approaches, but one that is sorely needed. Equally, it should be viewed by political theorists as a particular way of doing political theory, alongside the likes of *feminist* political theory. Though these approaches to political theory start with a particular issue, it would be a disservice to thinkers within them to claim that such thought *ends with* claims about said issue. So it must be with AR and food; while AR approaches to food will begin with the relatively simple claim that we must adopt veganism, they cannot simply stop there.

Beyond vegan

Having indicated that a political turn in animal ethics has taken place, I will now outline three ways in which an AR approach to food and food policy, especially a *political* AR approach to food, must move "beyond vegan." By this, I mean three ways in which *merely* stating that veganism is a moral imperative or demand of justice does not reflect all that AR approaches to food can, and must, say. First, the political face of AR is particularly well-situated to talk about the inclusion of NHAs within systems of distribution. This is something that has been marginalized in traditional AR philosophy. Second, we have to ask about the extent to which our food-related practices *indirectly* impact upon NHAs; though this debate has been had within traditional animal ethics, a move to political theory gives us tools to demand the kinds of changes that this line of thought may entail. Third, we must ask what AR approaches might say about, or could offer to, existing discussions in the normative food literature. It is in this final question that an AR philosophy *of* food is most sharply distinguished from merely AR philosophy *about* food.

The first way we can move "beyond vegan" is to think about the distribution of food to NHAs. If NHAs are to be recognized as co-citizens, or at least as members of a political community, then it is natural that they be included in questions about the distribution of food. Sue Donaldson and Will Kymlicka develop an account of political rights for NHAs by conceptualizing NHAs variously as *citizens* of a mixed human/NHA community, *denizens* of a mixed community, or *sovereign* over their own communities. The authors claim unambiguously that "[r]ecognizing domesticated animals as members of the community includes accepting their equal right to communal resources and the social bases of well-being" (2013: 142), which would include food distribution. It would be difficult to challenge this conclusion on the grounds that NHA members of a mixed community have less interest in access to distributive institutions than humans, as it is far from obvious that they do. Given the relative vulnerability of NHAs to the whims of their guardians, we might draw a parallel with children; while guardians have primary responsibility for ensuring the appropriate feeding of a given individual, the state has the responsibility to ensure that the guardian is satisfactorily carrying out their duty, and to provide an alternative should the guardian fail. One need not accept the somewhat-statist paradigm in which Donaldson and Kymlicka operate to recognize these kinds of obligations. Alasdair Cochrane, who takes a more cosmopolitan approach, accuses the pair of unjustifiably privileging the rights of "domestic" NHAs (2013), and a number of authors already stress the duty humans have to assist free-living NHAs in need (e.g., Hadley 2006; Horta 2013). In certain environments or on certain occasions, it may be that the most valuable assistance that humans can offer free-living NHAs is the provision of food, similar to how it is already recognized by a wide variety of normative thinkers that we have an obligation to help starving humans, even if they live on the other side of the world. Of course, it may be that a particular AR approach does not support the provision of food aid to some or all NHAs. The *laissez faire* intuition – the idea that we have a duty not to (or at least no duty to) intervene in nature – may continue to be defended by political AR thinkers (cf. Palmer 2010). Alternatively, a focus upon non-ideal theory might stress that the priority should be in ensuring that NHAs' negative, rather than positive, rights be respected. The point is not so much that an AR approach to food necessarily *endorses* the provision of food aid to NHAs, but that this is the kind of question that should be given thought.

The second way we can move "beyond vegan" is to think about the *indirect* effects of our food practices on NHAs. If all humans were to adopt vegan diets tomorrow, this would hugely limit, though not eliminate, NHA suffering caused by our food-related practices. In order to *eliminate* this suffering, we would also have to ask about the indirect impact of the practices. While vegan diets are certainly far less environmentally damaging than typical high- or even low-meat diets, a debate about NHA deaths in the harvesting process has arisen in the academic and popular literature (cf. Davis 2003; Lamey 2007). While this is by no means a vindication of current meat-eating practices or much of a challenge to veganism, it does raise questions for AR thinkers wishing to examine human diets. Given our causal (and moral?) responsibility for these deaths, it is arguably a more pressing concern than other suffering of free-living NHAs. While acknowledgement of this problem is relatively easy, offering practical solutions is somewhat harder. It seems likely, however, that this would require top-down change, such as legislation on appropriate food-production methods to limit (or, preferably, *eliminate*) accidental negative impact on free-living NHAs; it is hard to imagine the individual moral choices of consumers or farmers being able to resolve the problem, even if we *could* imagine individual moral choices leading to widespread veganism. As such, this is a good example of the kind of food policy issue with which AR theorists should be concerned above and beyond mere veganism, and, indeed, may be a food policy concern that non-AR food theorists have overlooked. Furthermore, it is a good example of the kind of problem with which political approaches to AR are better equipped to deal than the traditional moral approaches to AR.

The third way we can move "beyond vegan" is to ask what an AR approach to food can say about non-AR issues. If there is to be an AR approach to food, we must also ask what this perspective can offer to, or say about, existing issues in the literature on the philosophy of food, even (or especially) those not obviously related to AR issues. For instance, questions about the metaphysics of food should not be considered independently of the AR approach, or, minimally, the AR approach has something to offer to these debates. David Kaplan (2012: 3–4) offers a non-exhaustive list of seven metaphysics of food: food as *nutrition*; food as *nature*; food as *culture*; food as *social good*; food as *spirituality*; food as *desideratum*; and food as *aesthetic object*. Each of these approaches could be seen to have advantages and disadvantages from the perspective of an AR approach to food. For example, a focus on food as a cultural practice may serve to obscure or downplay issues of justice related to food choices, and thus risk legitimizing (or at least failing to challenge) unjust food practices. In this sense, *food as culture* might be considered a dangerous metaphysic for AR approaches to food. On the other hand, framing food in cultural terms stresses that there is nothing necessary about current food practices – inherent to the idea of culture is *difference* and *change*. As AR approaches to food will challenge many existing food systems, an acceptance that there is nothing necessary about current practices and an acknowledgement that these practices can change is necessary. This example should show that AR approaches to food and the metaphysics of food should not be considered independently, and I hope more work in this area will be forthcoming. If AR is to be a philosophy *of* food, rather than just philosophy *about* food, these are the kinds of questions that proponents must examine.

A final point to consider is that an AR approach to food must nonetheless be required to accommodate issues not directly related to the rights of NHAs; it cannot, to put it another way, exist in a vacuum. This is particularly true of the potential human consequences of realizing an AR vision of food production. Allow me to offer three examples. First, there are potential public health consequences. Certain major health problems – such as cardiovascular disease, obesity, high blood pressure, some cancers, and diabetes – are much less associated with veganism than with "normal" diets, but some nutrients, including vitamin D and vitamin B12, can be lacking in badly planned vegan diets (Craig 2009; Craig and Mangels 2009). The extent to which these kinds of deficiencies could be a problem, as well as possible solutions, should be explored by bioethicists and other health experts. Second, there are economic questions worth considering. The end of animal agriculture would result in an economic shift, potentially leaving large numbers of people out of work. The likelihood of and solutions to this issue need to be explored by political theorists and economists. Third, the environmental impact of adopting an AR approach to food policy could be very large. The environmental merits of veganism are well known (Scarborough et al. 2014; Singer and Mason 2006: 231–240), and include concerns about land use, water use, local-ized pollution, and greenhouse gas emissions. That said, a shift from pastoral to arable farming, as well as the end of hunting and fishing, would have a dramatic effect on landscapes and ecosystems, and perhaps even the biosphere. Consideration of the extent to which this would or could be a positive (or, at least, unproblematic) change would be valuable.

Animal rights without veganism?

I have illustrated how an AR approach to food could and should extend beyond mere veganism, especially when one considers AR from a political perspective. However, I now wish to suggest that veganism, as normally understood, may not be the only option for an AR-respecting diet and thus illustrate a particularly surprising way that AR philosophy can step "beyond vegan." First, however, it is worth saying that Gary Francione (2012) is right, given currently existing food structures, in saying that veganism must be endorsed as a moral baseline. AR without veganism, like human rights without the abolition of slavery, is not worthy of the name. Even if one favors (say) Cochrane's interest-based rights approach (2012) over Francione's abolitionist approach (2010), one must still recognize that the real-world practices of farming, hunting, fishing, or "harvesting" NHAs for flesh, eggs, or milk involve the infliction of horrific suffering (including physical pain and mental anguish) and death, and so must recognize that respecting NHAs' rights requires abstention – economically, politically, socially – from support of these industries. Given the horrific suffering and early, gruesome deaths inflicted upon NHAs as a matter of course in the pursuit of NHA-derived foods, anyone who holds that sensitive NHAs have a right not to have suffering or death inflicted upon them (that is, anyone who endorses AR) displays a baffling dissonance between their professed beliefs and their actions if they do not practice and endorse dietary veganism.

Despite this, questions may be raised about NHA-derived foods concerning certain unusual cases or plausible practices, and, if AR theory is going to engage with food theory, these issues are central. This is because if food theorists who do not endorse an AR framework are going to challenge veganism in AR theory, it is on these kinds of grounds that they are most likely to succeed. To that end, I now offer six kinds of issues that could challenge the claim that the abstention from all food products derived from NHAs is *necessary* given an AR approach to food. I do not claim that this list is exhaustive, and constraints of space mean that the issues these questions involve can only be sketched. Nonetheless, I hope that the topic can be explored more fully in the coming years.

1) *Non-sentient animals.* AR theorists, to borrow a phrase from Francione (2008: 129–147), now "take sentience seriously," meaning that sentience (the capacity for pleasure and pain) is seen as a *sufficient* condition for the attribution of rights. If it is also a *necessary* condition, then it follows that any non-sentient animal (NSA) could be utilized for food purposes. For example, imagine we could say *with certainty* that oysters were NSAs. This would mean that we would do no wrong to an oyster in eating "it." AR advocates, though, may nonetheless seek to restrict the exploitation of NSAs; perhaps there is some reason to endorse a moral line between animals and non-animals – a kind of thought more commonly used *against* AR thinkers. Contrarily, it may be plausible to say that AR advocates not only *may* eat NSAs, but *should*. Chris Meyers (2013) argues that, given insect non-sentience and given the environmental impact of certain forms of arable agriculture, vegans may have an obligation to adopt entomophagy. Though Meyers's premises are questionable (insect non-sentience is not as clear-cut as he argues, and a greater defense is needed of entomophagy's environmental merits), this kind of thought does warrant attention from AR theorists. AR approaches to food, then, may well be non-vegan insofar as they could permit (or endorse) the consumption of NSAs.

2) *Plausibly-sentient animals.* Between the NSAs and obviously-sentient NHAs are plausibly-sentient animals (PSAs). The most obvious way to address this question is with a kind of precautionary principle: as we do not know for sure whether these animals are sentient, and thus whether they have rights, it is better to treat them as if they are, and so do. This means that we should not eat them. However, I have elsewhere (Milburn 2015) argued that simply endorsing a principle prohibiting the killing of PSAs might be to oversimplify. Instead, I argued that we might plausibly endorse the killing of PSAs for food *if sufficiently important ends* were furthered. Specifically, I argued that mere gustatory pleasure could not justify the killing of PSAs, but feeding carnivorous members of a mixed human/NHA society might. A similar line of argument *might* be applicable in other cases. Say a whole cultural identity revolved around flesh-eating. While an AR position could never endorse allowing members of that culture to continue to kill (say) cattle, chickens, or fish, *perhaps* it could allow that members of these cultures could continue to eat PSAs. This is worth exploring, and is a possible way that AR theory might accommodate claims about the *value* of particular food practices (cf. Barnhill et al. 2014; Lomasky 2013) without compromising its central principles.

3) *Technological solutions.* One key issue at the intersection of food ethics/policy and AR philosophy is the possibility of technological solutions to "animal agriculture." *In vitro* flesh has been shown to be technologically (if not yet economically) viable, and so offers us a vision of a non-vegan food that nonetheless respects the rights of NHAs. Milk produced without cows (Pandya 2014), too, is on the scientific horizon. A number of ethical challenges to lab-grown flesh from outside of AR philosophy are conceivable but unconvincing (for reviews and responses, see Hopkins and Dacey 2008; Schaefer and Savulescu 2014), but questions may be raised from *within* AR philosophy. These include, but are likely not limited to, the extent to which NHAs would have to remain a part of the "food industry" (for the harvesting of genetic material) and their treatment, as well as questions of respect. This latter point is raised by Donaldson and Kymlicka; perhaps producing NHA, but not human, flesh in this way would reaffirm false ideas about

human superiority, by extending to humans a respect that we do not extend to NHAs (2013: 152). Similar concerns could be raised about other technological sources of meat. It is conceivable that we could genetically engineer some NHAs to be non-sentient (Shriver 2009), but the genetic engineering of NHAs raises a host of other ethical problems (cf. Cochrane 2012: ch. 5), which require consideration by AR theorists. Though they require further scrutiny, the various plausible technological solutions give hope for a non-vegan AR approach to food policy.

4) *Scavenging.* The question of to what extent it may be ethically permissible to eat "scavenged" flesh is a point of contention within vegan discourse. "Freeganism," at least partially, grew out of veganism, and is mostly associated with "dumpster-diving," or living off food (including NHA-derived products) taken from supermarket bins (Singer and Mason 2006: 267–268). Even if supermarkets stopped selling NHA-derived foodstuffs, freegans might still eat scavenged flesh, such as "roadkill." Leaving aside that we have an obligation to start designing our roadways to minimize NHA deaths (Donaldson and Kymlicka 2013: 201), it remains an open question whether AR philosophy might permit the scavenging of corpses.

5) *Genuinely ethical "farming."* Donaldson and Kymlicka (2013: 138) sketch a picture of genuinely ethical egg production. Chicken citizens could be left to incubate some eggs, but some excess eggs could be taken for human consumption. The process could not be commercialized (as this would exacerbate the chance of abuse) and the abusive practices standard in egg production (forced starvation, chick-culling, beak-trimming, slaughter, etc.) would not be permitted. Though rights-respecting dairy production seems somewhat more difficult, Cochrane offers the idea of farming NHAs for their corpses, indicating that a meat industry without slaughterhouses is possible (2012: 87); the extent to which such an industry could be consistent with AR positions is worth exploration. Francione objects to these kinds of ideas in principle, as, for him, recognition of AR requires the rejection of all *use* of NHAs (Francione 2008: 1–66; Francione 2010). There have been a variety of challenges to Francione's position, but perhaps most interesting is the claim that his approach has unacceptable consequences concerning the treatment of the disabled. Katherine Wayne (2013), who endorses a conception of AR similar to Donaldson and Kymlicka's, argues that the relationship between some disabled humans and caregivers is similar to a conceivable relationship between dependent NHAs and human caregivers. Wayne shows that certain modes of interaction between disabled humans and their guardians that are consistent with full respect of the former party's rights involve the "use" of the dependent party by the caregiver. As such, unless Francione wishes to make some deeply questionable claims about the relationships people might have with certain disabled humans, he would have to concede that there are some ways in which NHAs can be "used" that are consistent with full respect. It should be made clear, though, that these debates are theoretical, and do not absolve the meat, dairy, and egg industries of wrongdoing. "Happy" meat and "free-range" eggs are produced using processes inimical to the goals of AR. To repeat: *even if* an AR-consistent farm can be imagined in theory, abstention from NHA-derived foodstuffs would remain an obligation today for those who endorse AR.

6) *Subsistence hunting.* AR approaches to food can expect criticism due to what may be perceived as support for an imperialistic imposition of a particular (Western?) norm of justice on those who do not recognize that norm. Specifically, AR approaches demand that the food practices of almost all cultures, including the most oppressed cultures, change drastically. AR theorists should not and do not try to hide this aspect of their thought. Very few people hold that the most fundamental rights of humans can be ignored in the name of cultural autonomy or tradition, and, equally, we should not hold that the most fundamental rights of NHAs can be. Cultures change and adapt, and part of this evolution involves the acceptance of moral truths that were unthinkable, unclear, or neglected before. If some hypothetical culture is so

connected to the killing of NHAs that acceptance of AR amounts to the end of the culture in a recognizable form, then, while this may be regrettable, one has to ask how valuable that culture was to start with (Cochrane 2012: 192; Horta 2013: 377). A more difficult question arises in the case of subsistence hunting. AR theorists generally do not say that engaging in subsistence hunting is wrong (e.g., Cochrane 2012: 191; Donaldson and Kymlicka 2013: 41; Linzey 2009: 134). Alternatively, it is conceivable that, *if* subsistence hunting is wrong, it is an *excusable* wrong. Similarly, it may be the case that AR theory is open to humans eating NHAs in the ubiquitous desert island scenario; this does not tell us much of interest, as we might equally be open to the killing and eating of *humans* in these cases (Charlton and Francione 2013: 50–54; Francione 2007: ch. 7). Importantly, though, AR approaches to food should not simply accept subsistence hunting as unproblematic. We can ask to what extent particular practices are *genuinely* instances of subsistence hunting – Andrew Linzey, for example, refutes the claim that Canadian coastal communities rely on seal hunting (2009: 134–136) – and ask what can be done to bring genuine subsistence hunters out of their current situation.

The above list is indicative of how AR approaches may move beyond veganism. Here, and contrary to my prior use, I mean that as we explore the issues at the intersection of AR – especially political conceptions of AR – and food theory, we see that there are ways in which dietary veganism, understood simply as abstention from all NHA-derived food products, may *theoretically* be unnecessary.

Conclusion

Animal ethics has recently seen a political turn – a shift away from the traditional moral focus and towards political theory. In this sense, animal ethics has moved "beyond Regan." Animal rights philosophy, whether in its traditional *moral* or newer *political* form, has always had much to say about food, especially with regard to food ethics and food policy. However, and especially with the emergence of much normative work on food, it must be realized that there is more to AR and food than simply an endorsement of veganism, and the time is now ripe for a distinctive animal-rights philosophy *of* food. This perspective will move beyond veganism in a number of ways. Importantly, it will recognize that our food-related obligations to NHAs extend beyond merely not eating them, and it will address issues that are not obviously related to NHAs. Perhaps most interestingly of all, an AR approach to food will address the question of whether NHA-derived foods might be acquired in a just way at some point in the future. While further research on this issue is required, this is precisely what an AR approach to food will be best situated to offer. Despite this, whatever promise developments in AR theory hold, and even if an AR approach to food must move beyond this claim, the central demand remains constant. We must go vegan, and we must encourage those around us to do the same. To do anything less is to fail to respect the rights of nonhuman animals.

Acknowledgements

I would like to thank David Archard, Jeremy Watkins, Matteo Bonotti, and Simon Jenkins for reading drafts of this chapter. I would also like to thank Matteo Bonotti and Emanuela Ceva for including an animal ethics panel in their section on food and political theory at the ECPR Annual Conference, University of Glasgow, 2014, and Mary Rawlinson for inviting me to contribute this chapter. Finally, I would like to thank my supervisors, David Archard and Jeremy Watkins, and funder, the Department for Employment and Learning, Northern Ireland, for their support of my PhD research.

References

Barnhill, A., King, K. F., Kass, N., Faden, R. (2014) "The Value of Unhealthy Eating and the Ethics of Healthy Eating Policies," *Kennedy Institute of Ethics Journal* 24(3): 187–217.

Charlton, A., Francione, G. L. (2013) *Eat Like You Care*, Logan, UT: Exemplar Press.

Cochrane, A. (2010) *An Introduction to Animals and Political Theory*, Basingstoke, United Kingdom: Palgrave Macmillan.

——. (2012) *Animal Rights Without Liberation*, New York: Columbia University Press.

——. (2013) "Cosmozoopolis: The Case Against Group-Differentiated Animal Rights," *Law, Ethics and Philosophy* 1(1): 127–41.

Cooke, S. (2014) "Perpetual Strangers: Animals and the Cosmopolitan Right," *Political Studies* 62(4): 930–44.

Craig, W. J. (2009) "Health Effects of Vegan Diets," *The American Journal of Clinical Nutrition* 89(5): 1627S–33S.

Craig, W. J., Mangels, A. R. (2009) "Position of the American Dietetic Association: Vegetarian Diets," *Journal of the American Dietetic Association* 109(7): 1266–82.

Davis, S. L. (2003) "The Least Harm Principle May Require that Humans Consume a Diet Containing Large Herbivores, Not a Vegan Diet," *Journal of Agricultural and Environmental Ethics* 16(4): 387–94.

Donaldson, S., Kymlicka, W. (2013) *Zoopolis*, Oxford: Oxford University Press.

Ebert, R., Machan, T. R. (2012) "Innocent Threats and the Moral Problem of Carnivorous Animals," *Journal of Applied Philosophy* 29(2): 146–59.

Francione, G. L. (2007) *Introduction to Animal Rights*, Philadelphia, PA: Temple University Press.

——. (2008) *Animals as Persons*, New York: Columbia University Press.

——. (2010) "The Abolition of Animal Exploitation," in G. L. Francione and R. Garner, *The Animal Rights Debate*, New York: Columbia University Press, pp. 1–102.

——. (2012) "Animal Welfare, Happy Meat, and Veganism as the Moral Baseline," in D. M. Kaplan (ed.), *The Philosophy of Food*, Berkeley, CA: University of California Press, pp. 169–89.

Garner, R. (2012a) "Much Ado about Nothing?: Barry, Justice and Animals," *Critical Review of International Social and Political Philosophy* 15(3): 363–76.

——. (2012b) "Rawls, Animals and Justice: New Literature, Same Response," *Res Publica* 18(2): 159–72.

——. (2013) *A Theory of Justice for Animals*, Oxford: Oxford University Press.

Godlovitch, S., Godlovitch, R., Harris, J. (eds.) (1972) *Animals, Men, and Morals*, New York: Grove Press.

Hadley, J. (2006) "The Duty to Aid Nonhuman Animals in Dire Need," *Journal of Applied Philosophy* 23(4): 445–51.

Hopkins, P. D., Dacey, A. (2008) "Vegetarian Meat: Could Technology Save Animals and Satisfy Meat Eaters?" *Journal of Agricultural and Environmental Ethics* 21(6): 579–96.

Horta, O. (2013) "Expanding Global Justice: The Case for the International Protection of Animals," *Global Policy* 4(4): 371–80.

Kaplan, D. M. (2012) "Introduction: The Philosophy of Food," in D. M. Kaplan (ed.), *The Philosophy of Food*, Berkeley, CA: University of California Press, pp. 1–23.

Lamey, A. (2007) "Food Fight! Davis Versus Regan on the Ethics of Eating Beef," *Journal of Social Philosophy* 38(2): 331–48.

Linzey, A. (2009) *Why Animal Suffering Matters*, Oxford: Oxford University Press.

Lomasky, L. (2013) "Is It Wrong to Eat Animals?" *Social Philosophy and Policy* 30(1/2): 177–200.

Meyers, C. D. (2013) "Why It Is Morally Good to Eat (Certain Kinds of) Meat: The Case for Entomophagy," *Southwest Philosophy Review* 29(1): 119–26.

Milburn, J. (2014 [OnlineFirst]) "The Demandingness of Nozick's 'Lockean' Proviso," *European Journal of Political Theory*: 1–17. doi:10.1177/1474885114562978.

——. (2015) "Not Only Humans Eat Meat: Companions, Sentience and Vegan Politics," *Journal of Social Philosophy* 46(4): 449–62.

Milligan, T. (2015) "The Political Turn in Animal Rights," *Politics and Animals*, 1(1): 6–15.

Nussbaum, M. (2006) *Frontiers of Justice*, Cambridge, MA: Harvard University Press.

Palmer, C. (2010) *Animal Ethics in Context*, New York: Columbia University Press.

Pandya, R. (2014) "Milk Without the Moo," *New Scientist* 222(2975): 28–9.

Rowlands, M. (2009) *Animal Rights*, Basingstoke, United Kingdom: Palgrave Macmillan.

Scarborough, P., Appleby, P. N., Mizdrak, A., Briggs, A.D. M., Travis, R. C., Bradbury, K. E., Key, T. J. (2014) "Dietary Greenhouse Gas Emissions of Meat-Eaters, Fish-Eaters, Vegetarians and Vegans in the UK," *Climatic Change* 125(2): 179–92.

Schaefer, G. O., Savulescu, J. (2014) "The Ethics of Producing *In Vitro* Meat," *Journal of Applied Philosophy* 31(2): 188–202.

Shriver, A. (2009) "Knocking Out Pain in Livestock: Can Technology Succeed Where Morality has Stalled?" *Neuroethics* 2(3): 115–24.

Singer, P. (1975) *Animal Liberation*, New York: Random House.

Singer, P., Mason, J. (2006) *The Way We Eat*, Emmaus, PA: Rodale.

Smith, K. K. (2012) *Governing Animals*, Oxford: Oxford University Press.

Torres, B. (2007) *Making a Killing*, Oakland, CA: AK Press.

Valentini, L. (2014) "Canine Justice: An Associative Account," *Political Studies* 62(1): 37–52.

Wayne, K. (2013) "Permissible Use and Interdependence: Against Principled Veganism," *Journal of Applied Philosophy* 30(2): 160–75.

Wissenburg, M., Schlosberg, D. (2014) "Introducing Animal Politics and Political Animals," in M. Wissenburg and D. Schlosberg (eds.), *Animal Politics and Political Animals*, Basingstoke, United Kingdom: Palgrave Macmillan, pp. 1–14.

28

VEGANISM WITHOUT ANIMAL RIGHTS[1]

Gary L. Francione and Anna Charlton

Animals: our conventional wisdom

With respect to our moral obligations to nonhuman animals, there are three groups of people in the world. First, there are those who think that animals have no moral value whatsoever and are just *things*.[2] This first group is itself further subdivided into two groups. The first subgroup includes people like René Descartes, who argues that animals are literally machines made by God (as distinguished from machines made by humans), and that animals only appear to have interests. According to the Cartesian view, nothing we do to and with animals is morally problematic (as long as the animal is not someone else's property) because, as an empirical matter, animals, like clocks or other mechanical devices, have no interests that we can adversely affect (Francione 2000: 104–106; Francione 2008: 3).

The second subgroup includes Thomas Aquinas, Immanuel Kant, John Locke, and others, who recognize that animals are not mere machines and do have interests but claim that we can ignore those interests and treat animals as if they were mere Cartesian things because of their spiritual or cognitive inferiority to humans (Francione 2000: 106–113; Francione 2008: 3–5). That is, this view accepts on some level that animals are *sentient*, or subjectively aware, and can suffer, but it argues that humans can ignore animal interests because: animals were not created in the image of God; they are not rational; they are not able to use symbolic communication; they are unable to think in terms of abstractions; they lack cognitive characteristics; or they suffer from some combination of these spiritual and cognitive "defects." These spiritual or cognitive defects, according to this view, mean that animals do not matter morally at all. Most of those in this second subgroup maintain that we have an obligation to not treat animals in ways that will result in mistreatment of other humans. However, that obligation is owed to other humans and not to animals, and it is an obligation that does not in any way significantly limit our use and treatment of animals. So whether one subscribes to the Cartesian or to the alternative version of this view, the result is the same: humans do not owe any moral obligations to animals. Animals don't matter morally; they are just things.

Second, there are those, like the authors, who claim that all sentient beings – and that means just about all animals we routinely eat and otherwise use – have equal moral value for the purpose of not being used exclusively as a resource. This does not mean that we must treat animals in exactly the same way that we treat humans. We are not, for instance, required to allow animals to vote. It does, however, mean that, just as we all reject human slavery, we must accord to non-humans the fundamental right not to be used as the property of humans. And that requires that we abolish all institutionalized animal exploitation, which rests on the notion that animals are property. This is what we characterize as the *animal rights* position (Francione 2000; 2008).

Third, there is everyone else. Those in this third group accept some version of the *animal welfare* view, which represents conventional wisdom concerning animals (Francione 2000: xxi–xxii). According to this conventional wisdom, animals are not things and they *do* matter morally, but they don't matter as much as humans. Conventional wisdom is in agreement with Aquinas, Kant, and Locke in that it maintains that animals are spiritually or cognitively inferior to humans. However, conventional wisdom rejects that this inferiority means that animals are things that do not matter morally. Rather, the conventional view reflects the views of Jeremy Bentham and other nineteenth-century thinkers who agree that animals are cognitively inferior because they cannot reason, use symbolic communication, or think in abstractions – but who also maintain that, as long as animals are sentient and can suffer, humans have a moral obligation that they owe directly to animals to give appropriate weight to animal interests in deciding whether to use and kill them (Francione 2000: 5–6; Francione 2008: 5–9). In situations in which human interests conflict with the interests of nonhumans, the latter lose because their lives have lesser moral value. Humans can use and kill animals when necessary but they have an obligation to not inflict unnecessary suffering on the animals they use.

We believe it fair to say that some version of the animal welfare view is the default position for most people. Indeed, we maintain that many of those who are usually thought to subscribe to an animal rights position really embrace an animal welfare position (Francione 1996; Francione 2008: 67–128; Francione and Garner 2010: 1–102). That is, they agree that animals have moral value, but less moral value than do humans, who may use and kill animals if they do so with "compassion." The primary difference between many animal advocates and everyone else is that the former think that more needs to be done to satisfy the unnecessary suffering standard. This is why many animal advocacy organizations campaign for more "humane" standards of animal treatment and slaughter and promote animal products that are supposedly produced more "humanely."

We are going to defend what may appear to be a controversial position: that our rejection on moral grounds of meat, dairy, eggs, and all other animal products as food is *required* according to our conventional morality concerning animals. That is, our rejection of the idea that animals are just things with respect to which we can have no moral obligations commits us to adopting a vegan diet. It is not necessary to embrace a theory of animal rights to be logically committed to this position.

Consider the following hypothetical situation. Fred keeps a number of animals in his home, and he routinely causes them to suffer physical pain, fear, and distress. He also kills them. Fred is otherwise a lovely person; his penchant for mistreating and killing animals does not affect his dealings with other humans in any way. When asked about why he does this, Fred explains that he derives pleasure and amusement from these actions.

We would all agree that Fred's actions are morally reprehensible. We might even think that Fred should be institutionalized, although we may differ as to whether the appropriate institution is a psychiatric facility or a prison. But we would all agree that what Fred is doing is wrong because he is imposing suffering and death on animals without any good reason. There is no necessity for Fred's use. Fred is engaging in action that contravenes our conventional morality: he is imposing unnecessary suffering on animals.

Would such a reaction require acceptance of the animal rights position and consequent agreement that humans and nonhumans have equal moral value? No. Even if we think that animals have lesser moral value than humans, we would still object to Fred's fetish as long as we believe that animals have *some* moral value and are not just things. If you are in agreement with us that Fred is morally odious, we argue here that you are committed to veganism. No theory of animal rights is necessary.

"Unnecessary" suffering

Everyone who subscribes to conventional morality agrees that it is wrong to impose unnecessary suffering on animals. But how are we to interpret what suffering is necessary? If conventional wisdom is going to make any sense, then necessary suffering *must* exclude suffering imposed for pleasure, amusement, or convenience. If imposing pain for pleasure, amusement, or convenience may be considered as necessary, then there is *nothing* that can be considered as unnecessary. Indeed, if suffering can be imposed for reasons of pleasure, amusement, or convenience, then the conventional wisdom about animals is that we can use animals as long as we don't impose *unnecessary* unnecessary – or wholly gratuitous – suffering. So in Fred's case, conventional wisdom would say that Fred should not impose more harm than is necessary for him to derive the pleasure and amusement he seeks. But would anyone regard that as a plausible understanding of "necessity"? No, of course not. No one would say that, as long as Fred does not torture animals more than he needs to derive the pleasure he seeks, he is conforming to conventional morality.

This is precisely why many people object to blood sports such as fox hunting and bullfighting, and to other forms of "entertainment" where animals are maimed or killed. These uses of animals are, by definition, unnecessary – they involve imposing suffering and death on animals for the purposes of pleasure and amusement. There is a constant stream of stories in the news about people who inflict gratuitous harm on animals, and a good part of why the media features such stories is precisely that the public responds so very strongly. For example, in 2007, American football player Michael Vick was arrested on charges arising from a dog-fighting ring that he operated. He served time in prison in connection with this activity. The public reaction at the time of the incident was ferocious, and, to this day, Vick's public appearances elicit angry reactions from members of the public who continue to reprehend him for his conduct. Why does Vick elicit so strong a reaction? The answer is simple: Vick is a real-life Fred, and we regard all Freds – whether real or imagined – to be morally odious (Francione 2011). The reaction may be more intense or take on a different dimension if the particular Fred is a person of color, as was the case with Michael Vick. But the reaction is present whenever we learn about *any* Fred.

Consuming animals: we are all Fred

So the question becomes: on what basis can we justifiably kill animals for food – approximately 60 billion animals (not counting fish) per year worldwide? Under the best conditions – the most "humane" of circumstances – the amount of suffering we impose on animals in the process of using them for food is staggering. If we believe that unnecessary suffering is wrong, how can we justify that level of suffering? Indeed, even if we made animal agriculture much more "humane" than it presently is, there would still be suffering, fear, distress, and death – and we are not talking just about animals used for meat. Animals used for dairy and eggs suffer, and they are all ultimately slaughtered, just as those animals used only for meat are slaughtered. Most animals used for dairy and eggs are, like animals used exclusively for meat, kept in the intensive confinement and otherwise horrendous conditions of factory farms.

Contrary to popular belief, cows don't produce milk automatically and consider it a big favor that we milk them. Like other mammals, cows don't give milk unless and until they become pregnant. They are artificially and forcibly impregnated every year so that they are continually lactating. In order for humans to drink cow's milk, it is necessary that the calves for whom it was intended do not drink it. Newborn calves are taken away from their mothers shortly after birth, and no one seriously disputes that this causes great suffering and distress to mother and baby alike. Many of the female calves will become dairy cows (they are fed formula so that they do not take the milk); the rest of the females, and all the males, will become "meat" animals, with some slaughtered after about six months to be sold as veal. All cattle, whether raised for meat or milk, will eventually end up in the slaughterhouse. Dairy cows, who can live for up to 30 years, are usually slaughtered after four or five years when productivity starts to wane. Dairy cows suffer from lameness, mastitis (a painful inflammation of the udder), reproductive problems, and severe viral and bacterial diarrhea. They are often given drugs to cause them to produce more milk. They are mutilated; their horns are removed and tails are docked, or cut off, often without pain management.

As for the egg industry, after hatching, chicks are separated into males and females. Because male chicks will not be able to produce eggs, and because farmed laying chickens are specific breeds unsuitable to be "meat" animals, more than 100 million male chicks are killed in the United States alone every year. This slaughter is achieved by throwing chicks alive into grinding machines, suffocating them in garbage bags, or gassing them. Laying hens are confined in tiny battery cages where they get, on average, 67 square inches of space, or about the size of a single sheet of letter-sized paper, to live their entire lives. Most laying hens are subjected to forced molting, where the birds are starved for a period, causing them to lose their feathers and forcing their reproductive processes to rejuvenate, and to debeaking to stop the birds from injuring each other. Those hens not confined in battery cages are raised in "cage-free" or "free-range" circumstances that still result in horrible suffering. And laying hens are all slaughtered once their egg-producing capacity decreases, usually after one or two laying cycles. If you eat eggs, you are responsible not only for enormous animal suffering but also for more animal deaths than if you consumed beef or pork (Galef 2011).

The bottom line: there is as much suffering in a glass of milk, or in an egg, as in a steak. Indeed, there is no morally coherent distinction between meat and other animal-produced foods. For all of us who agree that Fred, Michael Vick, and similar types are reprehensible, there are two – and only two – choices. We either must conclude that we, too, are reprehensible, or we must be able to distinguish our use of animals for food from what these reprehensible people do. We must be able to argue that, unlike the situations in which we would all agree that there is no necessity, there is necessity in the situation involving the use of animals for food.

The problem is that we cannot make this argument.

Until recently, most people believed that it was necessary to consume animal foods, and that, without some animal protein, humans would shrivel up and die. Many people still believe this, but such a belief is not justifiable. We have known for centuries that humans can live without consuming any animal protein. To the extent that anyone holds that belief today, it is a testament to the combined power of advertising and a corporate-controlled media to reinforce our desire for eating what we are used to and what tastes good to us in light of our past experience.

The view that we need animal foods for human nutrition is clearly and unequivocally false. It is now acknowledged by virtually every respected professional organization, including the American Heart Association and the Mayo Clinic, as well as by many governmental agencies, that a diet consisting only of plant foods can be perfectly healthy. Indeed, there is mounting evidence that a vegan diet is almost certainly healthier than a diet heavy in meat, dairy, and eggs. We could now embark on a long discussion of the many studies that show that animal products are harming our health, but we do not need to do so; whether or not you agree that consuming animal foods is detrimental, there is certainly no argument that animal foods are *necessary* for optimal health. That is, even if we do not believe that we will be healthier if we eat a sensible vegan diet, we cannot reasonably believe that we will be less healthy. And, as a result, we come to the realization that consumption of animal foods is not necessary for human health.

There is also broad consensus that animal agriculture is an ecological disaster. Although estimates vary, there is no question that animal foods represent an inefficient use of plant protein in that animals have to consume many pounds of grain or forage to produce one pound of meat or eggs, and it takes much more water to produce meat, milk, and eggs than it does to produce plants with comparable nutritional content (Institute of Mechanical Engineers 2013; Pimentel and Pimentel 2003).

The Food and Agriculture Organization of the United Nations states that animal agriculture contributes more greenhouse gases – which are linked directly to global warming – to the atmosphere than does burning fossil fuels for transportation. According to Worldwatch Institute (2009), animal agriculture produces an estimated 51 percent of the worldwide total of greenhouse gas emissions from human activity. Moreover, a significant amount of fossil energy is required to yield an animal-based product. The average fossil energy input for all animal protein sources is 25 kcal of fossil energy input to one kcal of animal protein produced; this is more than 11 times greater than for grain protein production (Pimentel and Pimentel 2003).

Modern intensive animal agriculture techniques, known as "factory farming," have evolved to produce a large number of animals for market at a faster rate, at a lower cost, and by using far less land. This, of course, does not take into account the land that must be used to grow the grains and soy that must be fed to these animals; with this consideration factory farming represents anything but an efficient use of land. An acre of land can provide food for many more people who consume a vegan diet than for those who consume animal products.

While these practices produce cheaper food, factory farms, or concentrated animal feeding operations (CAFOs), as the United States Environmental Protection Agency (EPA) refers to them, have serious environmental implications. For example, the United States Department of Agriculture reports that 1.37 billion tons of solid animal waste is produced annually in the United States (130 times greater than the human waste produced in the country). The excess quantities of nitrogen found in this manure can easily convert into nitrates, which, according to EPA, contaminate the drinking water of approximately 4.5 million people. When nitrates exist in the groundwater, they can be fatal to infants (Pew Commission 2006).

The runoff into water and soil from factory farms is also responsible for the pollution of groundwater and the widespread dissemination of hormones. Antibiotics are routinely added to the feed and water of poultry, cattle, and pigs to promote growth and prevent infection caused by unsanitary, intensive confinement; approximately 80 percent of the antibiotics produced are fed to animals used for food. The use of antibiotics in animal agriculture and the resulting dissemination of antibiotics can contribute to antibiotic resistance in humans.

Animal agriculture is also responsible for other kinds of water pollution, deforestation, soil erosion, and all sorts of unhappy environmental consequences (see FAO 2006). Again, you may dispute some of the details, but no one can credibly maintain that animal agriculture is not a significant net negative as far as the environment is concerned.

So, what is our best justification for imposing suffering and death on approximately 60 billion land animals and at least a trillion aquatic animals – animals we do not need to consume for nutritional purposes and where the result of that consumption is ecological devastation? Animal foods taste good. We enjoy the taste of animal flesh and animal products. We find eating animal foods to be convenient. It's a habit.

And how exactly is our consumption of animal products any different from Fred's behavior? It is not. Palate pleasure is no different morally from any other sort of pleasure. How are we any different from Fred or his real-life counterpart, Michael Vick? We are not.

Pulling the trigger or paying someone else to pull it: it's murder in both cases

You may, at this point, be outraged, thinking to yourself or even saying out loud, "Of course there's a difference! Fred, Vick, and similar morally reprehensible characters participate directly in harming animals, and they enjoy the suffering of animals." You just buy animal products at the store. You certainly enjoy the results of animal suffering and death, but, unlike those who engage in the conduct directly, you don't enjoy the actual *process* of suffering and death. Although this may be true, it is irrelevant from a moral point of view.

As any first-year law student will tell you, criminal law is clear in that it does not matter whether you pull the trigger or whether you hire someone else to pull the trigger; it is murder in both cases. It may be true that the person who pulls the trigger, plunges the knife, or swings the hatchet is a less "nice" person in some sense than the one who just pays the fee. After all, it takes a certain sort of person to engage in the physical act of killing another person. The person who actually does the act may be a sadist who enjoys watching other humans suffer. But it is still murder both for the person who does the act and sadistically enjoys doing so, and for the person who pays for the homicide. We treat them the same legally because, from a moral point of view, they *are* the same. Similarly, the person who enjoys killing animals or watching them kill each other may be a more personally brutal person than the one who pays another to do the killing. So there may be a psychological difference between the person who pays another to kill and the person who kills, but as far as moral culpability is concerned, there is *no* difference.

Would your assessment of Fred be any different if he financed a dog-torturing operation but never participated personally? There may be a psychological difference between the person who participates in harming animals and those who otherwise make it possible. But there is no moral difference. There is no moral difference between person X, who kills the dog, and person Y, who says to X, "Kill the dog but wait until I leave because I am squeamish." The fact that we pay others to impose the suffering and death on animals does not get us off the moral hook. Many people who consume meat object to hunting. When we ask them why they object given that they eat meat, dairy, eggs, etc., they often reply, "Because there's something worse about killing the animal yourself. I would never be able to look at an animal and just shoot it with a bullet or an arrow."

Again, that response identifies a psychological fact and not anything that is morally relevant. Indeed, the animal raised and killed to make the hamburger probably had, on balance, a much worse life than the animal killed by the hunter. So, although killing the animal in both situations is not necessary, if there is any difference between these two situations, it is that the former is actually worse because it involves *more* suffering. There is no psychological or moral difference between a sport hunter and people like Fred. Sport hunters often say that they don't really enjoy the killing, and that they hunt just so that they can enjoy the tranquility and splendor of the outdoors. But if that were the case, they could take a walk in the woods. Killing an animal with a gun or an arrow is not necessary to enjoy tranquility or natural splendor.

Happy exploitation?

You may at this point be thinking that you agree that the horrible practices of intensive or "factory" farming are, indeed, immoral, but what if all that were changed? Couldn't we go from factory farms to Old MacDonald's farm and abolish intensive confinement in favor of better conditions?

That is exactly what some so-called animal advocates propose. In fact, most of the large animal organizations in the United States, Britain, and elsewhere campaign for larger cages for egg-laying hens, more space for nursing pigs and veal calves, and more "humane" slaughterhouses. Many of these animal organizations endorse and promote various labeling schemes that inform consumers that they are supposedly buying a "higher welfare" product (Francione 2008: 67–128; Francione and Garner 2010: 1–102).

There are two serious problems with this position. First, it completely misses the point. Even if the reforms proposed by animal advocates would significantly improve animal welfare – which, as we explain below, is not the case – the result would be a reduction in suffering. But, since the use of animals for food is not necessary at all, this would still not make our consumption of animal foods consistent with the moral principle that we claim to accept: that imposing *any* suffering and death on animals requires some justification based on an element of necessity or compulsion.

If we reformed dog fighting to be less violent, there may be a reduction of the suffering of the dogs. However, no one who thinks that Michael Vick's behavior was wrong would change her mind and support Vick's engagement in "humane" dog fighting. Dog fighting is wrong because, as a practice, it results in unnecessary suffering and death. Consuming animal foods is wrong because, as a practice, it results in unnecessary suffering and death. Making either practice more "humane" does not result in either practice conforming to our moral intuitions on the need to justify animal suffering and death. The fact that animal advocates are joining with industry to support and praise "happy" meat, eggs, and dairy does not mean that the consumption of those products is morally acceptable, just as a religious person declaring an act of violence to be the will of God does not make it morally right to kill.

Second, the reforms being proposed by animal organizations hardly mean the abolition of factory farming or a return to the nineteenth-century family farm. On the contrary, most of what animal organizations are proposing involves reforms that increase production efficiency. For example, animal advocates promote controlled-atmosphere killing of poultry, which involves exposing the birds to a mixture of gases that lead to suffocation, as an alternative to immobilizing the birds with an electric current and slitting their throats. Controlled-atmosphere killing reduces carcass damage and worker injuries and, as present equipment becomes obsolete, the industry will undoubtedly adopt this practice. Animal advocates similarly promote increasing space for pigs and veal calves, which may involve capital expenditures but also results in a decrease in stress suffered by the animals, which translates into lower veterinary costs. In any event, whether reforms increase production efficiency or not, these reforms are *very* modest. They are to animal ethics what padded water boards for use at Guantanamo Bay are to human rights.

The most "humanely" raised animals are still kept and killed in horrible circumstances. All of this talk about "happy" animal products is about *us*; it is about making us feel more comfortable about doing something that nags at us. It's about keeping us from having to recognize that we are all really no different from Fred. It really has nothing to do with the animals. They continue to suffer horribly, irrespective of what "happy" label – "free-range," "cage-free," "organic," "Certified Humane Raised and Handled," or "Freedom Food" – is slapped on their carcasses or the products we make from them. And the situation is made even worse when large animal organizations praise and support these "happy" products.

It costs money to protect animal interests. Of course, it is possible in theory that we might all be willing to pay many times more for animal products, and that standards could then improve in significant ways. However, very few people could actually afford animal products that were produced in a way that provided significantly more protection to animal interests. And to be perfectly clear: even if we *completely* eliminated every vestige of factory farming, which is an economic impossibility, and went back to a system of what we think of as the idyllic family farm, there would still be a great deal of animal suffering and death.

Moreover, anyone who would care enough to pay the significantly higher cost of such production would probably care enough to not eat animal products at all. Additionally, given economic realities and free-trade rules, even if welfare standards were raised significantly in one place, demand for lower-priced, lower-welfare products would force the higher-welfare producers out of business except, perhaps, to serve a very small and affluent niche market.

You may well ask about laws that purport to prohibit the infliction of unnecessary suffering, but the law does not prohibit the use of animals for food and for other purposes as long as the animals are treated "humanely." Why isn't the law interpreted to require veganism? These laws do not prohibit *uses* that are unnecessary; they supposedly prohibit only *treatment* that is not necessary to achieve a given use (Francione 2008: 1–23). We have seen that eating animals and animal products is not necessary for human health. Therefore, *all* of the suffering incidental to using animals as food is unnecessary. It runs afoul of what we claim to embrace as an uncontroversial moral principle: that animals matter morally and that we need some justification for imposing suffering and death on them. The pleasure of taste cannot suffice as a justification for consuming animal products, just as the pleasure of imposing suffering on animals cannot justify Fred's behavior.

So if we think that laws requiring "humane" treatment are morally relevant, we have misunderstood the issue. Even if these laws were effective, which, as we have discussed elsewhere, they are not (Francione 1995; Francione 2008; Francione and Garner 2010: 1–102), there would still be a great deal of animal suffering. A situation of merely reducing *unnecessary* suffering is still in conflict with the notion that we claim to accept that we can only justify *necessary* suffering. "Necessary" suffering requires some conflict, some compulsion. Our palate pleasure fails on that score, just as Fred's pleasure in making animals suffer fails.

The moment we start talking about a law that prohibits imposing "unnecessary" suffering in the context of an activity that is itself not necessary, we are talking nonsense. A rule prohibiting "unnecessary" suffering or requiring "humane" treatment in the context of, for example, dog fighting would make no sense, because *all* of the suffering incidental to dog fighting is unnecessary. So to talk about the "humane" treatment of animals we eat or use for purposes that are not themselves necessary is nothing more than to require that we not impose gratuitous suffering on animals. And that is surely not what our conventional wisdom says.

But isn't eating animals a tradition?

You may see your options disappearing and, as you contemplate your moral obligation to go vegan, you may find yourself resisting the conclusion to which you *are* committed and reach for the last straw of hope: "Yes, this is all logical, but it is tradition to eat animal products."

There is one word that, whenever you hear it in the context of an argument in favor of some position, you know with certainty that the person using the word to defend the position has nothing substantive to say. That word is *tradition*. To use tradition or culture to justify a position is simply another way of saying that we have done something for a long time, so we are justified in continuing to do it. In other words, it does not allow for any critiques of the practice being challenged.

We *know* that people have been eating animal foods for a long time. That's the point. We are challenging that behavior as inconsistent with our conventional wisdom – that we must be justified to impose suffering or death on animals. So, it is completely useless to the argument to repeat the fact that people have been eating animal foods for a long time. It merely re-states the problem under discussion and does not provide any resolution.

Virtually anything worth talking about from a moral point of view has been going on for a long time and is part of *someone's* tradition. For example, female genital mutilation is traditional in some cultures. Does this mean that it is automatically justified? Yes, people may claim that their particular ethnic animal foods are part of their group identity, but that is like saying that a particular sort of pornography is part of the identity of a group that practices sexism.

A similar response is to say, "These arguments are all logical, but it's natural to consume animal products." This is like saying God wants us to eat animals, but we don't even need to bother with God. Something else that is big and important – nature – wants us to eat animals. If we don't eat animals, we are acting against nature. We are behaving in an *unnatural* way. That is powerful stuff – even if you are an atheist.

But why do we think that nature intends (whatever that means) that we eat animals? The usual response is to say that we are physically adapted to eat meat and other animal products, so to not do so represents some sort of rebellion against nature. Putting aside that many people are lactose intolerant, and that many physicians are pointing out that animal products are detrimental to human health, the *most* we can say is that we *can* eat animal products; there is nothing about our bodies that suggests they require us to do so. Humans compare physically much more to herbivores than to carnivores. Carnivores have well-developed claws. We don't have claws. We also lack the sharp front teeth carnivorous animals need. Although we still have canine teeth, they are not sharp and cannot be used in the way carnivorous animals use their sharp canine teeth. We have flat molar teeth, as seen in herbivores, that we use for grinding. Carnivores have a short intestinal tract to quickly expel decaying meat. Herbivores have a much longer intestinal tract, as do humans. Herbivores and humans have weak stomach acid relative to carnivores that have strong hydrochloric acid in their stomachs to digest meat.

Herbivorous animals have well-developed salivary glands for pre-digesting fruits and grains and have alkaline saliva that is needed to pre-digest grains, as do humans. Carnivorous animals do not have similar salivary glands, and they have acidic saliva.

We are told by advocates of the Paleo diet that we should eat the way our "ancestors" ate. But how did they eat? As biologist Rob Dunn (2012) wrote in *Scientific American:*

> for most of the last twenty million years of the evolution of our bodies, through most of the big changes, we were eating fruit, nuts, leaves and the occasional bit of insect, frog, bird or mouse. While some of us might do well with milk, some might do better than others with starch and some might do better or worse with alcohol, we all have the basic machinery to get fruity or nutty without trouble.

And, as we stated earlier, the evidence is quite clear that animal products are not necessary for us to be optimally healthy. You would think that if we were intended to eat animal products, those of us who don't (and haven't for decades) would suffer deleterious health effects. But we do just fine. We have to make sure that we get vitamin B-12. Although some vitamin B-12 is made by bacteria in the human body, not enough is reliably made for our needs, and unhealthy human habits prevent maximum production and absorption of the endogenous B-12. Therefore, it is necessary to supplement B-12 from external sources, whether you consume a vegan diet or a diet of animal foods. So all humans need to get B-12 from somewhere outside their bodies. We get B-12 from yeast; omnivores get it from meat. All B-12 comes from bacteria, whether in the gut of ruminating animals fermenting plant material, or in certain strains of nutritional yeast. So, a vegan diet without an alternative source of B-12, such as yeast, may make a person ill. But there are many people who have B-12 deficiencies despite consumption of animal products.

Humans also need fatty acids that they cannot manufacture. Most people get essential fatty acids from eating fish, and the fish get fatty acids from consuming algae. Vegans can get these fatty acids directly from an algae supplement, and they can also eat flaxseeds and walnuts, which provide these nutrients.

So, while there is considerable evidence that animal foods are detrimental to human health, we do not want to start a battle of studies to convince the reader that it is healthier not to eat animal products. We do, however, want to make clear that the very best a consumer of animal products can say is that her diet is no better than that of someone who eats a balanced diet of non-animal foods.

In sum, there is no evidence that nature requires that we eat animal products. Indeed, the extant evidence is to the contrary.

There are many other responses that people offer when confronted by the contradiction between their reactions to Fred and their non-veganism. These range from developing a concern that plants are sentient (they aren't) to a claim that Hitler was a vegetarian (he wasn't, but if he had been, so what?). We have discussed these and many other responses elsewhere (Francione and Charlton 2013), and we cannot go into them further here.

Conclusion: when are you going vegan?

We have shown that, unless you are in the first group that regards animals as things that have no moral value, you are committed to veganism. And we have made this argument without mentioning animal rights. This is because that concept is only morally relevant when we are talking about situations in which there is a plausible claim of necessity, and we need a rights analysis to understand and resolve the conflict. But 99 percent of our uses of animals, including our numerically most significant use of them – for food – do not involve any sort of necessity or any real conflict between human and nonhuman interests. Indeed, the only use of animals we make that is not transparently frivolous involves using animals in biomedical research concerning serious human illnesses. While we do not think such use is morally justifiable, it at least requires a more complicated analysis because of the ostensible compulsion involved.

But, as far as our other uses of animals are concerned, only conventional wisdom is required to conclude that they cannot be morally justified.

Notes

1 The argument presented in this essay is discussed at greater length in Gary L. Francione and Anna Charlton (2013).
2 For an excellent discussion of the moral status of animals, see Gary Steiner (2005).

References

Dunn, Rob. (2012) "Human Ancestors Were Nearly All Vegetarians," *Scientific American Guest Blog*, http://blogs.scientificamerican.com/guest-blog/2012/07/23/human-ancestors-were-nearly-all-vegetarians/.
Food and Agriculture Organization of the United Nations. (2006) "Livestock a Major Threat to Environment," *FAO Newsroom*, http://www.fao.org/newsroom/en/news/2006/1000448/.
Francione, Gary L. (1995) *Animals, Property, and the Law*, Philadelphia, PA: Temple University Press.
——. (1996) *Rain Without Thunder: The Ideology of the Animal Rights Movement*, Philadelphia, PA: Temple University Press.
——. (2000) *Introduction to Animal Rights: Your Child or the Dog?* Philadelphia, PA: Temple University Press.
——. (2008) *Animals as Persons: Essays on the Abolition of Animal Exploitation*, New York: Columbia University Press.
——. (2011) *What Michael Vick Taught Us*, http://www.abolitionistapproach.com/what-michael-vick-taught-us/.

Francione, Gary L. & Charlton, Anna. (2013) *Eat Like You Care: An Examination of the Morality of Eating Animals*, Newark, NJ: Exempla Press.

Francione, Gary L. & Garner, Robert. (2010) *The Animal Rights Debate: Abolition or Regulation?*, New York: Columbia University Press.

Galef, J. (2011) "Want to Kill Fewer Animals? Give Up Eggs," *Scientific American Guest Blog*, http://blogs.scientificamerican.com/guest-blog/want-to-kill-fewer-animals-give-up-eggs-not-meat/.

Goodland, Robert & Anhang, Jeff. (2009) "Livestock and Climate Change," *Worldwatch Institute*, http://www.worldwatch.org/node/6294.

Institution of Mechanical Engineers. (2013) *Global Food: Waste Not, Want Not*, http://www.imeche.org/docs/default-source/reports/Global_Food_Report.pdf?sfvrsn=0.

Pew Commission on Industrial Farm Production. (2006) http://www.ncifap.org/issues/environment.

Pimentel, D. & Pimentel, M. (2003) "Sustainability of Meat-Based and Plant-Based Diets and the Environment," *American Journal of Clinical Nutrition* 78(suppl): 660S–663S, http://ajcn.nutrition.org/content/78/3/660S.full.pdf.

Steiner, Gary. (2005) *Anthropocentrism and Its Discontents: The Moral Status of Animals in the History of Western Philosophy*, Pittsburgh, PA: University of Pittsburgh Press.

29

RITUAL SLAUGHTERING VS. ANIMAL WELFARE

A utilitarian example of (moral) conflict management*

Francesco Ferraro

A factual conflict

European legal systems, as well as many others around the world, recognize the need to minimize animal suffering, both in livestock farming and in animal slaughtering, at least since directive 74/577/ EEC (later replaced by directive 93/119/EC). Regarding slaughtering, this concern mainly calls for the pre-stunning of animals using appropriate techniques in order to spare them from unnecessary suffering. This is meant as a "first step" in Europe's action to prevent all forms of cruelty to animals. The European Convention for the Protection of Animals for Slaughter restates the mandatory rule of pre-stunning and also explicitly forbids some traditional methods of stunning that are deemed to be inadequate or cruel (i.e., the use of the "puntilla," hammer, and pole-axe). The Convention also prescribes choosing only among the following stunning methods: mechanical instruments that administer a blow or penetrate at the level of the brain (i.e., captive bolt pistol), electro-narcosis, or gas anesthesia. However, such a concern for animal welfare finds explicit limitations in religious rituals. Directive 74/577/EEC did not affect national provisions related to "special methods of slaughter" required by religious rites. Although successive conventions, directives, and regulations also submitted religious slaughtering to the general rule of sparing animals from all unnecessary and avoidable pain, they still admit to having religiously grounded exceptions to pre-stunning. Such exceptions are usually normatively grounded in the general principle of religious freedom and the freedom to manifest one's religious beliefs in worship, teaching, practice, and observance (as per article 10 of the Charter of Fundamental Rights of the European Union).

This is a genuine case of moral conflict – on the one hand, we find a very widespread moral concern for the minimization of the suffering of sentient beings, while on the other hand, we find an equally widespread and legitimate concern for human freedom, and more specifically, for the freedom to express one's religious beliefs and shape one's own life in accordance with such beliefs. As is well known, both Jewish *shechitah* (ritual slaughtering) and Islamic *halal* slaughtering (using the *dhabihah* method) forbid the pre-stunning of animals. This leads to a *factual* conflict with legal prescriptions to the contrary. The conflict is a factual, rather than a principled, one, since neither religion disregards animal welfare and the minimization of animal suffering. On the contrary, the methods of slaughtering prescribed by such rites partly originated from an authentic concern for humane slaughtering. The method of jugulation, for instance, is to be performed in one single cut by skilled and trained professionals, and was the less painful way of killing animals known in ancient times. The religious obligation to only slaughter healthy and physically intact animals also seems to be derived from the preoccupation with avoiding excessive and prolonged suffering. However, the conflict between such prescriptions and the minimization of animal suffering now-adays seems factually unavoidable. The most effective and widespread methods of pre-stunning permanently damage the animal's body and thereby conflict, for instance, with the Islamic pre-scription that the heart of the animal still be beating until bleeding begins. It is true that some Jewish and Islamic authorities have consented to some methods of stunning that do not irre-versibly damage the animal's body; in New Zealand and Australia, for example, the adoption of very sophisticated instruments for electro-narcosis that leave the animal's brain intact and would permit swift regaining of consciousness has allowed those two countries to export their meat to Islamic countries. Moreover, mostly Islamic nations, such as Malaysia, have permitted the use of non-penetrating captive bolt pistols, which do not permanently damage the animal's encephalon.

However, the most effective methods of stunning – that is, those which cause the least suffering and are most likely to work – are still prohibited by religious prescriptions. A conflict between animal welfare concerns and religious freedom, therefore, cannot be ignored. The claim that ritual slaughtering causes no more pain to animals than does post-stunning slaughtering seems uncon-vincing. The main sources of suffering for non-stunned animals are the restraint systems, the pain from the cutting of the throat, and the pain of bleeding. Although appropriate restraint systems can minimize distress (Grandin and Regenstein 1994), the pain from the cut and the bleeding seems unavoidable in non-stunned animals. In addition, the claim that jugulation would grant a quicker loss of consciousness than would other methods is widely contested (among others, by the Federation of Veterinarians of Europe, as in FVE 2002). Moreover, today's meat industry requires large slaughterhouses to minimize the amount of butchering time spent per animal, thereby making it very difficult to comply with the strict regulations that avoid causing unneces-sary suffering to ritually slaughtered animals (Singer and Mason 2006).

A factual conflict, then, is unavoidable, unless we want to affirm the thesis that ritual slaughter-ing is not covered by the freedom "to manifest religion or belief, in worship, teaching, practice and observance" (European Convention on Human Rights, art. 9). This would seem odd, as the way people eat and how they prepare their food is of paramount importance to them and actually expresses cultural, national, and religious identities much more strongly and evidently than do many other aspects of human life. Religious practice obviously also includes regulations concerning nourishment. Moreover, the German constitutional court has already acknowledged *halal* slaughtering as falling under the protection given by the German *Grundgesetz* for freedom of religious expression (January 15, 2002), and the Hebraic *shechitah* was already recognized as legitimate. Although the conflict was not a principled one from the outset – since religious prac-titioners also do not oppose, nor disregard, the principle of minimizing animal suffering – it has recently evolved into a principled ethical dilemma: should human religious freedom count more than animal welfare – or, more precisely, than the minimization of animal suffering? Recent cases in the European Union (UK, Netherlands, Poland, and Denmark) show that public opinion is actually split between those who think that religious freedom comes first and those who believe animal rights should have precedence. In Denmark, minister for agriculture and food Dan Jør-gensen famously declared that animal rights come before religion (Withnall 2015). Countries like Denmark, Norway, Sweden, and Switzerland have altogether banned non-stun methods of slaughtering, and others, like Estonia, Finland, and Latvia have imposed rules regarding stunning right after the cut (Needham 2012).

Animal rights?

It is very tempting to adopt, in this respect, a Nozickian approach. After all, very few challenge the view that humans have moral rights that should never be trumped, among which we find the right to religious freedom. Legal systems should turn those rights into legal ones by granting them the protection of the law. The concern for minimizing non-human suffering is clearly legitimate and, indeed, mandatory, as long as it does not lead to actions that violate human rights. This approach has been famously described as "Kantianism for humans, utilitarianism for animals" (Nozick 1974: 39). However, such a stance is obviously irreconcilable with animalism, which does not admit to methods of slaughter that are unable to spare animals from unnecessary suffering, even on the grounds of the human right to freedom of religion. The Kantian-Nozickian approach falls under the definition of *speciesism*, that is, an attitude of bias or preference towards the interests of those belonging to our same species (Singer 1995: 6). If we see rights or, at least, fundamental rights, as "trump cards" (in a Dworkinian fashion), and we only ascribe rights to humans, it is quite clear that a right to religious freedom will always have precedence over animal welfare. Such speciesist outcomes stem from the Kantian concept of *dignity*: dignity stems from autonomy and from the moral law. The only beings capable of acting morally and, therefore, autonomously, are human beings. The dignity stemming from being the only possible "carriers" of the moral law calls for respect for humanity (which also includes respect, on every individual's part, for her/his humanity – that is, respect for one's self). Respect manifests itself as the non-violation of certain deontological restraints, which Kant summarizes in the imperative of not treating other humans as mere means, but also always as ends-in-themselves.

Although it is not always easy to fully comprehend the practical implications of such a maxim, we can say that respecting the dignity of other human beings also means taking into account their needs and interests, refraining from acting towards them in ways that they would not approve of, and not curbing their freedom of choice. Under such a view, non-rational beings cannot be ascribed dignity and are not ends-in-themselves. Of course, this does not mean that we cannot build upon Kantian grounds to also acknowledge animal rights, or at least human obligations towards animals (as in Korsgaard 2004 and Regan 1983). The "pure" Kantian-Nozickian perspective does not seem very attractive with regard to the problem at hand, since it opposes – at least prima facie – growing concerns for minimizing animal suffering. Simply claiming that animalist concerns are misplaced would solve the conflict between animalist and religious-freedom-related positions. If we reject this conclusion and its speciesist outcomes, we could also assume that non-human animals have moral rights and they should be entitled to certain protections against mistreatment and the infliction of unnecessary suffering. This does not compel us to ascribe a right to life to them that would absolutely forbid their slaughtering. We could simply recognize their right not to suffer pointlessly and contrast it with rights of religious freedom, which include the right to eat in compliance with religious prescriptions.

However, this is arguably not the most promising way of taking into account the animalist point of view. Rights are suitable for the protection of the interests of human beings because humans can (at least potentially) claim them and build their plans of life and expectations according to the rights they know they have. They can be seen as *valid claims*, that is, they morally authorize their holders to claim something as their due (Feinberg 1980: 151).

Rights are of no similar use to animals. Moreover, the strongly individualistic roots of rights language make it useful to express the needs and interests of beings who are, at the very least, rational and, to a certain degree, autonomous. Beings who are incapable of rational consideration of their interests and, moreover, are factually dependent on other beings, can, of course, be ascribed rights, but they will probably be more effectively protected by speaking of duties and responsibilities of other beings towards them. This, of course, also applies to children and adults under medical care (Wolgast 1987).

So, although animal rights talk has become more and more popular, it is, at the very least, highly debatable as to whether it suits the protection of animals' interests. It should be noted that the rejection of animal rights stems from the adoption of the so-called "Interest Theory" of rights, according to which the specific function of rights is that of benefiting their owners by promoting their interests (see, for instance, Kramer 1998). We could also adopt a "Choice Theory" of rights, according to which a right makes its holder a "small-scale sovereign" (Hart 1982: 183) by endowing her/him with a certain measure of control over the duties of other people, thereby protecting his/her freedom of choice (see also, for instance, Steiner 1994; 1998). However, by adopting this view, we would be really compelled to reject the ascription of rights to animals, as they do not possess the ability to exercise their freedom of choice to control the duties of others. This is also what makes moral and legal rights, on Kant's account, so difficult to apply to non-humans (Korsgaard 2012). What is said above does not imply that animals cannot be ascribed rights, since the ability to understand what a right is and what rights we have, as well as the ability to claim their enforcement, is not a necessary condition for the possession of legal rights (Lamont 1946: 83–85). This probably also holds true for the use of rights in moral language. My point is that, just like for children and incapacitated adults, the ascription of rights is not always the best way – much less the only way – to express our moral consideration of animals. Moreover, with respect to the case at hand, animal rights would still conflict with human rights to religious freedom, and we would still be left with the problem of solving that conflict.

Utilitarian conflict management

A different and maybe more promising approach to the problem is the utilitarian way, by which I mean the classic, hedonistic utilitarian ethical theory with its fundamental prescription of maximizing total pleasure and minimizing total pain. According to this view, the characteristic that makes a being the appropriate object of moral consideration is not rationality, nor the mere belonging to the human race, but *sentience* (Singer 1993). Utilitarianism, then, is typically non-speciesist, since it allows the taking into account of every being capable of experiencing pain and pleasure.

The concept of dignity as "intrinsic moral worth" is by no means discarded within such a perspective; it is rather extended to include all beings capable of experiencing pain (and pleasure). Utilitarians see no reason for ascribing to all human beings, but not to members of any other species, moral dignity understood as an entitlement to equal moral consideration. After all, it is very difficult to see why elephants, pigs, or chimpanzees should be denied the same kind of moral consideration we give, for instance, humans with profound intellectual disabilities and infants – not to mention despicable human beings, like serial killers or merciless dictators (Singer 1986: 228). As Jeremy Bentham, the father of modern utilitarianism, famously said, the "insuperable line," which includes a living being among those worthy of moral consideration, cannot be traced in "the faculty of reason," nor "in the faculty of discourse," unless we are ready to acknowledge that

> a full-grown horse or dog is beyond comparison more rational, as well as a more conversable animal, than an infant of a day, or a week, or even a month, old. But suppose they were otherwise, what would it avail? The question is not, Can they reason?, nor Can they *talk*? but, *Can they suffer*?
>
> (Bentham 1996: 282–283 n.)

Until recently, Peter Singer has defended a form of *preference utilitarianism*, that is, a consequential-ist theory that considers as good or just what leads to maximizing the satisfaction of preferences. Within this perspective, we should regard self-conscious beings as possessing a different moral status with respect to merely sentient (i.e., conscious, but not self-conscious) beings, because only the former are able to perceive the continuity of their existence through time and thereby fully qualify as persons. Persons have strong future-oriented preferences, among which – it may safely be assumed – the preference to keep on living, which is usually of paramount importance. Killing persons is wrong because it treads upon this preference. Self-conscious beings are irreplaceable and their killing is, in itself, wrong, even if it were completely painless.

Singer complements his view of what a person is and what value people's lives have with Michael Tooley's account of the "right to life." To be entitled to a right to life, living beings must at least be capable of desiring to continue existing as a distinct entity; of course, in order to do so, they need to understand the concept of their continued existence (or to be capable, or to have been capable of, understanding it). This involves the notion that killing beings who are structur-ally incapable of such a concept, like human infants and graver mental defectives, is not in itself wrong, and it is certainly preferable to killing creatures like the higher mammals who do display such capacity (Singer 1993: 95–99; Tooley 1986).

The utilitarian approach adopted here is different from this kind of preference utilitarianism, because the latter seems ill-suited for the case at hand; it simply leads to regarding as wrong the killing of all higher animals, i.e., of animals capable of preferences regarding their future. Such animals are, in the sense explained above, persons, and they should be endowed with a right to life. Not unlike our pets, most or all of our cattle qualify as persons much more than do human infants and those people with grave intellectual impairment. The concern for pre-stunning would be misplaced: eating meat would simply be wrong, whatever the method used for slaughtering. Utilitarianism would prescribe vegetarianism (or maybe veganism) as the only ethical option regarding human nutrition (Singer 1980). A purely hedonistic utilitarian approach, on the contrary, would just leave the moral question regarding the *killing* open, while maintaining a non-speciesist regard for every sentient being's suffering. This view makes it possible to see the problem posed by ritual slaughtering as a genuinely moral one, presenting us with a choice between different moral options, not between an ethical stance (for instance, vegetarianism) and unprincipled caprice.

Each alternative option would be supported by moral reasons, but would also involve some moral costs. For instance, a flat prohibition on ritual slaughtering would surely be recommend-able on account of concern for animal suffering, but it would have undeniable costs in terms of human suffering. Moreover, purely hedonistic utilitarianism seems comprehensive enough to also accommodate Singer's concern that animals capable of anticipating their future – and having preferences regarding it – should be differentiated from lower species that possess sentience, but no sense of their existence in time. It was Bentham's contention that, as long as little or no pain is inflicted on them, it is perfectly admissible to eat animals: "we are the better for it, and they are never the worse. They have none of those long-protracted anticipations of future misery which we have" (Bentham 1838–43: 142–143 n.; see also Dardenne 2010). Of course, we need not accept the contention that only humans are capable of feeling pain (or, for that matter, pleasure) by anticipation. We may assume the more plausible view that no sharp distinction could be made and that differences between (most) humans and non-humans in this respect, though undeni-able, are only a matter of degree. This would allow us both to take into account the religious practitioner's suffering that would issue from the impossibility of eating meat in compliance with her/his cult – a kind of sophisticated, all-too-human pain – and the necessity for reducing to a minimum animal suffering issuing from fear at the moment of slaughter.

In contemporary pluralist societies, many different ethical standards and conceptions of a good life have to live elbow-to-elbow and find political solutions to moral conflicts. Such moral pluralism and necessity for conciliation and compromise is clearly exemplified by the case of religious practitioners asking for ritual slaughter coexisting with people who include the concern for animal welfare among their ethical priorities. The form of hedonistic utilitarianism that is advocated here seems well suited to provide a common ground for discussion. In its best form, utilitarianism should not be thought of as an ethical theory prescribing the rejection of all other moral stances that conflict with the immediate minimization of pain (or maximization of pleasure). What it urges us to do is simply to translate those moral questions involving the making of decisions for large communities into terms of pain and pleasure. All public policies, regulations, institutions, etc., should be tested according to the suffering they help to avoid and the welfare they promise to bring about.

Although this seems to be a typically monistic approach to ethics, in the sense that it reduces all ethics to the pursuance of one single value (Brandt 1979: 271–285; Broad 1979: 280), it is in truth compatible with ethical pluralism in modern societies, as it attempts to find a common language or *lingua franca* to make dialogue between different moral stances possible. The idea behind this is that everybody can relate to pleasurable and painful experiences, and this makes them suitable as a solid common ground for ethical discussion.

Regarding the problem at hand, the importance of their rites and beliefs for religious practitioners would be taken into account in the global utilitarian calculations, as it is very easy to translate into terms of pains and pleasures. The impossibility of eating food that has been prepared in accordance with one's beliefs is, obviously, a source of major distress.

Anyway, it should be noted that meat is no longer regarded as a necessary part of human nutrition, and its deprivation is no longer considered incompatible with a healthy diet (provided, of course, that other conditions for balanced nourishment are met). This does not mean that those requiring ritual slaughtering for their meat should convert to vegetarianism. It may very well be that, in eating non-human animals, we "regard their life and well-being as subordinate to our taste for a particular kind of dish [. . .] this is purely a matter of pleasing our palate" (Singer 1986: 222). However, it would inevitably cause much suffering to be forced to choose between a radical change in one's dietary habits and renouncing personal religious prescriptions. One major source of such suffering would arguably be the feeling of disrespect on the part of public institutions imposing such a choice, as well as the feeling of being treated unequally with respect to people who hold different religious beliefs or hold none at all. Moreover, it must be remembered that bans on ritual slaughter throughout history have often been the result of anti-Semitic campaigns at the outset of wider, large-scale racial persecutions. It is no wonder that those who consume ritually slaughtered meat can come to see themselves as being the members of a despised minority. It would not be unreasonable for such people to fear flat bans of non-stun methods as the possible beginning of harsher discriminatory policies, and to see supporting campaigns as a disguise for hostility against them, based on religious or racial grounds.

On the "animal side," we should note that animal suffering related to slaughter without pre-stunning is only a minimal part of the whole of suffering caused by industrial livestock farming. Moreover, large slaughterhouses that butcher for the meat market are generally less able to provide the conditions for the proper performance of ritual slaughtering, which would cause animals only slightly more prolonged and more intense suffering than does post-stunning slaughter. This makes ritual slaughtering the cause of a very small amount of the pain caused to animals by the modern meat industry. It appears to not make sense to worry about the stunning prior to killing without regarding whether or not the animals were raised in conditions compatible with a decent life, i.e., in ways that avoid all unnecessary suffering. This is not the case of the vast majority of animals raised in industrial farming. Utilitarianism would probably only allow for the consumption of meat from traditional free-range farming (Frey 1983: 32, 174–183), although this would make meat consumption so expensive that most people would expunge it almost completely from their diet.

While livestock farming should gradually be abolished, this should not prevent us from addressing the conflict between animalist concerns and religious freedom in the meantime. Utilitarianism would prescribe a progressive reduction of non-stun killings, without, at the same time, curbing religious freedom and without instilling in religious practitioners the idea that they are being discriminated against.

Such a result could be obtained, for instance, with taxation on meat coming from ritually slaughtered animals. Such taxation should be sufficient to reduce the number of this type of slaughters, without making the purchase of the meat prohibitive for most people. It may be argued that this kind of measure would be perceived as discriminatory by those affected, but this objection could be rebutted by underlining that what is being taxed – and, no doubt, discouraged – here is not a specific religious cult, nor compliance with religious regulations in general, but a certain *lifestyle*. By "lifestyle," it is meant here the embracing of a set of coherent practices on the part of individuals who consider those practices to be the tangible expression of their self-identity (Giddens 1991: 81). Following an omnivorous diet, then, can be seen as one of the practices by which consumers express, and construct, their self-identity (Beekman 2000: 188).

Making some lifestyles more expensive than others, on account of concern for public ends and interests, is something that governments worldwide already do, and it is generally accepted. This occurs, for instance, with tobacco and alcohol taxes (at least when they are justified not on paternalist grounds, but because of the public costs of diseases related to their consumption). Should all such measures be regarded as discriminatory? The answer to this leads to reflection on the use of the concept of discrimination. A very plausible definition of "discrimination" would refer to it as a moralized concept, not a neutral one: discrimination is wrong, regardless of the grounds for such judgment of moral wrongness. If we expand on the definition, we will most likely tie discrimination to (wrong) inequality and (wrong) disadvantage for certain persons or groups. Presumptive discrimination here would be of the *direct* kind, that is, it would issue from the aims and purposes of the discriminating agent (i.e., legislatures and governments) and it would not merely be the undesired outcome of policies not aimed at creating inequalities.

Now, of course, the proposed "ritual-slaughter tax" would establish some kind of inequality between people that could eat non-religiously compliant meat and people that could not because of their creed. It would also, in a certain sense, disadvantage religious practitioners, at least by reducing their freedom of alimentary choice in comparison with others. But it can be doubted that inequality and relative disadvantage should be regarded as *wrong* in this case. If we assume that there is no principled religious objection to the concern for animal suffering, then we can expect, on the part of religious practitioners, an attitude open to consideration of the increased pain for ritually slaughtered animals. They should be made aware that the imposition of a small restriction on their alimentary options does not stem from disrespect towards their beliefs and practices. Moreover, making meat from ritual slaughters more expensive adjusts to the origins of ritual slaughter as a practice directly derived from animal sacrifices, which sacralizes the killing of a living being. Current rates of slaughters in meat production are by no means compatible with such sacralization of death.

It could also be argued that public intervention in this field would be illiberal because it would restrain the consumers' freedom of choice, thereby violating the autonomy-right to decide what lifestyle to pursue, that is, how to live one's own life (Feinberg 1986: 54). Political liberalism would leave an area as vast as possible for the consumers to make their choices free from governmental intervention. Moreover, by making a certain lifestyle (the one including an omnivorous diet in compliance with religious rules) more costly than others (i.e., those that allow for the consumption of non-ritually slaughtered animals), the government would violate the liberal principle of neutrality among conceptions of the good life (Raz 1986). With reference to government intervention in promoting conversion from meat to "novel protein foods," it has been argued that such intervention would be compatible with political liberalism.

In fact, political liberalism does acknowledge the legitimacy of public attempts at discouraging certain lifestyles if they harm others (the "harm principle"), if they violate distributive justice, or if they stem from irrational/uninformed choices. In particular, due to the huge environmental costs of animal husbandry, meat-eaters could be said to harm prospective future generations (Beekman 2000). This line of argumentation can easily be adopted for supporting the need for a ritual-slaughter tax. If the principle of harm can be used to protect the needs and interests of future human generations – who are not real individuals and might never be – it can obviously fit the case of living beings with actual interests, such as cows, pigs, etc. And, as has already been observed, there is little doubt that ritual slaughter actually increases the pain felt by the dying animal.

Taxation on ritual slaughter could also serve as a means to avoid the sale of meat coming from non-stunned animals to the large public, often with no awareness on the part of the consumers. In the UK and in Australia, for instance, it has recently caused public scandal that a considerable (though debated) percentage of the meat sold into supermarkets and restaurants actually comes from non-stun killing methods – mainly in compliance with Islamic *halal* slaughtering – and, predictably enough, this has sparked widespread indignation. Apparently, the percentage of such meat outnumbers by a huge ratio the percentage of Muslims living in those countries. Moreover, a statistical report in 2010 showed that the majority of the Muslims living in the UK would look for an express declaration of the *halal* status of the meat before buying it. More generally, Muslim consumers seem to be wedded to using small Muslim-run butcher shops and value the butcher's Islamic faith as the best validation of the religious compliance of the product (AHDB 2010). If the supply of *halal* meat outstrips demand, then its unlabeled sale is merely due to the simplicity and cost-effectiveness (both for large abattoirs and big supermarket chains) of incrementing ritual slaughters much beyond the demand and then selling all the meat undifferentiated to the mass market (Arnett 2014). Another cause for this is the presence of non-*kosher* or non-*halal* parts in the slaughtered animals. For example, the sciatic nerve in the hindquarters of beef is non-*kosher*. As it is difficult to remove, usually all the cuts from the back part of the animal end up on sale in the general market (Singer 1995: 155).

Of course, it would constitute a significant economic loss for producers to not be able to sell some of the choicest cuts, like filet mignon and sirloin steak. The practice of selling this meat unlabeled is an obvious violation of many people's consumer choices. To be sure, as said above, it appears as a display of moral incoherence to be concerned solely with the stunning of animals, while many or most animals have not lived lives with an acceptable level of well-being due to the current characteristics of meat industry. However, such worry cannot be regarded as merely uninformed or irrational and, therefore, as unworthy of public respect. To be entitled to respect of their lifestyle choices, people need not always be required to take fully coherent stances and to be able to support those stances with rational ethical argumentation. Although some may, after deeper reflection, decide to switch to a diet that excludes meat from industrial farming, or even choose vegetarianism, those who choose to stay omnivorous should be respected in their wish not to eat meat from pre-stunned animals. Their preference may very well be sentimental and unprincipled, but it should not be disregarded and ignored on that account; many would really feel bad at the thought of eating an animal that has been killed in a way that they find unacceptable, and many others have actually felt outraged when they found out that they were *deceived* by being routinely sold such meat with no notice. At the very least, most consumers would feel that they are being unduly deprived of the possibility to choose. Arguably, they would contend that they are being discriminated against. It comes as no surprise that such feelings have been utilized in recent political campaigns against presumptive "Islamization" of originally non-Muslim societies.

Part of the income from the taxation of meat from non-stun methods could be used to refund producers for the loss of profit determined by not being able to sell a considerable amount of the meat – of course, alongside increased controls on the meat chain. However, it should be remembered that the proposed solution is only provisional and adapts to an unideal situation, in which animal husbandry's methods still largely tread upon animal well-being (as well as impacting negatively the global environment). Public discussion should be encouraged in order to make public opinion and religious practitioners more and more aware of all the grave issues related to the human consumption of meat.

Modern utilitarianism, deeply imbued with the Enlightenment spirit, seems to suit such a perspective of ethical progress. Current moral codes, including religious ones, should not be taken as immutable matters of fact. The progressive and reforming spirit of utilitarianism will show up in public discussion to help mutual comprehension between animalists and religious practitioners and to enhance sensibility and sympathy for the suffering of non-humans, something that will hopefully lead to a change in eating habits both for religious practitioners and for all other humans.

Related topics

The Challenges of Dietary Pluralism
The Ethics of Humane Animal Agriculture
Animal Welfare
Animal Rights and Food: Beyond Regan, Beyond Vegan?

Note

* Research for this chapter was carried out within the framework of the FIRB Research Project "Feeding Respect," funded by the Italian Ministry of Education, University and Research.

References

AHDB. (2010) "The Halal Meat Market," *AHDB Beef & Lamb*, viewed 4 November 2015, http://beefand-lamb.ahdb.org.uk/wp/wp-content/uploads/2013/05/p_cp_eblex_halal_meat_final_111110.pdf.

Arnett, G. (2014) "Why Does the Supply of Halal Meat Outstrip Demand?," *The Guardian*, viewed 4 November 2015, http://www.theguardian.com/news/datablog/2014/may/08/why-does-supply-halal-meat-outstrip-demand.

Beekman, V. (2000) "You Are What You Eat: Meat, Novel Protein Foods, and Consumptive Freedom," *Journal of Agricultural and Environmental Ethics* 12: 185–196.

Bentham, J. (1838–43) *The Complete Works of Jeremy Bentham*, Vol. I, published under the superintendence of his executor, John Bowring, Edinburgh-London: Tait-Simpkin, Marshall, and Co.

———. (1996 [1789]) *An Introduction to the Principles of Morals and Legislation*, edited by J. H. Burns and H.L.A. Hart, with a new introduction by F. Rosen, Oxford: Clarendon Press.

Brandt, R. (1979) *A Theory of the Good and the Right*, Oxford: Clarendon Press.

Broad, C. D. (1979) *Five Types of Ethical Theory*, London: Routledge & Kegan Paul.

Dardenne, E. (2010) "From Jeremy Bentham to Peter Singer," *Revue d'études benthamiennes* 7, viewed 28 May 2015, http://etudes-benthamiennes.revues.org/197.

Feinberg, J. (1980 [1970]) "The Nature and Value of Rights," in *Rights, Justice, and the Bounds of Liberty: Essays in Social Philosophy*, Princeton: Princeton University Press, pp. 143–158.

——. (1986) *Harm to Self*, Oxford: Oxford University Press.

Frey, R. (1983) *Rights, Killing, and Suffering: Moral Vegetarianism and Applied Ethics*, Oxford: Basil Blackwell.

FVE. (2002) "Slaughter of Animals Without Prior Stunning," Federation of Veterinarians of Europe, viewed 4 November 2015, http://www.fve.org/news/position_papers/animal_welfare/fve_02_104_slaughter_prior_stunning.pdf.

Giddens, A. (1991) *Modernity and Self-Identity: Self and Society in the Late Modern Age*, Cambridge: Polity.

Grandin, T. and J. M. Regenstein. (1994) "Religious Slaughter and Animal Welfare: A Discussion for Meat Scientists," *Meat Focus International*, March, 115–123.

Hart, H.L.A. (1982) *Essays on Bentham: Studies in Jurisprudence and Political Theory*, Oxford: Clarendon.

Korsgaard, C. (2004) "Fellow Creatures: Kantian Ethics and Our Duties to Animals," in G. B. Peterson (Ed.), *The Tanner Lectures on Human Values*, Vol. 25/26, Salt Lake City: University of Utah Press, pp. 77–110.

——. (2012) "A Kantian Case for Animal Rights," in M. Michel, D. Kühne, and J. Hänni (Eds.), *Animal Law: Developments and Perspectives in the 21st Century/Tier und Recht. Entwicklungen un Perspektiven im 21. Jahrhundert*, Zürich–St. Gallen: Dike, pp. 3–27.

Kramer, M. H. (1998) "Rights Without Trimmings," in M. H. Kramer, N. E. Simmonds, and H. Steiner (Eds.), *A Debate Over Rights*, Oxford: Oxford University Press, pp. 7–111.

Lamont, W. D. (1946) *Principles of Moral Judgment*, Oxford: Clarendon Press.

Needham, C. (2012) "Religious Slaughter of Animals in the EU," European Parliament Website, viewed 4 November 2015, http://www.europarl.europa.eu/RegData/bibliotheque/briefing/2012/120375/LDM_BRI%282012%29120375_REV2_EN.pdf.

Nozick, R. (1974) *Anarchy, State, and Utopia*, New York: Basic Books.

Raz, J. (1986) *The Morality of Freedom*, Oxford: Clarendon Press.

Regan, T. (1983) *The Case for Animal Rights*, London: Routledge & Kegan Paul.

Singer, P. (1980) "Utilitarianism and Vegetarianism," *Philosophy and Public Affairs* 9(4): 325–337.

——. (1986) "All Animals are Equal," in P. Singer (Ed.), *Applied Ethics*, Oxford: Oxford University Press, pp. 215–228.

——. (1993) *Practical Ethics*, 2nd ed., Cambridge: Cambridge University Press.

——. (1995) *Animal Liberation*, 2nd ed., with a new preface by the author, London: Pimlico.

—— and J. Mason. (2006) *The Way We Eat: Why Our Food Choices Matter*, New York: Rodale.

Steiner, H. (1994) *An Essay on Rights*, Oxford, UK–Cambridge, USA: Basil Blackwell.

——. (1998) "Working Rights," in M. H. Kramer, N. E. Simmonds, and H. Steiner (Eds.), *A Debate Over Rights*, Oxford: Oxford University Press, pp. 233–301.

Tooley, M. (1986 [1972]) "Abortion and Infanticide," in P. Singer (Ed.), *Applied Ethics*, Oxford: Oxford University Press, pp. 57–85.

Withnall, A. (2015) "Denmark bans kosher and halal slaughter as minister says 'animal rights come before religion'," The Independent, viewed 4 November 2015, http://www.independent.co.uk/news/world/europe/denmark-bans-halal-and-kosher-slaughter-as-minister-says-animal-rights-come-before-religion-9135580.html.

Wolgast, E. (1987) "Wrong Rights," *Hypatia* 2(1): 25–43.

30

SEAFOOD ETHICS

The normative trials of Neptune's treasure

Craig K. Harris

Introduction

In the early part of the 20th century, locales in various countries began to organize fishing derbies or fishing tournaments. These ranged in orientation from highly professional competitions to opportunities for novices to experience the pleasure of catching fish. Whatever their specific orientation, they were happy, celebratory occasions. But by 1980, these derbies and tournaments began to be the targets of protests. Salmon tournaments were protested because the salmon stocks were severely depleted. By 1993 People for the Ethical Treatment of Animals (PETA) were protesting that the derbies were inhumane and cruel to the fish. What had been an occasion for merriment and celebration was alleged to be unethical and immoral excess. In the decades since, that ethical tension has increased and has spread to all aspects of recreational and commercial fisheries.

This paper takes the perspective that ethics is about actors who have interests and how those actors relate to each other. The field of ethics, then, concerns the norms that apply to those relationships. This paper follows the approach of Latour (2004) and others, that actors can be humans at different scales of aggregation (from individual to global), other biological creatures at different scales of aggregation, or biophysical systems at different scales of organization. Given the diversity of relevant actors, it is not surprising that the paper will consider a wide variety of interests – material well-being, rights and freedoms, autonomy, sovereignty, development, self-actualization, sustainability, and resilience.

This paper will focus on fisheries as the harvesting and production of seafood. In this paper, fisheries will be divided into three types – subsistence, recreational, and commercial – based on the purposes of the human organizers of the activity. Subsistence fisheries occur in urban and rural areas of more developed countries, and throughout less developed countries. Recreational fisheries include both personal leisure activities (usually smaller scale), and commercial sport fisheries (e.g., charter boats, guides). More frequent and larger-scale recreational fisheries are more common in more developed countries; recreational fisheries in less developed countries are more likely to be upper class and expatriate specialty fishing rather than domestic working-class leisure activities. Commercial fisheries are the most diverse of the three types, ranging from boats and nets fished by one person to large factory ships; harvesting a range of species from the smallest krill to the largest tunas, sharks, and whales; and handling the harvest via modalities ranging from direct sales at the dock to further processing for wholesale distribution, or for use as feed in aquaculture. All three of these types of fisheries may include rights granted to indigenous peoples by treaties with national or colonial governments (e.g., Michigan, Oregon, Washington, New Zealand), and the aboriginal fisheries may be more likely to emphasize the spiritual and ceremonial aspects of the activity (Cooke and Murchie 2013).

Each type of fishery implicates a variety of ethical issues. Some of these issues are particular to that type of fishery; others are more general. Cooke and Murchie (2013) note that all three types have to deal with overexploitation, collateral mortality, intersectoral conflict, climate change, water availability, invasive species, and habitat alteration. Thus, the ethical issues that are implicated in the fisheries include both relationships among the harvesters, relationships between the harvesters and the targeted fish, relationships between the harvesters and other aquatic species and interests, and relationships between other human actors and the harvesters.

Seafood includes a wide variety of human food and animal feed that is harvested from freshwater and marine bodies of water. In general, seafood includes the edible seaweeds (e.g., wakame), the smallest animals (e.g., krill), the smallest fish (e.g., menhaden, anchovy), the largest animals (e.g., tuna, sharks, whales), and the largest shellfish (e.g., crab, lobster). Given the limitations of space, this article will cover only fish and shellfish and their byproducts (e.g., caviar). The ethical dimensions of seafood discussed in the paper will include a variety of final destinations for consumption – feed for farm animals and aquaculture, pet food, mass consumption items like fish sticks and tuna salad, and more upscale, luxurious items like bluefin tuna sushi and sharkfin soup and caviar.

The next three sections of the paper will discuss respectively the major ethical issues in the three fisheries. The following section of the paper will consider efforts to respond to these ethical issues. The remaining sections of the paper will look across the three fisheries to examine ethical issues involving access, labor, processing, marketing, management, and consumption.

Subsistence fisheries

Subsistence fishing is common among low-income persons and households in both urban and rural areas of more developed countries (West 1992). Many people in coastal and shoreline locations in less developed countries rely on subsistence fishing for a significant portion of their protein consumption (Harris et al. 1995). Thus ethical issues concerning subsistence fishing are often framed as the right to food (De Schutter 2010). Further, subsistence fishing includes members of groups protected by treaties (Native Americans, aboriginals in New Zealand) or by government policies (e.g., tribal groups in Brazil). It is often difficult to distinguish subsistence fisheries from small-scale commercial fisheries; if we could imagine a Chayanovian peasant fisher (Harrison 1977), his/her harvest of fish might be split roughly equally between household consumption and the market. And it can be difficult to distinguish between subsistence fisheries and small-scale recreational fisheries: if the employment and household demands on one's time leave one with time to go fishing, one is both enjoying a leisure activity and contributing to household subsistence.

One of the major ethical issues with fisheries is the impact of a fishery on the aquatic ecosystem. In general, subsistence fisheries are seen as conserving their aquatic ecosystems. Both in more developed and in less developed countries, subsistence fisheries tend not to use very powerful harvesting technology. Generally, a subsistence fisher keeps whatever s/he catches, and takes it home to be eaten. While some ethical issues exist with the harvesting techniques in some subsistence fisheries, they will be discussed under the rubric of the commercial fisheries. In one instance where potential overfishing was perceived to be an issue, an indigenous community on the island of Molokai created a community-based subsistence fishing area with a management arrangement to ensure the long-term sustainability of the fishery (Maui Now 2013).

With subsistence fisheries, ethical issues more frequently occur with respect to limitations on the availability of, or access to, fish and shellfish that would be desired by subsistence fishers and feasible for them to harvest. In Latin America and Southeast Asia, the conversion of mangrove swamps to aquaculture and beachfront for tourism facilities has deprived subsistence fishers of access to harvestable resources (Skladany and Harris 1995). In locations in the US and other more developed countries, the removal of dams changes the riverine habitat from slow-moving warm water favoring subsistence species (e.g., catfish) to faster-moving, cooler water favoring recreational species (e.g., trout). But this negative impact on the access of local low-income people to food for subsistence is rarely considered when decisions are made about removing aging dams. Further, water pollution from mining activities and petroleum production kills or contaminates subsistence species on which local people have depended for subsistence.

Not only is the anthropogenic toxic contamination of seafood an ethical issue, but the ways management agencies respond to the contaminated seafood also pose ethical problems for both subsistence and recreational fisheries. Recreational and subsistence fisheries are one of the main ways governments at various levels generate public political support. When the seafood in a fishery becomes contaminated, the natural resource management agency is reluctant to shut down the fishery totally. At the same time, to allow the fishery to continue without any warning or limitation would itself raise ethical issues. To deal with this dilemma, agencies have developed fish consumption advisories to inform anglers in what quantities and in what ways the contaminated fish can be consumed safely. However, the acceptable consumption levels in advisories are usually calculated from the perspective of an occasional recreational fishery and not from the perspective of a regular subsistence fishery (Fox Besek 2015), and even then, the advisory does not consider perinatal exposure (Binnington et al. 2014). To deal with this issue, the Spokane Tribe has established stricter water quality standards so that the fish do not become contaminated (Kramer 2014).

Recreational fisheries

Recreational fisheries range in scale from individuals seeking leisure and relaxation to commercially organized charter fisheries and guided fishing. The technologies utilized also range, somewhat in parallel, from simple hooks and lines to elaborate and powerful devices for finding fish, reeling in a line from great depths, and landing the catch. The diversity in recreational fisheries ranges from a young child on a riverbank with a pole and a line, to luxurious upscale tourism on yachts that have been outfitted for fishing. Given this great diversity, it is not surprising that social scientists allocate much effort to increasing the perceived well-being of recreational fishers (Hunt et al. 2013).

For many decades, recreational fishing has been viewed in Europe and North America as promoting the conservation of natural resources. Much of the writing about fishing in the late 19th through 20th centuries emphasized that spending time fishing both cleansed the soul and increased one's appreciation for nature (Andersen 2001). For Leopold (1949), fishing was one of the ways that one cultivated an environmental ethic, and an interest in recreational fishing has led to organized efforts for environmental conservation (e.g., the Izaak Walton League, Trout Unlimited).

Despite this longstanding positive view of the impacts of recreational fishing, by the middle of the 20th century a competing literature was emerging that argued that many aspects of recreational fisheries raise severe ethical problems (see Arlinghaus and Schwab 2011). These problems revolve around five issues. First, do animals in nature have interests? Second, if so, do humans have a duty to care for those interests? Third, to what extent do fish and shellfish experience sensations similar to pain (Elwood and Appel 2009; Magee and Elwood 2013; Rose et al. 2014)? To the extent that fish have interests (including perhaps freedom from pain), issues arise concerning whether the killing of fish for human nutrition can justify the negative impacts on the interests of the fish. Finally, there is the question whether those negative impacts can be justified by the pleasure and prestige the fisher gets from catching the fish. This last question became increasingly relevant as catch and release regulations were imposed for conservation purposes and for public relations purposes at fishing derbies. The policy and/or practice of catch and release became additionally contested because of allegations that fish did not survive after being released, especially after being brought rapidly to the surface from great depths. One effort to deal with this was a device called the Seaqualizer that was designed to avert the damage caused by the rapid change in depth (Kerr 2015).

The potential conflict between the interests of subsistence fishery and of recreational fishery was noted above. Here we would add the additional consideration that the interests of recreational fishing may also conflict with the interests of commercial fishing. This latter conflict may involve competition for the same species, or the negative impacts of the commercial fishery on the habitats of species targeted by the recreational fishery. In some cases, specific fisheries have been allocated either to recreational or commercial uses, either by government decision or by public referendum. As noted above, recreational fisheries are a major source of public political support for governments. In addition, it is often the case that recreational fishing generates more income in the local community than does commercial fishing (Monbiot 2014).

Commercial fisheries

Both globally and nationally, commercial fisheries account for the majority of the seafood harvest (Preble 2001). Thus it is not surprising that commercial fisheries raise the most, and the most pressing, ethical issues (Clover 2006; Wigans 1999). Commercial fishing outfits range in organizational scale from individuals and households (the Chayanovian piscatorial peasantry described above) to multi-billion-dollar corporations, which may be either primarily industrial or primarily financial, and in spatial scale from a local beach to the high seas of three or four oceans. The literature distinguishes small scale (Cordell 1990), intermediate scale (Freeman 1969), and large industrial scale (Fricke 1973). They range in harvesting technology from a simple net or longline to giant trawl nets, spotter aircraft, and fish-aggregating devices. Processing technology ranges from outdoor solar driers and small smoking kilns to mammoth factory ships, flash freezers, and canning machines. Distribution technology ranges from bicycles and sales at the beach to refrigerated trucks, rail cars, and air freight. While wild harvest is distinguished from aquacultural production, both have a large range of organizational, spatial, and technological scales.

Given the diversity of the commercial fisheries, it is not surprising that the ethical issues associated with the commercial fisheries are very diverse as well. The United Nations Food and Agriculture Organization (2005) distinguishes eight dimensions of the ethics of fisheries – fish stocks, ecosystems, fisheries, fishers, fishing communities, other stakeholders, consumers, and politicians. The first three of those dimensions will be discussed in this section. The other five dimensions will be considered in the remainder of the paper.

The issue of overfishing and depletion of fish stocks is one of the greatest concerns. The Patagonian toothfish, renamed the sea bass for commercial purposes, became so popular that in a matter of years it came to be overfished. An effort to establish a sustainable harvest was met with a large amount of poaching, which in turn gave rise to a public-private partnership to control poaching. While that has been successful, more recently Chilean fishers have had to sue the national government to reduce an excessive quota. Similarly, a large demand has been created for the minute shrimp called krill, for feed for fish farms and other farm animals, so concerns are being expressed about how to control the krill harvest.

It is important to be clear about the extent to which and the ways in which overfishing is an ethical issue. One ethical dimension of overfishing is that it is *IUU* – illegal, unreported, and done by unregistered vessels. But this legalistic approach raises questions both about corruption and about the responsibility for the enforcement of the relevant maritime codes (Martini 2013). Currently, the European Union is pressing Thailand to improve its enforcement of these regulations. In one case, a vessel belonging to the conservation organization Sea Shepherd pursued an IUU vessel until the sailors on the latter simply scuttled the ship and were picked up by the Sea Shepherd vessel. This case brings together the ethical issues of overfishing, illegal fishing, and vigilantism. But a significant amount of overfishing occurs in areas beyond national jurisdiction, so the legalistic approach cannot resolve all of the ethical issues with overfishing.

If a fish stock were depleted to virtually nothing, the interests harmed might include fishers whose operations are not highly mobile and flexible, future generations who might want to continue this fishery activity, local processors and marketers who depend on the supply of this species, and consumers who do not have access to alternative substitutes for this species. These ethical issues become particularly acute (Pramod 2014) when a fish stock in a less developed country (e.g., the countries of West Africa and the South Pacific) is being overfished by outfits from more developed countries (e.g., the European Union, China) because many less developed countries lack the capacity to control access to their territorial waters.

Another major ethical issue with commercial fisheries concerns impacts on species of fish and shellfish and other animals that are not the target of the fishery – nontarget species. Most commercial fishing technology is only partially selective, so usually the harvest includes some *bycatch* – species that the fishers do not want to keep because there is a strict quota or prohibition on their harvest, because there is not a sufficiently remunerative market for them at the boat's port, or because they would take up space on the vessel and displace the more valuable target species. Often the nontarget species have died during the harvesting process so they are discarded, or they are put back in the water alive but may fail to survive because of the high stress from being harvested.[1]

Bycatch and nontarget species pose several ethical issues. One is the wastefulness of discarding good food in a world where many people do not have secure access to food. Another is the negative impact on the harvested animals themselves. In some cases the nontarget species is a target for another fishery: in Alaska, the pollock fishery negatively impacts the halibut stock, which is the target for both commercial and recreational fisheries. In other cases the bycatch is a species on which humans have placed a high conservation value, either because of its scarcity or because of its "higher" evolutionary status. In the US, the two original bycatch issues were dolphins that were caught in purse seines for tuna, and turtles that were caught in trawls for shrimp. US law requires that marine mammals be protected, so the Department of Commerce has established a program to ensure that tuna has been produced without harm to dolphins, and the National Marine Fisheries Service requires that shrimp trawls be equipped with turtle excluder devices (TEDs). Outside the US, there is concern for the impacts of longline and driftnet fisheries on seabirds (Jackson 2013), sharks (Dapp et al. 2013), and turtles (Žydelis 2013).

Nontarget species issues also arise in connection with harvesting. When salmon congregate in nearshore areas before beginning their run upstream, they become easier prey for predatory birds. In aquaculture production, egrets and other piscivorous birds take advantage of the availability of fish. In both of these situations, the US Fish and Wildlife Service has authorized the killing of the birds to maintain the value of the harvest. On the other hand, one Spanish aquaculture enterprise simply allows predation by the birds as a cost of doing business (Klein 2013).

The third major ethical dimension listed by the United Nations Food and Agriculture Organization (FAO) concerns the impacts of commercial fishing on ecosystem functioning and ecosystem services. One specific example involves the large quantities of sardines that are harvested off the US west coast, which in turn impairs the viability of species that forage on sardines. Two more general examples involve the technologies of bottom trawling and aquaculture. The ecological impacts of bottom trawling are highly contested, with groups like the World Wide Fund for Nature (WWF)[2] posting videos of totally destroyed sea floors, and organizations like the Marine Stewardship Council citing research that shows minimal impacts from the technique.

A number of major ethical issues involve aquacultural production. When aquaculture was gaining traction in the middle of the 20th century, it was seen as an environmentally benign way of producing protein for a growing population, and as solving the problem that the world's fisheries were approaching maximum sustainable yields. With adaptable, fast-growing species like tilapia, the blue revolution could transform seafood production. In the decades since, potential problems with aquaculture have become evident, along with more potential benefits (e.g., labor safety). With the exception of China, most aquaculture has been implemented by private investors in capitalist societies, so most aquaculture has been oriented toward maximizing return on investment rather than toward production of affordable and accessible protein. Thus, most aquaculture has produced salmon and tilapia for higher-income consumers; currently, tuna and lobster aquaculture are being developed.

Fish are grown in ponds on land or in large net pens in the water at very high densities that raise issues of animal welfare. The aquacultural operations use a large amount of antibiotics and generate large amounts of fecal waste, both of which are released into the aquatic environment. Both with ponds and net pens, it is very common that the fish escape as a result of storms and floods; this raises issues concerning both the introduction of invasive species and interbreeding with native fish stocks (Volpe et al. 2000). In Southeast Asia and Central America it was very common to convert mangrove swamps into aquaculture ponds; this often transferred the property from long-term local communities to nonlocal investors, and it deprived the local people of the protection that the mangrove swamps had provided them against storms and tsunamis (Stonich 1995). In some cases the construction of the ponds displaced traditional local subsistence farms (Islam 2014). In Chile the Norwegian firm Marine Harvest expanded its operations despite opposition from indigenous Mapuche communities. The efforts of Red Lobster to develop lobster aquaculture in Indonesia were very explicitly an attempt to eliminate its dependence on developing country harvesters.

Aquaculture transfers genotypes from the wild to the farm, and then raises those genotypes in biophysical environments that are almost totally different from what they would have encountered in the wild. The density is much higher, the feed is totally different, mobility is highly restricted, water temperature and chemistry are different, and antibiotics are applied. These conditions raise the ethical issue: is this really a salmon?

The ethical issues concerning commercial fisheries provoke contentious questions (Mulvaney and Zivian 2013). At what point does a technology like a fish-aggregating device become so powerful that it violates some sense of fairness in wild harvest? At what point does the genetic modification of fish (e.g., salmon, grouper) become so great that it poses a likely possibility of significantly restructuring the aquatic ecosystem? If superfast growing salmon are raised only in open-ocean netpens far from shore, does that alleviate the ethical issues? At what point does a flash-processing supertrawler from a more developed country become so powerful that it would be unethical for it to harvest fish species that currently provide the livelihoods for smaller-scale harvesters in less developed countries?

Efforts to promote ethical systems and behaviors

In the global village of the 21st century, any significant perception of injustice and ethical lapse has the potential to threaten prestige and profitability. Thus it is not surprising that a variety of efforts have been undertaken to avert or alleviate the perceived ethical issues. One of the most common types of efforts has been to establish systems of standards for ethical conduct (Busch 2000). A standards system consists of a process for establishing the standard, a way of assessing compliance with the standard, and some means of enforcing the standard. One of the first standards for commercial fisheries was established by the Marine Stewardship Council (MSC), a partnership of the food corporation Unilever and the environmental organization World Wide Fund for Nature. The goal of the MSC was to certify fisheries for commercial species as being managed for sustainability, and then to allow firms to put the MSC logo on the packages of fish that came from certified fisheries.

This effort to deal with ethical issues in commercial fisheries has itself been accused of ethical breaches with regard to participation by all fishery stakeholders (especially fishers) and with regard to social sustainability (Bonnano and Constance 1996). The MSC certification process does not consider the social impacts of the management arrangements; for example, the certification of pollock and halibut fisheries in Alaska does not consider the impacts of the management arrangements on the native fishing communities. Fair-trade certification does consider the social and economic dimensions of compensation (Hatanaka 2010). Similarly, the efforts of the US government to ensure dolphin-safe tuna and turtle-safe shrimp have been challenged at the World Trade Organization by Mexico as unfair restrictions on trade. At this point Mexico and the US have agreed that Mexico's efforts to protect turtles are satisfactory, but the two countries are continuing to disagree about the fairness of the US regulations concerning dolphins.

A second type of effort has involved chefs in the US and the UK forming collectives with the commitment to offer in their restaurants fish without ethical issues. In some cases these efforts emphasized particular kinds of fish (e.g., avoiding Chilean sea bass before it was certified). In other cases the efforts involved eating smaller species of fish (Gulbrandsen 2010), eating less popular fish, eating lesser-known fish procured directly from local harvesters (Thorn 2015), and eating lower on the seafood chain. Nevertheless, even eating lower on the seafood chain raised ethical issues concerning overharvesting of fish that are the forage species for larger fish. In Turkey the *slowfish movement* convinced the government to raise the minimum size for harvesting bluefish by almost 50 percent. An offshoot of this effort in the UK was the Fishlove Project[3] that published pictures of nude celebrities hugging large fish. Although the project was relatively successful, it raised ethical issues of using female nudity to advance a social cause.

A third type of effort has involved the creation of marine reserve areas (MRAs) where no, or only a very low level, harvest is allowed. MRAs provide refugia where the stocks of overexploited species can recover, and these restored stocks then spill over into adjoining areas where they can be harvested. However, with MRAs there are ethical issues concerning the creation of the MRA without the involvement of the people living in the coastal zone of the MRA, and of the exclusion of those people from fishing in the MRA, again without their consent (López-Angarita et al. 2014).

There have been attempts to apply technical fixes to some of the ethical issues in fisheries. The use of TEDs was noted above. Circle hooks that increase the survival rate for catch and release, and for bycatch on longlines, are now required in Ecuador. Precision seafood harvesting is a way to focus effort only on the target species, and sustainable trawling techniques have been developed. As cobia became a popular species for aquaculture in the early years of the 21st century, concern was raised about the large amount of forage fish that had to be captured for feed; this led to a successful effort to convert the cobia to a vegetarian diet. Finally, aquaponic systems where both animals (fish, shellfish) and plants are raised in circulating water have been developed and implemented.

Technology to assess compliance with fisheries' ethical norms has also been developed. New Zealand requires cameras on fishing boats, and Mexico uses drones to verify the use of TEDs. Various social actors use satellite images to assess ethical behavior, and the vigilante activities of Sea Shepherd were noted above.

Finally, it is noteworthy that various corporate actors have emphasized ethical behavior with respect to fisheries. Some airlines have refused to transport shark fins. Some distributors have collaborated on seafood sustainability. Some food companies have specifically included due diligence for fisheries in their programs for corporate social responsibility. The Walton Family Foundation (Walmart) and Darden (Red Lobster) have established fisheries improvement projects to avert the depletion of fisheries. And the MSC has established the Global Fisheries Sustainability Fund to support research and outreach that will assist small-scale fisheries in achieving sustainability certification.[4]

Access

In the introduction to this chapter, it was noted that access is one of the fundamental ethical issues in all fisheries. Problems concerning access in the subsistence and recreational fisheries were mentioned briefly in the two sections above. This section will focus more on the variety of ethical issues concerning access in the commercial fishery.

McCay and Acheson (1990) suggest that access is one of the fundamental ways of organizing the management of fisheries across a broad spectrum of social formations. Ownership of riparian property (Faris 1972) and allocation of open water territories (Acheson 1988) have been ways of limiting access to harvesting opportunities to members of the local community. More recently, many governments have considered the establishment of Individual Transferable Quotas (ITQs) as a way of rationalizing investment and effort in commercial fisheries; Russia is using this approach to reduce the size of its Pacific fleet. Critics acknowledge the environmental and economic rationales, but they raise the ethical issue that ITQs convert what had been an open-access common-property resource to private property (Carothers and Chambers 2012). A World Bank panel has suggested that partial privatization is acceptable if it is done in conjunction with community control (Kinver 2013).

One aspect of the ethical problems with ITQs is the question of what interests wind up with control of the quota (Pinkerton and Davis 2015). In South America, the large-scale industrial fishing outfits have tended to crowd out the artisanal operations. In the UK, the government reallocated quota from large-scale operations to smaller-scale outfits, and the courts upheld this policy. The FAO has issued guidelines that emphasize the sustainability of small-scale operations. Many ethical questions have been raised about Israeli control of the Gaza fisheries.

Issues concerning access depend in part on the capacities of governments to control access to their aquatic territories. The government of Palau has begun burning Vietnamese fishing boats to discourage poaching in Palauan waters. Issues of seafood sovereignty (Harris 2013) lead to ethical questions about ocean grabbing (Bennett et al. 2015) – the exploitation of the seafood resources of less developed countries by fishing operations from more developed countries. Although such arrangements are permitted under the surplus clause in the United Nations Convention on the Law of the Sea, they become ethically problematic when they are made possible by subsidies from the governments of the more developed countries.

Labor

Television shows like *The Deadliest Catch* and movies like *A Perfect Storm* have raised public awareness of the occupational safety and health issues associated with the production of seafood.

Harvesting seafood on the open oceans or large lakes is inherently risky, so the ethical issue is more a question of whether the occupation has been made as safe as possible. This includes scheduling trips to avoid the most dangerous weather and carrying gear to maximize the likelihood of surviving an accident. One of the arguments in favor of ITQs is that they diminish the incentive to go out in very rough weather, especially early in the year when the weather is the most dangerous. Although the International Labor Organization has established conventions governing working conditions in the seafood industries, occupational safety and health issues persist even in the most modern processing plants (Barry 2013).

While the ethical issues of occupational safety and health apply in fisheries in both more and less developed countries, in the latter one is also likely to encounter ethical issues dealing with basic human rights. The fisheries of both Thailand and Kampuchea are perceived as relying on kidnapping and slavery, especially of the indigenous Rohingya, to work on the boats and on the shrimp farms. Along with forced labor, lack of promised compensation and child labor are common; while the International Labor Organization addresses compensation abuses,[5] the FAO has published guidelines on child labor.[6] Although very few fisheries workers belong to a labor union, recently the largest tuna company in Europe, Albacora, signed a collective agreement with the International Transport Workers Federation, the first agreement to cover workers on EU boats who are not EU nationals. Even though shrimp aquaculture shows some of the most advanced forms of capitalist exploitation of labor (Das 2014), unionization is very uncommon. Organizations like Fairfood do try to be certain that the shrimp processors they certify are treating workers fairly.

Processing and marketing

While some of the ethical issues involving labor in the processing and marketing sectors were noted in the preceding section, this section will focus on other types of ethical problems. In 2013, PETA released a video showing lobsters and crabs being killed by inhumane methods at a processing plant in Maine (PETA n.d.). In response, the Commissioner of the Maine Department of Marine Resources stated that the techniques shown in the video were compliant with state and federal laws and regulations (World Fishing and Aquaculture 2013). Turning to more social ethical questions, one of the issues with seafood processing is that the seafood is harvested from the waters of less developed countries and then frozen on the factory ship for processing later in more developed countries. This deprives the less developed country of the industrial development and the value added that comes from the processing.

Some of the ethical issues concerning seafood marketing apply generally to all food marketing; for example, one industry observer has suggested that Walmart pushed some US producers to lower their prices so much that the producers went bankrupt. At the same time, two or three ethical problems are specific to seafood. During the past couple of years in the US there has been concern about seafood products being mislabeled and about less expensive fish and shellfish being substituted for the more expensive product on the label. But even when the seafood is correctly labeled, one might raise ethical questions about the naming of the product. Indeed it is to some extent standard practice in the industry to rename a product with a more desirable name. When Clarence Birdseye developed flash freezing of fish fillets in the 1930s, "rockfish" had no name recognition; but many people in the US and Europe were accustomed to eating perch, so "ocean perch" was born. It was noted above that "Patagonian toothfish" sounded very unappealing, but "sea bass" resonated positively with the more familiar freshwater bass. Because some common names can refer to as many as 64 different species, the environmental group Oceana is advocating that the Department of Commerce should implement a policy of "one species, one name," so that buyers will get what they want and know what they are getting.

Management of the fishery

All fishery stakeholders and interests want management to "do the right thing." But is "the right thing" determined by consensus among biophysical scientists, or political power at the state or national level, or justice and fairness, or social power at the local level? Most commonly, managers balance conservation and food security (Hall et al. 2013). In the US, the Magnuson-Stevens Act mandates that federal fisheries management balance sustainable yield, economic return, community and social well-being, and seafood supply. Other governability schemes place greater emphasis on livelihood (Johnson 2013) or social justice (Fabinyi 2012; Jentoft 2013). Allison (2012) and Pullin (2013) call for a human-rights-based approach, while Charles (2013) divides this into harvest rights and management rights. In all of these approaches, the inclusion of indigenous perspectives is ethically important (Clifton and Majors 2012). Some of the most vexing problems in the management of US fisheries come from deciding what fraction of the stock of a target species to allocate for other predators, e.g., what share of the pollock stock should be allocated for marine mammals in general and for Steller's sea lion (an endangered species) in particular.

Some efforts to accomplish ethical management involve co-management – the inclusion of multiple perspectives and interests in the management process (Verelst 2013). Given the complexity of the situation, it is not surprising that different forms of co-management produce different outcomes (Cinner and Huchery 2015). While co-management often responds to fishery community activism and advocacy (Sundar 2012), it is not surprising that even in co-management, the distribution of power may leave fishers at a disadvantage (Njaya et al. 2011).

Within these broad normative issues, specific ethical questions arise. At the national level, how can compliance be ensured in an equitable fashion (Gezelius and Hauck 2011)? Whereas the government of Scotland provides assistance in complying with emerging regulations, the government of Indonesia imposed a regulation that made it impossible for small-scale outfits to fish for several months. How can nation-states and subnational units resolve differences in management approaches that significantly affect access? For example, the US government treats Gulf red snapper as a small-scale commercial harvest, but the states treat it as a recreational fish. In Alaska, some groups want to restrict the salmon in some areas to recreational harvest only.

Internationally, the vexing issues concern highly migratory species, IUU fishing, how to deal with a failed state, and how to implement the United Nations Convention on the Law of the Sea on the high seas in areas beyond national jurisdiction (Druel et al. 2013). In some cases one nation has detained and impounded boats of another nation that were violating an international agreement; in other cases, NGO actors have engaged in vigilantism.

Finally, the 500-pound sea monster in the management room is subsidies. More developed countries are able to provide their fishers with significant subsidies, which disadvantage the fishers of less developed countries when the former fish in the waters of the latter. The Doha trade negotiations are beginning their 15th year, and fishery subsidies have always been under discussion. This may be a paradigmatic instance of domestic politics trumping international ethics at the expense of public goods (Squires et al. 2014).

Gender

Gender is certainly one of the major ethical dimensions of fisheries. All aspects of fisheries – harvesting, aquaculture, processing, marketing, managing – are structured in gendered ways. The ethical aspects of gender in fisheries have been thoroughly addressed in two existing publications. Monfort (2014) summarizes the current state of knowledge concerning gender in fisheries and identifies the specific needs for further investigation concerning gender and fisheries. Further, Burton (2012) presents ten comparative perspectives on gender, representation, and agency in coastal communities.

An ethics of consumption

Part of the food movement in the US in recent years has been the admonition for consumers to be more mindful about the ethical dimensions of food – the labor processes, the environmental impacts, and the sociocultural elements of eating. Seafood has certainly been included in mindful eating. Both the Monterey Bay Aquarium and the New England Aquarium have made electronically available ratings of different seafoods in terms like "avoid," "good substitute," and "best choice." One of the goals of WWF and Unilever in establishing the Marine Stewardship Council was to make it possible for consumers to choose seafood products that were environmentally sustainable. More recently Bumble Bee Seafoods, the largest shelf-stable seafood company in North America, initiated the Superfresh and Wild Selections lines that are sourced from sustainably managed fisheries.

There is, of course, another end of the spectrum. Bluefin tuna continues to be overfished and sold as a luxury item for sushi. The finning of sharks continues in some locations to supply the prestigious consumption of sharkfin soup. Almas Iranian beluga caviar has not been constrained by the trade embargo. But even in their traditional cultures, these are increasingly seen as ostentatious, conspicuous consumption and not as models for society.

One of the most interesting issues of seafood ethics has concerned the consumption of fish by pregnant and breastfeeding women and women intending to become pregnant. In the 1990s, it became generally known that many of the large ocean fish (e.g., tuna) and some larger freshwater fish had high levels of mercury in their flesh from Asian and North American power plants. It was generally accepted that mercury had negative neurological impacts, and that fetuses and infants would be especially susceptible to these impacts. So it was recommended that pregnant, nursing, and childbearing women not consume fish. Then research supported by the seafood industry showed that the health benefits for women and children from the consumption of fish oils outweighed the negative neurological impacts from the mercury. So now it is recommended that such women eat fish. Lost in this whole saga is the ethical issue of whether women of childbearing age should have to choose between two very suboptimal alternatives, and the point that the ethical course of action is to eliminate the mercury from the diets of the fish as quickly as possible.

Conclusion

This paper has argued that ethical issues are alive and well in the fisheries of the world. In a paper of this length it has not been possible to cover ethical issues involving either fishery-dependent communities or global climate change, but the interests and actors that generate these problems, often the same actors who are working on the solutions, have been highlighted. The fisheries of the world live in interesting times.

Notes

1 When dealing with unwanted bycatch that is still alive, many fishers do try to behave ethically by puncturing the swim bladder of the fish so that it is not trapped at the surface of the water. It is not clear what impact this has on the survival of the fish in the intermediate term.
2 The World Wide Fund for Nature was formerly known as the World Wildlife Fund, which remains its name in Canada and the US.
3 For information, see <https://fishlove.co.uk/>.
4 See <https://www.msc.org/newsroom/news/msc-launches-global-fisheries-sustainability-fund> for information.
5 See <http://www.ilo.org/ilc/ILCSessions/103/reports/reports-to-the-conference/WCMS_235287/lang--en/index.htm>.
6 See <www.fao.org/docrep/018/i3318e/i3318e.pdf>.

References

Acheson, J. (1988) *The Lobster Gangs of Maine*, Lebanon: University Press of New England.

Allison, E. H., B. D. Ratner, B. Åsgård, R. Willmann, R. Pomeroy and J. Kurien, (2012) "Rights-based Fisheries Governance," *Fish and Fisheries* 13(1): 14–29.

Andersen, T. (2001) *The Application of a Co-Evolutionary Perspective to the Case of Deer Hunting Ethoses*, Ph.D. dissertation, Michigan State University Department of Sociology.

Arlinghaus, R. and A. Schwab. (2011) "Five Ethical Challenges to Recreational Fishing," *American Fisheries Society Symposium*.

Barry, F. (2013) "Herring "Fog" Puts Workers at Risk for Asthma and Allergies," *Food Quality News*, 22 August.

Bennett, N.J., H. Govan and T. Satterfield. (2015) "Ocean Grabbing," *Marine Policy* 57(July): 61–68.

Binnington, M.J., C.L. Quinn, M.S. McLachlan and F. Wania. (2014) "Evaluating the Effectiveness of Fish Consumption Advisories," *Environmental Health Perspectives*.

Bonnano, A. and D. Constance. (1996) *Caught In the Net*, Lawrence: University Press of Kansas.

Burton, V. (ed.) (2012) "Fish/Wives: Gender, Representation, and Agency in Coastal Communities," *Signs* 37(3): 527–536.

Busch, L. (2000) "The Moral Economy of Grades and Standards," *Journal of Rural Studies* 16(3): 273–283.

Carothers, C. and C. Chambers. (2012) "Fisheries Privatization and the Remaking of Fishery Systems," *Environment and Society* 3(1): 39–59.

Charles, A. (2013) "Governance of Tenure In Small Scale Fisheries," *Land Tenure Journal* 1(13): 9–37.

Cinner, J. and C. Huchery. (2015) "A Comparison of Social Outcomes Associated with Different Fisheries Co-management Institutions," *Conservation Letters* 7(3): 224–232.

Clifton, J. and C. Majors. (2012) "Culture, Conservation, and Conflict," *Society & Natural Resources* 25(7): 716–725.

Clover, C. (2006) *The End of the Line*, New York: The New Press.

Cooke, S. and K. Murchie. (2013) "Status of Aboriginal, Commercial and Recreational Inland Fisheries in North America," *Fisheries Management and Ecology* 22(1): 1–13.

Cordell, J. (1990) *A Sea of Small Boats*, Cambridge, MA: Cultural Survival.

Dapp, D., R. Arauz, J.R. Spotila and M.P. O'Connor. (2013) "Impact of Costa Rican Longline Fishery on its Bycatch of Sharks, Stingrays, Bony Fish and Olive Ridley Turtles (Lepidochelysolivacea)," *Journal of Experimental Marine Biology and Ecology* 448: 228–239.

Das, R. (2014) "Low-Wage Capitalism, Social Difference, and Nature-Dependent Production," *Human Geography* 7(1), http://www.hugeog.com/index.php/component/content/article?id=307:v7n1-das.

De Schutter, O. (2010) *International Human Rights Law: Cases, Materials, Commentary*, Cambridge: Cambridge University Press.

Druel, E., R. Billé and J. Rochette. (2013) *Getting to Yes? Discussions Towards an Implementing Agreement to UNCLOS on Biodiversity in ABNJ*, IDDRI (Institut du développement durable et des relations internationals), policy brief No. 10.

Elwood, R. and M. Appel. (2009) "Pain Experience in Hermit Crabs?," *Animal Behaviour* 77(5): 1243–1246.

Fabinyi, M. (2012) *Fishing for Fairness*, Australian National University Press.

Faris, J. (1972) *Cat Harbour*, St. Johns, NL: Memorial University of Newfoundland.

Fox Besek, J. (2015) "Neoliberal Niagara?," *Environment and Planning D* 33(2): 281–295.

Freeman, M. (1969) *Intermediate Adaptation in Newfoundland and the Arctic*, St. Johns, NL: Memorial University of Newfoundland.

Fricke, P. (1973) *Seafarer and Community*, London: Croom Helm.

Gezelius, S. and M. Hauck. (2011) "Toward a Theory of Compliance in State-Regulated Livelihoods," *Law & Society Review* 45(2): 435–470.

Gulbrandsen, L. (2010) *Transnational Environmental Governance*, Cheltenham, UK: Edward Elgar Publishing.

Hall, S.J., R. Hilborn, N.L. Andrew and E.H. Allison. (2013) "Innovations in Capture Fisheries are an Imperative for Nutrition Security in the Developing World," *Proceedings of the National Academy of Sciences* 110(21): 8393–8398.

Harris, C. (2013) "King of the Sea," *Food Sovereignty*, 14–15 September, http://www.iss.nl/fileadmin/ASSETS/iss/Research_and_projects/Research_networks/ICAS/61_Harris_2013.pdf.

——, D.S. Wiley and D.C. Wilson. (1995) "Socio-Economic Impacts of Introduced Species In Lake Victoria Fisheries," in T. Pitcher and P. Hart (eds.), *The Impact of Species Changes In African Lakes*, London: Chapman and Hall, pp. 215–242.

Harrison, M. (1977) "The Peasant Mode of Production in the Work of A.V. Chayanov," *The Journal of Peasant Studies* 4(4): 323–336.

Hatanaka, M. (2010) "Certification, Partnership, and Morality in an Organic Shrimp Network," *World Development* 38(5): 706–716.

Hunt, L.M., S.G. Sutton and R. Arlinghaus. (2013) "Illustrating the critical role of human dimensions research," *Fisheries Management and Ecology* 20(2–3): 111–124.

Islam, M. (2014) *Confronting the Blue Revolution*, Toronto: The University of Toronto Press.

Jackson, S. (2013) "Fishermen Work to Reduce Albatross Deaths," *National Geographic Ocean Views*, 2 December.

Jentoft, S. (2013) "Social Justice in the Context of Fisheries," in M. Bavinck, R. Chuenpagdee, S. Jentoft and J. Kooiman (eds.), *Governability of Fisheries and Aquaculture*, Amsterdam: MARE Publication Series, pp. 45–65.

Johnson, D. (2013) "Livelihoods in the Context of Fisheries," in M. Bavinck, R. Chuenpagdee, S. Jentoft and J. Kooiman (eds.), *Governability of Fisheries and Aquaculture*, Amsterdam: MARE Publication Series, pp. 67–86.

Kerr, M. (2015) "The SeaQualizer Gives Doomed Fish a Fighting Chance," *Gear*, 21 June.

Kinver, M. (2013) "Collective Rights 'Offer Hope for Global Fisheries,'" *BBC News*, 24 September.

Klein, D. (2013) "This Fish Farm gives a Portion of its Product to Predators," *Grist*, 7 July 2013, http://grist.org/food/this-fish-farm-gives-a-portion-of-its-product-to-predators/.

Kramer, B. (2014) "Tribe Sets New Spokane River Pollution Standards," *The Spokesman-Review*, 6 January, http://www.spokesman.com/stories/2014/jan/06/tribe-sets-new-spokane-river-pollution-standards/.

Latour, B. (2004) *Reassembling the Social: An Introduction to Actor–Network Theory*, Oxford: Oxford University Press.

Leopold, A. (1949) *A Sand County Almanac*, Oxford: Oxford University Press.

López-Angarita, J., R. Moreno-Sánchez, J.H. Maldonado and J.A. Sánchez. (2014) "Evaluating Linked Social-ecological Systems in Marine Protected Areas," *Conservation Letters* 7(3): 241–252.

Magee, B. and R. Elwood. (2013) "Shock Avoidance by Discrimination Learning in the Shore Crab (*Carcinusmaenas*) is Consistent with a Key Criterion for Pain," *Journal of Experimental Biology* 216: 353–358.

Martini, M. (2013) "Illegal, Unreported and Unregulated Fishing and Corruption," *Transparency International*, 5 September, http://www.transparency.org/whatwedo/answer/illegal_unreported_and_unregulated_fishing_and_corruption.

Maui Now. (2013) "Moʻomomi Community-Based Subsistence Fishing Area Proposed," 31 December, http://mauinow.com/2013/12/31/moomomi-community-based-subsistence-fishing-area-proposed/.

McCay, B. and J. Acheson. (1990) *The Question of the Commons*, Tucson: University of Arizona Press.

Monbiot, G. (2014) "Anglers are Our Allies Against Unsustainable Industrial Fishing," *The Guardian*, 24 January, http://www.theguardian.com/environment/georgemonbiot/2014/jan/24/anglers-sport-fishers-fishing-george-monbiot.

Monfort, M. (2014) *The Role of Women in the Seafood Industry*, United Nations Food and Agriculture Organization Globefish Research Programme, Volume 119.

Mulvaney, D. and A. Zivian. (2013) "Sowing Seeds of Hope in California's Fields of Resistance to Pharm Rice and Frankenfish," *Journal of Political Ecology* 20: 70–179.

Njaya, F., S. Donda and C. Béné. (2011) "Analysis of Power in Fisheries Co-Management," *Society & Natural Resources* 25(7): 652–666.

Office of Director General. (2005) *Ethical Issues in Fisheries*, United Nations Food and Agriculture Organization, http://www.fao.org/docrep/008/y6634e/y6634e00.htm.

PETA (People for the Ethical Treatment of Animals). (n.d.) "Undercover Exposé Reveals Live Lobsters, Crabs Torn Apart!" *PETA.com*, viewed 13 October 2015, http://www.peta.org/action/action-alerts/undercover-expose-reveals-live-lobsters-crabs-torn-apart-2/.

Pramod, G., K. Nakamura, T.J. Pitcher and L. Delagran. (2014) "Estimates of Illegal and Unreported Fish in Seafood Imports to the USA," *Marine Policy* 48: 102–113.

Preble, D. (2001) *The Fishes of the Sea: Commercial and Sport Fishing in New England*, Dobbs Ferry: Sheridan House.

Pinkerton, E. and R. Davis. (2015) "Neoliberalism and the Politics of Enclosure in North American Small-scale Fisheries," *Marine Policy*, 11 April, http://www.sciencedirect.com/science/article/pii/S0308597X15000743.

Pullin, R. (2013) "Food Security in the Context of Fisheries and Aquaculture," in M. Bavinck, R. Chuenpagdee, S. Jentoft and J. Kooiman (eds.), *Governability of Fisheries and Aquaculture*, Amsterdam: MARE Publication Series, pp. 87–109.

Rose, J.D., R. Arlinghaus, S.J. Cooke, B.K. Diggles, W. Sawynok, E.D. Stevens and C.D.L. Wynne. (2014) "Can Fish Really Feel Pain?" *Fish and Fisheries* 15(1): 97–133.

Skladany, M. and C. Harris. (1995) "On Global Pond," in P. McMichael (ed.), *Food and Agricultural Systems in the World Economy*, Westport: Greenwood Press, pp. 169–192.

Squires, D., R. Clarke and V. Chan. (2014) "Subsidies, Public Goods, and External Benefits in Fisheries," *Marine Policy* 45: 222–227.

Stonich, S. (1995) "The Environmental Quality and Social Justice Implications of Shrimp Mariculture Development in Honduras," *Human Ecology* 23(2): 143–168.

Sundar, A. (2012) "Alternatives to Crisis," *Human Geography* 5(2), http://www.hugeog.com/index.php/component/content/article?id=221:globalfisheries-5–2.

Thorn, B. (2015) "Chef Applies Farm-to-Table Approach to Seafood," *Nation's Restaurant News*, 15 June, http://nrn.com/seafood-trends/chef-applies-farm-table-approach-seafood.

Verelst, B. (2013) "Managing Inequality," *Journal of Political Ecology* 20: 14–36.

Volpe, J.P., E.B. Taylor, D.W. Rimmer and B.W. Glickman. (2000) "Evidence of Natural Reproduction of Aquaculture-escaped Atlantic Salmon in a Coastal British Columbia River," *Conservation Biology* 14(3): 899–903.

West, P. (1992) "Minority Anglers and Toxic Fish Consumption," in B. Bryant and P. Mohai (eds.), *Race and the Incidence of Environmental Hazards*, Boulder: Westview Press, pp. 100–113.

Wigans, M. (1999) *The Last of the Hunter Gatherers*, Minneapolis: Voyageur Press.

World Fishing and Aquaculture. (2013) "'Extreme' Lobster Killing Is Compliant with Regulations," 19 September, http://www.worldfishing.net/news101/industry-news/extreme-lobster-killing-is-compliant-with-regulations.

Žydelis, R., C. Small and G. French. (2013) "The Incidental Catch of Seabirds in Gillnet Fisheries," *Biological Conservation* 162: 76–88.

PART VII
Food justice

31

SAVING A DYNAMIC SYSTEM

Sustainable adaptation and the Balinese subak

Thomas C. Hilde, Matthew R. G. Regan, and Wiwik Dharmiasih

Introduction

Set against a background of widespread, unsustainable resource use, sustainable development is aspirational, a normative ideal or set of goals to be achieved. The United Nations Sustainable Development Goals reflected this aspiration in 2015, as did the Brundtland Report, *Our Common Future*, in 1987.[1] Whatever the object of sustainability under discussion – a non-polluting practice, a healthy-forest ecosystem, management of petroleum reserves, a local agricultural community, the planet – we are not there yet.

Ideals have very real impacts on how we think about, critique, and change practices. An ideal of sustainability, whether global or local, helps us determine what is unsustainable. Fixed, stubbornly held ideals can be dangerous, especially when they cloud our ability to see what is in front of us. General conceptions of sustainability risk losing usefulness as normative ideals; what works in one socio-cultural and ecological context might be irrelevant in another. Furthermore, the temporal horizon for policy-making is impeded by both the problem of long-term projection and near-term political exigencies.

Outside the usual sphere for discussions of sustainability, however, resilient, sustainable systems do exist. Local systems that may in practice comprise general conceptions of sustainability are sometimes concealed by the institutional and conceptual frameworks of the larger discourse. This essay does not address how to build better sustainable systems; rather, it is about how to manage disruptions of already-existing systems that have demonstrated resilient sustainability. We discuss one such system, a rice cultivation and irrigation system that has existed for a millennium, the *subak* water temple system of Bali, Indonesia. This case allows us to see what an actual sustainable system looks like and consider the source of its resilience. The subaks are currently threatened with radical change and potential collapse from endogenous and exogenous forces. We discuss these disruptions and the interventions intended to mitigate them. We argue that any intervention that exogenously sets out to manage the system from an a priori conception of sustainability will fail. The complexity of subak resource management and ritual impels us to look in a very different direction.

The Balinese subak

Bali is a remarkably transformed landscape, sculpted with intricate hillside terraces and dotted with ornate temples. Its picturesque vistas, however, conceal the complex interactions that have shaped them, including one that, ironically, was largely a mystery even to most Balinese, until it nearly collapsed: the complex network of irrigation associations known as subaks. Studied by anthropologist Stephen Lansing (Lansing 1991; 1995), the near-collapse that followed the introduction of high-yield, fast-growing Green Revolution rice strains by the government in the 1970s, and the nearly catastrophic blight of pests that followed the abandonment of traditional cultivation methods for modern, "scientific" ones, demonstrated just how far-reaching the subak system really was. Rather than "simply" a traditional way of growing rice, the subak system incorporated a whole range of concepts and relationships, summarized into what the Balinese call *tri hita karana* (THK) – the three sources of goodness, understood as harmonious relationships between humans and the spiritual realms *(parhyangan)*, between humans and other humans *(pawongan)*, and between humans and nature *(palemahan)*.

The three dimensions of THK play out intimately in the relationships covered by the subak system. The most obvious, the relationship between humans and nature, is inherent to a degree in every agricultural system. Agriculture occurs on a precipice of chaos, as human cultivators, the organisms they cultivate, and the various other features of the natural landscape tread the difficult path to a successful harvest. In the subak system, resources – most notably water – are allocated through a complex series of religious and social institutions (the other two dimensions of THK). On a small volcanic island like Bali, the actions of upstream farmers can have serious impacts on those downstream. Likewise, flooding, draining, and harvesting patterns have remarkable effects on the control of rice pests. Lansing (2006) found that the behavior of subaks can be modeled with a few simple rules, and when iterated over many generations can even produce astonishingly similar cropping patterns to those found in the field.

Unlike Lansing's automated subaks, however, real subaks make their decisions through a system of deliberation and egalitarian consensus, bringing us to the second dimension of THK, the relationship between humans. The subak itself is a social unit, an association of farmers who all own plots of land related to a specific node in the irrigation network. These farmers, whether they own a few hectares or many, are all entitled to participate in subak meetings, where decisions about planting, flooding, and fallowing are made. Unlike other social institutions in Bali, caste does not determine authority in the subak assembly, although from our discussions with the farmers, there seems to be a system of social norms that nudges decisions towards consensus.

Once a decision has been reached, a religious ceremony occurs, which serves not only to ensure the proper spiritual conditions for the task at hand – every major event in the cultivation cycle has an associated ceremony – but also to further strengthen the bonds among members. Thus enters the third dimension of THK, the spiritual. Just as Lansing's computer model showed that the application of simple cropping principles can transmit data across the irrigation system, affecting farmers who might never meet face-to-face, so too can the ritual life of the subaks be seen as connecting each individual field within the dense matrix of Balinese cosmology. In Balinese Hinduism, all goodness derives ultimately from God, who manifests in various forms depending on cosmological function: subak farmers worship at *Ulun Danu* temples to give thanks to the goddess of the lake, Dewi Danu, who resides in and gives the blessing of life through its water; shrines to Dewi Sri, goddess of rice, who is believed to inhabit the rice fields and grants life and prosperity through the paddies; *Ulun Suwi* or *Bedugul* temples located at every dam and division point in the irrigation system sharing the same water source; and of course every individual rice field, each of which has its own shrine. Farmers perform individual offerings and communal ceremonies organized by their subak. While this dimension might not seem as intuitive as the environmental and social dimensions, to the Balinese farmers, the connection between a good harvest and maintenance of the proper rituals and spiritual practices is not trivial – it is vital.

The subak as complex adaptive social-ecological system

The most influential anthropologists to study Bali, Clifford Geertz (1980) and Lansing (1991; 2006), both caution against applying orthodox social science models to Bali, approaching it as either pre-modern or modern, hierarchical or egalitarian. Lansing writes:

> The more we understand about Balinese society, the more the Balinese people seem to be marching off in both directions at once, adding new embellishments to their ancient rituals of status while also devoting themselves to the perfection of formal systems of self-governance.
>
> (Lansing 2006: 5)[2]

Elsewhere he notes, "the water temples inhabit a world largely outside the domain of social theory as it is presently constituted" (Lansing 1991: 8). To understand the subaks and temple network we must understand that a subak is at once a technological unit, physical unit, social unit, legal unit, and religious unit, on multiple ecological scales, fitting within a larger system of associations of customary villages *(desa adat)*, hamlets *(banjar)*, temple congregations *(pemaksan)*, and kinship groups *(dadia)* (Lorenzen and Lorenzen 2011), not to mention the Bali provincial government, the Indonesian state, and global society. In short, we must understand the subak as a social-ecological system (SES).

We use the term SES in two senses. First, the concept implies a transactional relationship between culture and nature, one in which human values are shaped by ecological features in the process of reshaping those features. Human beings are inescapably organisms in an environment, which renders the distinction between environmental and social systems artificial and arbitrary (Berkes and Folke 1998: 4). For the Balinese, for example, water is much more than an environmental resource to be managed by society. Water is a sacred substance that plays a vital role in nearly every aspect of social and ritual life.

Second, as Elinor Ostrom puts it, SESs:

> ... are composed of multiple subsystems and internal variables within these subsystems at multiple levels analogous to organisms composed of organs, organs of tissues, tissues of cells, cells of proteins, etc.... In a complex SES, subsystems such as a resource system ..., resource units ..., users ..., and governance systems ... are relatively separable but interact to produce outcomes at the SES level, which in turn feed back to affect these subsystems and their components, as well other larger or smaller SESs.
>
> (Ostrom 2009: 419)

We can distinguish functional nodes within the broader system, but their inputs and outputs are ultimately determined relationally on different temporal and spatial scales. In the Balinese case, they coevolved. As Geertz writes, "a complex ecological order was both reflected in and shaped by an equally complex ritual order, which at once grew out of it and was imposed upon it" (Geertz 1980: 82). The continuity and iterations of the democratic, consensus-based decision-making[3] of subak farmers is influenced by the empirical results of rice cultivation. These are dependent on collective management of the common resource of sacred water through subak irrigation systems, which are in turn embedded in a context of religious ritual, political patronage, and myriad overlapping social groups. This complex, in turn, provides resources for and meaning to rice farming in both the tangible *(sekala)* and intangible *(niskala)* realms.

The subaks and water temples form a "group of actors or agents engaged in a process of coadaptation, in which adaptive moves by individuals have consequences for their neighbors" (Lansing 2006: 83). Among other features, a complex adaptive system is typically characterized by the diversity and connectivity of its components, simple rules of interaction, constant change, self-organization rather than planning, and emergence or system-wide features that result unpredictably from the interaction of individual components. Classic examples are termite mounds, stock markets, and the brain (Norberg and Cumming 2008).

One of the most important elements in the ecology of Balinese rice paddies is pest control. Using his simulation model along with survey data, Lansing and his team found that individual farmers act in response to the success or failure of neighboring farmers' cultivation practices, who likewise act in response to other neighboring farmers, yielding system-wide self-organization through simple information sharing. Small adaptations in one subak can have broad effects across a range of subaks. The cooperative interactions of individual farmers and subaks generated synchronized flooding and fallowing schedules across a broad network of distant subaks without top-down planning (Lansing 2006: 67–87). Lansing's insight addresses the question of why upstream farms would share water with downstream farms. Coordinated irrigation schedules and synchronized fallow periods essentially created a landscape in which pests have few places to go, rather than hopping from one set of flooded terraces to another set of terraces with ripening rice. Downstream farmers required a steady flow of water, but upstream farmers required downstream farmers to coordinate cropping patterns in order to control pests. Thus, multi-scale coordination occurs across the landscape. Furthermore, Bali's rugged landscape features hundreds of lush ravines, creating myriad microclimates or microecosystems. Although broad patterns of crop management develop at the system level, the system comprises local variations in planting and harvesting across different ecological features to which some individual farms and subaks are better adapted than others. While there is systemic coordination, there is also local variety.

An understanding of the subaks as a complex adaptive SES allows us to see how sustainability emerges at a systems level rather than through central planning or other programmatic efforts. Drawing on Paul Thompson's work on sustainable agriculture (Thompson 2010), we might regard the features of a sustainable food system as three interlinked aspects: sufficient production to meet the desired goal (resource sufficiency), agricultural practices that are not destructive of the larger social-ecological context (functional integrity), and the socio-cultural values associated with agricultural practices (sustainability as "nonsubstantive" norm). Moving from these *character traits* to a functional understanding of a system's sustainability, however, requires a sort of examination that even many accounts of sustainability do not fully envision. The Brundtland Report and similar macro-level models of sustainability – as generalized activity occurring in linear progression towards an idealized future state – are of little help in describing and understanding a system of active agents in a dynamic social-ecological context that requires constant cooperation and adaptation within a non-linear conception of time (Eiseman 1990; Lansing 1991). While macro-level models have much to offer in terms of parsimony and conceptual completeness, when overlapped with the dynamic conditions of the field, the neat edges and clean lines that make them so appealing actually dull their applicability. Given such a challenge, it is tempting to dismiss micro-level features as elements in the system that, although they must have some role in the final tally, can be abstracted away with a cursory nod to local variability or systemic randomness.

While such a tactic can provide much-needed clarity, it can also obscure critical details of a system's operation. To frame our discussion of the sustainability of the subak system, then, we turn to Ostrom's design principles drawn from empirical study of long-term, common-pool resource systems (Ostrom 1990; 2005).

The sustainable subak?

Ostrom outlines what she refers to as *design principles* for robust SESs and the management of common-pool resources in two major works (Ostrom 1990; 2005). Since her initial statement of the principles in 1990, they have been explored by others in numerous field studies across the world. Armed with this new data, Ostrom updated the principles in 2005. Without the space here to detail Ostrom's own analyses of these principles and the field studies, we borrow them to sketch an outline of the features of the subak system that we find integral to its longevity and resilience.

Clearly defined boundaries

For Ostrom, boundaries address the problem of free riding on the use of a common-pool resource. In Bali, this resource is water. As a sacred resource, there exist rights of use, but not rights of exclusion (Caponera and Nanni 2007: 90–91). As water runs from its upland sources into rivers, it goes through a series of engineered diversions to different groups of subaks. Given the rugged topography, this has often involved creating tunnels through the rock, some of which date back centuries. As water joins particular groupings of farmers' paddies – through, perhaps, a network of channels and tunnels coming from a river – the boundaries of a subak are given definition. The boundaries are demarcated by a shared water source, but there is always an outflow so that the water may return to other subak fields or the river, and ultimately flow to the sea. Temples mark these "boundaries." As water moves through one terrace to another in a subak, smaller temples also mark individual farmers' fields. The temples do not, however, demarcate claims to ownership as we typically understand this in Western property schemes: "Each shrine or temple is associated with some particular component of the irrigated landscape" (Lansing 1991: 52). Subak and larger temples are sites of congregation and worship. Since many subaks share the same water source further upstream – the same river or ultimately the crater lake for all subaks – inter-subak associations and the holiest temples mark these sources. All are responsible for offerings to these temples. Temples at different scales serve as coordinating devices for the entire network, while authority over the irrigation systems is retained by farmers in "a bottom-up system of irrigation management [functioning] in the absence of hierarchical control" (Lansing 2000: 310). Ostrom's concerns about boundaries stem from the Tragedy of the Commons myth,[4] for which the typical responses are privatization of the resource, a coercive external authority, or a system of direct reciprocity. According to Lansing, none of these response types explain subak cooperation, nor do models like the Prisoner's Dilemma. Rather, cooperation emerges from practical needs, such as controlling pests through synchronized fallowing, flooding, and planting periods (Lansing 2006: 68–87). "The water temples derive all the authority they need from their practical success in managing the ecology of the rice terraces, and their symbolic association with the gods" (Lansing 2006: 87). The water temple network allows for information sharing, communication, and coordination of the relevant schedules. Fidelity to coordination and cooperation is a function of the pragmatic success of the system. The temples serve as nodes in a multi-scalar complex adaptive SES, "awaken[ing] the powers of the collective, not the individual, by emphasizing not the singular but the universal and stereotypical" (Lansing 2006: 128).

Proportional equivalence between benefits and costs

This principle involves finding a fair balance between individuals' inputs into a system and the benefits received from those efforts, along with rules devised to ensure fair apportionment. Subaks have sets of rules codified as *awig-awig.* "These laws regulate rights and duties among the members of the subak. Such rights and duties include public obligations, regulations concerning land and water use, legal transactions of land transfer, and collective religious ceremonies" (Lorenzen et al. 2005: 1). The formal process involved in consulting *awig-awig,* however, is rarely pursued and even considered impolite (Lorenzen et al. 2005: 1–3). The same goes for using more than one's share of water. A farmer may need to use more water and request to "borrow" it from another farmer by opening the inlet to his field. When needed, farmers allow the subak head *(pekaseh* or *klian subak)* to determine the fair allotment of water. The *pekaseh* also monitors other features of the rice terraces, such as size and contours (there is an aesthetic dimension to the job, hence the subak's contributions to the beauty of Bali). Much of this borrowing is negotiated between farmers, however. According to Lorenzen and Lorenzen, shame is the normative check on potential advantages taken in the balance between inputs and benefits. The result is near-universal cooperation (Lorenzen and Lorenzen 2001). In Balinese society, shame will have an effect not only in the relationship between individual subak farmers but in the other forms of association through which farmers and their families interact in both the material and spiritual realms. Furthermore:

> . . . the acceptance of borrowing water gives the *subak* heads and the farmers the necessary flexibility to instantly respond to water stresses. Formal avenues or strict regulations hinder spontaneity. Informal arrangements and formal regulations complement each other and strengthen the system. Social, cultural, and religious values bind the farmers in a way that the social consequences for non-compliance seem unbearable.
>
> (Lorenzen et al. 2005: 5)

Collective choice arrangements

One reason subak farmers so readily follow basic norms of sharing and decision-making is that normative rules are themselves collectively determined and modified. Ostrom writes:

> resource regimes that use this principle are both better able to tailor rules to local circumstance and to devise rules that are considered fair by participants. As environments change over time, being able to craft local rules is particularly important as officials located far away do not know of the change.
>
> (Ostrom 2005: 263)

Each subak holds meetings, usually once per month, where decisions are made democratically regarding planting, water management, dam maintenance, and the management of funds. There is a leadership structure within the subak, but all decisions, including the setting of simple rules, are made by subak farmers themselves. One can say that, because of the participatory nature of rule formation and modification, they are manifestations of farmers' agency. Perhaps this explains why it is said that *awig-awig* needs rarely to be consulted. Lansing has long insisted that subak rule-making and network governance is ultimately a bottom-up affair, despite some criticism of this view (Hauser-Schäublin 2012; Helmreich 1999; Lansing 1991; 2000). He notes that "the democracy of the water temples expects failures, because it is based on an attempt to mobilize the resources of fallible human community" (Lansing 2006: 150).

Monitoring

Ostrom maintains that few long-term common-pool resource regimes can survive only on communal trust – they require exogenous monitoring and rule enforcement (Ostrom 2005: 265). In the subak case, formal monitoring and enforcement of the rules of water distribution, rice terrace construction, and such is also the role of the *pekaseh* and his deputies. Much of what is said above about costs, benefits, and collective choice holds here. Two further elements are important, however. Norms are not merely internalized rules given in the tangible world *(sekala)*. They are reinforced by the intangible, occult realm *(niskala)*, populated by gods and demons that manifest themselves in omens, accidents, emotions, family struggles, and so on. While the tendency in the West is to view policing the rules as a role of the state, the subaks are different. Lansing writes:

> . . . [the subaks] sought ways to enhance the ability of individuals to master their own emotions. This was a much more ambitious goal, and required a different kind of social institution. The elaborate rituals of the water temples convey a powerful message: that when individuals and subaks succeed in mastering themselves, the world (or at least the microcosm controlled by the subak) becomes more orderly. The flooded terraces resemble sparkling jewels, there are no plagues of pests, and the social life of families and communities is harmonious. . . . [W]hen Reason gives way to destructive emotions, the effects are soon seen in quarreling families, disorderly fields, sickness, poverty, and pests. . . . Implicit in such beliefs is an enhanced sense of efficacy – an assumption that if a subak can manage to achieve a state of collective harmony, the effects will permeate the living world.
>
> (Lansing 2006: 196)

An ordered self and community reflect an ordered landscape, and vice versa. Thus, ecological signals do not merely convey data important for farmers' economic livelihoods, but provide feedback information into the state of one's self and one's community as itself a monitoring mechanism. In this respect, ecological failures are less failures of resource-management rule violations as they are failures of piety.

Graduated sanctions and conflict resolution mechanisms

Graduated sanctions serve the role of providing information to the rule-breaker and the community regarding the act and its consequences. They allow for errors in judgment. Moreover, "[i]n a regime that uses graduated punishments . . . a person who purposely or by error breaks a rule is notified that others notice the infraction (thereby increasing the individual's confidence that others will be caught)" (Ostrom 2009: 267). Lighter initial sanctions, therefore, can serve to engender trust rather than resentment on the part of both the violator and the community. Balinese believe that human beings must constantly struggle to maintain a balance between ever-present good and evil in themselves and the world. When individuals violate norms, they are out of psychical and cosmological balance. As such, individual actions cannot be evaluated solely by the intentions of the offender, but also their supernatural context (Hornbacher 2009: 43).

Expulsion from a subak for a violation of the rules is possible, but rare (Lorenzen et al. 2005). A subak can also fail. Lansing reports that members of some subaks viewed their collective as weak when powerful individuals were allowed to become dominant (Lansing 2006: 89). Again, the pragmatic upshot is that productive harvests demand cooperative self-governance, which the farmers have understood for centuries.

One might say that the subak is itself a conflict resolution mechanism. The elected subak head arranges planting and irrigation schedules after discussions in subak meetings. Dewi et al. (2014) see this as the basis for conflict resolution in the subaks, at least for Lodtunduh, the subak in their study. Those who take more water than allowed are fined; mutual borrowing of water is allowed on a rotation system monitored by the subak head; and there are three meetings before each planting season to resolve any outstanding disagreements over water distribution (Dewi et al. 2014). One of the central elements for mitigating conflict is engineered. At Lodtunduh, there is one inlet and one outlet for all the water that runs through each field and the entire subak itself. This allows for the subak to measure, however informally, the total fair amount of water per farmer.

Minimal recognition of rights to organize

This principle is a function of a community's placement within a larger institutional structure. Ostrom finds that the longevity of a social-ecological, common-pool resource system "is affected by whether [its users] have at least minimal recognition of the right to organize by a national or local government" (Ostrom 2005: 268). The self-governing subaks have not created formal structures of government on a larger scale; they have always existed within a governmental framework. When Bali was ruled by local kings, the subaks operated autonomously within a system of royal patronage (a practice that continues today in a mostly ceremonial fashion). Under Dutch colonial rule, they were largely ignored as long as production continued. After Indonesian independence, the government urged the subaks to take on new cultivars and production techniques to render Indonesia a net rice exporter. Until the Green Revolution period, the subaks had been a resource-sufficient system and, as such, were allowed to continue more or less as they always had. The work of Lansing and others eventually led to acknowledgement by the Asian Development Bank and government that the subaks did indeed manage their environment and rice production better than the "high technology and bureaucratic" approach of the Green Revolution (Lansing 1991).

Disruption and adaptation: UNESCO World Heritage designation

The features of sustainable management detailed above enabled the Balinese to provide themselves with a reliable agricultural base for many generations. As Wayan Windia quipped to a group of students we brought to Lodtunduh, the system is "not [necessarily] efficient, but effective." The past two centuries, however, have brought some of the most serious challenges to the subak system. Any system that has managed to remain viable over the span of a millennium, of course, has encountered a vast number of challenges. Two recent ones, the arrival of tourism and modern agricultural techniques, seem to be having the most detrimental effect on the subaks in their long history. Even after the Green Revolution experiment, subak farmers have continued to use chemical inputs and other innovations – adapting and innovating in the face of changing conditions, after all, is what subaks do best. Indeed, one critique suggests that the subaks may be an obstacle to other Balinese efforts towards environmental sustainability (MacRae and Arthawiguna 2011). Tourism has proved an even bigger danger, as hotels and other tourist properties, in a drive to capture the beautiful vistas of the rice fields, have integrated themselves into land and water systems that were not developed with their demanding needs in mind. Furthermore, real estate development for tourism (an estimated loss of 1,000 hectares of farmland per year) elevates land tax rates, since these rates are based on market value. Farmers and other poor Balinese, many surviving on less than $2 per day, can scarcely afford the taxes or rents. There is intense economic pressure to sell land. As we have seen, however, land is not just a material asset for Balinese; it is invested with spiritual, aesthetic, and social values (Warren 2009). To give up land is to surrender a place of family temples, where one's ancestors abide and, perhaps, much of Balinese memory and ritual meaning. In a tragic case of "loving Bali to death," as Lansing often puts it, the picturesque beauty of the system's terraced fields might ultimately lead to the consumption of its lifeblood by tourists and developers. Beyond the cost in resources, however, come opportunities for young Balinese to seek employment and worth outside of the immediate context of a traditional agricultural lifestyle. Wet rice cultivation is by no means easy work, and many younger Balinese express a desire to "get out of the mud" (Lorenzen and Lorenzen 2011). Herein lies the dilemma. If we are to simply accept the subaks as a heuristic mechanism, one designed to solve the problems endemic to growing rice in Bali, then we must accept that whatever result the subaks collectively arrive at must be the "best" outcome – even if it is collapse. If, however, there is value to keeping the subaks operating in a similar form to that which has been maintained for centuries, some kind of intervention is needed. For those who seek to preserve the subaks as something approximating their historic configuration, the question becomes: What changes can the system tolerate while still maintaining its most pertinent features, precisely where one of its defining features is intractable complexity?

One recent effort to bulwark the subaks against the challenges of modernity is the designation of part of the system as a UNESCO World Heritage site. In 2012, after many years of work, the subaks were added to the list under the title "Cultural Landscape of Bali Province: the *Subak* System as a Manifestation of the *Tri Hita Karana* Philosophy" (UNESCO 2012) making it one of the few man-made features on the list that represents an active, ongoing social system, as opposed to the relatively static cultural artifacts (temples, historical buildings, archaeological sites) that require preservation but not necessarily the performance of its primary function, such as the Buddhist ruins of Bamiyan in Afghanistan.

The 2012 listing was not the result of a unified effort to list the subaks, but rather the final phase of a long episode of contention and negotiation, not just between UNESCO and the Indonesian government, but also between the government and the Balinese. Putra and Hitchcock detail how Jakarta's proposal to list Pura Besakih temple met with "stiff local resistance" (Putra and Hitchcock 2005: 225) in the 1990s and 2000s, and ultimately failed. The primary source of local resistance was the fear that, as important temples like Besakih were designated as heritage sites, tourists would push out local worshipers. In the nomination document of the successful bid (Indonesian Ministry of Tourism and Government of Bali Province 2011),[5] which includes both temple networks and swathes of subak-managed farmland, pains are made to present the subak system as an integrated landscape, which cannot be reduced to temples and terraced farmland. The nomination document and the official description of the site (UNESCO 2012)[6] make explicit reference to THK as the reason for the site's uniqueness. By presenting the cultural landscape as the living embodiment of THK, created not by the locations alone, but by the nexus of place, people, and relationships, the World Heritage listing presents the site as an organic system rather than merely a collection of interesting places to visit.

If emphasizing the relationship between the components of the system was essential to finally securing World Heritage status for the subaks, however, it also lies at the heart of its management difficulties. Unlike the temples of Borobudur or Prambanan, which are essentially the fossilized remains of previous Javanese Hindu–Buddhist society, the living nature of the subak World Heritage site is one that presents unique management challenges. For it to work, farmers must actually farm, subaks must actually meet, and priests must actually perform their rituals. And yet, somehow, tourists must also be able to visit and experience the site, bringing further income to farmers. This navigation between the needs of the community and the needs of the tourist seems to have been accomplished most successfully at the temple sites, where tourists can purchase entrance tickets and, depending on the cycle of religious time, mingle with and respectfully observe everyday Balinese as they worship. But for the fields themselves, the transition has been more difficult to achieve. As one subak leader lamented:

> We hope the UNESCO acknowledgement will bring a positive impact to us, as many more tourists will come to our village. Nowadays, we haven't got any benefit from the tourism around our rice fields. Tourists only [come] to see our activities, but we've got nothing.
>
> (Erviani 2012)

If the World Heritage site is unable to find some way for the farmers themselves to reap some benefit from tourism, designation might actually exacerbate the problem it proposed to solve – providing Balinese farmers and their children with other viable non-farming opportunities, thus endangering the critical human dimension of subaks.

But even if the resource allocation hurdle can be cleared, there remains another aspect of World Heritage status that might prove problematic for the subaks. The *preservation* of the subaks through a World Heritage site potentially provides exactly the opposite of what has made the subaks successful and sustainable: a clear blueprint and top-down command and control. If World Heritage status is applied as an "out-of-the-box" solution, it may share many of the features of the Green Revolution intervention, one that proved to undervalue some aspects of the subaks at the expense of what was viewed as its primary feature, rice production. By viewing the subaks as a purely agricultural system, the Green Revolution experiment failed to consider their extensive cultural and social dimensions. That is not to say that the Green Revolution intervention entirely failed. After all, many Balinese farmers continue to use the chemical inputs introduced during the Green Revolution, some out of habit, but others because they see them producing tangible benefits (MacRae and Arthawiguna 2011). Could this be an example of the subaks' information-processing function in action? Given the changing conditions of Balinese agriculture, the availability of inputs, and other incentives faced by farmers (market forces, fertilizer subsidies), neither "never use new technology" nor "always use new technology" is a suitable answer.

Likewise, the danger of World Heritage status is to deny the very real role the subaks have in the livelihoods of ordinary Balinese. If the subaks are viewed merely as a cultural artifact, something that can be vacuum-sealed and preserved under glass, then UNESCO status too will fail. Even the conception of the subaks as a manifestation of THK is more an invented tradition than a natural one (Roth and Sedana 2015). The concept itself does not derive from any single authoritative Balinese or Indic source, but rather it was constructed in the twentieth century as an approximation of what the subaks do and the relationships and norms the subak farmers observe (Pedersen and Dharmiasih 2015). If UNESCO status provides space for Balinese to seek new livelihoods within the framework of culturally protected, subak-managed rice cultivation, either as a pursuit for farm produce or as a means of participating in a wide sense of community related to heritage tourism, then it will succeed in preserving the spirit of the subak system, even if its form is due to modify and adapt. Preserving the form of the subaks without safeguarding the lives of those Balinese who depend on it – be it materially from the production of rice, spiritually from the manifest connections between the subaks and Balinese religion, or even as an internationally visible symbol of their homeland – would be the highest betrayal of the processes and norms that have yielded the system's longevity.

Conclusion

As Geertz remarked of the nineteenth-century theater state, "imagination for the Balinese was not a mode of fantasy, of notional make-believe, but a mode of perception, representation, and actualization" (Geertz 1980: 130). Look at any Balinese art and you are likely to see depictions or symbols of the system of rice cultivation, whether bucolic subak terraces, flows of sacred water *(tirtha)* from the mountains, the holy mountain itself, or representations of goddesses. Balinese Hinduism is often referred to as *Agama Tirtha*, the religion of holy water. Not all temples on this island of perhaps tens of thousands of temples are connected to rice cultivation and its sacred water, but the most important temples are, as are the small farmers' shrines dotting the rice terraces.

Bali has long been portrayed, both to outsiders and to many who live there, as a fantastic and romantic paradise of peace and harmony.[7] Rice cultivation has always been precarious as a livelihood, however, and the farmers often poor (MacRae 2011). The subak system may be located at the heart of Balinese culture, society, and politics, and it may be the life-source of the philosophy of THK, but it is also a food-production system that has been weakening under the social, economic, and political pressures of a globalized world. Its sustainability as an SES has been due to its complexity and its adaptive and emergent characteristics, scaled into a mandala (to use Lansing's trope) of interactive agents, activities, and beliefs. Emergent phenomena, like the important pest control system of the subaks, cannot be planned. Yet, could it be the case that the UNESCO World Heritage designation, with its recognition of both the subak water temple network as a complex system and the farmers as agents, is another adaptation for the system, one that places it fully in a polycentric world?

There is a paradox in the developing arrangement: the subaks developed as a food system, and must continue to be one if they are to be "preserved" in a sense meaningful to UNESCO and the Balinese. The success of the World Heritage site requires balancing the tension between food as a viable local economic product and food as an embedded component of a global cultural system. Do we go from the sustainable system of the past to the globalized rice bowl aspirations of the Green Revolution to arrive at boutique rice cultivation?

Saving the subaks involves a broadening of what we think a food system is. UNESCO's goal is to preserve the subaks' values and technical features while enabling the farmers to *eat*, whether it is the rice they grow or goods they buy with the proceeds of tourism. Try as we might, we cannot separate the food element from the other elements of the system. In the spirit of the subaks, can we really say, "These are the food parts" and "These are the non-food parts"? To create sustainable agricultural development, the subaks force us to look beyond farms and fields and markets and plates, and take a look at food, water, and livelihood relationships in very new ways.

What makes a sustainable, resilient system good or not? Certainly resource sufficiency, ecological integrity, and principles-in-action (such as Ostrom's) that characterize long-term social-ecological management of common resources. But a more germane response is that the relevant community at the relevant scale – agents who are implicated in the system – has judged it to be so and developed in local context the meanings of sufficiency or integrity. We know that agricultural food-production systems are usually about more than the production of a commodity (although much of the current discussion about crises in the global food system stems from the economics of commodity-oriented food systems). Food and water systems reproduce communities in more ways than sustenance or profit, as we see clearly in the case of the subaks. Reproduction is at the very core of the subak – iterative democratic deliberation and decision-making, collaborative labor, ecological feedback, and the networked ritual life that sustains the meaning of what it is to be Balinese. Instead of World Heritage status involving preservation of the subaks, perhaps it could provide sufficient space at the level of globalizing forces for the system to reconfigure to face the challenges of modernity, while providing protection for those features deemed by participants to be the most valuable, following the design principles of THK. Its best resource for doing so is not an international discourse on aspirational sustainability, but coevolution and actualization of the subaks' own history and agency.

Notes

1 See <https://sustainabledevelopment.un.org/topics/sustainabledevelopmentgoals>. The classic definition of sustainability from *Our Common Future* (the Brundtland Report) is "development that meets the needs of the present without compromising the ability of future generations to meet their own needs" (World Commission on Environment and Development 1987).
2 See also Geertz (1980).
3 Wayan Windia, professor of agriculture at Udayana University and a leading expert on the subaks, says of Lodtunduh subak that the farmers *always* reach consensus on decisions about planting or harvesting, the division of water to individual fields, or how to spend subak funds. Consistent consensus may be difficult to understand for Westerners, but it is based on a local understanding that individual farmers' crops succeed only in collaborative management of water and cropping patterns.
4 The Tragedy of the Commons is the situation famously outlined by Garrett Hardin in his 1968 article of the same name. The situation involves use of a common-pool resource that is open to all (i.e., a non-excludable but rivalrous resource). Hardin uses a cattle pasture as an example, but the same could apply to forests, fisheries, or the global atmosphere. Each individual resource user seeks to maximize individual gain by continuing to take more from the resource, since the individual benefits of doing so outweigh the individual costs, as the burden is shared by all the users. The tragedy, Hardin concludes, is that each individual user of a common-pool resource will continue to take more of the resource for himself until the resource is depleted to the detriment of all.
5 See <http://whc.unesco.org/uploads/nominations/1194rev.pdf>.
6 See <http://whc.unesco.org/en/list/1194>.
7 The island's history, however, is also one of violent conflict, from rivalries between kings to colonization and occupation to the massacres of the mid-1960s. For an overview of violence in Bali in the twentieth century, see Robinson (1995).

References

Berkes, F. and C. Folke (eds.) (1998) *Linking Social and Ecological Systems: Management Practices and Social Mechanisms for Building Resilience*, Cambridge: Cambridge University Press.
Caponera, D. and M. Nanni. (2007) *Principles of Water Law and Administration: National and International*, 2nd ed., Boca Raton, FL: CRC Press.
Dewi, R. K., W. Windia, D. P. Darmawan, and I. W. Budiasa. (2014) "Simulation Subak Management Function Optimally in Subak Lodtunduh, Bali, Indonesia," *Journal of Economics and Sustainable Development* 5(28): 111–118.
Eiseman, F. B. (1990) *Bali: Sekala and Niskala, Vol. 1*, Berkeley: Periplus Editions.
Erviani, N. (2012) "'Subak' Inscribed on UNESCO World Heritage List," *Bali Daily–Jakarta Post*, 3 July.
Geertz, C. (1980) *Negara: The Theatre State in Nineteenth-Century Bali*, Princeton: Princeton University Press.
Hardin, G. (1968) "The Tragedy of the Commons," *Science* 162(3859): 1243–1248.
Hauser-Schäublin, B. (2012) "Comment on Lansing/de Vet's Paper," *Human Ecology* 40: 473–474.
Helmreich, S. (1999) "Digitizing 'Development': Balinese Water Temples, Complexity and the Politics of Simulation," *Critique of Anthropology* 19(3): 249–265.
Hornbacher, A. (2009) "Global Conflict in Cosmocentric Perspective: A Balinese Approach to Reconciliation," in B. Bräuchler (ed.), *Reconciling Indonesia: Grassroots Agency for Peace*, London: Routledge, pp. 34–53.
Indonesian Ministry of Tourism and Government of Bali Province. (2011) "Nomination for Inscription on the UNESCO World Heritage List: Cultural Landscape of Bali Province," *UNESCO.org*, viewed 1 November 2015, http://whc.unesco.org/uploads/nominations/1194rev.pdf.
Lansing, J. S. (1991) *Priests and Programmers: Technologies of Power in the Engineered Landscape of Bali*, Princeton: Princeton University Press.

——. (1995) *The Balinese*, Belmont, CA: Wadsworth Cengage Learning.

——. (2000) "Foucault and the Water Temples: A Reply to Helmreich," *Critique of Anthropology* 20(3): 309–318.

——. (2003) "Complex Adaptive Systems," *Annual Review of Anthropology* 32: 183–204.

——. (2006) *Perfect Order: Recognizing Complexity in Bali*, Princeton, NJ: Princeton University Press.

Lorenzen, R. and S. Lorenzen. (2011) "Changing Realities – Perspectives on Balinese Rice Cultivation," *Human Ecology* 39(1): 29–42.

Lorenzen, S., R. Lorenzen, and P. Perez. (2005) "'I Am Just Borrowing Water But I Will Return It in an Hour': How Balinese Farmers Negotiate Their Use of Water," presentation at *International Symposium on Eco-hydrology*, Bali, 21–25 November.

MacRae, G. (2011) "Rice Farming in Bali: Organic Production and Marketing Challenges," *Critical Asian Studies* 43(1): 69–92.

MacRae, G. and A. Arthawiguna. (2011) "Sustainable Agricultural Development in Bali: Is the Subak an Obstacle, an Agent or Subject?," *Human Ecology* 39: 11–20.

Norberg, J. and G. S. Cumming (eds.) (2008) *Complexity Theory for a Sustainable Future*, New York: Columbia University Press.

Ostrom, E. (1990) *Governing the Commons: The Evolution of Institutions for Collective Action*, Cambridge: Cambridge University Press.

——. (2005) *Understanding Institutional Diversity*, Princeton, NJ: Princeton University Press.

——. (2009) "A General Framework for Analyzing Sustainability of Social-Ecological Systems," *Science* 325(5939): 419–422.

Pedersen, L. and W. Dharmiasih. (2015) "The Enchantment of Agriculture: State Decentering and Irrigated Rice Production in Bali," *Asia Pacific Journal of Anthropology* 16(2): 141–156.

Putra, N. and M. Hitchcock. (2005) "Pura Besakih: World Heritage Site Contested," *Indonesia and the Malay World* 33(96): 225–238.

Robinson, G. (1995) *The Dark Side of Paradise: Political Violence in Bali*, Ithaca, NY: Cornell University Press.

Roth, D. and G. Sedana. (2015) "Reframing *Tri Hita Karana*: From 'Balinese Culture' to Politics," *Asia Pacific Journal of Anthropology* 16(2): 157–175.

Thompson, P. B. (2010) *The Agrarian Vision: Sustainability and Environmental Ethics*, Lexington, KY, USA: University Press of Kentucky.

UNESCO. (2012) Decision: 36 COM 8B.26, *Cultural Properties – Cultural Landscape of Bali Province: The Subak System as a Manifestation of the Tri Hita Karana Philosophy (Indonesia)*, http://whc.unesco.org/en/decisions/4797.

Warren, C. (2009) "Off the Market? Elusive Links in Community-Based Sustainable Development Initiatives in Bali," in C. Warren and J. F. McCarthy (eds.), *Community, Environment and Local Governance in Indonesia*, London: Oxford University Press, pp. 197–226.

World Commission on Environment and Development. (1987) *Our Common Future*, Oxford: Oxford University Press.

32

LABOR AND LOCAL FOOD

Farmworkers on smaller farms

Margaret Gray

Introduction

Often lionized in the pages of foodie magazines and the travel sections of major US newspapers, local farmers are depicted as practicing a dying trade and preserving open space for the cultural and environmental good. Food writers help consumers sustain the belief that local agricultural activity is superior in almost every respect compared to the industrial food system. Local farmers are depicted as much more than merely businesspeople; they are rural heroes saving the land and promoting sustainability. Moreover, popular writing often conflates alternative, sustainable, and fair as features of local food. For example, food movement leader Michael Pollan argued in *The Omnivore's Dilemma* that there are two essential categories of farming: industrial and pastoral. The latter is part of the alternative food chain, which, he states, has been described as "'organic,' 'local,' 'biological,' and 'beyond organic'" (Pollan 2006: 8). Where does farm labor fit into this framework?

When food writers discuss the wages and conditions of farmworkers, it is usually only in reference to the industrial food system and in contradistinction to local and alternative food (Kingsolver 2007: 306; Schlosser 2003; 2001).[1] Workers in the local food system are hidden from popular food writing and from academic studies,[2] just as they are invisible to consumers due to their rural isolation. The farmworkers I interviewed were housed on the farms where they worked, segregated from local communities in farm labor camps. A discussion of the conditions of workers on local farms is particularly relevant to the local food movement, which has been widely celebrated as an engine for economic revitalization in part due to the jobs it is helping to create. Those new jobs are portrayed not only as supportive of a field defined by environmental sustainability, but they are also held up as a model of sustainable employment (Farm to Institution Summit 2015; Feenstra 2002; Hird 1997; NYSERDA 2012; Schroeder 2013; Unger and Wooten 2006).

My research contradicts the assumptions about local food and demonstrates that the structure of farm jobs and the poor working conditions faced by local agricultural workers largely mimic those of farmworkers on industrial farms. In addition, workers on local farms tend to experience a management regime characterized by a complicated form of paternalism. This paternalism, unique on smaller farms, serves as a vital and effective form of labor control. Finally, I argue that romantic agrarianism is a vehicle not only for marketing local agriculture, but also for masking labor concerns, and this helps explain why it has been easy to overlook the farmworkers behind local food.

There is no doubt that the Hudson Valley is a premier local food region. The region's food identity is anchored by the Culinary Institute of America (CIA), a prestigious culinary college in lower Dutchess County that has trained many of the area's chefs. *The Hudson River Valley Cookbook*, written by one important graduate, Waldy Malouf, made the *New York Times* 1995 roundup of top cookbooks of the year, helping to promote the region's food culture. Moreover, Laura Pensiero, the proprietor of Gigi Trattoria in Rhinebeck, penned the cookbook, *Hudson Valley Mediterranean*, a 2009 paean to the region's local foods. One chef in particular who has shaped ideas about the region's local food is Dan Barber, chef and co-owner of Manhattan's Blue Hill restaurant and proprietor of Blue Hill at Stone Barns at Westchester County's Stone Barns Center for Food and Agriculture, which includes a working farm, restaurant, and education center. In addition, nonprofits advocate for local agriculture by promoting local farming, matching farmers with land, and fostering dialogue through events, publications, and local programs. These include the Glynwood Institute for Sustainable Food and Farming, the Local Economies Project and its Hudson Valley Farm Hub, and the Columbia Land Conservancy. Finally, publications are vital for promoting local food; the *Valley Table* and *Edible Hudson Valley* are two examples.

Of all the changes to Hudson Valley farming in the last few decades, the "buy local" movement seems the most promising for sustaining regional farms. As a *New York Times* travel article declared, "Food has been the great engine in the region's revival," and the Hudson Valley "has now gone thoroughly locavore" (Shteyngart 2010). Amtrak's onboard magazine *Arrive* (which I picked up on the Hudson River line) proclaimed the Hudson Valley a "culinary destination" (Johnson 2008). These are examples of the promotional apparatus that helped give birth to the Hudson Valley's distinct food culture, which is rooted in local food sales, artisanal value-added products, and the pastoral, rural vernacular of the landscape that connects the era of yeomanry to today's greenmarket-focused growers.

New York is exceeded only by California in the market value of "local" agricultural sales, and the six counties covered by my research account for more than 20 percent of those sales (Diamond and Soto 2009). Moreover, it is distinctive for its concentration of small farms – 92 percent of the state's farms are considered small-scale, with a gross income less than $250,000 a year (USDA, National Agricultural Statistics Service 2007). Farmers' markets have proliferated all over the region, and numerous restaurants tout local products on their menus. These factors make the Hudson Valley a robust case study for the local food movement.

This research is based on more than fifteen years of field research – primarily in-depth interviews and participant observation – in New York's Hudson Valley and other regions in New York State. In addition to interviewing farmworkers, I interviewed farmers, statewide farmworker advocates, government employees, state legislators and aides, lobbyists, representatives from farmer organizations, consumers, and a range of farmworker service providers. My participant observation involved active attendance at a wide range of public events – rallies, marches, delegations, public forums, fundraising events, community meetings, legislative sessions and hearings, farmers' markets, and food and farm conferences. I also supplemented and compared my primary data with journalistic accounts, government information, nonprofit reports, management texts, and scholarly research on the state's agriculture industry.

Farmworker conditions

There is a long history of robust studies and reporting on US farmworkers, almost all of which is focused on industrial agriculture and not on smaller, local farms.[3] This work dates back to Carey McWilliams, whose *Factories in the Fields* (1935) was a groundbreaking work on the conditions of California farmworkers and the exploitation of a succession of vulnerable immigrant groups.

Public understanding and outcry about farmworker conditions increased when the plight of white workers was depicted – as in John Steinbeck's fictional *Grapes of Wrath* (1939), which pro-filed white dustbowl migrants struggling and competing with immigrant workers on California farms, as well as Dorothea Lange's depression era photos of the same population. Probably the defining moment for raising awareness about farmworker conditions was the landmark *CBS Reports* documentary *Harvest of Shame* (Friendly 1960), which aired on Thanksgiving Day in 1960. In the broadcast, Edward R. Murrow introduced television viewers to the "forgotten peo-ple" who labored on farms, and he prodded policy makers to address the concerns of seasonal and migrant workers, an effort championed by Bobby Kennedy (Schlesinger 2002).

Due to the nature of the tasks, the wages, the hours, and the seasonality of farm work, this sec-tor of labor has historically been filled by immigrants of one description or another. When grow-ers did hire citizen workers, they were generally those who were already marginalized socially and economically because of poverty and racism. The evolution of the farmworker job category has been shaped by the vulnerability of those who were hired to its ranks. An important cause *and* effect of their poor treatment is the lack of political influence wielded by workers themselves. Today's workers are largely undocumented immigrants who experience poverty at a rate of more than twice that of other salary and wage workers. However, to understand the reproduction of farm labor inequality as based solely on the prior poverty and desperation of its prospective work-force would be to ignore other factors that have coalesced to define this job category.

The issues confronting most agricultural workers on factory and local farms are not gross abuses and human trafficking – although these problems do exist – but that their jobs are struc-tured in such a way that poor labor treatment is institutionalized, inscribed, and perpetuated through both the law and through practice. Farm laborers lack protective labor laws due to racist policies written during the New Deal (Perea 2011), which excluded them from overtime pay requirements, a day of rest, and collective bargaining protections (Telega and Maloney 2010: 23–27). They suffer labor-law violations (Gray 2007; Kandel 2008) including endemic wage theft and minimum-wage violations (Kutz 2009; McMillan 2012; Robinson et al. 2011). Workers face overcrowded and rundown housing, pesticide exposure, heat exhaustion, stroke, and a lack of medical coverage or sick days (Kandel 2008). In addition, female farmworkers, about one-fifth of the farm labor force, experience worse conditions than their male counterparts, including lower wages, sexual harassment, and sexual abuse on the job (Bauer and Ramírez 2010). One study of California female farmworkers found that 80 percent experienced sexual harassment, in compari-son to an estimated 25 percent of all women in US jobs (Waugh 2010).

My research revealed that on local farms in the Hudson Valley, similar conditions exist (Gray 2007). The workforce consists almost entirely of non-citizens – the undocumented and guest-workers. Such workers are often unfamiliar with the labor laws that apply to them and are gener-ally too afraid to complain about poor working conditions. In addition, poor English-language skills, low levels of formal education, and a lack of job skills constrain workers' employment opportunities. In general, these factors seem to lead to a mentality of self-sacrifice that militates against plans for the future. Food writers are fond of the notion that local farms play a role in creating community (Berry 2002; 1977; Lyson 2004), but such communitarianism clearly does not extend to the laborers. Because the undocumented prefer not to be noticed, they inhabit an underworld concealed from local communities and cut off from any avenue for accumulating social capital (Lichter 2012).

In my research, I found that some workers logged excessive hours. Harvesters reported 80- to 90-hour workweeks for several months in a row. On one such farm, the bookkeeper informed me that hours above 50 or so were not on the books and would never appear in official data. Many workers – both field workers and packinghouse workers – reported being yelled at or rushed when on break, while the American-born members of the labor force could take breaks whenever they wanted. The average total annual income reported by the workers surveyed was $8,163 in 2001 and $8,078 in 2002. These figures include wages from Hudson Valley farm work, and, for 36 percent of respondents, additional income. This income level was well below the 2002 US Federal Poverty Guidelines for a family of three, $15,020 (United States Department of Health and Human Services 2002). When I interviewed workers again in 2008 and 2009, their wages were slightly higher. Despite poverty wages, 95 percent of workers reported sending money home, and two-thirds did so on a monthly basis or even more frequently. The average remittance was $513 a month, a figure representing roughly half of an average worker's monthly take-home pay.

None of the workers I met received paid sick days. Although the consensus was that employers were generally understanding when it came to employees needing time off when they were sick or had a family emergency, workers admitted that they rarely missed work. Several mentioned that their bosses were annoyed or angry when anyone was too sick to show up. I heard again and again about those who went to work with a fever or a severe cold. This corresponds with nationwide data that show that 53 percent of US food workers go to work ill (Jayaraman 2012: 63). Immigrant workers also compared their situations to the native-born, white counterparts with whom they worked. Whites usually did not harvest or pack, but worked as mechanics, tractor drivers, or in other similar positions. An apple packer mentioned that whites could go home without a problem if they were feeling even a little sick. One worker told me that he lost his job when he hurt his back, while an American co-worker was allowed to return and take it easy after an injury. Guestworkers reported that their peers had been sent back to the home country after being injured on the job, and that they had to fight to be reimbursed for medical expenses.

Almost all the workers that I met lived in farmer-provided housing. In the labor camps I visited, housing types varied widely, ranging from trailers and cement-block barracks to large rooming houses, sometimes divided into apartments. Some were well maintained and offered ample space for dwellers, but many were rundown and crowded, with windows replaced with cardboard, missing screens, broken outdoor lights, mold in bathrooms and kitchens, peeling or missing flooring, and leaky roofs. The popular public radio program *This American Life* offered a vignette featuring New York dairy workers who did not even have their own beds – they worked opposite shifts and shared the same bed. Meanwhile, a co-worker slept on a mattress positioned over the bathtub (Chase and Glass 2015).

A significant research finding revealed by my fieldwork that seems unique to smaller farms was the paternalism and accompanying forms of labor discipline that made it difficult for the agricultural workers to challenge their substandard conditions. Paternalism is more likely to exist when farmers have a direct role in supervising workers, as is common on smaller farms.[4] Workplace paternalism by employers can be understood as an intimate but extremely hierarchical relationship in which an employer's control extends into workers' everyday lives, affecting even their personal and recreational habits (Norris 1978). In a paternalistic setting, employers typically extend benefits to workers in return for good behavior and loyalty (Bennett 1968). On the small family farms I surveyed, the system of paternalism was relatively complex. For example, workers could take farm products for free, use farm vehicles, live with non-worker family members in employer-provided housing, and receive advances on their salaries. More extreme examples of paternalism included farmers telling workers that they were trying to secure green cards for them, and farmers discussing with workers the possibility of giving them land to establish their own farms.

The varying degrees of paternalistic benefits resulted in different levels of involvement in and control over worker habits and behavior. The benefits themselves were a form of labor control, as workers felt indebted to their employers, and they believed the only way they could reciprocate was by not complaining about their jobs or asking for work improvements. When I asked workers what they would do if they had a problem with their employer, one characteristic response was: "I'm not sure what I would do, he is good to us." Such systems of paternalism are complex, because it is difficult to separate farmers' generosity from labor control; and farmworkers usually consent to these arrangements to secure material and psychological benefits. This personal attention in the workplace is the flip side of the intimacy championed by food writers as integral to the virtues of local food.

I encountered a great deal of ambivalence among workers about whether their sacrifices were worth the wages and whether the economic benefits outweighed the social deficits. One apple packer attested to what he had gained and lost while employed as a farm hand:

> I have built a house; well I should say a mansion because I made it to my liking. It cost me a lot of money, a lot of money. But it also cost me separation from my family, which is the thing I love the most.

Another felt equally compromised: "It's complicated. I know that I am better economically here, but we are so lonely, it is depressing." He went on to describe feeling alienated from American culture. No workers harbored illusions about the US as a land of opportunity. As a former farm hand summarized it: "Everyone talks about the American dream, but for us it's more of a nightmare."

Agrarian romanticism

Underpinning the romance with local farms, popular and scholarly commentators promote an automatic equation of geographic proximity with goodness. This is the "local trap," since scale – whether local or global – is always socially constructed and non-uniform (Born and Purcell 2006). The conflation of localness and wholesomeness prevents further scrutiny of this phenomenon, and of labor conditions in particular. In addition, much of the praise for local food is linked to nostalgia for an agrarian ideal (Hofstadter 1955). Julie Guthman (2004) demonstrates how big agriculture co-opted the USDA organic standards, and die-hard organic farmers responded by calling for a new strategy to promote their farm products, arguing that scale was a vital component. According to their logic, the "small-scale family farm" became "a proxy for social justice" (Guthman 2004: 171). Such a vision obstructs an analysis of farmworker conditions.

Romantic agrarianism encompasses three main beliefs: (1) farmers are economically independent and self-sufficient; (2) farming is intrinsically a natural and moral activity; and (3) farming is the fundamental industry of society. These three tenets reinforce one another. For example, discussions about farmers' self-reliance are often seeded with ideas about their virtuous characters and simple, humble lives, even though there is no inherent connection between these qualities. In addition, naïve beliefs about the wholesomeness, reliability, honesty, and hard manual work of farmers, as well as overestimations of the role they play in defending agricultural traditions, feed into the nobility bestowed on their self-reliance.[5] These ideals help consumers relate to and sympathize with farmers, while perpetuating the invisibility of farm laborers.

Today the Hudson Valley signifies a respite from the ills of corporate agriculture. The Valley's landscape itself elicits nostalgia. Scattered throughout the region's small communities, farms and farm stands not only advertise their local products but also offer visual reminders of the scale and diversity of the industry. Today's local food gets linked to "community capitalism," a kinder, gentler approach to business that incorporates civic engagement (Lyson and Green 1999). In the popular *Animal, Vegetable, Miracle: A Year of Food Life*, Barbara Kingsolver goes even further to suggest that "'locally grown' is a denomination whose meaning is incorruptible" (Kingsolver 2007: 123). Such writing offers florid descriptions of farmers' markets, glowing profiles of local purveyors, and anecdotes of happy farm animals put a gloss on the public image of the food movement. This is typified in an article in the magazine *Edible Hudson Valley*, which claims, "Traditional agricultural values of generosity and cooperation, rooted in the Hudson Valley, seem infused in each batch of cheese produced" (Barritt 2012). Such writing helps reinforce the positive, nostalgic, and romantic role of farmers, and it rarely mentions workers.

Given the incredible emphasis on praising local and small farmers, it is easy to see why consumers and foodies might not question labor conditions. Agricultural exceptionalism has driven public attitudes and policy decisions about farming for more than two hundred years (Pedersen 1990). The public elaboration of agrarian beliefs has been prolific and pervasive; more than one agrarian writer has claimed that these beliefs don't need to be learned by those growing up in the country, but instead they are simply absorbed (Berry 2002: 238; Paarlberg 1980). Agrarianism still resonates today, and writers trade on the romance of agrarian ideals (Carlson 2008; Sheingate 2000). For example, in a 2004 op-ed in the *New York Times*, Victor Davis Hanson, writer, farmer, and senior fellow at the Hoover Institution, wrote: "Agriculture is more than just feeding people; it is the historic center of bedrock American social and cultural values. . . . In this most dangerous period in our nation's history, agriculture remains our most precious resource" (Hanson 2004). *New York Times* columnist Nicholas Kristof, in an article criticizing corporate monoculture farming and the government's support for it, tapped into his own childhood experiences on a farm to argue that "the family farm traditionally was the most soulful place imaginable" (Kristof 2009).

Conclusion

Consumers have been told repeatedly to vote with their forks and to use their food dollars to promote a more just and sustainable food system (see in this volume, "Ethical Consumerism: A Defense"). The problem is the difficulty of determining the labor conditions behind the food. It is now possible to buy a Fair Food, US-grown tomato at Whole Foods, but such transparency is a rarity: almost none of our food is labeled based on labor standards. Moreover, even shopping at your local farmers' market does not ensure better labor conditions. For example, farmworkers in the Hudson Valley who serve the local food market may experience the same sort of labor conditions as agricultural workers in the industrial food system, as well as a complex system of paternalism (Gray 2014). We should also contrast the lack of attention to labor standards with initiatives to promote animal welfare (see in this volume, "Animal Rights and Food" and "Animal Welfare"). Whole Foods, for example, has implemented the Five-Step Animal Welfare Rating, which includes making sure animals are grass-fed, free range, offered shade protection, and more (Whole Foods, n.d.).

In the history of farmworker studies, similar issues have come up repeatedly. These issues are often shared for workers on small and large farms, corporate monoculture farms, and local diverse farms: long hours, low wages, poverty, exploitation of immigrant non-citizen workers, the lack of labor protections, wage theft, poor housing, health risks including pesticide exposure and heat exhaustion, lack of medical coverage and sick days, sexual harassment and abuse, and lack of respect. Decade after decade we see farm jobs filled by workers who lack social, economic, and political power, creating conditions for the imposition of systems of paternalism and other forms of labor control. The poor conditions of workers in large agricultural operations are evident throughout the world, and there is a growing body of study showing that exploitation in local food systems is also not confined to the US (Aznar-Sánchez et al. 2014; Fairey et al. 2008; Hennebry et al. 2012; Sippel and Gertel 2014).

Romantic agrarianism is one of the main factors we must examine to understand why the conditions of workers on smaller and local farms are not scrutinized. In the sentimental conflation of local, small, sustainable, and wholesome, there is an embedded lack of concern for farmworkers. Romantic agrarianism also helps perpetuate the notion that labor is treated better on organic farms, if for no other reason than that labor concerns largely are not addressed outside of factory farms. Indeed, like the local foods many of us enjoy daily, the perceptions of the agrarian realm as a modern-day Eden rely on the invisibility of migrant workers.

Notes

1 Even Michael Pollan has recently begun to address labor on farms (Mark Bittman et al. 2014; Pollan 2013).
2 A generation of scholars has expounded on the positive aspects of local food systems, which include economic and social benefits (Feenstra 1997; Norberg-Hodge et al. 2002; Pacione 1997), the promotion of justice and community through face-to-face interactions with food producers (Murdoch et al. 2000), and the capacity of alternative agrisystems to promote civic engagement and enhance democracy (Allen et al. 2003; DuPuis and Goodman 2005; Hinrichs et al. 1998; Lyson 2004; Weatherell et al. 2003; Winter 2003). For scholars that call for an inclusion of farmworkers in food systems research, see Alle (2004; 2008); Besky and Brown (2015); Brown and Getz (2008); Garcia (2007); Guthman (2004).
3 See Besky and Brown (2015) for a review of labor studies including those focused on the spatial marginalization of workers, labor mobilization, the role of gender, race, and ethnicity, and theoretical work. The contemporary hardship faced by agricultural workers is documented in reports by the National Center for Farmworker Health (see fact sheets and reports on the website of the National Center for Farmworker Health: http://www.ncfh.org/fact-sheets--research.html), Bon Appetit and the UFW (Fojo et al. 2011), Farmworker Justice and Oxfam (Goldstein et al. 2010), the Southern Poverty Law Center (Bauer and Ramírez, 2010), the Food Chain Workers Alliance (Jayaraman 2012), and the USDA (Kandel 2008). Also documented is the growing phenomenon of human trafficking on US farms, most prominently in Immokalee, Florida (Bowe 2007; Estabrook 2011). In addition, *Food Chains*, directed by Sanjay Rawal (Rawal 2014), focuses on the invisible food chains that keep Florida's tomato workers oppressed, as well as the successful work of the Coalition of Immokalee Workers (CIW) to combat that oppression and improve workers' conditions and pay (Espinoza 2014).
4 For a more comprehensive discussion of paternalism on small farms, see Gray (2014: 53–61).
5 This paragraph draws on the work of Hofstadter (1955) and Johnstone (1940). It is worth noting that there is no definitive version of agrarianism; rather it has been revised over time by those who employ it to serve various purposes. See Flinn and Johnson (1974).

References

Allen, P. (2004) *Together at the Table: Sustainability and Sustenance in the American Agrifood System*, University Park: Pennsylvania State University Press.
Allen, P. (2008) "Mining for Justice in the Food System: Perceptions, Practices, and Possibilities," *Agriculture and Human Values* 25: 157–161.
Allen, P., FitzSimmons, M., Goodman, M., Warner, K. (2003) "Shifting Plates in the Agrifood Landscape: The Tectonics of Alternative Agrifood Initiatives in California," *Journal of Rural Studies* 19: 61–75.
Aznar-Sánchez, J. Á., Belmonte-Ureña, L. J., Tapia-León, J. J. (2014) "The Industrial Agriculture: A 'Model for Modernization' from Almería?," in J. Gertel and S. R. Sippel (eds.), *Seasonal Workers in Mediterranean Agriculture: The Social Costs of Eating Fresh*, London: Routledge, pp. 112–120.
Barritt, T. W. (2012) "Food for Thought: A Sense of Place," *Edible Hudson Valley*, viewed 3 August 2015, http://ediblehudsonvalley.com/editorial/spring-2012/food-for-thought-791/.
Bauer, M., Ramírez, M. (2010) *Injustice on Our Plates: Immigrant Women in the U.S. Food Industry*, Montgomerym AL: Southern Poverty Law Center.
Bennett, J. W. (1968) "Paternalism," in D. Sills (ed.), *International Encyclopedia of the Social Sciences*, New York: Macmillan, pp. 472–477.
Berry, W. (1977) *The Unsettling of America: Culture and Agriculture*, San Francisco: Sierra Club Books.

Berry, W. (2002) "The Whole Horse," in N. Wirzba (ed.), *The Art of the Common-Place: The Agrarian Essays of Wendell Berry*, Washington, DC: Counterpoint, pp. 236–48.

Besky, S., Brown, S. (2015) "Looking for Work: Placing Labor in Food Studies," *Labor Studies in Working-Class History in the Americas* 12: 19–43.

Bittman, M., Pollan, M., Salvador, R., de Schutter, O. (2014) "How a National Food Policy Could Save Millions of American Lives," *The Washington Post*, viewed 3 August 2014, https://www.washingtonpost.com/opinions/how-a-national-food-policy-could-save-millions-of-american-lives/2014/11/07/89c55e16–6 37f-11e4–836c-83bc4f26eb67_story.html.

Born, B., Purcell, M. (2006) "Avoiding the Local Trap: Scale and Food Systems in Planning Research," *Journal of Planning Education & Research* 26: 195–207.

Bowe, J. (2007) *Nobodies: Modern American Slavery and the Dark Side of New Global Economy*, New York: Random House.

Brown, S., Getz, C. (2008) "Toward Domestic Fair Trade? Farm Labor, Food Localism, and the 'Family Scale' Farm," *GeoJournal* 73: 11–22.

Carlson, A. (2008) "Agrarianism Reborn: On the Curious Return of the Small Family Farm," *The Intercollegiate Review* 43: 13–23.

Chase, Z., Glass, I. (2015) "Same Bed, Different Dreams," *This American Life*, No. 556, Chicago Public Media, 4 May.

Diamond, A., Soto, R. (2009) "Facts on Direct-to-Consumer Food Marketing: Incorporating Data from the (2007) Census of Agriculture," Washington DC: United States Department of Agriculture, Agricultural Marketing Service.

DuPuis, E. M., Goodman, D. (2005) "Should We Go 'Home' to Eat?: Toward a Reflexive Politics of Localism," *Journal of Rural Studies* 21: 357–71.

Espinoza, L. S. (2014) "Fair Food Program 2014 Annual Report," Sarasota, FL: Fair Food Standards Council.

Estabrook, B. (2011) *Tomatoland: How Modern Industrial Agriculture Destroyed our Most Alluring Fruit*, Kansas City, MO: Andrews McMeel Publishing, LLC.

Fairey, D., Hanson, C., MacInnes, G., McLaren, A. T., Otero, G., Preibisch, K., Thompson, M. (2008) "Cultivating Farmworker Rights: Ending the Exploitation of Immigrant and Migrant Farmworkers in BC," Vancouver, BC: Canadian Centre for Policy Alternatives – BC Office, Justicia for Migrant Workers, Progressive Intercultural Community Services, and the BC Federation of Labour.

Farm to Institution Summit. (2015) "2015 Program Guide," viewed 19 November 2015 http://www.farmtoinstitution.org/sites/default/files/imce/uploads/F2I%20Summit%20Program%20Guide_0.pdf.

Feenstra, G. (1997) "Local Food Systems and Sustainable Communities," *American Journal of Alternative Agriculture* 12: 28–36.

——. (2002) "Creating Space for Sustainable Food Systems: Lessons from the Field," *Agriculture and Human Values*, 19: 99–106.

Flinn, W. L., Johnson, D. E. (1974) "Agrarianism among Wisconsin Farmers," *Rural Sociology* 39: 187–204.

Fojo, C., Burtness, D., Chang, V. (2011) "Inventory of Farmworker Issues and Protections in the United States," Palo Alto, CA: Bon Appétit Management Company Foundation and The United Farmworkers.

Friendly, F. (1960) "Harvest of Shame," *CBS Reports*, 5 November.

Garcia, M. (2007) "Labor, Migration, and Social Justice in the Age of the Grape Boycott," *Gastronomica: The Journal of Food and Culture* 7: 68–74.

Goldstein, B., Howe, B., Tamir, I. (2010) "Weeding Out Abuses: Recommendations for a Law-Abiding Farm Labor System," Washington DC: Farmworker Justice and Oxfam America.

Gray, M. (2007) *The Hudson Valley Farmworker Report: Understanding the Needs and Aspirations of a Voiceless Population*, Annandale-on-Hudson, NY: Bard College.

Gray, M. (2014) *Labor and the Locavore: The Making of a Comprehensive Food Ethic*, Berkeley: University of California Press.

Guthman, J. (2004) *Agrarian Dreams: The Paradox of Organic Farming in California*, Berkeley: University of California Press.

Hanson, V. D. (2004) "A Secretary for Farmland Security," *The New York Times*, December 9: 41.

Hennebry, J., Preibisch, K., McLaughlin, J. (2012) *Health Across Borders: Health Status, Risks and Care Among Transnational Migrant Farm Workers in Ontario*, Toronto, ON: CERIS The Ontario Metropolis Centre.

Hinrichs, C., Kloppenburg, J., Stevenson, S., Lezberg, S., Hendrickson, J., DeMaster, K. (1998) "Moving Beyond Global and Local," Regional Research Project NE-185 Working Statement, October 2, Washington DC: United States Department of Agriculture.

Hird, V. (1997) *Double Yield Jobs and Sustainable Food Production*, London: SAFE Alliance.

Hofstadter, R. (1955) *The Age of Reform: From Bryan to F.D.R.*, New York: Vintage Books.

Jayaraman, S. (2012) *The Hands that Feed Us: Challenges and Opportunities for Workers along the Food Chain*, Los Angeles: Food Chain Workers Alliance.

Johnson, L. (2008) "Garden of Eating," *Arrive: The Magazine for Northeast Business Travelers*, September/October: 68–74.

Johnstone, P. H. (1940) "Old Ideals Versus New Ideas in Farm Life," in G. Hambidge (ed.), *Farmers in a Changing World: The Yearbook of Agriculture*, Washington, DC: U.S. Government Printing Office, pp. 111–170.

Kandel, W. (2008) "Profile of Hired Farmworkers, a (2008) Update," Economic Research Report No. 60, Washington, DC: Economic Research Service, U.S. Department of Agriculture.

Kingsolver, B. (2007) *Animal, Vegetable, Miracle: A Year of Food Life*, New York: HarperCollins Publishers.

Kristof, N. D. (2009) "Food for the Soul," *The New York Times*, 22 August: WK10.

Kutz, G. D. (2009) "Wage and Hour Division's Complaint Intake and Investigative Processes Leave Low Wage Workers Vulnerable to Wage Theft," No. GAO-09-458T, 25 March, Washington, DC: Government Accountability Office.

Lichter, D. T. (2012) "Immigration and the New Racial Diversity in Rural America," *Rural Sociology* 77: 3–35.

Lyson, T. A. (2004) *Civic Agriculture: Reconnecting Farm, Food, and Community*, Medford, MA: Tufts University Press.

Lyson, T. A., Green, J. (1999) "The Agricultural Marketscape: A Framework for Sustaining Agriculture and Communities in the Northeast," *Journal of Sustainable Agriculture* 15: 133–50.

McMillan, T. (2012) "As Common As Dirt," *The American Prospect*, viewed 3 August 2015, http://prospect.org/article/common-dirt-0.

McWilliams, C. (1935) *Factories in the Field: The Story of Migratory Farm Labor in California*, Boston: Little, Brown and Company.

Murdoch, J., Marsden, T., Banks, J. (2000) "Quality, Nature, and Embeddedness: Some Theoretical Considerations in the Context of the Food Sector," *Economic Geography* 76: 107–25.

Norberg-Hodge, H., Merrifield, T., Gorelick, S. (2002) *Bringing the Food Economy Home: Local Alternatives to Global Agribusiness*, London: Zed.

Norris, G. M. (1978) "Industrial Paternalist Capitalism and Local Labour Markets," *Sociology* 12: 469–489.

NYSERDA. (2012) *Capital Region Sustainability Plan*, Albany, NY: New York State Energy Research and Development Authority.

Paarlberg, D. (1980) *Farm and Food Policy: Issues of the 1980s*, Lincoln: University of Nebraska Press.

Pacione, M. (1997) "Local Exchange Trading Systems – A Rural Response to the Globalization of Capitalism?" *Journal of Rural Studies* 13: 415–27.

Pedersen, D. B. (1990) "Introduction to the Agricultural Law Symposium," *University of California Davis Law Review* 23: 401–14.

Perea, J. F. (2011) "The Echoes of Slavery: Recognizing the Racist Origins of the Agricultural and Domestic Worker Exclusion from the National Labor Relations Act," *Ohio State Law Journal* 72: 95–138.

Pollan, M. (2006) *The Omnivore's Dilemma: A Natural History of Four Meals*, New York: Penguin Press.

Pollan, M. (2013) "The Most Important Fight in the Struggle for Food Justice," MoveOn.Org, viewed 2 August 2015, http://front.moveon.org/the-most-important-fight-in-the-struggle-for-food-justice/.

Rawal, S. (2014) "Food Chains," Screen Media Films.

Robinson, E., Nguyen, H. T., Isom, S., Quandt, S. A., Grzywacz, J. G., Chen, H., Arcury, T. A. (2011) "Wages, Wage Violations, and Pesticide Safety Experienced by Migrant Farmworkers in North Carolina," *New Solutions* 21: 251–68.

Schlesinger, A. M. (2002) *Robert Kennedy and His Times*, Boston: Houghton Mifflin Harcourt.

Schlosser, E. (2001) *Fast Food Nation*, Boston: Houghton Mifflin.

Schlosser, E. (2003) *Reefer Madness: Sex, Drugs, and Cheap Labor in the American Black Market*, Boston: Mariner Books.

Schroeder, A. R. (2013) *Local Food Local Jobs: Job Growth and Creation in the Pioneer Valley Food System*, Boston: Massachusetts Workforce Alliance, February.

Sheingate, A. D. (2000) "Institutions and Interest Group Power: Agricultural Policy in the United States, France, and Japan," *Studies in American Political Development* 14: 184–211.

Shteyngart, G. (2010) "Escape to New York's Hudson Valley," *Travel + Leisure*, September 15, viewed 3 August 2015, http://www.travelandleisure.com/articles/escape-to-new-yorks-hudson-valley.

Sippel, S. R., Gertel, J. (2014) "Shared Insecurities? Farmers and Workers in Bouches-du-Rhône," in J. Gertel and S. R. Sippel (eds.), *Seasonal Workers in Mediterranean Agriculture: The Social Costs of Eating Fresh*, London: Routledge, pp. 37–48.

Steinbeck, J. (1939) *Grapes of Wrath*, New York: Viking.

Telega, S. W., Maloney, T. R. (2010) "Legislative Actions on Overtime Pay and Collective Bargaining and their Implications for Farm Employers in New York State, 2009–2010," (No. 121660) Ithaca, NY: Cornell University, Department of Applied Economics and Management.

Unger, S., Wooten H. (2006) "A Food Systems Assessment for Oakland, CA: Toward a Sustainable Food Plan," Oakland, CA: Oakland Mayor's Office of Sustainability and University of California, Berkeley, Department of City and Regional Planning, June 21.

United States Department of Health and Human Services. (2002) "The (2002) HHS Poverty Guidelines," viewed 3 August 2015, http://aspe.hhs.gov/poverty/02poverty.htm.

USDA, National Agricultural Statistics Service. (2007) Table 1. Historical Highlights: 2007 and Earlier Census Years (New York)," Washington, DC: United States Department of Agriculture.

Waugh, I. M. (2010) "Examining the Sexual Harassment Experiences of Mexican Immigrant Farmworking Women," *Violence Against Women* 16: 237–61.

Weatherell, C. Tregear, A., Allinson, J. (2003) "In Search of the Concerned Consumer: UK Public Perceptions of Food, Farming and Buying Local," *Journal of Rural Studies* 19: 233–44.

Whole Foods n.d. "Five-Step Animal Welfare Rating," viewed 3 August 2015 http://www.wholefoods market.com/mission-values/animal-welfare/5-step-animal-welfare-rating.

Winter, M. (2003) "Embeddedness, the New Food Economy and Defensive Localism," *Journal of Rural Studies* 19: 23–32.

33

INDIGENOUS FOOD SOVEREIGNTY, RENEWAL, AND US SETTLER COLONIALISM

Kyle Powys Whyte

Introduction

Indigenous peoples often embrace different concepts of food sovereignty to frame their ongoing efforts to achieve self-determination and justice. Yet concepts of food sovereignty can come across as so many impossible ideals of community food self-sufficiency and cultural autonomy. I will suggest in this essay that for some North American Indigenous peoples, food sovereignty movements are not really based on such ideals, even though they invoke concepts of cultural revitalization and political sovereignty in relation to food. Instead, food sovereignty should be seen – at least in part – as a strategic process of Indigenous resurgence that negotiates structures of settler colonialism that erase what I will call the ecological value of certain foods for Indigenous peoples.

The strategic process involves prioritizing certain foods for renewal. These foods can motivate Indigenous collective capacities to address multiple health, cultural, educational, and political issues associated with settler-colonial erasure. To understand this concept of food sovereignty, it is critical to be able to connect settler colonialism with the ecological value of food. I will begin by discussing criticisms of food sovereignty based on concerns that it represents impractical ideals, before moving on to cover the ideas of the ecological value of food, settler colonialism, and food sovereignty as a strategic process.

Food sovereignty and food self-sufficiency

There are many concepts of food sovereignty that express diverse themes about the relationship between communities and food systems. Often, concepts of food sovereignty emphasize food-production systems characterized by community food self-sufficiency or cultural autonomy in relation to food. These concepts refer to community-based control over the major dimensions of food production, distribution, and consumption, and the recycling or disposal of food refuse – from cultural customs to political institutions. The Detroit Food Justice Task Force, for example, describes food sovereignty as "liberating land . . . for the production of food for communities," "hosting collective meals in our communities as a way of connecting people across generations and cultural backgrounds," and "forging new models of collective control of land and waterways" (Detroit Food Justice Task Force 2014). The Indigenous Circle of the People's Food Policy

Project in Canada describes food sovereignty as embodying the idea of "food as sacred, part of the web of relationships with the natural world that define culture and community" (People's Food Policy Project 2014). The International Institute for Development claims that realizing food sovereignty involves "reclaiming autonomous food systems" (Pimbert 2009).

Ideas of food self-sufficiency and cultural autonomy appear across the variety of sovereigns that are referenced through the several origins of concepts of food sovereignty cited by scholars. Some scholars see the origin of food sovereignty in La Vía Campesina's (LVC) 1996 involvement in the World Food Summit. LVC defined food sovereignty as the "right of each nation to maintain and develop their own capacity to produce foods that are crucial to national and community food security, respecting cultural diversity and diversity of production methods" (cited in Hospes 2014: 120).[1] Other scholars suggest that food sovereignty originated in earlier instances, such as Mexico's 1983 National Food Program that used the concept as a form of national control, as opposed to the control of local communities, over the food system (Edelman 2014).

Some scholars are concerned that food sovereignty suggests so many unreasonable or impossible ideals of a community's complete control over its own food system. Bernstein (2014), for example, argues that food sovereignty discourses invoke:

> emblematic instances of the virtues of peasant/small-scale/family farming as capital's other. The two are often connected, so that the individual peasant farm (and community) exemplifies the way forward to save the planet, to feed its population in socially more equitable and ecologically more sustainable ways.
>
> (Bernstein 2014: 1032)

The challenge posed by Bernstein, as I read the essay, is that the viability of some concepts of food sovereignty rests on whether we can claim that communities can live up to this ideal. But this ideal is of course rather problematic. Many communities cannot extricate themselves from dependency on trade or aid stemming from globalized food systems. Nor is it clear whether farming based on peasant "virtues" could provide sufficient food quality and quantity for either feeding local communities or trading with other local communities.

Thompson (2015) discusses how if food sovereignty refers to the idea of a nation feeding its entire population, there will be "some degree of skepticism about food sovereignty among the policy specialists that have focused on getting nutritionally adequate diets to poor people for the last fifty years" (75). Though Thompson also suggests that:

> the idea points to the way entire rural communities, local cultures, and longstanding social relations are brought together through the production, preparation, and consumption of food. . . . The continuance of community depends upon people to care for one another. . . . The survival and maintenance of these food practices is critical to the sustainability of these communities in every sense of the word.
>
> (Thompson 2015: 75–76)

For Thompson, concepts of food sovereignty are useful for cultural continuance and identity, but they are too idealistic for dealing with the challenges of food security in the context of globalization.

Other scholars emphasize that many local communities do not embody enough of the values and tastes associated with the food self-sufficiency and cultural autonomy aspects of food sovereignty. For example, some communities have developed tastes for and dependencies on nonlocal foods, so that today it is incorrect to suggest that there is a resounding distaste for foreign foods by some communities that embrace food sovereignty (Steckley 2015). Moreover, food sovereignty and local agrarian reform movements often rely on problematic, whether ahistorical or "traditional," class and gender categories that are oppressive for some community members (Bernstein 2010; Minkoff-Zern 2013; Park et al. 2015). There are also concerns raised that certain ideals of local food fail to consider the responsibilities that different sovereigns and groups have to aid and trade equitably with one another (Navin 2014).

Much of the literature just described addresses the uses of food sovereignty by groups outside of North American/US-sphere Indigenous contexts. Though the exact term "food sovereignty" in English was rarely used in this region until recently, we should consider that North American Indigenous peoples, going back several hundred years, were using English-language concepts and frames associated with concepts of inherent sovereignty, self-determination, cultural integrity, subsistence harvesting, and treaty rights as ways of justifying their own control over foods that matter culturally, economically, and nutritionally. For example, in the process of treaty-making in the 19th century, many Indigenous peoples ensured their retention of rights to continue harvesting foods in the territories they ceded to the US. Well over a century after signing these treaties, the same Indigenous groups continue to protect and exercise these rights, often working with the US court system and co-management arrangements with the US federal and state governments (Brown 1994; Nesper 2002; Weaver 1996; Wilkinson 2005).

As a Potawatomi scholar-activist, I began to wonder whether Indigenous North American food sovereignties were just so many ideals with little practical value for true change and transformation of our food systems. Upon further reflection, I realized that these concerns were not taking into account how Indigenous peoples often understand the value of food that uses of food sovereignty seek to invoke. Moreover, the concerns did not seem to address a particular form of oppression that many Indigenous peoples face in North America, namely settler colonialism. In the rest of this essay, I will connect these missing pieces in order to suggest that concepts of food sovereignty need not always be ideals, but may be strategic processes for negotiating structures of settler colonialism that promote Indigenous resurgence.

The hub-like or ecological value of food

North American Indigenous peoples living in the US settler sphere are visible actors addressing the impacts of colonialism on the food systems that affect them. Food systems are complex chains of food production, distribution, consumption, and the recirculation of refuse. Indigenous organizations, such as the *Indigenous Environmental Network* and *Honor the Earth*, are at the forefront of many food debates, such as the debate over the ethics of genetically modified organisms. Through organizations such as the Great Lakes Indian Fish and Wildlife Commission (GLIFWC) and the Northwest Indian Fish Commission (NWIFC), Tribes and First Nations in North America have resisted US and Canadian attempts to deny Indigenous persons their rights to harvest in treaty areas. Various Indigenous peoples in North America have formed large networks and cooperative organizations, such as the Intertribal Agriculture Council, to protect native seeds, to cultivate supply chains separate from capture by powerful corporations, and to protect subsistence and sacred foods from pollution and other forms of ecological degradation. Indigenous persons have sought to redefine the connections among nutrition, colonialism, and conditions such as diabetes and hypertension that affect Indigenous peoples disproportionately (Arquette et al. 2002; Walters and Simoni 2002). In many of these anti-colonial food movements, Indigenous persons claim that the issues they face concern values associated with food that are not reducible to the taste, quantity, or nutrient content of food. Consider the following examples.

Speaking on the relation between treaty rights and mining, genetic modification, and other threats to wild rice agriculture, Norman Deschampe, former Minnesota Chippewa Tribal President, said:

> We are of the opinion that the wild rice rights assured by treaty accrue not only to individual grains of rice, but to the very essence of the resource. We were not promised just any wild rice; that promise could be kept by delivering sacks of grain to our members each year. We were promised the rice that grew in the waters of our people, and all the value that rice holds.
>
> (Andow et al. 2009: 3)

Here, Deschampe references the value of the rice connected to a particular kind of habitat, with intrinsic value to Ojibwe people that cannot be replaced by importing rice from somewhere else.

In Alaska, extraction industries, especially oil and gas, pose threats to many foods that Indigenous communities there depend on. In an article on the threat of oil drilling to the whaling tradition of a particular Alaska Native village, Edward Itta, former mayor of that village, describes whaling as not merely important for distribution of nutrition:

> No one person can catch a whale. It takes a whole community. Because of the whale, we share, we are very close, we come together. Without it, our way of life – what we pass on to our kids and grandkids – would be diminished.
>
> (Birger 2012)

Again, we see reference to a value of food that extends beyond its taste and nutrient content. For communities with comprehensive practices associated with particular foods, immediate threats to those foods are also threats to the fabric of the communities.

In another case, involving threats from the oil industry to Indigenous peoples in the Yukon Territory, Norma Kassi says of her Gwich'in community:

> We cannot, however, simply change our diet. If we were to change suddenly and start eating store-bought foods more, then disease would increase and our rate of death would be higher, because it would be too rapid a change, too much of a shock to our systems.
>
> (Kassi 1996: 80)

For Kassi, while adaptation is always possible, food nonetheless has a special value that makes certain rapid adaptations harmful for communities.

Winona LaDuke, writing on the restoration of sturgeon, which figures importantly as part of her Ojibwe community's culture and subsistence, writes about the words of a fellow tribal member: "As Holzkamm surmises, . . . 'We are lucky that [sturgeon] are coming back to White Earth. The fish themselves never knew that invisible border of the US, Canada, or any of the counties' (or any other jurisdictions)." LaDuke writes, "Maybe the fish will help a diverse set of people work together to make something right. . . . The fish help us remember all of those relations, and in their own way, help us recover ourselves" (LaDuke 1999: 41–42). Sturgeon has the type of value that can serve the collective renewal of Ojibwe people – a complex form of remembering that is suitable for today's challenges.

Elizabeth Hoover's work, describing issues with pollution and fish, quotes Haudenosaunee community leader Henry Lickers on the language and culture of tying knots, the continuance of which is being challenged as the fishery is affected by pollution:

> People forget, in their own culture, what you call the knot that you tie in a net. And so, a whole section of your language and culture is lost because no one is tying those nets anymore. The interrelation between men and women, when they tied nets, the relationship between adults or elders and young people, as they tied nets together, the stories . . . that whole social infrastructure that was around the fabrication of that net disappeared.
>
> (Hoover 2013: 5)

Lickers focuses heavily on the value of fish in relation to the intergenerational connections that keep communities vibrant and self-supporting.

The Diné Policy Institute recently put out a report on food sovereignty in the Navajo Nation. The report states:

> In relation to cultivated plants, it is said that the Holy People shared with the Diné people the teachings of how to plant, nurture, prepare, eat and store our sacred cultivated crops, such as corn. The importance of these teachings to our well-being was made clear in that the Holy People shared that we would be safe and healthy until the day that we forgot our seeds, our farms, and our agriculture. It was said that when we forgot these things, we would be afflicted by disease and hardship again, which is what some elders point to as the onset of diabetes, obesity and other ills facing Diné people today.
>
> (Diné Policy Institute 2014: 38)

The value of sacred crops serves as an indicator of people's collective health and well-being today according to the report.

In these examples, Indigenous persons are articulating a distinct value for food that is not reducible to scientifically assessable nutritional qualities or the quantities of food produced by or administered to particular populations. For the voices just featured, food production, labor, preparation, consumption, and disposal are woven tightly with land tenure, a community's way of life, reciprocal gift giving and life sustenance, connecting people in a community, and respect for nonhuman life. In these ways, food's value is that it serves as a type of hub. For food can somehow bring together, or convene, many of the relationships required for people to live well and make plans for the future. The hub-like value of certain foods, such as whale or sturgeon, allows them to convene biological, environmental, cultural, social, economic, political, and spiritual aspects of communities. While social institutions such as harvesting groups, ceremonies, and treaty organizations help to distribute goods associated with many of the foods described above, from nutrition to cultural preference fulfillment, the Indigenous persons quoted earlier believe that these social institutions would not be able to thrive if another food were substituted too quickly.

Food's value is hub-like, in the sense of a centripetal force pulling certain people, nonhumans, and ecosystems together in ways that promote collective action. More generally, food serves as a particular kind of motivator of the collective capacities of particular Indigenous peoples to cultivate and tend, produce, distribute, and consume their own foods, to recirculate refuse, and to acquire trusted foods and ingredients from other populations. The concept of collective capacities aims to describe an ecology, i.e., an ecological system, of interacting humans, nonhuman beings (animals, plants, etc.), entities (spiritual, inanimate, etc.), and landscapes (climate regions, boreal zones, etc.) that are conceptualized and operate purposefully to facilitate a collective's range of adaptation options to metascale forces. Metascale forces refer to disruptions and perturbations to systems that require those systems to adapt and adjust. They may be associated with changes in rainfall patterns (i.e., climate change) or with invasions by other populations brought about through global forces (e.g., the gold rushes and the fur trade). So, they can be either anthropogenic or based on complex earth systems over which humans exercise little influence. Like most conceptions of ecology (including agroecology) today, I use the term *ecology* not to designate a system always seeking to return to a particular equilibrium. Rather, ecology refers to systems that are organized in ways that reflect perspectives on more or less suitable ranges of adaptations to various metascale forces that have acted over time (Whyte 2015).

We can understand an ecology as another way of describing a people's homeland. For food to express its role as a hub-like value, then, the entire ecology of the place where human communities live, work, worship, and play has to have certain aquatic, terrestrial, and climatic conditions in which humans are actively engaged socially, culturally, economically, and politically. In this sense, I will refer to the hub-like value of food as its ecological value. The ecological value of certain foods involves the ways in which those foods are irreplaceable elements of a community's range of collective capacities to adapt to change. That is, in many cases food systems have evolved so that they are resilient to many of the challenges they have faced over time. But newer challenges that fall outside that range, especially intervention of other human groups, may interfere with, perturb, or degrade the ability of a system to provide valued aspects of a collective's quality of life, such as cultural integrity, freedom, food security, or public health, among others. A people's homeland is a place where they can participate in an ecology that is conducive to a range of options for adaptation.

Food injustice and settler colonialism

To understand some of the senses of Indigenous food sovereignty with which I am concerned here, we first have to understand how a particular form of colonialism in North America specifically targets the ecological, or homeland, value of food. The ecological value of food is connected to the range of adaptation options to local and metascale forces that groups have. *Settler colonialism* is a structure of oppression that wrongfully interferes with Indigenous capacities to maintain an adaptive capacity in their homelands. I will discuss how the structure of interference is a settlement-driven homeland-inscription process that motivates settler populations to erase Indigenous homelands, replacing them with their own homelands and futurity. In this sense, *settler colonization* is a structured process of erasing another population's range of adaptation options. My brief description in this section only touches on some of the themes from the diverse literature on settler colonialism (Lefevre 2015). My own interpretations of settler colonialism draw from literatures in Indigenous gender studies, feminism, environmental and climate justice, and education, some of which have developed concepts of settler colonialism as a structure of oppression before "settler colonialism" became coined academically in more recent times (Calhoun et al. 2007; Goeman and Denetdale 2009; Grinde and Johansen 1995; LaDuke 1993; Tuck and Gaztambide-Fernández 2013; Walker et al. 2013; Whyte 2015).

Settlers come to permanently inscribe – that is, incise or physically engrave – a homeland for themselves into Indigenous ecologies or homelands. While part of the motivation for settlement involves capitalist extraction of resources to the place settlers originate from and labor exploitation of Indigenous populations, the ultimate desire is to create a homeland in the "new" territory so that the settlers will never have to return permanently. Making a homeland is a process of inscription, that is, it is an ecological endeavor in the sense in which I have been using the concept of ecology. A territory will only emerge as a settler homeland if the origin, religious and cultural narratives, social ways of life, and political and economic systems (e.g., property) are physically incised and engraved into the waters, soils, air, and other environmental dimensions of the landscape. Settler *ecologies* are inscribed so that settlers can activate their own cultural, economic, and political aspirations and collective capacities. In this sense, waves of settlement seek to embed ecologies required for their own collective capacities to flourish in the landscapes they seek to occupy permanently.

As discussed earlier, the ecologies on which Indigenous collective capacities are based have their own origin, religious and cultural narratives, societal ways of life, and political and economic systems. For settlers, Indigenous ecologies can impede settler tactics to establish the legitimacy of their homelands, including settlers' claims to have title to land, morally praiseworthy religious missions, and exclusive political and cultural sovereignty. So as to eradicate any markers or physical obstacles challenging their legitimacy, settlers seek to erase the ecologies required for Indigenous capacity to adapt to change.

Settlement, then, actively erases Indigenous peoples' collective capacities as a means of inscribing settler ecologies into Indigenous homelands. In this way, settlers actually seek to eliminate themselves *as settlers*. Settlers seek to render the territory *their* homeland in every dimension – cultural, social, economic, political, and so on. Settlers engage in a process, then, that seeks to make their ecologies permanent and inevitable. They do so in a number of ways, from creating origin stories and myths that seek to justify their arrival and development of the land (e.g., "the pilgrims") to forming their own polities, from national governments to municipal and subnational governments, that serve to shelter the homeland-inscription process through laws, policies, and military and economic force.

In the US and Canada, settler inscription and replacement engenders settler collective capacities through what are now known to be rather unsustainable, industrial means: deforestation, mineral and fossil fuel extraction, petrochemical and other industries producing water and air pollution, commodity agriculture, urban sprawl and widespread automobile use, and so on. These means are built into the settler narratives of homeland, such as in narratives of the "Americanness" and wholesomeness of industrious "blue collar" work that built the economy. They are sometimes hidden in plain sight, such as in narratives of recreation and the natural beauty of parts of the US that mask histories of how people of color – Indigenous and other communities – have been forcibly relocated and made to live in places with disproportionately greater levels of risk from pollution and radiation.

The erasure, through industrial means, of Indigenous food systems is particularly pronounced. As a large literature on environmental injustice in North America shows, industrial technologies, from weaponry to mining to petrochemical facilities, have polluted and destroyed terrestrial and aquatic habitats that Indigenous peoples cultivated for food (Agyeman et al. 2010; Grijalva 2008; Grinde and Johansen 1995; Hoover et al. 2012). The examples from the previous section each testified to the hub-like or ecological value of food for particular Indigenous peoples, pushing back against industrial technologies and practices that curtailed the cultivated-habitats and cultivated-landscapes Indigenous peoples maintained in order for certain foods to express this form of value. Industrialization was and continues to be part of a settlement process aimed at erasing Indigenous homelands that developed around the ecological value of certain foods.

Food sovereignty, ecologies, and renewal

Settlement, then, refers to processes of ecological, or homeland, inscription that combine military, commercial, and cultural structures. The fallout of the homeland-inscription process is that, as Indigenous peoples, we continue to exercise political and cultural self-determination, even though there are now these states, such as the US and Canada, that are perceived by many people as the major sovereigns in the places where Indigenous peoples live, work, and play. Settlement has altered North American Indigenous ecologies to such a degree that it is hard to recognize any dimensions of historic or contemporary Indigenous homelands in them.

Though one important form of settler erasure is to motivate Indigenous assimilation, Indigenous populations do not even gain the same privileges and benefits as understood from a settler worldview through the assimilation process. Indeed, the outcomes of the settler inscription process are higher health-risk factors for many Indigenous peoples from relatively high environmental exposures to natural and industrial toxins (Grijalva 2008), diabetes from inadequate or improper diets (Milburn 2004), and mental health concerns from historical and personal trauma (Evans-Campbell 2008). Socioeconomic factors can magnify health risks for Indigenous persons living in impoverished urban, rural, or remote communities with high suicide, alcoholism, or infant/child mortality rates (Kuhnlein and Receveur 1996; Kuhnlein et al. 2004; Sarche and Spicer 2008).

At base, settler erasure challenges the very root of Indigenous touchstones for planning for future generations, because the future embedded within the landscape becomes a settler one (Tuck and Gaztambide-Fernández 2013; Walker et al. 2013). If we go along with the settler ecologies, we face numerous immediate problems that are hard to solve (e.g., suicide) and that can be divisive (poverty and drug abuse). Yet the habitats and landscapes needed to establish more beneficial collective capacities and trade with other groups are degraded beyond our ability to fully adapt them to our contemporary needs. Our range of adaptive options has been substantially curtailed. In the face of settler colonialism, one of the primary issues Indigenous peoples face concerns how to design, plan, and implement ecologies that can create physical, cultural, and social well-being in our societies. Food sovereignty represents a particular strategy for how to live under this structure of oppression that prioritizes certain foods for renewal.

Consider, for example, *Anishinaabek*[2] food sovereignty in relation to wild rice in the Great Lakes region in North America. Anishinaabek have a complex heritage of adaptive, seasonal, group activities of tending, cultivating, gathering, harvesting, processing, distributing, storing, and consuming diverse animal and plant foods, recirculating the refuse and unharvested materials within the ecosystem. These activities form Anishinaabe ecologies. Foods in this systematic cycle that are still harvested today include walleye, blueberries, deer, hare, maple, sturgeon, and wild rice, among others – for there were many more foods and medicinal plants in this system historically. As an ecology, the activities associated with the seasonal round renew the family, community, cultural, economic, social, and political relationships that connect Anishinaabe persons with one another and with all the plants, animals, and other entities in the environment, even the water itself. As Frances Van Zile, a Sokaogon Chippewa member, puts it, describing a future without wild rice: "My whole way of being as an Indian would be destroyed. I can't imagine being without it. And there is no substitute for this lake's rice" (Great Lakes Indian Fish and Wildlife Commission 1995). According to these words, wild rice has ecological value.

In the case of wild rice, Anishinaabek have prioritized its revitalization or renewal, as settler Americans have done quite a bit to threaten wild rice. For example, in Minnesota, wild rice has declined by half in the last 100 years (Andow et al. 2009). Neighboring settler American groups engage in activities such as mining, damming, growing commercial paddy rice for mass distribution, and recreational boating that directly affect wild rice and its habitat – particularly the relationship between water and wild rice. These activities can modify water levels, water flow, water quality, and the diversity of plants and animals in the lake. Many Anishinaabek are also concerned that settler Americans who breed and grow varieties of commercial paddy rice for mass harvest are not careful enough to ensure that these strains avoid affecting wild rice. Settler Americans also began to adopt "wild rice" as their own, and some Anishinaabe people adapted by selling their harvest to others who would process it off reservation. The Anishinaabe rice was sold at a premium price as a hand-harvested product. In the 1960s and 1970s, when settler Americans determined how to domesticate wild rice, the price dropped, shutting Anishinaabek out of the market. Settler Americans further captured the market through accepting the idea that it is appropriate for settler companies to market wild rice as if it were harvested and processed by Anishinaabek (LaDuke 2007; Wallwork 1997).

Declines and threats to wild rice in such a short time period put immense and rapid pressures on the ecological value of food for Anishinaabek – forcing them to adapt at a harmful pace that disrupted the maintenance of a range of adaptation options. Without wild rice, Anishinaabek lose an integral glue holding together biological, family, social, cultural, economic, ecological, political, and spiritual dimensions of group life. Anishinaabe nations today face many challenges, including relatively higher rights of diabetes, food insecurity, and hunger (Cho et al. 2014; Sarche and Spicer 2008). Culturally, certain ceremonies are becoming less common (Wallwork 1997). Though, according to some, the US has improved the quality and distribution of commodity foods on reservations, Anishinaabe persons in nations such as White Earth see the protection and revitalization of wild rice as integral to fully addressing problems of nutrition, cultural decline, and poverty (Siple 2011).

Motivation to protect wild rice has produced an incredibly diverse set of strategic responses that support the protection of Anishinaabek from numerous problems associated with settler colonialism. The responses seek to establish institutions that renew and restore cultural, social, and political systems associated with wild rice. In this way, wild rice is an invaluable motivator for institutional and community responses to create a range of adaptation options that do not require Anishinaabek to succumb to settler erasure.

Consider some examples. The natural resources and environmental agencies of many Anishinaabe Tribal governments, such as the Leech Lake Band of Ojibwe or the Little Traverse Bay Bands of Odawa Indians, devote institutional and staff resources to learning about the biology and ecology of wild rice through connecting with elders and ricers and performing in-house scientific research and habitat restoration (Circle of Flight and Great Lakes Restoration Initiative 2014). Anishinaabe treaty organizations, such as the Great Lakes Indian Fish and Wildlife Commission (GLIFWC) and Chippewa Ottawa Resource Authority (CORA), engage in research and advocate for law and policy reforms that protect wild rice in ceded territories, where many Anishinaabe communities exercise stewardship and harvesting rights. For example:

> GLIFWC focuses on the preservation and enhancement of wild rice in ceded territory lakes. Annual surveys are performed on existing beds to determine density and overall health of bed. Select lakes are also reseeded for the purpose of enhancement or re-establishing old beds. Recently, GLIFWC completed a comprehensive wild rice lake inventory in the ceded territories with documentation necessary to develop and launch a comprehensive wild rice management plan.
> (Great Lakes Indian Fish and Wildlife Commission 2013; 1995)

This information is often used in law and policy contexts as evidence that environmental threats, such as mining, are harming rice populations.

Anishinaabe-led nongovernmental organizations, such as the White Earth Land Recovery Project (LaDuke and Carlson 2003) or the Native Wild Rice Coalition, are involved in many projects promoting cultural life and economic viability around wild rice. Some of these organizations seek to create markets for wild rice on terms that are financially viable for Anishinaabek and to educate settler populations. The *Nibi and Manoomin* (water and rice) *Symposium*, which is held every two years, attempts to bring together different parties that can affect wild rice, from paddy rice growers and representatives of mining companies to Anishinaabe leaders, family members, elders, and representatives of Indigenous organizations. The symposium seeks to create cross-cultural education so that people sharing the Great Lakes can respect each other's ways of life and act ethically toward one another. The symposium is hosted by an Ojibwe Tribe in the region (Andow et al. 2009).

In these examples, wild rice has the power to convene Anishinaabek around a number of strategic responses to settler erasure of their ecologies, or homelands. Other foods, such as the commodity cheese and spam distributed through US food assistance programs, or microwave meals, cannot replace wild rice as comparable contributors to the establishment and maintenance of such an array of institutional responses. Wild rice continues to have an ecological value that, if prioritized, can support the renewal of both the rice itself and of Anishinaabek well-being, even though much of the settler damage to the Indigenous food system is permanent in the sense that Anishinaabek will likely continue to eat mixed diets of different foods, from Indigenous and local foods to industrially produced foods.

Food sovereignty for some North American Indigenous persons, in my view, is not really based on ideals of food self-sufficiency and cultural autonomy. Indeed, food sovereignty is a practical response to a particular structure of oppression that seeks to erase the ecologies that constitute Indigenous homelands. In the case of wild rice, Anishinaabe people prioritize rice as a way of adapting to today's circumstances, planning for the future, finding new terms of trade and exchange, and educating and reconciling with the settler society. Food sovereignty, then, serves more as a strategic process whereby foods that are renewed serve to engender ranges of adaptive options that are appropriate when confronted with the challenges of Indigenous erasure in settler landscapes.

Notes

1 I wish to note here that LVC has developed a complex and evolving concept of food sovereignty and that the definition quoted here is just an excerpt.
2 I tried to use English spellings of words in Anishinaabemowin (the language of the Anishinaabek) that can be identified by diverse Ojibwe, Potawatomi, and Odawa people and people who work in relation to this language. I recognize that there are many accents and spelling systems, and that the one I am using is in some ways the least similar to how members of my Tribe (Potawatomi) engage in English-language spelling.

References

Agyeman, J., P. Cole, R. Haluza-Delay, and P. O'Riley. (2010) *Speaking for Ourselves: Environmental Justice in Canada*, Vancouver: University of British Columbia Press.
Andow, D., T. Bauer, M. Belcourt, P. Bloom, B. Child, J. Doerfler, A. Eule-Nashoba, T. Heidel, A. Kokotovich, A. Lodge, J. Lagarde, K. Lorenz, L. Mendoza, E. Mohl, J. Osborne, K. Prescott, P. Schultz, D. Smith, S. Solarz, and R. Walker. (2009) "Wild Rice White Paper: Preserving the Integrity of Manoomin in Minnesota," People Protecting Manoomin: Manoomin Protecting People – A Symposium Bridging Opposing Worldviews.
Arquette, M., M. Cole, K. Cook, B. LaFrance, M. Peters, J. Ransom, E. Sargent, V. Smoke, and A. Stairs. (2002) "Holistic Risk-Based Environmental Decision-making: A Native Perspective," *Environmental Health Perspectives* 110: 259–264.
Bernstein, H. (2010) *Class Dynamics of Agrarian Change*, Sterling, VA: Kumarian Press.
——. (2014) "Food Sovereignty via the 'Peasant Way': A Sceptical View," *Journal of Peasant Studies* 41: 1031–1063.

Birger, J. (2012) "Why Shell Is Betting Billions to Drill for Oil in Alaska," *Fortune*, May 24, viewed 13 May 2016, http://fortune.com/2012/05/24/why-shell-is-betting-billions-to-drill-for-oil-in-alaska/.

Brown, J. J. (1994) "Treaty Rights: Twenty Years After the Boldt Decision," *Wicazo Sa Review*: 1–16.

Calhoun, A., M. Goeman, and M. Tsethlikai. (2007) "Achieving Gender Equity for American Indians," in S. S. Klein, B. Richardson, D. A. Grayson, L. H. Fox, C. Kramarae, D. S. Pollard, and C. A. Dwyer (eds.), *Handbook for Achieving Gender Equity through Education*, New York: Routledge, pp. 525–552.

Cho, P., L. S. Geiss, N. R. Burrows, D. L. Roberts, A. K. Bullock, and M. E. Toedt. (2014) "Diabetes-Related Mortality Among American Indians and Alaska Natives, 1990–2009," *American Journal of Public Health* 104: S496–S503.

Circle of Flight and Great Lakes Restoration Initiative. (2014) "Tribal Habitat: Restoration and Invasive Species Control," Midwest Region Report.

Detroit Food Justice Task Force. (2014) *Food Justice* [Online], http://www.detroitfoodjustice.org/.

Diné Policy Institute. (2014) "Diné Food Sovereignty," Report.

Edelman, M. (2014) "Food Sovereignty: Forgotten Genealogies and Future Regulatory Challenges," *Journal of Peasant Studies* 41: 959–978.

Evans-Campbell, T. (2008) "Historical Trauma in American Indian/Native Alaska Communities: A Multilevel Framework for Exploring Impacts on Individuals, Families, and Communities," *Journal of Interpersonal Violence* 23: 316–338.

Goeman, M. and J. Denetdale. (2009) "Native Feminisms: Legacies, Interventions, and Indigenous Sovereignties," *Wicazo Sa Review* 24(2): 9–13.

Great Lakes Indian Fish and Wildlife Commission. (1995) *Sulfide Mining: The Process and the Price, A Tribal and Ecological Perspective*, Odana, WI: Great Lakes Indian Fish and Wildlife Commission.

———. (2013) *Manoomin (Wild Rice)* [Online], viewed 15 October 2013, www.glifwc.org/WildRice/wildrice.html.

Grijalva, J. M. (2008) *Closing the Circle: Environmental Justice in Indian Country*, Durham, NC: Carolina Academic Press.

Grinde, D. A. and B. E. Johansen. (1995) *Ecocide of Native America: Environmental Destruction of Indian Lands and Peoples*, Sante Fe: Clear Light.

Hoover, E. (2013) "Cultural and Health Implications of Fish Advisories in a Native American Community," *Ecological Processes* 2: 1–12.

Hoover, E., K. Cook, R. Plain, K. Sanchez, V. Waghiyi, P. Miller, R. Dufault, C. Sislin, and D. O. Carpenter. (2012) "Indigenous Peoples of North America: Environmental Exposures and Reproductive Justice," *Environmental Health Perspectives* 120: 1645–1649.

Hospes, O. (2014) "Food Sovereignty: The Debate, the Deadlock, and a Suggested Detour," *Agriculture and Human Values* 31: 119–130.

Kassi, N. (1996) "A Legacy of Maldevelopment," in J. Weaver (ed.), *Defending Mother Earth: Native American Perspectives on Environmental Justice*, Maryknoll, New York: Orbis Books, pp. 72–84.

Kuhnlein, H. V. and O. Receveur. (1996) "Dietary Change and Traditional Food Systems of Indigenous Peoples," *Annual Review of Nutrition* 16: 417–442.

Kuhnlein, H. V., O. Receveur, R. Soueida, and G. M. Egeland. (2004) "Arctic Indigenous Peoples Experience The Nutrition Transition with Changing Dietary Patterns and Obesity," *The Journal of Nutrition* 134: 1447–1453.

LaDuke, W. (1993) "A Society Based on Conquest Cannot Be Sustained," in R. Hofrichter (ed.), *Toxic Struggles: The Theory and Practice of Environmental Justice*, Philadelphia: New Society Publishers, pp. 98–106.

———. (1999) "Return of the Sturgeon: Namewag Bi-Azhegiiwewaad," *News from Indian Country*, 31 August.

———. (2007) "Ricekeepers: A Struggle to Protect Biodiversity and a Native American way of Life," *Orion* 26: 18–23.

——— and B. Carlson. (2003) *Our Manoomin, Our Life: The Anishinaabeg Struggle to Protect Wild Rice*, White Earth Land Recovery Project.

Lefevre, T. A. (2015) "Settler Colonialism," in J. Jackson (ed.), *Oxford Bibliographies in Anthropology*, Oxford, UK: Oxford University Press, pp. 1–26.

Milburn, M. P. (2004) "Indigenous Nutrition: Using Traditional Food Knowledge to Solve Contemporary Health Problems," *The American Indian Quarterly* 28: 411–434.

Minkoff-Zern, L. (2013) "The New American Farmer: The Agrarian Question, Food Sovereignty and Immigrant Mexican Growers in the United States," in *Food Sovereignty: A Critical Dialogue*, 14–15 September, New Haven.

Navin, M. C. (2014) "Local Food and International Ethics," *Journal of Agricultural and Environmental Ethics* 27: 349–368.

Nesper, L. (2002) *The Walleye War: The Struggle for Ojibwe Spearfishing and Treaty Rights*, Lincoln: University of Nebraska Press.

Park, C.M.Y., B. White, and J. White. (2015) "We Are Not All The Same: Taking Gender Seriously in Food Sovereignty Discourse," *Third World Quarterly* 36: 584–599.

People's Food Policy Project. (2014) *Resetting The Table: A People's Food Policy For Canada*, Montreal: People's Food Policy Project and Food Secure Canada.

Pimbert, M. (2009) *Towards Food Sovereignty*, London: International Institute for Environment and Development.

Sarche, M. and P. Spicer. (2008) "Poverty and Health Disparities for American Indian and Alaska Native Children," *Annals of the New York Academy of Sciences* 1136: 126–136.

Siple, J. (2011) "A Return to Traditional Foods Helps Some Fight Hunger on White Earth Reservation," *Minnesota Public Radio News*, 4 October.

Steckley, M. (2015) "Eating Up The Social Ladder: The Problem Of Dietary Aspirations For Food Sovereignty," *Agriculture and Human Values*, Online First: 1–14.

Thompson, P. B. (2015) *From Field to Fork: Food Ethics for Everyone*, Oxford: Oxford University Press.

Tuck, E. and R. A. Gaztambide-Fernández. (2013) "Curriculum, Replacement, and Settler Futurity," *Journal of Curriculum Theorizing* 29: 72–89.

Walker, R., D. Natcher, and T. Jojola. (2013) *Reclaiming Indigenous Planning*, Montreal: McGill–Queen's Press.

Wallwork, D. (director) (1997) *The Good Life: Mino-Bimadiziwin*, Saint Paul, MN: RedEye Video.

Walters, K. L. and J. M. Simoni. (2002) "Reconceptualizing Native Women's Health: An 'Indigenist' Stress-coping Model," *American Journal of Public Health* 92: 520–524.

Weaver, J. (1996) *Defending Mother Earth: Native American Perspectives On Environmental Justice*, Maryknoll, NY: Orbis Books.

Whyte, K. P. (2015) "Indigenous Food Systems, Environmental Justice, and Settler-Industrial States," in M. C. Rawlinson and C. Ward (eds.), *Global Food, Global Justice: Essays on Eating under Globalization*, Newcastle upon Tyne, UK: Cambridge Scholars Publishing, pp. 143–166.

Wilkinson, C. F. (2005) *Blood Struggle: The Rise of Modern Indian Nations*, New York: Norton.

34

CASE STUDIES OF FOOD SOVEREIGNTY INITIATIVES AMONG THE MĀORI OF *AOTEAROA* (NEW ZEALAND)

Karyn Stein, Miranda Mirosa, Lynette Carter, and Marion Johnson

Introduction

The industrial food system, which is based on the commodification of food and corporate control of food production and distribution, has failed to combat world hunger and malnutrition. According to the World Food Program, over 90% of the world's hungry are simply too poor to buy enough food (Holt-Giménez and Patel 2012). Holt-Giménez (2014) concludes that there is already enough food to feed everyone on the planet; hunger is not a problem of production, but rather the result of poverty and inequality. Similarly, Timmer (2012) contends that the problem is not with food production, but rather food produced solely for profit. Food is being produced for the market as a commodity, while families that are financially unable to participate in the market system go hungry (Timmer 2012). The "destructive neo-liberal market path-dependency" of the global, industrial food system has led to rising energy and food prices, unstable communities that are no longer self-sufficient, and adverse environmental impacts, including climate change and water and air pollution (McMichael 2014: 951). Environmental degradation has been unprecedented in the last 60 years, at a rate unseen in the last 10,000 years (Milman 2015). There is widespread consensus that the food system is in need of transformation in order to become more sustainable, equitable, and just. There is an urgent need for alternatives, and the focus is shifting towards "the question of stewardship of the land as an act of social provisioning and human survival" (McMichael 2014: 951). The true heroes that are transforming the food system from the ground up include Indigenous women producing food while reviving traditional ways, preserving biodiversity, and conserving their culture. Through a variety of approaches, their actions represent local solutions to global problems presented by an unsustainable and unjust global food system.

This article explores how Māori women and local communities in *Aotearoa* (New Zealand) are actively taking control of their food systems through community gardens and farms. The research contextualizes local food struggles within the framework of food sovereignty. This research is part of a "counter-narrative" that, as McMichael states, "underscores the importance of regenerative local farming practices as solutions to the combined crises facing the planet" (2014: 952). Through these case studies we can better understand the many manifestations of food sovereignty in practice. As food producers, these women are practicing food sovereignty by "exercising their rights to control their food system, including where food comes from and how land is used to produce food; sustainability; building a food-based community; and expressing culture and tradition" (Larder et al. 2014: 70). Through these examples we find inspiration in community-based agriculture that is both ecologically sustainable and socially just (Wittman et al. 2010).

The need for food sovereignty

Food sovereignty represents a viable and democratic solution to food poverty, hunger, and malnutrition. Food sovereignty recognizes the right to define one's own food system, as well as the collective control of the local food system (Borras and Franco 2012; Claeys 2013). Hunger and malnutrition are the "ultimate symbols of powerlessness," caused not by "food or land scarcity, but a scarcity of democracy" (Boucher 1999: 6). Thus, the concept of food sovereignty focuses on power dynamics and control of the food system and captures the multidimensional nature of food, including its cultural connection and historical roots.

Food sovereignty aims "to combat the neoliberalization of food production and consumption" (Slocum and Saldanha 2013: 8), and is distinct from food security, which deepens food dependency and fails to address corporate control of the food system and the prevalence of unhealthy, cheap processed food (Bové and Dufour 2001). Instead, food and nutritional sovereignty emphasizes the right to food and critically examines all aspects of food production, distribution, and consumption, including the type and quality of food that is produced, where, how, by whom, and at what scale (McMichael 2009; Patel 2009). According to La Vía Campesina, "food sovereignty is a precondition to genuine food security" (1996: 1), and "it draws attention to the deceit of feeding the world with the claim of providing food security through a marketplace in which a minority of the world's population participates" (McMichael 2014: 937).

Food poverty in New Zealand

The employment rate for Māori is 59%, compared to 67.3% of Pākehā (NZ European) aged 15 and over (Statistics New Zealand 2014). Māori, along with Pacific Island population groups, have the poorest health of all in New Zealand (Ministry of Health 2006). Health inequalities between ethnic groups are a result of "differences in power relationships, as well as historical and social factors such as colonization and racism" (Earle 2011: 37). Ill health and poverty reflect the failure of the state to protect Indigenous Peoples' rights (Damman et al. 2008).

Food poverty is also highest among Māori and Pacific people (Carter et al. 2010; Parnell et al. 2001; 2003). According to the 2008/09 Adult Nutritional Survey, 18.3% of Māori women were food insecure, as compared to 6.6% New Zealand European women with low food security (Ministry of Health 2008). As research has shown, food poverty impacts the choice and quantity of foods consumed (Stevenson 2011). Cheap, processed food contributes to obesity, as it is high in fat and sugar (Rush and Rusk 2009; Te Hotu Manawa Māori 2007). Levels of obesity correspond to wealth, and there are higher levels of obesity in New Zealand's poorer communities (University of Otago and Ministry of Health 2011). The prevalence of obesity is 26.5% among the general population, one of the highest obesity rates internationally, with 42% of Māori adults classified as obese (International Association of the Study of Obesity 2011; Ministry of Health 2008; Ono et al. 2010). The relationship between food poverty and obesity is strongest in women, as well as among Māori and Pacific populations (Stevenson 2011). Sixty-one percent of Māori women are obese or overweight (Grigg and Macrae 2000), which has implications for future generations.

Research shows that food prices have an influence on the well-being of low-income consumers in developed countries (Beatty 2010; Broda et al. 2009). Clearly, there is a considerable price differential between the cost of a healthy diet versus an energy-dense but nutrient-poor diet (Wynd 2005). The prices of healthy foods, such as fruits and vegetables, are higher (Drewnowski and Darmon 2005), and prices of fast food were inversely associated with fast-food intake (Gordon-Larsen et al. 2011). In addition, those facing food poverty and low food security are more likely to consume cheap, processed fatty cuts of meat (sausages and saveloys) than leaner, more expensive cuts (beef/veal) (Parnell 2005).

Fast-food consumption is associated with a diet high in energy, but low in essential micronutrient density, thus contributing to weight gain (Bowman and Vinyard 2004). Cheap, processed foods are also higher in saturated fats, a risk factor for obesity, diabetes, and coronary heart disease (Parillo and Riccardi 2004). These are ailments disproportionately affecting the poor in New Zealand (Ministry of Health 2008). Not only are processed foods less nutritious, but they also include artificial ingredients and added flavors that can further compromise health (Wilkie 2014). Cheap, processed food can be toxic, "unsafe," and "hazardous," as can be seen in India's recent ban of Nestlé's Maggi instant noodles, a staple for many low-income households, after tests found excessive levels of lead (Agence France-Presse 2015).

As the above statistics reveal, the inequality that pervades the food system reflects racial and gender disparities. As Slocum and Saldanha point out, "race is endemic to the global food system in the aftermath of colonialism" (2013: 1). The food system reflects structural inequalities and social stratification based on the type, quality, and cost of food that people are able to consume, which has devastating implications for health and well-being, including for future generations. Phillips emphasizes the need to examine "markers of inclusion and exclusion" with regard to food, and why such markers are being maintained (2006).

Food sovereignty and food justice

Food sovereignty and food justice overlap and are often used interchangeably (Cadieux and Slocum 2015; Holt-Giménez and Shattuck 2011). Both terms encompass a rights-based approach and address inequalities in the food system (Slocum and Saldanha 2013). *Food justice* represents "a transformation of the current food system, including but not limited to eliminating disparities and inequities" (Gottlieb and Joshi 2010: ix). *Food sovereignty* is "the right of peoples and governments to choose the way food is produced and consumed in order to respect livelihoods, as well as the policies that support this choice" (La Vía Campesina 2009: 57). According to Cadieux and Slocum, the four areas around which organizing for food justice and food sovereignty occurs include: (1) confronting historical injustice and race, class, and gender inequalities; (2) building communal reliance and control; (3) practicing agroecological land-use practices that benefit the whole ecosystem and build on diverse knowledge systems to grow food; and (4) guaranteeing a minimum income (2015: 13).

Food sovereignty is a response to the market focus of a global food system. The aim is to empower communities to take back or retain control of their local, autonomous food systems (Patel 2009), based on local knowledge and culture (Pimbert 2008). This involves a shift towards empowering communities, protecting agro-biodiversity, promoting organic agriculture, and fostering self-sufficiency (Altieri and Toledo 2011). Agroecology is a key strategy for achieving food sovereignty (Martínez-Torres and Rosset 2010; Altieri and Toledo 2011). A key tenet of agroecology is agro-biodiversity, and thus environmental resiliency. Species diversification is an important strategy for reducing risk (Altieri and Koohafkan 2013).

Organic farming, in particular agroecological systems, builds rather than depletes soil organic matter and ensures a balanced ecosystem (Rodale Institute 2011). Over the long term, organic yields match conventional yields; are more sustainable; outperform conventional systems in years of drought; are more efficient, using 45% less energy; and produce less greenhouse gases (conventional systems produce 40% more greenhouse gases) (Rodale Institute 2011).

Research also supports the claim that organic food is more healthy and nutritious than food grown using pesticides and fertilizers, as it has significantly higher levels of antioxidants, which reduce the risk of cancer and chronic disease (Barański et al. 2014). Conventional crops had significantly higher levels of the toxic heavy metal cadmium, and the levels of pesticide residues were four times higher (Barański et al. 2014). Food grown with chemicals harms our bodies, depletes the soil, pollutes water sources, and harms wildlife, such as bees.

Alternative food systems, including community gardens and local farms, are growing in popularity and visibility (Burch and Lawrence 2007). Such local food movements often take a community-based approach to decision-making and are commonly based on the "principles of organics, care for the environment, and social equity within the food system" (Bittermann 2007: 24). Feenstra defines the "localisation of food as a collaborative effort to build more locally-based, self-reliant food economies, one in which sustainable food production, processing, distribution and consumption is integrated to enhance the economic, environmental and social health of a particular place" (2002: 100).

Parihaka and Indigenous food sovereignty

Parihaka is a small Māori settlement in the Taranaki region of *Aotearoa* (New Zealand), located between Mount Taranaki and the Tasman Sea. Historically, it was a pacifist haven and a symbol of protest against British colonizers taking Māori land. Te Whiti-o-Rongomai and Tohu Kākahi were leaders of the non-violent movement and used tactics such as repairing fences and cultivating land to prevent land confiscations. On November 5–7, 1881, Parihaka was attacked by around 1,600 troops. The village was plundered, houses ransacked, crops uprooted, livestock pillaged, women raped, and men arrested. Te Whiti, Tohu, and many others were arrested and exiled until 1883.

Parihaka has a long history of *maara* (food gardens), especially as a peaceful means of protecting land. In 1881, up to 1,300 inhabitants were residing in the village (Sinclair 1991). Approximately 2,000 people routinely attended meetings on the 17th of each month, where huge amounts of food were provided. Land was, and still is, considered sacred. The *maara* (garden), at the entrance to the Parihaka *pa* (Māori village), is much more than a place where food is cultivated. It is a symbol of peace and historical significance. It is a symbol of culture, history, and land *occupation*.[1] Indigenous understandings of place and their surrounding environment should be respected and acknowledged (Bawaka Country et al. 2013; Moreton-Robinson and Walter 2009). Gardens and food cultivation areas are important spaces for Indigenous well-being. Food sovereignty "resonates closely with their claims to land and with their struggles for self-determination" (Cadieux and Slocum 2015: 12).

As Charissa Waerea, coordinator of the community gardens at Parihaka explains, *kaitiakitanga* (guardianship) means it is our job to protect, maintain, and look after the land – leave it in a better state. The Māori, as *tangata whenua* (people of the land), therefore have an obligation to protect the natural environment and natural resources (treasures or *taonga*) for future generations (Durie 1998). Charissa is the mother of five *tamariki* (children), and is concerned about what her *whānau* (family) put into their bodies. To her, the garden is about education of the youth, thinking about future generations, and planting for the future. Furthermore, the garden brings people closer to their *tipuna* (ancestors) through working the land.

A variety of *kai* (food) is grown in the gardens. There are native trees and fruit trees. Vegetables include kumara, cucumbers, tomatoes, garlic, asparagus, water cress, strawberries, blueberries, broad beans, kale, beetroot, spring onions, celery, brassicas, onions, zucchini, and lettuce, as well as less-common crops like *taro* (starchy root crop), *kōkihi* (New Zealand spinach), *kamokamo* (marrow or Māori squash), *kaanga maa* (white corn), pumpkins, and gourds. Many different types of potatoes are grown, including Māori heritage varieties such as *tutaekuri, huakaroro,* and *kowiniwini.* Medicinal herbs, such as calendula, peppermint, thyme, rosemary, sage, parsley, and lavender are also grown. The soil is fed with nitrogen-fixing crops and enriched through composting organic matter such as seaweed, manure, wood ash, blood, and bone. Surplus vegetables are offered to the community for *koha* (gift/donation), with an honesty box in front of the garden.

The *whakapapa* (genealogy) of the seed is important – heritage seeds are often sourced and the best seed from the garden saved. Charissa talks about the *tikanga* (cultural protocols) among the gardeners for respecting each others' seed. *Tikanga* refers to a set of moral behaviors that people follow, and "within an environmental context, refers to a preferred way of protecting natural resources, exercising *kaitiakitanga* (guardianship), and upholding the responsibility and obligation to protect the environment for future generations" (Durie 1998: 21). "Local knowledge and cultural memory is crucial for the conservation of biodiversity" (Nazarea 2006: 318), as monocultures have caused a depletion of local species and varieties (Negri 2005).

Some of the food that is grown in the garden is used for significant events, commemorations, and *tangi* (funerals). On the 18th and the 19th of each month the Parihaka prophets Te Whiti-o-Rongomai and Tohu Kākahi are commemorated, with visitors from all over New Zealand taking part and food partly supplied by the garden. The sacking of Parihaka on November 5th, 1881 – called *Te Pahuatanga o Parihaka* – is also marked each year, with people coming together to remember this time. It is hoped in the future the garden will provide *kumara* (sweet potato), pumpkin, and potatoes for Pahuatanga and other significant events, but land is needed to expand the garden. The plan is to reuse kumara pits and have horses plough the land, like it was done in the past. The goal is to have as much food production within the *papakainga* (Māori housing development on ancestral land, literally meaning "a nurturing place to return to") and to become self-sufficient and able to meet community needs, especially during significant events.

The garden also faces many obstacles. One of the main issues is access to productive land, especially for future expansion. Manpower is another big problem, as many residents are elderly or very young. As with other rural communities, many young adults have left for cities to work. Families in Parihaka are very busy juggling work and family. However, garden volunteers have come up with some creative and innovative ways of overcoming obstacles by, for example, collaborating with other gardens and organizations in the region for joint working bees, which fosters a sense of community and interdependence, truly reviving the spirit of food cultivation in Parihaka.

Awhi farm and sustainable living

Awhi Farm is a demonstration center for sustainable living in Turangi, a small town located along the Tangariro River and on the North Island Volcanic Plateau. *Awhi* means to cherish, embrace, and care for in *te reo Māori* (the Māori language). It is located on land that is owned by Ngāti Tūwharetoa's Kawakawa Trust and is run by the bicultural Awhi Turangi Trust, composed of Lisa Isherwood, Joanna Pearsall, and Bryan Innes. The Board of Trustees has an egalitarian structure and also manages the farm. Lisa is of Tuwharetoa descent and lives on site.

When Lisa, Joanna, and Bryan started the farm in 2009, the land was covered in blackberry, gorse, heather, cotoneaster, and other weeds. The roughly 10-acre parcel was previously used by the Ministry of Works for a men's camp and then to store gravel for roads and for vehicle maintenance. The previously degraded land is now a thriving permaculture farm promoting self-sufficiency and agro-biodiversity. The mission of the farm is to inspire people to make changes on the path to sustainable practice. It is influenced by permaculture practices and demonstrates organic agriculture, waste reduction, sustainable building, and alternative-energy practices.

The farm is located in Turangi, a small town at the southern end of Lake Taupo on the Tongariro River on the North Island's Volcanic Plateau of *Aotearoa* (New Zealand). The farm is run by volunteers. There are gardens, orchards, and food forests, which mimic natural forest ecosystems while producing food, medicine, and fuel, and building up the soil. The farm includes 30 two-person huts for accommodation, an outdoor kitchen, composting toilets, and compost-heated/solar showers. Sustainable buildings include a dome/vault building made with earth bricks and local materials, an earth-bag building, portable round pallet houses, and a cordwood house. Chickens are reared for free-range eggs, and bees are kept for honey. A variety of vegetables are produced, like garlic, kale, potatoes, beetroot, carrots, cabbage, silverbeet, and lettuces. Orchards have fruit and nut trees, such as chestnuts, walnuts, apples, pears, figs, nectarines, and feijoas. During the Australasian Permaculture Convention of 2012 in Turangi, Awhi Farm provided most of the food (fruits and vegetables) for close to 500 people.

Education is the foundation of the farm, learning and sharing information the ethos. The local Michael Park Steiner School uses the farm as a base for their summer camps. Lisa also believes strongly in community outreach, and volunteers do gardening and prepare beds with local schools, including at *Te Kura o Hirangi* (a Māori-language immersion school). They are currently involved with a tree-planting project with the local *kura* (Māori-language immersion schools) and community, planting fruit and nut trees at schools and along residential roads with community members. Volunteers learn by doing, live collectively, and share communal meals from the farm. They come from the local community and are international, including WWOOFers (Willing Workers on Organic Farms). Visiting school groups, universities, and school workshops have been held on topics including permaculture design principles, bee keeping, debt-free living, seed saving, whole and raw foods, bicultural living, Māori immersion, food forests, gardening, plant propagation, community wealth systems, etc. The farm hosts a weekly organic market during the warmer months, selling its organic produce, as well as eggs, garden tools, and seedlings. The market is also open to locals selling their goods. It is about increasing access to local organic food, while also generating employment and building community connections and resiliency.

The farm embraces permaculture principles, which is an approach to landscape design that mimics natural ecosystems. The foundation of permaculture is based on three ethical principles, including: (1) care for the earth; (2) care for the people; and (3) fair share – principles found in most traditional societies (Holmgren 2002). Permaculture is also about regenerating damaged land. This resonates with *kaitiaki* (the Māori concept of guardianship for the sky, sea, and land), "a holistic approach that provides for the restoration of damaged ecosystems and ecological harmony for the sake of future generations" (Durie 1998).

Lisa is a self-proclaimed "solutionist" and believes in like-minded people from different countries, cultures, and backgrounds coming together and working towards common solutions. Lisa is also concerned with the impact of fast foods on Māori communities and believes education of the youth is key, as well as promoting access to organic fruits and vegetables. Not only does the variety of crops and medicinal plants provide nutritional benefits and act as a potential source of income, but the "gardens are important social and cultural spaces where knowledge related to agriculture is transmitted" (Galluzzi et al. 2010: 3635).

Motueka Community Garden and seeing for the future

The Motueka Community Garden is located in the town of Motueka at the top of the South Island of *Aotearoa* (New Zealand), close to the mouth of the Motueka River on the shore of the Tasman Bay. The garden began in 2010 with a group of local people who wanted to share the benefits of growing food. A charitable trust, which is run voluntarily, makes collective decisions regarding the management of the garden.

Ellen Baldwin, a Māori elder, is one of the original founders of the community garden and is currently a trust member. She is originally from King Country in the North Island. Ellen is extremely active in the garden, where you can find her at least five days a week, coordinating the volunteers for the two working bees each week. The garden site is located on Council land just out of town in a recreational area with walkways, parks, and the skate park – an area once used as a landfill, loaded with chunks of concrete and stone. The garden includes over 25 plots, which include community and private allotments – the latter are maintained by individuals for a small fee of $1 per sq. meter per year. Although many in the garden would like to see all private allotments, for Ellen it is very important to maintain the community plots. Excess produce from the communal plots is donated regularly to the local food bank, to people in need, and to the elderly in the community.

A variety of cultivation techniques are practiced in the garden, including biodynamic gardening, double digging, "no-dig" gardens, mulching, etc. The garden is 100% organic. There were aphids initially, but after diversifying over about seven years, the garden is much more in balance, with the pest problem controlled. The garden actually won an award in the community for the most agro-biodiversity. Traditional agro-ecosystems had high levels of agro-biodiversity, contributing to the "conservation of agricultural heritage systems" (Altieri and Koohafkan 2013: 56). In addition, seed saving contributes significantly to the conservation of biodiversity in-vivo, showcasing "conservation as a way of life" (Nazarea 2005: x)

The plots include lots of peppers, potatoes, brassicas, kales, turnips, silverbeet, kumara, turnips, beans, corn, pumpkins, rhubarb, asparagus, and taro. Heritage seeds are sought, if possible. There are also fruit trees, native trees, and berries. The soil is fed through composting, liquid manure, seaweed, and mulching. Irrigation is the most important thing to consider, and luckily a water system is connected to town water. There is a strong focus on education. A diverse range of workshops on a variety of topics are held at the gardens, including what, when, and how to grow. Community and school groups are also welcome on tours of the gardens.

Ellen has a strong interest in *rongoa* (Māori traditional medicine), which she used with her children and now her grandchildren. "It's very easy to come by, plant medicine," says Ellen. "A lot of the plants we see as weeds, we have been eating as medicine for years." She wants to learn more about *rongoa*, but there are not many people left to learn from. This underscores the importance of "cultural memory as a means to conserve biodiversity" (Nazarea 2005: x). A *rongoa* trail is planned along the periphery of the garden.

Ellen, at 71 years old, is of the age group that participated in the traditional ways. As a child, she and *whānau* (family) were brought up on a farm and lived off the land. According to Ellen, "there were acres and acres of food for *whānau* – now, the current generation has lost their knowledge." The idea with gardens is to keep that memory alive. For Ellen it is "important to get the younger generations involved." She has a vision and always looks forward 20 years. Ellen is very concerned about the high cost of food, with organic food unaffordable at the local health food store. Consideration of future generations is a strong Māori principle related to sustainable environmental management (Durie 1998).

Conclusion

The case studies above explore what food sovereignty means in a variety of contexts. A participant at the Nyéléni food sovereignty forum in Mali in 2007 stated:

> while it is important to define food sovereignty in a way that is understandable to the public, the most powerful way of communicating the message of food sovereignty is by doing – for instance, by engaging citizens directly in transformation of the food system.
>
> (Quoted in Schiavoni 2009: 685)

Our research aims to bring attention to Indigenous women who are doing the work that matters most: taking back control of their food systems. These examples illustrate how people and Māori women in particular are connecting with their environment, history, and culture by producing healthy *kai*, a healthy environment, and healthy communities.

As is the case around the world, the Indigenous Peoples of *Aotearoa* New Zealand, the Māori, are losing their traditional ways. The Māori, as *tangata whenua* (people of the land), have an obligation to protect the natural environment or *taonga* (treasure) for future generations (Durie 1998). Indigenous knowledge systems are often devalued in the face of modernity and science. However, the preservation and promotion of Indigenous knowledge and values with respect to traditional food systems and *rongoa* (traditional medicine) is crucial, not only for the empowerment of local and Indigenous communities, but as an important element in achieving sustainable development for all.

Through community gardens and small farms, people are reconnecting with their food and the environment, and truly democratizing the food system. Communities "are developing adaptive strategies that intersect with food sovereignty visioning, whether they call it food sovereignty or not" (McMichael 2014: 952). Ultimately, food sovereignty speaks to a food system that is "community-driven" and "transforms knowledge and important ways of knowing" (Wittman 2011: 98).

According to Bové and Dufour:

> the strength of food sovereignty is precisely that it differs from place to place. . . . The world is a complex place, and it would be a mistake to look for a single answer to complex and different phenomena. . . . We have to provide answers at different levels – not just the international level, but local and national levels too.
>
> (2001: 168)

As demonstrated by these examples, food sovereignty is seen in a variety of forms, from Indigenous communities taking back their power, to permaculture farms epitomizing sustainable living, to community gardens that are truly community driven. Seed saving, food cultivation, community outreach, sustainability education, cultural diversity, concern for the environment and future generations, and community empowerment are what food sovereignty means in action.

Note

1 Māori did not believe that land could be owned.

References

Agence France-Presse. (2015) "India Bans 'Hazardous' Maggi Noodles," *The New Zealand Herald*, 6 June, viewed on 13 August 2015, http://www.New Zealandherald.co.NewZealand/lifestyle/news/article.cfm?c_id=6&objectid=11459325.

Altieri, M. and Koohafkan, P. (2013) "Strengthening Resilience of Farming Systems: A Prerequisite for Sustainable Agricultural Production," in Global Research Partnership for a Food Secure Future (ed.), *United Nations Trade and Environment Review: Wake Up Before It's Too Late*, Geneva: United Nations Publication, pp. 56–60.

Altieri, M. A. and Toledo, V. M. (2011) "The Agroecological Revolution in Latin America: Rescuing Nature, Ensuring Food Sovereignty and Empowering Peasants," *Journal of Peasant Studies* 38(3): 587–612.

Barański, M., Srednicka-Tober, D., Volakakis, N., Seal, C., Sanderson, R., Stewart, G. B., and Leifert, C. (2014) "Higher Antioxidant and Lower Cadmium Concentrations and Lower Incidence of Pesticide Residues in Organically Grown Crops: A Systematic Literature Review and Meta-analyses," *British Journal of Nutrition* 112(05): 794–811.

Bawaka Country (including Suchet-Pearson, S., Wright, S., Lloyd, K., and Burarrwanga, L.). (2013) "Caring as Country: Towards an Ontology of Co-becoming in Natural Resource Management," *Asia Pacific Viewpoint* 54(2): 185–197.

Beatty, T. (2010) "Do the Poor Pay More for Food? Evidence from the United Kingdom," *American Journal of Agricultural Economics* 92: 608–621.

Bittermann, V. (2007) *Civic Agriculture: An Analysis of Citizen and Community Engagement in Vermont's Food System*, unpublished Masters thesis, Boston: Tufts University.

Borras Jr., S.M. and Franco, J.C. (2012) *A 'Land Sovereignty' Alternative? Towards a Peoples' Counter-Enclosure*, Amsterdam: Transnational Institute.

Boucher, D. M. (1999) *The Paradox of Plenty: Hunger in a Bountiful World*, Oakland, CA: Food First Books.

Bové, J. and Dufour, F. (2001) *The World is Not For Sale*, London: Verso.

Bowman, S. A. and Vinyard, B. T. (2004) "Fast Food Consumption of US Adults: Impact on Energy and Nutrient Intakes and Overweight Status," *Journal of the American College of Nutrition* 23(2): 163–168.

Broda, C., Leibtag, E., and Weinstein, D. (2009) "The Role of Prices in Measuring the Poor's Living Standards," *Journal of Economic Perspectives* 23(2): 77–97.

Burch, D. and Lawrence, G. (eds.) (2007) *Supermarkets and Agri-food Supply Chains: Transformations in the Production and Consumption of Food*, Northampton: Edward Elgar.

Cadieux, K. V. and Slocum, R. (2015) "What does it Mean to Do Food Justice," *Journal of Political Ecology* 22: 1–26.

Carter, K. N., Lanumata, T., Kruse, K., and Gorton, D. (2010) "What are the Determinants of Food Insecurity in New Zealand and does this Differ for Males and Females?" *Australian and New Zealand Journal of Public Health* 34(6): 602–608.

Claeys, P. (2013) "From Food Sovereignty to Peasants' Rights: An Overview of Via Campesina's Struggle for New Human Rights," *La Vía Campesina's Open Book: Celebrating 20 Years of Struggle and Hope*, http://viacampesina.org/downloads/pdf/openbooks/EN-02.pdf.

Damman, S., Eide, W. B., and Kuhnlein, H. V. (2008) "Indigenous Peoples' Nutrition Transition in a Right to Food Perspective," *Food Policy* 33(2): 135–155.

Drewnowski, N. and Darmon, N. (2005) "The Economics of Obesity: Dietary Energy Density and Energy Cost," *The American Journal of Clinical Nutrition* 82: 265S–273S.

Durie, M. (1998) *Te Mana, Te Kāwanatanga: The Politics of Self Determination*, Auckland: Oxford University Press.

Earle, M. D. (2011) *Cultivating Health: Community Gardening as a Public Health Intervention*, Thesis, Master of Public Health, University of Otago, http://hdl.handle.net/10523/2078.

Feenstra, G. (2002) "Creating Space for Sustainable Food Systems: Lessons from the Field," *Agriculture and Human Values* 19(2): 99–106.

Galluzzi, G., Eyzaguirre, P., and Negri, V. (2010) "Home Gardens: Neglected Hotspots of Agro-biodiversity and Cultural Diversity," *Biodiversity and Conservation* 19(13): 3635–3654.

Gordon-Larsen, P., Guilkey, D. K., and Popkin, B. M. (2011) "An Economic Analysis of Community-level Fast Food Prices and Individual-level Fast Food Intake: A Longitudinal Study," *Health & Place* 17(6): 1235–1241.

Gottlieb, R. and Joshi, A. (2010) *Food Justice*, Cambridge: MIT Press.

Grigg, M. C. and Macrae, B. (2000) *Tikanga Oranga Hauora, Monitoring and Evaluation*, Te Puni Kōkiri (Ministry of Māori Development).

Holmgren, D. (2002) *Principles & Pathways Beyond Sustainability*, Hampshire, UK: Permanent Publications.

Holt-Giménez, E. (2014) "We Already Grow Enough Food for 10 Billion People – and Still Can't End Hunger," *Huffington Post*, 30 March, viewed on 10 August 2015, http://www.huffingtonpost.com/eric-holt-gimenez/world-hunger_b_1463429.html.

Holt-Giménez, E. and Patel, R. (eds.) (2012) *Food Rebellions: Crisis and the Hunger for Justice*, Oakland, CA: Food First Books.

Holt-Giménez, E. and Shattuck, A. (2011) "Food Crises, Food Regimes and Food Movements: Rumblings of Reform or Tides of Transformation?," *The Journal of Peasant Studies* 38(1): 109–144.

International Association for the Study of Obesity. (2011) *Global Prevalence of Adult Obesity*, viewed on 10 August 2015, http://www.worldobesity.org/site_media/uploads/Global_Prevalence_of_Adult_Obesity_January_2011.pdf.

La Vía Campesina. (1996) *Food Sovereignty: A Future without Hunger*, Rome, 11–17 November, viewed on 4 August 2015, http://www.voiceoftheturtle.org/library/1996%20Declaration%20of%20Food%20Sovereignty.pdf.

——. (2009) *La Vía Campesina Policy Documents*, viewed on 4 July 2015, http://viacampesina.org/downloads/pdf/policydocuments/POLICYDOCUMENTS-EN-FINAL.pdf.

Larder, N., Lyons, K., and Woolcock, G. (2014) "Enacting Food Sovereignty: Values and Meanings in the Act of Domestic Food Production in Urban Australia," *Local Environment* 19(1): 56–76.

Martínez-Torres, M. E., and Rosset, P. (2010) "La Vía Campesina: The Birth and Evolution of a Transnational Peasant Movement," *Journal of Peasant Studies* 37: 149–176.

McMichael, P. (2009) "Global Citizenship and Multiple Sovereignties: Reconstituting Modernity," in Y. Atasoy (ed.), *Hegemonic Transitions, the State and Crisis in Neoliberal Capitalism*, Oxon: Routledge, pp. 25–42.

——. (2014) "Historicizing Food Sovereignty," *Journal of Peasant Studies* 41(6): 933–957.

Milman, O. (2015) "Rate of Environmental Degradation Puts Life on Earth at Risk, Say Scientists," *The Guardian*, 15 January, viewed on 24 July 2015, http://www.theguardian.com/environment/2015/jan/15/rate-of-environmental-degradation-puts-life-on-earth-at-risk-say-scientists.

Moreton-Robinson, A.M. and Walter, M. (2009) "Indigenous Methodologies in Social Research," in M. Walter (ed.), *Social Research Methods*, Australia: Oxford University Press, pp. 1–18.

Nazarea, V. D. (2005) *Heirloom Seeds and Their Keepers: Marginality and Memory in the Conservation of Biological Diversity*, Tucson: University of Arizona Press.

Nazarea, V. D. (2006) "Local Knowledge and Memory in Biodiversity Conservation," *Annual Review of Anthropology* 35: 317–335.

Negri, V. (2005) "Agro-biodiversity Conservation in Europe: Ethical Issues," *Journal of Agricultural and Environmental Ethics* 18(1): 3–25.

New Zealand Ministry of Health. (2006) "Tatau Kahukura: Māori Health Chart Book," *Public Health Intelligence of Monitoring Report No. 5*, Wellington: Ministry of Health.

——. (2008) *A Portrait of Health: Key Results of the 2006/2007 New Zealand Health Survey*, Wellington: Ministry of Health.

Ono, T., Guthold, R., and Strong, K. (2010) "Estimated Obesity Prevalence, Females, Aged 15+, 2010 and Estimated Obesity Prevalence, Males, Aged 15+," *WHO Global Comparable Estimates*, viewed on 13 May 2016, https://apps.who.int/infobase/.

Parillo, M. and Riccardi, G. (2004) "Diet Composition and the Risk of Type-2 Diabetes: Epidemiological and Clinical Evidence," *British Journal of Nutrition* 92(01): 7–19.

Parnell, W. (2005) *Food Security in New Zealand*, unpublished PhD thesis, University of Otago: Dunedin.

Parnell, W. R., Reid, J., Wilson, N. C., McKenzie, J., and Russell, D. G. (2001) "Food Security: Is New Zealand a Land of Plenty?" *The New Zealand Medical Journal* 114(1128): 141–145.

Parnell, W. R., Scragg, R. K. R., Wilson, N. C., Schaaf, D., and Fitzgerald, E. D. H. (2003) *NEW ZEALAND Food: NEW ZEALAND Children: Key Results of the 2002 National Children's Nutrition Survey*, Wellington: Ministry of Health.

Patel, R. (2009) "What does Food Sovereignty Look Like?," *Journal of Peasant Studies* 36(3): 663–706.

Phillips, L. (2006) "Food and Globalization," *Annual Review of Anthropology* 35(1): 37–57.

Pimbert, M. (2008) *The Role of Local Organizations in Sustaining Local Food Systems, Livelihoods and the Environment*, London: Institute for Environment and Development.

Rodale Institute. (2011) *The Farming Systems Trial: Celebrating 30 Years*, Kutztown: Rodale Institute.

Rush, E. and Rusk, I. (2009) *Food Security for Pacific Peoples in New Zealand: A Report for the Obesity Action Coalition*, Wellington: Obesity Action Coalition.

Schiavoni, C. (2009) "The Global Struggle for Food Sovereignty: From Nyéléni to New York in Food Sovereignty," *The Journal of Peasant Studies* 36(3): 663–706.

Sinclair, K. (1991) *Kinds of Peace: Maori People after the Wars, 1870–85*, Auckland: Auckland University Press.

Slocum, R. and Saldanha, A. (2013) *Geographies of Race and Food*, Farnham: Ashgate.

Statistics New Zealand. (2014) New Zealand Social Indicators – He kete tatauranga – Labour Market, Wellington: Statistics New Zealand, viewed on November 11, 2015, http://www.stats.govt.nz/browse_for_stats/snapshots-of-nz/nz-social-indicators/Home/Labour%20market/employment.aspx.

Stevenson, S. (2011) *Edible Impact: Food Security Policy Literature Review*, Whakatane: Toi Te Ora – Public Health Service, BOPDHB.

Te Hotu Manawa Māori. (2007) *Food Security Among Māori in Aotearoa*, Auckland: Te Hotu Manawa Māori.

Timmer, P. C. (2012) "One Billion Hungry: Can We Feed the World?," *The Wilson Quarterly* 36(4): 131–134.

University of Otago and Ministry of Health. (2011) *A Focus on Nutrition: Key Findings of the 2008/09 New Zealand Adult Nutrition Survey*, Wellington: University of Otago.

Wilkie, K. (2014) "Families Feel Bite of Food Cost," *Stuff.co.nz*, 7 December, http://www.stuff.co.New Zealand/national/10260101/Families-feel-bite-of-food-cost.

Wittman, H. (2011) "Food Sovereignty: A New Rights Framework for Food and Nature?," *Environment and Society: Advances in Research* 2: 87–105.

Wittman, H., Desmarais, A, and Wiebe, N. (2010) *Food Sovereignty: Reconnecting Food, Nature and Community*, Halifax: Fernwood.

Wynd, D. (2005) *Hard to Swallow: Foodbank use in New Zealand*, Auckland: Child Poverty Action Group.

35

INDIVIDUAL AND COMMUNITY IDENTITY IN FOOD SOVEREIGNTY

The possibilities and pitfalls of translating a rural social movement

Ian Werkheiser

Food sovereignty is a growing, vibrant discourse in food justice. International organizations such as La Vía Campesina connect hundreds of local food sovereignty groups all over the world; food sovereignty as a concept has been included in the Ecuadorian and Venezuelan constitutions; and it has gained increasing currency among academics. However, food sovereignty has its critics. Some argue that the movement, which addresses a wide variety of environmental and social ills, is too diverse to be sensibly described as being about food. Activists respond in part that due to certain characteristics of food, truly reforming the food system without addressing these wider issues is impossible. Further, certain characteristics of food allow it to act as a central boundary object, making it an ideal candidate to provide a frame with which to address a wide range of injustices. Food sovereignty, they argue, must push toward a radical re-imagining of society. Another objection arises in response to this view. Some worry that these connections between food and wider issues might only be natural ones to make for the rural subsistence food producers who started the food sovereignty movement; food sovereignty as it is pursued by activists may be less salient for other peoples in other places. If this is right, then food sovereignty may be an effective social movement in some contexts, but it would not be as promising a candidate for a global movement as it is purported to be.

This chapter addresses these concerns by exploring what food sovereignty is, and how it uses an imaginary of food to ground and motivate the movement. It then looks at how and how well food sovereignty translates into contexts other than those in which the discourse first emerged. Ultimately, this chapter argues that food sovereignty can be a global social movement, but the successful translation of food sovereignty into the contexts of communities in wealthy countries will look far different from what is usually supposed by both advocates and critics of the movement.

Food sovereignty

The term "food sovereignty" was introduced to the world stage in 1996 by La Vía Campesina (henceforth, Vía) at the World Food Summit for the Food and Agriculture Organization of the

United Nations (FAO) (Patel 2009).[1] Vía is an organization of self-described "peasants" who see their food practices as essential to their communities' identities and survival and further see threats to their food practices as arising in large part from the exploitative institutions of global capitalism (Nyéléni Declaration 2007; Our World is Not For Sale 2001; Tlaxcala Declaration 1996).

There are multiple senses of the term "food sovereignty," and these senses reflect differing goals and commitments within the movement. This chapter will focus on the way in which the term is employed in transnational and local social-justice activism. For activists, the term denotes how people and communities should have sovereignty over their food systems.[2] This amounts to the following definition of food sovereignty:

> The right of peoples to define their own food and agriculture; to protect and regulate domestic agricultural production and trade in order to achieve sustainable development objectives; to determine the extent to which they want to be self reliant; to restrict the dumping of products in their markets; and to provide local fisheries-based communities the priority in managing the use of and the rights to aquatic resources. Food sovereignty does not negate trade, but rather, it promotes the formulation of trade policies and practices that serve the rights of peoples to safe, healthy and ecologically sustainable production.
>
> (Our World is Not for Sale 2001)

This transnational justice sense of food sovereignty captures a broad range of concerns. One set of criticisms sees this diversity of concerns and aims within the movement as problematic. Food sovereignty is a diverse discourse, bringing together concerns about the rights of indigenous people, women, and the environment. Food sovereignty focuses on reforms to the economy, land use, international trade, and a host of other issues. For some critics, incorporating "all manner of movements for liberation from oppression, from the Zapatistas to the women's movement" (Flora 2011: 545) under the banner of food sovereignty is too great a burden for one idea, especially one merely about food.

For advocates within the food sovereignty discourse, these seemingly disparate issues are inherently interconnected and inseparable. This is because, on the one hand, the food system is deeply interwoven into the fabric of modern global capitalism. Thus, advocates of food sovereignty contend that to try to deal in isolation with the challenges surrounding food will likely be doomed to failure, as the system in which food is embedded will remain unchanged. On the other hand, the various ways that we intend food, both when it is present in front of us and in our imaginations, are a central part of people's concepts of themselves and of their communities. For these advocates, it will inevitably support currently existing (and unjust) power structures that harm individual and community flourishing if we ignore the ways in which food is co-constituted with individual and community identity and instead think of the problem merely in terms of access to food (Nyéléni Declaration 2007; Our World is Not For Sale 2001; Tlaxcala 1996). For food sovereignty activists, the recognition of the interconnectedness of food with economic, political, and cultural systems, and the concomitant need to address them as a whole, is a virtue, not a vice, of food sovereignty. In addition to its promise for finally making headway against the perennial problems of food insecurity, this framing enables food to be a single boundary object (Star and Greisemer 1989) that grounds and motivates a host of other concerns. In other words, our desire to ensure food security for all can force us to deal with other injustices.

This concept of the centrality of food to our community and individual identities underlies both the practices and commitments of food sovereignty activists. In terms of practice, food sovereignty activists are not interested only in petitioning the state and powerful social institutions for redress, but rather to engage in the prefigurative politics of "propaganda of the deed" (Breines

1989; Graeber 2004), by showing that food practices and more just social relations can co-exist by beginning to create them. As Menser (2008) points out, food sovereignty in this sense "aims to cultivate and proliferate an alternative model of agricultural *production* and a corresponding political program," one that "draws upon local and traditional knowledge in combination with laboratory studies to farm in such a way as to meet local cultural needs, provide for human health, and conserve biodiversity" (31).

In terms of commitments, this means that for food sovereignty activists, fixing injustices in the food system requires more just social relationships generally, and vice versa. A good example of this is the importance of justice for women for many food sovereignty activists. Vía, for example, has Assemblies of Women that meet regularly to discuss women's issues, and these assemblies release important declarations and policy statements. This is not just a separate good that is also of interest to members of La Vía Campesina; rather, it is seen as playing a central role for communities to achieve food justice and for Vía to be an effective organization. As Wiebe says in her 2013 article, "Side by side and in solidarity with the men of La Vía Campesina, we bring political analysis, experience, and energy to the shared goal of creating a future that is more just, egalitarian, peaceful, ecologically healthy, and life-giving" (5). Justice for women within Vía strengthens the community and makes it more effective at pursuing its goals, both by making consensus decisions better informed, and by making such decisions actually consensual, and thus more likely to be adopted by community members, including women. Vía is engaged in a number of programs to aid the lives of women, and it pays particular attention to their participation in the food sovereignty movement. Indeed, members of Vía often say that it was the incorporation of women's voices into Vía – which happened only after the organization had been an active peasant-rights group for some time – that allowed it to realize the importance of sovereignty and of food as uniting themes for the many issues facing small-scale farmers in the global South. These members say that the decisive Nyéléni Declaration came about only because of participation by women, who had taken important leadership roles prior to that meeting (Wittman et al. 2010).[3]

It makes sense that the usefulness of food as a central boundary object could be intuitive for the subsistence farmers and for other (self-described) peasants who made up the bulk of the founders of the movement. For people intimately familiar with food in all stages, from production to distribution to preparation to consumption to disposal, it may well be possible to sit at a meal and have that experience evoke a web of interrelations, which can be evaluated in terms of their justness. It may further be possible to think about justice issues and have food present itself as an obvious example, a thread running through those various issues, and ultimately as a frame for understanding complex problems. Taking food to be centrally constitutive to identity and to justice might then, as advocates suggest, be an effective means of motivating a transnational, radical, social-justice movement addressing systemic problems in the food system as well as community and individual flourishing more generally.

However, it is possible that this social imaginary surrounding food might be a product only of the communities and people initially engaged in food sovereignty – rural subsistence farmers – and therefore not translatable to a global movement. As Thompson (2015) says, "[food sovereignty] points to the way entire rural communities, local cultures, and longstanding social relations are brought together through the production, preparation, and consumption of food" (75). However, as he goes on to argue, "unfortunately, as compelling as this argument is for the small farmers that Vía Campesina represents, it is not an idea that necessarily travels well" (Thompson 2015: 75). The widely used Nyéléni Declaration, for example, lays out principles of food sovereignty that call for a focus on food producers, and the Declaration goes into significant detail about particular means of production such as farming and fishing (see Declaration's appendix). These details point to the lived experiences of the authors, but they may not resonate as central issues to people from other contexts.

Food sovereignty has been taken up by activists in contexts quite different from its origin, including among people fighting for better wages for service workers in the food system in the US, people fighting for more control over their food systems in relatively affluent Vermont, and people fighting to protect heritage food traditions in Italy (sometimes against international fast-food chain stores, sometimes against immigrants to the country selling local food from their home cultures) (Alkon and Mares 2012; Ayres and Bosia 2011; Fairbairn 2012). Of course, many details and applications of food sovereignty need to change in these different contexts. Perhaps the translation is no more difficult than translating food sovereignty into the contexts of disparate peasant communities around the world, with their different food production methods and the cultures around them. On the other hand, if there is some unique problem of translation for food sovereignty from rural subsistence communities in poor countries to communities of food consumers – by and large – in relatively affluent countries, it is worth exploring what that problem may be.

For some critics, this concern about the movement not "traveling well" might be predicated on a misunderstanding of the concept of food sovereignty that is used by many activists. Namely, there is a tendency among some critics to think that food sovereignty is necessarily committed to a kind of food self-sufficiency, or food independence. Perhaps this derives from the meaning of "food sovereignty" as sometimes used by states in contexts often focused on food independence and national security (Koont 2011; La Vía Campesina 1996). If food sovereignty necessarily entailed this ideal of independence, it would not be a useful or even possible goal for many groups, such as urban dwellers. However, though food sovereignty activists have stressed the importance of the integrity of producers and food production processes, they do not argue for isolated communities to be able to produce all their own food. Rather, the ideal of food sovereignty entails maximally local control over communities' food systems (Menser 2008). Those systems will often – perhaps always – include connections with other communities to share food, tools, skills, and so on. Urban communities fighting for food sovereignty may well envision a system that includes affordable grocery stores along with urban gardens and other elements in a complex food system; for food sovereignty the important characteristic of that overall system is that it is determined by the affected communities through processes that are as democratic as possible. Thus understood, many of the actual overarching principles of food sovereignty – e.g., community and individual flourishing, maximally local and democratic decision-making, broad transnational networks of solidarity and mutual aid – seem like plausible candidates for a large, transnational social movement.

There is another, deeper version of the concern about translation and portability of food sovereignty to other contexts. It is an open question whether food plays or can play the same role in communities that do not produce much food, as compared to the central role it has among self-described peasants. In particular, for non-rural communities food is less obviously connected to other justice issues, such as gender justice, land reform, economic justice, and so on. Even if it is the case in non-rural communities that fixing food injustices requires addressing other issues in society and culture, food might not serve as the best rallying cry for making those changes. To address this concern, it is worth exploring the phenomenal nature of food for people not as immediately, materially connected to its production.

Food

It is not a new idea to argue that food carries enough meaning for its producers that it can motivate movements for justice. Indeed, the idea occurs at many points throughout history. From the Tiller movement in ancient China, 700 BCE, to the Diggers in 17th Century, to the Farmers Movement in the US in the 19th Century, many social movements have taken the practices around food as a model for social reform. The experiences of producing food – working with the land, cooperating with one another by necessity, watching something grow and caring for it without being able to control the process directly – encourage particular types of values and cultural practices for many who work as producers.

Such examples highlight the roles of producers and show how models for justice emerge based on valuing food production. For consumers, particularly in the modern age, the commodification and fetishization of food may render the production process and its values opaque; this is why many have advocated for an engagement with food production to some extent in all sectors of society (e.g., Berry 1977; Thompson 1994; 2010). However, there is a possibility that engagement with the phenomenon of food as experienced by modern consumers will not only fail to connect them with these justice-related values of production, but connect them instead with the efficiency- and consumption-based values of the current global industrial food system – the opposite of the reaction food sovereignty activists are hoping for. As the activist and writer Derrick Jensen worries:

> If your experience – far deeper than belief or perception – is that your food comes from the grocery store (and your water from the tap), from the economic system, from the social system we call civilization, it is to this you will pledge back your life. . . . You will defend this social system to your very death.
>
> (2006: 696)

The question, then, is whether food can serve as a boundary object for those not engaged in "the peasants' way" (as "La Vía Campesina" translates in English) to motivate a transnational, radical, social-justice movement. A sign that it may is that, as put by Dena Hoff, the North American coordinator of La Vía Campesina, "Everybody eats" (Ridberg 2013). By this she means that food is something everyone engages with every day, at least in consumption, and often in preparation and distribution, even if they do not engage with it as a producer. There are two elements of our experience of food as eaters that hold some support for Hoff's vision – food's material connection to justice and ethics, and food's phenomenological connection to justice and ethics.

First, eating food can be experientially as well as materially tied to ethics and justice. It is widely agreed that eating has a material connection to ethical and justice-based issues, even for those who disagree on which food system would be more ethical, or on the relative importance of eating compared to other activities. This material, ethical connection is what undergirds the Fair Trade movement (e.g., Goodman 2004), ethical vegetarianism/veganism (e.g., Plumwood 2000; Singer 1975), appeals for sustainable fish consumption (e.g., Jacquet and Pauly 2006), food-miles labeling (e.g., Singer and Mason 2006), many boycotts of particular food products or producers (e.g., Singer and Mason 2006), and a host of other social movements around the consumption of food. In all such cases, the act of consuming particular foods is seen as lending material support and reinforcement to ethically charged practices by producers. Thus, for many people and communities not focused on food production, food nevertheless serves as a tangible, salient reminder of ethical and justice issues. For urban communities, a lack of access to fresh, healthy, affordable food can be a constant reminder of social inequity and its material consequences.

Phenomenally, it seems to be the case that, even for consumers, food can be bound up with awareness of where it came from, how it was produced, and other salient interconnections. When we eat (as marketers and menu-writers well know), knowing something about how it was prepared, where the recipe or ingredients come from, and other narrative details about the food can be as much a part of the enjoyment of the meal as the feeling in the mouth, the information registered by the tongue, the smell, the appearance, the location of the experience, the company, the sounds during the event, and other elements that help build up into the overall taste. This narrative aspect of the experience of eating has a distinctly normative flavor – some narratives are good and taste good, while others are bad and taste bad. For example, for many people in our culture, authenticity and naturalness (whatever those might mean) have strongly positive connotations and enhance the taste of the food with which they associated, while artificiality has more negative connotations and can have a deleterious effect on the taste of our food. This is well known by marketers who often try to create a sense of authenticity and naturalness for their products (see, e.g., Cloud 2008; Molleda and Roberts 2008).

While this account runs the risk of making narratives into aesthetic experiences consumed by the eater, a narrative understanding of our relationship with food also creates the possibility for something more. This normative component can sometimes be bound up to ethics and justice. The rise of fair-trade, organic, shade-grown, vegetarian, and other such monikers (however ineffective these particular labels might be at correctly indicating the qualities they promise) shows that for many, there is a profound preference for food that is part of ethical and just processes. Further, people do not enjoy being told about unethical aspects of foods they enjoy – such as the harvesting process for much of the chocolate we consume (see Mustapha 2010) – particularly while they are eating. (Perhaps this is because they are thus prevented from conveniently forgetting these facts.) It seems to be the case that such information is more distasteful to people than discussion of other injustices, which do not directly pertain to the food they are eating; thus such hesitance is not merely a desire to focus on the pleasurable experiences of eating without being reminded of injustice generally. Rather, in a sense, it seems that ethical food tastes better and unethical food tastes worse (Kaplan 2015). We can see this with stark clarity in the case of people for whom ethical considerations render many foods entirely inedible, such as moral vegetarians or vegans. Speaking from personal experience, it was not long after becoming a vegetarian for moral reasons that meat became not only something I chose not to eat, but indeed something I found deeply unappetizing. The unethical nature (as I perceived it) of meat made it taste and smell bad.

There are times when an eater knows of ethical and justice concerns, but those concerns appear not to affect the eater's enjoyment of a food. In such cases I would argue that the ethical narrative content of the food is still one aspect of the experience, but that aspect does not become salient due to being overwhelmed by other aspects. For example, sometimes food is rejected on ethical grounds due to the material effects of consuming the food, without much thought given to what the experience of eating the food would be like, as was likely the case for many who engaged in the boycotts of particular grape farms as part of the United Farm Workers' campaigns in California in the late 1950s and early 1960s (see Ganz 2009). Other times, eaters enjoy a food despite knowing the ways in which it is unethical, such as for those who understand and decry the treatment of workers in banana plantations, yet enjoy bananas, or those who are disturbed by the production methods of foie gras and yet enjoy it. However, in these cases, it seems probable that most people who actually hold those values would enjoy an ethical and just version of those foods more, much as bland food can be enjoyable despite the fact that properly seasoned food might be enjoyed even more. If not, we would have normative grounds to criticize their enjoyment of the food as revealing either an insensitivity toward or endorsement of the unethical aspects of the food (as happens in some discussions between vegetarians and meat eaters). This phenomenon of the ethical or justice-based aspects of eating has potential as a source of normativity to be harnessed in support of the food-sovereignty movement. If eating highlights ethical and justice concerns, then food could be an excellent candidate for a framework to understand and address the concerns of food sovereignty activists, as the act of eating connects a host of justice and ethics issues that are not otherwise easily put into a single framework.

A food-sovereignty movement may also be supported by another salient element of our experience of food as eaters: the ways in which food is bound up with our identities, values, and practices, both as individuals and as communities. The experience of eating is an experience of one's culture and of bonding with one's community, particularly when we sit down to eat with others. In a sense we are eating culture when we sit down to the table. This is both an experience of identity and a performance of identity for anyone eating at the same table.

This is most obvious in people whose eating practices differ significantly from mainstream cultural norms. The ways in which food is co-constituted with community identity is relatively clear when communities must work to actively preserve their food practices, such as in the case of kosher practices for observant Jews. It is not necessary to be a kosher slaughterer to recognize that your kosher food values and practices as a consumer are inseparable parts of your community's culture and identity in a shared social imaginary. This phenomenon is less apparent for members of cultures in which food plays a less explicit role, and particularly for members of dominant cultures for which cultural practices and values are made invisible rather than brought into relief by the most prominent food distribution and production systems. However, despite this invisibility, this cultural component of food is also salient for those dominant cultures with less explicit dietary values. For example, the social imaginary around meat in Western culture is bound up with what we imagine as a culture of masculinity, patriotism, and so forth (Adams 1990). This cultural orientation would make it difficult for many North Americans to change their eating habits overnight to abandon meat in favor of a plant-based diet; combined with other dominant ideologies, this cultural identity ensures a high level of resistance to institutional changes that put ranchers out of business or otherwise make eating meat difficult.

At the level of individual identity, too, the co-constitution of food and identity becomes more visible in cases where an eater's food practices significantly differ from the norms of her larger society, such as for someone on a severely restricted diet, someone who refuses to eat a food on moral or religious grounds, or someone who considers herself a wine connoisseur. In such cases, the eater's identity and its interconnections with food become salient at every meal, and this identity is performed to others, whose responses may differ in the degree to which they ignore, comment upon, or police the behavior against deviation from the societal norm.

This co-constitution of identity and food is a double-edged sword. On the one hand, it means that structural change to the dominant food system is difficult, as that system reinforces and is reinforced by culture and by food practices. (For this point, it is instructive to return to the idea of cultural allegiances expressed by Jensen [2006] quoted above.) On the other hand, it means that food is a daily act of engaging with one's culture and community, and thus a vivid place to begin or to reinforce a conversation about justice and community flourishing. If that conversation can begin to change food habits, those changes can have quite profound ripple effects on people's attitudes toward other institutions. Sometimes this "conversation" is not a verbal one, but instead a silent change in the discourse. Food choices by one party can often ethically charge a situation that previously was seen as unproblematic – what Adams (1990) calls standing in for the absent referent of the victims of particular food choices. While Adams refers to the non-human animals being eaten after being symbolically and materially reduced to meat, it is also the case that the producers of the food are also often an absent referent.

We can see the power of food as a resonant aspect of larger social change, even for mere consumers, in the historical example of sugar and the slave trade in England. The push for a boycott of sugar – produced on slave plantations through particularly brutal practices – accomplished several important goals. Materially, it affected slaveholders by hurting their economic interests. In accomplishing this goal it also made every teatime and meal an opportunity to show solidarity with victims of the slave trade, beginning or reinforcing conversations about the abhorrent nature of slavery among those sitting at the same table. This helped reinforce the identity of being an Abolitionist for those who participated in the boycott. It was thus an act of pressure against the slave trade, a recruitment and retention mechanism for Abolitionists, and a lever to change the culture.[4]

Translating food sovereignty

It seems at least possible that food sovereignty as a movement could resonate in contexts far removed from those in which it first emerged, even for those people whose primary interactions with food are as consumers and perhaps preparers. This is true both for food sovereignty's argument that addressing food insecurity requires fixing deeper problems in society, and also for the argument that food is a good frame within which to work toward radical change. However, this does not mean that casual adoption of the framework of food sovereignty will be successful for groups interested in food and justice in the US and other wealthy economies. Such adoptions have been attempted, but they sometimes diffuse the radical political potential of food sovereignty, properly understood, by reducing it to a simplistic – and sometimes even jingoistic – argument for local food (Fairbairn 2012) to the exclusion of other concerns such as immigrant communities (Alkon and Mares 2012) or solidarity and support for distant communities (Navin 2014). These attempts to use the rhetoric of food sovereignty without sufficient self-reflection in a US context also run the risk of reinforcing neoliberal discourse, such as by focusing on market-based approaches, even if it means pricing food-insecure individuals and communities out of the healthy food market (Alkon and Mares 2012).

In these cases, problems arise when food sovereignty is reduced to a call to be closer to the production of food, on the one hand – either by growing some food oneself or by minimizing food miles for purchased food – and, on the other hand, a vague sympathy toward producers in poorer countries. This flattening of food sovereignty allows it to stand alongside so-called "happy meat," "paleo" diets, and other such food choices, to be added to the list of options available to privileged people living as consumers in a neoliberal system of industrial capitalism. This translation loses the resistance to neoliberal globalization that is fundamental to food sovereignty. Instead, it is precisely that element of resistance that the work of translation ought to preserve. Thus, the expansion of food sovereignty as a framework for justice should move from the model provided by subsistence food producers resisting neoliberal globalization in poor countries to the model of communities in rich countries, producing some food but to a much lesser extent, figuring out how they can best resist neoliberal globalization from their position of relative privilege – especially by identifying and creating opportunities for radical solidarity and mutual aid with other, less privileged communities.

It is not possible for this chapter to define exactly what that translation should look like. Rather, such a translation must occur in democratic dialogue within and between communities. To do otherwise would undercut the commitment to maximally local, democratic decision-making, which is the hallmark of food sovereignty (Menser 2008). Such a democratic, justly conducted conversation utilizes the "propaganda of the deed" (Breines 1989; Graeber 2004) to prefigure the kind of food sovereignty movement that is its goal, and indeed to prefigure the society that food sovereignty activists ultimately aim to achieve.

Conclusion

It is perhaps ironic that the worries about translating food sovereignty into other contexts are usually expressed about moving from a context of production to one of consumption, yet it is precisely the retention of the production aspect of food sovereignty, as opposed to its radical political aims, that has caused failures of translation into more privileged contexts. It is perfectly consistent with dominant US culture, for example, to value the production of food as a noble goal, and even to value more abstractly the producers of food. Indeed, the celebration of cowboys and the use of phrases such as the "heartland" show that this valorization is already a part of mainstream US culture. If this symbolic appreciation is the meaning of food sovereignty in a US context, then food movements seem destined to ignore or even support current unjust institutions. Much more challenging to translate into mainstream US culture is the resistance to current global economic and political systems, radical solidarity, and maximally local yet transnationally linked democracy. It is important to stress that this work will require translation, rather than simple importation – for example, it is an open question what maximally local, democratic decision-making around food systems means in the US, with its dependence on large numbers of migrant and immigrant agricultural laborers. Addressing questions such as this one would be of benefit not only to the US food system, but also to the movement of food sovereignty as a whole, in part because many laborers in the US food production and distribution system come from the same subsistence food production communities that originated the food sovereignty movement, and in part because accelerating climate change will vastly increase the volume of migration and immigration in the future.

Fortunately, such translations may be possible. It is certainly the case that food is a fetishized commodity for many, cut off from the labor and materials that created it. Yet even in this fetishized state there is a phenomenal character of food that ties it to its origins, and this embeds our cultures and our communities and individual identities within our experiences as eaters, not only as producers. That these connections can emerge every day with such vividness makes food a promising vehicle for critical self-reflection and change, and one that cannot be avoided or entirely ignored in any community that is striving for justice.

Notes

1 For recent scholarly work delving into the complex history of food sovereignty, see McMichael (2014) and Edelman (2014). While some disagree as to the origin of the term, all sources agree that Vía was one of its most prominent early exponents, and Vía has continued to play a prominent role in advocating for and developing the concept in the years since its inception.
2 Even within this discourse of transnational social justice there are differences in conceptions of what these goals require. For a discussion of different conceptions of food sovereignty as either reformist or revolutionary, see Werkheiser et al. (2015).
3 For a good discussion of gender in food sovereignty generally and in Vía in particular, see Navin (2015).
4 See Hochschild (2005) for a good discussion of the sugar boycott in the Abolition movement in England.

References

Adams, C. (1990) *The Sexual Politics of Meat: A Feminist-Vegetarian Critical Theory*, New York: Bloomsbury Academic.

Alkon, A. H. and T. M. Mares. (2012) "Food Sovereignty in US Food Movements: Radical Visions and Neo-liberal Constraints," *Agriculture and Human Values* 29(3): 347–359.

Ayres, J. and M. J. Bosia. (2011) "Beyond Global Summitry: Food Sovereignty as Localized Resistance to Globalization," *Globalizations* 8(1): 47–63.

Berry, W. (1977) *The Unsettling of America: Culture and Agriculture*, San Francisco: Sierra Club.

Breines, W. (1989) *Community and Organization in the New Left, 1962–1968: The Great Refusal*, New Brunswick, NJ: Rutgers University Press.

Cloud, B. (2008) "Synthetic Authenticity," *Time Magazine*, viewed on 10 November 2015, http://content.time.com/time/specials/2007/article/0,28804,1720049_1720050_1722070,00.html.

Edelman, M. (2014) "Food Sovereignty: Forgotten Genealogies and Future Regulatory Challenges," *The Journal of Peasant Studies* 41(6): 959–978.

Fairbairn, M. (2012) "Framing Transformation: The Counter-Hegemonic Potential of Food Sovereignty in the US Context," *Agriculture and Human Values* 29(2): 217–230.

Flora, C. B. (2011) (Book Review) Schanbacher, W. D.: "The Politics of Food: The Global Conflict Between Food Security and Food Sovereignty," *Journal of Agricultural and Environmental Ethics* 24: 545–547.

Ganz, M. (2009) *Why David Sometimes Wins: Leadership, Organization, and Strategy in the California Farm Worker Movement*, Oxford: Oxford University Press.

Goodman, M. K. (2004) "Reading Fair Trade: Political Ecological Imaginary and the Moral Economy of Fair Trade Foods," *Political Geography* 23(7): 891–915.

Graeber, D. (2004) *Fragments of an Anarchist Anthropology*, Chicago: Prickly Paradigm Press.

Hochschild, A. (2005) *Bury the Chains: Prophets and Rebels in the Fight to Free an Empire's Slaves*, Boston: Houghton Mifflin Company.

Jacquet, J. L. and D. Pauly. (2006) "The Rise of Seafood Awareness Campaigns in an Era of Collapsing Fisheries," *Marine Policy* 31(3): 308–313.

Jensen, D. (2006) *Endgame, Volume 2: Resistance*, New York: Seven Stories Press.

Kaplan, D. (2015) "What Does Ethics Taste Like?" *Moral Cultures of Food* (Keynote Address). University of North Texas, March 20.

Koont, S. (2011) *Sustainable Urban Agriculture in Cuba*, Gainesville: University Press of Florida.

La Vía Campesina. (1996) "Declaration of Food Sovereignty," viewed on 10 November 2015, http://www.voiceoftheturtle.org/library/1996%20Declaration%20of%20Food%20Sovereignty.pdf.

McMichael, P. (2014) "Historicizing Food Sovereignty," *The Journal of Peasant Studies* 41(6): 933–957.

Menser, M. (2008) "Transnational Participatory Democracy in Action: The Case of La Vía Campesina," *Journal of Social Philosophy* 39(1): 20–41.

Molleda, J. C. and M. Roberts. (2008) "The Value of 'Authenticity' in 'Glocal' Strategic Communication: The New Juan Valdez Campaign," *International Journal of Strategic Communications* 2(3): 154–174.

Mustapha, K. (2010) "Taste of Child Labor Not So Sweet: A Critique of Regulatory Approaches to Combating Child Labor Abuses by the U.S. Chocolate Industry," *Washington University Law Review* 87(5): 1163–1195.

Navin, M. (2014) "Local Food and International Ethics," *Journal of Agricultural and Environmental Ethics* 27(3): 349–368.

——. (2015) "Food Sovereignty and Gender Justice: The Case of La Vía Campesina," in Jill Dieterle (ed.), *Just Food: Philosophy, Food and Justice*, New York: Rowman and Littlefield, pp. 87–100.

Nyéléni Declaration. (2007) *Nyéléni 2007—Forum for Food Sovereignty*, viewed on 10 November 2015, http://nyeleni.org/spip.php?article290.

Our World is Not for Sale – Priority to People's Food Sovereignty, WTO Out of Agriculture. (2001) *La Vía Campesina: International Peasant's Movement*, viewed on 15 Oct 2015, http://viacampesina.org/en/index.php/main-issues-mainmenu-27/food-sovereignty-and-trade-mainmenu-38/396-peoples-food-sovereignty-wto-out-of-agriculture.

Patel, R. (2009) "Grassroots Voices: Food Sovereignty." *The Journal of Peasant Studies* 36(3): 663–706.

Plumwood, V. (2000) "Integrating Ethical Frameworks for Animals, Humans, and Nature: A Critical Feminist Eco-Socialist Analysis," *Ethics and the Environment* 5(2): 285–322.

Ridberg, R. (2013) "Leading the Fight for Food Sovereignty, An Interview with La Vía Campesina's Dena Hoff," *World Watch Institute*, viewed 10 November 2015, http://www.worldwatch.org/node/6514.

Singer, P. (1975) *Animal Liberation*, New York: Random House.

Singer, P. and J. Mason. (2006) *The Ethics of What We Eat: Why Our Food Choices Matter*, Emmaus, PA: Rodale Inc.

Star, S. L. and J. R. Greisemer. (1989) "Institutional Ecology, 'Translations' and Boundary Objects: Amateurs and Professionals on Berkeley's Museum of Vertebrate Zoology," *Social Studies of Science* 19(3): 387–420.

Thompson, P. B. (1994) *The Spirit of the Soil: Agriculture and Environmental Ethics*, New York: Routledge.

———. (2010) *The Agrarian Vision: Sustainability and Environmental Ethics*, Lexington: University of Kentucky Press.

———. (2015) *From Field to Fork: Food Ethics for Everyone.* Oxford: Oxford University Press.

Tlaxcala Declaration of the Vía Campesina. (1996) viewed 10 November 2015, http://viacampesina.org/en/index.php/our-conferences-mainmenu-28/2-tlaxcala-1996-mainmenu-48/425-ii-international-conference-of-the-via-campesina-tlaxcala-mexico-april-18–21.

Werkheiser, I., S. Tyler, and P. B. Thompson. (2015) "Food Sovereignty: Two Conceptions of Food Justice," in Jill Dieterle (ed.), *Just Food: Philosophy, Food and Justice*, New York: Rowman and Littlefield, pp. 71–86.

Wiebe, N. (2013) "Women of La Vía Campesina: Creating and Occupying Our Rightful Spaces," in *La Vía Campesina's Open Book: Celebrating 20 Years of Struggle and Hope*, viewed 10 November 2015, http://viacampesina.org/en/index.php/publications-mainmenu-30/1409-la-vía-campesina-s-open-book-celebrating-20-years-of-struggle-and-hope.

Wittman, H., A. Desmarais, and N. Wiebe. (2010) *Food Sovereignty: Reconnecting Food, Nature, and Community*, Oakland, CA: Food First Books.

36

RESPONSIBILITY FOR HUNGER IN LIBERAL DEMOCRACIES

David Reynolds and Miranda Mirosa

Honesty is all out of fashion.

—Martin Carthy, "Rigs of the Time"

Introduction

This chapter is concerned with responses to hunger in liberal democracies – the United Kingdom (UK), the United States of America (USA), Canada, Australia, and New Zealand. These countries are economically developed, industrialized, and have some form of welfare provision for citizens. They also have plenty of food, as Janet Poppendieck (1998b: 563) observes: "Collectively, and for the most part individually, we have too much food, not too little." Despite this, there are citizens in these countries who go hungry. This chapter examines significant perspectives regarding hunger and situates these in the context of liberal democratic societies. The significance of hunger as an affliction of sections of the populations in these countries means that the ways in which hunger is responded to are important. As the perspective taken renders particular responses legitimate and others illegitimate, how hunger is viewed is significant.

The conception of hunger as a problem afflicting citizens of economically developing countries is at odds with the phenomenon of "want in the midst of abundance" (Poppendieck 1998b). As Amartya Sen (Sen 1981; Drèze and Sen 1989) argues, famine is not inherently caused by food shortage, though this may certainly be a contributing factor. The production or supply of food is only one of many "factors that affect the capacity of particular households and social groups to establish entitlement over food" (Sobhan 1991: 79). Social and economic structures and relations, and people's relative location in these, affect their ability to acquire food.

With the understanding that the phenomenon of hunger has a social dimension, the particular way in which hunger is problematized becomes significant. Bacchi (2009) makes a distinction between the phenomenon of a problem, identified as a "social condition," and the "problem" as it is understood to exist. Problems are social constructions, and examining these can be informative, clarifying the assumptions and conditions present in the background of a particular problem. Problems are also significant because a particular understanding of the nature of a social condition informs the manner of any solution that is considered viable or legitimate. In other words, the way that a social condition is problematized is important – in that the construction of a problem influences how that social condition is conceived of and subsequently acted on.

A key aspect of the construction of a problem, and subsequent responses to it, is the allocation of responsibility for the social condition. Remedying a problem requires some form of change, and the site of change is necessarily designated by the site of responsibility. Given the influence of the particular construction of hunger as a problem on responses to the social condition of hunger, the allocation of responsibility is very important. Effective action against the social condition of hunger in liberal democracies is driven or blocked by the constructed allocation of responsibility. Responsibility, or "moral responsibility," is a fundamentally social concept. A person is responsible for an action (or inaction) where it is worthy of a reaction by another person, such as praise or blame (Eshleman 2014). What is worthy of a reaction, and what kind of reaction, is judged by people with expectations shaped by their social context and by social expectations. Thus, the attribution or allocation of responsibility is socially contingent. For, while the social condition of hunger may be broadly understood to be problematic, this neither entails a particular problem, nor a specific location of responsibility.

Indeed, it is apparent that the understood nature of the problem of hunger in liberal democracies is contested. Positions evident in political, media, and public forums include: that it does not exist; that only people who make poor choices could possibly go hungry; that governments are breaching their human rights commitments to hungry citizens; that hunger and an obesity epidemic cannot co-exist; that food banks sufficiently address hunger; that hungry people should grow their own vegetables; that food banks encourage dependence on handouts; and so on. These conflicting reactions to the social condition of hunger, based on a range of sets of beliefs and information, illustrate differences in the construction of hunger as a problem, and the accompanying variable attribution of responsibility.

This chapter examines the responses of three significant perspectives on the social condition of hunger in liberal democracies and locates these with reference to economic, social, and political conditions in liberal democracies. In doing so, it covers the substantial issues surrounding responsibility for hunger in the midst of plenty. First, the importance of addressing the phenomenon of hunger is framed in empirical terms.

The "social condition": hunger

Data on the incidence of hunger, or on the related concept "food security," is produced at a range of intervals across liberal democracies using a range of measures. It is clear, however, that hunger exists in all liberal democracies. Hunger is a severe outcome of "food insecurity" (for a definition, see Anderson 1990: 1576), which has been associated with a wide and significant range of negative physical and mental health outcomes. The vast amount of research into the health outcomes of food insecurity carried out across liberal democracies will receive only a brief treatment here. Hunger falls at the severe end of outcomes of food insecurity, so the negative health outcomes of food insecurity are relevant in demonstrating its significant consequences.

Gundersen and Kreider (2009) provide a useful summary of findings relating food insecurity to the health of children, including: poor health, psychosocial problems, worse developmental outcomes, more chronic illnesses, a higher likelihood of obesity, impaired mental proficiency, frequent stomach aches and headaches, and behavior problems. Food insecurity infringes on children's education, impacting cognition, classroom behavior, social skills, weight gain, and longitudinal test results as an indicator of development (Jyoti et al. 2005).

Adults living in food-insecure households, as compared to those living in food-secure households, have poorer physical and mental health, with other factors controlled (Stuff et al. 2004). Such adults also have nutrient inadequacy (Kirkpatrick and Tarasuk 2008) and are "significantly more likely to report having heart disease, diabetes, high blood pressure and food allergies"

(Vozoris and Tarasuk 2003: 122). Food insecurity is also associated with having type-2 diabetes among adults, even allowing for body mass index (Seligman et al. 2007).

Reporting on a non-causal link between food insecurity and overweight and obesity in adults living in poverty, Martin and Ferris note that "poverty alone is not a risk factor for obesity; there appears to be something specific about not being able to consistently have access to enough food that contributes to adult obesity" (2007: 34). Regarding mental health, Carter and co-workers found that with other variables controlled for, there exists "a 60% (males) to 110% (females) elevated odds of psychological distress among those reporting food insecurity" (Carter et al. 2011: 1468).

The body of empirical evidence about hunger in these countries, which continues to grow, prompts the observation that "the need to address issues of food insecurity in high-income countries seems pressing" (Gorton et al. 2010: 2). Building on this idea, this chapter draws attention to the complexity of the social and political context of "the need to address." It examines responses to hunger in liberal democracies through three significant perspectives. The response of a neoliberal perspective is included because this is the dominant political rationality in economically developed liberal democracies. The response of a human rights perspective is included because of the commitments to United Nations (UN) agreements by those countries. Charity responses are included because of the widespread efforts of a huge number of charitable organizations to address hunger in liberal democracies.

The next three sections will examine significant responses to hunger. Following that, these responses will be reconciled with the wider economic, social, and political situation of the social condition of hunger in liberal democracies. Finally, this chapter will reflect on the practical implications for the need to address hunger.

Neoliberalism: assuming individual responsibility

Neoliberalism refers to "forms of political-economic governance premised on the extension of market relationships" (Larner 2000: 5). Neoliberalism views the market "as the model for the state and for the overall organization of society" (Oksala 2011: 480, in Foster et al. 2014: 231), following the belief that "the social good will be maximized by maximizing the reach and frequency of market transactions" (Harvey 2005: 3). Larner (2000) describes five values as underlying the neoliberal political framework: "the individual; freedom of choice; market security; laissez faire; and minimal government" (7). These drive the "active export" of market logic to other social domains (Shamir 2008: 6), so that "[a]ll conduct is economic conduct; all spheres of existence are framed and measured by economic terms and metrics" (Brown 2015: 10).

In this way, neoliberalism is more than an ideology, a particular set of policies, or the incorporation of market mechanisms into the operation of the state – it is "a normative order of reason developed over three decades into a widely and deeply disseminated governing rationality" (Brown 2015: 9). In other words, neoliberalism constitutes, and is constituted through, a particular way of thinking. The neoliberal way of thinking about hunger in economically developed liberal democracies is as a problem of self-responsibility.

This is a function of the "responsibilization of the self" under neoliberalism, which Peters characterizes as a simultaneously economic and moral process (2001: 91). The neoliberal citizen is an autonomous individual with a sovereign power to make choices in the marketplace,

> imbued with a seemingly enhanced capacity and responsibility for managing choices and decisions … [and with] an equally enhanced capacity to incur the risk of making the 'wrong' choices, given that the consequences of their actions are to be borne by the subject alone.
>
> (Foster et al. 2014: 232)

In line with the adage "with great power comes great responsibility," the (apparent) *freedom* of the neoliberal citizen to choose their way to well-being – how to live; what to do with one's time; how to "invest in one's health, education, security, employability, and retirement" (Peters 2001: 92) – entails the *responsibility* to do so, and to do so well. An individual's inadequate welfare is thus a moral failure by that individual. The "enterprising self" (Peters 2001: 85) is responsible for "self-care" against social risks such as unemployment, poverty, and illness – and hunger (Lemke 2001: 201).

The other three values listed by Larner above pertain to the free market; this is the necessary partner of the autonomous, self-responsible and enterprising consumer-citizen. For neoliberalism, then, hunger is thought of as an outcome of individuals not sufficiently or effectively being empowered-responsible citizens. It is something for which hungry people are themselves responsible.

Human rights: insufficient state action

Human rights are "rights inherent to all human beings. . . . These rights are all interrelated, interdependent and indivisible" (OHCHR 2015a). A human rights response to hunger "provides a mechanism for reanalysing and renaming 'problems' as 'violations,' and, as such, something that need not and should not be tolerated" (Jochnick 1997: 60, in Dowler and O'Connor 2012: 46). Elizabeth Dowler and Hannah Lambie-Mumford have examined food insecurity in the UK, including from a human rights perspective (e.g., Dowler 2002; Dowler and O'Connor 2012; Lambie 2011; Lambie-Mumford and Dowler 2014).

Several of the core human rights treaties are relevant to a human rights perspective on hunger. The *Universal Declaration of Human Rights*, which Member States, including New Zealand, Australia, Canada, the UK, and the USA, pledged to achieve, addresses food. Article 25 includes the assertion that:

> Everyone has *the right to a standard of living adequate for the health and well-being of himself and of his family, including food* . . . and the right to security in the event of unemployment, sickness, disability, widowhood, old age or other lack of livelihood in circumstances beyond his control.
>
> (United Nations 1948, italics added)

The *International Covenant on Economic, Social and Cultural Rights (ICESCR)*, signed and ratified by states including New Zealand, Australia, Canada, and the UK, and signed but not ratified by the USA, asserts "the fundamental right of everyone to be free from hunger" in Article 11 (United Nations 1966). The agreed means to achieve this are "(a) To improve methods of production, conservation and distribution of food . . . and (b) to . . . ensure an equitable distribution of world food supplies in relation to need" around the globe (United Nations 1966).

The United Nations also founded the role of *Special Rapporteur on the Right to Food*, who frames the human right to food as:

> The right to have regular, permanent and unrestricted access, either directly or by means of financial purchases, to quantitatively and qualitatively adequate and sufficient food corresponding to the cultural traditions of the people to which the consumer belongs, and which ensure a physical and mental, individual and collective, fulfilling and dignified life free of fear.
>
> (OHCHR 2014)

Dowler and O'Connor (2012) explain the responsibilities accepted by states under the *Covenant*: States have the responsibility to respect, protect, and fulfill (facilitate) the rights asserted in the *Covenant* for their citizens. The responsibility to "respect" concerns existing access to adequate food; states are obliged not to diminish that access through their actions, such as the removal of entitlements to welfare payments without providing alternative means of access to adequate food. The "protection" of the right to adequate food involves ensuring that other individuals or enterprises do not impede access. The obligation to "fulfill" (facilitate) requires states to pro-actively implement measures to "strengthen people's access to, and utilization of, resources and means to ensure their livelihood to enable food purchase," as well as to fulfill (provide for) access to adequate food, where an individual or group is unable to do so themselves for reasons beyond their control (Dowler and O'Connor 2012: 46).

In the context of the rise of food banks in Canada, Riches (1986) observes that "[t]echnologi-cal, demographic and other forces helped to create large scale unemployment" (102). Given the commitments made by liberal democratic states to the human rights of their citizens, it seems that "[w]hat matters is how the state responds to the social and economic dislocation of these struc-tural determinants. All social and economic policies rest on values and assumptions[:] ... political priorities. Spending is choosing" (Riches 1986: 102). The policy choices being made by liberal democratic states appear to be abandoning the human right to freedom from hunger.

Charity: a helping hand

In liberal democracies, the re-emergence of hunger since the 1980s has produced a significant charitable response. This might be characterized as rooted in concern, "intrinsic human desires of compassion and caring for those in need" (Booth 2014: 15), as opposed to the more devel-oped conceptual frameworks behind neoliberal and human rights responses to hunger. In liberal democracies, a huge number of charitable organizations have mobilized resources to provide "emergency food" to people who are unable to provide it for themselves.

In Canada and the USA, food banking operates on a massive scale, in a corporate-style struc-ture. Graham Riches (e.g., 1986; 1997c; 1999; 2002) and Janet Poppendieck (1994; 1998a; 1998b) have documented the emergence, expansion, and entrenchment of charitable emergency food aid and its implications in Canada and the USA, respectively. Valarie Tarasuk has researched many dimensions of charitable food aid in Canada (e.g., 2001; Davis and Tarasuk 1994; Tarasuk et al. 2014; Tarasuk and Dachner 2009; Tarasuk and Eakin 2003).

Emergency food aid in Australia took off in the early 1990s (Booth 2014; Wilson 1997) and in New Zealand in 1980 (Uttley 1997). In the UK, the expansion of emergency food aid has occurred more recently; there was only one reported food bank in the UK in 2000, but very rapid growth has followed "global economic austerity" (Wells and Caraher 2014: 1426). Emergency food aid operations, including food banks, food pantries, and soup kitchens, tend to begin with the intention of providing emergency, not longer-term support (Riches 1986: 48). In Canada, as in other liberal democracies, food banks emerged and expanded in the 1980s, "initially perceived as temporary, 'emergency' responses to needs arising from the economic recession of that period" (Tarasuk et al. 2014: 1405).

Despite providing emergency aid, food banks and similar organizations have continued to expand and provide food to people struggling to feed themselves (Lambie-Mumford and Dowler 2014; Tarasuk et al. 2014; Wilson 1997). Tarasuk and colleagues observe that "the problems of poverty and unemployment that characterized the lives of those using food banks did not abate as the economy improved, and food bank activity continued to expand" (2014: 1405). Poppendieck notes that the "'emergency' to which emergency food providers have responded" continues, as "[t]hrough recessions and recoveries, the demand for emergency food has continued to grow" (Poppendieck 1994: 71). Consequently, "this approach to poverty is now quite thoroughly institutionalized" (Poppendieck 1994: 71).

The limits of a popular, but ultimately *ad hoc* and inadequately resourced, system of responding to hunger has been highlighted by the research of Riches and Tarasuk in Canada. Despite the fact that "food banks in Canada today enjoy broad government, business and media support and a high degree of public legitimacy" (Riches 2002: 653), their approach "has failed to stem the growth of hunger" (Riches 1997a: 71). The reason for this is an inadequacy inherent in the system: "food banks lack the capacity to respond to the food needs of those who seek assistance" (Tarasuk and Eakin 2003: 1513). The "countless acts of altruism" on which food banks operate are insufficient to cope with the problem of widespread hunger (Riches 1986: 121). Food banks are supply- (donor-) driven, so that demand for emergency food aid cannot be expected to be solved through their operation (Tarasuk and Beaton 1999: 112). As a result, "while charitable food assistance may have alleviated *some* of the absolute food deprivation in the households studied, it clearly did not *prevent* members from going hungry" in Canada in the late 1990s (Tarasuk and Beaton 1999: 112, in Riches 2002: 657, italics in original).

Tarasuk and Eakin term the "limited and highly variable" nature of donations to food banks "the problem of supply" (2003: 1507). This problem is one of quality as well as quantity: the ability of food banks to distribute food is contingent upon donations, as is the selection and quality of food given out, despite the best efforts of staff in some food banks (Tarasuk and Eakin 2003). Tarasuk and Eakin conclude that donating to food banks is a "symbolic gesture," because the distribution of food parcels is dissociated from the real or stated needs of food bank users (2003: 1512). Warshawsky (2010) argues that this constitutes "an important moral safety valve" for those who support the operations of food banks by donating or volunteering (Warshawsky 2010: 765).

As a manifestation of "community altruism," food banks enjoy "significant community legitimacy" (Riches 1997a: 62) and this continues to support the success of emergency food aid provision. Many food bank volunteers view hunger as a solvable problem (Poppendieck 1998b), and thus see their work as contributing to a solution to hunger in liberal democracies. However, despite the best intentions of organizers, volunteers, and donors, charitable emergency food aid has not provided a solution to the social condition of hunger in liberal democracies.

Contextualizing responsibility

This section contextualizes neoliberal, human rights, and charity responses to hunger within the wider circumstances of liberal democracies. It details the limitations of the responses to hunger from the three perspectives and highlights how the attribution of responsibility for hunger takes shape in the interplay between them.

A neoliberal perspective on hunger in liberal democracies erases structural influences as a contributor to the hunger of citizens, locating responsibility with those suffering hunger. This is problematic for two reasons. First, it is incompatible with reality; structural influences on people's lives are significant. As Marx put it, "[people] make their own history, but they do not make it as they please; they do not make it under self-selected circumstances, but under circumstances existing already, given and transmitted from the past" (Marx 1995 [1852]). Second, this erasure has a major impact on how hunger is thought about, due to the dominance of neoliberal rationality in liberal democracies.

Watts and Bohle (1993) offer a way of understanding the circumstances existing already for hunger. They map the "space of vulnerability" to hunger with "social, political, economic and structural-historical co-ordinates" (117), extending Sen's concept of "entitlement failure" to cover structures affecting "entitlement and capability," "empowerment and enfranchisement," and "class and crisis." The overlap of these structural influences, they argue, explains why, while it is "mainly the poor who suffer from famine, hunger and malnutrition[,] . . . not all poor people are equally vulnerable to hunger; indeed it is not necessarily the poorest who face the greatest risk" (Watts and Bohle 1993: 117).

The three structural influences operate to influence people's location relative to the three basic co-ordinates of vulnerability:

1) The risk of exposure to crises, stress, and shocks;
2) The risk of inadequate capacities to cope with stress, crises, and shocks;
3) The risk of severe consequences of, and the attendant risks of slow or limited recovery (resiliency) from crises, risk, and shocks. (Watts and Bohle 1993: 118)

An individual person could be considered responsible for reducing their capacity to cope with a crisis, perhaps through "unnecessary" spending. However, it is ridiculous to argue that a person is responsible for the shocks that they are exposed to, such as the Global Financial Crisis initiated in 2008. The susceptibility of sections of middle-class society to this shock emphasizes that deprivation is not driven by the perceived deviant behavior by poor people, but by vulnerability, inherently involving structural forces. This is not to say that individuals' behavior – alcoholism, drug use, or gambling habits tend to be suggested – are never a factor in financial difficulties or hunger. These are social problems that need attention themselves, but they are neither the major drivers of poverty, nor of hunger. It is disingenuous as well as unjust to blame the victims of circumstance for their predicament. A person's location in the space of vulnerability – how vulnerable they are to hunger – is far from exclusively their own responsibility.

A stark example of the impact of structural factors on the vulnerability to hunger of a section of the New Zealand population followed the benefit cuts of the 1991 budget. This also illustrates how neoliberal policies contribute to the vulnerability of a population to hunger, reducing both ability to cope with, and resilience following, shocks. The number of food parcels distributed by the Salvation Army in New Zealand jumped from 2,124 in 1991 to 10,261 in 1992 (Uttley 1997: 81). While food bank use is not an ideal proxy for rates of hunger, these data are compelling. It is clear that the cause of the increase in demand for food assistance from this charitable organization was the reduction in state provision. The change in the number of food parcels was not due to a sudden increase in the number of people in New Zealand who were lazy, feckless, or inhibited by other personal faults. Nor was it driven by more food banks operating, causing more people to use them, as British Conservative MP Lord Freud suggested of his country in 2013 (Morris 2013).

Adherence to the idea of self-responsibility here obfuscates the strong link between the structural change in welfare policy, reliance on markets to deliver well-being, and the increased deprivation of the poor. Erasing this link is essential to the retreat of the welfare state, which has been taking place in liberal democracies since the "neoliberal turn" of the 1980s. The consequences of this narrow focus on the individual serves to drive hunger in liberal democracies. With what seems to be willful disregard for inconvenient empirical evidence, neoliberalism shapes the social context of liberal democracies, with implications for "the fundamental right of everyone to be free from hunger."

The gap between neoliberal notions of self-responsibility and empirical evidence is reflected in the gap between notions of the responsibility of states for their citizens' human rights and the existing practices of the liberal democratic states. States are required, for instance, to take steps "to the maximum of their available resources to achieve progressively the full realization of economic, social and cultural rights" under the *ICESCR* (OHCHR 2015b).

However, as Harvey (2005) succinctly observes, "[i]f political power is not willing, then notions of rights remain empty" (189). The operationalization of human rights – their existence as something more than abstract concepts – is reliant on actions, especially those of states. The articulation of human rights constitutes a set of ideals, rather than particular concrete actions to be undertaken. The incompatibility of certain human rights with neoliberal values dominant in policy-making restricts the full realization of the human right to be free from hunger at the state level.

As already noted, it is important to recognize that there is more to neoliberalism than a policy regime – neoliberalism is a way of thinking, a rationality (Brown 2015; Larner 2000). This way of thinking is founded upon certain human rights – those that guarantee "negative freedoms," i.e., freedoms from restriction or obstruction. In contrast, the neoliberal way of thinking conflicts with the "positive freedoms" guaranteed by certain other human rights enacted through enablement. Freedom from hunger, requiring the maintenance of access to food, is a positive freedom; the right to this freedom thus conflicts with the neoliberal rationality.

In liberal democracies, the dominant and quotidian rationality of neoliberalism hails some human rights as essential, while disparaging others as inconveniently expensive, reliant on inefficient market interference, or involving overbearing government (the "Nanny state"). Neoliberal rationality understands the guarantees of many positive human rights as things to be earned by individuals, unencumbered by structural restraints, in competitive markets. Thus, notions such as a right to be free from hunger, or the right to food, remain empty in liberal democracies. Riches suggests the consequences of this: "If the right to food security is to be constrained by people's ability to participate fully in the marketplace, particularly in societies which show little inclination to support full employment, the future is one of increasing risk and vulnerability" (Riches 1997b: 5).

It is significant that the means of addressing food insecurity in part (b) of Article 11 of the *ICESCR* are conceived as "technical and scientific knowledge," focused on problems in the "production, conservation and distribution of food." The international distribution of food is mentioned as significant, but the idea that hunger might be "primarily an issue of distributional justice" within an economically developed country (Riches 1997d: 170) escaped consideration when the *ICESCR* was written. The intentions of peace and goodwill, upon which the foundations of the United Nations and the international human rights framework were built, appear to have been eclipsed by market logic in defining the obligations of states. The limited acknowledgement of the implications of this shift in rationality by liberal democratic states is disingenuous; appearing to support human rights, while abandoning their implementation to the operation of markets – which a large amount of empirical evidence shows to be a regressive move for the rights of at least some citizens – amounts to dishonesty through purposive ignorance. The consequences of these contradictions and dishonesty are written in the lives of the vulnerable, generally the poor, in liberal democracies.

Charity responses to hunger appear to exist outside of the market, sanctioned in liberal democracies by neoliberal support for the voluntary action of "neighbor helping neighbor" (Riches 1986: 26). With perhaps the best intentions, it has two limitations: it is unable to provide sufficient support for hungry people, and it enables the state to turn a blind eye on hunger (Riches 1986; 1997a).

Janet Poppendieck (1994) outlines two models of responses to hunger that compete "for public endorsement: charity and justice" (69). In characterizing this dichotomy, Poppendieck suggests that emergency food aid poses "a dilemma that confronts all thoughtful persons who approach issues of food security from the perspective of a commitment to justice and basic human

rights" (1994: 71).That is, the dilemma of choosing either to respond to need while perpetuating systemic drivers of that need, or to neglect aid to people suffering hunger while seeking to
address underlying causes of that suffering (see Poppendieck 1994; 1998a; 1998b; Riches 1986;
2002).

The proliferation of food charity, Poppendieck (1998a) argues, contributes to the USA's cultural and political "failure to grapple in meaningful ways with poverty" (5–6). Similarly, Riches
argues that "food banks have served to depoliticise the issue of hunger . . . [by] undermining the
governments' legislated obligations to guarantee adequate welfare benefits and by obviating the
need for responsible public action" (1997a: 62). Riches (1986) details the rise of food banks in
Canada as a result of neoconservative policies implemented in the 1980s, drawing attention to
the growth of charitable emergency food aid "alongside a broad sweep of social policy reforms"
(Tarasuk et al. 2014: 1405).As such, "the growth and entrenchment of emergency food provision"
must be understood in the context of social policy developments (Lambie-Mumford 2013: 71) –
in particular the withdrawal of the neoliberal state from welfare provision, and the abandonment
of human rights and the aspiration to banish hunger from liberal democracies (Riches 1997a;
Robertson 1989–1990).

The evident inadequacy of emergency food aid, including food banks, to address hunger in
liberal democracies, in the context of neoliberal reforms of the welfare state and broad social
policy changes, makes food banks "inadequate replacements for governmental emergency food
programs" (Warshawsky 2010: 765).Tarasuk and MacLean (1990) characterize the institutionalization of food banks as a shift in the role of provision by food banks from emergency relief to a
resource upon which vulnerable people rely repeatedly and regularly, forming a dependency (in
Riches 2002: 653).This is evident in Canada and the USA, and increasingly in other economically developed countries (see, e.g., Silvasti 2015).

Despite this inadequacy, by emphasizing the provision of "a short-term emergency supplement" while effectively providing a substitute for state welfare payments, emergency food aid
generates the public belief that an *ad hoc* charitable system is "capable of handling the crisis"
of hunger (Riches 1986: 120–121). However, referrals to food banks from state welfare agencies highlight their filling the role of "the true service of last resort" (Riches 1986: 121). For
many of those involved in the operation of emergency food aid, the "issues are seen as practical and immediate, not ideological" (Riches 1986: 65).This masks the "real debate" about the
dismantling of the welfare state, while hunger "is not even seen as a controversial political issue"
(Riches 1986: 121).

The assumed individual responsibility for hunger by the neoliberal perspective dominates the
view that hunger is a violation of citizens' human rights, supported by the well-intentioned but
ultimately insufficient charitable emergency food aid. The sentiment behind the human rights
perspective and the charitable response to hunger is congruent: people shouldn't go hungry,
especially when the means are readily available to prevent it.The difference between the two
responses is that the former sees responsibility as lying with a powerful, well-resourced actor
that operates a system to support citizen welfare, while the latter sees responsibility as falling on
citizens who are able to assist those vulnerable to hunger, through a generous, caring, *ad hoc*, insufficient, and "fundamentally reactive" (Riches 1997a: 73) system.

May I have some more?

This short examination of responsibility for hunger in liberal democracies highlights the complexities of this issue. Hunger remains a social condition that demands remedy.What form that
remedy takes, and what it is intended to achieve, depends on how the problem of hunger is

constructed. It is apparent that a neoliberal perspective is incompatible with the empirical evidence. A human rights perspective offers aspiration, but given the present dominance of neoliberal rationality, notions of rights may continue to remain empty, with empty stomachs following. As laudable, generous, and aspirational as charity responses to hunger are, they operate to bring the illusory comfort of an insufficiently capable *ad hoc* system attempting to provide for the effects of systemic drivers of hunger in liberal democracies, propping up inadequate state welfare provision (Riches 1986: 127).

In liberal democracies, there is a disconnect between allocating responsibility for hunger and taking responsibility for hunger, possibly a cynical one. In the context of an economic environment with too few jobs and a welfare state with inadequate and shrinking benefits, market-based access to food will produce hungry people (Riches 1997d). Who is taking responsibility for this? Hunger in liberal democracies is the suffering of adults and children, the violation of human rights, and a burden on health systems. Who is taking responsibility for this? Something has to change.

References

Anderson, S. A. (1990) "Core Indicators of Nutritional State for Difficult-to-Sample Populations," *The Journal of Nutrition* 120: 1555–1600.

Bacchi, C. L. (2009) *Analysing Policy: What's the Problem Represented to Be?* Frenchs Forest, NSW: Pearson.

Booth, S. (2014) "Food Banks in Australia: Discouraging the Right to Food," in Riches, G. & Silvasti, T. (eds.), *First World Hunger Revisited*, second ed., Basingstoke: Palgrave Macmillan, pp. 15–28.

Brown, W. (2015) *Undoing the Demos*, Cambridge, MA: The MIT Press.

Carter, K.N., Kruse, K., Blakely, T. & Collings, S. (2011) "The Association of Food Security with Psychological Distress in New Zealand and Any Gender Differences," *Social Science & Medicine* 72(9): 1463–1471.

Davis, B. & Tarasuk, V. (1994) "Hunger in Canada," *Agriculture and Human Values* 11: 50–57.

Dowler, E. (2002) "Food and Poverty in Britain: Rights and Responsibilities," *Social Policy & Administration* 36: 698–717.

Dowler, E. A. & O'Connor, D. (2012) "Rights-Based Approaches to Addressing Food Poverty and Food Insecurity in Ireland and UK," *Social Science & Medicine* 74: 44–51.

Drèze, J. & Sen, A. (1989) *Hunger and Public Action*, New York: Oxford University Press.

Eshleman, A. (2014) "Moral Responsibility," in Zalta, E. N. (ed.), *The Stanford Encyclopedia of Philosophy*, Summer 2014 ed., viewed 18 July 2015, http://plato.stanford.edu/archives/sum2014/entries/moral-responsibility/.

Foster, E. A., Kerr, P. & Byrne, C. (2014) "Rolling Back to Roll Forward: Depoliticisation and the Extension of Government," *Policy & Politics* 42: 225–241.

Gorton, D., Bullen, C.R. & Mhurchu, C.N. (2010) "Environmental Influences on Food Security in High-Income Countries," *Nutrition Reviews* 68(1): 1–29.

Gundersen, C. & Kreider, B. (2009) "Bounding the Effects of Food Insecurity on Children's Health Outcomes," *Journal of Health Economics* 28: 971–983.

Harvey, D. (2005) *A Brief History of Neoliberalism*, Oxford: Oxford University Press.

Jochnick, C. (1997) *Unleashing Human Rights to Address Global Poverty*, Quito, Ecuador: Center for Economic and Social Rights.

Jyoti, D. F., Frongillo, E. A. & Jones, S. J. (2005) "Food Insecurity Affects School Children's Academic Performance, Weight Gain, and Social Skills," *The Journal of Nutrition* 135: 2831–2839.

Kirkpatrick, S. I. & Tarasuk, V. (2008) "Food Insecurity is Associated with Nutrient Inadequacies among Canadian Adults and Adolescents," *The Journal of Nutrition* 138: 604–612.

Lambie, H. (2011) "The Trussell Trust Foodbank Network: Exploring the Growth of Foodbanks Across the UK," *Final Report*, Coventry, Coventry University.

Lambie-Mumford, H. (2013) "'Every Town Should Have One': Emergency Food Banking in the UK," *Journal of Social Policy* 42: 73–89.

Lambie-Mumford, H. & Dowler, E. (2014) "Rising Use of 'Food Aid' in the United Kingdom," *British Food Journal* 116: 1418–1425.

Larner, W. (2000) "Neo-liberalism: Policy, Ideology, Governmentality," *Studies in Political Economy* 63: 5–25.

Lemke, T. (2001) "'The Birth of Bio-politics': Michel Foucault's Lecture at the Collège de France on Neo-liberal Governmentality," *Economy and Society* 30: 190–207.

Martin, K. S. & Ferris, A.M. (2007) "Food Insecurity and Gender are Risk Factors for Obesity," *Journal of Nutrition Education and Behavior* 39: 31–36.

Marx, K. (1995 [1852]) *The Eighteenth Brumaire of Louis Bonaparte* [Online], Marxists Internet Archive, viewed 10 April 2015, https://www.marxists.org/archive/marx/works/1852/18th-brumaire/ch01.htm.

Morris, N. (2013) "Demand for Food Banks has Nothing to do with Benefits Squeeze, says Work Minister Lord Freud," *The Independent*, viewed 27 July 2015, http://www.independent.co.uk/news/uk/politics/demand-for-food-banks-has-nothing-to-do-with-benefits-squeeze-says-work-minister-lord-freud-8684005.html.

OHCHR. (2014) *Special Rapporteur on the Right to Food* [Online], New York: United Nations, viewed 21 July 2014, http://www.ohchr.org/EN/Issues/Food/Pages/FoodIndex.aspx.

——. (2015a) *What are Human Rights?* [Online], New York: United Nations, viewed 11 July 2015, http://www.ohchr.org/EN/Issues/Pages/WhatareHumanRights.aspx.

——. (2015b) *What are the Obligations of States on Economic, Social and Cultural Rights?* [Online], New York: United Nations, viewed 11 July 2015, http://www.ohchr.org/EN/Issues/ESCR/Pages/Whatarethe obligationsofStatesonESCR.aspx.

Oksala, J. (2011) "Violence and Neoliberal Governmentality," *Constellations* 18(3): 474–486.

Peters, M. A. (2001) *Poststructuralism, Marxism, and Neoliberalism: Between Theory and Politics*, Lanham, MD: Rowman & Littlefield Publishers.

Poppendieck, J. (1994) "Dilemmas of Emergency Food: A Guide for the Perplexed," *Agriculture and Human Values* 11: 69–76.

——. (1998a) *Sweet Charity? Emergency Food and the End of Entitlement*, New York: Viking Penguin.

——. (1998b) "Want Amid Plenty: From Hunger to Inequality," *Monthly Review: An Independent Socialist Magazine* 50: 125.

Riches, G. (1986) *Food Banks and the Welfare Crisis*, Toronto: James Lorimer & Company.

——. (1997a) "Canada: Abandoning the Right to Food," in Riches, G. (ed.), *First World Hunger: Food Security and Welfare Politics*, Toronto: University of Toronto Press, pp. 46–77.

——. (1997b) "Comparative Perspectives," in Riches, G. (ed.), *First World Hunger: Food Security and Welfare Politics*, Toronto: University of Toronto Press, pp. 1–13.

——. (1997c) "Hunger, Food Security and Welfare Policies: Issues and Debates in First World Societies," *Proceedings of the Nutrition Society* 56: 63–74.

——. (1997d) "Hunger, Welfare and Food Security: Emerging Strategies," in Riches, G. (ed.), *First World Hunger: Food Security and Welfare Politics.* Toronto: University of Toronto Press, pp. 165–178.

Riches, G. (1999) "Advancing the Human Right to Food in Canada: Social Policy and the Politics of Hunger, Welfare, and Food Security," *Agriculture and Human Values* 16: 203–211.

Riches, G. (2002) "Food Banks and Food Security: Welfare Reform, Human Rights and Social Policy. Lessons from Canada?," *Social Policy & Administration* 36: 648–663.

Robertson, R. E. (1989–1990) "The Right to Food – Canada's Broken Covenant," *Canadian Human Rights Yearbook*: 185–215.

Seligman, H., Bindman, A., Vittinghoff, E., Kanaya, A. & Kushel, M. (2007) "Food Insecurity is Associated with Diabetes Mellitus: Results from the National Health Examination and Nutrition Examination Survey (NHANES) 1999–2002," *Journal of General Internal Medicine* 22: 1018–1023.

Sen, A. (1981) *Poverty and Famines: An Essay on Entitlement and Deprivation*, Oxford: Clarendon.

Shamir, R. (2008) "The Age of Responsibilization: On Market-embedded Morality," *Economy and Society* 37: 1–19.

Silvasti, T. (2015) "Food Aid – Normalising the Abnormal in Finland," *Social Policy and Society* 14: 471–482.

Sobhan, R. (1991) "The Politics of Hunger and Entitlement," in Drèze, J. & Sen, A. (eds.), *The Political Economy of Hunger: Volume 1: Entitlement and Well-being, Volume 1*, New York: Oxford University Press, pp. 79–111.

Stuff, J. E., Casey, P. H., Szeto, K. L., Gossett, J. M., Robbins, J. M., Simpson, P.M., Connell, C. & Bogle, M. L. (2004) "Household Food Insecurity is Associated with Adult Health Status," *The Journal of Nutrition* 134: 2330–2335.

Tarasuk, V. S. (2001) "Household Food Insecurity with Hunger Is Associated with Women's Food Intakes, Health and Household Circumstances," *The Journal of Nutrition* 131: 2670–2676.

Tarasuk, V. S. & Beaton, G. H. (1999) "Household Food Insecurity and Hunger Among Families Using Food Banks," *Canadian Journal of Public Health = Revue Canadienne de Sante Publique* 90: 109–113.

Tarasuk, V. S. & Dachner, N. (2009) "The Proliferation of Charitable Meal Programs in Toronto," *Canadian Public Policy / Analyse de Politiques* 35: 433–450.

Tarasuk, V., Dachner, N. & Loopstra, R. (2014) "Food Banks, Welfare, and Food Insecurity in Canada," *British Food Journal* 116: 1405–1417.

Tarasuk, V. S. & Eakin, J. M. (2003) "Charitable Food Assistance as Symbolic Gesture: An Ethnographic Study of Food Banks in Ontario," *Social Science & Medicine* 56: 1505–1515.

Tarasuk, V.S. & MacLean, H. (1990) "The Institutionalization of Food Banks in Canada: A Public Health Concern," *Canadian Journal of Public Health* 81(4): 331–332.

United Nations. (1948) *The Universal Declaration of Human Rights*, New York: United Nations.

——. (1966) *International Covenant on Economic, Social and Cultural Rights*, New York: United Nations.

Uttley, S. (1997) "New Zealand: A Question of Rights?," in Riches, G. (ed.), *First World Hunger: Food Security and Welfare Politics*, Toronto: University of Toronto Press, pp. 78–107.

Vozoris, N. T. & Tarasuk, V. S. (2003) "Household Food Insufficiency Is Associated with Poorer Health," *The Journal of Nutrition* 133: 120–126.

Warshawsky, D. N. (2010) "New Power Relations Served Here: The growth of food banking in Chicago," *Geoforum* 41: 763–775.

Watts, M. J. & Bohle, H. G. (1993) "Hunger, Famine and the Space of Vulnerability," *GeoJournal* 30(2): 117–125.

Wells, R. & Caraher, M. (2014) "UK Print Media Coverage of the Food Bank Phenomenon: From Food Welfare to Food Charity?" *British Food Journal* 116: 1426–1445.

Wilson, J. (1997) "Australia: Lucky Country/Hungry Silence," in Riches, G. (ed.), *First World Hunger: Food Security and Welfare Politics*, Toronto: University of Toronto Press, pp. 14–45.

Further Reading

E. A. Dowler and D. O'Connor, "Rights-Based Approaches to Addressing Food Poverty and Food Insecurity in Ireland and UK," *Social Science & Medicine* 74(2012): 44–51, concisely examines a human rights perspective on food insecurity, with a focus on health. B. Shepherd, "Thinking Critically About Food Security," *Security Dialogue* 43(2012): 195–212, provides a provocative reframing of food (in)security. J. Poppendieck, *Sweet Charity?: Emergency Food and the End of Entitlement* (New York: Viking Penguin, 1998), unpacks the context and implications of the charitable model of response to food insecurity. G. Riches, *Food Banks and the Welfare Crisis* (Toronto: James Lorimer & Company, 1986) gives a historically and geographically specific account of neoliberal/neoconservative policies, food insecurity, and food bank responses, which is unfortunately relevant today across many rich countries. The book edited by G. Riches, *First World Hunger: Food Security and Welfare Politics* (Toronto: University of Toronto Press, 1997) and its expanded second edition, edited by G. Riches and T. Silvasti, *First World Hunger Revisited* (Basingstoke: Palgrave Macmillan, 2014), are composed of chapters examining food insecurity in particular rich countries, and both offer some analysis of commonalities across these case studies.

37

ETHICS OF FOOD WASTE

Miranda Mirosa, David Pearson, and Rory Pearson

Introduction

Recent reports indicate that 30 to 50 percent of all food produced for human consumption is wasted and not eaten by humans (FAO 2011; IME 2013). Thus individuals and businesses continue to make decisions that result in this massive amount of food waste (Pearson et al. 2013). Although food losses occur throughout the supply chain, in developing countries most of this is prior to purchase by consumers – mainly due to limited investment in efficient storage, transport, and processing infrastructure, whilst in industrialized countries most is wasted by consumers – mainly due to food being relatively abundant and economically cheap (FAO 2011). Thus the magnitude, pervasiveness, and persistence of food waste suggest that it remains a complicated issue.

In order to investigate the ethical implications of the food waste issue, this chapter first considers the wider role of ethics in society (section 2) before moving on to discuss general ethical issues in relation to food (section 3). The case is made in these sections that an ethical food system would strive to supply all individuals with regular supply of a variety of healthy foods. Further, the production, distribution, and retailing would be carried out in an environmentally sustainable manner in which the welfare of animals is also upheld. In a more specific exploration of the ethics of food waste (section 4), it is suggested that food waste reduction is linked to reducing hunger, reducing obesity, and reducing environmental degradation. The links in each of these three areas are reviewed in turn. Responses to food waste are highlighted (section 5) prior to concluding comments (section 6).

Consideration of ethics in society

Ethics is considered by many to be the study of morality (see, for example, Williams 2012). In this sense it includes consideration of issues around what is "right" and consequently what is "wrong." As thousands of years of philosophical scholarship and debate demonstrate, there are no clear answers.

However, these endeavors have investigated questions of "the best way for people to live" (Grayling 2011), and what actions by individuals support the collective "best way to live," and hence are either "right" or "wrong" in a particular circumstance. Thus ethics has evolved to help us understand the inherent tension between the individual and continuation of the community in which he or she is a member. This interdependence pits the instincts in an individual that encourage selfish competitive actions against those that recognize the benefits from cooperation that facilitates continuation of a robust community.

It is important to note that "right" conduct may or may not be in accordance with existing behavior such as social conventions, religious beliefs, or even the law (Paul and Elder 2006). Thus ethics encourages removing cultural habits and personal beliefs to undertake independent thought involving analyzing and recommending concepts for "right" or "wrong" conduct. Although it is common to pose opposites, such as guilty or innocent, issues where ethics dominate are often much more complicated. As such most ethical analysis requires careful consideration of many facets that are integral to the issue. For example, phrasing an issue, "Is wasting food always wrong?" leads to recognition of the fact that there may be circumstances where wasting food is right or permissible. Thus ethics offers an approach to explore the array of interrelated and potentially conflicting circumstances around the enduring challenge of reducing food waste.

Ethical issues in relation to food

Alongside sophisticated technological and scientific developments in food production and nutrition, efficient means of food distribution, and unprecedented availability of food in some parts of the world, food is contested like never before (Lien and Anthony 2007). In a multicultural society it is natural to assume that there will be vastly differing ethical grounds for food-related behaviors of individuals. Vegetarian, kosher, halal, and vegan diets offer just some examples (Hepting et al. 2014). In addition to the differing ethical standpoints of individuals, there is the question of whether they, in spite of living in the information age, have access to information that enables them to make informed choices, on ethical issues among other things.

Food has been loaded with cultural meaning and immersed in ethical boundaries for thousands of years. In a brief chronology of significant ethical issues in relation to food, Zwart (2000) notes the following:

- Ancient Greeks used the term "dietetics" to describe living and acting in accordance with nature, where, due to the faculty of reason, mankind is forced to participate in a conscious manner.
- The Hebrew Bible identifies those foods that are allowed to be eaten and others that are not. For example, "Of all the larger land animals you may eat any hoofed animal which has cloven hoofs and also chews the cud; those which only have cloven hoofs or only chew the cud you must not eat" (Leviticus 11:1–4). The author continues by noting that efforts have been made to explain why these seemingly arbitrary laws exist, which have looked into health, hygiene, and other utilitarian concerns, finding limited evidence to support them.
- The New Testament offers an alternative by removing such constraints on food. For example, "No one is defiled by what goes into his mouth; only by what comes out of it. . . . Do you not see that whatever goes in by the mouth passes into the stomach and so is discharged at a certain place? But what comes out of the mouth has its origins in the heart; and that is what defiles a person." (Matthew 15:11–17)
- Medieval and Renaissance times added another food ethic in terms of prescribing times of fasting or regulations for special fasting-days, such as abstention from meat intake on Fridays and the forty-day period of fasting during Lent.

Pressing ethical issues of concern in contemporary society include animal welfare, food security, equity of consumption – as both hunger and obesity coexist – and finally environmental sustainability (Hepting et al. 2014).

The treatment of animals (embodying both animal welfare and animal rights) is a major ethical issue in relation to food. For example, some consumers are concerned about how animals are raised and slaughtered. Live export of animals and concentrated animal feeding operations (CAFOs), also known as factory farms, are considered especially inhumane and major sources of concern. Adopting more vegetarian and plant-based diets is a common response to such ethical concerns.

Consideration of food supply leads to identification of some individuals being more food secure than others, such as those who are more affluent. Food security is defined by United Nations Food and Agriculture Organization as "when all people, at all times, have physical, social and economic access to sufficient, safe and nutritious food which meets their dietary needs and food preferences for an active and healthy life" (UNFAO 2015). Food self-sufficiency, on the other hand, refers to the concept of sufficient food production to feed those living in the area under consideration, whether that is the local community or the whole country. The contention is that dependence on other areas to supply food creates vulnerability should supply lines be interrupted for reasons such as international tensions.

Consideration of the distribution of food leads to identification of significant inequities in food consumption. Some, often those who are marginalized, consume less food and, of even more importance, food of lower nutritional value. For example, those on lower incomes are more likely to buy higher quantities of energy-dense foods that are high in fat and sugar, because they are more affordable and accessible. This is further demonstrated by Sustainable Organic Local Ethical (SOLE) products, in that the economically disadvantaged may not have practical access to the full array of choices afforded to more affluent consumers (Hepting et al. 2014). This has led to the suggestion that ethical consumption of food may be an elite social practice, especially since some niche markets are positioned to serve wealthy, educated consumers (Johnston et al. 2011). Thus the ethical issues in relation to food are largely dependent on the part of the food chain put under scrutiny. Attention is now focused on the food wasted across the food chain and the ethical issues related to this waste, from farm to fork and beyond.

Ethics of food waste

When considered on a global scale the amount of food wasted is staggering – as previously mentioned around 30 to 50 percent. Theoretically this food could be used to feed those who are hungry today, contributing significantly to meeting the anticipated increase in demand for food that will accompany the growth in global population. In addition, and not often discussed, there is the issue of food being wasted due to excessive consumption by some individuals. This over-nutrition is evident in the prevalence of obesity around the world. Furthermore, the resources used to produce, transport, process, and store the food that is wasted have also been wasted when food is discarded. In an era of increasing concern about environmental sustainability, this waste of productive agricultural land, clean water, agricultural chemicals, and non-renewable energy resources – particularly those that contribute to greenhouse gas emissions – is of particular concern. The ethical issues of each of these, namely, the role that food waste reduction could play in reducing world hunger, reducing obesity, and reducing environmental degradation, will now be discussed in turn.

Reducing world hunger

According to the United Nations Universal Declaration of Human Rights, "All human beings are born free and equal in dignity and rights. They are endowed with reason and conscience and should act towards one another in a spirit of brotherhood" (Article 1) and "Everyone has the right to a standard of living adequate for the health and well-being of himself and of his family, including food ..." (Article 25) (UN 2015). These foundations for societal workings and processes include explicit noting of a food system that provides all people with safe and healthy food, while ensuring those working in the food system an adequate income. Further elaboration on this concept of a rights-based approach to food security can be found in this handbook, in "Responsibility for Hunger in Liberal Democracies."

However, despite this right to food, nearly 800 million people worldwide do not have enough to eat. This means that one in nine people are suffering from hunger (UNFAO 2015). Hunger and malnutrition are the number one risk to health worldwide. Hunger is not just an issue for developing countries. Kirkpatrick and Tarasuk (2011), for example, report that food insecurity is not uncommon in North America, where it affected 8 percent of Canadian households in 2007/2008 and 15 percent of US households in 2008.[1] Addressing global hunger is an incredibly urgent development challenge. However, it is not an easy challenge given the multifaceted nature of the causes of the problem. Contributing factors include, but are not limited to: poverty, natural disasters, conflict, poor agricultural infrastructure, lack of access to the marketplace, economic crises and volatile food prices, politics, and a person's socioeconomic status. One thing that is clear, however, is that people are not hungry because of a shortage of global food supply. The world is producing more than enough food to feed every single person on this planet. The Food and Agriculture Organization (2011) estimate that recovering just half of the food that is lost or wasted could feed the world alone.

Therefore, addressing world hunger is not simply a challenge of increasing food production; it is also a challenge to reduce the amount of food produced that is wasted. Of course, reducing food waste does not automatically translate into fewer hungry people. Sometimes it might result in just the opposite if, for example, people are relying on this discarded waste for their survival (Stuart 2009). However, "since the food supply has become a global phenomenon, and particularly where demand outstrips supply, putting food in the bin really is equivalent to taking it off the world market and out of the mouths of the starving" (Stuart 2009: 82).

One problem is that it is obviously not simply a matter of taking food waste and redistributing it to people that are hungry. Although there are initiatives underway to do just this (i.e., recover unwanted food from retail and redistribute it to food banks; see "Responses to Food Waste" section), these sorts of initiatives alone will not feed the nearly 800 million people worldwide that do not have enough to eat, most of whom are in developing countries and not in the industrialized countries where the food waste is produced.

This then leads us to the ethical issue of responsibility for addressing food waste: Are humans obligated, and if so, to what extent, to change their consumption patterns in order to benefit others who are not as privileged as them (Aiken and LaFollette 1996)? Remembering that the right to food is recognized as a fundamental human right, this would suggest that there should be obligation somewhere.

Research repeatedly shows that most people do feel guilty about wasting food (see, e.g., WasteMINZ 2014, in which 89 percent of the people surveyed agreed that wasting food felt wrong to them). As food waste advocate Stuart (2009) suggests, rather than feeling guilty about wasting food, people should feel empowered by the sense of responsibility, knowing that by making small adjustments in their everyday food habits, they can play a part in helping to improve the lives of people who are currently hungry. Other food waste scholars are quick to point out, though, that the issue of food waste cannot be conceptualized as a problem of individual consumer behavior, and therefore that it is of no use to simply blame consumers (Evans 2011). Such arguments are followed by suggestions that meaningful reductions in food waste will occur only when policies and interventions are targeted at the social and material conditions in which food is provisioned (Evans 2011).

Reducing obesity

Just as the inextricable links between public health concerns about hunger and food waste are clear, so too are the links between public health concerns about obesity and food waste. Global scale statistics highlight an apparent paradox – how can almost one billion people who do not have sufficient food be living on the same planet as over a billion people who are eating an excess of food? Whilst this massive imbalance remains – that is, some eating too much whilst others do not have enough – more detailed investigation identifies that obesity is determined not only by how much is eaten; rather, it is the particular foods that are eaten that contributes to this paradox.

It may be seen as a contrast between obesity and malnutrition – too much food as opposed to too little. Yet, obesity is both a problem of too much food and too much of the wrong food. The modern industrial food system has created some products that contribute to the enjoyment of life whilst making only limited contribution to human health. These are often processed convenience foods that have high levels of salt, sugar, and fat – also known by the colloquial term, junk foods. Obesity and to a lesser extent malnutrition are exacerbated when individuals increase the amount of junk food eaten, from being an occasional treat to being a regular staple component in their diet. The overconsumption of low-value, processed junk foods that contribute to poor nutritional outcomes is particularly prevalent in low-income and marginalized populations (Lang et al. 2009).

Whilst the practice of eating special food for special events can lead to feasts, where an excess of food that is ultimately wasted may be used – perhaps as a means to show power and wealth – the amount of food eaten on a daily basis is often in excess of the individual's requirements. Obesity caused by overconsumption of food, and its associated prevalence of junk food, thus represents a waste of food. Smil (2004) explicitly includes over-nutrition – the gap between the energy value of consumed food per capita and the energy value of food needed per capita – in his definitions of food waste. Scholars Blair and Sobal (2006) have defined the term "luxus consumption" to mean food waste and overconsumption, leading to storage of body fat, health problems, and excess resource utilization. They estimate that 18 percent of land and ocean hectares used to support the US diet is used to produce this luxus consumption.

Reducing environmental degradation

To consider the ethical issues relating to reducing food waste, we must consider the relationship between human beings and the natural environment. To a large extent increases in food production have emerged from increases in agricultural productivity, which have taken place at the expense of the natural environment. Historically these "costs" have been viewed as externalities in that they have not been reflected in an appropriate increase in the price of food.

Food production in the modern era has a massive impact on the local environment. Its impact has progressively increased since the first move from a nomadic hunter-gatherer lifestyle to fixed settlements, supported by what is now referred to as agriculture, around 10,000 years ago. The domestication of livestock and commencement of organized planting transforms local ecologies by encouraging a limited number of dominant and often new species. This has resulted in the reduction and even extinction of much native flora and fauna. Loss of biodiversity is of concern because it removes a gene bank that may include currently unexploited opportunities, and it can also be argued to have intrinsic worth that does not exist solely for human pleasure and taking. The emergence of coordinated maintenance for protected areas, such as National Parks and wildlife corridors, over the last 100 years aims to maintain limited areas of native habitat whilst allowing production of food to continue. Thus there is a loss of native ecosystems for the land that is used to produce food that is wasted.

Most production of food, with the exception of that produced in domestic gardens, occurs in peri-urban and rural areas outside of cities. Thus food producers, often referred to as farmers, and the rural communities that support them play a critical role in the management of natural resources. From the perspective of maintaining and enhancing the natural environment, it is desirable for these rural residents to be active stewards of the landscape in both coordinated and individual efforts.

In addition to the use of land, the food production systems that dominate around the globe are based on an industrial model. This requires significant external inputs of potentially scarce resources, such as clean, fresh water, agricultural chemicals, and energy. It is worth noting that some production systems, such as Certified Organic food, actively seek to reduce their use of these external inputs (see, for example, Pearson et al. 2011). However, other than a pure renewable harvest of food from areas where production has occurred without input from humans, such as "wild" harvests from wilderness areas, all food production still requires external inputs to a greater or lesser extent.

The production of large amounts of food from the use of land and external inputs using the industrial model of agriculture tends to result in some other outputs that have a negative impact on the natural environment. These include contamination of soil and waterways with agricultural chemicals and accumulation of other materials that are not recyclable, such as plastics. Collectively these may be seen as pollution.

There is concern that using industrial methods to produce meat, in particular, has a number of negative consequences. The ethical issues associated with eating meat and those relating to animal welfare are discussed elsewhere. Whilst being an excellent source of nutrition, the economic efficiencies of "industrial" production of meat has resulted in it becoming relatively cheaper, and as a result more is consumed. When meat production allows animals to forage for their food, animal welfare issues are reduced, and in many cases this provides food from an otherwise unproductive landscape – such as sheep feeding off hilly landscapes that could not be used for cropping. However, when the livestock are confined and their nutrients are brought to them – such as intensive chicken or pig production – the use of external inputs per unit of production increases massively, as does the environmental degradation.

And finally, there is concern with the increasing proportion of animal-based protein in human diets, particularly when this protein comes from high-external-input systems. Such systems require harvesting crops that are then fed to animals, which are then eaten by humans. This process is inherently inefficient due to the loss of energy embedded in the food. For example, a human would derive significantly more energy, as measured in kilojoules or calories, if she or he ate the edible component of the crop, rather than that of the animal that has eaten the crop. Thus the waste of proteins derived from animals is of particular concern.

In summary, any food that is wasted squanders the resources used in its production. In terms of reducing environmental degradation, of particular concern are reducing greenhouse gas emissions, mainly from energy derived from fossil fuels, whilst also aiming to reduce use of clean, fresh water. These environmental costs are present at every stage of the food chain – from production, processing, distribution, and consumption. And these costs escalate; the higher up the food system the food waste occurs from farm to fork, the more detrimental the waste is to the environment.

In addition to the abovementioned negative environmental consequences of wasted food along the supply chain, the disposal of the food waste itself is also problematic. Food that is landfilled is generally compacted down and covered, which removes the oxygen, causing it to break down in an anaerobic process. This rotting food produces methane, a greenhouse gas. Pound for pound, the comparative impact of methane on climate change is 25 times greater than carbon dioxide over a 100-year period (EPA 2015). The implications of landfilling food waste therefore are severe for global warming and climate change. Some countries, including Taiwan and South Korea, have already banned landfilling food. While reducing the volume of food waste generated at the source is preferable, if food waste is created, there are other less environmentally damaging ways of disposing of it, including feeding it to people or to animals, or using it for industrial purposes. Composting eliminates many of the problems of landfilling food, and in the process it recycles essential yet finite nutrients. Putting waste in digesters to produce energy in the form of a biogas is another option. However, while some disposal methods are obviously better for the environment than others, the fact remains that food that is not eaten has unnecessarily wasted the resources that have gone into growing, transporting, storing, selling, buying, and cooking the food, and it thus has caused much needless environmental degradation.

Responses to food waste

As more of the global population seeks increasing convenience in their "income rich, time poor" lifestyles, it is likely that some food will continue to be wasted. However, there are also interesting developments that are aiming to reduce food waste at various food waste hotspots along the food system. Downstream in the supply chain, initiatives are underway to cut crop waste. Crops that were previously left to rot in the fields, because of bad weather, market imperfections, or canceled supply contracts with buyers, are now instead being harvested by groups of gleaners – volunteers that collect excess fresh foods direct from the farmers' fields to donate to people in need. Scientists are working on advancing post-harvest technologies to control quality and extend the shelf life of fresh products. The food-processing and logistics industries are finding solutions for their waste with innovations that range from new packaging and storage technologies to finding ways to create value from byproducts. Food retailers are selling "ugly" fresh produce for cheaper, removing promotions that explicitly encourage overconsumption, such as "two-for-one" deals, and selling nearly expired food for a discount as well. The food hospitality industry is experimenting with waste-reduction initiatives such as downsizing meals, reducing menu options, providing doggy bags, and charging diners extra that leave food on their plates. Food that is not able to be sold by retailers and caterers is increasingly being donated to food-rescue organizations that divert unwanted food from supermarkets and catering organizations to help feed the hungry. If not donated to such organizations, wasted food from the retail and hospitality sectors is often targeted by dumpster divers who eat food collected from waste bins. Further up the food supply chain, there are significant efforts contributing to reducing consumer food waste by providing information, education, and inspiration for individuals in their private and professional lives. One of the high-profile activities in this area is the Waste Resources Action Program, based in the UK, which works with individuals, community groups, and businesses to reduce food waste through its Love Food Hate Waste community engagement program (WRAP 2015).

Concluding comments

The waste of food in society is not a new phenomenon. Nor are efforts to reduce it. Citizens in countries on both sides of WWI and WWII were encouraged in government-sponsored, social marketing campaigns to be patriotic by not wasting food. Predating this in the 19th century, food waste prevention advice was plentiful in the household manuals and cookbooks of the time (Strasser 1999). However, over recent decades food waste is being (re)subjected to scrutiny as the importance of both food security and environmental degradation are increasing on the national and international political agendas. In addition, recent investigations have highlighted the massive negative impact that the food system is having on the natural environment, and food waste is one area in which individuals are likely to make changes (Pearson et al. 2014).

Although there may be some economic reasons, such as reducing costs, pursuing behaviors that aim to reduce food waste is essentially an ethical choice. It requires individuals and organizations to behave in ways that meet their own pleasures and aspirations whilst simultaneously minimizing the harm done to individuals, animals, and the natural environment more generally.

This chapter has highlighted the fundamental ties between food waste, human health, and the health of our planet. The scale of global food waste is shocking, and this wasted food results in a number of ethically questionable implications. As the impacts of food insecurity, obesity, and climate change really start to hit home, food waste looks set to become one of the major social justice, public health, and environmental issues of our time. The upside of the food waste reduction challenge is that there is enormous scope for improvement by all players in the food system. There has been an increasing amount of noise about the food waste issue in recent years, which is a signal that major changes are on the way. A common thread in these food waste conversations is that food waste is morally outrageous. As such, addressing food waste is likely to be an effective way to initiate some of the other more general pro-environmental/social behavior changes required in our food system if we are to be able to ethically and sustainably feed the predicted nine billion people that will live on this planet by 2050.

Note

1 Note that these data are not directly comparable due to differences in measures used to determine food security status.

References

Aiken, W., & LaFollette, H. (1996) *World Hunger and Morality*, 2nd ed., Upper Saddle River, NJ: Prentice Hall, Inc.

Blair, D., & Sobal, J. (2006) "Luxus Consumption: Wasting Food Resources Through Overeating," *Agriculture and Human Values* 23(1): 63–74.

Environmental Protection Agency. (2015) *Overview of Greenhouse Gases, Methane Emissions*, viewed 17 July 2015, http://epa.gov/climatechange/ghgemissions/gases/ch4.html.

Evans, D. (2011) "Blaming the Consumer–Once Again: The Social and Material Contexts of Everyday Food Waste Practices in Some English Households," *Critical Public Health* 21(4): 429–440.

FAO (Food and Agriculture Organization). (2011) *Global Food Losses and Food Waste*, Rome: United Nations.

Grayling, A. C. (2011) *What Is Good? The Search for the Best Way to Live*, London: Phoenix.

Hepting, D. H., Jaffe, J., & Maciag, T. (2014) "Operationalizing Ethics in Food Choice Decisions," *Journal of Agricultural and Environmental Ethics* 27(3): 453–469.

IME (Institute of Mechanical Engineers). (2013) *Global Food: Waste Not, Want Not*, viewed 17 July 2015, http://www.imeche.org/docs/default-source/reports/Global_Food_Report.pdf.

Johnston, J., Szabo, M., & Rodney, A. (2011) "Good Food, Good People: Understanding the Cultural Repertoire of Ethical Eating," *Journal of Consumer Culture* 11(3): 293–318.

Kirkpatrick, S. I., & Tarasuk, V. (2011) "Housing Circumstances are Associated with Household Food Access Among Low-Income Urban Families," *Journal of Urban Health* 88(2): 284–296.

Lang, T., Barling, D., & Caraher, M. (2009) *Food Policy: Integrating Health, Environment and Society*. Oxford: Oxford University Press.

Lien, M. E., & Anthony, R. (2007) "Ethics and the Politics of Food," *Journal of Agricultural and Environmental Ethics* 20(5): 413–417.

Paul, R., & Elder, L. (2006) *The Miniature Guide to Understanding the Foundations of Ethical Reasoning*, Tomales, CA, United States: Foundation for Critical Thinking Free Press.

Pearson, D., Friel, S., & Lawrence, M. (2014) "Building Environmentally Sustainable Food Systems on Informed Citizen Choices: Evidence from Australia," *Biological Agriculture and Horticulture* 30(3): 183–197.

Pearson, D., Henryks, J., & Jones, H. (2011) "Organic Food: What we Know (and do not know) about Consumers," *Renewable Agriculture and Food Systems* 26(2): 171–177.

Pearson, D., Minehan, M., & Wakefield-Rann, R. (2013) "Food Waste in Australian Households: Why does it Occur?," *Locale: The Pacific Journal of Regional Food Studies* 3: 118–132.

Smil, V. (2004) "Improving Efficiency and Reducing Waste in our Food System," *Environmental Sciences* 1(1): 17–26.

Strasser, S. (1999) *Waste and Want: A Social History of Trash*, New York: Metropolitan Book.

Stuart, T. (2009) *Waste: Uncovering the Global Food Scandal*, New York: Norton.

UN (United Nations). (2015) *The Universal Declaration of Human Rights*, viewed 17 July 2015, http://www.un.org/en/documents/udhr/.

UNFAO (United Nations Food and Agriculture Organization). (2015) *Food Security Statistics*, viewed 17 July 2015, http://www.fao.org/economic/ess/ess-fs/en/.

WasteMINZ. (2014) *National Food Waste Prevention Study: National Report New Zealand*, viewed 17 July 2015, http://www.wasteminz.org.nz/pubs/national-food-waste-prevention-study-into-attidutes-towards-food-waste/.

Williams, B. (2012) *Morality: An Introduction to Ethics*, Cambridge: Cambridge University Press.

WRAP (Waste Resources Action Plan). (2015) *Save More Evaluation Report*, Banbury, UK.

Zwart, H. (2000) "A Short History of Food Ethics," *Journal of Agricultural and Environmental Ethics* 12(2), 113–126.

38

FOOD SECURITY AND ETHICS

Marko Ahteensuu and Helena Siipi[1]

Introduction

The world is far from being food secure. The current food systems fail to satisfy the nutritional needs of the human population. According to the estimates of the Food and Agriculture Organization of the United Nations (FAO 2015), globally 795 million people are undernourished between 2014 and 2016. This means that hundreds of millions of individuals live in hunger and do not get sufficient calories from the food they consume. Furthermore, an even greater number suffers from lack of necessary micronutrients. It has been estimated, for example, that around two billion people are iron deficient (see, e.g., Pinstrup-Andersen 2009: 7) and that almost a third of the world's population fail to get enough iodine from their food (see, e.g., Korthals 2015: 243).

The international community has set goals to enhance food security and to fight hunger in the world. Among the most well-known are the *1996 Rome Declaration on World Food Security* target to halve the *number* of hungry people and the *2001 Millennium Development Goal 1C* (MDG 1C)[2] target to halve the *proportion* of hungry people in the total population, both by 2015. The FAO (2015: 9) reports that the proportion of hungry people in 2015 is significantly smaller than in 2001 and that the Millennium Development Goal 1C target "can be considered as having been achieved." Because of high rates of *population growth* in many hunger-affected areas, the goal of the Rome Declaration, however, will be missed by a large margin. Yet, FAO announces "significant progress in fighting hunger over the past decade" (FAO 2015: 9).[3]

In addition to population growth (see, e.g., Misselhorn 2012), several other factors make enhancing global food security a difficult task. These include increased wealth, which is strongly associated with *higher levels of consumption* (Agarwal 2015: 275), *loss of agricultural land* through urbanization and soil erosion (Godfray et al. 2010), *climate change* (Schmidhuber and Tubiello 2007), and *overexploitation of natural resources and ecosystem services* (Godfray et al. 2010). Together these challenges necessitate modifying food production and consumption as old practices simply become unsuccessful. Crop plants, for example, may no longer succeed in the new climates of the areas where they are currently grown (Lever-Tracy 2014). Poppy and colleagues (2014: 1) conclude that "[w]e must increase food security sustainably and in a climate change-resilient manner, while also reducing greenhouse gas emissions, alleviating poverty and conserving biodiversity: perhaps the greatest challenge that we have ever faced."

Proposed ways to reduce global food insecurity include (1) reducing world population growth, (2) increasing agricultural productivity, (3) reducing wastage, (4) fighting poverty, (5) changing the ways of food distribution, and (6) changing the world diet (Cribb 2011; Godfray et al. 2010; Sandler 2015: 52–58). Most experts agree that none of these undertakings alone can solve the problem. Where they differ, however, is which one or ones should be prioritized. Furthermore, it is not only the proposed solutions that vary, but also the views regarding the best means to achieve them. For example, should reducing population growth be achieved by policies such as China's one child policy or by increasing the level of education in developing countries? Could a significant increase in productivity be achieved by a large-scale use of GM crop varieties (Newell-McLoughlin 2015) or by agroecological approaches (Uphoff 2015)?

In this chapter, we will take a step back and pose the following questions: What does food security mean? Why does food security matter? What kinds of obligations pertain to the goal of increasing global food security, and to whom do they apply? Answers to these questions are interrelated: what is understood by food security delineates the scope of reasons for why it matters and whether there are obligations related to enhancing it. Definitions of food security are far from insignificant wordplay as they carry momentous policy implications. For example, the fact that the current definitions focus on the quality of food (e.g., the availability of micronutrients), and not merely its amount, has important consequences for suitable policy alternatives. Moreover, the definitions fix not only what is aimed at, but also how food secure the world appears to be. The more demanding the definition adopted, the lower the level of food security measured by indicators.[4]

What does food security mean?

The term *food security* was coined at the *World Food Conference* in 1974. According to the definition given then, it means "availability at all times of adequate world food supplies of basic food-stuffs to sustain a steady expansion of food consumption and to offset fluctuations in production and prices" (UN 1975: 6). The definition focuses on availability of food in terms of food supply. Sufficiency of food is seen as a global concern, which corresponds to efforts in the seventies to create international systems of grain reserves. Nevertheless, food security was first applied at the national level, and it was strongly connected to the ideals of national self-sufficiency and food systems as a matter of national policies (Cardwell 2014: 965; Pinstrup-Andersen 2009: 5).

Since the early seventies, a plethora of definitions for food security has been put forth. Answers to the questions "Who or what can be food secure?" and "What does it imply to be food secure?" have changed. Two trends have been to widen the sphere of (individual and collective) agents that can be considered food secure and to add new requirements. The mere existence of large amounts of food, certainly, is no longer considered sufficient for food security. In particular, four important developments have taken place in the past forty years (see, e.g., Cardwell 2014; Hadiprayitno 2014).

First, the interest has turned from national food security to food security of households and individuals (Maxwell 1996: 157). The fundamental drawback of the focus (solely) on the national food supply is that the food available is not necessarily distributed equally among citizens. Even when the supply appears sufficient from the point of view of per capita calculations, this does not guarantee that all households or individuals get enough to eat (Cardwell 2014: 965). The focus is also problematic in failing to acknowledge the global nature of the current food markets and food systems. The country in which food is consumed often differs from the one in which it is produced. As a result, the macro-level interest is today mostly in global food security (Pinstrup-Andersen 2009: 7).

A second and related development is that, from concentrating on the amount of food, the interest has shifted toward access to food, owing largely to the seminal work by Amartya Sen. Food insecurity connects to *extreme poverty:* some people just do not have enough money to buy food, the means to produce it, or a possibility to access food sources in safe and socially acceptable ways (McDonald 2010: 15).[5]

Third, requirements for food security have been broadened to include safety and nutritional quality of food. A group (or an individual) should not be considered food secure if the food it (or he/she) has access to fails to be safe or lacks necessary nutrients. The level of food security of even an obese individual can be low, if he or she has access only to low-quality food. In fact, a low level of food security in industrialized countries is often associated with obesity (Cardwell 2014: 965; Renzaho and Mellor 2010: 7).

The fourth change has been the introduction of indicators that admit the inclusion of subjective experiences. Access to safe and nutritious food is not sufficient for food security if the food is such that one *considers* it unacceptable or inedible, that is, against one's religious, cultural, or personal values (Pinstrup-Andersen 2009: 6). The experienced level of food security has also been suggested to be central: "people are food secure [only] when a food system operates in such a way as to remove the fear that there will not be enough to eat" (Maxwell 1996: 159).

Currently, the most commonly employed definition of food security accommodates virtually all of these developments; it states that food security exists "when all people, at all times, have physical and economic access to sufficient, safe and nutritious food to meet their dietary needs and food preferences for an active and healthy life" (FAO 1996). The definition is typically understood to describe *four dimensions* of food security: availability, access, utilization, and stability. The dimensions are hierarchical. Without availability of food, access to it is never possible. Availability and access are necessary, but not sufficient, for efficient utilization. The question of stability arises only with respect to the other three dimensions (Barrett 2010: 825; see also Misselhorn et al. 2012).

Availability refers to the quantity, quality, diversity, and desirability of food supply. A high level of food availability implies the existence of a sufficient supply of safe and nutritious food that is compatible with people's preferences (Pinstrup-Andersen 2009: 5–6). On a *global level*, availability is a question of the amount of food in relation to the world population: is there enough for all? On a *local level*, availability is concerned with the existence of food in a certain area (e.g., a state, region, or village). On the level of a *household* or an *individual*, availability pertains to the existence of food in places sufficiently near to one's household (or a living environment when homeless or staying in a temporary shelter).

Access concerns the affordability and allocation of the food supply. While it highlights food insecurity's close relationship to *poverty*, lack of money is not the sole cause of a lack of access. Rather, access is contingent on a large web of socio-economic determinants (Dilley and Boudreau 2001: 233). Even when food exists near to a household, its members may lack safe, tolerable, and dignified means to reach it.

Utilization divides into physical and biological components. *Physical* utilization refers to the infrastructure needed for transporting food, as well as to the facilities needed for storing and preparing it. It also concerns food-related workload and time available for cooking. *Biological* utilization refers to the human body's capacity to use the nutrients of the food consumed. Infections and diseases can diminish it and, thus, biological utilization is strongly dependent on access to clean water, sanitation, and health care (Barrett 2010: 825; Misselhorn et al. 2012: 7–8; Renzaho and Mellor 2010: 6). It is noteworthy that both types of utilization hinge partly on the knowledge and skills of individuals and can sometimes be enhanced by education (Keenan et al. 2001).

Stability draws on the fact that food availability, access, and utilization are dynamic and changing states of affairs dependent on various factors.[6] Not all food-secure individuals, households, and areas remain such at all times, and food-insecure agents may turn into food-secure ones. Some households and areas are nonetheless more stable than others. A low level of stability is related to *vulnerability*, which is increasingly shaped by climate change: "The number of extreme events such as droughts, floods and hurricanes has increased in recent years, as has the unpredictability of weather patterns, leading to substantial losses in production and lower incomes in vulnerable areas" (FAO 2013: 22; see also Brown and Funk 2008).

While the result of over forty years of refinement, the current FAO definition of food security and its four dimensions are not unproblematic. With the inclusion of the requirements for safety and food preferences, for instance, food security has become a complex state of affairs, far removed from simple lack of hunger. The definition thus raises questions concerning the sufficient degree of safety and the relevance of different kinds of preferences. Pinstrup-Andersen (2009: 6) poses the question whether the definition "can be used to guide policies and programs or whether there is a need to disaggregate the concept into different kinds of food insecurity depending on the nature and severity of the problem and the type of solution required." Indeed, food insecurity for people in *industrialized countries*, especially when linked to obesity accompanied by the lack of micronutrients, is very different from food insecurity for the poorest people in *developing countries*, where it often means undernourishment that results in *wasting* (i.e., being too thin for one's height) and the permanent condition of *stunting* (i.e., being too short for one's age) of children.

Why does food security matter?

Why is increasing food security of value? As every human being needs nutritionally adequate and safe food, and as for many this basic need remains unfulfilled, the legitimacy of the goal to enhance food security appears self-evident (Cardwell 2014: 964).[7] But food security actually contributes to a number of ends. To begin with, the motives to enhance food security can be moral or non-moral (Hadiprayitno 2014). An example of a *non-moral motivation* is the belief that achieving the goal is economically beneficial. *Moral motivations* may follow from rights-based, consequentialist, and virtue-based approaches to ethics.[8] According to the moral motivations, food security has *instrumental value* as it helps people to pursue a meaningful life and to attain other things valuable in themselves.

From the point of view of rights-based ethics, the answer to the question posed is that food insecurity infringes basic rights (Eide 2015). Human beings have a right to nutritious, safe food that is sufficient and acceptable for them, and a high level of food security protects that right at different levels, from individuals and households to the world population. In particular, food security protects *the right to food* that was enshrined in Article 25 of the United Nations' *Universal Declaration of Human Rights* in 1948 and listed together with housing, clothing, medical care, and other basic necessities for individuals' health and wellbeing. This right to food has later been included in many other international human rights declarations and conventions.

Food security and the right to food can be seen as closely related – both, for example, have been considered to emphasize food availability, access, safety, and cultural acceptability – and the notions have sometimes been used as synonyms. However, a closer look reveals their differences. While food security is a goal of national and international policies, the right to food is a legal and moral concept. As a legal right, the latter can be violated, and its violation can be the subject of juridical remedies. Another difference is that food security can be pursued on non-moral grounds, whereas the right to food as a human right is based on human dignity and autonomy, and thus renders all other considerations secondary (Hadiprayitno 2014: 961).

According to a consequentialist view, morality requires enhancing the overall wellbeing of humans, and a high level of food security contributes to this aim. A high quality of life is thus considered intrinsically valuable, a good thing in itself. Increasing food security carries further instrumental value because it alleviates human suffering (which, according to negative utilitarianism, is the morally right thing to do) and because it is necessary for welfare (which is the sole moral concern according to certain forms of positive utilitarianism). Following the Aristotelian virtue ethics tradition, food security may be thought to further human flourishing as it enables us to move closer to human telos, *eudaimonia*.

It may, moreover, be argued that food security contributes to other valuable things, such as peace and stability (McDonald 2010: 17). Food security also makes possible autonomous choices with regard to food and other things. In particular, food security enables individuals to choose (buy or produce) their food according to their deeply held ethical values, in socially and culturally acceptable ways, and consistently with religious prescriptions. A certain level of adequate nutrition and energy intake are, needless to say, preconditions to be met before most other personal projects even become possible.

Increasing food security also enhances distributive justice. While it may do so in the relative sense of the term by narrowing welfare differences (globally or within a society), it always does so in the absolute sense that the worst-off people are brought up to a minimum standard of living. Furthermore, efforts to erase food insecurity help to target marginalized and vulnerable groups, such as children, that are often hit the hardest by extreme poverty and disasters (e.g., Barrett 2010: 827). This is in line with prioritarianism, the view that the worse off a person the more important, morally speaking, are benefits for him or her.

It is noteworthy, however, that in a broader understanding of food justice, food security alone seems insufficient. This is because of its mere focus on distribution and blindness to recognition and participation, both of which arguably are necessary for justice in a wider sense of the term. This shortcoming could be remedied by, as has been suggested, combining the goal of food security with that of food sovereignty (Murdock and Noll 2015).

What food-security-related obligations are there?

Given the basic right(s) that food security protects and ethical values to which it contributes, the enhancement of food security can be considered morally necessary. But who has the duty to bring about the required changes in the food systems? And what are the duty-bearers obligated to do? Possible answers to the first question include nation-states and individuals – which form our focus here – but also the international community, as well as corporations running the global food markets.

Nation-states

Historically, it is the nation-state that has been considered the primary duty-bearer: "[l]ike many other human rights, the state is the duty-bearer of the right to food" (Hadiprayitno 2014: 960; see also Eide 2015: 65–67). Nation-states certainly have duties toward their own citizens, but often they are taken also to have duties toward other nation-states and their citizens. As discussed by Irene Hadiprayitno (2014), Wenche Barth Eide (2015), and Claire Debucquois (2014), the duties of states regarding the food security of their own citizens can be divided into three duties as follows.

First, a state has a negative duty to *respect* the food security of its citizens. According to a strict understanding, states may never take measures that hinder any citizen from having access to safe and nutritious food. This, however, seems not to be feasible in practice. Alternatively, the duty might be understood as an obligation not to diminish a nation's overall food security, not to opt for policies that can be (fore)seen to reduce someone's food security, or not to accept policies that are likely to diminish the food security of some citizen(s) below a certain level. A problem with these alternative ways to interpret the duty is that they seem to fail to sufficiently protect citizens' rights.

Second, states have a duty to *protect* the food security of their citizens. They should act in ways that ensure that third parties (e.g., other states or corporations) do not deprive citizens of access to safe and nutritious food. A challenge with this kind of obligation is that, in some cases, consequences of the actions of third parties may be hard to detect. One cannot say, for example, that trade of agricultural products always increases or decreases local food security (Cardwell 2014). "Trade, in itself, is neither a threat nor a panacea when it comes to food security" (FAO 2015: 35).

The third duty is:

> the obligation to *fulfill* (facilitate) [food security, which] means that states must proactively engage in activities intended to *strengthen* people's access to and utilization of resources and means to ensure their livelihood and food security. Whenever an individual or a group is unable, for reasons beyond their control, to enjoy the right to adequate food by the means at their disposal, states have an obligation to fulfill (provide) that right directly.
>
> (Debucquois 2014: 9; italics added)

As can be seen from the quotation, states are not usually thought to have an absolute obligation to provide food to their citizens. Their role is to promote conditions in which everybody is able to feed themselves or their households. In addition to this, states have an obligation to provide food when someone is at risk of suffering hunger for "reasons beyond their control." What constitutes these reasons, however, leaves room for different interpretations.

Sometimes nation-states do not or are unable to carry out their duties regarding the food security of their own citizens. In such cases, what kinds of duties, if any, do other states have? Especially, what kinds of duties do the well-off states have regarding the citizens of food-insecure nations? The duty to respect food security, explained above, is a negative duty *not to harm others*. From the human rights and justice points of view, there appears to be no obvious moral justification for restricting this duty to citizens of one's own country. This concerns both non-citizens in one's own country and people in other countries. In the era of global food markets, the practical implications of this duty regarding the latter pertain, at least, to acceptable forms of trade of agricultural products and the farmland.

Duties of the well-off nations need not be restricted to the negative sort. Several arguments have been presented for the claim that well-off states have a duty to *facilitate* food security in poor countries. *Historical arguments* point to the fact the affluent countries have had a major contribution in bringing about food insecurity by their past actions (e.g., by colonialism, slave trade, and armed conflicts). According to the so-called *international-order arguments*, the current international order often works against the interests of the poorer countries. On similar lines, the *shared-benefits argument* is based on the thesis that the poverty of developing countries gives affluent countries access to inexpensive labor, cheap food, and agricultural land (Sandler 2015: 60–61; see also Pogge 2005). One instance of this is *land-grabbing*, which means either that farmers (or farm workers) in developing countries receive so little money from the food produced that it is not sufficient for the food security of their families, or that a global corporation or another nation-state buys or rents land from a developing country and thus takes it away from local food production (Tscharntke 2012: 55).

All three arguments above are intended to justify *contribution-related obligations*. Actions of well-off states are at least part of the cause (and, thus, the states are responsible) for food insecurity. Therefore, they have a duty to correct and minimize the damage caused. It is important to note that nation-states may have *positive obligations* even when they have not contributed to food insecurity. This follows from human rights – such as the right to food – being universal. They should be protected worldwide. Furthermore, opportunities for people born in affluent countries and those born in food-insecure countries differ dramatically. This is not fair and, thus, nation-states and the international community have an obligation to try to equalize the opportunities people have. As a low level of food security dramatically circumscribes one's possibilities, affluent states have an obligation to protect and facilitate food security in food-insecure countries (Gilabert 2004; Sandler 2015: 61).

Individuals

Do individuals have obligations related to enhancing global food security? Affluent individuals could contribute to it through (1) changes to their own consumption habits, (2) charity, and (3) political action and political consumerism (e.g., voting, being active in NGOs, boycotts, and purchasing choices). The distinction between respecting, protecting, and facilitating proves helpful also in regard to these three forms of action.

In practice, respecting food security implies omitting ways of consumption that jeopardize the food security of others. Because of the highly complicated causal chains (or nets) in the global food system, it may often be practically impossible for individual consumers to find out the effects of their purchasing choices. Yet, some causal chains are known and well documented, and it may be argued that it follows from the duty of respect that affluent individuals should, for example, reduce their meat consumption and food wastage. Compared to other sources of protein, meat production is typically inefficient. Land used for growing feed could instead be used for food crops. Meat production further contributes to climate change, which, in turn, threatens global food security (see, e.g., Godfray 2010: 816–817; Martindale 2015: 45; McDonald 2010: 58–59, 68–69). Meat is not just eaten; like other food, it is wasted by affluent individuals who throw it away, over-consume it, and process it in ways that strip its nutrients. In short, "waste and over-consumption of inappropriate foods have knock-on effects in global food systems" (Christoplos and Pain 2015: 3).

Do affluent individuals have a duty to *facilitate* global food security by donating money to development and food aid organizations? Peter Singer famously argues for a duty to help others when one is in a position to do so and the cost of helping is not too high. In Singer's thought experiment, a person sees a child who is drowning in a pond. Most of us intuitively agree that this person has a duty to (try to) save the child, even if it will have some cost (of lesser moral importance) for him – it will, for example, ruin his new suit. Singer continues by noting that distance between a helper and the one helped is not an *ethically relevant factor*, that is, a factor that would justify different moral judgment when the child in need of help is far away. Thus, according to Singer, our ethical intuitions regarding the pond case show that affluent individuals have a duty to help food-insecure individuals in distant countries. The thought experiment has been much debated ever since, often with a goal to point out an ethically relevant difference between helping the drowning child and food aid. This has, however, proved to be a rather challenging task (see, e.g., Sandler 2015: 66; Wenar 2010).

An important goal of political consumerism is to *protect* food security of less well-off individuals and groups. *Political consumerism* refers to consumer choices of products that are, at least partly, motivated by ethical views and by a desire to shape food markets accordingly. Presumably, the most common actions are boycotts against corporations that are considered to behave in morally questionable ways. Such purchasing choices are meant to compel food companies to act in accordance with consumer demand and support morally preferable policies in the food markets (Micheletti et al. 2004; Stolle et al. 2005: 246). Political consumerism and action seems to be needed since the current global food system, and the multinational corporations' control over it, can worsen the position of the poorest: "[t]he global system for pricing farm products and farming inputs acts strongly against the long-term interests of food security" (Cribb 2011: 124).

Conclusion

Enhancing food security has, in various policy documents, been listed among the most important goals and greatest challenges of humankind in the coming decades. In this paper, we asked: What exactly does food security mean? Why does it matter ethically? And, are there food-security-related obligations?

We have argued first that different definitions of food security carry momentous policy implications. In line with this, Hadiprayitno (2014: 958) notes that "[t]he changes in defining the substantive meaning of food security are to a certain extent reflected in the transformation regarding the ways in which international community addresses the issues of feeding the world."

Second, food security is instrumentally valuable as it protects the right to food and contributes to a number of ends, such as alleviating human suffering. Some of these valuable things benefit an individual, while others (such as peace) benefit a society more generally. This is related to an immensely difficult question in ethics: to what extent, if any, can benefits to some justify burdens on others? A further point is that food security, as currently defined, is a complex and highly demanding state of affairs, much broader than the lack of hunger. Yet, part of its instrumental value does not require this inclusive notion of food security, but follows from the basic need for adequate nutrition and sufficient energy intake.

Finally, states and individuals have obligations to enhance global food security. It is problematic, however, to consider them the sole duty-bearers. In keeping with the Kantian principle that *ought implies can*, since the food markets and systems are global, it may well be that the weightiest duties rest on the international community and multinational corporations. They may have the greatest ability to bring about change on the global scale that is necessary.

Notes

1 Contribution of the authors is equal.
2 There are eight Millennium Development Goals. The first goal is to "eradicate extreme poverty and hunger" and its sub-goal C reads: "halve, between 1990 and 2015, the proportion of people who suffer from hunger" (United Nations 2015).
3 Not all agree that the success has been as great as presented by the FAO. Thomas Pogge (2013) argues that the decreases in numbers of the hungry are partly due to changes made to the methodology of counting as well as to the definition of being hungry.
4 As food security is measured by a suite of proxy indicators (see, e.g., Barrett 2010; Headey and Ecker 2013) that focus on particular aspects or dimensions of food security, the link also works in another direction: the choice of an indicator partially determines how food (in)secure the current situation appears and which policy interventions seem appropriate. In line with this, Christopher B. Barrett (2010: 827) writes that food security "[m]easurement drives diagnosis and response."
5 The connection between poverty and food security is not simple. In Nepal and Vietnam, for instance, levels of undernourishment are relatively low despite high levels of extreme poverty (FAO 2013: 27). At the same time, economic growth does not lead to improved food security in all countries (FAO 2015: 28–30).
6 Instead of the stability dimension, Andre M. N. Renzaho and David Mellor (2010) speak about *asset creation*, i.e., people's own abilities and *coping strategies*.

7 Even if security is necessary for one to enjoy his/her freedoms and rights, the rhetoric of security can also be (mis-)used to "justify" actions that curb personal freedoms and rights, e.g., privacy. The crucial questions are: How secure is secure enough? And to what extent can other valuable things (i.e., goods and rights) be justifiably sacrificed in order to achieve that level of security?

8 Other approaches within which food security may also be considered to include, for example, deontology and ethics of care (because providing someone food is an important part of taking care of him/her).

References

Agarwal, B. (2015) "Food Security, Productivity, and Gender Inequality," in R. J. Herring (ed.), *The Oxford Handbook of Food, Politics, and Society*, New York: Oxford University Press, pp. 273–300.

Barrett, C. B. (2010) "Measuring Food Insecurity," *Science* 327(12 February): 825–828.

Brown, M. B. & Funk, C. C. (2008) "Food Security Under Climate Change," *Science* 319(5863): 580–581.

Cardwell, R. (2014) "Food Security and International Trade," in P. B. Thompson & D. M. Kaplan (eds.), *Encyclopedia of Food and Agricultural Ethics*, New York: Springer, pp. 964–972.

Christoplos, I. & Pain, A., eds. (2015) *New Challenges to Food Security: From Climate Change to Fragile States*, London: Routledge.

Cribb, J.H.J. (2011) "Food Security: What Are the Priorities?," *Food Security* 3: 123–125.

Debucquois, C. (2014) "Access to Land and the Right to Food," in P. B. Thompson & D. M. Kaplan (eds.), *Encyclopedia of Food and Agricultural Ethics*, New York: Springer, pp. 8–11.

Dilley, M. & Boudreau, T. E. (2001) "Coming to Terms with Vulnerability: A Critique of the Food Security Definition," *Food Policy* 26: 229–247.

Eide, W. B. (2015) "Strengthening Food Security Through Human Rights: A Moral and Legal Imperative and Practical Opportunity," in I. Christoplos & A. Pain (eds.), *New Challenges to Food Security: From Climate Change to Fragile States*, London: Routledge, pp. 63–84.

Food and Agriculture Organization of United Nations. (1996) *Rome Declaration on World Food Security and World Food Summit Plan for Action*, viewed 24 June 2015, http://www.fao.org/docrep/003/w3613e/w3613e00.HTM.

———. (2013) *The State of Food Insecurity in the World: The Multiple Dimensions of Food Security*, viewed 24 June 2015, http://www.fao.org/docrep/018/i3434e/i3434e.pdf.

———. (2015) *The State of Food Insecurity in the World*, viewed 24 June 2015, www.fao.org/publications.

Gilabert, P. (2004) "The Duty to Eradicate Global Poverty: Positive or Negative," *Ethical Theory and Moral Practice* 7: 537–550.

Godfray, H.C.J., Beddington, J.R., Crute, I.R., Haddad, L., Lawrence, D.L., Muir, J.F., Pretty, J., Robinson, S., Thomas, S.M. & Toulmin, C. (2010) "Food Security: The Challenge of Feeding 9 Billion People," *Science* 327(12 Feb.): 812–818.

Hadiprayitno, I. (2014) "Food Security," in P. B. Thompson & D. M. Kaplan (eds.), *Encyclopedia of Food and Agricultural Ethics*, New York: Springer, pp. 957–964.

Headey, D. & Ecker, O. (2013) "Rethinking the Measurement of Food Security: From First Principles to Best Practice," *Food Security* 5: 327–343.

Keenan, D. P., Olson, C., Hersey, J.C. & Parmer, S.M. (2001) "Measures of Food Insecurity/Security," *Journal of Nutrition Education* 33: S49–S58.

Korthals, M. (2015) "Ethics of Food Production and Consumption," in R. J. Herring (ed.), *The Oxford Handbook of Food, Politics, and Society*, New York: Oxford University Press, pp. 231–252.

Lever-Tracy, C. (2014) "Climate Change, Ethics, and Food Production," in P. B. Thompson & D. M. Kaplan (eds.), *Encyclopedia of Food and Agricultural Ethics*, New York: Springer, pp. 364–371.

Martindale, W. (2015) *Global Food Security and Supply*, Oxford: Wiley Blackwell.

Maxwell, D. G. (1996) "Measuring Food Insecurity: The Frequency and Severity of 'Coping Strategies,'" *Food Policy* 21: 291–303.

McDonald, B. L. (2010) *Food Security*, Cambridge: Polity.

Micheletti, M., Follesdahl, A. & Stolle, D. (2004) "Introduction," in M. Micheletti, A. Follesdahl & D. Stolle (eds.), *Politics, Products and Markets: Exploring Political Consumerism Past and Present*, New Brunswick: Transaction Publishers, pp. ix–xxvi.

Misselhorn, A., Aggarwal, P., Ericksen, P., Gregory, P., Horn-Phathanothai, L., Ingram, J. & Wiebe, K. (2012) "A Vision for Attaining Food Security," *Current Opinion in Environmental Sustainability* 4: 7–17.

Murdock, E. & Noll, S. (2015) "Beyond Access: Integrating Food Security and Food Sovereignty Models of Justice," in E. Dumitras, I. M. Jitea & S. Aerts (eds.), *Know Your Food: Food Ethics and Innovation*, Wageningen: Wageningen Academic Publishers, pp. 327–332.

Newell-McLoughlin, M. (2015) "Genetically Improved Crops," in R. J. Herring (ed.), *The Oxford Handbook of Food, Politics, and Society*, New York: Oxford University Press, pp. 65–104.

Pinstrup-Andersen, P. (2009) "Food Security: Definition and Measurement," *Food Security* 1: 5–7.

Pogge, T. (2005) "Reply to the Critics: Severe Poverty as a Violation of Negative Duties," *Ethics and International Affairs* 19: 55–83.

——. (2013) "Poverty, Hunger and Cosmetic Progress," in M. Langford, A. Sumner & A. E. Yamin (eds.), *The Millennium Development Goals and Human Rights: Past, Present and Future*, New York: Oxford University Press, pp. 209–232.

Poppy, G. M., Jepson, P. C., Pickett, J. A. & Birkett, M. A. (2014) "Achieving Food and Environmental Security: New Approaches to Close the Gap," *Philosophical Transaction of the Royal Society* 369: 1–6.

Renzaho, A. M. N. & Mellor, D. (2010) "Food Security Measurement in Cultural Pluralism: Missing the Point or Conceptual Misunderstanding?", *Nutrition* 26: 1–9.

Sandler, R. L. (2015) *Food Ethics: The Basics*, London: Routledge.

Schmidhuber, J. & Tubiello, F. N. (2007) "Global Food Security under Climate Change," *PNAS* 104(50): 19703–19708.

Stolle, D., Hooghe, M. & Micheletti, M. (2005) "Politics in the Supermarket: Political Consumerism as a Form of Political Participation," *International Political Science Review* 26(2): 245–269.

Tscharntke, T., Clough, Y., Wanger, T. C., Jackson, L., Motzke, I., Perfecto, I., Vandermeer, J. & Whitbread, A. (2012) "Global Food Security, Biodiversity Conservation and the Future of Agricultural Intensification," *Biological Conservation* 151: 53–59.

United Nations. (1948) *The Universal Declaration of Human Rights*, viewed 24 June 2015, http://www.un.org/en/documents/udhr/.

——. (1975) *World Food Conference*, Rome, 5–16 November 1974.

——. (2015) *Millennium Goals*, viewed 24 June 2015, http://www.un.org/millenniumgoals.

Uphoff, N. (2015) "Alternative Paths to Food Security," in R. J. Herring (ed.), *The Oxford Handbook of Food, Politics, and Society*, New York: Oxford University Press, pp. 202–228.

Wenar, L. (2010) "Poverty Is Not a Pond," in P. Illingworth, T. Pogge & L. Wenar (eds.), *Giving Well: The Ethics of Philanthropy*, Oxford: Oxford University Press, pp. 104–132.

Further Reading

T. Pogge, *World Poverty and Human Rights: Cosmopolitan Responsibilities and Reforms*, 2nd edition (Cambridge: Polity Press, 2008) is a highly informative reading on world poverty, social justice, and human rights. A. Sen, *Poverty and Famines: An Essay on Entitlement and Deprivation* (Oxford: Oxford University Press, 1981) is a seminal work on the causes of famines. P. Singer, "Famine, Affluence, and Morality," *Philosophy and Public Affairs* 1(1972): 229–243 (revised edition) is a much-discussed paper on ethics of charity that introduces the pond thought experiment.

39

THE NEW
THREE-LEGGED STOOL

Agroecology, food sovereignty, and food justice

M. Jahi Chappell and Mindi Schneider

Introduction: why we need a new three-legged stool

Sustainability and sustainability science have come to be characterized by a "tripartite model" that heuristically and epistemologically separates the subject into social, economic, and environmental dimensions. Variously called the "three pillars," the "three-legged stool," or the "triple-bottom line" (3BL) of sustainability, this model is a mainstream and mainstay of sustainability discussions (Global Reporting Initiative 2013; Raar 2002; Shnayder et al. 2015).[1] It has further been adopted in business management circles as a corporate social responsibility strategy to ensure long-term benefits for "profit, people, and the planet" (Elkington 1997). However, despite the model's staying power and increasing popularity over the past three decades, it has obscured and muddied issues surrounding sustainability more than it has clarified them. At best, the model provides a way to divide complex issues into manageable categories that allow for (over-)simplified analyses. At worst, it becomes a mere public relations strategy that firms use to increase profits, under the guise of balancing goals for economic growth with wider social and environmental concerns (Norman and MacDonald 2004). In between these two poles, the concept of "sustainability" and the tools proposed for how to achieve it are increasingly politicized.

Given these and other challenges, the tripartite model needs a radical reformulation. A new model should maintain a focus on the multiple (and often contested) dimensions of sustainability, without creating artificial divisions that manifest as barriers to trans-disciplinary research and discussion, and that facilitate corporate cooptation and "green washing" (e.g., Friedmann 2005). In this light, we propose a new tripartite approach, rooted in agrifood systems. In industrial form, agrifood systems are major drivers of biodiversity loss, climate change, declining public health, smallholder dispossession, corporate concentration, and environmental degradation (Lang et al. 2009; Tilman et al. 2002; Weis 2007). At the same time, research increasingly shows the regenerative and restorative potential of small-scale agroecological farming, which reach far beyond the realm of food and farming (e.g., IAASTD 2009; Lin et al. 2011). Agrifood systems, in other words, are important components of sustainability *problems*, as well as their *solutions*: food and farming constitute two of the most important ways that humans interact with the environment and support – or detract from – sustainability (Chappell and LaValle 2011; Tilman et al. 2002).

Based on our analysis of the classical tripartite model and our established work in agrifood systems, we suggest replacing social, economic, and environmental sustainability with three new legs calling for research and action based on (1) agroecology, (2) food sovereignty, and (3) food justice. Furthermore, we argue that it is the character of the connections and relations between and among these legs that are most important, not the individual legs themselves. We take a systems approach that integrates rather than separates, proposing sustainability as a process rather than a state of being.

Although we will draw on existing and important critiques of the tripartite model (e.g., Adams 2006; Schoolman et al. 2012), our intention here is not simply to add to this list. Instead, we offer a new conceptualization of sustainability in order to remedy some of the deficiencies of the traditional model as it applies to food security and the sustainability of food and farming systems. While our approach is not directly transferable to other systems, we believe it offers insights that may help refine definitions of sustainability beyond the agrifood context.

A critique of the classical tripartite model of sustainability

Of all critiques of the classical "three-legged stool" of sustainability, perhaps the most important is the foundational question of whether or not the model provides a viable or useful taxonomy of sustainability. Adams's (2006) critique of sustainability and sustainable development as a whole applies equally to the division of each into the three legs of economic, social, and environmental sustainability: it is "holistic, attractive, elastic but imprecise," and it has been widely accepted ". . . precisely [because of] this looseness. It can be used to cover very divergent ideas." Most damningly, the ideas "may bring people together but it does not necessarily help them to agree on goals" (3). This is a fatal problem with the classical model, we argue, on two grounds. First, different communities (for example, of farmers, scholars, urban workers, economic and political elites, civil society) bring disparate goals and ideals into sustainability conversations. And although each group may agree that all three legs are vital, how to define and measure social, economic, and environmental sustainability is often contested between and among groups, and occupies thoroughly different discursive spaces. This leaves little room for the substantive talk and listening that can uncover crucial shared or conflicting values and interests, and potentially reconcile them (Erdman and Susskind 2008: 15–26; Prugh et al. 2000: 107–108, 111–120). Second, defining and operationalizing the multiple dimensions of sustainability is a highly political process in which different actors occupy starkly different positions of power. We return to this issue below.

The importance of this disconnect between the conceptualization and operationalization of the stool model can be seen in both the epistemological critiques of the classical model, and the critical evaluations of how its conceptualization has played out in practice. The classic three-legged stool's divisions between social, economic, and environmental concerns defies an appropriate epistemological understanding of the systems of interest, given that the three legs are inevitably related in complex ways and are not readily or realistically reducible to this kind of discrete categorization. The clearest example of this is the fact, long pointed out by ecological economists, that social and economic systems are inevitably subsets of environmental systems – humans do not and cannot supersede or, indeed, exist without environmental systems (Costanza et al. 2014; Daly and Farley 2010). To illustrate, although estimates of the total economic value of the environment have been ventured (e.g., Costanza et al. 2014), the "true" value (if such a thing exists) would be infinite: there is no amount of money we would not pay to maintain the environment as a whole, because without it, we would not exist. This may superficially appear compatible with the classical three-legged stool – after all, the idea is that without any one leg, the whole stool falls over – but there is an important difference between a stool falling over onto the floor, and there being no floor in the first place (Dawe and Ryan 2003).

These issues related to "natural limits" bring to the fore further conceptual and political road-blocks that the classic model is not necessarily well-equipped to deal with. For example, numerous such roadblocks can be found in the legacy and continuing prevalence of Malthusian logic, with its racialized and racist orientation, which creates a challenging context within which to define and address "natural limits" of any kind (cf. Harvey 1974). Still, as proponents of the "degrowth" social movement (*décroissance* in France, where the movement originated) emphasize, the ideology and drive for continual growth is itself unsustainable (e.g., Demaria et al. 2013). Instead,

> Sustainable degrowth may be defined as an equitable downscaling of production and consumption that increases human wellbeing and enhances ecological conditions at the local and global level, in the short and long term. The adjective sustainable does not mean that degrowth should be sustained indefinitely (which would be absurd) but rather that the process of transition/transformation and the end-state should be sustainable in the sense of being environmentally and socially beneficial. The paradigmatic proposition of degrowth is therefore that human progress without economic growth is possible.
>
> (Schneider et al. 2010: 512)

"Sustainability," then, is not the same as "sustainable development," despite the gradual elision of differences between the two as the conceptual lines separating the "three-legged stool" and the "triple-bottom line" have become largely indistinct. Sustainable development, which has been adopted by international institutes of global governance as well as the corporate social responsibility camp (Norman and MacDonald 2004; Shnayder et al. 2015), leaves the capitalist logic of continual economic growth and capital accumulation unexamined. This kind of tunnel vision is made possible by the artificial separation of social and environmental issues; of human and natural systems; and of humans and nature more generally. Building on Karl Marx's notion of an "irreparable rift in the interdependent process of social metabolism" under capitalism,[2] John Bellamy Foster (1999; 2009) proposed the concept of *metabolic rift* to understand and analyze these separations. As a theory of capital's ecological crises, the metabolic rift takes the separation of people from the land as a primary focus. With enclosure of the commons (and other forms of agrarian dispossession), connections between people and land are unsettled and distanced. As a result, human–nature relations are ruptured, along with the flows of energy between them. Industrialization of agriculture further exacerbates this rift, as long-distance trade and the separation of crop and livestock agriculture disrupts soil nutrient cycles, creating a lack of nutrients on the farm, with the corollary of excess nutrients in cities or wherever "wastes" are disposed of (Foster and Magdoff 2000; Schneider and McMichael 2010).

The metabolic rift expresses a crisis of capitalist development, and of epistemologies that separate humans and nature in thought and action. But economic and social systems are intensely intertwined, with economic thought and practice invariably prefigured and conceived within specific social contexts. In this way, the metabolic rift can also be thought of as emblematic of rifts in humans' relations with one another: the ability and readiness to engage in genuine conversation and decision-making across barriers of socioeconomic inequality, and segregation by race, class, and culture within many societies has been eroded (Prugh et al. 2000; Putnam 2001), and continuing inequality makes decision-making in complex systems more difficult yet (Farrell and Shalizi forthcoming). Further, and as many have previously observed, the classic three-legged stool has tended to focus on the economy to the detriment of social and environmental relations, ossifying the artificial separation of the three legs rather than challenging it. Continuing in the example of "natural limits," it would take the resources of several Earths in order for everyone in the world to consume at the level of the average US citizen, but conversely, if the ~4,600 kcal/person/day of edible food harvest in the world were distributed evenly, without waste or conversion to livestock or biofuels, then we could nominally support a world human population of 12–14 billion people today (UNCTAD 2013). Similarly, economic growth without explicit consideration of equity is much less able to improve human well-being (Haddad 2015). These considerations, which barely scrape the surface of economic–social–environmental interactions, illustrate how separating these into three legs can beggar rather than enrich rational conversation. How do we decide – and who gets to decide – to pursue intensified agricultural production instead of, or in addition to, seeking to redistribute the food already produced? How – and to whom – can it be justified to continue to expand current food and agriculture systems, with the inevitable costs to the environment rather than taking less resource-intensive paths of redistribution and social and economic empowerment?

Despite real and profound challenges in negotiating these kinds of conflicting interests, the conversation of sustainability is not well served by sublimating them or making them so vague as to avoid conflict altogether (Adams 2006; Prugh et al. 2000). The non-obvious nature of both the meaning and measurement of sustainability in the classical model further distances it from being a useful centerpiece for societal conversations of broad interest and import (Norman and MacDonald 2004; Shnayder et al. 2015). Correspondingly, ill-defined problems with unclear metrics have substantial difficulty in gaining purchase in wider society and within policy agendas (Kingdon 2003). Thus, the classical model fits into and reinforces existing problems and hierarchies of knowledge, making conversations on sustainability amenable to elite experts' "*de-facto* authority to declare proper public meanings" (Welsh and Wynne 2013: 544). In short, neither the conceptual nor political processes of understanding, defining, and operationalizing sustainability are well served by the classical model.

One could conceivably retort that food justice, agroecology, and food sovereignty are not themselves terribly accessible or measurable concepts, and that the bodies of scholarship around them bear the same threat of opacity and elite/expert fiats. However, as we argue in the next section, we believe that our proposed integrative approach to our three legs is in fact more readily intelligible as grounds for societal conversations, and that further evidence that they are better terrains for functional discourse is already ready at hand.

Standing on its own three legs: rationale for a new approach

Given the shortcomings outlined above, we need a new heuristic device that takes a systems approach to long-term, equitable, and inclusive socio-environmental sustainability. We need a new three-legged stool based on integration rather than separation, and one that allows for critical analysis of how sustainability has become part of the "business as usual" approach to food security and agrifood governance (e.g., McMichael and Schneider 2011). Our new conceptualization calls for research and action in food and agriculture considering a stool that stands on the integration of agroecology, food sovereignty, and food justice. Below, we provide elementary definitions of each leg.

Agroecology

Agroecology has come to be understood as a science, a set of practices, and a social movement (or movements) (Wezel et al. 2009). Its academic roots go back nearly one hundred years, drawing on (and co-evolving with) the fields of agronomy, horticulture, and ecology. From these fields, it

draws much of its scientific and practical roots, using the burgeoning science of ecology to understand how different agricultural systems function (and where they may be improved) by viewing agricultural areas as ecosystems themselves that therefore must follow the same patterns and
processes gleaned from the study of non-agricultural environments. Agroecology, however, does
not simply integrate the three natural sciences above: its provenance in traditions from Europe
and Latin America has also lent agroecology an emphasis on the livelihoods, culture, and social
contexts of farmers, with a high priority on understanding and addressing the repeated patterns of
exploitation and expropriation of small-scale farmers around the world (Wezel et al. 2009). Thus,
in a technical sense, agroecology includes agricultural practices grounded in academic social and
natural sciences and animated by reflection and action to continuously evaluate environmental
and socioeconomic impacts of agrifood systems.

Beyond the science and the practices validated or motivated by it, there has been a growing
social movement advocating the potential of agroecology to improve linked human and environmental health and well-being. Farmers around the world have claimed the term "agroecology" as central to their survival, and they note that much of agroecology in fact stems from their
ingenuity: ecological science has validated the efficiency and low-impact systematic approach of
many "traditional" farming practices (Chappell and LaValle 2011). So-called peasant farmers have
also reminded academic ecologists that many practices (indeed, nearly all of them for most of the
10,000 years of human agriculture) have come from the experimentation, culture, and heritage
of small-scale farmers, who continue to innovate and adapt. Academic science in some (possibly
many) cases is "discovering" (or rediscovering) the validity of numerous traditional practices,
adding (in the best of cases) an academic epistemology to the practical "metis" of farmers in a
dialectical process of exchange and refinement (Perfecto et al. 2009).

This connects agroecology to two tendencies that are useful for our new three-legged model.
First, the increasing interest in and support for agroecology has led many academic agroecologists
to go beyond the biophysical sciences and inquire about the social dynamics affecting farming and
agriculture, particularly the marginalization and assumed "backwardness" of pre-industrial farming.
The modern push for "scientific agriculture" has usually not been to the benefit of the majority
of farmers, and in some cases it has even abetted their marginalization and the destruction of their
livelihoods (Perfecto et al. 2009; Weis 2007). The classic finding of Walter Goldschmidt – that rural
communities with more, smaller farms saw higher well-being than those with fewer, larger farms –
has been questioned by modernist scholars, but has also seen numerous studies supporting its conclusions, and it certainly has never been strongly refuted (Chappell and LaValle 2011). The irony of
an increasingly (and rhetorically) "science-based" approach to agriculture that ignores an empirical examination of what kind and scale of farming actually produces the greatest well-being for
society has driven many agroecologists to politically engage in farmers' struggles. Thus, the second
tendency: even as the large peasant farmers' movement La Vía Campesina has outlined agroecology's
foundational importance for peasant livelihoods, they have also brought to prominence another leg
of our stool, *food sovereignty*, as an inseparable partner to agroecology.

Food sovereignty

Food sovereignty, a concept developed by civil society actors, is about the rights of communities to decide what they eat, what they grow, and how they grow it. It is a social movement that
requires (re)consideration of the political-economic systems governing food and agriculture, and
demands full democratic participation and control in building sustainable agrifood systems. If
agroecology defines the farming practices and desired ecological outcomes for long-term sustainability, food sovereignty defines part of the social process that is necessary to get there.

As a social movement and a conceptual apparatus, food sovereignty is a thing in motion. Since La Vía Campesina first introduced the concept at the World Food Summit in 1996, exponents of food sovereignty have adjusted the particularities of its meaning and application to changing social contexts, and across political jurisdictions (Iles and Montenegro de Wit 2015; Schiavoni 2015; Trauger 2014). As Raj Patel (2009: 663) states, "Food sovereignty is, if anything, over defined." Still, through its various incarnations, food sovereignty has been unified in bringing social control of the agrifood system to the fore, urging that achieving global food security will require democratic participation, agrarian reform, and the elevation of social and environmental values above market logics and the profit motive. Today, the leading definition of food sovereignty is La Vía Campesina's Nyéléni Declaration from 2007, which states:

> Food sovereignty is the right of peoples to healthy and culturally appropriate food produced through ecologically sound and sustainable methods, and their right to define their own food and agriculture systems. It puts the aspirations and needs of those who produce, distribute and consume food at the heart of food systems and policies rather than the demands of markets and corporations. It defends the interests and inclusion of the next generation. It offers a strategy to resist and dismantle the current corporate trade and food regime, and directions for food, farming, pastoral and fisheries systems determined by local producers and users. Food sovereignty prioritises local and national economies and markets and empowers peasant and family farmer-driven agriculture, artisanal fishing, pastoralist-led grazing, and food production, distribution and consumption based on environmental, social and economic sustainability. Food sovereignty promotes transparent trade that guarantees just incomes to all peoples as well as the rights of consumers to control their food and nutrition. It ensures that the rights to use and manage lands, territories, waters, seeds, livestock and biodiversity are in the hands of those of us who produce food. Food sovereignty implies new social relations free of oppression and inequality between men and women, peoples, racial groups, social and economic classes and generations.

Food sovereignty has been a largely peasant-led and rural-based movement, arguably strongest in the so-called Global South. While activists and scholars are working to translate and situate the ideologies and goals of food sovereignty into contexts in the Global North (see, for example, Alkon and Mares 2012; Fairbairn 2011; McMichael 2014; Schiavoni 2009), the movement remains largely rooted in agrarian issues and politics. Recognizing the transnational nature of the food sovereignty movement, and efforts to bridge global political geographies, we nonetheless argue that a third conceptual leg that directly tackles urban and rural–urban inequalities is necessary for sustainability. That leg is *food justice*, and in particular, the way it addresses how "stark conditions of racial, gendered and class-based urban inequality produce significant barriers to accessing affordable and healthy food for many inner city residents" (Heynen et al. 2012).

Food justice

Food justice, then, provides a final prism through which to view and analyze the outcomes of food and agricultural system endeavors. It presents the requirement that any intervention not only support environmentally sustainable practices and democratic processes, but must also provide dignified and equitable access to safe, sufficient, affordable, culturally appropriate, and healthy food for all – from food producers, to workers, to consumers in rural and urban places. As a concept and a movement, food justice places food access in the context of uneven historical and ongoing race, gender, and class relations, highlighting "food insecurity and high rates of diet-related diseases not as the result of poor individual choices, but from institutionalized racism" (and patriarchy and capitalism) (Alkon and Norgaard 2009: 289). In this way, food justice more directly engages with the needs and struggles of people for whom agrifood systems are just one more realm of marginalization, discrimination, and oppression, rather than the primary site of inequality. Examples of "unaffordable, unhealthy, and unsustainable urban foodscapes" (Heynen et al. 2012: 305) abound, the result of uneven food distribution systems, the withdrawal of supermarkets from central cities, the proliferation of fast and durable foods (Alkon et al. 2013; Friedmann 1992; Nestle 2002), and more general processes of racialized and gendered capitalist development.

In their book, *Cultivating Food Justice: Race, Class, and Sustainability*, Alkon and Agyeman (2011: 8) provide the following definition of food justice:

> [t]he food justice movement mirrors . . . two key concerns through the concepts of food access and food sovereignty. Food access is the ability to produce and consume healthy food. While the environmental justice movement is primarily concerned with preventing disproportionate exposure to toxic environmental burdens, the food justice movement works to ensure equal access to the environmental benefit of healthy food. Food sovereignty is a community's "right to define their own food and agriculture systems" (Vía Campesina 2002). Like procedural justice, food sovereignty moves beyond the distribution of benefits and burdens to call for a greater distribution of power in the management of food and environmental systems.

There are clear links between food justice and food sovereignty, both conceptually and politically. However, as Heynen et al. (2012) caution, "for *food justice* to have intellectual and political value, it must both take advantage of the robust history of food politics and then move these politics forward toward more emancipatory goals" (306). In their work on urban hunger and malnutrition, Heynen et al. (2012) propose that urban agriculture can link *community food security* to *food sovereignty* in order to realize *food justice*. Our approach is similar, but we argue that *agroecology* is a more robust accompaniment to sovereignty and justice that captures agrifood systems in both rural and urban areas.

The new three legs: putting sustainability on solid footing

This new three-legged stool provides a framework that serves as an analytical and evaluative tool for scholars, policy makers, and civil society organizations involved in agrifood systems and politics. The key strength of the approach is that it places socially just and ecologically embedded practices at the heart of the analysis, while explicitly recognizing the necessity of social action for envisioning and creating renewable and sustainable food and farming systems.

The immediate advantage of our approach is that agroecology, food sovereignty, and food justice imply specific values, ideas, practices, and standards. Although each of these concepts are themselves the object of ongoing development and debate, they serve the immediate function of *foregrounding* the important conversations necessary for collective action, rather than trying to smuggle in collective action through superficial consensus. While there is an important role for *strategic ambiguity* within movements (Mische 2003), this does not mean effective change can be made without grappling at all with identity and definitions. Unlike the vague "social, economic, and environmental" legs, each of our legs represent specific communities of concepts and can already boast multi-sectoral conversations within (and between) each leg. And indeed, we do not suggest that our framework will – or even should – necessarily be the precise one adopted going forward. Rather, it should serve as a template for the debate and deliberation on conceptual commitments and ideals in a way that should provide space for coalition-building across sectors, and therefore improve the chance of advancing a sustainability agenda.

To wit, within each of our three proposed legs, active conversations and actions around justice and social change are already taking place. For example, Perfecto et al. (2009) powerfully connect ecological and social sciences in their book, *Nature's Matrix: Linking Agriculture, Conservation and Food Sovereignty*. They argue that biodiversity conservation, agroecological farming, and grassroots political mobilization among smallholder farmers are intricately related, and that all three are necessary for achieving food security without devastating human and non-human communities. Similarly, Méndez et al. (2013) propose an integrative approach to agroecology, defining it as necessarily "transdisciplinary, participatory and action-oriented" (3), and stating that "a transformative agroecology incorporates a critique of the political economic structures that shape the current agro-food system" (11). What is more, as noted above, the international peasant movement La Vía Campesina sees agroecology as central to food sovereignty. At the First Assembly of the Alliance for Food Sovereignty of Latin America and the Caribbean in 2013,

> Agroecology was chosen as "a way of life that recovers all we have lost, a connection with ancient knowledge," as it rescues local markets and knowledge of communities, raises debate about the prices and encourages exchange and barter as a model of a social and solidary economy based on sustainability, redistribution and reciprocity.
>
> (La Vía Campesina 2013)

It is true, however, that conversations linking race and racism to agroecology and sovereignty have been less pronounced. Procedural and distributional justice, while originally included in definitions of sustainability (Loos et al. 2014), get lost or overlooked in the traditional stool. But given a finite world, decisions of distribution must be countenanced. As we reviewed above, such questions are inextricably and simultaneously economic, social, and environmental – choices around economic growth, or degrowth, distribution and empowerment, and resource use determine who benefits, and how much, from processes with varying environmental implications and "costs." And because neither economics, nor social relations, nor the environment are static, a just approach to these decisions must not only contemplate final distributions, but also the process of making the pertinent decisions – in other words, both procedural and distributive justice must be deliberately considered and implemented in an ongoing manner (Farrell and Shalizi forthcoming; Loos et al. 2014).[3]

In the model we propose, we argue that the three legs – or goals – can be meaningfully self-reinforcing. Agroecology is aided by sovereignty because food sovereignty acknowledges and respects farmers' and communities' knowledge, which can then be more equitably incorporated into improved agroecological practices. Food justice in turn can expand democratic participation in agrifood systems to include the needs and struggles of marginalized communities who may not live and work directly *in* the agrifood system, but who are impacted by its control and operation nonetheless. Although we do not claim our new model solves all the problems of sustainability – far from it – we do think this approach, which foregrounds the values and putative goals of sustainability, offers a significant improvement on an otherwise somewhat stalled sustainability discourse. Further, agroecology, food justice, and food sovereignty, unlike the classic three-legged stool, represent concepts that are being actively defined by and with a variety of communities, from a variety of backgrounds and social classes, around the world. In this way, the very dialogue we believe is necessary to sustainability is in many ways already embodied by our proposed model. Integrating these dialogues as a purposeful model within society and the academy may therefore in fact serve as a vehicle to advance the sustainability discourse beyond its current impasses.

Notes

1 The approach has become so common as to apparently no longer need identification by name: the Global Reporting Initiative's *G4 Sustainability Reporting Guidelines* lists three categories in its chapter on "Specific standard disclosures": Economic, Environmental, and Social. But there is no reference to the provenance of these categories in the document, or use of the terms "three-legged stool" or "triple-bottom line."
2 As quoted in Foster (1999: 379).
3 Farrell and Shalizi (forthcoming) argue that social systems combining diversity and a large degree of substantive equality are more likely to generate workable solutions to complex problems, and many have argued that political and social inequalities lead to less optimal decision-making and problem-solving as the more powerful can use their power to block socially desirable solutions in favor of their own interests.

References

Adams, W. M. (2006) *The Future of Sustainability: Re-thinking Environment and Development in the Twenty-first Century*, Gland, Switzerland: IUCN, retrieved from http://cmsdata.iucn.org/downloads/iucn_future_of_sustainability.pdf.

Alkon, A. H. & Agyeman, J. (2011) *Cultivating Food Justice: Race, Class, and Sustainability*, Cambridge: MIT Press.

Alkon, A. H., Block, D., Moore, K., Gillis, C., DiNuccio, N., & Chavez, N. (2013) "Foodways of the Urban Poor," *Geoforum* 48: 126–135.

Alkon, A. H. & Mares, T. M. (2012) "Food Sovereignty in US Food Movements: Radical Visions and Neo-liberal Constraints," *Agriculture and Human Values* 29(3): 347–359.

Alkon, A. H. & Norgaard, K. M. (2009) "Breaking the Food Chains: An Investigation of Food Justice Activism," *Sociological Inquiry* 79(3): 289–305.

Chappell, M. J. & LaValle, L. A. (2011) "Food Security and Biodiversity: Can We Have Both? An Agroecological Analysis," *Agriculture and Human Values* 28(1): 3–26.

Costanza, R., de Groot, R., Sutton, P., van der Ploeg, S., Anderson, S. J., Kubiszewski, I., Farber, S., & Turner, R. K. (2014) "Changes in the Global Value of Ecosystem Services," *Global Environmental Change* 26: 152–158.

Daly, H. E. & Farley, J. (2010) *Ecological Economics: Principles and Applications* (2nd ed.), Washington, D.C.: Island Press.

Dawe, N. K. & Ryan, K. L. (2003). "The Faulty Three-Legged-Stool Model of Sustainable Development," *Conservation Biology* 17(5): 1458–1460.

Demaria, F., Schneider, F., Sekulova, F., & Martínez-Alier, J. (2013) "What Is Degrowth? From an Activist Slogan to a Social Movement," *Environmental Values* 22: 191–215.

Elkington, J. (1997) *Cannibals with Forks: Triple Bottom Line of the 21st Century Business*, Oxford: Capstone.

Erdman, S. & Susskind, L. (2008) *The Cure For Our Broken Political System: How We Can Get Our Politicians To Resolve the Issues Tearing Our Country Apart*, Dulles, Virginia: Potomac Books.

Fairbairn, M. (2011) "Framing Transformation: The Counter-Hegemonic Potential of Food Sovereignty in the US Context," *Agriculture and Human Values* 27(2): 217–230.

Farrell, H. & Shalizi, C. (forthcoming 2016) "Cognitive Democracy," in D. Allen & J. Light (eds.), *Youth, New Media and Political Participation*, Cambridge: The MIT Press.

Foster, J. B. (1999) "Marx's Theory of Metabolic Rift: Classical Foundations for Environmental Sociology," *American Journal of Sociology* 105(2): 366–405.

Foster, J. B. (2009) *The Ecological Revolution: Making Peace with the Planet*, New York: Monthly Review Press.

Foster, J. B. & Magdoff, F. (2000) "Liebig, Marx, and the Depletion of Soil Fertility: Relevance for Today's Agriculture," in F. Magdoff, J. B. Foster, & F. H. Buttel (eds.), *Hungry for Profit: The Agribusiness Threat to Farmers, Food, And the Environment*, New York: Monthly Review Press, pp. 43–60.

Friedmann, H. (1992) "Distance and Durability: Shaky Foundations of the World Food Economy," *Third World Quarterly* 13(2): 371–383.

Friedmann, H. (2005) "From Colonialism to Green Capitalism: Social Movements and Emergence of Food Regimes," in F. H. Buttel, & P. McMichael (eds.), *New Directions in the Sociology of Global Development*, London: Emerald Group Publishing Limited, pp. 227–264.

Global Reporting Initiative. (2013) "G4 Sustainability Reporting Guidelines: Reporting Principles and Standard Disclosures," viewed on 29 October 2015, https://www.globalreporting.org/resourcelibrary/GRIG4-Part1-Reporting-Principles-and-Standard-Disclosures.pdf.

Haddad, L. (2015) "Equity: Not Only For Idealists," *Development Policy Review* 33(1): 5–13.

Harvey, D. (1974) "Population, Resources and the Ideology of Science," *Economic Geography* 50: 256–277.

Heynen, N., Kurtz, H. E., & Trauger, A. (2012) "Food Justice, Hunger and the City," *Geography Compass* 6(5): 304–311.

Iles, A. & Montenegro de Wit, M. (2015) "Sovereignty at What Scale? An Inquiry into Multiple Dimensions of Food Sovereignty," *Globalizations* 12(4): 481–497.

International Assessment of Agricultural Knowledge Science and Technology for Development (IAASTD). (2009) *Agriculture at a Crossroads: International Assessment of Agricultural Knowledge, Science and Technology for Development*, Washington, DC: Island Press.

Kingdon, J. W. (2003) *Agendas, Alternatives, and Public Policies*, 2nd ed., New York: Harper Collins.

Lang, T., Barling, D., & Caraher, M. (2009) *Food Policy: Integrating Health, Environment & Society*, New York: Oxford University Press.

La Vía Campesina. (2007) "Declaration of the Forum for Food Sovereignty, Nyéléni 2007," viewed on 29 October 2015, http://nyeleni.org/spip.php?article290.

——. (2013) "*Agroecology as a Way of Life*," viewed on 29 October 2015, http://viacampesina.org/en/index.php/main-issues-mainmenu-27/sustainable-peasants-agriculture-mainmenu-42/1480-agroecology-as-a-way-of-life.

Lin, B. B., Chappell, M. J., Vandermeer, J., Smith, G., Quintero, E., Bezner-Kerr, R., Griffith, D. M., Ketcham, S., Latta, S. C., McMichael, P., McGuire, K. L., Nigh, R., Rocheleau, D., Soluri, J., & Perfecto. I. (2011) "Effects of Industrial Agriculture on Climate Change and the Mitigation Potential of Small-Scale Agro-Ecological Farms," *CAB Reviews: Perspectives in Agriculture, Veterinary Science, Nutrition, and Natural Resources* 6(20): 1–18.

Loos, J., Abson, D. J., Chappell, M. J., Hanspach, J., Mikulcak, F., Tichit, M., & Fischer, J. (2014) "Putting Meaning Back into 'Sustainable Intensification'," *Frontiers in Ecology and the Environment* 12(6): 356–361.

McMichael, P. (2014) "Historicizing Food Sovereignty," *Journal of Peasant Studies* 41(6): 933–957.

McMichael, P. & Schneider, M. (2011) "Food Security Politics and the Millennium Development Goals," *Third World Quarterly* 32(1): 119–139.

Méndez, V. E., Bacon, C. M., & Cohen, R. (2013) "Agroecology as a Transdisciplinary, Participatory, and Action-Oriented Approach," *Agroecology and Sustainable Food Systems* 37(1): 3–18.

Mische, A. (2003) "Cross-Talk in Movements: Reconceiving the Culture-Network Link," in M. Diani, & D. McAdam (eds.), *Social Movements and Networks Relational Approaches to Collective Action*, New York: Oxford University Press, pp. 258–280.

Nestle, M. (2002) *Food Politics: How the Food Industry Influences Nutrition and Health*, Berkeley, CA: University of California Press.

Norman, W. & MacDonald, C. (2004) "Getting to the Bottom of 'Triple Bottom Line'," *Business Ethics Quarterly* 14(02): 243–262.

Patel, R. (2009) "What Does Food Sovereignty Look Like?" *Journal of Peasant Studies* 36(3): 663–673.

Perfecto, I., Vandermeer, J., & Wright, A. (2009) *Nature's Matrix: Linking Agriculture, Conservation and Food Sovereignty*, Washington D.C.: Earthscan Press.

Prugh, T., Costanza, R., & Daly, H. E. (2000) *The Local Politics of Global Sustainability*, Washington, DC: Island Press.

Putnam, R. D. (2001) *Bowling Alone: The Collapse and Revival of American Community*, New York: Simon and Schuster.

Raar, J. (2002) "Environmental Initiatives: Towards Triple-Bottom Line Reporting," *Corporate Communications: An International Journal* 7(3): 169–183.

Schiavoni, C. (2009) "The Global Struggle for Food Sovereignty: From Nyéléni to New York," *Journal of Peasant Studies* 36(3): 682–689.

Schiavoni, C. (2015) "Competing Sovereignties, Contested Processes: Insights from the Venezuelan Food Sovereignty Experiment," *Globalizations* 12(4): 466–480.

Schneider, F., Kallis, G., & Martínez-Alier, J. (2010) "Crisis or Opportunity? Economic Degrowth for Social Equity and Ecological Sustainability. Introduction to this Special Issue," *Journal of Cleaner Production* 18(6): 511–518.

Schneider, M. & McMichael, P. (2010) "Deepening, and Repairing, the Metabolic Rift," *Journal of Peasant Studies* 37(3): 461–484.

Schoolman, E., Guest, J., Bush, K., & Bell, A. (2012) "How Interdisciplinary is Sustainability Research? Analyzing the Structure of an Emerging Scientific Field," *Sustainability Science* 7(1): 67–80.

Shnayder, L., van Rijnsoever, F. J., & Hekkert, M. P. (2015) "Putting Your Money Where Your Mouth Is: Why Sustainability Reporting Based on the Triple Bottom Line Can Be Misleading," *PLoS ONE* 10(3): e0119036.

Tilman, D., Cassman, K. G., Matson, P. A., Naylor, R., & Polasky, S. (2002) "Agricultural Sustainability and Intensive Production Practices," *Nature* 418(6898): 671–677.

Trauger, A. (2014) "Toward a Political Geography of Food Sovereignty: Transforming Territory, Exchange and Power in the Liberal Sovereign State," *Journal of Peasant Studies* 41(6): 131–1152.

UNCTAD (United Nations Conference on Trade and Development). (2013) *Trade And Environment Review 2013: Wake Up Before It Is Too Late: Make Agriculture Truly Sustainable Now For Food Security In A Changing Climate*, Geneva: United Nations.

Weis, A. J. (2007) *The Global Food Economy: The Battle for the Future of Farming*, New York: Zed Books.

Welsh, I. & Wynne, B. (2013) "Science, Scientism and Imaginaries of Publics in the UK: Passive Objects, Incipient Threats," *Science as Culture* 22(4): 540–566.

Wezel, A., Bellon, S., Dore, T., Francis, C., Vallod, D., & David, C. (2009) "Agroecology as a Science, a Movement and a Practice: A Review," *Agronomy for Sustainable Development* 39: 503–515.

40

PARTICIPATIVE INEQUALITIES AND FOOD JUSTICE

Clement Loo

Introduction

There has been a tendency within both the academic and activist literatures to treat food justice as primarily a matter of distributional disparities (Loo 2014). This chapter will argue that such a conception of food justice is limited and that creating or promoting equitable food systems requires attention to participative inequalities. Such is the case because there is reason to suspect that distributional injustices are related to barriers to fair participation on the part of marginalized communities in the governance of food.

To ensure that the reader has adequate background to appreciate the thesis of this chapter, I begin by reviewing the distinction between participative and distributive justice. Next, I outline two examples drawn from the environmental justice literature: (a) the mistreatment of farmworkers, and (b) the development of food deserts within inner cities and more remote rural locales. These two examples demonstrate that some of the key unfair distributions discussed in the food justice literature are in fact the result of participative disparities. I conclude by arguing that if paradigmatic cases of distributive injustice are, in fact, cases of participative injustice, then those who are concerned about food justice should consider how participation is relevant to their work.

The participative/distributive distinction

The distinction between distributive and participative justice can likely be traced to the work of Walzer (1983), Young (1990), and Shrader-Frechette (2002). One way to think of this distinction is in terms of an emphasis on outcome or process in regards to the distribution of a given set of benefits or burdens (Loo 2014).

For those concerned primarily with distributive justice, a just system is one that ensures that goods and harms are distributed fairly across a given group of individuals or communities. The emphasis in such an approach is clearly on outcome. What is most important for one who is focused solely, or perhaps even mainly, on distributive justice is that material goods and the costs associated with those goods are shared in such a way that no individual or group is left carrying the burden of costs in excess of receiving the boon offered by the goods.

On the other hand, those who are focused on participative justice are more concerned with process. That is, they would likely be most interested in the actual decision-making process or system of distribution that determines how benefits and costs are apportioned across persons or communities. One who is concerned with participation will endorse and promote methods of apportioning that allow all stakeholders fair opportunity to influence how the various benefits and costs in question are divided across parties. So, while one who is concerned primarily with distribution would focus on the actual goods and costs and *to whom* they are allotted, one who is concerned more with participation would focus on *how* goods and costs are allotted and would likely pay attention to whether systems responsible for distribution are democratic to ensure that no groups are marginalized or excluded from playing a role in negotiations regarding that allotment.

In the context of food justice, those who believe distribution is more central will focus most on questions such as: (a) Who earns the most profits from growing food relative to who contributes the most labor or experiences the most associated hardships? (b) Who experiences the most environmental harms associated with agriculture relative to who has the most access to the food grown? Or (c) who has access to food, who does not have access to food, for which communities is food available, and for which is food not available?

On the other hand, one who has more of a focus on participative food justice would instead seek answers for questions such as: (1) Who owns and has most control of the land that food is grown on? (2) Whose opinions are the most influential in regards to agricultural, food, and development policy, and whose opinions are heeded the least? (3) Who owns, manages, or otherwise has the most control of the markets where food is sold, and who does not? Or (4) are there particular interest groups that exert more influence than others in regards to selecting the food grown or determining how crops are distributed, and are there interest groups that exert less influence?

Now that I have reviewed, albeit somewhat quickly and roughly, the distinction between participative food justice and distributive food justice, I will move on to demonstrate that even some problems that have traditionally been understood primarily as distributive are in fact participative. This suggests that we ought to think of food justice in a much broader and encompassing way than is usual, and our strategies should attend to participative disparities as well as distributive ones.

Two key distributional injustices and their participative underpinnings

It is impossible to comprehensively review every distributive injustice associated with food systems and to conclusively demonstrate that they should also be considered in participative terms. Instead I will consider a small number of arguably representative cases and highlight how they have importantly participative elements. And, in doing this, I hope to demonstrate that it is possible and perhaps plausible to think that other similar cases may have importantly participative elements as well.

I will discuss two cases: the first regards the poor conditions experienced by itinerant workers who comprise the primary labor force for the American agricultural system; the second focuses on food deserts found in inner cities and isolated rural communities throughout North America and Western Europe.

There are at least three reasons to think that that these two cases are particularly appropriate for the purposes of this chapter. One, they are both prima facie very much distributional problems. In the first case the poor conditions of farmworkers involve low pay and limited access to goods such as shelter, health care, and education, a situation that seems particularly inequitable in light of the large profits earned by the firms that contract them. In the case of food deserts the key problem attended to by activists and scholars is the distribution and availability of various food products relative to geographic location and socio-economic status. Two, they are commonly discussed in the canonical literature regarding food justice. For example, if one examines the most frequently cited, recently published books regarding food justice – such as Alkon and Agyeman (2011a) and Gottlieb and Joshi (2010) – one will find substantial attention paid to these cases. Such is also true of a great number of article-length publications as well – a cursory review of article-length works regarding food justice will reveal that many are concerned with either the treatment of farmworkers or with limited access on the part of various communities to healthy food. This would suggest that the treatment of food workers and food deserts are central the field of food justice. And, three, these two cases encompass both production-based and consumption-based inequalities; the example of the poor working conditions of agricultural labor highlights inequalities related to the growing of food, while food deserts are a manner in which the distributing of food to eaters can occur in manifestly unjust ways. Thus, these two cases cover a fairly broad range of the domain of food justice.

Justice and farmworkers

One of the topics most often discussed by activists and scholars working on food justice regards the poor conditions experienced by agricultural workers in the United States. Descriptions of these conditions can be found in the work of Brown and Getz (2011) and Gottlieb and Joshi (2010). They note that farmworkers, particularly itinerant ones, are often mistreated in a number of ways.

First, farmworkers are usually paid wages that are much lower than would be expected given the hours they work and the dangers they encounter at their jobs. While agribusiness is a booming industry within the United States, garnering sales of over $35 billion a year in just the state of California alone, the average farm laborer earns between $5,000 and $8,500 annually (Brown and Getz 2011). This is the case despite the fact that most these farm laborers work around 1,000 hours during the few weeks of the planting and harvesting season (Brown and Getz 2011).

Second, in addition to, or perhaps because of, earning as little as $5 per hour for grueling labor, agricultural laborers also find themselves with little access to adequate housing, health care, or other services (Brown and Getz 2011). Indeed, while the American agricultural system has achieved increasing yields – the cost of food has dropped so much that the average American household spends less than 8 percent of its annual income on food, in contrast to 20 percent in 1900 – more than half of those whose labor makes such yields possible experience food insecurity in a given year (Brown and Getz 2011). Further, the informal nature of farm work tends to prevent workers from gaining access to health insurance, and thus they have little access to health care. Low incomes also often force workers to live in crowded, poor-quality housing (Gottlieb and Joshi 2010).

Third, farmworkers are also exposed to a number of occupational hazards. The physical difficulty of the work itself contributes to chronic injuries (Brown and Getz 2011; Gottlieb and Joshi 2010) and exposures to agricultural chemicals result in elevated rates of cancer (Zahm and Blair 1993), asthma (do Pico 1992), miscarriage (Payan-Renteria et al. 2012), birth defects (Schwartz et al. 1986), and Parkinson's disease (Semchuk et al. 1993).

Finally, many farmworkers in the United States encounter workplace violence and/or forced labor. As recently as 2002 there have been multiple known – and prosecuted – cases of slave labor within agriculture in the United States (Gottlieb 2010). Indeed, while a common perception is that the majority of trafficked persons are forced into the sex industry, such is not the case (Feingold 2005). Rather, most trafficked persons become involved in forced labor (Feingold 2005), and agriculture is one of the sectors where forced labor is the most common within the United States (Belser 2005).

Some estimates suggest that up to 90 percent of the farm labor within the United States consists of undocumented immigrants from Asia and Latin America (Gottlieb and Joshi 2010). Approximately 70 percent of these undocumented farmworkers within the United States work under "gangmasters" who act as intermediaries and contractors between farm owners and their labor force (Belser 2005). Many of these contractor gangmasters are also human smugglers who are contracted by landowners to provide labor (Gottlieb and Joshi 2010; United States Department of State 2013).

These farm labor contractors/human smugglers often recruit their labor force from impoverished regions with limited economic opportunity by suggesting to potential workers that wages for farmworkers are high, that debts incurred during the smuggling process can be rapidly repaid, and that the workers will be settled near family or friends (Gottlieb and Joshi 2010). However, when the immigrants are brought to the United States they often find themselves dropped off at unexpected locations where they have no previous social contacts, are unable to earn sufficient wages to purchase food or obtain adequate housing, and are unable to repay debts to smugglers and criminal organizations (Gottlieb and Joshi 2010).

Because of such debt, smuggled individuals find themselves in positions in which they are forced to become de facto indentured laborers, accepting whatever conditions they are offered by traffickers. Given the often-poor treatment that such workers experience, some resist their gangmasters, incurring threats and actual violence from their captors (Gottlieb and Joshi 2010). There are a number of reports of farm laborers forced to work at gunpoint, workers being beaten, and even workers being killed for non-compliance (Bales et al. 2004; Gottlieb and Joshi 2010).

It might appear, at least on the surface, that the above listed ways that farmworkers are mistreated are distributive injustices, and indeed they have often been treated as such in the existing literature. For example, low wages, poor housing, lack of health care, increased risk of injury and illness, and exposure to violence have all been understood as indicators that farmworkers receive a lion's share of the material harms and burdens, while not receiving an adequate share of the material benefits associated with the US food system (Brown and Getz 2011; Gottlieb and Joshi 2010). However, there is reason to suspect that behind such distribution inequity are participative disparities.

In the case of the United States, the current conditions experienced by food and farmworkers are arguable due to a confluence of factors that together result in participative disparities, thereby limiting the ability of those workers to argue for improved conditions. These factors include immigration status and its effect on ability to recruit the help of police and other authorities, the ability and willingness of employers to resort to violence, and the relative replaceability of labor. Working together, these result in the inability of food and farmworkers to demand that their concerns be addressed.

The immigrant status of many agricultural workers interferes with their self-determination in at least two ways.

First, undocumented immigrants face the constant threat of deportation if they are discovered. Thus, many farmworkers have limited ability to bring concerns regarding their employers to authorities such as the police, OSHA, or the Department of Labor. The immigration status of farmworkers often makes it nearly impossible for them to take action to ensure that they are treated well by their employers. The result is that they are particularly vulnerable to exploitation and abuse, a position that is manifested in the low wages, poor safety conditions, and workplace violence so often faced by agricultural laborers.

Second, as noted earlier, reports suggest that human traffickers often mislead potential migrants/farmworkers regarding the sort of work they will have, the remuneration they will receive for that work, and the access to resources that they will have when they are brought to the United States

(Gottlieb and Joshi 2010). This limits the ability of potential farmworkers to make informed decisions based on their needs and interests. Without the ability to make informed decisions, it is impossible for farmworkers to fairly participate in decisions regarding their employment (Loo 2014). In this case, not having knowledge about the real consequences of their choices makes it practically impossible for potential workers to avoid the poor working conditions they will likely face.

Violence on the part of contractor/gangmasters also serves to limit participation of workers in determining their work conditions, contributing to the burdens faced by so many of those working in US fields. Fear of this violence prevents farmworkers from individually resisting or organizing to communally resist the poor treatment they receive from their employers. The inability to actively advocate for self-interest is another form of participative disparity and, in this case, it serves to allow contractor/gangmasters to mistreat their workers in the ways described earlier in this section.

Finally, in addition to the undocumented farmworkers' limited ability to self-advocate due to immigration status and the willingness of contractors to respond to dissent with violence, farm work is often unskilled labor, and farmworkers are for the most part replaceable by anyone willing to do the work. As such, if a worker refuses to work under the conditions presented – despite lacking formal protections against wrongful dismissal and facing the risk of violence for the reasons described above – contractors can readily replace them with other trafficked workers. Further, given the prevalence of poverty throughout Asia and Latin America, there is likely to be a constantly available pool of potential persons to be trafficked to fulfill this purpose. This condition of replaceability also limits the ability of farmworkers to participate in determining their working conditions. Because they can be immediately dismissed and replaced with other workers if they attempt to strike or take other job actions, workers have no substantive means of protesting unfair treatment. This again provides contractors with a fair amount of liberty to mistreat and underpay their workers.

It should be noted that attention to participative disparities is not only important for diagnosing problems associated with the mistreatment of farm labor. It is also a means of identifying solutions and interventions for such mistreatment. This is evident when one considers examples such as the work of the Coalition of Immokalee Workers (CIW).

The CIW (2012) is a self-described worker-based farm labor rights movement that was formed by a small group of tomato pickers in 1993. It began as a small group of workers who began organizing work stoppages, hunger strikes, marches, and boycotts as a response to low wages, poor working conditions, and workplace violence (CIW 2012). What began as a relatively small labor movement within 20 years grew into an international organization, the efforts of which have had a number of results that have ended the abuses experienced by and substantively improved the conditions for farmworkers in Florida (where the CIW is based) (Greenhouse 2014). These results include: several federal investigations that have led to arrests of farm labor contractors for violating anti-slavery laws (CIW 2012); agreements by McDonald's, Yum Brands, Walmart, Subway, Bon Appétit Management Company, Aramark, and Sodexo to demand that growers treat workers fairly (Greenhouse 2014); and substantial increases of farmworker wages (CIW 2012).

Cases such as the CIW demonstrate that one key means to improve distributional disparities in the realm of agricultural labor is through ensuring that workers can voice their grievances and have the leverage to negotiate with their employers. Responding to and ameliorating distributional injustice within the agricultural system then involves protecting and promoting the ability of workers to organize, to strike, and to take other action to more effectively demand fair terms from their employers. More concretely, this suggests that what seems to be a matter regarding distribution is in fact a matter that requires solutions such as strong union protections, protections against employer retaliation, and other interventions that improve participative equity.

However, the importance of participative justice for distributive justice is not limited to those who work to grow food. Participation and participative fairness is also important for those who consume food. There is reason to think that there are also participative elements at the root of the apparently distributive problem posed by food deserts.

Justice and access to fresh food

In the last three decades "food deserts," areas of limited access to fresh meat and produce, have been discovered in both inner-city and rural low-income areas throughout the United States and Europe (Gottlieb and Joshi 2010; Ornelas 2010). The advent and spread of food deserts in inner cities and in the rural countryside are due to the growing dominance of "big-box stores" (e.g., Walmart, Sam's, Costco) relative to traditional independent grocers in both settings. With the efficiencies of scale and vertical integration available to large franchises, smaller traditional grocers are unable to compete in the marketplace. Indeed, in the past two decades great numbers of traditional independent grocers have been forced out of business throughout the US and the United Kingdom (Walker et al. 2010).

However, while big-box stores have the advantage of efficiencies of scale and the ability to sell at much lower prices than their traditional counterparts, they require two things: first, they require large customer bases to be profitable, and second, they require large amounts of land. That being the case, rural areas, with their lower population densities, and the inner city, with little available land, are two regions that find themselves particularly poorly suited for the introduction of big-box stores. Yet, while big-box stores tend not to serve either inner cities or small rural towns, they still draw enough customers from those communities to undermine the viability of local independent grocers (Bailey 2010). And, as such, one finds that with the rise of big-box stores – which tend to site their franchises in the suburbs – and the concomitant shuttering of smaller grocers, those living in inner cities and rural communities now often have become reliant upon fast-food restaurants, gas stations, bodegas, and even liquor stores as their primary sources of food (Gottlieb and Joshi 2010; Ornelas 2010).

This shift is worrisome because fast-food restaurants, gas stations, and bodegas often serve little in the way of fresh produce. Instead, they tend to offer foods that are heavily processed and have a relatively high ratio of fats and simple carbohydrates to other nutrients. That being so, without nearby grocers, residents of rural and inner-city communities without access to transportation find themselves unable to easily purchase fresh food and are forced to rely on the processed foods that are available in their neighborhoods. This has resulted in the development of a marked disparity in health outcomes between those who live in the suburbs, where fresh foods are available, and those living in rural and inner-city food deserts (Gottlieb and Joshi 2010; Ornelas 2010). Indeed, when one contrasts those living where fresh produce is plentiful with those living in food deserts, those with access to fresh produce are half as likely to suffer metabolic disorders such as cardiovascular disease or diabetes (Ornelas 2010). Further, those who have fresh produce available, when they do develop metabolic disorders, tend to develop them later in life (Ornelas 2010).

The problem of food deserts may initially seem to be primarily a distributive issue, a matter of how fresh produce is distributed or maldistributed across different segments of society. However, I argue that this hides what is also importantly a participative issue.

First, though perhaps more superficially, it is clear that the origin and spread of food deserts is the result of a shift in who controls community food markets, from individuals living within those communities to large national (or even multinational) corporations. As noted above, in the past, the primary sources of food for most communities were local independent grocers (Walker et al. 2010). The problem of food deserts arose when franchise big-box stores began replacing those local independent grocers (Gottlieb and Joshi 2010; Ornelas 2010; Walker et al. 2010). The loss of access to produce and other fresh foods in inner cities and the countryside was the result of the loss of local control of food markets and the concentration of food distribution networks into the hands of the firms operating the big-box franchises.

Second, and more importantly, there is a broad consensus in the literature that the solution to food deserts involves empowering communities to regain control of their food systems (Alkon and Agyeman 2011b; The Community Alliance for Global Justice 2013; Gottlieb and Joshi 2010; Just Food 2010). More specifically, the intervention that has become the most common for returning fresh produce to food deserts is – depending on context – the development of one or more of the following: community gardens, farmers markets, community-supported agriculture, and urban agriculture (Alkon and Agyeman 2011a; The Community Alliance for Global Justice 2013; Gottlieb and Joshi 2010; Just Food 2010).

For example, in the United States, the Agricultural Act of 2014 includes a number of programs intended to reduce the impact of food deserts. These programs include: the Local Foods Promotion Program (LFPP), the Healthy Food Financing Initiative (HFFI), the Food Insecurity Nutrition Incentive (FINI), and the Farmers Market Promotion Program (FMPP). All of these programs are designed to provide resources and incentives to promote the development of localized food systems centered around community-run farmers markets.

The LFPP will offer 25 percent matching funds up to $100,000 to support "the development and expansion of local and regional food business enterprises to increase domestic consumption of, and access to, locally and regionally produced agricultural products, and to develop new market opportunities for farm and ranch operations serving local markets" (USDA 2014a).

The FMPP will provide several $15,000–$100,000 grants (with an annual total of $30 million) to businesses or programs that:

> develop new market opportunities for farm and ranch operations serving local markets by developing, improving, expanding, and providing outreach, training, and technical assistance to, or assisting in the development, improvement, and expansion of, domestic farmers markets, roadside stands, community-supported agriculture programs, agritourism activities, and other direct producer-to-consumer market opportunities.
>
> (USDA 2014b)

FINI would promote the development of local food systems by providing matching funds to shoppers who use the Supplemental Nutritional Assistance Program (SNAP) at farmers markets. Finally, the HFFI, if funded by the US Congress, would do something similar and provide funds for community stores in areas that have been designated food deserts, enabling stores to purchase equipment to allow for the selling of fresh meat and produce.

In all these cases, it clear that the underlying, albeit perhaps unspoken, understanding is that the best way to ensure that those living in food deserts have access to nutritious food is to support the development of local infrastructure to promote the local growing and marketing of food. This promotion of localizing the food system is, in effect, the promotion of localizing control and participation within the food system. In that they create markets that only involve individuals that are neighbors living within the same community, farmers markets and direct farmer-to-consumer sales are ways local communities can take control of food from outside vendors.

What the above section demonstrates is that fair participation is an important element for food justice. Even if one is primarily concerned with distributive justice in the context of fair treatment for food workers or the fair distribution of food despite poverty, race, or region, one must still be concerned about participation; fair participation is, at the very least, one factor impacting distribution.

The participative element

The above two examples, the poor conditions of farmworkers and the problem of food deserts, should make it clear to the reader that problems that may seem prima facie to be primarily a matter of distributive disparities can be importantly participative. That is, distributive disparities can be the result of participative disparities, and they thus can require participative interventions to solve. In the case of farmworkers, artifacts of immigration status, the replaceability of unskilled laborers, and the willingness of contractors to threaten or commit violence all add to the difficulty for workers to promote their own interests. This in turn results in workers being particularly vulnerable to exploitation, which likely contributes to the remarkably poor conditions that are experienced by so much of the agricultural labor in the United States.

Such being the case, it is likely the most effective interventions intended to improve conditions for workers will have to address the participative disparities listed above that prevent workers from being able to fairly negotiate with their employers. Similarly, in the case of food deserts, participation is at the root of disparities regarding distribution, and solving distributive disparities requires that we address participative ones.

Specifically, in the case of food deserts, the reduction in the availability of fresh food in low-income urban and rural areas was the result of the shift in food systems from locally owned and operated grocers to large national (or even multinational) franchises. As such, most proposals for ameliorating the effects of food deserts involve the development of alternative, more local food networks that empower communities to better control their own food systems.

The lesson that one ought to take away from this is that those who are concerned with food justice should not be concerned solely with distribution. Rather, food justice requires attention to both distribution as well as participation.

What this means practically is that those seeking to promote fair food systems must consider how various stakeholders are involved in decisions affecting the disposition of food systems and whether all relevant stakeholders are fairly recognized in those decisions. If it is the case that some stakeholders tend to be marginalized, excluded, or otherwise have their participation limited, proponents of food justice must consider how to promote the ability of those stakeholders to empower themselves or to find alternative systems that can ensure that their interests and needs are met. In terms of policy, promotion of food justice should be understood as democratization and localization of food systems.

The current model, in which a small number of agribusiness firms are the primary source of food for most people, is one that limits the ability of eaters to express their interests and preferences in regards to their food systems. As such, individuals currently have a relatively limited ability to participate in deciding how their food is grown and distributed. Food systems that involve a wider range of producers and distributors, including local farmers, community-supported agriculture, neighborhood gardens, and other alternatives, at the very least provide for more choice and may provide means for individuals to become directly involved in the production and distribution of their own food.

With greater control on the part of the general public in regards to food production and distribution, those who may not currently be priority customers or stakeholders from the perspectives of the firms that presently dominate the global food system would be able to better assert themselves by being able to reject the received system in favor of alternatives. This would allow those who are marginalized to better resist the systems of distribution that marginalize them. Returning to the examples discussed above – the conditions faced by farmworkers and the problem of food deserts – democratization and localization of food systems would be helpful in several ways.

In the case of food deserts, the potential positive impact of democratization and localization is fairly obvious. Introducing community-based agriculture and markets would provide for the small-scale, relatively cheap-to-operate sources of fresh food that are currently so rare in inner cities and isolated rural locales. In the case of farmworkers, alternative community-based food systems would provide alternatives for those wishing to stand in solidarity with farmworkers and boycott producers who abuse their labor force. Further, promotion of local agriculture in impoverished areas in low- and middle-income countries might provide sufficient economic opportunity to prevent some individuals from becoming involved with human traffickers. Finally, in places such as the United States, alternative agriculture and food markets might provide alternative sources of employment to enable some mistreated workers to have the option of leaving their employers.

Conclusion

To summarize, the main argument of this chapter is that participative inequalities ought to be a central concern to those who are interested in promoting food justice. Appealing to two examples, the mistreatment of farmworkers and food deserts, I suggest that even problems that initially appear to be primarily distributive may also fundamentally involve participative disparities. This, in turn, indicates that bringing about food justice entails ensuring that marginalized individuals have adequate capacity to play a role in governing the food systems on which they are reliant.

References

Alkon, A. H., & Agyeman, J. (2011a) *Cultivating Food Justice: Race, Class, and Sustainability*, Cambridge: MIT Press.
Alkon, A. H., & Agyeman, J. (2011b) "Introduction: The Food Movement as Polyculture," in A. H. Alkon & J. Agyeman (eds.), *Cultivating Food Justice: Race, Class, and Sustainability*, Cambridge: MIT Press, pp. 1–20.
Bailey, J. M. (2010) *Rural Grocery Stores: Importance and Challenges*, Lyons: Center for Rural Affairs.
Bales, K., Fletcher, L., & Stover, E. (2004) *Hidden Slaves: Forced Labor in the United States*, Berkeley: Human Rights Center.
Belser, P. (2005) *Forced Labor and Human Trafficking: Estimating the Profits*, Geneva: International Labour Office
Brown, S., & Getz, C. (2011) "Farmworker Food Insecurity and the Production of Hunger in California," in A. H. Alkon & J. Agyeman (eds.), *Cultivating Food Justice: Race, Class, and Sustainability*, Cambridge: MIT Press, pp. 121–146.
Coalition of Immokalee Workers. (2012) "About CIW," viewed 11 November 2015, http://www.ciw-online.org/about/.
The Community Alliance for Global Justice. (2013) "Food Justice Project," viewed 9 November 2015, http://www.seattleglobaljustice.org/food-justice/.
do Pico, G.A. (1992) "Hazardous Exposure and Lung Disease among Farm Workers," *Clinics in Chest Medicine* 13: 311–328.
Feingold, D. A. (2005) "Human Trafficking," *Foreign Policy* 150: 26–30.
Gottlieb, R., & Joshi, A. (2010) *Food Justice*, Cambridge: MIT Press.
Greenhouse, S. (2014) "In Florida Tomato Fields, a Penny Buys Progress," *The New York Times*, 24 April.
Just Food. (2010) "Just Food," viewed 3 April 2016, http://www.justfood.org.
Loo, C. (2014) "Towards a More Participative Definition of Food Justice," *The Journal of Agricultural and Environmental Ethics* 27: 787–809.
Ornelas, L. (2010) *Shining a Light on the Valley of Heart's Delight: Taking a Look at Access to Healthy Foods in Santa Clara County's Communities of Color and Low-Income Communities*, San Jose: Food Empowerment Project.
Payan-Renteria, R., Garibay-Chavez, G., Rangel-Ascencio, R., Preciado-Martinez, V., Munoz-Islas, L., Beltran-Miranda, C., Mena-Mungia, S., Jave-Suarez, L., Feria-Velasco, A., & De Celis, R. (2012) "Effect of Chronic Pesticide Exposure in Farm Workers of a Mexico Community," *Archives of Environmental & Occupational Health* 67: 22–30.

Schwartz, D.A., Newsum, L.A., & Heifetz, R.M. (1986) "Parental Occupation and Birth Outcome in an Agricultural Community," *Scandinavian Journal of Work, Environment & Health* 12: 51–54.

Semchuk, K.M., Love, E.J., & Lee, R.G. (1993) "Parkinson's Disease: A Test of the Multifactorial Etiologic Hypothesis," *Neurology* 43: 1173–1180.

Shrader-Frechette, K. (2002) *Environmental Justice: Creating Equity, Reclaiming Democracy*, Oxford: Oxford University Press.

United States Department of State. (2013) *Trafficking in Persons Report 2013*, Washington: Government Printing Office.

USDA. (2014a) "Local Food Promotion Program," viewed 9 November 2015, http://www.ams.usda.gov/AMSv1.0/lfpp.

USDA. (2014b) "Farmers Market Promotion Program," *USDA Agricultural Marketing Service*, viewed 9 November 2015, http://www.ams.usda.gov/AMSv1.0/fmpp.

Walker, R.E., Butler, J., Kriska, A., Keane, C., Fryer, C.S., & Burke, J.G. (2010) "How Does Food Security Impact Residents of a Food Desert and a Food Oasis?" *Journal of Hunger & Environmental Nutrition* 5: 454–470.

Walzer, M. (1983) *Spheres of Justice*, New York: Basic Books.

Young, I. M. (1990) *Justice and the Politics of Difference*, Princeton: Princeton University Press.

Zahm, S.H., & Blair, A. (1993) "Cancer among Migrant and Seasonal Farmworkers: An Epidemiological Review and Research Agenda," *American Journal of Industrial Medicine* 24: 753–766.

INDEX

Note: Page numbers in *italics* indicate figures.